BANK PROFITABILITY

RENTABILITÉ DES BANQUES

FINANCIAL STATEMENTS OF BANKS

COMPTES DES BANQUES

1999

ORGANISATION FOR ECONOMIC CO-OPERATION AND DEVELOPMENT
ORGANISATION DE COOPÉRATION ET DE DÉVELOPPEMENT ÉCONOMIQUES

ORGANISATION FOR ECONOMIC CO-OPERATION AND DEVELOPMENT

Pursuant to Article 1 of the Convention signed in Paris on 14th December 1960, and which came into force on 30th September 1961, the Organisation for Economic Co-operation and Development (OECD) shall promote policies designed:

- to achieve the highest sustainable economic growth and employment and a rising standard of living in Member countries, while maintaining financial stability, and thus to contribute to the development of the world economy;
- to contribute to sound economic expansion in Member as well as non-member countries in the process of economic development; and
- to contribute to the expansion of world trade on a multilateral, non-discriminatory basis in accordance with international obligations.

The original Member countries of the OECD are Austria, Belgium, Canada, Denmark, France, Germany, Greece, Iceland, Ireland, Italy, Luxembourg, the Netherlands, Norway, Portugal, Spain, Sweden, Switzerland, Turkey, the United Kingdom and the United States. The following countries became Members subsequently through accession at the dates indicated hereafter: Japan (28th April 1964), Finland (28th January 1969), Australia (7th June 1971), New Zealand (29th May 1973), Mexico (18th May 1994), the Czech Republic (21st December 1995), Hungary (7th May 1996), Poland (22nd November 1996) and Korea (12th December 1996). The Commission of the European Communities takes part in the work of the OECD (Article 13 of the OECD Convention).

ORGANISATION DE COOPÉRATION ET DE DÉVELOPPEMENT ÉCONOMIQUES

En vertu de l'article 1er de la Convention signée le 14 décembre 1960, à Paris, et entrée en vigueur le 30 septembre 1961, l'Organisation de Coopération et de Développement Économiques (OCDE) a pour objectif de promouvoir des politiques visant :

- à réaliser la plus forte expansion de l'économie et de l'emploi et une progression du niveau de vie dans les pays Membres, tout en maintenant la stabilité financière, et à contribuer ainsi au développement de l'économie mondiale ;
- à contribuer à une saine expansion économique dans les pays Membres, ainsi que les pays non membres, en voie de développement économique ;
- à contribuer à l'expansion du commerce mondial sur une base multilatérale et non discriminatoire conformément aux obligations internationales.

Les pays Membres originaires de l'OCDE sont : l'Allemagne, l'Autriche, la Belgique, le Canada, le Danemark, l'Espagne, les États-Unis, la France, la Grèce, l'Irlande, l'Islande, l'Italie, le Luxembourg, la Norvège, les Pays-Bas, le Portugal, le Royaume-Uni, la Suède, la Suisse et la Turquie. Les pays suivants sont ultérieurement devenus Membres par adhésion aux dates indiquées ci-après : le Japon (28 avril 1964), la Finlande (28 janvier 1969), l'Australie (7 juin 1971), la Nouvelle-Zélande (29 mai 1973), le Mexique (18 mai 1994), la République tchèque (21 décembre 1995), la Hongrie (7 mai 1996), la Pologne (22 novembre 1996) et la Corée (12 décembre 1996). La Commission des Communautés européennes participe aux travaux de l'OCDE (article 13 de la Convention de l'OCDE).

FOREWORD

This publication provides information on financial statements of banks in all OECD countries. The coverage of banks in this volume is not the same in each country, though the objective is to include all institutions which conduct ordinary banking business, namely institutions which primarily take deposits from the public at large and provide finance for a wide range of purposes. Some supplementary information on the number of reporting banks, their branches and staff is also included.

The institutional coverage of the tables has been largely dictated by the availability of data on income and expenditure accounts of banks. As a result of the reporting methods which are being used in OECD countries, the tables are not integrated in the system of national accounts and are, therefore, not compatible with the *Financial Accounts of OECD Countries*. International comparisons in the field of income and expenditure accounts of banks are particularly difficult due to considerable differences in OECD countries as regards structural and regulatory features of national banking systems, accounting rules and practices, and reporting methods.

The standard framework used for presenting the statistics was modified following the recommendations of the Task Force on Bank Profitability. The preparation of this publication benefited from the work of Financial Statistics Section (of Financial Affairs Division) but could not have been accomplished without the assistance of the members of the OECD Working Party on Financial Statistics and the national administrations which they represent. It is published on the responsibility of the Secretary-General of the OECD.

AVANT-PROPOS

Cet ouvrage présente les informations relatives aux comptes des banques dans tous les pays de l'OCDE. La couverture des banques figurant dans ces statistiques n'est pas la même dans chaque pays, bien que l'objectif reste d'inclure toutes les institutions qui effectuent des opérations courantes de banque, c'est-à-dire qui reçoivent des dépôts du public et offrent des concours financiers à des fins très diverses. Des informations complémentaires sur le nombre de banques, celui de leurs succursales et de leurs salariés figurent également dans cet ouvrage.

La couverture institutionnelle des tableaux a été largement dictée par la disponibilité des données sur les comptes de revenus et de dépenses des banques. Du fait des modes de communication des données en vigueur dans les pays de l'OCDE, ces tableaux ne sont pas intégrés dans le Système de comptabilité nationale et ne sont donc pas compatibles avec les Comptes financiers des pays de l'OCDE. Les comparaisons internationales dans le domaine des comptes de revenus et de dépenses des banques sont particulièrement délicates étant donné les différences importantes qui existent entre les pays de l'OCDE en ce qui concerne la structure du système bancaire et la réglementation des banques, les règles et pratiques comptables et le système de communication des données.

Le cadre de référence utilisé pour la présentation des statistiques a été modifié suivant les recommandations du Groupe de projet sur la Rentabilité des banques. Cet ouvrage a bénéficié des travaux de la Section des Statistiques financières (de la Division des Affaires financières), mais n'aurait pu être réalisé sans l'aide des membres du Groupe de travail de l'OCDE sur les statistiques financières et des administrations nationales qu'ils représentent. Cet ouvrage est publié sous la responsabilité du Secrétaire général de l'OCDE.

TABLE OF CONTENTS

Part II **GENERAL TABLES**[1]

1. a. Structure of the Financial System
   b. Resident/Non-resident and Domestic/Foreign Currency Classification of Bank Assets and Liabilities

CONVENTIONAL SIGNS

..	*Not available*
-	*Nil or negligible*
·	*Decimal point*

TABLE DES MATIÈRES

Partie II TABLEAUX GÉNÉRAUX[1]

1. a. Structure du système financier
   b. Résident/non résident et monnaie nationale/étrangère classification de l'actif et du passif des banques

SIGNES CONVENTIONNELS

..	*Non disponible*
-	*Nul ou négligeable*
·	*Point décimal (sépare les unités des décimale)*

INTRODUCTION

The present volume provides statistics updating the earlier editions of *Bank Profitability -- Financial Statements of Banks.*

1. Standard framework for detailed statistics by country

National data are grouped and, where necessary, re-classified to fit as far as possible into the following standard framework of presentation.

Income statement

1. *Interest income*

   This item generally includes income on interest-bearing assets, fee income related to lending operations, and dividend income on shares and participations. In some cases it may also include income on bonds calculated as the difference between the book value and the redemption value of bonds.

2. *Interest expenses*

   This item generally includes interest paid on liabilities, fee expenses related to borrowing operations and may include in some cases the difference between the issue price on debt instruments and their par value.

3. *Net interest income* (item 1 minus item 2)

4. *Non-interest income (net)*

   a. Fees and commissions receivable

   b. Fees and commissions payable

   c. Net profit or loss on financial operations

   d. Other

   This item is generally the net result of a number of different income and expense items (other than those included in items 1 and 2) such as the following: commissions received and paid in connection with payments services, securities transactions and related services (new issues, trading, portfolio management, safe-custody) and foreign exchange transactions in the banks own name and on behalf of clients. Other income and expenses resulting from special transactions which do not represent ordinary and regular banking business may also be included. Realised losses and gains on foreign-exchange operations and securities transactions are generally included as well.

5. *Gross income* (item 3 plus item 4)

6. *Operating expenses*

   a. Staff costs

   b. Property costs

   c. Other

   This item includes all expenses relating to the ordinary and regular banking business other than those included in items 2 and 4, particularly salaries and other employee benefits, including transfers to pension reserves (staff costs), and expenses for property and equipment and related depreciation expenses. Taxes other than income or corporate taxes are also included.

7. *Net income* (item 5 minus item 6)

8. *Provisions (net)*

   a. Provisions on loans

   b. Provisions on securities

   c. Other

   This item includes, in part or in full, charges for value adjustments in respect of loans, credits and securities, book gains from such adjustments, losses on loans and transfers to and from reserves for possible losses on such assets. Realised gains or losses from foreign exchange transactions and securities transactions are, however, generally included under *Non-interest income (net)* (item 4).

9. *Profit before tax* (item 7 minus item 8)

10. *Income tax*

11. *Profit after tax* (item 9 minus item 10)

12. *Distributed profit*

13. *Retained profit* (item 11 minus item 12)

Balance sheet

Assets

14.Cash and balance with Central bank

15.Interbank deposits

16.Loans

17.Securities

18.Other assets

Liabilities

19.Capital and reserves

20.Borrowing from Central bank

21.Interbank deposits

22.Non-bank deposits

23.Bonds

24.Other liabilities

Balance sheet total

25.End-year total (sum of items 14 to 18 or 19 to 24)

26.Average total

Method of calculation varies between countries. The majority is the average of two end-year totals. Others are based on 13-month averages.

Memorandum items

27.Short-term securities (included in item 17)

Following the definition used in the European System of Integrated Accounts (paragraph 539), short-term securities with an original maturity of usually up to 12 months, but with a maximum maturity of two years.

28.Bonds (included in item 17)

Following the definition of the European System of Integrated Accounts (paragraph 542), this item includes fixed or variable-interest rate securities with an original maturity of several years.

29.Shares and participations (included in item 17)

30.Claims on non-residents (included in items 15 to 18)

31.Liabilities to non-residents (included in items 21 to 24)

Capital Adequacy

32.Tier 1 Capital: paid up shared capital/common stocks, disclosed reserves

33.Tier 2 Capital: undisclosed reserves, asset revaluation reserves, general provision/general loan loss reserves, debt/equity capital instruments, subordinated term debt.

34.Supervisory deductions

35.Total net capital resources (item 32 plus item 33 minus item 34)

36.Risk-weighted assets

Supplementary information

37.Number of institutions (covered by the data)

38.Number of branches (covered by the data)

39.Number of staff ('000) (of the institutions covered by the data)

2. Standard presentations for general tables

Structure of the financial system

Year

	Number of institutions	Number of branches	Number of employees	Total assets or liabilities	Total financial assets	
				in national currency	in national currency	%
Central bank						
Other monetary institutions						
Commercial banks						
Foreign owned banks						
Savings banks						
Co-operative banks						
Other financial institutions						
Mortgage credit institutions						
Development credit institutions						
Finance companies						
Others						
Insurance institutions						
Insurance companies						
Pension funds and foundations						
Others						
All financial institutions						

Resident/non-resident and domestic/foreign currency classification of bank assets and liabilities

Year

in national currency

	Residents	Non-residents	Total
Assets			
Domestic currency			
Foreign currencies			
Total			
Liabilities			
Domestic currency			
Foreign currencies			
Total			

3. Methodological information

In order to facilitate the interpretation and analysis of the data included in the present publication and to enable the user of the data to judge how cautiously the figures should be used for comparative purposes, methodological country notes provide detailed information[1] on the following:

- Institutional coverage, and the relative importance of the institutions covered as compared with the whole financial system;

- Geographical coverage and degree of consolidation indicating whether domestic or foreign financial or non-financial subsidiaries of the reporting banks are covered by the data and whether branches and/or subsidiaries of foreign banks are included;

- Structure of the banking system including information on the regulatory framework;

- Summary description of activities of banks: payment facilities, deposit business, lending business, savings instruments, money market business, security business, foreign exchange business, non-bank business.

- Explanations on individual items and reconciliation tables for income statement and balance sheet items giving detailed information on the way in which the data included in the present publication are derived from generally more detailed national data;

- Sources of data.

1. Revised methodological country notes will be published in the second half of 1999.

INTRODUCTION

Le présent volume fournit des statistiques mettant à jour les éditions antérieures de *Rentabilité des banques -- Comptes des banques.*

1. Modèle de présentation des statistiques détaillées par pays

Les données communiquées par les pays ont été groupées et, lorsque nécessaire, reclassées afin de cadrer, autant que possible, avec le modèle de présentation ci-après.

Compte de résultats

1. Produits financiers

Ce poste comprend, en principe, les revenus des actifs porteurs d'intérêts, les commissions afférentes aux opérations de prêt, ainsi que les dividendes d'actions et titres de participation. Dans certains cas, il peut comprendre aussi les revenus d'obligations définis comme la différence entre la valeur comptable et la valeur de remboursement des titres.

2. Frais financiers

Ce poste comprend, en principe, les intérêts versés sur les éléments du passif et les commissions versées sur les opérations d'emprunt. Il peut comprendre aussi, dans certains cas, la différence entre la valeur d'émission des instruments de dette et leur valeur nominale.

3. Produits financiers nets (poste 1 moins poste 2)

4. Produits non financiers (nets)

a. Frais et commissions à recevoir

b. Frais et commissions à payer

c. Profits ou pertes nets sur opérations financières

d. Autres

Ce poste est en principe le résultat net d'un certain nombre de produits et frais différents (autres que ceux figurant aux postes 1 et 2) tels que : commissions reçues et versées en paiement de services, opérations sur titres et services y afférents (nouvelles émissions, transactions, gestion de portefeuille, garde de titres), et opérations de change effectuées par les banques pour leur propre compte ou pour celui de leurs clients. Figurent aussi à ce poste, les produits et les charges résultant d'opérations exceptionnelles et non des activités courantes des banques. Les gains et pertes de change réalisées et les plus-values et moins-values réalisées sur les opérations sur titres y figurent également.

5. *Résultat brut* (poste 3 plus poste 4)

6. *Frais d'exploitation*

   a. Dépenses en personnel

   b. Dépenses afférentes à l'immobilier

   c. Autres

   Ce poste comprend toutes les dépenses afférentes aux activités courantes des banques (à l'exclusion de celles reprises aux postes 2 et 4), en particulier les salaires et autres avantages perçus par les salariés, y compris les dotations au fonds de pension (dépenses en personnel) et les charges afférentes aux terrains et immeubles et aux matériels, mobilier et installations ainsi que les amortissements. Sont aussi comptabilisés à ce poste les impôts autres que l'impôt sur le revenu ou les sociétés.

7. *Résultat net* (poste 5 moins poste 6)

8. *Provisions (nettes)*

   a. Provisions sur prêts

   b. Provisions sur titres

   c. Autres

   Ce poste comprend, en partie ou en totalité, les charges pour ajustement de la valeur comptable des prêts, crédits et titres de placement, les plus-values comptables découlant de cet ajustement, les pertes sur prêts, les dotations aux provisions pour pertes éventuelles sur ces éléments d'actif et les reprises de provisions. En revanche, les gains ou pertes de change réalisés et les plus-values ou moins-values réalisées sur les opérations sur titres de placement figurent normalement au poste *Produits non financiers (nets)* (poste 4).

9. *Bénéfices avant impôt* (poste 7 moins poste 8)

10. *Impôt sur le revenu*

11. *Bénéfices après impôt* (poste 9 moins poste 10)

12. *Bénéfices distribués*

13. *Bénéfices mis en réserve* (poste 11 moins poste 12)

Bilan

Actif

14. Caisse et soldes auprès de la Banque centrale

15. Dépôts interbancaires

16. Prêts

17. Valeurs mobilières

18. Autres actifs

Passif

19. Capital et réserves

20. Emprunts auprès de la Banque centrale

21. Dépôts interbancaires

22. Dépôts non bancaires

23. Obligations

24. Autres engagements

Total du bilan

25. Total en fin d'exercice (somme des postes 14 à 18 ou 19 à 24)

26. Total moyen

Les méthodes de calcul varient selon les pays. La moyenne sur deux fins d'exercices constitue la majorité. Les autres sont basées sur des moyennes de 13 mois.

Pour mémoire

27. Titres à court terme (comptabilisés au poste 17)

Ce poste comprend, selon la définition du Système européen de comptes économiques intégrés (paragraphe 539), les titres dont l'échéance initiale est normalement fixée jusqu'à 12 mois, mais avec une échéance maximum de deux ans.

28. Obligations (comptabilisées au poste 17)

Ce poste comprend, selon la définition du Système européen de comptes économiques intégrés (paragraphe 542), les titres à revenu fixe ou variable avec une échéance initiale de plusieurs années.

29.*Actions et participations* (comptabilisées au poste 17)

30.*Créances sur des non résidents* (comptabilisées aux postes 15 à 18)

31.*Engagements envers des non résidents* (comptabilisés aux postes 21 à 24)

Solvabilité

32. *Fonds propres de base:* capital social libéré/actions ordinaires, réserves publiées.

33.*Fonds propres complémentaires:* réserves non publiées, réserves de réévaluation des actifs, provisions générales/réserves générales pour créances douteuses, instruments dette/capital, dette subordonnée à terme.

34. *Eléments à déduire des fonds propres*

35. *Total net des ressources en capital* (poste 32 plus poste 33 moins poste 34)

36. *Actifs pondérés des risques*

Renseignements complémentaires

35.*Nombre d'institutions* (prises en compte)

36.*Nombre de succursales* (prises en compte)

37.*Nombre de salariés* (en milliers) (des institutions prises en compte)

2. Modèle de présentation pour les tableaux généraux

Structure du système financier

Année

	Nombre d'institutions	Nombre de succursales	Nombres de salariés	Total des actifs ou des passifs	Total des actifs financiers	
				en monnaie nationale	en monnaie nationale	%
Banque centrale						
Autres institutions monétaires						
Banques commerciales						
Banques étrangères						
Caisses d'épargne						
Banques mutualistes						
Autres institutions financières						
Institutions de crédit hypothécaire						
Institutions de crédit de développement						
Sociétés financières						
Autres						
Institutions d'assurance						
Sociétés d'assurance						
Fonds de pension et fondations						
Autres						
Ensemble des institutions financières						

Résident/non résident et monnaie nationale/étrangère classification de l'actif et du passif des banques

Année

Monnaie nationale

	Résidents	Non résidents	Total
Actif			
Monnaie nationale			
Monnaies étrangères			
Total			
Passif			
Monnaie nationale			
Monnaies étrangères			
Total			

3. Informations méthodologiques

Pour faciliter l'interprétation et l'analyse des données reprises dans la présente publication et pour inciter l'utilisateur à être prudent dans l'utilisation des statistiques à des fins de comparaisons internationales, les notes méthodologiques[1] par pays apportent des précisions sur les points suivants :

- Les institutions sur lesquelles portent les statistiques et leur importance par rapport à l'ensemble du système financier;
- Le champ géographique et le degré de consolidation indiquant si les filiales financières ou non financières nationales ou étrangères des banques déclarantes sont couvertes par les données et si les succursales et/ou les filiales des banques étrangères sont incluses ;
- La structure du système bancaire, y compris des informations sur la réglementation;
- Une description succincte des activités des banques : facilités de paiement, opérations de dépôts, de prêts, instruments d'épargne, marché monétaire, opérations sur titre, change, activités non-bancaires;
- Des explications sur les postes et des tableaux de concordance des comptes de résultats et des bilans comprenant des renseignements précis sur la façon dont les bilans reproduits dans cette publication ont été construits à partir des données plus détaillées fournies par les pays;
- Les sources des données

1. La version révisée des notes méthodologiques par pays sera publiée au cours du second semestre de 1999.

Part I

STATISTICS ON FINANCIAL STATEMENTS OF BANKS

STATISTIQUES SUR LES COMPTES DES BANQUES

AUSTRALIA / AUSTRALIE

All banks / Ensemble des banques

	1988	1989	1990	1991	1992	1993	1994	1995	1996	1997	
Million Australian dollars											*Millions de dollars australiens*
INCOME STATEMENT											**COMPTE DE RESULTATS**
1. Interest income	27384	37341	48101	42744	33653	29136	28844	34634	39089	39477	1. Produits financiers
2. Interest expenses	19173	27691	37442	31712	23306	18300	16909	22031	25547	25930	2. Frais financiers
3. Net interest income	8211	9650	10659	11032	10347	10836	11935	12603	13542	13546	3. Produits financiers nets
4. Non-interest income (net)	5327	5948	7129	10075	8111	7762	8409	7024	8626	10101	4. Produits non financiers (nets)
a. Fees and commissions receivable	..	..	..	..	..	..	..	..	..	..	*a. Frais et commissions à recevoir*
b. Fees and commissions payable	..	..	..	..	..	..	..	..	..	..	*b. Frais et commissions à payer*
c. Net profits or loss on financial operations	..	..	..	..	..	..	..	..	..	..	*c. Profits ou pertes nets sur opérations financières*
d. Other	..	..	..	..	..	..	..	..	..	..	*d. Autres*
5. Gross income	13538	15598	17788	21107	18458	18598	20344	19627	22168	23647	5. Résultat brut
6. Operating expenses	8770	10144	11748	12672	13635	12409	12854	12684	13708	15268	6. Frais d'exploitation
a. Staff costs	..	..	..	..	..	..	..	..	..	..	*a. Dépenses en personnel*
b. Property costs	..	..	..	..	..	..	..	..	..	..	*b. Dépenses en immobilier*
c. Other	..	..	..	..	..	..	..	..	..	..	*c. Autres*
7. Net income	4768	5454	6040	8435	4823	6189	7490	6943	8460	8379	7. Résultat net
8. Provisions (net)	1052	1709	3402	5117	4900	2560	1437	836	571	693	8. Provisions (nettes)
a. Provisions on loans	..	..	..	..	..	..	..	..	..	..	*a. Provisions sur prêts*
b. Provisions on securities	..	..	..	..	..	..	..	..	..	..	*b. Provisions sur titres*
c. Other	..	..	..	..	..	..	..	..	..	..	*c. Autres*
9. Profit before tax	3716	3745	2638	3318	-77	3629	6053	6106	7889	7686	9. Bénéfices avant impôt
10. Income tax	1703	1446	1079	1500	336	1440	1703	1611	2040	1983	10. Impôt sur le revenu
11. Profit after tax	2013	2299	1559	1818	-413	2189	4350	4495	5849	5703	11. Bénéfices après impôt
12. Distributed profit	1220	2102	1742	1390	1627	2101	2790	3713	4509	5143	12. Bénéfices distribués
13. Retained profit	793	197	-183	428	-2040	88	1560	782	1340	560	13. Bénéfices mis en réserve
BALANCE SHEET											**BILAN**
Assets											**Actif**
14. Cash & balance with Central bank	4714	4376	4197	3919	4215	4363	4768	6467	9036	8185	14. Caisse & solde auprès de la Banque centrale
15. Interbank deposits	19191	31833	34483	32884	34770	28707	24597	23675	31039	30775	15. Dépôts interbancaires
16. Loans (1)	161963	206300	239051	249425	256501	271828	284599	298961	336345	380423	16. Prêts (1)
17. Securities (1)	46875	49597	30852	35460	40438	37524	38298	42567	40880	39972	17. Valeurs mobilières (1)
18. Other assets (1)	68955	82233	109737	111918	118047	118955	113827	138356	160769	185206	18. Autres actifs (1)
Liabilities											**Passif**
19. Capital & reserves	22953	28363	39300	43289	45221	46779	48803	50583	61310	64483	19. Capital et réserves
20. Borrowing from Central bank	..	..	..	..	..	..	..	..	..	..	20. Emprunts auprès de la Banque centrale
21. Interbank deposits	26175	38352	36263	36914	42222	35436	33052	32462	33935	32337	21. Dépôts interbancaires
22. Non-bank deposits (1)	..	..	228711	232934	245237	260154	269323	285323	326443	366137	22. Dépôts non bancaires (1)
23. Bonds	..	..	..	..	..	..	..	..	..	..	23. Obligations
24. Other liabilities (1)	252568	307624	114046	120471	121294	119008	114911	141658	156382	181601	24. Autres engagements (1)
Balance sheet total											**Total du bilan**
25. End-year total	301697	374339	418322	433608	453971	461377	466089	510026	578069	644559	25. En fin d'exercice
26. Average total	274685	338018	396331	425965	443790	457674	463733	488058	544048	611314	26. Moyen

AUSTRALIA
All banks

AUSTRALIE
Ensemble des banques

	1988	1989	1990	1991	1992	1993	1994	1995	1996	1997	
Million Australian dollars											*Millions de dollars australiens*
Memorandum items											**Pour mémoire**
27. Short-term securities	*7712*	*8958*	*5919*	*10780*	*10212*	*9412*	*11262*	*10006*	*7773*	*7147*	*27. Titres à court terme*
28. Bonds	*19443*	*14369*	*17160*	*14159*	*16024*	*15621*	*15674*	*19824*	*19033*	*16693*	*28. Obligations*
29. Shares and participations (1)	*13508*	*14219*	..	..	..	..	..	..	..	..	*29. Actions et participations (1)*
30. Claims on non-residents	..	..	..	..	..	..	..	..	..	..	*30. Créances sur des non-résidents*
31. Liabilities to non-residents	..	..	..	..	..	..	..	..	..	..	*31. Engagements envers des non-résidents*
Capital adequacy (2)											**Solvabilité (2)**
32. Tier 1 Capital	..	..	*25859*	*26839*	*28929*	*29708*	*33882*	*38650*	*40131*	*42893*	*32. Fonds propres de base*
33. Tier 2 Capital	..	..	*13734*	*15506*	*13955*	*15014*	*14080*	*13709*	*14291*	*15863*	*33. Fonds propres complémentaires*
34. Supervisory deductions	..	..	*25*	*133*	*955*	*457*	*508*	*757*	*1452*	*3097*	*34. Eléments à déduire des fonds propres*
35. Total net capital resources	..	..	*39568*	*42212*	*41929*	*44265*	*47454*	*51602*	*52970*	*55659*	*35. Total net des ressources en capital*
36. Risk-weighted assets	..	..	*425601*	*419342*	*412080*	*409427*	*398071*	*427006*	*475804*	*540981*	*36. Actifs pondérés des risques*
SUPPLEMENTARY INFORMATION											**RENSEIGNEMENTS COMPLEMENTAIRES**
37. Number of institutions	32	32	32	29	28	29	29	31	28	29	37. Nombre d'institutions
38. Number of branches	14381	15009	14617	14203	13491	13338	12832	12519	13415	13072	38. Nombre de succursales
39. Number of employees (x 1000)	..	..	..	..	..	..	..	..	..	..	39. Nombre de salariés (x 1000)

1. Change in methodology.
2. Capital adequacy data (items 32 through 36) are consolidated worldwide and include banks' domestic and overseas non-bank subsidiaries.

Change in methodology:

- Introduction of revised statistical collection in 1990 resulted in reclassification of shares and participations from Securities (item 17) to Loans and Other Assets (item 16 and item 18).
- Until 1990, Non-bank deposits (item 22) were included under Other liabilities (item 24). This item includes a small proportion of interbank deposits.
- As from 1990, Shares and participations (item 29) are not separately available following the introduction of revised statistical collection.

1. Changement méthodologique.
2. Les données sur la solvabilité (poste 32 à poste 36) sont regroupées sur une base mondiale y compris les filiales non-bancaires dans le pays et à l'étranger.

Changement méthodologique :

- La reclassification des actions et participations du poste 17 Titres au poste 16 Prêts et poste 18 Autres actifs est consécutive à l'introduction en 1990 d'une révision de la collecte statistique.
- Jusqu'en 1990, les Dépôts non bancaires (poste 22) étaient inclus sous Autres engagements (poste 24). Ce poste inclut une petite partie des dépôts interbancaires.
- A partir de 1990, les Actions et participations (poste 29) ne sont plus disponibles séparément suite à l'introduction d'une révision de la collecte statistique.

AUSTRALIA
All banks

AUSTRALIE
Ensemble des banques

	1988	1989	1990	1991	1992	1993	1994	1995	1996	1997	
Per cent											*Pourcentage*
INCOME STATEMENT ANALYSIS											**ANALYSE DU COMPTE DE RESULTATS**
% of average balance sheet total											**% du total moyen du bilan**
40. Interest income	9.97	11.05	12.14	10.03	7.58	6.37	6.22	7.10	7.18	6.46	40. Produits financiers
41. Interest expenses	6.98	8.19	9.45	7.44	5.25	4.00	3.65	4.51	4.70	4.24	41. Frais financiers
42. Net interest income	2.99	2.85	2.69	2.59	2.33	2.37	2.57	2.58	2.49	2.22	42. Produits financiers nets
43. Non-interest income (net)	1.94	1.76	1.80	2.37	1.83	1.70	1.81	1.44	1.59	1.65	43. Produits non financiers (nets)
a. Fees and commissions receivable	..	..	..	..	..	..	..	..	..	..	*a. Frais et commissions à recevoir*
b. Fees and commissions payable	..	..	..	..	..	..	..	..	..	..	*b. Frais et commissions à payer*
c. Net profits or loss on financial operations	..	..	..	..	..	..	..	..	..	..	*c. Profits ou pertes nets sur opérations financières*
d. Other	..	..	..	..	..	..	..	..	..	..	*d. Autres*
44. Gross income	4.93	4.61	4.49	4.96	4.16	4.06	4.39	4.02	4.07	3.87	44. Résultat brut
45. Operating expenses	3.19	3.00	2.96	2.97	3.07	2.71	2.77	2.60	2.52	2.50	45. Frais d'exploitation
a. Staff costs	..	..	..	..	..	..	..	..	..	..	*a. Dépenses en personnel*
b. Property costs	..	..	..	..	..	..	..	..	..	..	*b. Dépenses en immobilier*
c. Other	..	..	..	..	..	..	..	..	..	..	*c. Autres*
46. Net income	1.74	1.61	1.52	1.98	1.09	1.35	1.62	1.42	1.56	1.37	46. Résultat net
47. Provisions (net)	0.38	0.51	0.86	1.20	1.10	0.56	0.31	0.17	0.10	0.11	47. Provisions (nettes)
a. Provisions on loans	..	..	..	..	..	..	..	..	..	..	*a. Provisions sur prêts*
b. Provisions on securities	..	..	..	..	..	..	..	..	..	..	*b. Provisions sur titres*
c. Other	..	..	..	..	..	..	..	..	..	..	*c. Autres*
48. Profit before tax	1.35	1.11	0.67	0.78	-0.02	0.79	1.31	1.25	1.45	1.26	48. Bénéfices avant impôt
49. Income tax	0.62	0.43	0.27	0.35	0.08	0.31	0.37	0.33	0.37	0.32	49. Impôt sur le revenu
50. Profit after tax	0.73	0.68	0.39	0.43	-0.09	0.48	0.94	0.92	1.08	0.93	50. Bénéfices après impôt
51. Distributed profit	0.44	0.62	0.44	0.33	0.37	0.46	0.60	0.76	0.83	0.84	51. Bénéfices distribués
52. Retained profit	0.29	0.06	-0.05	0.10	-0.46	0.02	0.34	0.16	0.25	0.09	52. Bénéfices mis en réserve
% of gross income											**% du total du résultat brut**
53. Net interest income	60.65	61.87	59.92	52.27	56.06	58.26	58.67	64.21	61.09	57.28	53. Produits financiers nets
54. Non-interest income (net)	39.35	38.13	40.08	47.73	43.94	41.74	41.33	35.79	38.91	42.72	54. Produits non financiers (nets)
a. Fees and commissions receivable	..	..	..	..	..	..	..	..	..	..	*a. Frais et commissions à recevoir*
b. Fees and commissions payable	..	..	..	..	..	..	..	..	..	..	*b. Frais et commissions à payer*
c. Net profits or loss on financial operations	..	..	..	..	..	..	..	..	..	..	*c. Profits ou pertes nets sur opérations financières*
d. Other	..	..	..	..	..	..	..	..	..	..	*d. Autres*
55. Operating expenses	64.78	65.03	66.04	60.04	73.87	66.72	63.18	64.63	61.84	64.57	55. Frais d'exploitation
a. Staff costs	..	..	..	..	..	..	..	..	..	..	*a. Dépenses en personnel*
b. Property costs	..	..	..	..	..	..	..	..	..	..	*b. Dépenses en immobilier*
c. Other	..	..	..	..	..	..	..	..	..	..	*c. Autres*
56. Net income	35.22	34.97	33.96	39.96	26.13	33.28	36.82	35.37	38.16	35.43	56. Résultat net
57. Provisions (net)	7.77	10.96	19.13	24.24	26.55	13.76	7.06	4.26	2.58	2.93	57. Provisions (nettes)
a. Provisions on loans	..	..	..	..	..	..	..	..	..	..	*a. Provisions sur prêts*
b. Provisions on securities	..	..	..	..	..	..	..	..	..	..	*b. Provisions sur titres*
c. Other	..	..	..	..	..	..	..	..	..	..	*c. Autres*
58. Profit before tax	27.45	24.01	14.83	15.72	-0.42	19.51	29.75	31.11	35.59	32.50	58. Bénéfices avant impôt
59. Income tax	12.58	9.27	6.07	7.11	1.82	7.74	8.37	8.21	9.20	8.39	59. Impôt sur le revenu
60. Profit after tax	14.87	14.74	8.76	8.61	-2.24	11.77	21.38	22.90	26.38	24.12	60. Bénéfices après impôt
% of net income											**% du total du résultat net**
61. Provisions (net)	22.06	31.33	56.32	60.66	101.60	41.36	19.19	12.04	6.75	8.27	61. Provisions (nettes)
a. Provisions on loans	..	..	..	..	..	..	..	..	..	..	*a. Provisions sur prêts*
b. Provisions on securities	..	..	..	..	..	..	..	..	..	..	*b. Provisions sur titres*
c. Other	..	..	..	..	..	..	..	..	..	..	*c. Autres*
62. Profit before tax	77.94	68.67	43.68	39.34	-1.60	58.64	80.81	87.94	93.25	91.73	62. Bénéfices avant impôt
63. Income tax	35.72	26.51	17.86	17.78	6.97	23.27	22.74	23.20	24.11	23.67	63. Impôt sur le revenu
64. Profit after tax	42.22	42.15	25.81	21.55	-8.56	35.37	58.08	64.74	69.14	68.06	64. Bénéfices après impôt

AUSTRALIA
All banks

AUSTRALIE
Ensemble des banques

	1988	1989	1990	1991	1992	1993	1994	1995	1996	1997	
Per cent											*Pourcentage*
BALANCE SHEET ANALYSIS											**ANALYSE DU BILAN**
% of year-end balance sheet total											**% du total du bilan en fin d'exercice**
Assets											**Actif**
65. Cash & balance with Central bank	1.56	1.17	1.00	0.90	0.93	0.95	1.02	1.27	1.56	1.27	65. Caisse & solde auprès de la Banque centrale
66. Interbank deposits	6.36	8.50	8.24	7.58	7.66	6.22	5.28	4.64	5.37	4.77	66. Dépôts interbancaires
67. Loans	53.68	55.11	57.15	57.52	56.50	58.92	61.06	58.62	58.18	59.02	67. Prêts
68. Securities	15.54	13.25	7.38	8.18	8.91	8.13	8.22	8.35	7.07	6.20	68. Valeurs mobilières
69. Other assets	22.86	21.97	26.23	25.81	26.00	25.78	24.42	27.13	27.81	28.73	69. Autres actifs
Liabilities											**Passif**
70. Capital & reserves	7.61	7.58	9.39	9.98	9.96	10.14	10.47	9.92	10.61	10.00	70. Capital et réserves
71. Borrowing from Central bank	..	..	..	..	..	..	..	..	..	..	71. Emprunts auprès de la Banque centrale
72. Interbank deposits	8.68	10.25	8.67	8.51	9.30	7.68	7.09	6.36	5.87	5.02	72. Dépôts interbancaires
73. Non-bank deposits	..	..	54.67	53.72	54.02	56.39	57.78	55.94	56.47	56.80	73. Dépôts non bancaires
74. Bonds	..	..	..	..	..	..	..	..	..	..	74. Obligations
75. Other liabilities	83.72	82.18	27.26	27.78	26.72	25.79	24.65	27.77	27.05	28.17	75. Autres engagements
Memorandum items											***Pour mémoire***
76. Short-term securities	*2.56*	*2.39*	*1.41*	*2.49*	*2.25*	*2.04*	*2.42*	*1.96*	*1.34*	*1.11*	*76. Titres à court terme*
77. Bonds	*6.44*	*3.84*	*4.10*	*3.27*	*3.53*	*3.39*	*3.36*	*3.89*	*3.29*	*2.59*	*77. Obligations*
78. Shares and participations	*4.48*	*3.80*	..	..	..	..	..	..	..	..	*78. Actions et participations*
79. Claims on non-residents	..	..	..	..	..	..	..	..	..	..	*79. Créances sur des non-résidents*
80. Liabilities to non-residents	..	..	..	..	..	..	..	..	..	..	*80. Engagements envers des non-résidents*

* See notes on previous pages.

* Voir les notes en pages précédentes.

AUSTRIA — AUTRICHE

All banks — Ensemble des banques

Million schillings	1988	1989	1990	1991	1992	1993	1994	1995	1996	1997	Millions de schillings
INCOME STATEMENT											**COMPTE DE RESULTATS**
1. Interest income	229896	275916	327360	347980	355738	332995	315878	330936	303032	307339	1. Produits financiers
2. Interest expenses	166908	210562	256357	271594	273939	241563	221898	241033	211748	218063	2. Frais financiers
3. Net interest income	62988	65354	71003	76386	81799	91432	93980	89903	91284	89276	3. Produits financiers nets
4. Non-interest income (net)	17415	25226	31767	36158	41005	35430	37905	58386	63556	67348	4. Produits non financiers (nets)
a. Fees and commissions receivable	*15610*	*19363*	*23306*	*23928*	*25861*	*30115*	*32780*	*30438*	*33887*	*37578*	*a. Frais et commissions à recevoir*
b. Fees and commissions payable	*3361*	*4387*	*6096*	*5534*	*5902*	*6376*	*6908*	*6192*	*6928*	*8110*	*b. Frais et commissions à payer*
c. Net profits or loss on financial operations	..	..	..	..	..	..	..	*7887*	*8462*	*8471*	*c. Profits ou pertes nets sur opérations financières*
d. Other	..	..	..	..	..	..	..	*26253*	*28135*	*29410*	*d. Autres*
5. Gross income	80403	90580	102770	112544	122804	126862	131885	148289	154840	156624	5. Résultat brut
6. Operating expenses	55047	59340	66661	73061	78573	80545	85851	102987	107066	108667	6. Frais d'exploitation
a. Staff costs	*32181*	*34696*	*39547*	*43379*	*46817*	*47343*	*50668*	*54226*	*56218*	*57208*	*a. Dépenses en personnel*
b. Property costs	..	..	..	..	..	..	..	*30021*	*32011*	*33309*	*b. Dépenses en immobilier*
c. Other	..	..	..	..	..	..	..	*18740*	*18837*	*18150*	*c. Autres*
7. Net income	25356	31240	36109	39483	44231	46317	46034	45302	47774	47957	7. Résultat net
8. Provisions (net)	-	14813	20032	22077	29108	25284	25287	23188	24211	22774	8. Provisions (nettes)
a. Provisions on loans	..	*6566*	*8050*	*11875*	*17857*	*19344*	*18167*	*26544*	*25653*	*25233*	*a. Provisions sur prêts*
b. Provisions on securities	..	*5789*	*7348*	*3206*	*3749*	*1107*	*4741*	*-3356*	*-1442*	*-2459*	*b. Provisions sur titres*
c. Other	..	..	..	..	..	..	..	..	..	..	*c. Autres*
9. Profit before tax (1)	25356	16427	16077	17406	15123	21033	20747	20351	23563	25183	9. Bénéfices avant impôt (1)
10. Income tax	3103	3157	3032	2911	2600	2725	2434	4243	4997	4656	10. Impôt sur le revenu
11. Profit after tax	22253	13270	13045	14495	12523	18308	18313	16108	18566	20527	11. Bénéfices après impôt
12. Distributed profit	..	..	..	..	..	..	..	..	..	..	12. Bénéfices distribués
13. Retained profit	..	..	..	..	..	..	..	..	..	..	13. Bénéfices mis en réserve
BALANCE SHEET											**BILAN**
Assets											**Actif**
14. Cash & balance with Central bank	67199	76883	73166	68441	83827	86601	93228	77396	89837	87091	14. Caisse & solde auprès de la Banque centrale
15. Interbank deposits	1231639	1223461	1235092	1242533	1303640	1437018	1472119	1628364	1652507	1679639	15. Dépôts interbancaires
16. Loans	1710902	1884902	2048063	2213849	2379219	2467115	2562296	2736711	2883060	3061696	16. Prêts
17. Securities	424417	445993	468099	492964	476684	539811	638953	767744	866396	961972	17. Valeurs mobilières
18. Other assets	183171	199619	216056	258405	297082	296131	312130	168457	172616	186687	18. Autres actifs
Liabilities											**Passif**
19. Capital & reserves	141636	163595	186199	202114	220564	241649	263679	249820	245291	269237	19. Capital et réserves
20. Borrowing from Central bank	2792	1144	1533	1103	557	598	1378	181	297	805	20. Emprunts auprès de la Banque centrale
21. Interbank deposits	1287885	1286495	1280553	1315567	1359228	1418268	1472380	1578207	1697770	1798600	21. Dépôts interbancaires
22. Non-bank deposits	1452911	1569986	1725712	1876343	2029440	2144613	2272048	2364034	2445911	2511400	22. Dépôts non bancaires
23. Bonds	593320	659477	692662	705669	737231	815018	847944	935807	976461	1066459	23. Obligations
24. Other liabilities	138785	150162	153816	175396	193432	206529	221298	250624	298686	330584	24. Autres engagements
Balance sheet total											**Total du bilan**
25. End-year total	3617329	3830858	4040476	4276192	4540452	4826676	5078727	5378672	5664416	5977085	25. En fin d'exercice
26. Average total	3543249	3769759	4012331	4228420	4414568	4335612	4946920	5220513	5505312	5885155	26. Moyen

AUSTRIA
All banks

AUTRICHE
Ensemble des banques

	1988	1989	1990	1991	1992	1993	1994	1995	1996	1997	
Million schillings											*Millions de schillings*
Memorandum items											***Pour mémoire***
27. Short-term securities	*8439*	*5951*	*6807*	*6088*	*5468*	*5516*	*5716*	*5474*	*5556*	*4040*	*27. Titres à court terme*
28. Bonds	*334051*	*348443*	*352728*	*366784*	*361695*	*408885*	*493859*	*546977*	*606048*	*674308*	*28. Obligations*
29. Shares and participations	*62326*	*76772*	*93973*	*112789*	*127830*	*133843*	*139862*	*205394*	*225855*	*283624*	*29. Actions et participations*
30. Claims on non-residents	*816929*	*842040*	*843875*	*846806*	*915883*	*1012407*	*1039462*	*1129898*	*1252278*	*1443786*	*30. Créances sur des non-résidents*
31. Liabilities to non-residents	*877311*	*926274*	*932278*	*958893*	*1045004*	*1084039*	*1110421*	*1190110*	*1379605*	*1637216*	*31. Engagements envers des non-résidents*
Capital adequacy											***Solvabilité***
32. Tier 1 Capital	..	..	..	..	..	..	*221504*	*236216*	*254398*	*276206*	*32. Fonds propres de base*
33. Tier 2 Capital	..	..	..	..	..	..	*86673*	*91627*	*104571*	*132564*	*33. Fonds propres complémentaires*
34. Supervisory deductions	..	..	..	..	..	..	*12000*	*12607*	*12221*	*12482*	*34. Eléments à déduire des fonds propres*
35. Total net capital resources	..	..	..	..	..	..	*296177*	*315236*	*346748*	*396288*	*35. Total net des ressources en capital*
36. Risk-weighted assets	..	..	..	..	..	..	*2272899*	*2385682*	*2517748*	*2719628*	*36. Actifs pondérés des risques*
SUPPLEMENTARY INFORMATION											**RENSEIGNEMENTS COMPLEMENTAIRES**
37. Number of institutions	1250	1240	1210	1165	1104	1063	1053	1041	1019	995	37. Nombre d'institutions
38. Number of branches	4295	4373	4497	4594	4667	4691	4683	4686	4694	4691	38. Nombre de succursales
39. Number of employees (x 1000)	70.2	66.6	68.5	69.9	70.0	68.9	71.2	71.0	71.0	71.0	39. Nombre de salariés (x 1000)

1. For 1995, Profit before tax (item 9) includes "extraordinary profit or loss (net)" in the amount of -1764 million schillings.

Notes

- Average balance sheet totals (item 26) are based on twelve end-month data.

1. Pour l'année 1995, les Bénéfices avant impôt (poste 9) comprennent des "pertes ou profits extraordinaires (net)" d'un montant de -1764 millions de schillings

Notes

- La moyenne du total des actifs/passifs (poste 26) est basée sur douze données de fin de mois.

AUSTRIA
All banks

AUTRICHE
Ensemble des banques

	1988	1989	1990	1991	1992	1993	1994	1995	1996	1997	
Per cent											*Pourcentage*
INCOME STATEMENT ANALYSIS											**ANALYSE DU COMPTE DE RESULTATS**
% of average balance sheet total											**% du total moyen du bilan**
40. Interest income	6.49	7.32	8.16	8.23	8.06	7.68	6.39	6.34	5.50	5.22	40. Produits financiers
41. Interest expenses	4.71	5.59	6.39	6.42	6.21	5.57	4.49	4.62	3.85	3.71	41. Frais financiers
42. Net interest income	1.78	1.73	1.77	1.81	1.85	2.11	1.90	1.72	1.66	1.52	42. Produits financiers nets
43. Non-interest income (net)	0.49	0.67	0.79	0.86	0.93	0.82	0.77	1.12	1.15	1.14	43. Produits non financiers (nets)
a. Fees and commissions receivable	*0.44*	*0.51*	*0.58*	*0.57*	*0.59*	*0.69*	*0.66*	*0.58*	*0.62*	*0.64*	*a. Frais et commissions à recevoir*
b. Fees and commissions payable	*0.09*	*0.12*	*0.15*	*0.13*	*0.13*	*0.15*	*0.14*	*0.12*	*0.13*	*0.14*	*b. Frais et commissions à payer*
c. Net profits or loss on financial operations	..	..	..	..	..	..	..	*0.15*	*0.15*	*0.14*	*c. Profits ou pertes nets sur opérations financières*
d. Other	..	..	..	..	..	..	..	*0.50*	*0.51*	*0.50*	*d. Autres*
44. Gross income	2.27	2.40	2.56	2.66	2.78	2.93	2.67	2.84	2.81	2.66	44. Résultat brut
45. Operating expenses	1.55	1.57	1.66	1.73	1.78	1.86	1.74	1.97	1.94	1.85	45. Frais d'exploitation
a. Staff costs	*0.91*	*0.92*	*0.99*	*1.03*	*1.06*	*1.09*	*1.02*	*1.04*	*1.02*	*0.97*	*a. Dépenses en personnel*
b. Property costs	..	..	..	..	..	..	..	*0.58*	*0.58*	*0.57*	*b. Dépenses en immobilier*
c. Other	..	..	..	..	..	..	..	*0.36*	*0.34*	*0.31*	*c. Autres*
46. Net income	0.72	0.83	0.90	0.93	1.00	1.07	0.93	0.87	0.87	0.81	46. Résultat net
47. Provisions (net)	-	0.39	0.50	0.52	0.66	0.58	0.51	0.44	0.44	0.39	47. Provisions (nettes)
a. Provisions on loans	..	*0.17*	*0.20*	*0.28*	*0.40*	*0.45*	*0.37*	*0.51*	*0.47*	*0.43*	*a. Provisions sur prêts*
b. Provisions on securities	..	*0.15*	*0.18*	*0.08*	*0.08*	*0.03*	*0.10*	*-0.06*	*-0.03*	*-0.04*	*b. Provisions sur titres*
c. Other	..	..	..	..	..	..	..	..	..	..	*c. Autres*
48. Profit before tax	0.72	0.44	0.40	0.41	0.34	0.49	0.42	0.39	0.43	0.43	48. Bénéfices avant impôt
49. Income tax	0.09	0.08	0.08	0.07	0.06	0.06	0.05	0.08	0.09	0.08	49. Impôt sur le revenu
50. Profit after tax	0.63	0.35	0.33	0.34	0.28	0.42	0.37	0.31	0.34	0.35	50. Bénéfices après impôt
51. Distributed profit	..	..	..	..	..	..	..	..	..	..	51. Bénéfices distribués
52. Retained profit	..	..	..	..	..	..	..	..	..	..	52. Bénéfices mis en réserve
% of gross income											**% du total du résultat brut**
53. Net interest income	78.34	72.15	69.09	67.87	66.61	72.07	71.26	60.63	58.95	57.00	53. Produits financiers nets
54. Non-interest income (net)	21.66	27.85	30.91	32.13	33.39	27.93	28.74	39.37	41.05	43.00	54. Produits non financiers (nets)
a. Fees and commissions receivable	*19.41*	*21.38*	*22.68*	*21.26*	*21.06*	*23.74*	*24.85*	*20.53*	*21.89*	*23.99*	*a. Frais et commissions à recevoir*
b. Fees and commissions payable	*4.18*	*4.84*	*5.93*	*4.92*	*4.81*	*5.03*	*5.24*	*4.18*	*4.47*	*5.18*	*b. Frais et commissions à payer*
c. Net profits or loss on financial operations	..	..	..	..	..	..	..	*5.32*	*5.46*	*5.41*	*c. Profits ou pertes nets sur opérations financières*
d. Other	..	..	..	..	..	..	..	*17.70*	*18.17*	*18.78*	*d. Autres*
55. Operating expenses	68.46	65.51	64.86	64.92	63.98	63.49	65.10	69.45	69.15	69.38	55. Frais d'exploitation
a. Staff costs	*40.02*	*38.30*	*38.48*	*38.54*	*38.12*	*37.32*	*38.42*	*36.57*	*36.31*	*36.53*	*a. Dépenses en personnel*
b. Property costs	..	..	..	..	..	..	..	*20.24*	*20.67*	*21.27*	*b. Dépenses en immobilier*
c. Other	..	..	..	..	..	..	..	*12.64*	*12.17*	*11.59*	*c. Autres*
56. Net income	31.54	34.49	35.14	35.08	36.02	36.51	34.90	30.55	30.85	30.62	56. Résultat net
57. Provisions (net)	-	16.35	19.49	19.62	23.70	19.93	19.17	15.64	15.64	14.54	57. Provisions (nettes)
a. Provisions on loans	..	*7.25*	*7.83*	*10.55*	*14.54*	*15.25*	*13.77*	*17.90*	*16.57*	*16.11*	*a. Provisions sur prêts*
b. Provisions on securities	..	*6.39*	*7.15*	*2.85*	*3.05*	*0.87*	*3.59*	*-2.26*	*-0.93*	*-1.57*	*b. Provisions sur titres*
c. Other	..	..	..	..	..	..	..	..	..	..	*c. Autres*
58. Profit before tax	31.54	18.14	15.64	15.47	12.31	16.58	15.73	13.72	15.22	16.08	58. Bénéfices avant impôt
59. Income tax	3.86	3.49	2.95	2.59	2.12	2.15	1.85	2.86	3.23	2.97	59. Impôt sur le revenu
60. Profit after tax	27.68	14.65	12.69	12.88	10.20	14.43	13.89	10.86	11.99	13.11	60. Bénéfices après impôt
% of net income											**% du total du résultat net**
61. Provisions (net)	-	47.42	55.48	55.92	65.81	54.59	54.93	51.19	50.68	47.49	61. Provisions (nettes)
a. Provisions on loans	..	*21.02*	*22.29*	*30.08*	*40.37*	*41.76*	*39.46*	*58.59*	*53.70*	*52.62*	*a. Provisions sur prêts*
b. Provisions on securities	..	*18.53*	*20.35*	*8.12*	*8.48*	*2.39*	*10.30*	*-7.41*	*-3.02*	*-5.13*	*b. Provisions sur titres*
c. Other	..	..	..	..	..	..	..	..	..	..	*c. Autres*
62. Profit before tax	100.00	52.58	44.52	44.08	34.19	45.41	45.07	44.92	49.32	52.51	62. Bénéfices avant impôt
63. Income tax	12.24	10.11	8.40	7.37	5.88	5.88	5.29	9.37	10.46	9.71	63. Impôt sur le revenu
64. Profit after tax	87.76	42.48	36.13	36.71	28.31	39.53	39.78	35.56	38.86	42.80	64. Bénéfices après impôt

AUSTRIA — AUTRICHE
All banks — Ensemble des banques

	1988	1989	1990	1991	1992	1993	1994	1995	1996	1997	
Per cent											*Pourcentage*
BALANCE SHEET ANALYSIS											**ANALYSE DU BILAN**
% of year-end balance sheet total											**% du total du bilan en fin d'exercice**
Assets											**Actif**
65. Cash & balance with Central bank	1.86	2.01	1.81	1.60	1.85	1.79	1.84	1.44	1.59	1.46	65. Caisse & solde auprès de la Banque centrale
66. Interbank deposits	34.05	31.94	30.57	29.06	28.71	29.77	28.99	30.27	29.17	28.10	66. Dépôts interbancaires
67. Loans	47.30	49.20	50.69	51.77	52.40	51.11	50.45	50.88	50.90	51.22	67. Prêts
68. Securities	11.73	11.64	11.59	11.53	10.50	11.18	12.58	14.27	15.30	16.09	68. Valeurs mobilières
69. Other assets	5.06	5.21	5.35	6.04	6.54	6.14	6.15	3.13	3.05	3.12	69. Autres actifs
Liabilities											**Passif**
70. Capital & reserves	3.92	4.27	4.61	4.73	4.86	5.01	5.19	4.64	4.33	4.50	70. Capital et réserves
71. Borrowing from Central bank	0.08	0.03	0.04	0.03	0.01	0.01	0.03	-	0.01	0.01	71. Emprunts auprès de la Banque centrale
72. Interbank deposits	35.60	33.58	31.69	30.76	29.94	29.38	28.99	29.34	29.97	30.09	72. Dépôts interbancaires
73. Non-bank deposits	40.17	40.98	42.71	43.88	44.70	44.43	44.74	43.95	43.18	42.02	73. Dépôts non bancaires
74. Bonds	16.40	17.21	17.14	16.50	16.24	16.89	16.70	17.40	17.24	17.84	74. Obligations
75. Other liabilities	3.84	3.92	3.81	4.10	4.26	4.28	4.36	4.66	5.27	5.53	75. Autres engagements
Memorandum items											***Pour mémoire***
76. Short-term securities	*0.23*	*0.16*	*0.17*	*0.14*	*0.12*	*0.11*	*0.11*	*0.10*	*0.10*	*0.07*	*76. Titres à court terme*
77. Bonds	*9.23*	*9.10*	*8.73*	*8.58*	*7.97*	*8.47*	*9.72*	*10.17*	*10.70*	*11.28*	*77. Obligations*
78. Shares and participations	*1.72*	*2.00*	*2.33*	*2.64*	*2.82*	*2.77*	*2.75*	*3.82*	*3.99*	*4.75*	*78. Actions et participations*
79. Claims on non-residents	*22.58*	*21.98*	*20.89*	*19.80*	*20.17*	*20.98*	*20.47*	*21.01*	*22.11*	*24.16*	*79. Créances sur des non-résidents*
80. Liabilities to non-residents	*24.25*	*24.18*	*23.07*	*22.42*	*23.02*	*22.46*	*21.86*	*22.13*	*24.36*	*27.39*	*80. Engagements envers des non-résidents*

* See notes on previous pages.

* Voir les notes en pages précédentes.

BELGIUM
All banks

BELGIQUE
Ensemble des banques

	1988	1989	1990	1991	1992	1993	1994	1995	1996	1997	
Million Belgian francs											*Millions de francs belges*
INCOME STATEMENT (1)											**COMPTE DE RESULTATS (1)**
1. Interest income	1329265	1682787	1895521	1952442	2005480	2315019	2132827	2283358	2197837	2434592	1. Produits financiers
2. Interest expenses	1080027	1416434	1624356	1672337	1705669	2014514	1835239	1977125	1869955	2113030	2. Frais financiers
3. Net interest income	249238	266353	271165	280105	299811	300505	297588	306234	327882	321562	3. Produits financiers nets
4. Non-interest income (net)	80695	78157	61232	73190	82626	120098	105695	126311	144962	189547	4. Produits non financiers (nets)
a. Fees and commissions receivable	..	..	..	..	..	*56685*	*64519*	*59256*	*71632*	*85962*	*a. Frais et commissions à recevoir*
b. Fees and commissions payable	..	..	..	..	..	*29672*	*35303*	*36274*	*38668*	*40896*	*b. Frais et commissions à payer*
c. Net profits or loss on financial operations	..	..	..	..	..	*63883*	*52076*	*76708*	*93487*	*97745*	*c. Profits ou pertes nets sur opérations financières*
d. Other	..	..	..	..	..	*29203*	*24404*	*26621*	*18510*	*46736*	*d. Autres*
5. Gross income	329933	344510	332397	353295	382437	420603	403283	432544	472844	511110	5. Résultat brut
6. Operating expenses	212760	230194	240333	247535	261115	285399	289217	292405	310662	326747	6. Frais d'exploitation
a. Staff costs (2)	*107866*	*114791*	*121940*	*125381*	*131918*	*174100*	*175976*	*177990*	*186721*	*187080*	*a. Dépenses en personnel (2)*
b. Property costs	..	..	..	..	..	*21841*	*22245*	*22324*	*23506*	*25293*	*b. Dépenses en immobilier*
c. Other	..	..	..	..	..	*89458*	*90996*	*92091*	*100435*	*114374*	*c. Autres*
7. Net income	117173	114316	92064	105760	121322	135204	114066	140139	162181	184363	7. Résultat net
8. Provisions (net)	67740	78687	39603	58965	75207	53610	33824	58595	57933	69593	8. Provisions (nettes)
a. Provisions on loans (3)	..	..	..	..	..	*47001*	*30522*	*37899*	*42393*	*27124*	*a. Provisions sur prêts (3)*
b. Provisions on securities (3)	..	..	..	..	..	*-1340*	*1298*	*-149*	*-44*	*983*	*b. Provisions sur titres (3)*
c. Other (3)	..	..	..	..	..	*6066*	*3602*	*20175*	*14634*	*36316*	*c. Autres (3)*
9. Profit before tax	49433	35629	52461	46795	46115	81595	80242	81544	104248	114770	9. Bénéfices avant impôt
10. Income tax	14125	13666	12569	13611	17336	23997	25186	29874	34762	39458	10. Impôt sur le revenu
11. Profit after tax	35308	21963	39892	33184	28779	57597	55056	51670	69487	75312	11. Bénéfices après impôt
12. Distributed profit (3)	..	..	..	..	..	26421	28612	27724	36046	38007	12. Bénéfices distribués (3)
13. Retained profit (3)	..	..	..	..	..	24273	21232	20963	32063	37590	13. Bénéfices mis en réserve (3)
BALANCE SHEET											**BILAN**
Assets											**Actif**
14. Cash & balance with Central bank	35067	41994	37856	55718	42907	39917	42867	45535	46769	57280	14. Caisse & solde auprès de la Banque centrale
15. Interbank deposits	5353508	5582422	6005165	6060663	6378056	7383496	7414043	8152849	8893637	9332314	15. Dépôts interbancaires
16. Loans	5221802	6018525	6380491	6733063	7129799	7578940	7942512	8137199	8627597	9293965	16. Prêts
17. Securities	4960616	5126815	5355436	5373426	5987508	6473389	6830544	7241355	8097481	8842524	17. Valeurs mobilières
18. Other assets	746342	835262	916069	939793	907116	1233296	1144407	1276004	1396835	1679228	18. Autres actifs
Liabilities											**Passif**
19. Capital & reserves	502301	594211	632723	722028	809018	577566	606290	632528	682414	759013	19. Capital et réserves
20. Borrowing from Central bank (2)	-	500	3000	4703	4710	1460	3010	144	3543	7032	20. Emprunts auprès de la Banque centrale (2)
21. Interbank deposits	7325812	7697079	8018769	7595140	7980658	9025249	9103159	10123046	11149706	11919446	21. Dépôts interbancaires
22. Non-bank deposits	5365347	5962446	6366836	6807430	7410378	7488836	7759118	8255435	9182088	10321693	22. Dépôts non bancaires
23. Bonds (4)	2271121	2316290	2632235	2929716	3066669	4079097	4242544	4068550	4052033	3849625	23. Obligations (4)
24. Other liabilities	852754	1034492	1041454	1103646	1173953	1536830	1660253	1773239	1992535	2348501	24. Autres engagements
Balance sheet total											**Total du bilan**
25. End-year total	16317335	17605018	18695017	19162663	20445386	22709038	23374374	24852942	27062319	29205310	25. En fin d'exercice
26. Average total (2)	15544881	16961177	18150018	18928840	19804025	22338475	23450655	24804448	26844638	29991071	26. Moyen (2)

BELGIUM
All banks

BELGIQUE
Ensemble des banques

	1988	1989	1990	1991	1992	1993	1994	1995	1996	1997	
Million Belgian francs											*Millions de francs belges*
Memorandum items											***Pour mémoire***
27. Short-term securities (2)	*911849*	*1013808*	*1073607*	*850297*	*872936*	*1150415*	*1505065*	*1152531*	*1113411*	*1004075*	*27. Titres à court terme(2)*
28. Bonds (2)	*2512578*	*2520453*	*2693915*	*2876444*	*3201526*	*5024732*	*5027663*	*5720084*	*6578329*	*7347277*	*28. Obligations (2)*
29. Shares and participations (2)	*104694*	*122660*	*114820*	*128649*	*127618*	*298241*	*297816*	*368741*	*405742*	*491171*	*29. Actions et participations (2)*
30. Claims on non-residents (2)	*5962069*	*6316380*	*6454242*	*6607820*	*6876595*	*8797310*	*8788407*	*9626972*	*10525588*	*12558296*	*30. Créances sur des non-résidents (2)*
31. Liabilities to non-residents (2)	*7067369*	*7545517*	*7708313*	*7506927*	*7806888*	*9533417*	*9847162*	*10812142*	*11721433*	*13631721*	*31. Engagements envers des non-résidents (2)*
Capital adequacy (3)											***Solvabilité (3)***
32. Tier 1 Capital	..	..	..	..	..	*571677*	*603701*	*648734*	*701387*	*786068*	*32. Fonds propres de base*
33. Tier 2 Capital	..	..	..	..	..	*268621*	*297262*	*320535*	*374005*	*430813*	*33. Fonds propres complémentaires*
34. Supervisory deductions	..	..	..	..	..	*107942*	*115888*	*171660*	*199220*	*271415*	*34. Eléments à déduire des fonds propres*
35. Total net capital resources	..	..	..	..	..	*732356*	*785075*	*797608*	*876172*	*945466*	*35. Total net des ressources en capital*
36. Risk-weighted assets	..	..	..	..	..	*5639469*	*5700938*	*6000763*	*6392740*	*6999456*	*36. Actifs pondérés des risques*
SUPPLEMENTARY INFORMATION											**RENSEIGNEMENTS COMPLEMENTAIRES**
37. Number of institutions	122	120	115	119	121	150	147	143	140	131	37. Nombre d'institutions
38. Number of branches	22231	19211	18389	17078	16405	19888	19159	18304	17963	17259	38. Nombre de succursales
39. Number of employees (x 1000)	76.0	79.0	79.0	77.0	76.0	76.3	76.2	76.5	76.9	76.9	39. Nombre de salariés (x 1000)

1. The Income Statement reporting period is the fiscal year ending 30 June of the following year.
2. Change in methodology.
3. The subitems (a., b., and c.) of item 8, Provisions (net), Distributed and Retained profit (items 12 and 13), and data on Capital adequacy (items 32 to 36) cover only credit institutions governed by Belgian law.
4. Bonds (item 23) include CD's.

Notes

- All banks: All credit institutions.

Change in methodology

- Up to 1992, Staff costs (item 6.a) and Short-term securities, Bonds, Shares and participations, Claims on non-residents, Liabilities to non-residents (items 27 through 31) cover only Commercial banks and Savings banks.
- Up to 1992, Borrowing from Central bank (item 20) covers only the Savings banks; and for the Commercial banks, Borrowing from Central bank is included under Interbank deposits (item 21).
- Beginning 1993, Average balance sheet totals (item 26) are the average of monthly data within the calendar year.

1. La période couverte pour le Compte de résultats est l'année fiscale se terminant le 30 juin de l'année suivante.
2. Changement méthodologique.
3. Seuls les établissements de crédit de droit belge sont inclus dans les sous-catégories (a., b., et c.) des Provisions (nettes) (poste 8), dans les Bénéfices distribués et Bénéfices mis en réserve (postes 12 et 13), et dans les données relatives à la Solvabilité (postes 32 à 36).
4. Les Obligations (poste 23) comprennent les certificats de dépôt.

Notes

- Ensemble des banques : Ensemble des établissements de crédit.

Changement méthodologique

- Jusqu'en 1992, seules les Banques commerciales et les Caisses d'épargne sont incluses dans les Dépenses en personnel (poste 6.a.) et les Titres à court terme, les Obligations, les Actions et participations, les Créances sur des non-résidents et les Engagements envers des non-résidents (postes 27 à 31).
- Jusqu'en 1992, seules les Caisses d'épargne sont incluses dans les Emprunts auprès de la Banque centrale (poste 20) ; les Emprunts auprès de la Banque centrale sont repris, pour les Banques commerciales, sous la rubrique Dépôts interbancaires (poste 21).
- A partir de 1993, la moyenne du total des actifs/passifs (poste 26) est la moyenne des données mensuelles de l'année calendrier.

BELGIUM — BELGIQUE

All banks — Ensemble des banques

	1988	1989	1990	1991	1992	1993	1994	1995	1996	1997	
Per cent											*Pourcentage*
INCOME STATEMENT ANALYSIS											**ANALYSE DU COMPTE DE RESULTATS**
% of average balance sheet total											**% du total moyen du bilan**
40. Interest income	8.55	9.92	10.44	10.31	10.13	10.36	9.09	9.21	8.19	8.12	40. Produits financiers
41. Interest expenses	6.95	8.35	8.95	8.83	8.61	9.02	7.83	7.97	6.97	7.05	41. Frais financiers
42. Net interest income	1.60	1.57	1.49	1.48	1.51	1.35	1.27	1.23	1.22	1.07	42. Produits financiers nets
43. Non-interest income (net)	0.52	0.46	0.34	0.39	0.42	0.54	0.45	0.51	0.54	0.63	43. Produits non financiers (nets)
a. Fees and commissions receivable	..	..	..	..	..	*0.25*	*0.28*	*0.24*	*0.27*	*0.29*	*a. Frais et commissions à recevoir*
b. Fees and commissions payable	..	..	..	..	..	*0.13*	*0.15*	*0.15*	*0.14*	*0.14*	*b. Frais et commissions à payer*
c. Net profits or loss on financial operations	..	..	..	..	..	*0.29*	*0.22*	*0.31*	*0.35*	*0.33*	*c. Profits ou pertes nets sur opérations financières*
d. Other	..	..	..	..	..	*0.13*	*0.10*	*0.11*	*0.07*	*0.16*	*d. Autres*
44. Gross income	2.12	2.03	1.83	1.87	1.93	1.88	1.72	1.74	1.76	1.70	44. Résultat brut
45. Operating expenses	1.37	1.36	1.32	1.31	1.32	1.28	1.23	1.18	1.16	1.09	45. Frais d'exploitation
a. Staff costs	*0.69*	*0.68*	*0.67*	*0.66*	*0.67*	*0.78*	*0.75*	*0.72*	*0.70*	*0.62*	*a. Dépenses en personnel*
b. Property costs	..	..	..	..	..	*0.10*	*0.09*	*0.09*	*0.09*	*0.08*	*b. Dépenses en immobilier*
c. Other	..	..	..	..	..	*0.40*	*0.39*	*0.37*	*0.37*	*0.38*	*c. Autres*
46. Net income	0.75	0.67	0.51	0.56	0.61	0.61	0.49	0.56	0.60	0.61	46. Résultat net
47. Provisions (net)	0.44	0.46	0.22	0.31	0.38	0.24	0.14	0.24	0.22	0.23	47. Provisions (nettes)
a. Provisions on loans	..	..	..	..	..	*0.21*	*0.13*	*0.15*	*0.16*	*0.09*	*a. Provisions sur prêts*
b. Provisions on securities	..	..	..	..	..	*-0.01*	*0.01*	-	-	-	*b. Provisions sur titres*
c. Other	..	..	..	..	..	*0.03*	*0.02*	*0.08*	*0.05*	*0.12*	*c. Autres*
48. Profit before tax	0.32	0.21	0.29	0.25	0.23	0.37	0.34	0.33	0.39	0.38	48. Bénéfices avant impôt
49. Income tax	0.09	0.08	0.07	0.07	0.09	0.11	0.11	0.12	0.13	0.13	49. Impôt sur le revenu
50. Profit after tax	0.23	0.13	0.22	0.18	0.15	0.26	0.23	0.21	0.26	0.25	50. Bénéfices après impôt
51. Distributed profit	..	..	..	..	..	0.12	0.12	0.11	0.13	0.13	51. Bénéfices distribués
52. Retained profit	..	..	..	..	..	0.11	0.09	0.08	0.12	0.13	52. Bénéfices mis en réserve
% of gross income											**% du total du résultat brut**
53. Net interest income	75.54	77.31	81.58	79.28	78.39	71.45	73.79	70.80	69.34	62.91	53. Produits financiers nets
54. Non-interest income (net)	24.46	22.69	18.42	20.72	21.61	28.55	26.21	29.20	30.66	37.09	54. Produits non financiers (nets)
a. Fees and commissions receivable	..	..	..	..	..	*13.48*	*16.00*	*13.70*	*15.15*	*16.82*	*a. Frais et commissions à recevoir*
b. Fees and commissions payable	..	..	..	..	..	*7.05*	*8.75*	*8.39*	*8.18*	*8.00*	*b. Frais et commissions à payer*
c. Net profits or loss on financial operations	..	..	..	..	..	*15.19*	*12.91*	*17.73*	*19.77*	*19.12*	*c. Profits ou pertes nets sur opérations financières*
d. Other	..	..	..	..	..	*6.94*	*6.05*	*6.15*	*3.91*	*9.14*	*d. Autres*
55. Operating expenses	64.49	66.82	72.30	70.06	68.28	67.85	71.72	67.60	65.70	63.93	55. Frais d'exploitation
a. Staff costs	*32.69*	*33.32*	*36.69*	*35.49*	*34.49*	*41.39*	*43.64*	*41.15*	*39.49*	*36.60*	*a. Dépenses en personnel*
b. Property costs	..	..	..	..	..	*5.19*	*5.52*	*5.16*	*4.97*	*4.95*	*b. Dépenses en immobilier*
c. Other	..	..	..	..	..	*21.27*	*22.56*	*21.29*	*21.24*	*22.38*	*c. Autres*
56. Net income	35.51	33.18	27.70	29.94	31.72	32.15	28.28	32.40	34.30	36.07	56. Résultat net
57. Provisions (net)	20.53	22.84	11.91	16.69	19.67	12.75	8.39	13.55	12.25	13.62	57. Provisions (nettes)
a. Provisions on loans	..	..	..	..	..	*11.17*	*7.57*	*8.76*	*8.97*	*5.31*	*a. Provisions sur prêts*
b. Provisions on securities	..	..	..	..	..	*-0.32*	*0.32*	*-0.03*	*-0.01*	*0.19*	*b. Provisions sur titres*
c. Other	..	..	..	..	..	*1.44*	*0.89*	*4.66*	*3.09*	*7.11*	*c. Autres*
58. Profit before tax	14.98	10.34	15.78	13.25	12.06	19.40	19.90	18.85	22.05	22.46	58. Bénéfices avant impôt
59. Income tax	4.28	3.97	3.78	3.85	4.53	5.71	6.25	6.91	7.35	7.72	59. Impôt sur le revenu
60. Profit after tax	10.70	6.38	12.00	9.39	7.53	13.69	13.65	11.95	14.70	14.73	60. Bénéfices après impôt
% of net income											**% du total du résultat net**
61. Provisions (net)	57.81	68.83	43.02	55.75	61.99	39.65	29.65	41.81	35.72	37.75	61. Provisions (nettes)
a. Provisions on loans	..	..	..	..	..	*34.76*	*26.76*	*27.04*	*26.14*	*14.71*	*a. Provisions sur prêts*
b. Provisions on securities	..	..	..	..	..	*-0.99*	*1.14*	*-0.11*	*-0.03*	*0.53*	*b. Provisions sur titres*
c. Other	..	..	..	..	..	*4.49*	*3.16*	*14.40*	*9.02*	*19.70*	*c. Autres*
62. Profit before tax	42.19	31.17	56.98	44.25	38.01	60.35	70.35	58.19	64.28	62.25	62. Bénéfices avant impôt
63. Income tax	12.05	11.95	13.65	12.87	14.29	17.75	22.08	21.32	21.43	21.40	63. Impôt sur le revenu
64. Profit after tax	30.13	19.21	43.33	31.38	23.72	42.60	48.27	36.87	42.85	40.85	64. Bénéfices après impôt

BELGIUM
All banks

BELGIQUE
Ensemble des banques

	1988	1989	1990	1991	1992	1993	1994	1995	1996	1997	
Per cent											*Pourcentage*
BALANCE SHEET ANALYSIS											**ANALYSE DU BILAN**
% of year-end balance sheet total											**% du total du bilan en fin d'exercice**
Assets											**Actif**
65. Cash & balance with Central bank	0.21	0.24	0.20	0.29	0.21	0.18	0.18	0.18	0.17	0.20	65. Caisse & solde auprès de la Banque centrale
66. Interbank deposits	32.81	31.71	32.12	31.63	31.20	32.51	31.72	32.80	32.86	31.95	66. Dépôts interbancaires
67. Loans	32.00	34.19	34.13	35.14	34.87	33.37	33.98	32.74	31.88	31.82	67. Prêts
68. Securities	30.40	29.12	28.65	28.04	29.29	28.51	29.22	29.14	29.92	30.28	68. Valeurs mobilières
69. Other assets	4.57	4.74	4.90	4.90	4.44	5.43	4.90	5.13	5.16	5.75	69. Autres actifs
Liabilities											**Passif**
70. Capital & reserves	3.08	3.38	3.38	3.77	3.96	2.54	2.59	2.55	2.52	2.60	70. Capital et réserves
71. Borrowing from Central bank	-	-	0.02	0.02	0.02	0.01	0.01	-	0.01	0.02	71. Emprunts auprès de la Banque centrale
72. Interbank deposits	44.90	43.72	42.89	39.64	39.03	39.74	38.95	40.73	41.20	40.81	72. Dépôts interbancaires
73. Non-bank deposits	32.88	33.87	34.06	35.52	36.24	32.98	33.19	33.22	33.93	35.34	73. Dépôts non bancaires
74. Bonds	13.92	13.16	14.08	15.29	15.00	17.96	18.15	16.37	14.97	13.18	74. Obligations
75. Other liabilities	5.23	5.88	5.57	5.76	5.74	6.77	7.10	7.13	7.36	8.04	75. Autres engagements
Memorandum items											***Pour mémoire***
76. Short-term securities	*5.59*	*5.76*	*5.74*	*4.44*	*4.27*	*5.07*	*6.44*	*4.64*	*4.11*	*3.44*	*76. Titres à court terme*
77. Bonds	*15.40*	*14.32*	*14.41*	*15.01*	*15.66*	*22.13*	*21.51*	*23.02*	*24.31*	*25.16*	*77. Obligations*
78. Shares and participations	*0.64*	*0.70*	*0.61*	*0.67*	*0.62*	*1.31*	*1.27*	*1.48*	*1.50*	*1.68*	*78. Actions et participations*
79. Claims on non-residents	*36.54*	*35.88*	*34.52*	*34.48*	*33.63*	*38.74*	*37.60*	*38.74*	*38.89*	*43.00*	*79. Créances sur des non-résidents*
80. Liabilities to non-residents	*43.31*	*42.86*	*41.23*	*39.17*	*38.18*	*41.98*	*42.13*	*43.50*	*43.31*	*46.68*	*80. Engagements envers des non-résidents*

* See notes on previous pages.

* Voir les notes en pages précédentes.

BELGIUM / BELGIQUE

Large commercial banks / Grandes banques commerciales

	1993	1994	1995	1996	1997	
Million Belgian francs						*Millions de francs belges*
INCOME STATEMENT (1)						**COMPTE DE RESULTATS (1)**
1. Interest income	1281150	1217040	1360429	1341374	1535176	1. Produits financiers
2. Interest expenses	1087225	1013271	1145661	1114836	1310484	2. Frais financiers
3. Net interest income	193926	203769	214769	226538	224692	3. Produits financiers nets
4. Non-interest income (net)	91249	73694	86398	108113	138325	4. Produits non financiers (nets)
a. Fees and commissions receivable	*39361*	*45316*	*41837*	*49616*	*61179*	*a. Frais et commissions à recevoir*
b. Fees and commissions payable	*15185*	*18355*	*18523*	*18952*	*22667*	*b. Frais et commissions à payer*
c. Net profits or loss on financial operations	*50990*	*37673*	*55617*	*73634*	*74790*	*c. Profits ou pertes nets sur opérations financières*
d. Other	*16083*	*9060*	*7467*	*3815*	*25024*	*d. Autres*
5. Gross income	285175	277463	301167	334651	363017	5. Résultat brut
6. Operating expenses	196494	201892	206124	218834	235211	6. Frais d'exploitation
a. Staff costs	*128992*	*131646*	*133451*	*140160*	*141674*	*a. Dépenses en personnel*
b. Property costs	*16004*	*16555*	*16968*	*18135*	*19962*	*b. Dépenses en immobilier*
c. Other	*51498*	*53691*	*55705*	*60539*	*73575*	*c. Autres*
7. Net income	88681	75571	95042	115817	127806	7. Résultat net
8. Provisions (net)	37552	23395	34607	40396	45521	8. Provisions (nettes)
a. Provisions on loans	*32769*	*20943*	*18266*	*29828*	*17498*	*a. Provisions sur prêts*
b. Provisions on securities	*-718*	*652*	*147*	*77*	*728*	*b. Provisions sur titres*
c. Other	*5502*	*1800*	*16194*	*10491*	*27295*	*c. Autres*
9. Profit before tax	51128	52175	60436	75421	82285	9. Bénéfices avant impôt
10. Income tax	13198	17317	19853	24095	26413	10. Impôt sur le revenu
11. Profit after tax	37931	34858	40583	51326	55872	11. Bénéfices après impôt
12. Distributed profit	19224	20141	20804	27683	24818	12. Bénéfices distribués
13. Retained profit	18707	14717	19779	23643	31054	13. Bénéfices mis en réserve
BALANCE SHEET						**BILAN**
Assets						**Actif**
14. Cash & balance with Central bank	30228	31777	33670	34993	44930	14. Caisse & solde auprès de la Banque centrale
15. Interbank deposits	3059133	3402542	4182238	4811522	5092948	15. Dépôts interbancaires
16. Loans	5147328	5492457	5859360	6390336	7149489	16. Prêts
17. Securities	4061679	4334893	4779033	5429732	6209422	17. Valeurs mobilières
18. Other assets	706483	636347	734500	847890	1218442	18. Autres actifs
Liabilities						**Passif**
19. Capital & reserves	363098	385581	408750	451876	538281	19. Capital et réserves
20. Borrowing from Central bank	71	2557	5	2788	5369	20. Emprunts auprès de la Banque centrale
21. Interbank deposits	3574888	4056504	5220195	6277841	6780530	21. Dépôts interbancaires
22. Non-bank deposits	5198454	5421379	5827810	6515317	7602799	22. Dépôts non bancaires
23. Bonds (2)	2936188	3027136	2986817	2977916	3083098	23. Obligations (2)
24. Other liabilities	932150	1004858	1145223	1288733	1705153	24. Autres engagements
Balance sheet total						**Total du bilan**
25. End-year total	13004850	13898017	15588799	17514472	19715231	25. En fin d'exercice
26. Average total	12833218	13802110	15117061	17008015	19657810	26. Moyen

BELGIUM
Large commercial banks

BELGIQUE
Grandes banques commerciales

	1993	1994	1995	1996	1997	
Million Belgian francs						*Millions de francs belges*
Memorandum items						***Pour mémoire***
27. Short-term securities	*651818*	*985783*	*856287*	*791256*	*650475*	*27. Titres à court terme*
28. Bonds	*3159493*	*3098200*	*3601259*	*4292608*	*5137679*	*28. Obligations*
29. Shares and participations	*250368*	*250910*	*321487*	*345869*	*421269*	*29. Actions et participations*
30. Claims on non-residents	*4234801*	*4422209*	*5371526*	*6240641*	*7843543*	*30. Créances sur des non-résidents*
31. Liabilities to non-residents	*4639942*	*5012838*	*6214828*	*7009011*	*8633945*	*31. Engagements envers des non-résidents*
Capital adequacy						***Solvabilité***
32. Tier 1 Capital	*383364*	*407611*	*439279*	*483362*	*574870*	*32. Fonds propres de base*
33. Tier 2 Capital	*210356*	*234527*	*261832*	*311438*	*368716*	*33. Fonds propres complémentaires*
34. Supervisory deductions	*96367*	*101063*	*152905*	*171545*	*237483*	*34. Eléments à déduire des fonds propres*
35. Total net capital resources	*497353*	*541076*	*548207*	*623255*	*706103*	*35. Total net des ressources en capital*
36. Risk-weighted assets	*3992668*	*4001959*	*4339477*	*4684826*	*5389788*	*36. Actifs pondérés des risques*
SUPPLEMENTARY INFORMATION						**RENSEIGNEMENTS COMPLEMENTAIRES**
37. Number of institutions	7	7	7	7	7	37. Nombre d'institutions
38. Number of branches	..	..	..	..	..	38. Nombre de succursales
39. Number of employees (x 1000)	..	..	..	..	..	39. Nombre de salariés (x 1000)

1. The Income Statement reporting period is the fiscal year ending 30 June of the following year.
2. Bonds (item 23) include CD's.

Notes

- Large commercial banks: 7 large credit institutions governed by Belgian law.
- Average balance sheet totals (item 26) are the average of monthly data within the calendar year.

1. La période couverte pour le Compte de résultats est l'année fiscale se terminant le 30 juin de l'année suivante.
2. Les Obligations (poste 23) comprennent les certificats de dépôt.

Notes

- Grandes banques commerciales : 7 grands établissements de crédit de droit belge.
- La moyenne du total des actifs/passifs (poste 26) est la moyenne des données mensuelles de l'année calendrier.

BELGIUM

Large commercial banks

BELGIQUE

Grandes banques commerciales

	1993	1994	1995	1996	1997	
Per cent						*Pourcentage*
INCOME STATEMENT ANALYSIS						**ANALYSE DU COMPTE DE RESULTATS**
% of average balance sheet total						**% du total moyen du bilan**
40. Interest income	9.98	8.82	9.00	7.89	7.81	40. Produits financiers
41. Interest expenses	8.47	7.34	7.58	6.55	6.67	41. Frais financiers
42. Net interest income	1.51	1.48	1.42	1.33	1.14	42. Produits financiers nets
43. Non-interest income (net)	0.71	0.53	0.57	0.64	0.70	43. Produits non financiers (nets)
a. Fees and commissions receivable	*0.31*	*0.33*	*0.28*	*0.29*	*0.31*	*a. Frais et commissions à recevoir*
b. Fees and commissions payable	*0.12*	*0.13*	*0.12*	*0.11*	*0.12*	*b. Frais et commissions à payer*
c. Net profits or loss on financial operations	*0.40*	*0.27*	*0.37*	*0.43*	*0.38*	*c. Profits ou pertes nets sur opérations financières*
d. Other	*0.13*	*0.07*	*0.05*	*0.02*	*0.13*	*d. Autres*
44. Gross income	2.22	2.01	1.99	1.97	1.85	44. Résultat brut
45. Operating expenses	1.53	1.46	1.36	1.29	1.20	45. Frais d'exploitation
a. Staff costs	*1.01*	*0.95*	*0.88*	*0.82*	*0.72*	*a. Dépenses en personnel*
b. Property costs	*0.12*	*0.12*	*0.11*	*0.11*	*0.10*	*b. Dépenses en immobilier*
c. Other	*0.40*	*0.39*	*0.37*	*0.36*	*0.37*	*c. Autres*
46. Net income	0.69	0.55	0.63	0.68	0.65	46. Résultat net
47. Provisions (net)	0.29	0.17	0.23	0.24	0.23	47. Provisions (nettes)
a. Provisions on loans	*0.26*	*0.15*	*0.12*	*0.18*	*0.09*	*a. Provisions sur prêts*
b. Provisions on securities	*-0.01*	-	-	-	-	*b. Provisions sur titres*
c. Other	*0.04*	*0.01*	*0.11*	*0.06*	*0.14*	*c. Autres*
48. Profit before tax	0.40	0.38	0.40	0.44	0.42	48. Bénéfices avant impôt
49. Income tax	0.10	0.13	0.13	0.14	0.13	49. Impôt sur le revenu
50. Profit after tax	0.30	0.25	0.27	0.30	0.28	50. Bénéfices après impôt
51. Distributed profit	0.15	0.15	0.14	0.16	0.13	51. Bénéfices distribués
52. Retained profit	0.15	0.11	0.13	0.14	0.16	52. Bénéfices mis en réserve
% of gross income						**% du total du résultat brut**
53. Net interest income	68.00	73.44	71.31	67.69	61.90	53. Produits financiers nets
54. Non-interest income (net)	32.00	26.56	28.69	32.31	38.10	54. Produits non financiers (nets)
a. Fees and commissions receivable	*13.80*	*16.33*	*13.89*	*14.83*	*16.85*	*a. Frais et commissions à recevoir*
b. Fees and commissions payable	*5.32*	*6.62*	*6.15*	*5.66*	*6.24*	*b. Frais et commissions à payer*
c. Net profits or loss on financial operations	*17.88*	*13.58*	*18.47*	*22.00*	*20.60*	*c. Profits ou pertes nets sur opérations financières*
d. Other	*5.64*	*3.27*	*2.48*	*1.14*	*6.89*	*d. Autres*
55. Operating expenses	68.90	72.76	68.44	65.39	64.79	55. Frais d'exploitation
a. Staff costs	*45.23*	*47.45*	*44.31*	*41.88*	*39.03*	*a. Dépenses en personnel*
b. Property costs	*5.61*	*5.97*	*5.63*	*5.42*	*5.50*	*b. Dépenses en immobilier*
c. Other	*18.06*	*19.35*	*18.50*	*18.09*	*20.27*	*c. Autres*
56. Net income	31.10	27.24	31.56	34.61	35.21	56. Résultat net
57. Provisions (net)	13.17	8.43	11.49	12.07	12.54	57. Provisions (nettes)
a. Provisions on loans	*11.49*	*7.55*	*6.07*	*8.91*	*4.82*	*a. Provisions sur prêts*
b. Provisions on securities	*-0.25*	*0.23*	*0.05*	*0.02*	*0.20*	*b. Provisions sur titres*
c. Other	*1.93*	*0.65*	*5.38*	*3.13*	*7.52*	*c. Autres*
58. Profit before tax	17.93	18.80	20.07	22.54	22.67	58. Bénéfices avant impôt
59. Income tax	4.63	6.24	6.59	7.20	7.28	59. Impôt sur le revenu
60. Profit after tax	13.30	12.56	13.48	15.34	15.39	60. Bénéfices après impôt
% of net income						**% du total du résultat net**
61. Provisions (net)	42.35	30.96	36.41	34.88	35.62	61. Provisions (nettes)
a. Provisions on loans	*36.95*	*27.71*	*19.22*	*25.75*	*13.69*	*a. Provisions sur prêts*
b. Provisions on securities	*-0.81*	*0.86*	*0.15*	*0.07*	*0.57*	*b. Provisions sur titres*
c. Other	*6.20*	*2.38*	*17.04*	*9.06*	*21.36*	*c. Autres*
62. Profit before tax	57.65	69.04	63.59	65.12	64.38	62. Bénéfices avant impôt
63. Income tax	14.88	22.91	20.89	20.80	20.67	63. Impôt sur le revenu
64. Profit after tax	42.77	46.13	42.70	44.32	43.72	64. Bénéfices après impôt

BELGIUM / BELGIQUE

Large commercial banks / Grandes banques commerciales

	1993	1994	1995	1996	1997	
Per cent						*Pourcentage*
BALANCE SHEET ANALYSIS						**ANALYSE DU BILAN**
% of year-end balance sheet total						**% du total du bilan en fin d'exercice**
Assets						**Actif**
65. Cash & balance with Central bank	0.23	0.23	0.22	0.20	0.23	65. Caisse & solde auprès de la Banque centrale
66. Interbank deposits	23.52	24.48	26.83	27.47	25.83	66. Dépôts interbancaires
67. Loans	39.58	39.52	37.59	36.49	36.26	67. Prêts
68. Securities	31.23	31.19	30.66	31.00	31.50	68. Valeurs mobilières
69. Other assets	5.43	4.58	4.71	4.84	6.18	69. Autres actifs
Liabilities						**Passif**
70. Capital & reserves	2.79	2.77	2.62	2.58	2.73	70. Capital et réserves
71. Borrowing from Central bank	-	0.02	-	0.02	0.03	71. Emprunts auprès de la Banque centrale
72. Interbank deposits	27.49	29.19	33.49	35.84	34.39	72. Dépôts interbancaires
73. Non-bank deposits	39.97	39.01	37.38	37.20	38.56	73. Dépôts non bancaires
74. Bonds	22.58	21.78	19.16	17.00	15.64	74. Obligations
75. Other liabilities	7.17	7.23	7.35	7.36	8.65	75. Autres engagements
Memorandum items						***Pour mémoire***
76. Short-term securities	*5.01*	*7.09*	*5.49*	*4.52*	*3.30*	*76. Titres à court terme*
77. Bonds	*24.29*	*22.29*	*23.10*	*24.51*	*26.06*	*77. Obligations*
78. Shares and participations	*1.93*	*1.81*	*2.06*	*1.97*	*2.14*	*78. Actions et participations*
79. Claims on non-residents	*32.56*	*31.82*	*34.46*	*35.63*	*39.78*	*79. Créances sur des non-résidents*
80. Liabilities to non-residents	*35.68*	*36.07*	*39.87*	*40.02*	*43.79*	*80. Engagements envers des non-résidents*

* See notes on previous pages.

* Voir les notes en pages précédentes.

BELGIUM
Other commercial banks

BELGIQUE
Autres banques commerciales

	1993	1994	1995	1996	1997	
Million Belgian francs						*Millions de francs belges*
INCOME STATEMENT (1)						**COMPTE DE RESULTATS (1)**
1. Interest income	627827	590269	608121	584084	546677	1. Produits financiers
2. Interest expenses	555498	511289	529893	495404	465501	2. Frais financiers
3. Net interest income	72329	78980	78228	88681	81176	3. Produits financiers nets
4. Non-interest income (net)	25844	16045	23666	19474	30603	4. Produits non financiers (nets)
a. Fees and commissions receivable	*11686*	*13904*	*12942*	*15273*	*17053*	*a. Frais et commissions à recevoir*
b. Fees and commissions payable	*12670*	*14668*	*15640*	*16432*	*15758*	*b. Frais et commissions à payer*
c. Net profits or loss on financial operations	*22743*	*11306*	*17521*	*16728*	*18660*	*c. Profits ou pertes nets sur opérations financières*
d. Other	*4085*	*5503*	*8843*	*3905*	*10649*	*d. Autres*
5. Gross income	98173	95024	101893	108154	111779	5. Résultat brut
6. Operating expenses	65114	62108	62810	65716	64201	6. Frais d'exploitation
a. Staff costs	*36710*	*35693*	*35911*	*37382*	*35708*	*a. Dépenses en personnel*
b. Property costs	*4904*	*4632*	*4392*	*4452*	*4537*	*b. Dépenses en immobilier*
c. Other	*23500*	*21783*	*22507*	*23881*	*23955*	*c. Autres*
7. Net income	33059	32917	39083	42439	47579	7. Résultat net
8. Provisions (net)	14174	12027	23318	16587	18901	8. Provisions (nettes)
a. Provisions on loans	*14232*	*9579*	*19634*	*12565*	*9626*	*a. Provisions sur prêts*
b. Provisions on securities	*-622*	*646*	*-296*	*-121*	*254*	*b. Provisions sur titres*
c. Other	*564*	*1802*	*3981*	*4143*	*9020*	*c. Autres*
9. Profit before tax	18885	20890	15764	25852	28678	9. Bénéfices avant impôt
10. Income tax	6122	5904	7660	9068	8954	10. Impôt sur le revenu
11. Profit after tax	12763	14986	8104	16784	19724	11. Bénéfices après impôt
12. Distributed profit	7196	8471	6920	8364	13189	12. Bénéfices distribués
13. Retained profit	5566	6515	1185	8420	6536	13. Bénéfices mis en réserve
BALANCE SHEET						**BILAN**
Assets						**Actif**
14. Cash & balance with Central bank	9575	10721	11518	11674	12206	14. Caisse & solde auprès de la Banque centrale
15. Interbank deposits	1118246	1023831	1184998	1287170	1221981	15. Dépôts interbancaires
16. Loans	1833655	1944078	1762703	1764628	1620883	16. Prêts
17. Securities	1916079	2131886	2162660	2304041	2285369	17. Valeurs mobilières
18. Other assets	347028	317977	356139	346811	298535	18. Autres actifs
Liabilities						**Passif**
19. Capital & reserves	182772	190108	198338	205803	197317	19. Capital et réserves
20. Borrowing from Central bank	296	105	115	335	686	20. Emprunts auprès de la Banque centrale
21. Interbank deposits	1713207	1722631	1793719	1799817	1911957	21. Dépôts interbancaires
22. Non-bank deposits	1773010	1860848	1961619	2176752	2158423	22. Dépôts non bancaires
23. Bonds (2)	1137472	1210938	1080300	1068315	760938	23. Obligations (2)
24. Other liabilities	417826	443863	443927	463303	409653	24. Autres engagements
Balance sheet total						**Total du bilan**
25. End-year total	5224582	5428493	5478017	5714325	5438974	25. En fin d'exercice
26. Average total	5196893	5467253	5578690	5798668	5918897	26. Moyen

BELGIUM
Other commercial banks

BELGIQUE
Autres banques commerciales

	1993	1994	1995	1996	1997	
Million Belgian francs						*Millions de francs belges*
Memorandum items						***Pour mémoire***
27. Short-term securities	*282895*	*332652*	*210696*	*199221*	*257233*	*27. Titres à court terme*
28. Bonds	*1587012*	*1754107*	*1906494*	*2046236*	*1960028*	*28. Obligations*
29. Shares and participations	*46172*	*45127*	*45469*	*58584*	*68108*	*29. Actions et participations*
30. Claims on non-residents	*1367087*	*1429363*	*1559219*	*1590035*	*1720590*	*30. Créances sur des non-résidents*
31. Liabilities to non-residents	*1270527*	*1474170*	*1551397*	*1546559*	*1564324*	*31. Engagements envers des non-résidents*
Capital adequacy						***Solvabilité***
32. Tier 1 Capital	*188313*	*196090*	*209455*	*218026*	*211198*	*32. Fonds propres de base*
33. Tier 2 Capital	*58265*	*62735*	*58702*	*62567*	*62097*	*33. Fonds propres complémentaires*
34. Supervisory deductions	*11575*	*14826*	*18756*	*27675*	*33932*	*34. Eléments à déduire des fonds propres*
35. Total net capital resources	*235003*	*243999*	*249401*	*252917*	*239363*	*35. Total net des ressources en capital*
36. Risk-weighted assets	*1646802*	*1698979*	*1661285*	*1707913*	*1609668*	*36. Actifs pondérés des risques*
SUPPLEMENTARY INFORMATION						**RENSEIGNEMENTS COMPLEMENTAIRES**
37. Number of institutions	105	100	97	93	86	37. Nombre d'institutions
38. Number of branches	..	..	..	..	..	38. Nombre de succursales
39. Number of employees (x 1000)	..	..	..	..	..	39. Nombre de salariés (x 1000)

1. The Income Statement reporting period is the fiscal year ending 30 June of the following year.

2. Bonds (item 23) include CD's.

Notes

- Other commercial banks: Other credit institutions governed by Belgian law.
- Average balance sheet totals (item 26) are the average of monthly data within the calendar year.

1. La période couverte pour le Compte de résultats est l'année fiscale se terminant le 30 juin de l'année suivante.

2. Les Obligations (poste 23) comprennent les certificats de dépôt.

Notes

- Autres banques commerciales : Autres établissements de crédit de droit belge.
- La moyenne du total des actifs/passifs (poste 26) est la moyenne des données mensuelles de l'année calendrier.

BELGIUM
Other commercial banks

BELGIQUE
Autres banques commerciales

	1993	1994	1995	1996	1997	
Per cent						*Pourcentage*
INCOME STATEMENT ANALYSIS						**ANALYSE DU COMPTE DE RESULTATS**
% of average balance sheet total						**% du total moyen du bilan**
40. Interest income	12.08	10.80	10.90	10.07	9.24	40. Produits financiers
41. Interest expenses	10.69	9.35	9.50	8.54	7.86	41. Frais financiers
42. Net interest income	1.39	1.44	1.40	1.53	1.37	42. Produits financiers nets
43. Non-interest income (net)	0.50	0.29	0.42	0.34	0.52	43. Produits non financiers (nets)
a. Fees and commissions receivable	*0.22*	*0.25*	*0.23*	*0.26*	*0.29*	*a. Frais et commissions à recevoir*
b. Fees and commissions payable	*0.24*	*0.27*	*0.28*	*0.28*	*0.27*	*b. Frais et commissions à payer*
c. Net profits or loss on financial operations	*0.44*	*0.21*	*0.31*	*0.29*	*0.32*	*c. Profits ou pertes nets sur opérations financières*
d. Other	*0.08*	*0.10*	*0.16*	*0.07*	*0.18*	*d. Autres*
44. Gross income	1.89	1.74	1.83	1.87	1.89	44. Résultat brut
45. Operating expenses	1.25	1.14	1.13	1.13	1.08	45. Frais d'exploitation
a. Staff costs	*0.71*	*0.65*	*0.64*	*0.64*	*0.60*	*a. Dépenses en personnel*
b. Property costs	*0.09*	*0.08*	*0.08*	*0.08*	*0.08*	*b. Dépenses en immobilier*
c. Other	*0.45*	*0.40*	*0.40*	*0.41*	*0.40*	*c. Autres*
46. Net income	0.64	0.60	0.70	0.73	0.80	46. Résultat net
47. Provisions (net)	0.27	0.22	0.42	0.29	0.32	47. Provisions (nettes)
a. Provisions on loans	*0.27*	*0.18*	*0.35*	*0.22*	*0.16*	*a. Provisions sur prêts*
b. Provisions on securities	*-0.01*	*0.01*	*-0.01*	-	-	*b. Provisions sur titres*
c. Other	*0.01*	*0.03*	*0.07*	*0.07*	*0.15*	*c. Autres*
48. Profit before tax	0.36	0.38	0.28	0.45	0.48	48. Bénéfices avant impôt
49. Income tax	0.12	0.11	0.14	0.16	0.15	49. Impôt sur le revenu
50. Profit after tax	0.25	0.27	0.15	0.29	0.33	50. Bénéfices après impôt
51. Distributed profit	0.14	0.15	0.12	0.14	0.22	51. Bénéfices distribués
52. Retained profit	0.11	0.12	0.02	0.15	0.11	52. Bénéfices mis en réserve
% of gross income						**% du total du résultat brut**
53. Net interest income	73.68	83.12	76.77	82.00	72.62	53. Produits financiers nets
54. Non-interest income (net)	26.32	16.89	23.23	18.01	27.38	54. Produits non financiers (nets)
a. Fees and commissions receivable	*11.90*	*14.63*	*12.70*	*14.12*	*15.26*	*a. Frais et commissions à recevoir*
b. Fees and commissions payable	*12.91*	*15.44*	*15.35*	*15.19*	*14.10*	*b. Frais et commissions à payer*
c. Net profits or loss on financial operations	*23.17*	*11.90*	*17.20*	*15.47*	*16.69*	*c. Profits ou pertes nets sur opérations financières*
d. Other	*4.16*	*5.79*	*8.68*	*3.61*	*9.53*	*d. Autres*
55. Operating expenses	66.33	65.36	61.64	60.76	57.44	55. Frais d'exploitation
a. Staff costs	*37.39*	*37.56*	*35.24*	*34.56*	*31.95*	*a. Dépenses en personnel*
b. Property costs	*5.00*	*4.87*	*4.31*	*4.12*	*4.06*	*b. Dépenses en immobilier*
c. Other	*23.94*	*22.92*	*22.09*	*22.08*	*21.43*	*c. Autres*
56. Net income	33.67	34.64	38.36	39.24	42.57	56. Résultat net
57. Provisions (net)	14.44	12.66	22.88	15.34	16.91	57. Provisions (nettes)
a. Provisions on loans	*14.50*	*10.08*	*19.27*	*11.62*	*8.61*	*a. Provisions sur prêts*
b. Provisions on securities	*-0.63*	*0.68*	*-0.29*	*-0.11*	*0.23*	*b. Provisions sur titres*
c. Other	*0.57*	*1.90*	*3.91*	*3.83*	*8.07*	*c. Autres*
58. Profit before tax	19.24	21.98	15.47	23.90	25.66	58. Bénéfices avant impôt
59. Income tax	6.24	6.21	7.52	8.38	8.01	59. Impôt sur le revenu
60. Profit after tax	13.00	15.77	7.95	15.52	17.65	60. Bénéfices après impôt
% of net income						**% du total du résultat net**
61. Provisions (net)	42.87	36.54	59.66	39.08	39.73	61. Provisions (nettes)
a. Provisions on loans	*43.05*	*29.10*	*50.24*	*29.61*	*20.23*	*a. Provisions sur prêts*
b. Provisions on securities	*-1.88*	*1.96*	*-0.76*	*-0.29*	*0.53*	*b. Provisions sur titres*
c. Other	*1.71*	*5.47*	*10.19*	*9.76*	*18.96*	*c. Autres*
62. Profit before tax	57.13	63.46	40.33	60.92	60.27	62. Bénéfices avant impôt
63. Income tax	18.52	17.94	19.60	21.37	18.82	63. Impôt sur le revenu
64. Profit after tax	38.61	45.53	20.74	39.55	41.46	64. Bénéfices après impôt

BELGIUM
Other commercial banks

BELGIQUE
Autres banques commerciales

	1993	1994	1995	1996	1997	
Per cent						*Pourcentage*
BALANCE SHEET ANALYSIS						**ANALYSE DU BILAN**
% of year-end balance sheet total						**% du total du bilan en fin d'exercice**
Assets						**Actif**
65. Cash & balance with Central bank	0.18	0.20	0.21	0.20	0.22	65. Caisse & solde auprès de la Banque centrale
66. Interbank deposits	21.40	18.86	21.63	22.53	22.47	66. Dépôts interbancaires
67. Loans	35.10	35.81	32.18	30.88	29.80	67. Prêts
68. Securities	36.67	39.27	39.48	40.32	42.02	68. Valeurs mobilières
69. Other assets	6.64	5.86	6.50	6.07	5.49	69. Autres actifs
Liabilities						**Passif**
70. Capital & reserves	3.50	3.50	3.62	3.60	3.63	70. Capital et réserves
71. Borrowing from Central bank	0.01	-	-	0.01	0.01	71. Emprunts auprès de la Banque centrale
72. Interbank deposits	32.79	31.73	32.74	31.50	35.15	72. Dépôts interbancaires
73. Non-bank deposits	33.94	34.28	35.81	38.09	39.68	73. Dépôts non bancaires
74. Bonds	21.77	22.31	19.72	18.70	13.99	74. Obligations
75. Other liabilities	8.00	8.18	8.10	8.11	7.53	75. Autres engagements
Memorandum items						***Pour mémoire***
76. Short-term securities	*5.41*	*6.13*	*3.85*	*3.49*	*4.73*	*76. Titres à court terme*
77. Bonds	*30.38*	*32.31*	*34.80*	*35.81*	*36.04*	*77. Obligations*
78. Shares and participations	*0.88*	*0.83*	*0.83*	*1.03*	*1.25*	*78. Actions et participations*
79. Claims on non-residents	*26.17*	*26.33*	*28.46*	*27.83*	*31.63*	*79. Créances sur des non-résidents*
80. Liabilities to non-residents	*24.32*	*27.16*	*28.32*	*27.06*	*28.76*	*80. Engagements envers des non-résidents*

* See notes on previous pages.

* Voir les notes en pages précédentes.

BELGIUM
Foreign commercial banks

BELGIQUE
Banques commerciales étrangères

	1993	1994	1995	1996	1997	
Million Belgian francs						*Millions de francs belges*
INCOME STATEMENT (1)						**COMPTE DE RESULTATS (1)**
1. Interest income	406042	325518	314808	272379	352739	1. Produits financiers
2. Interest expenses	371791	310678	301571	259716	337045	2. Frais financiers
3. Net interest income	34250	14840	13237	12663	15694	3. Produits financiers nets
4. Non-interest income (net)	3005	15957	16247	17375	20619	4. Produits non financiers (nets)
a. Fees and commissions receivable	*5638*	*5299*	*4476*	*6743*	*7731*	*a. Frais et commissions à recevoir*
b. Fees and commissions payable	*1817*	*2280*	*2111*	*3284*	*2470*	*b. Frais et commissions à payer*
c. Net profits or loss on financial operations	*-9850*	*3097*	*3570*	*3125*	*4295*	*c. Profits ou pertes nets sur opérations financières*
d. Other	*9035*	*9842*	*10311*	*10791*	*11064*	*d. Autres*
5. Gross income	37256	30796	29484	30038	36313	5. Résultat brut
6. Operating expenses	23791	25217	23471	26112	27335	6. Frais d'exploitation
a. Staff costs	*8398*	*8637*	*8628*	*9179*	*9698*	*a. Dépenses en personnel*
b. Property costs	*933*	*1058*	*964*	*920*	*794*	*b. Dépenses en immobilier*
c. Other	*14460*	*15522*	*13879*	*16014*	*16844*	*c. Autres*
7. Net income	13465	5579	6014	3926	8978	7. Résultat net
8. Provisions (net)	1883	-1598	670	950	5171	8. Provisions (nettes)
a. Provisions on loans	..	..	..	..	..	*a. Provisions sur prêts*
b. Provisions on securities	..	..	..	..	..	*b. Provisions sur titres*
c. Other	..	..	..	..	..	*c. Autres*
9. Profit before tax	11582	7177	5344	2976	3807	9. Bénéfices avant impôt
10. Income tax	4678	1965	2361	1599	4091	10. Impôt sur le revenu
11. Profit after tax	6904	5212	2983	1377	-284	11. Bénéfices après impôt
12. Distributed profit	..	..	..	..	..	12. Bénéfices distribués
13. Retained profit	..	..	..	..	..	13. Bénéfices mis en réserve
BALANCE SHEET						**BILAN**
Assets						**Actif**
14. Cash & balance with Central bank	113	369	348	102	144	14. Caisse & solde auprès de la Banque centrale
15. Interbank deposits	3206118	2987670	2785613	2794945	3017385	15. Dépôts interbancaires
16. Loans	597958	505977	515136	472633	523592	16. Prêts
17. Securities	495631	363765	299662	363708	347733	17. Valeurs mobilières
18. Other assets	179786	190083	185366	202134	162252	18. Autres actifs
Liabilities						**Passif**
19. Capital & reserves	31696	30600	25440	24734	23414	19. Capital et réserves
20. Borrowing from Central bank	1092	348	24	420	977	20. Emprunts auprès de la Banque centrale
21. Interbank deposits	3737154	3324024	3109132	3072048	3226959	21. Dépôts interbancaires
22. Non-bank deposits	517372	476891	466007	490019	560471	22. Dépôts non bancaires
23. Bonds (2)	5437	4469	1433	5802	5589	23. Obligations (2)
24. Other liabilities	186854	211532	184089	240499	233695	24. Autres engagements
Balance sheet total						**Total du bilan**
25. End-year total	4479606	4047864	3786126	3833522	4051106	25. En fin d'exercice
26. Average total	4308364	4181292	4108698	4037955	4414364	26. Moyen

BELGIUM
Foreign commercial banks

BELGIQUE
Banques commerciales étrangères

	1993	1994	1995	1996	1997	
Million Belgian francs						*Millions de francs belges*
Memorandum items						***Pour mémoire***
27. Short-term securities	*215702*	*186629*	*85548*	*122934*	*96367*	*27. Titres à court terme*
28. Bonds	*278227*	*175356*	*212331*	*239485*	*249571*	*28. Obligations*
29. Shares and participations	*1701*	*1779*	*1783*	*1289*	*1795*	*29. Actions et participations*
30. Claims on non-residents	*3195423*	*2936836*	*2696228*	*2694912*	*2994163*	*30. Créances sur des non-résidents*
31. Liabilities to non-residents	*3622948*	*3360155*	*3045918*	*3165863*	*3433453*	*31. Engagements envers des non-résidents*
Capital adequacy						***Solvabilité***
32. Tier 1 Capital	..	..	..	..	..	*32. Fonds propres de base*
33. Tier 2 Capital	..	..	..	..	..	*33. Fonds propres complémentaires*
34. Supervisory deductions	..	..	..	..	..	*34. Eléments à déduire des fonds propres*
35. Total net capital resources	..	..	..	..	..	*35. Total net des ressources en capital*
36. Risk-weighted assets	..	..	..	..	..	*36. Actifs pondérés des risques*
SUPPLEMENTARY INFORMATION						**RENSEIGNEMENTS COMPLEMENTAIRES**
37. Number of institutions	38	40	39	40	38	37. Nombre d'institutions
38. Number of branches	..	..	..	..	..	38. Nombre de succursales
39. Number of employees (x 1000)	..	..	..	..	..	39. Nombre de salariés (x 1000)

1. The Income Statement reporting period is the fiscal year ending 30 June of the following year.

2. Bonds (item 23) include CD's.

Notes

- Foreign commercial banks: Branches of credit institutions governed by foreign law.

- Average balance sheet totals (item 26) are the average of monthly data within the calendar year.

1. La période couverte pour le Compte de résultats est l'année fiscale se terminant le 30 juin de l'année suivante.

2. Les Obligations (poste 23) comprennent les certificats de dépôt.

Notes

- Banques commerciales étrangères : Succursales d'établissements de crédit de droit étranger.

- La moyenne du total des actifs/passifs (poste 26) est la moyenne des données mensuelles de l'année calendrier.

BELGIUM — BELGIQUE

Foreign commercial banks — Banques commerciales étrangères

	1993	1994	1995	1996	1997	
Per cent						*Pourcentage*
INCOME STATEMENT ANALYSIS						**ANALYSE DU COMPTE DE RESULTATS**
% of average balance sheet total						**% du total moyen du bilan**
40. Interest income	9.42	7.79	7.66	6.75	7.99	40. Produits financiers
41. Interest expenses	8.63	7.43	7.34	6.43	7.64	41. Frais financiers
42. Net interest income	0.79	0.35	0.32	0.31	0.36	42. Produits financiers nets
43. Non-interest income (net)	0.07	0.38	0.40	0.43	0.47	43. Produits non financiers (nets)
a. Fees and commissions receivable	*0.13*	*0.13*	*0.11*	*0.17*	*0.18*	*a. Frais et commissions à recevoir*
b. Fees and commissions payable	*0.04*	*0.05*	*0.05*	*0.08*	*0.06*	*b. Frais et commissions à payer*
c. Net profits or loss on financial operations	*-0.23*	*0.07*	*0.09*	*0.08*	*0.10*	*c. Profits ou pertes nets sur opérations financières*
d. Other	*0.21*	*0.24*	*0.25*	*0.27*	*0.25*	*d. Autres*
44. Gross income	0.86	0.74	0.72	0.74	0.82	44. Résultat brut
45. Operating expenses	0.55	0.60	0.57	0.65	0.62	45. Frais d'exploitation
a. Staff costs	*0.19*	*0.21*	*0.21*	*0.23*	*0.22*	*a. Dépenses en personnel*
b. Property costs	*0.02*	*0.03*	*0.02*	*0.02*	*0.02*	*b. Dépenses en immobilier*
c. Other	*0.34*	*0.37*	*0.34*	*0.40*	*0.38*	*c. Autres*
46. Net income	0.31	0.13	0.15	0.10	0.20	46. Résultat net
47. Provisions (net)	0.04	-0.04	0.02	0.02	0.12	47. Provisions (nettes)
a. Provisions on loans	..	..	..	..	..	*a. Provisions sur prêts*
b. Provisions on securities	..	..	..	..	..	*b. Provisions sur titres*
c. Other	..	..	..	..	..	*c. Autres*
48. Profit before tax	0.27	0.17	0.13	0.07	0.09	48. Bénéfices avant impôt
49. Income tax	0.11	0.05	0.06	0.04	0.09	49. Impôt sur le revenu
50. Profit after tax	0.16	0.12	0.07	0.03	-0.01	50. Bénéfices après impôt
51. Distributed profit	..	..	..	..	..	51. Bénéfices distribués
52. Retained profit	..	..	..	..	..	52. Bénéfices mis en réserve
% of gross income						**% du total du résultat brut**
53. Net interest income	91.93	48.19	44.90	42.16	43.22	53. Produits financiers nets
54. Non-interest income (net)	8.07	51.82	55.10	57.84	56.78	54. Produits non financiers (nets)
a. Fees and commissions receivable	*15.13*	*17.21*	*15.18*	*22.45*	*21.29*	*a. Frais et commissions à recevoir*
b. Fees and commissions payable	*4.88*	*7.40*	*7.16*	*10.93*	*6.80*	*b. Frais et commissions à payer*
c. Net profits or loss on financial operations	*-26.44*	*10.06*	*12.11*	*10.40*	*11.83*	*c. Profits ou pertes nets sur opérations financières*
d. Other	*24.25*	*31.96*	*34.97*	*35.92*	*30.47*	*d. Autres*
55. Operating expenses	63.86	81.88	79.61	86.93	75.28	55. Frais d'exploitation
a. Staff costs	*22.54*	*28.05*	*29.26*	*30.56*	*26.71*	*a. Dépenses en personnel*
b. Property costs	*2.50*	*3.44*	*3.27*	*3.06*	*2.19*	*b. Dépenses en immobilier*
c. Other	*38.81*	*50.40*	*47.07*	*53.31*	*46.39*	*c. Autres*
56. Net income	36.14	18.12	20.40	13.07	24.72	56. Résultat net
57. Provisions (net)	5.05	-5.19	2.27	3.16	14.24	57. Provisions (nettes)
a. Provisions on loans	..	..	..	..	..	*a. Provisions sur prêts*
b. Provisions on securities	..	..	..	..	..	*b. Provisions sur titres*
c. Other	..	..	..	..	..	*c. Autres*
58. Profit before tax	31.09	23.30	18.13	9.91	10.48	58. Bénéfices avant impôt
59. Income tax	12.56	6.38	8.01	5.32	11.27	59. Impôt sur le revenu
60. Profit after tax	18.53	16.92	10.12	4.58	-0.78	60. Bénéfices après impôt
% of net income						**% du total du résultat net**
61. Provisions (net)	13.98	-28.64	11.14	24.20	57.60	61. Provisions (nettes)
a. Provisions on loans	..	..	..	..	..	*a. Provisions sur prêts*
b. Provisions on securities	..	..	..	..	..	*b. Provisions sur titres*
c. Other	..	..	..	..	..	*c. Autres*
62. Profit before tax	86.02	128.64	88.86	75.80	42.40	62. Bénéfices avant impôt
63. Income tax	34.74	35.22	39.26	40.73	45.57	63. Impôt sur le revenu
64. Profit after tax	51.27	93.42	49.60	35.07	-3.16	64. Bénéfices après impôt

BELGIUM
Foreign commercial banks

BELGIQUE
Banques commerciales étrangères

	1993	1994	1995	1996	1997	
Per cent						*Pourcentage*
BALANCE SHEET ANALYSIS						**ANALYSE DU BILAN**
% of year-end balance sheet total						**% du total du bilan en fin d'exercice**
Assets						**Actif**
65. Cash & balance with Central bank	-	0.01	0.01	-	-	65. Caisse & solde auprès de la Banque centrale
66. Interbank deposits	71.57	73.81	73.57	72.91	74.48	66. Dépôts interbancaires
67. Loans	13.35	12.50	13.61	12.33	12.92	67. Prêts
68. Securities	11.06	8.99	7.91	9.49	8.58	68. Valeurs mobilières
69. Other assets	4.01	4.70	4.90	5.27	4.01	69. Autres actifs
Liabilities						**Passif**
70. Capital & reserves	0.71	0.76	0.67	0.65	0.58	70. Capital et réserves
71. Borrowing from Central bank	0.02	0.01	-	0.01	0.02	71. Emprunts auprès de la Banque centrale
72. Interbank deposits	83.43	82.12	82.12	80.14	79.66	72. Dépôts interbancaires
73. Non-bank deposits	11.55	11.78	12.31	12.78	13.84	73. Dépôts non bancaires
74. Bonds	0.12	0.11	0.04	0.15	0.14	74. Obligations
75. Other liabilities	4.17	5.23	4.86	6.27	5.77	75. Autres engagements
Memorandum items						***Pour mémoire***
76. Short-term securities	*4.82*	*4.61*	*2.26*	*3.21*	*2.38*	*76. Titres à court terme*
77. Bonds	*6.21*	*4.33*	*5.61*	*6.25*	*6.16*	*77. Obligations*
78. Shares and participations	*0.04*	*0.04*	*0.05*	*0.03*	*0.04*	*78. Actions et participations*
79. Claims on non-residents	*71.33*	*72.55*	*71.21*	*70.30*	*73.91*	*79. Créances sur des non-résidents*
80. Liabilities to non-residents	*80.88*	*83.01*	*80.45*	*82.58*	*84.75*	*80. Engagements envers des non-résidents*

* See notes on previous pages.

* Voir les notes en pages précédentes.

CANADA
Commercial banks

CANADA
Banques commerciales

	1989	1990	1991	1992	1993	1994	1995	1996	1997	1998 p	
Million Canadian dollars											*Millions de dollars canadiens*
INCOME STATEMENT											**COMPTE DE RESULTATS**
1. Interest income	49671	54109	51530	44115	41878	44623	56376	58853	60147	71364	1. Produits financiers
2. Interest expenses	35516	40006	35688	27324	24122	25588	36854	37714	38347	48962	2. Frais financiers
3. Net interest income	14154	14102	15842	16791	17756	19035	19522	21139	21800	22402	3. Produits financiers nets
4. Non-interest income (net)	5831	6321	6821	7533	8419	10058	10395	12417	17828	20302	4. Produits non financiers (nets)
a. Fees and commissions receivable	..	..	..	..	..	..	..	..	..	..	*a. Frais et commissions à recevoir*
b. Fees and commissions payable	..	..	..	..	..	..	..	..	..	..	*b. Frais et commissions à payer*
c. Net profits or loss on financial operations	..	..	..	..	..	..	..	..	..	..	*c. Profits ou pertes nets sur opérations financières*
d. Other	..	..	..	..	..	..	..	..	..	..	*d. Autres*
5. Gross income	19985	20423	22663	24324	26175	29093	29917	33556	39628	42704	5. Résultat brut
6. Operating expenses	11798	12996	14063	15367	16713	18493	19041	21283	25385	28807	6. Frais d'exploitation
a. Staff costs	*6785*	*7433*	*7970*	*8502*	*9250*	*10269*	*10500*	*11882*	*14044*	*15975*	*a. Dépenses en personnel*
b. Property costs	..	..	..	..	..	..	..	..	..	..	*b. Dépenses en immobilier*
c. Other	..	..	..	..	..	..	..	..	..	..	*c. Autres*
7. Net income	8187	7427	8600	8957	9462	10600	10876	12273	14243	13897	7. Résultat net
8. Provisions (net)	5108	1692	2704	6035	4780	3469	2560	1950	1985	2453	8. Provisions (nettes)
a. Provisions on loans	*5108*	*1692*	*2704*	*6035*	*4780*	*3469*	*2560*	*1950*	*1985*	*2453*	*a. Provisions sur prêts*
b. Provisions on securities	..	..	..	..	..	..	..	..	..	..	*b. Provisions sur titres*
c. Other	..	..	..	..	..	..	..	..	..	..	*c. Autres*
9. Profit before tax	3079	5736	5896	2922	4682	7131	8316	10323	12258	11444	9. Bénéfices avant impôt
10. Income tax	1106	2127	2086	969	1666	2744	3028	3867	4529	4101	10. Impôt sur le revenu
11. Profit after tax	1974	3608	3810	1953	3016	4387	5288	6456	7729	7343	11. Bénéfices après impôt
12. Distributed profit	..	..	..	..	..	..	..	..	..	..	12. Bénéfices distribués
13. Retained profit	..	..	..	..	..	..	..	..	..	..	13. Bénéfices mis en réserve
BALANCE SHEET											**BILAN**
Assets											**Actif**
14. Cash & balance with Central bank	6446	5653	6113	5897	5179	4433	4381	5219	4385	4716	14. Caisse & solde auprès de la Banque centrale
15. Interbank deposits	33346	32947	33609	36007	38148	53801	75468	72336	86435	72528	15. Dépôts interbancaires
16. Loans	351748	375601	393693	421772	457155	501495	532732	607840	704624	752955	16. Prêts
17. Securities	46347	49147	68855	89920	115151	135128	157242	180259	193452	241177	17. Valeurs mobilières
18. Other assets	18914	20289	19457	22444	27208	28653	31609	35368	98997	157756	18. Autres actifs
Liabilities											**Passif**
19. Capital & reserves	24926	27326	31066	31899	35352	38635	41600	43817	51183	58485	19. Capital et réserves
20. Borrowing from Central bank	261	38	53	6	311	61	204	20	17	52	20. Emprunts auprès de la Banque centrale
21. Interbank deposits	54211	60214	60955	81352	81890	97693	113583	125943	133549	143576	21. Dépôts interbancaires
22. Non-bank deposits	339626	354773	381258	405925	445195	481651	516121	541764	629902	687118	22. Dépôts non bancaires
23. Bonds	8270	9212	10817	12376	15309	16208	16977	17695	22851	23919	23. Obligations
24. Other liabilities	29507	32074	37578	44482	64784	89262	112947	171784	250391	315983	24. Autres engagements
Balance sheet total											**Total du bilan**
25. End-year total	456801	483637	521727	576040	642841	723510	801432	901022	1087893	1229132	25. En fin d'exercice
26. Average total	439775	470219	502682	548883	609441	683176	762471	851227	994457	1158512	26. Moyen

CANADA
Commercial banks

CANADA
Banques commerciales

	1989	1990	1991	1992	1993	1994	1995	1996	1997	1998 p	
Million Canadian dollars											*Millions de dollars canadiens*
Memorandum items											***Pour mémoire***
27. Short-term securities	..	..	..	..	..	..	..	..	..	..	*27. Titres à court terme*
28. Bonds	..	..	..	..	..	..	..	..	..	..	*28. Obligations*
29. Shares and participations	..	..	..	..	..	..	..	..	..	..	*29. Actions et participations*
30. Claims on non-residents	..	..	..	..	..	..	..	..	..	..	*30. Créances sur des non-résidents*
31. Liabilities to non-residents	..	..	..	..	..	..	..	..	..	..	*31. Engagements envers des non-résidents*
Capital adequacy											***Solvabilité***
32. Tier 1 Capital	..	..	..	..	..	..	..	..	..	..	*32. Fonds propres de base*
33. Tier 2 Capital	..	..	..	..	..	..	..	..	..	..	*33. Fonds propres complémentaires*
34. Supervisory deductions	..	..	..	..	..	..	..	..	..	..	*34. Eléments à déduire des fonds propres*
35. Total net capital resources	..	..	..	..	..	..	..	..	..	..	*35. Total net des ressources en capital*
36. Risk-weighted assets	..	..	..	..	..	..	..	..	..	..	*36. Actifs pondérés des risques*
SUPPLEMENTARY INFORMATION											**RENSEIGNEMENTS COMPLEMENTAIRES**
37. Number of institutions	10	10	10	10	11	11	11	11	9	9	37. Nombre d'institutions
38. Number of branches	..	..	..	..	..	..	..	..	..	..	38. Nombre de succursales
39. Number of employees (x 1000)	..	..	..	..	..	..	..	..	..	..	39. Nombre de salariés (x 1000)

Notes

- The reporting period is the fiscal year ending 31 October.

Notes

- La période couverte est l'exercice financier qui se termine le 31 octobre

CANADA

Commercial banks

CANADA

Banques commerciales

	1989	1990	1991	1992	1993	1994	1995	1996	1997	1998 p	
Per cent											*Pourcentage*
INCOME STATEMENT ANALYSIS											**ANALYSE DU COMPTE DE RESULTATS**
% of average balance sheet total											**% du total moyen du bilan**
40. Interest income	11.29	11.51	10.25	8.04	6.87	6.53	7.39	6.91	6.05	6.16	40. Produits financiers
41. Interest expenses	8.08	8.51	7.10	4.98	3.96	3.75	4.83	4.43	3.86	4.23	41. Frais financiers
42. Net interest income	3.22	3.00	3.15	3.06	2.91	2.79	2.56	2.48	2.19	1.93	42. Produits financiers nets
43. Non-interest income (net)	1.33	1.34	1.36	1.37	1.38	1.47	1.36	1.46	1.79	1.75	43. Produits non financiers (nets)
a. Fees and commissions receivable	..	..	..	..	..	..	..	..	..	..	*a. Frais et commissions à recevoir*
b. Fees and commissions payable	..	..	..	..	..	..	..	..	..	..	*b. Frais et commissions à payer*
c. Net profits or loss on financial operations	..	..	..	..	..	..	..	..	..	..	*c. Profits ou pertes nets sur opérations financières*
d. Other	..	..	..	..	..	..	..	..	..	..	*d. Autres*
44. Gross income	4.54	4.34	4.51	4.43	4.29	4.26	3.92	3.94	3.98	3.69	44. Résultat brut
45. Operating expenses	2.68	2.76	2.80	2.80	2.74	2.71	2.50	2.50	2.55	2.49	45. Frais d'exploitation
a. Staff costs	*1.54*	*1.58*	*1.59*	*1.55*	*1.52*	*1.50*	*1.38*	*1.40*	*1.41*	*1.38*	*a. Dépenses en personnel*
b. Property costs	..	..	..	..	..	..	..	..	..	..	*b. Dépenses en immobilier*
c. Other	..	..	..	..	..	..	..	..	..	..	*c. Autres*
46. Net income	1.86	1.58	1.71	1.63	1.55	1.55	1.43	1.44	1.43	1.20	46. Résultat net
47. Provisions (net)	1.16	0.36	0.54	1.10	0.78	0.51	0.34	0.23	0.20	0.21	47. Provisions (nettes)
a. Provisions on loans	*1.16*	*0.36*	*0.54*	*1.10*	*0.78*	*0.51*	*0.34*	*0.23*	*0.20*	*0.21*	*a. Provisions sur prêts*
b. Provisions on securities	..	..	..	..	..	..	..	..	..	..	*b. Provisions sur titres*
c. Other	..	..	..	..	..	..	..	..	..	..	*c. Autres*
48. Profit before tax	0.70	1.22	1.17	0.53	0.77	1.04	1.09	1.21	1.23	0.99	48. Bénéfices avant impôt
49. Income tax	0.25	0.45	0.41	0.18	0.27	0.40	0.40	0.45	0.46	0.35	49. Impôt sur le revenu
50. Profit after tax	0.45	0.77	0.76	0.36	0.49	0.64	0.69	0.76	0.78	0.63	50. Bénéfices après impôt
51. Distributed profit	..	..	..	..	..	..	..	..	..	..	51. Bénéfices distribués
52. Retained profit	..	..	..	..	..	..	..	..	..	..	52. Bénéfices mis en réserve
% of gross income											**% du total du résultat brut**
53. Net interest income	70.82	69.05	69.90	69.03	67.84	65.43	65.25	63.00	55.01	52.46	53. Produits financiers nets
54. Non-interest income (net)	29.18	30.95	30.10	30.97	32.16	34.57	34.75	37.00	44.99	47.54	54. Produits non financiers (nets)
a. Fees and commissions receivable	..	..	..	..	..	..	..	..	..	..	*a. Frais et commissions à recevoir*
b. Fees and commissions payable	..	..	..	..	..	..	..	..	..	..	*b. Frais et commissions à payer*
c. Net profits or loss on financial operations	..	..	..	..	..	..	..	..	..	..	*c. Profits ou pertes nets sur opérations financières*
d. Other	..	..	..	..	..	..	..	..	..	..	*d. Autres*
55. Operating expenses	59.03	63.63	62.05	63.18	63.85	63.57	63.65	63.43	64.06	67.46	55. Frais d'exploitation
a. Staff costs	*33.95*	*36.40*	*35.17*	*34.95*	*35.34*	*35.30*	*35.10*	*35.41*	*35.44*	*37.41*	*a. Dépenses en personnel*
b. Property costs	..	..	..	..	..	..	..	..	..	..	*b. Dépenses en immobilier*
c. Other	..	..	..	..	..	..	..	..	..	..	*c. Autres*
56. Net income	40.97	36.37	37.95	36.82	36.15	36.43	36.35	36.57	35.94	32.54	56. Résultat net
57. Provisions (net)	25.56	8.28	11.93	24.81	18.26	11.92	8.56	5.81	5.01	5.74	57. Provisions (nettes)
a. Provisions on loans	*25.56*	*8.28*	*11.93*	*24.81*	*18.26*	*11.92*	*8.56*	*5.81*	*5.01*	*5.74*	*a. Provisions sur prêts*
b. Provisions on securities	..	..	..	..	..	..	..	..	..	..	*b. Provisions sur titres*
c. Other	..	..	..	..	..	..	..	..	..	..	*c. Autres*
58. Profit before tax	15.41	28.09	26.02	12.01	17.89	24.51	27.80	30.76	30.93	26.80	58. Bénéfices avant impôt
59. Income tax	5.53	10.41	9.20	3.98	6.36	9.43	10.12	11.52	11.43	9.60	59. Impôt sur le revenu
60. Profit after tax	9.88	17.67	16.81	8.03	11.52	15.08	17.68	19.24	19.50	17.20	60. Bénéfices après impôt
% of net income											**% du total du résultat net**
61. Provisions (net)	62.39	22.78	31.44	67.38	50.52	32.73	23.54	15.89	13.94	17.65	61. Provisions (nettes)
a. Provisions on loans	*62.39*	*22.78*	*31.44*	*67.38*	*50.52*	*32.73*	*23.54*	*15.89*	*13.94*	*17.65*	*a. Provisions sur prêts*
b. Provisions on securities	..	..	..	..	..	..	..	..	..	..	*b. Provisions sur titres*
c. Other	..	..	..	..	..	..	..	..	..	..	*c. Autres*
62. Profit before tax	37.61	77.23	68.56	32.62	49.48	67.27	76.46	84.11	86.06	82.35	62. Bénéfices avant impôt
63. Income tax	13.51	28.64	24.26	10.82	17.61	25.89	27.84	31.51	31.80	29.51	63. Impôt sur le revenu
64. Profit after tax	24.11	48.58	44.30	21.80	31.87	41.39	48.62	52.60	54.27	52.84	64. Bénéfices après impôt

CANADA

Commercial banks / Banques commerciales

	1989	1990	1991	1992	1993	1994	1995	1996	1997	1998 p	
Per cent											*Pourcentage*
BALANCE SHEET ANALYSIS											**ANALYSE DU BILAN**
% of year-end balance sheet total											**% du total du bilan en fin d'exercice**
Assets											**Actif**
65. Cash & balance with Central bank	1.41	1.17	1.17	1.02	0.81	0.61	0.55	0.58	0.40	0.38	65. Caisse & solde auprès de la Banque centrale
66. Interbank deposits	7.30	6.81	6.44	6.25	5.93	7.44	9.42	8.03	7.95	5.90	66. Dépôts interbancaires
67. Loans	77.00	77.66	75.46	73.22	71.11	69.31	66.47	67.46	64.77	61.26	67. Prêts
68. Securities	10.15	10.16	13.20	15.61	17.91	18.68	19.62	20.01	17.78	19.62	68. Valeurs mobilières
69. Other assets	4.14	4.20	3.73	3.90	4.23	3.96	3.94	3.93	9.10	12.83	69. Autres actifs
Liabilities											**Passif**
70. Capital & reserves	5.46	5.65	5.95	5.54	5.50	5.34	5.19	4.86	4.70	4.76	70. Capital et réserves
71. Borrowing from Central bank	0.06	0.01	0.01	-	0.05	0.01	0.03	-	-	-	71. Emprunts auprès de la Banque centrale
72. Interbank deposits	11.87	12.45	11.68	14.12	12.74	13.50	14.17	13.98	12.28	11.68	72. Dépôts interbancaires
73. Non-bank deposits	74.35	73.36	73.08	70.47	69.25	66.57	64.40	60.13	57.90	55.90	73. Dépôts non bancaires
74. Bonds	1.81	1.90	2.07	2.15	2.38	2.24	2.12	1.96	2.10	1.95	74. Obligations
75. Other liabilities	6.46	6.63	7.20	7.72	10.08	12.34	14.09	19.07	23.02	25.71	75. Autres engagements
Memorandum items											***Pour mémoire***
76. Short-term securities	..	..	..	..	..	..	..	..	..	..	*76. Titres à court terme*
77. Bonds	..	..	..	..	..	..	..	..	..	..	*77. Obligations*
78. Shares and participations	..	..	..	..	..	..	..	..	..	..	*78. Actions et participations*
79. Claims on non-residents	..	..	..	..	..	..	..	..	..	..	*79. Créances sur des non-résidents*
80. Liabilities to non-residents	..	..	..	..	..	..	..	..	..	..	*80. Engagements envers des non-résidents*

* See notes on previous pages.

* Voir les notes en pages précédentes.

CANADA
Foreign commercial banks

CANADA
Banques commerciales étrangères

	1989	1990	1991	1992	1993	1994	1995	1996	1997	1998 p	
Million Canadian dollars											*Millions de dollars canadiens*
INCOME STATEMENT											**COMPTE DE RESULTATS**
1. Interest income	4003	4945	4669	3792	3515	3608	4927	4530	4534	5945	1. Produits financiers
2. Interest expenses	3250	4030	3664	2908	2628	2580	3696	3161	3248	4483	2. Frais financiers
3. Net interest income	753	916	1005	884	887	1028	1231	1369	1286	1462	3. Produits financiers nets
4. Non-interest income (net)	378	511	775	787	884	935	769	884	1209	1326	4. Produits non financiers (nets)
a. Fees and commissions receivable	..	..	..	..	..	..	..	..	..	..	*a. Frais et commissions à recevoir*
b. Fees and commissions payable	..	..	..	..	..	..	..	..	..	..	*b. Frais et commissions à payer*
c. Net profits or loss on financial operations	..	..	..	..	..	..	..	..	..	..	*c. Profits ou pertes nets sur opérations financières*
d. Other	..	..	..	..	..	..	..	..	..	..	*d. Autres*
5. Gross income	1131	1427	1780	1671	1771	1963	2000	2252	2495	2788	5. Résultat brut
6. Operating expenses	626	865	1143	1168	1273	1311	1386	1541	1765	2066	6. Frais d'exploitation
a. Staff costs	*308*	*376*	*426*	*434*	*478*	*515*	*541*	*643*	*723*	*823*	*a. Dépenses en personnel*
b. Property costs	..	..	..	..	..	..	..	..	..	..	*b. Dépenses en immobilier*
c. Other	..	..	..	..	..	..	..	..	..	..	*c. Autres*
7. Net income	505	562	637	503	498	652	614	711	730	722	7. Résultat net
8. Provisions (net)	106	288	524	1102	628	451	241	189	95	384	8. Provisions (nettes)
a. Provisions on loans	*106*	*288*	*524*	*1102*	*628*	*451*	*241*	*189*	*95*	*384*	*a. Provisions sur prêts*
b. Provisions on securities	..	..	..	..	..	..	..	..	..	..	*b. Provisions sur titres*
c. Other	..	..	..	..	..	..	..	..	..	..	*c. Autres*
9. Profit before tax	398	274	113	-599	-130	201	373	522	635	338	9. Bénéfices avant impôt
10. Income tax	164	112	53	-212	13	150	163	216	255	121	10. Impôt sur le revenu
11. Profit after tax	235	162	60	-386	-143	51	210	306	380	217	11. Bénéfices après impôt
12. Distributed profit	..	..	..	..	..	..	..	..	..	..	12. Bénéfices distribués
13. Retained profit	..	..	..	..	..	..	..	..	..	..	13. Bénéfices mis en réserve
BALANCE SHEET											**BILAN**
Assets											**Actif**
14. Cash & balance with Central bank	267	123	146	103	162	204	228	190	257	306	14. Caisse & solde auprès de la Banque centrale
15. Interbank deposits	7221	6177	7427	8260	6230	8650	7450	7434	8707	6032	15. Dépôts interbancaires
16. Loans	31037	33987	34140	36285	37245	39464	43983	46071	53406	56927	16. Prêts
17. Securities	4664	5932	7071	9221	12474	11170	11599	12186	14501	15244	17. Valeurs mobilières
18. Other assets	1167	1507	1303	1736	2722	2053	2959	7300	10527	18061	18. Autres actifs
Liabilities											**Passif**
19. Capital & reserves	3416	3973	3952	3697	3830	4012	4176	4255	4983	5822	19. Capital et réserves
20. Borrowing from Central bank	-	-	-	-	-	-	-	-	-	-	20. Emprunts auprès de la Banque centrale
21. Interbank deposits	13080	15281	15530	17049	15202	18419	19746	15756	19821	18866	21. Dépôts interbancaires
22. Non-bank deposits	24545	23863	24857	27680	30565	30942	33492	37580	40076	43170	22. Dépôts non bancaires
23. Bonds	292	557	873	1147	1155	1272	1552	1540	1651	1849	23. Obligations
24. Other liabilities	3023	4052	4875	6032	8081	6896	7253	14050	20867	26863	24. Autres engagements
Balance sheet total											**Total du bilan**
25. End-year total	44356	47726	50087	55605	58833	61541	66219	73181	87398	96570	25. En fin d'exercice
26. Average total	42440	46041	48906	52846	57219	60187	63880	69700	80290	91984	26. Moyen

CANADA

Foreign commercial banks

CANADA

Banques commerciales étrangères

	1989	1990	1991	1992	1993	1994	1995	1996	1997	1998 p	
Million Canadian dollars											*Millions de dollars canadiens*
Memorandum items											***Pour mémoire***
27. Short-term securities	..	..	..	..	..	..	..	..	..	..	*27. Titres à court terme*
28. Bonds	..	..	..	..	..	..	..	..	..	..	*28. Obligations*
29. Shares and participations	..	..	..	..	..	..	..	..	..	..	*29. Actions et participations*
30. Claims on non-residents	..	..	..	..	..	..	..	..	..	..	*30. Créances sur des non-résidents*
31. Liabilities to non-residents	..	..	..	..	..	..	..	..	..	..	*31. Engagements envers des non-résidents*
Capital adequacy											***Solvabilité***
32. Tier 1 Capital	..	..	..	..	..	..	..	..	..	..	*32. Fonds propres de base*
33. Tier 2 Capital	..	..	..	..	..	..	..	..	..	..	*33. Fonds propres complémentaires*
34. Supervisory deductions	..	..	..	..	..	..	..	..	..	..	*34. Eléments à déduire des fonds propres*
35. Total net capital resources	..	..	..	..	..	..	..	..	..	..	*35. Total net des ressources en capital*
36. Risk-weighted assets	..	..	..	..	..	..	..	..	..	..	*36. Actifs pondérés des risques*
SUPPLEMENTARY INFORMATION											**RENSEIGNEMENTS COMPLEMENTAIRES**
37. Number of institutions	57	56	56	56	56	53	50	50	45	45	37. Nombre d'institutions
38. Number of branches	..	..	..	..	..	..	..	..	..	..	38. Nombre de succursales
39. Number of employees (x 1000)	..	..	..	..	..	..	..	..	..	..	39. Nombre de salariés (x 1000)

Notes

- The reporting period is the fiscal year ending 31 October.

Notes

- La période couverte est l'exercice financier qui se termine le 31 octobre

CANADA | CANADA

Foreign commercial banks | Banques commerciales étrangères

	1989	1990	1991	1992	1993	1994	1995	1996	1997	1998 p	
Per cent											*Pourcentage*
INCOME STATEMENT ANALYSIS											**ANALYSE DU COMPTE DE RESULTATS**
% of average balance sheet total											**% du total moyen du bilan**
40. Interest income	9.43	10.74	9.55	7.18	6.14	5.99	7.71	6.50	5.65	6.46	40. Produits financiers
41. Interest expenses	7.66	8.75	7.49	5.50	4.59	4.29	5.79	4.54	4.05	4.87	41. Frais financiers
42. Net interest income	1.77	1.99	2.05	1.67	1.55	1.71	1.93	1.96	1.60	1.59	42. Produits financiers nets
43. Non-interest income (net)	0.89	1.11	1.58	1.49	1.54	1.55	1.20	1.27	1.51	1.44	43. Produits non financiers (nets)
a. Fees and commissions receivable	..	..	..	..	..	..	..	..	..	..	*a. Frais et commissions à recevoir*
b. Fees and commissions payable	..	..	..	..	..	..	..	..	..	..	*b. Frais et commissions à payer*
c. Net profits or loss on financial operations	..	..	..	..	..	..	..	..	..	..	*c. Profits ou pertes nets sur opérations financières*
d. Other	..	..	..	..	..	..	..	..	..	..	*d. Autres*
44. Gross income	2.66	3.10	3.64	3.16	3.10	3.26	3.13	3.23	3.11	3.03	44. Résultat brut
45. Operating expenses	1.48	1.88	2.34	2.21	2.22	2.18	2.17	2.21	2.20	2.25	45. Frais d'exploitation
a. Staff costs	*0.73*	*0.82*	*0.87*	*0.82*	*0.84*	*0.86*	*0.85*	*0.92*	*0.90*	*0.89*	*a. Dépenses en personnel*
b. Property costs	..	..	..	..	..	..	..	..	..	..	*b. Dépenses en immobilier*
c. Other	..	..	..	..	..	..	..	..	..	..	*c. Autres*
46. Net income	1.19	1.22	1.30	0.95	0.87	1.08	0.96	1.02	0.91	0.78	46. Résultat net
47. Provisions (net)	0.25	0.63	1.07	2.09	1.10	0.75	0.38	0.27	0.12	0.42	47. Provisions (nettes)
a. Provisions on loans	*0.25*	*0.63*	*1.07*	*2.09*	*1.10*	*0.75*	*0.38*	*0.27*	*0.12*	*0.42*	*a. Provisions sur prêts*
b. Provisions on securities	..	..	..	..	..	..	..	..	..	..	*b. Provisions sur titres*
c. Other	..	..	..	..	..	..	..	..	..	..	*c. Autres*
48. Profit before tax	0.94	0.60	0.23	-1.13	-0.23	0.33	0.58	0.75	0.79	0.37	48. Bénéfices avant impôt
49. Income tax	0.39	0.24	0.11	-0.40	0.02	0.25	0.26	0.31	0.32	0.13	49. Impôt sur le revenu
50. Profit after tax	0.55	0.35	0.12	-0.73	-0.25	0.08	0.33	0.44	0.47	0.24	50. Bénéfices après impôt
51. Distributed profit	..	..	..	..	..	..	..	..	..	..	51. Bénéfices distribués
52. Retained profit	..	..	..	..	..	..	..	..	..	..	52. Bénéfices mis en réserve
% of gross income											**% du total du résultat brut**
53. Net interest income	66.58	64.19	56.46	52.90	50.08	52.37	61.55	60.79	51.54	52.44	53. Produits financiers nets
54. Non-interest income (net)	33.42	35.81	43.54	47.10	49.92	47.63	38.45	39.25	48.46	47.56	54. Produits non financiers (nets)
a. Fees and commissions receivable	..	..	..	..	..	..	..	..	..	..	*a. Frais et commissions à recevoir*
b. Fees and commissions payable	..	..	..	..	..	..	..	..	..	..	*b. Frais et commissions à payer*
c. Net profits or loss on financial operations	..	..	..	..	..	..	..	..	..	..	*c. Profits ou pertes nets sur opérations financières*
d. Other	..	..	..	..	..	..	..	..	..	..	*d. Autres*
55. Operating expenses	55.35	60.62	64.21	69.90	71.88	66.79	69.30	68.43	70.74	74.10	55. Frais d'exploitation
a. Staff costs	*27.23*	*26.35*	*23.93*	*25.97*	*26.99*	*26.24*	*27.05*	*28.55*	*28.98*	*29.52*	*a. Dépenses en personnel*
b. Property costs	..	..	..	..	..	..	..	..	..	..	*b. Dépenses en immobilier*
c. Other	..	..	..	..	..	..	..	..	..	..	*c. Autres*
56. Net income	44.65	39.38	35.79	30.10	28.12	33.21	30.70	31.57	29.26	25.90	56. Résultat net
57. Provisions (net)	9.37	20.18	29.44	65.95	35.46	22.98	12.05	8.39	3.81	13.77	57. Provisions (nettes)
a. Provisions on loans	*9.37*	*20.18*	*29.44*	*65.95*	*35.46*	*22.98*	*12.05*	*8.39*	*3.81*	*13.77*	*a. Provisions sur prêts*
b. Provisions on securities	..	..	..	..	..	..	..	..	..	..	*b. Provisions sur titres*
c. Other	..	..	..	..	..	..	..	..	..	..	*c. Autres*
58. Profit before tax	35.19	19.20	6.35	-35.85	-7.34	10.24	18.65	23.18	25.45	12.12	58. Bénéfices avant impôt
59. Income tax	14.50	7.85	2.98	-12.69	0.73	7.64	8.15	9.59	10.22	4.34	59. Impôt sur le revenu
60. Profit after tax	20.78	11.35	3.37	-23.10	-8.07	2.60	10.50	13.59	15.23	7.78	60. Bénéfices après impôt
% of net income											**% du total du résultat net**
61. Provisions (net)	20.99	51.25	82.26	219.09	126.10	69.17	39.25	26.58	13.01	53.19	61. Provisions (nettes)
a. Provisions on loans	*20.99*	*51.25*	*82.26*	*219.09*	*126.10*	*69.17*	*39.25*	*26.58*	*13.01*	*53.19*	*a. Provisions sur prêts*
b. Provisions on securities	..	..	..	..	..	..	..	..	..	..	*b. Provisions sur titres*
c. Other	..	..	..	..	..	..	..	..	..	..	*c. Autres*
62. Profit before tax	78.81	48.75	17.74	-119.09	-26.10	30.83	60.75	73.42	86.99	46.81	62. Bénéfices avant impôt
63. Income tax	32.48	19.93	8.32	-42.15	2.61	23.01	26.55	30.38	34.93	16.76	63. Impôt sur le revenu
64. Profit after tax	46.53	28.83	9.42	-76.74	-28.71	7.82	34.20	43.04	52.05	30.06	64. Bénéfices après impôt

CANADA
Foreign commercial banks

CANADA
Banques commerciales étrangères

	1989	1990	1991	1992	1993	1994	1995	1996	1997	1998 p	
Per cent											*Pourcentage*
BALANCE SHEET ANALYSIS											**ANALYSE DU BILAN**
% of year-end balance sheet total											**% du total du bilan en fin d'exercice**
Assets											**Actif**
65. Cash & balance with Central bank	0.60	0.26	0.29	0.19	0.28	0.33	0.34	0.26	0.29	0.32	65. Caisse & solde auprès de la Banque centrale
66. Interbank deposits	16.28	12.94	14.83	14.85	10.59	14.06	11.25	10.16	9.96	6.25	66. Dépôts interbancaires
67. Loans	69.97	71.21	68.16	65.25	63.31	64.13	66.42	62.95	61.11	58.95	67. Prêts
68. Securities	10.51	12.43	14.12	16.58	21.20	18.15	17.52	16.65	16.59	15.79	68. Valeurs mobilières
69. Other assets	2.63	3.16	2.60	3.12	4.63	3.34	4.47	9.98	12.04	18.70	69. Autres actifs
Liabilities											**Passif**
70. Capital & reserves	7.70	8.32	7.89	6.65	6.51	6.52	6.31	5.81	5.70	6.03	70. Capital et réserves
71. Borrowing from Central bank	-	-	-	-	-	-	-	-	-	-	71. Emprunts auprès de la Banque centrale
72. Interbank deposits	29.49	32.02	31.01	30.66	25.84	29.93	29.82	21.53	22.68	19.54	72. Dépôts interbancaires
73. Non-bank deposits	55.34	50.00	49.63	49.78	51.95	50.28	50.58	51.35	45.85	44.70	73. Dépôts non bancaires
74. Bonds	0.66	1.17	1.74	2.06	1.96	2.07	2.34	2.10	1.89	1.91	74. Obligations
75. Other liabilities	6.82	8.49	9.73	10.85	13.74	11.21	10.95	19.20	23.88	27.82	75. Autres engagements
Memorandum items											***Pour mémoire***
76. Short-term securities	..	..	..	..	..	..	..	..	..	..	*76. Titres à court terme*
77. Bonds	..	..	..	..	..	..	..	..	..	..	*77. Obligations*
78. Shares and participations	..	..	..	..	..	..	..	..	..	..	*78. Actions et participations*
79. Claims on non-residents	..	..	..	..	..	..	..	..	..	..	*79. Créances sur des non-résidents*
80. Liabilities to non-residents	..	..	..	..	..	..	..	..	..	..	*80. Engagements envers des non-résidents*

* See notes on previous pages.

* Voir les notes en pages précédentes.

CZECH REPUBLIC — REPUBLIQUE TCHEQUE

All banks — Ensemble des banques

	1993	1994	1995	1996	1997	
Million Czech koruna						*Millions de couronnes tchèques*
INCOME STATEMENT						**COMPTE DE RESULTATS**
1. Interest income	133675	139901	143807	155260	188327	1. Produits financiers
2. Interest expenses	85325	88669	96114	113799	141824	2. Frais financiers
3. Net interest income	48350	51232	47693	41461	46503	3. Produits financiers nets
4. Non-interest income (net)	66842	91521	116052	152644	238230	4. Produits non financiers (nets)
a. Fees and commissions receivable	*8283*	*9770*	*10655*	*13357*	*14028*	*a. Frais et commissions à recevoir*
b. Fees and commissions payable	*717*	*889*	*1149*	*1550*	*1716*	*b. Frais et commissions à payer*
c. Net profits or loss on financial operations	*9727*	*11142*	*15837*	*19164*	*27663*	*c. Profits ou pertes nets sur opérations financières*
d. Other	*49549*	*71498*	*90709*	*121673*	*198255*	*d. Autres*
5. Gross income	115192	142753	163745	194105	284733	5. Résultat brut
6. Operating expenses	70850	103918	134072	188722	263175	6. Frais d'exploitation
a. Staff costs	*8519*	*11446*	*14138*	*16776*	*18286*	*a. Dépenses en personnel*
b. Property costs	*14550*	*17836*	*22372*	*26024*	*28465*	*b. Dépenses en immobilier*
c. Other	*47781*	*74636*	*97562*	*145922*	*216425*	*c. Autres*
7. Net income	44342	38835	29673	5383	21558	7. Résultat net
8. Provisions (net)	36919	31591	23959	14533	27181	8. Provisions (nettes)
a. Provisions on loans	..	..	..	..	..	*a. Provisions sur prêts*
b. Provisions on securities	..	..	..	..	..	*b. Provisions sur titres*
c. Other	..	..	..	..	..	*c. Autres*
9. Profit before tax	7423	7244	5714	-9150	-5623	9. Bénéfices avant impôt
10. Income tax	3625	3492	3463	1542	798	10. Impôt sur le revenu
11. Profit after tax	3798	3752	2251	-10692	-6421	11. Bénéfices après impôt
12. Distributed profit	..	2649	4496	12833	14660	12. Bénéfices distribués
13. Retained profit	..	1103	-2245	-23525	-21081	13. Bénéfices mis en réserve
BALANCE SHEET						**BILAN**
Assets						**Actif**
14. Cash & balance with Central bank	81620	91634	173211	170233	228254	14. Caisse & solde auprès de la Banque centrale
15. Interbank deposits	279544	313736	328152	398807	485851	15. Dépôts interbancaires
16. Loans	720392	838940	915706	982668	1053477	16. Prêts
17. Securities	109256	186627	346168	329832	347509	17. Valeurs mobilières
18. Other assets	84960	107569	139802	221073	215743	18. Autres actifs
Liabilities						**Passif**
19. Capital & reserves	148914	195365	201686	204722	210104	19. Capital et réserves
20. Borrowing from Central bank	77836	77783	74078	79934	97071	20. Emprunts auprès de la Banque centrale
21. Interbank deposits	254535	306762	408997	486023	495723	21. Dépôts interbancaires
22. Non-bank deposits	730724	857672	973065	1045616	1154228	22. Dépôts non bancaires
23. Bonds	3784	27622	56159	63656	93140	23. Obligations
24. Other liabilities	59979	73302	189057	222662	280568	24. Autres engagements
Balance sheet total						**Total du bilan**
25. End-year total	1275772	1538506	1903042	2102613	2330834	25. En fin d'exercice
26. Average total	..	1407139	1572440	1704983	1830153	26. Moyen

CZECH REPUBLIC — REPUBLIQUE TCHEQUE

All banks — Ensemble des banques

	1993	1994	1995	1996	1997	
Million Czech koruna						*Millions de couronnes tchèques*
Memorandum items						***Pour mémoire***
27. Short-term securities	..	..	..	..	..	*27. Titres à court terme*
28. Bonds	..	..	..	..	..	*28. Obligations*
29. Shares and participations	..	..	..	..	..	*29. Actions et participations*
30. Claims on non-residents	*103838*	*114918*	*138507*	*189366*	*309206*	*30. Créances sur des non-résidents*
31. Liabilities to non-residents	*64176*	*95863*	*204386*	*265596*	*329758*	*31. Engagements envers des non-résidents*
Capital adequacy						***Solvabilité***
32. Tier 1 Capital	..	..	..	..	..	*32. Fonds propres de base*
33. Tier 2 Capital	..	..	..	..	..	*33. Fonds propres complémentaires*
34. Supervisory deductions	..	..	..	..	..	*34. Eléments à déduire des fonds propres*
35. Total net capital resources	..	..	..	..	..	*35. Total net des ressources en capital*
36. Risk-weighted assets	..	..	..	..	..	*36. Actifs pondérés des risques*
SUPPLEMENTARY INFORMATION						**RENSEIGNEMENTS COMPLEMENTAIRES**
37. Number of institutions	53	56	58	54	51	37. Nombre d'institutions
38. Number of branches	1497	1462	1481	2156	1570	38. Nombre de succursales
39. Number of employees (x 1000)	51	57	60	58	54	39. Nombre de salariés (x 1000)

CZECH REPUBLIC — REPUBLIQUE TCHEQUE

All banks — Ensemble des banques

	1993	1994	1995	1996	1997	
Per cent						*Pourcentage*
INCOME STATEMENT ANALYSIS						**ANALYSE DU COMPTE DE RESULTATS**
% of average balance sheet total						**% du total moyen du bilan**
40. Interest income	..	9.94	9.15	9.11	10.29	40. Produits financiers
41. Interest expenses	..	6.30	6.11	6.67	7.75	41. Frais financiers
42. Net interest income	..	3.64	3.03	2.43	2.54	42. Produits financiers nets
43. Non-interest income (net)	..	6.50	7.38	8.95	13.02	43. Produits non financiers (nets)
a. Fees and commissions receivable	..	*0.69*	*0.68*	*0.78*	*0.77*	*a. Frais et commissions à recevoir*
b. Fees and commissions payable	..	*0.06*	*0.07*	*0.09*	*0.09*	*b. Frais et commissions à payer*
c. Net profits or loss on financial operations	..	*0.79*	*1.01*	*1.12*	*1.51*	*c. Profits ou pertes nets sur opérations financières*
d. Other	..	*5.08*	*5.77*	*7.14*	*10.83*	*d. Autres*
44. Gross income	..	10.14	10.41	11.38	15.56	44. Résultat brut
45. Operating expenses	..	7.39	8.53	11.07	14.38	45. Frais d'exploitation
a. Staff costs	..	*0.81*	*0.90*	*0.98*	*1.00*	*a. Dépenses en personnel*
b. Property costs	..	*1.27*	*1.42*	*1.53*	*1.56*	*b. Dépenses en immobilier*
c. Other	..	*5.30*	*6.20*	*8.56*	*11.83*	*c. Autres*
46. Net income	..	2.76	1.89	0.32	1.18	46. Résultat net
47. Provisions (net)	..	2.25	1.52	0.85	1.49	47. Provisions (nettes)
a. Provisions on loans	..	..	..	..	..	*a. Provisions sur prêts*
b. Provisions on securities	..	..	..	..	..	*b. Provisions sur titres*
c. Other	..	..	..	..	..	*c. Autres*
48. Profit before tax	..	0.51	0.36	-0.54	-0.31	48. Bénéfices avant impôt
49. Income tax	..	0.25	0.22	0.09	0.04	49. Impôt sur le revenu
50. Profit after tax	..	0.27	0.14	-0.63	-0.35	50. Bénéfices après impôt
51. Distributed profit	..	0.19	0.29	0.75	0.80	51. Bénéfices distribués
52. Retained profit	..	0.08	-0.14	-1.38	-1.15	52. Bénéfices mis en réserve
% of gross income						**% du total du résultat brut**
53. Net interest income	41.97	35.89	29.13	21.36	16.33	53. Produits financiers nets
54. Non-interest income (net)	58.03	64.11	70.87	78.64	83.67	54. Produits non financiers (nets)
a. Fees and commissions receivable	*7.19*	*6.84*	*6.51*	*6.88*	*4.93*	*a. Frais et commissions à recevoir*
b. Fees and commissions payable	*0.62*	*0.62*	*0.70*	*0.80*	*0.60*	*b. Frais et commissions à payer*
c. Net profits or loss on financial operations	*8.44*	*7.81*	*9.67*	*9.87*	*9.72*	*c. Profits ou pertes nets sur opérations financières*
d. Other	*43.01*	*50.09*	*55.40*	*62.68*	*69.63*	*d. Autres*
55. Operating expenses	61.51	72.80	81.88	97.23	92.43	55. Frais d'exploitation
a. Staff costs	*7.40*	*8.02*	*8.63*	*8.64*	*6.42*	*a. Dépenses en personnel*
b. Property costs	*12.63*	*12.49*	*13.66*	*13.41*	*10.00*	*b. Dépenses en immobilier*
c. Other	*41.48*	*52.28*	*59.58*	*75.18*	*76.01*	*c. Autres*
56. Net income	38.49	27.20	18.12	2.77	7.57	56. Résultat net
57. Provisions (net)	32.05	22.13	14.63	7.49	9.55	57. Provisions (nettes)
a. Provisions on loans	..	..	..	..	..	*a. Provisions sur prêts*
b. Provisions on securities	..	..	..	..	..	*b. Provisions sur titres*
c. Other	..	..	..	..	..	*c. Autres*
58. Profit before tax	6.44	5.07	3.49	-4.71	-1.97	58. Bénéfices avant impôt
59. Income tax	3.15	2.45	2.11	0.79	0.28	59. Impôt sur le revenu
60. Profit after tax	3.30	2.63	1.37	-5.51	-2.26	60. Bénéfices après impôt
% of net income						**% du total du résultat net**
61. Provisions (net)	83.26	81.35	80.74	269.98	126.08	61. Provisions (nettes)
a. Provisions on loans	..	..	..	..	..	*a. Provisions sur prêts*
b. Provisions on securities	..	..	..	..	..	*b. Provisions sur titres*
c. Other	..	..	..	..	..	*c. Autres*
62. Profit before tax	16.74	18.65	19.26	-169.98	-26.08	62. Bénéfices avant impôt
63. Income tax	8.18	8.99	11.67	28.65	3.70	63. Impôt sur le revenu
64. Profit after tax	8.57	9.66	7.59	-198.63	-29.78	64. Bénéfices après impôt

CZECH REPUBLIC — REPUBLIQUE TCHEQUE
All banks — Ensemble des banques

	1993	1994	1995	1996	1997	
Per cent						*Pourcentage*
BALANCE SHEET ANALYSIS						**ANALYSE DU BILAN**
% of year-end balance sheet total						**% du total du bilan en fin d'exercice**
Assets						**Actif**
65. Cash & balance with Central bank	6.40	5.96	9.10	8.10	9.79	65. Caisse & solde auprès de la Banque centrale
66. Interbank deposits	21.91	20.39	17.24	18.97	20.84	66. Dépôts interbancaires
67. Loans	56.47	54.53	48.12	46.74	45.20	67. Prêts
68. Securities	8.56	12.13	18.19	15.69	14.91	68. Valeurs mobilières
69. Other assets	6.66	6.99	7.35	10.51	9.26	69. Autres actifs
Liabilities						**Passif**
70. Capital & reserves	11.67	12.70	10.60	9.74	9.01	70. Capital et réserves
71. Borrowing from Central bank	6.10	5.06	3.89	3.80	4.16	71. Emprunts auprès de la Banque centrale
72. Interbank deposits	19.95	19.94	21.49	23.12	21.27	72. Dépôts interbancaires
73. Non-bank deposits	57.28	55.75	51.13	49.73	49.52	73. Dépôts non bancaires
74. Bonds	0.30	1.80	2.95	3.03	4.00	74. Obligations
75. Other liabilities	4.70	4.76	9.93	10.59	12.04	75. Autres engagements
Memorandum items						***Pour mémoire***
76. Short-term securities	..	..	..	..	..	*76. Titres à court terme*
77. Bonds	..	..	..	..	..	*77. Obligations*
78. Shares and participations	..	..	..	..	..	*78. Actions et participations*
79. Claims on non-residents	*8.14*	*7.47*	*7.28*	*9.01*	*13.27*	*79. Créances sur des non-résidents*
80. Liabilities to non-residents	*5.03*	*6.23*	*10.74*	*12.63*	*14.15*	*80. Engagements envers des non-résidents*

DENMARK — DANEMARK

Commercial banks and savings banks — Banques commerciales et caisses d'épargne

	1988	1989	1990	1991(1)	1992	1993	1994	1995	1996	1997(1)	
Million Danish kroner											*Millions de couronnes danoises*
INCOME STATEMENT											**COMPTE DE RESULTATS**
1. Interest income	68776	87280	103599	100453	98915	96366	77135	69679	64411	67707	1. Produits financiers
2. Interest expenses	44703	61504	75254	66050	64453	59298	39070	40340	35937	39616	2. Frais financiers
3. Net interest income	24073	25776	28345	34403	34462	37068	38065	29339	28474	28091	3. Produits financiers nets
4. Non-interest income (net) (2)	13784	7170	4016	5728	-3984	9435	-5450	14289	13476	13078	4. Produits non financiers (nets) (2)
a. Fees and commissions receivable	..	..	..	..	..	..	..	*7296*	*8361*	*9206*	*a. Frais et commissions à recevoir*
b. Fees and commissions payable	..	..	..	..	..	..	..	*837*	*850*	*1171*	*b. Frais et commissions à payer*
c. Net profits or loss on financial operations	..	..	..	..	..	..	..	*9071*	*6880*	*4801*	*c. Profits ou pertes nets sur opérations financières*
d. Other	..	..	..	..	..	..	..	*-1241*	*-915*	*242*	*d. Autres*
5. Gross income	37857	32946	32361	40131	30478	46503	32615	43628	41950	41169	5. Résultat brut
6. Operating expenses	20135	21383	22200	25112	24800	23759	23650	23558	23860	24362	6. Frais d'exploitation
a. Staff costs	*12682*	*13340*	*13814*	*15165*	*15141*	*14497*	*14627*	*14477*	*14234*	*14313*	*a. Dépenses en personnel*
b. Property costs	..	..	..	..	..	..	..	..	..	..	*b. Dépenses en immobilier*
c. Other	..	..	..	..	..	..	..	..	..	..	*c. Autres*
7. Net income	17722	11563	10161	15019	5678	22744	8965	20070	18090	16807	7. Résultat net
8. Provisions (net)	9416	8777	13111	15113	17331	16651	8924	7042	5152	4088	8. Provisions (nettes)
a. Provisions on loans	*8043*	*7388*	*11408*	*13592*	*15826*	*15108*	*7382*	*5542*	*3681*	*2556*	*a. Provisions sur prêts*
b. Provisions on securities	..	..	..	..	..	..	..	..	..	..	*b. Provisions sur titres*
c. Other	..	..	..	..	..	..	..	..	..	..	*c. Autres*
9. Profit before tax	8306	2786	-2950	-94	-11653	6093	41	13028	12940	12720	9. Bénéfices avant impôt
10. Income tax	2572	522	-238	331	189	2114	361	2261	2107	1178	10. Impôt sur le revenu
11. Profit after tax	5734	2264	-2712	-425	-11842	3979	-320	10767	10832	11542	11. Bénéfices après impôt
12. Distributed profit	1274	1666	1320	1861	959	1141	1209	1980	2755	5225	12. Bénéfices distribués
13. Retained profit	4460	598	-4032	-2286	-12801	2838	-1529	8787	8076	6317	13. Bénéfices mis en réserve
BALANCE SHEET											**BILAN**
Assets											**Actif**
14. Cash & balance with Central bank	16180	17005	14341	19979	20858	37790	34464	41365	53117	70830	14. Caisse & solde auprès de la Banque centrale
15. Interbank deposits	169575	171700	170112	189185	160419	252109	183329	194171	241301	229259	15. Dépôts interbancaires
16. Loans	410545	456793	495821	508427	479976	478311	433769	440765	493336	576629	16. Prêts
17. Securities	200753	230152	212776	244309	227649	231968	251488	294531	330256	353120	17. Valeurs mobilières
18. Other assets	175828	184476	228538	47885	48069	41620	42668	45959	45869	58731	18. Autres actifs
Liabilities											**Passif**
19. Capital & reserves	87933	92470	88199	67564	55379	57424	62246	70419	80197	84294	19. Capital et réserves
20. Borrowing from Central bank	3513	19844	4880	19339	34573	83646	64046	47805	38620	32361	20. Emprunts auprès de la Banque centrale
21. Interbank deposits	233807	271829	292874	313462	242967	249313	204647	236165	302124	341318	21. Dépôts interbancaires
22. Non-bank deposits	471360	496049	526552	503260	499060	558750	537310	566019	620185	670476	22. Dépôts non bancaires
23. Bonds	-	-	-	42821	32761	22524	14051	20075	30143	51717	23. Obligations
24. Other liabilities	176268	179934	209083	63339	72231	70141	63418	76308	92610	108403	24. Autres engagements
Balance sheet total											**Total du bilan**
25. End-year total	972881	1060126	1121588	1009785	936971	1041798	945718	1016791	1163879	1288570	25. En fin d'exercice
26. Average total	867164	1010504	1084007	1016200	967878	943654	965284	924495	1053444	1206798	26. Moyen

DENMARK / DANEMARK

Commercial banks and savings banks / Banques commerciales et caisses d'épargne

	1988	1989	1990	1991(1)	1992	1993	1994	1995	1996	1997(1)	
Million Danish kroner											*Millions de couronnes danoises*
Memorandum items											***Pour mémoire***
27. Short-term securities	*34208*	*21240*	*23713*	*48935*	*73969*	*51710*	*67767*	*80905*	*67625*	*72899*	*27. Titres à court terme*
28. Bonds	*132322*	*165343*	*147593*	*159252*	*120665*	*142582*	*146079*	*171087*	*211053*	*217883*	*28. Obligations*
29. Shares and participations	*27553*	*36782*	*34341*	*36122*	*33015*	*37676*	*37642*	*42539*	*51578*	*62338*	*29. Actions et participations*
30. Claims on non-residents	*276874*	*324297*	*365812*	..	..	..	..	..	..	..	*30. Créances sur des non-résidents*
31. Liabilities to non-residents	*329555*	*386679*	*420807*	..	..	..	..	..	..	..	*31. Engagements envers des non-résidents*
Capital adequacy											***Solvabilité***
32. Tier 1 Capital	..	..	..	..	..	..	..	..	..	..	*32. Fonds propres de base*
33. Tier 2 Capital	..	..	..	..	..	..	..	..	..	..	*33. Fonds propres complémentaires*
34. Supervisory deductions	..	..	..	..	..	..	..	..	..	..	*34. Eléments à déduire des fonds propres*
35. Total net capital resources	..	..	..	..	..	..	..	..	..	..	*35. Total net des ressources en capital*
36. Risk-weighted assets	..	..	..	..	..	..	..	..	..	..	*36. Actifs pondérés des risques*
SUPPLEMENTARY INFORMATION											**RENSEIGNEMENTS COMPLEMENTAIRES**
37. Number of institutions	206	199	189	119	113	112	113	114	117	92	37. Nombre d'institutions
38. Number of branches	3159	3059	2884	2652	2467	2340	2245	2215	2203	2178	38. Nombre de succursales
39. Number of employees (x 1000)	56.0	56.0	55.0	56.0	52.0	50.0	49.0	47.0	44.0	42.5	39. Nombre de salariés (x 1000)

1. Break in series. See Change in methodology.

2. Non-interest income (net) (item 4) includes value adjustments on foreign currency assets and liabilities and on securities.

Notes

- Average balance sheet totals (item 26) are based on day-to-day data.

Change in methodology

- As from 1997, the statistics cover domestic banks with a working capital of more than DKr 250 million (DKr 100 million through 1996).

1. Rupture dans les séries. Voir Changement méthodologique.

2. Les Produits non financiers (net) (poste 4) contiennent des ajustements en valeurs concernant les actifs/passifs en monnaies étrangères et les valeurs mobilières.

Notes

- La moyenne du total des actifs/passifs (poste 26) est basée sur des données au jour le jour.

Changement méthodologique

- A partir de 1997, les données fournies englobent toutes les banques danoises dotées d'un fonds de roulement de plus 250 millions de KrD (100 millions de KrD jusqu'en 1996 inclus).

DENMARK / DANEMARK

Commercial banks and savings banks / Banques commerciales et caisses d'épargne

Per cent	1988	1989	1990	1991(1)	1992	1993	1994	1995	1996	1997(1)	Pourcentage
INCOME STATEMENT ANALYSIS											**ANALYSE DU COMPTE DE RESULTATS**
% of average balance sheet total											**% du total moyen du bilan**
40. Interest income	7.93	8.64	9.56	9.89	10.22	10.21	7.99	7.54	6.11	5.61	40. Produits financiers
41. Interest expenses	5.16	6.09	6.94	6.50	6.66	6.28	4.05	4.36	3.41	3.28	41. Frais financiers
42. Net interest income	2.78	2.55	2.61	3.39	3.56	3.93	3.94	3.17	2.70	2.33	42. Produits financiers nets
43. Non-interest income (net)	1.59	0.71	0.37	0.56	-0.41	1.00	-0.56	1.55	1.28	1.08	43. Produits non financiers (nets)
a. Fees and commissions receivable	..	..	..	..	..	..	..	*0.79*	*0.79*	*0.76*	*a. Frais et commissions à recevoir*
b. Fees and commissions payable	..	..	..	..	..	..	..	*0.09*	*0.08*	*0.10*	*b. Frais et commissions à payer*
c. Net profits or loss on financial operations	..	..	..	..	..	..	..	*0.98*	*0.65*	*0.40*	*c. Profits ou pertes nets sur opérations financières*
d. Other	..	..	..	..	..	..	..	*-0.13*	*-0.09*	*0.02*	*d. Autres*
44. Gross income	4.37	3.26	2.99	3.95	3.15	4.93	3.38	4.72	3.98	3.41	44. Résultat brut
45. Operating expenses	2.32	2.12	2.05	2.47	2.56	2.52	2.45	2.55	2.26	2.02	45. Frais d'exploitation
a. Staff costs	*1.46*	*1.32*	*1.27*	*1.49*	*1.56*	*1.54*	*1.52*	*1.57*	*1.35*	*1.19*	*a. Dépenses en personnel*
b. Property costs	..	..	..	..	..	..	..	..	..	..	*b. Dépenses en immobilier*
c. Other	..	..	..	..	..	..	..	..	..	..	*c. Autres*
46. Net income	2.04	1.14	0.94	1.48	0.59	2.41	0.93	2.17	1.72	1.39	46. Résultat net
47. Provisions (net)	1.09	0.87	1.21	1.49	1.79	1.76	0.92	0.76	0.49	0.34	47. Provisions (nettes)
a. Provisions on loans	*0.93*	*0.73*	*1.05*	*1.34*	*1.64*	*1.60*	*0.76*	*0.60*	*0.35*	*0.21*	*a. Provisions sur prêts*
b. Provisions on securities	..	..	..	..	..	..	..	..	..	..	*b. Provisions sur titres*
c. Other	..	..	..	..	..	..	..	..	..	..	*c. Autres*
48. Profit before tax	0.96	0.28	-0.27	-0.01	-1.20	0.65	-	1.41	1.23	1.05	48. Bénéfices avant impôt
49. Income tax	0.30	0.05	-0.02	0.03	0.02	0.22	0.04	0.24	0.20	0.10	49. Impôt sur le revenu
50. Profit after tax	0.66	0.22	-0.25	-0.04	-1.22	0.42	-0.03	1.16	1.03	0.96	50. Bénéfices après impôt
51. Distributed profit	0.15	0.16	0.12	0.18	0.10	0.12	0.13	0.21	0.26	0.43	51. Bénéfices distribués
52. Retained profit	0.51	0.06	-0.37	-0.22	-1.32	0.30	-0.16	0.95	0.77	0.52	52. Bénéfices mis en réserve
% of gross income											**% du total du résultat brut**
53. Net interest income	63.59	78.24	87.59	85.73	113.07	79.71	116.71	67.25	67.88	68.23	53. Produits financiers nets
54. Non-interest income (net)	36.41	21.76	12.41	14.27	-13.07	20.29	-16.71	32.75	32.12	31.77	54. Produits non financiers (nets)
a. Fees and commissions receivable	..	..	..	..	..	..	..	*16.72*	*19.93*	*22.36*	*a. Frais et commissions à recevoir*
b. Fees and commissions payable	..	..	..	..	..	..	..	*1.92*	*2.03*	*2.84*	*b. Frais et commissions à payer*
c. Net profits or loss on financial operations	..	..	..	..	..	..	..	*20.79*	*16.40*	*11.66*	*c. Profits ou pertes nets sur opérations financières*
d. Other	..	..	..	..	..	..	..	*-2.84*	*-2.18*	*0.59*	*d. Autres*
55. Operating expenses	53.19	64.90	68.60	62.58	81.37	51.09	72.51	54.00	56.88	59.18	55. Frais d'exploitation
a. Staff costs	*33.50*	*40.49*	*42.69*	*37.79*	*49.68*	*31.17*	*44.85*	*33.18*	*33.93*	*34.77*	*a. Dépenses en personnel*
b. Property costs	..	..	..	..	..	..	..	..	..	..	*b. Dépenses en immobilier*
c. Other	..	..	..	..	..	..	..	..	..	..	*c. Autres*
56. Net income	46.81	35.10	31.40	37.42	18.63	48.91	27.49	46.00	43.12	40.82	56. Résultat net
57. Provisions (net)	24.87	26.64	40.51	37.66	56.86	35.81	27.36	16.14	12.28	9.93	57. Provisions (nettes)
a. Provisions on loans	*21.25*	*22.42*	*35.25*	*33.87*	*51.93*	*32.49*	*22.63*	*12.70*	*8.77*	*6.21*	*a. Provisions sur prêts*
b. Provisions on securities	..	..	..	..	..	..	..	..	..	..	*b. Provisions sur titres*
c. Other	..	..	..	..	..	..	..	..	..	..	*c. Autres*
58. Profit before tax	21.94	8.46	-9.12	-0.23	-38.23	13.10	0.13	29.86	30.85	30.90	58. Bénéfices avant impôt
59. Income tax	6.79	1.58	-0.74	0.82	0.62	4.55	1.11	5.18	5.02	2.86	59. Impôt sur le revenu
60. Profit after tax	15.15	6.87	-8.38	-1.06	-38.85	8.56	-0.98	24.68	25.82	28.04	60. Bénéfices après impôt
% of net income											**% du total du résultat net**
61. Provisions (net)	53.13	75.91	129.03	100.63	..	73.21	99.54	35.09	28.48	24.32	61. Provisions (nettes)
a. Provisions on loans	*45.38*	*63.89*	*112.27*	*90.50*	..	*66.43*	*82.34*	*27.61*	*20.35*	*15.21*	*a. Provisions sur prêts*
b. Provisions on securities	..	..	..	..	..	..	..	..	..	..	*b. Provisions sur titres*
c. Other	..	..	..	..	..	..	..	..	..	..	*c. Autres*
62. Profit before tax	46.87	24.09	-29.03	-0.63	..	26.79	0.46	64.91	71.53	75.68	62. Bénéfices avant impôt
63. Income tax	14.51	4.51	-2.34	2.20	3.33	9.29	4.03	11.27	11.65	7.01	63. Impôt sur le revenu
64. Profit after tax	32.36	19.58	-26.69	-2.83	..	17.49	-3.57	53.65	59.88	68.67	64. Bénéfices après impôt

DENMARK / DANEMARK

Commercial banks and savings banks / Banques commerciales et caisses d'épargne

	1988	1989	1990	1991(1)	1992	1993	1994	1995	1996	1997(1)	
Per cent											*Pourcentage*
BALANCE SHEET ANALYSIS											**ANALYSE DU BILAN**
% of year-end balance sheet total											**% du total du bilan en fin d'exercice**
Assets											**Actif**
65. Cash & balance with Central bank	1.66	1.60	1.28	1.98	2.23	3.63	3.64	4.07	4.56	5.50	65. Caisse & solde auprès de la Banque centrale
66. Interbank deposits	17.43	16.20	15.17	18.74	17.12	24.20	19.39	19.10	20.73	17.79	66. Dépôts interbancaires
67. Loans	42.20	43.09	44.21	50.35	51.23	45.91	45.87	43.35	42.39	44.75	67. Prêts
68. Securities	20.63	21.71	18.97	24.19	24.30	22.27	26.59	28.97	28.38	27.40	68. Valeurs mobilières
69. Other assets	18.07	17.40	20.38	4.74	5.13	4.00	4.51	4.52	3.94	4.56	69. Autres actifs
Liabilities											**Passif**
70. Capital & reserves	9.04	8.72	7.86	6.69	5.91	5.51	6.58	6.93	6.89	6.54	70. Capital et réserves
71. Borrowing from Central bank	0.36	1.87	0.44	1.92	3.69	8.03	6.77	4.70	3.32	2.51	71. Emprunts auprès de la Banque centrale
72. Interbank deposits	24.03	25.64	26.11	31.04	25.93	23.93	21.64	23.23	25.96	26.49	72. Dépôts interbancaires
73. Non-bank deposits	48.45	46.79	46.95	49.84	53.26	53.63	56.82	55.67	53.29	52.03	73. Dépôts non bancaires
74. Bonds	-	-	-	4.24	3.50	2.16	1.49	1.97	2.59	4.01	74. Obligations
75. Other liabilities	18.12	16.97	18.64	6.27	7.71	6.73	6.71	7.50	7.96	8.41	75. Autres engagements
Memorandum items											***Pour mémoire***
76. Short-term securities	*3.52*	*2.00*	*2.11*	*4.85*	*7.89*	*4.96*	*7.17*	*7.96*	*5.81*	*5.66*	*76. Titres à court terme*
77. Bonds	*13.60*	*15.60*	*13.16*	*15.77*	*12.88*	*13.69*	*15.45*	*16.83*	*18.13*	*16.91*	*77. Obligations*
78. Shares and participations	*2.83*	*3.47*	*3.06*	*3.58*	*3.52*	*3.62*	*3.98*	*4.18*	*4.43*	*4.84*	*78. Actions et participations*
79. Claims on non-residents	*28.46*	*30.59*	*32.62*	..	..	..	..	..	..	..	*79. Créances sur des non-résidents*
80. Liabilities to non-residents	*33.87*	*36.47*	*37.52*	..	..	..	..	..	..	..	*80. Engagements envers des non-résidents*

* See notes on previous pages.

* Voir les notes en pages précédentes.

FINLAND
All banks

FINLANDE
Ensemble des banques

	1988	1989	1990	1991	1992	1993	1994	1995	1996	1997	
Million markkaa											*Millions de markkas*
INCOME STATEMENT											**COMPTE DE RESULTATS**
1. Interest income	43193	60507	74459	77567	72766	57372	41211	38921	30752	29180	1. Produits financiers
2. Interest expenses	32492	48838	60676	65331	63567	44912	29470	27117	19749	17625	2. Frais financiers
3. Net interest income	10701	11669	13783	12236	9199	12460	11741	11804	11003	11555	3. Produits financiers nets
4. Non-interest income (net)	12112	10977	11750	13228	13589	17181	10348	8975	10783	9676	4. Produits non financiers (nets)
a. Fees and commissions receivable	..	..	..	..	..	..	..	..	..	..	*a. Frais et commissions à recevoir*
b. Fees and commissions payable	..	..	..	..	..	..	..	..	..	..	*b. Frais et commissions à payer*
c. Net profits or loss on financial operations	..	..	..	..	..	..	..	..	..	..	*c. Profits ou pertes nets sur opérations financières*
d. Other	..	..	..	..	..	..	..	..	..	..	*d. Autres*
5. Gross income	22813	22646	25533	25464	22788	29641	22089	20779	21786	21231	5. Résultat brut
6. Operating expenses	16790	19199	20807	31372	43397	40444	30900	23314	19302	15575	6. Frais d'exploitation
a. Staff costs	*7357*	*8014*	*8015*	*8438*	*7947*	*7117*	*6809*	*5704*	*5857*	*4608*	*a. Dépenses en personnel*
b. Property costs	*1641*	*2285*	*2690*	*2893*	*2798*	*2887*	*2361*	*1848*	*1785*	*1634*	*b. Dépenses en immobilier*
c. Other	*7792*	*8900*	*10102*	*20041*	*32652*	*30440*	*21730*	*15762*	*11660*	*9333*	*c. Autres*
7. Net income	6023	3447	4726	-5908	-20609	-10803	-8811	-2535	2484	5656	7. Résultat net
8. Provisions (net)	2980	1618	1890	-53	-442	-42	-240	-97	-156	59	8. Provisions (nettes)
a. Provisions on loans	*2084*	*2231*	*2192*	*-10*	*-259*	*92*	*-203*	..	..	..	*a. Provisions sur prêts*
b. Provisions on securities	*675*	*-623*	*-973*	*-43*	*-182*	*-134*	*-37*	..	..	..	*b. Provisions sur titres*
c. Other	*227*	*11*	*671*	-	-	-	-	..	..	..	*c. Autres*
9. Profit before tax	3043	1829	2836	-5855	-20167	-10761	-8571	-2438	2640	5597	9. Bénéfices avant impôt
10. Income tax	457	602	961	475	263	179	163	342	488	775	10. Impôt sur le revenu
11. Profit after tax	2586	1227	1875	-6330	-20430	-10940	-8734	-2780	2152	4822	11. Bénéfices après impôt
12. Distributed profit	1052	1177	727	273	58	77	65	129	592	1108	12. Bénéfices distribués
13. Retained profit	1534	50	1148	-6603	-20488	-11017	-8799	-2909	1560	3714	13. Bénéfices mis en réserve
BALANCE SHEET											**BILAN**
Assets											**Actif**
14. Cash & balance with Central bank	24465	32085	24491	19090	26007	13416	11814	17266	10692	14441	14. Caisse & solde auprès de la Banque centrale
15. Interbank deposits	22749	24534	24072	22011	25911	51076	20044	19007	17458	23837	15. Dépôts interbancaires
16. Loans	367326	444797	483139	490581	464070	399735	348145	320702	315679	368222	16. Prêts
17. Securities	77809	89223	95149	130734	125917	155032	158305	170742	149908	147765	17. Valeurs mobilières
18. Other assets	91617	91812	107152	107975	118736	134830	142477	117040	135109	118411	18. Autres actifs
Liabilities											**Passif**
19. Capital & reserves	39098	45677	50563	53350	41264	37874	33999	30726	33159	36851	19. Capital et réserves
20. Borrowing from Central bank	4813	3871	3918	5804	8019	5732	881	7700	12609	2873	20. Emprunts auprès de la Banque centrale
21. Interbank deposits	16480	18075	17363	18828	22158	17046	19613	20868	20113	24960	21. Dépôts interbancaires
22. Non-bank deposits	328332	347022	378838	390247	393512	372121	360365	362347	354734	380174	22. Dépôts non bancaires
23. Bonds	29922	44580	62675	78444	75613	65159	63193	45372	33930	38094	23. Obligations
24. Other liabilities	165321	223226	220646	223718	220075	256157	202734	177744	174301	189724	24. Autres engagements
Balance sheet total											**Total du bilan**
25. End-year total	583966	682451	734003	770391	760641	754089	680785	644757	628846	672676	25. En fin d'exercice
26. Average total	518221	633209	708228	752198	765517	757366	717437	662771	636802	650761	26. Moyen

FINLAND
All banks

FINLANDE
Ensemble des banques

	1988	1989	1990	1991	1992	1993	1994	1995	1996	1997	
Million markkaa											*Millions de markkas*
Memorandum items											***Pour mémoire***
27. Short-term securities	*28582*	*30029*	*36176*	*50621*	*47230*	*66606*	*85634*	*64844*	*51120*	*53035*	*27. Titres à court terme*
28. Bonds	*38546*	*42763*	*42423*	*55802*	*64888*	*74528*	*58112*	*80133*	*72428*	*69906*	*28. Obligations*
29. Shares and participations	*10681*	*16431*	*16550*	*24311*	*13799*	*13898*	*14559*	*25765*	*26450*	*25031*	*29. Actions et participations*
30. Claims on non-residents	*88306*	*94136*	*102036*	*103688*	*116390*	*128716*	*107683*	*104990*	*125158*	*157420*	*30. Créances sur des non-résidents*
31. Liabilities to non-residents	*158315*	*176339*	*218019*	*221916*	*212036*	*185571*	*145536*	*127497*	*120205*	*139678*	*31. Engagements envers des non-résidents*
Capital adequacy											***Solvabilité***
32. Tier 1 Capital	..	..	..	..	..	..	..	..	..	..	*32. Fonds propres de base*
33. Tier 2 Capital	..	..	..	..	..	..	..	..	..	..	*33. Fonds propres complémentaires*
34. Supervisory deductions	..	..	..	..	..	..	..	..	..	..	*34. Eléments à déduire des fonds propres*
35. Total net capital resources	..	..	..	..	..	..	..	..	..	..	*35. Total net des ressources en capital*
36. Risk-weighted assets	..	..	..	..	..	..	..	..	..	..	*36. Actifs pondérés des risques*
SUPPLEMENTARY INFORMATION											**RENSEIGNEMENTS COMPLEMENTAIRES**
37. Number of institutions	589	553	523	438	370	358	357	351	350	348	37. Nombre d'institutions
38. Number of branches	2956	2977	2821	2662	2393	2200	1828	1612	1409	1306	38. Nombre de succursales
39. Number of employees (x 1000)	47.4	48.6	46.1	42.8	38.9	36.0	34.1	30.6	27.1	25.7	39. Nombre de salariés (x 1000)

Notes

- All banks include Commercial banks (including the Post office bank), Foreign commercial banks, Savings banks and Co-operative banks.

Notes

- L'Ensemble des banques comprend les Banques commerciales (y compris la Banque postale), les Banques commerciales étrangères, les Caisses d'épargne et les Banques mutualistes.

	1988	1989	1990	1991	1992	1993	1994	1995	1996	1997	
Per cent											*Pourcentage*
INCOME STATEMENT ANALYSIS											**ANALYSE DU COMPTE DE RESULTATS**
% of average balance sheet total											**% du total moyen du bilan**
40. Interest income	8.33	9.56	10.51	10.31	9.51	7.58	5.74	5.87	4.83	4.48	40. Produits financiers
41. Interest expenses	6.27	7.71	8.57	8.69	8.30	5.93	4.11	4.09	3.10	2.71	41. Frais financiers
42. Net interest income	2.06	1.84	1.95	1.63	1.20	1.65	1.64	1.78	1.73	1.78	42. Produits financiers nets
43. Non-interest income (net)	2.34	1.73	1.66	1.76	1.78	2.27	1.44	1.35	1.69	1.49	43. Produits non financiers (nets)
a. Fees and commissions receivable	..	..	..	..	..	..	..	..	..	..	*a. Frais et commissions à recevoir*
b. Fees and commissions payable	..	..	..	..	..	..	..	..	..	..	*b. Frais et commissions à payer*
c. Net profits or loss on financial operations	..	..	..	..	..	..	..	..	..	..	*c. Profits ou pertes nets sur opérations financières*
d. Other	..	..	..	..	..	..	..	..	..	..	*d. Autres*
44. Gross income	4.40	3.58	3.61	3.39	2.98	3.91	3.08	3.14	3.42	3.26	44. Résultat brut
45. Operating expenses	3.24	3.03	2.94	4.17	5.67	5.34	4.31	3.52	3.03	2.39	45. Frais d'exploitation
a. Staff costs	*1.42*	*1.27*	*1.13*	*1.12*	*1.04*	*0.94*	*0.95*	*0.86*	*0.92*	*0.71*	*a. Dépenses en personnel*
b. Property costs	*0.32*	*0.36*	*0.38*	*0.38*	*0.37*	*0.38*	*0.33*	*0.28*	*0.28*	*0.25*	*b. Dépenses en immobilier*
c. Other	*1.50*	*1.41*	*1.43*	*2.66*	*4.27*	*4.02*	*3.03*	*2.38*	*1.83*	*1.43*	*c. Autres*
46. Net income	1.16	0.54	0.67	-0.79	-2.69	-1.43	-1.23	-0.38	0.39	0.87	46. Résultat net
47. Provisions (net)	0.58	0.26	0.27	-0.01	-0.06	-0.01	-0.03	-0.01	-0.02	0.01	47. Provisions (nettes)
a. Provisions on loans	*0.40*	*0.35*	*0.31*	-	*-0.03*	*0.01*	*-0.03*	..	..	..	*a. Provisions sur prêts*
b. Provisions on securities	*0.13*	*-0.10*	*-0.14*	*-0.01*	*-0.02*	*-0.02*	*-0.01*	..	..	..	*b. Provisions sur titres*
c. Other	*0.04*	-	*0.09*	-	-	-	-	..	..	..	*c. Autres*
48. Profit before tax	0.59	0.29	0.40	-0.78	-2.63	-1.42	-1.19	-0.37	0.41	0.86	48. Bénéfices avant impôt
49. Income tax	0.09	0.10	0.14	0.06	0.03	0.02	0.02	0.05	0.08	0.12	49. Impôt sur le revenu
50. Profit after tax	0.50	0.19	0.26	-0.84	-2.67	-1.44	-1.22	-0.42	0.34	0.74	50. Bénéfices après impôt
51. Distributed profit	0.20	0.19	0.10	0.04	0.01	0.01	0.01	0.02	0.09	0.17	51. Bénéfices distribués
52. Retained profit	0.30	0.01	0.16	-0.88	-2.68	-1.45	-1.23	-0.44	0.24	0.57	52. Bénéfices mis en réserve
% of gross income											**% du total du résultat brut**
53. Net interest income	46.91	51.53	53.98	48.05	40.37	42.04	53.15	56.81	50.50	54.43	53. Produits financiers nets
54. Non-interest income (net)	53.09	48.47	46.02	51.95	59.63	57.96	46.85	43.19	49.50	45.57	54. Produits non financiers (nets)
a. Fees and commissions receivable	..	..	..	..	..	..	..	..	..	..	*a. Frais et commissions à recevoir*
b. Fees and commissions payable	..	..	..	..	..	..	..	..	..	..	*b. Frais et commissions à payer*
c. Net profits or loss on financial operations	..	..	..	..	..	..	..	..	..	..	*c. Profits ou pertes nets sur opérations financières*
d. Other	..	..	..	..	..	..	..	..	..	..	*d. Autres*
55. Operating expenses	73.60	84.78	81.49	123.20	190.44	136.45	139.89	112.20	88.60	73.36	55. Frais d'exploitation
a. Staff costs	*32.25*	*35.39*	*31.39*	*33.14*	*34.87*	*24.01*	*30.83*	*27.45*	*26.88*	*21.70*	*a. Dépenses en personnel*
b. Property costs	*7.19*	*10.09*	*10.54*	*11.36*	*12.28*	*9.74*	*10.69*	*8.89*	*8.19*	*7.70*	*b. Dépenses en immobilier*
c. Other	*34.16*	*39.30*	*39.56*	*78.70*	*143.29*	*102.70*	*98.37*	*75.86*	*53.52*	*43.96*	*c. Autres*
56. Net income	26.40	15.22	18.51	-23.20	-90.44	-36.45	-39.89	-12.20	11.40	26.64	56. Résultat net
57. Provisions (net)	13.06	7.14	7.40	-0.21	-1.94	-0.14	-1.09	-0.47	-0.72	0.28	57. Provisions (nettes)
a. Provisions on loans	*9.14*	*9.85*	*8.58*	*-0.04*	*-1.14*	*0.31*	*-0.92*	..	..	..	*a. Provisions sur prêts*
b. Provisions on securities	*2.96*	*-2.75*	*-3.81*	*-0.17*	*-0.80*	*-0.45*	*-0.17*	..	..	..	*b. Provisions sur titres*
c. Other	*1.00*	*0.05*	*2.63*	-	-	-	-	..	..	..	*c. Autres*
58. Profit before tax	13.34	8.08	11.11	-22.99	-88.50	-36.30	-38.80	-11.73	12.12	26.36	58. Bénéfices avant impôt
59. Income tax	2.00	2.66	3.76	1.87	1.15	0.60	0.74	1.65	2.24	3.65	59. Impôt sur le revenu
60. Profit after tax	11.34	5.42	7.34	-24.86	-89.65	-36.91	-39.54	-13.38	9.88	22.71	60. Bénéfices après impôt
% of net income											**% du total du résultat net**
61. Provisions (net)	49.48	46.94	39.99	0.90	2.14	0.39	2.72	3.83	-6.28	1.04	61. Provisions (nettes)
a. Provisions on loans	*34.60*	*64.72*	*46.38*	*0.17*	*1.26*	*-0.85*	*2.30*	..	..	..	*a. Provisions sur prêts*
b. Provisions on securities	*11.21*	*-18.07*	*-20.59*	*0.73*	*0.88*	*1.24*	*0.42*	..	..	..	*b. Provisions sur titres*
c. Other	*3.77*	*0.32*	*14.20*	-	-	-	-	..	..	..	*c. Autres*
62. Profit before tax	50.52	53.06	60.01	99.10	97.86	99.61	97.28	96.17	106.28	98.96	62. Bénéfices avant impôt
63. Income tax	7.59	17.46	20.33	-8.04	-1.28	-1.66	-1.85	-13.49	19.65	13.70	63. Impôt sur le revenu
64. Profit after tax	42.94	35.60	39.67	107.14	99.13	101.27	99.13	109.66	86.63	85.25	64. Bénéfices après impôt

FINLAND — FINLANDE
All banks — Ensemble des banques

	1988	1989	1990	1991	1992	1993	1994	1995	1996	1997	
Per cent											*Pourcentage*
BALANCE SHEET ANALYSIS											**ANALYSE DU BILAN**
% of year-end balance sheet total											**% du total du bilan en fin d'exercice**
Assets											**Actif**
65. Cash & balance with Central bank	4.19	4.70	3.34	2.48	3.42	1.78	1.74	2.68	1.70	2.15	65. Caisse & solde auprès de la Banque centrale
66. Interbank deposits	3.90	3.59	3.28	2.86	3.41	6.77	2.94	2.95	2.78	3.54	66. Dépôts interbancaires
67. Loans	62.90	65.18	65.82	63.68	61.01	53.01	51.14	49.74	50.20	54.74	67. Prêts
68. Securities	13.32	13.07	12.96	16.97	16.55	20.56	23.25	26.48	23.84	21.97	68. Valeurs mobilières
69. Other assets	15.69	13.45	14.60	14.02	15.61	17.88	20.93	18.15	21.49	17.60	69. Autres actifs
Liabilities											**Passif**
70. Capital & reserves	6.70	6.69	6.89	6.93	5.42	5.02	4.99	4.77	5.27	5.48	70. Capital et réserves
71. Borrowing from Central bank	0.82	0.57	0.53	0.75	1.05	0.76	0.13	1.19	2.01	0.43	71. Emprunts auprès de la Banque centrale
72. Interbank deposits	2.82	2.65	2.37	2.44	2.91	2.26	2.88	3.24	3.20	3.71	72. Dépôts interbancaires
73. Non-bank deposits	56.22	50.85	51.61	50.66	51.73	49.35	52.93	56.20	56.41	56.52	73. Dépôts non bancaires
74. Bonds	5.12	6.53	8.54	10.18	9.94	8.64	9.28	7.04	5.40	5.66	74. Obligations
75. Other liabilities	28.31	32.71	30.06	29.04	28.93	33.97	29.78	27.57	27.72	28.20	75. Autres engagements
Memorandum items											***Pour mémoire***
76. Short-term securities	*4.89*	*4.40*	*4.93*	*6.57*	*6.21*	*8.83*	*12.58*	*10.06*	*8.13*	*7.88*	*76. Titres à court terme*
77. Bonds	*6.60*	*6.27*	*5.78*	*7.24*	*8.53*	*9.88*	*8.54*	*12.43*	*11.52*	*10.39*	*77. Obligations*
78. Shares and participations	*1.83*	*2.41*	*2.25*	*3.16*	*1.81*	*1.84*	*2.14*	*4.00*	*4.21*	*3.72*	*78. Actions et participations*
79. Claims on non-residents	*15.12*	*13.79*	*13.90*	*13.46*	*15.30*	*17.07*	*15.82*	*16.28*	*19.90*	*23.40*	*79. Créances sur des non-résidents*
80. Liabilities to non-residents	*27.11*	*25.84*	*29.70*	*28.81*	*27.88*	*24.61*	*21.38*	*19.77*	*19.12*	*20.76*	*80. Engagements envers des non-résidents*

* See notes on previous pages.

* Voir les notes en pages précédentes.

FINLAND
Commercial banks

FINLANDE
Banques commerciales

	1988	1989	1990	1991	1992	1993	1994	1995	1996	1997	
Million markkaa											*Millions de markkas*
INCOME STATEMENT											**COMPTE DE RESULTATS**
1. Interest income	28941	41113	51091	52508	49389	38713	29219	27107	20844	20176	1. Produits financiers
2. Interest expenses	23252	35004	43382	46022	43463	31396	22152	20234	14622	13257	2. Frais financiers
3. Net interest income	5689	6109	7709	6486	5926	7317	7067	6873	6222	6919	3. Produits financiers nets
4. Non-interest income (net)	7703	7679	8060	8645	7221	7686	7486	6221	7409	6217	4. Produits non financiers (nets)
a. Fees and commissions receivable	..	..	..	..	..	..	..	..	..	..	*a. Frais et commissions à recevoir*
b. Fees and commissions payable	..	..	..	..	..	..	..	..	..	..	*b. Frais et commissions à payer*
c. Net profits or loss on financial operations	..	..	..	..	..	..	..	..	..	..	*c. Profits ou pertes nets sur opérations financières*
d. Other	..	..	..	..	..	..	..	..	..	..	*d. Autres*
5. Gross income	13392	13788	15769	15131	13147	15003	14553	13094	13631	13136	5. Résultat brut
6. Operating expenses	9951	11300	12589	20804	22942	24234	20658	15828	12161	8785	6. Frais d'exploitation
a. Staff costs	*3997*	*4500*	*4501*	*5013*	*4559*	*4108*	*4462*	*3764*	*3931*	*2746*	*a. Dépenses en personnel*
b. Property costs	*836*	*1077*	*1268*	*1338*	*1055*	*1260*	*1321*	*1059*	*1048*	*916*	*b. Dépenses en immobilier*
c. Other	*5118*	*5723*	*6820*	*14453*	*17328*	*18866*	*14875*	*11005*	*7182*	*5123*	*c. Autres*
7. Net income	3441	2488	3180	-5673	-9795	-9231	-6105	-2734	1470	4351	7. Résultat net
8. Provisions (net)	1407	1024	924	-54	-59	20	-250	-122	-216	56	8. Provisions (nettes)
a. Provisions on loans	*1355*	*1355*	*1225*	*-465*	*-47*	*43*	*-211*	..	..	..	*a. Provisions sur prêts*
b. Provisions on securities	*52*	*-331*	*-950*	*411*	*-12*	*-23*	*-39*	..	..	..	*b. Provisions sur titres*
c. Other	-	-	*649*	-	-	-	-	..	..	..	*c. Autres*
9. Profit before tax	2034	1464	2256	-5619	-9736	-9251	-5855	-2612	1686	4295	9. Bénéfices avant impôt
10. Income tax	326	421	735	272	127	39	18	98	186	393	10. Impôt sur le revenu
11. Profit after tax	1708	1043	1521	-5891	-9863	-9290	-5873	-2710	1500	3902	11. Bénéfices après impôt
12. Distributed profit	991	1111	665	223	30	57	63	102	555	1049	12. Bénéfices distribués
13. Retained profit	717	-68	856	-6114	-9893	-9347	-5936	-2812	945	2853	13. Bénéfices mis en réserve
BALANCE SHEET											**BILAN**
Assets											**Actif**
14. Cash & balance with Central bank	13457	16228	12485	10489	11440	9296	7947	13498	6762	10600	14. Caisse & solde auprès de la Banque centrale
15. Interbank deposits	7586	8034	6464	3232	8236	4573	4170	1617	3026	7104	15. Dépôts interbancaires
16. Loans	235294	289508	321154	327169	308638	293033	245139	219917	218652	266617	16. Prêts
17. Securities	64450	72232	77896	111357	109499	137389	143269	132160	118503	122008	17. Valeurs mobilières
18. Other assets	74991	74888	85839	80049	84579	100224	97814	87457	98944	73254	18. Autres actifs
Liabilities											**Passif**
19. Capital & reserves	28065	32255	36206	39140	27247	26411	24374	20831	22294	25062	19. Capital et réserves
20. Borrowing from Central bank	3283	2001	2292	4013	5436	5416	605	5553	12112	2873	20. Emprunts auprès de la Banque centrale
21. Interbank deposits	16142	17207	17139	18706	22060	16456	19589	20679	20101	24893	21. Dépôts interbancaires
22. Non-bank deposits	204387	212448	241785	245335	250665	266582	249732	243884	241551	264185	22. Dépôts non bancaires
23. Bonds	25529	37690	54424	63503	57863	48379	49753	37284	27613	32846	23. Obligations
24. Other liabilities	118372	159289	151992	161599	159121	181271	154286	126418	122216	129724	24. Autres engagements
Balance sheet total											**Total du bilan**
25. End-year total	395778	460890	503838	532296	522392	544515	498339	454649	445887	479583	25. En fin d'exercice
26. Average total	353724	428334	482364	518067	527344	533454	521427	476494	450268	462735	26. Moyen

FINLAND

Commercial banks

FINLANDE

Banques commerciales

	1988	1989	1990	1991	1992	1993	1994	1995	1996	1997	
Million markkaa											*Millions de markkas*
Memorandum items											***Pour mémoire***
27. Short-term securities	*24184*	*25650*	*31939*	*43075*	*39169*	*57799*	*73528*	*44008*	*36223*	*41500*	*27. Titres à court terme*
28. Bonds	*32844*	*36928*	*35860*	*50301*	*59575*	*68817*	*58112*	*64371*	*57934*	*57684*	*28. Obligations*
29. Shares and participations	*7422*	*9654*	*10097*	*17981*	*10755*	*10773*	*11629*	*23781*	*24346*	*22824*	*29. Actions et participations*
30. Claims on non-residents	*87112*	*92621*	*101667*	*102735*	*114403*	*127282*	*103937*	*94475*	*110259*	*132682*	*30. Créances sur des non-résidents*
31. Liabilities to non-residents	*154544*	*172104*	*215469*	*218400*	*205809*	*182759*	*142186*	*114923*	*110719*	*124976*	*31. Engagements envers des non-résidents*
Capital adequacy											***Solvabilité***
32. Tier 1 Capital	..	..	..	..	..	..	..	..	..	..	*32. Fonds propres de base*
33. Tier 2 Capital	..	..	..	..	..	..	..	..	..	..	*33. Fonds propres complémentaires*
34. Supervisory deductions	..	..	..	..	..	..	..	..	..	..	*34. Eléments à déduire des fonds propres*
35. Total net capital resources	..	..	..	..	..	..	..	..	..	..	*35. Total net des ressources en capital*
36. Risk-weighted assets	..	..	..	..	..	..	..	..	..	..	*36. Actifs pondérés des risques*
SUPPLEMENTARY INFORMATION											**RENSEIGNEMENTS COMPLEMENTAIRES**
37. Number of institutions	7	10	10	12	10	10	10	7	8	9	37. Nombre d'institutions
38. Number of branches	1004	1010	1037	948	860	1114	909	729	620	547	38. Nombre de succursales
39. Number of employees (x 1000)	26.2	26.9	26.5	24.2	22.3	20.1	23.1	20.2	17.6	16.6	39. Nombre de salariés (x 1000)

Notes

- Including the Post office bank (Postipankki).

Notes

- Y inclus la Banque postale (Postipankki).

FINLAND
Commercial banks

FINLANDE
Banques commerciales

Per cent	1988	1989	1990	1991	1992	1993	1994	1995	1996	1997	Pourcentage
INCOME STATEMENT ANALYSIS											**ANALYSE DU COMPTE DE RESULTATS**
% of average balance sheet total											**% du total moyen du bilan**
40. Interest income	8.18	9.60	10.59	10.14	9.37	7.26	5.60	5.69	4.63	4.36	40. Produits financiers
41. Interest expenses	6.57	8.17	8.99	8.88	8.24	5.89	4.25	4.25	3.25	2.86	41. Frais financiers
42. Net interest income	1.61	1.43	1.60	1.25	1.12	1.37	1.36	1.44	1.38	1.50	42. Produits financiers nets
43. Non-interest income (net)	2.18	1.79	1.67	1.67	1.37	1.44	1.44	1.31	1.65	1.34	43. Produits non financiers (nets)
a. Fees and commissions receivable	..	..	..	..	..	..	..	..	..	..	*a. Frais et commissions à recevoir*
b. Fees and commissions payable	..	..	..	..	..	..	..	..	..	..	*b. Frais et commissions à payer*
c. Net profits or loss on financial operations	..	..	..	..	..	..	..	..	..	..	*c. Profits ou pertes nets sur opérations financières*
d. Other	..	..	..	..	..	..	..	..	..	..	*d. Autres*
44. Gross income	3.79	3.22	3.27	2.92	2.49	2.81	2.79	2.75	3.03	2.84	44. Résultat brut
45. Operating expenses	2.81	2.64	2.61	4.02	4.35	4.54	3.96	3.32	2.70	1.90	45. Frais d'exploitation
a. Staff costs	*1.13*	*1.05*	*0.93*	*0.97*	*0.86*	*0.77*	*0.86*	*0.79*	*0.87*	*0.59*	*a. Dépenses en personnel*
b. Property costs	*0.24*	*0.25*	*0.26*	*0.26*	*0.20*	*0.24*	*0.25*	*0.22*	*0.23*	*0.20*	*b. Dépenses en immobilier*
c. Other	*1.45*	*1.34*	*1.41*	*2.79*	*3.29*	*3.54*	*2.85*	*2.31*	*1.60*	*1.11*	*c. Autres*
46. Net income	0.97	0.58	0.66	-1.10	-1.86	-1.73	-1.17	-0.57	0.33	0.94	46. Résultat net
47. Provisions (net)	0.40	0.24	0.19	-0.01	-0.01	-	-0.05	-0.03	-0.05	0.01	47. Provisions (nettes)
a. Provisions on loans	*0.38*	*0.32*	*0.25*	*-0.09*	*-0.01*	*0.01*	*-0.04*	..	..	..	*a. Provisions sur prêts*
b. Provisions on securities	*0.01*	*-0.08*	*-0.20*	*0.08*	-	-	*-0.01*	..	..	..	*b. Provisions sur titres*
c. Other	-	-	*0.13*	-	-	-	-	..	..	..	*c. Autres*
48. Profit before tax	0.58	0.34	0.47	-1.08	-1.85	-1.73	-1.12	-0.55	0.37	0.93	48. Bénéfices avant impôt
49. Income tax	0.09	0.10	0.15	0.05	0.02	0.01	-	0.02	0.04	0.08	49. Impôt sur le revenu
50. Profit after tax	0.48	0.24	0.32	-1.14	-1.87	-1.74	-1.13	-0.57	0.33	0.84	50. Bénéfices après impôt
51. Distributed profit	0.28	0.26	0.14	0.04	0.01	0.01	0.01	0.02	0.12	0.23	51. Bénéfices distribués
52. Retained profit	0.20	-0.02	0.18	-1.18	-1.88	-1.75	-1.14	-0.59	0.21	0.62	52. Bénéfices mis en réserve
% of gross income											**% du total du résultat brut**
53. Net interest income	42.48	44.31	48.89	42.87	45.07	48.77	48.56	52.49	45.65	52.67	53. Produits financiers nets
54. Non-interest income (net)	57.52	55.69	51.11	57.13	54.93	51.23	51.44	47.51	54.35	47.33	54. Produits non financiers (nets)
a. Fees and commissions receivable	..	..	..	..	..	..	..	..	..	..	*a. Frais et commissions à recevoir*
b. Fees and commissions payable	..	..	..	..	..	..	..	..	..	..	*b. Frais et commissions à payer*
c. Net profits or loss on financial operations	..	..	..	..	..	..	..	..	..	..	*c. Profits ou pertes nets sur opérations financières*
d. Other	..	..	..	..	..	..	..	..	..	..	*d. Autres*
55. Operating expenses	74.31	81.96	79.83	137.49	174.50	161.53	141.95	120.88	89.22	66.88	55. Frais d'exploitation
a. Staff costs	*29.85*	*32.64*	*28.54*	*33.13*	*34.68*	*27.38*	*30.66*	*28.75*	*28.84*	*20.90*	*a. Dépenses en personnel*
b. Property costs	*6.24*	*7.81*	*8.04*	*8.84*	*8.02*	*8.40*	*9.08*	*8.09*	*7.69*	*6.97*	*b. Dépenses en immobilier*
c. Other	*38.22*	*41.51*	*43.25*	*95.52*	*131.80*	*125.75*	*102.21*	*84.05*	*52.69*	*39.00*	*c. Autres*
56. Net income	25.69	18.04	20.17	-37.49	-74.50	-61.53	-41.95	-20.88	10.78	33.12	56. Résultat net
57. Provisions (net)	10.51	7.43	5.86	-0.36	-0.45	0.13	-1.72	-0.93	-1.58	0.43	57. Provisions (nettes)
a. Provisions on loans	*10.12*	*9.83*	*7.77*	*-3.07*	*-0.36*	*0.29*	*-1.45*	..	..	..	*a. Provisions sur prêts*
b. Provisions on securities	*0.39*	*-2.40*	*-6.02*	*2.72*	*-0.09*	*-0.15*	*-0.27*	..	..	..	*b. Provisions sur titres*
c. Other	-	-	*4.12*	-	-	-	-	..	..	..	*c. Autres*
58. Profit before tax	15.19	10.62	14.31	-37.14	-74.05	-61.66	-40.23	-19.95	12.37	32.70	58. Bénéfices avant impôt
59. Income tax	2.43	3.05	4.66	1.80	0.97	0.26	0.12	0.75	1.36	2.99	59. Impôt sur le revenu
60. Profit after tax	12.75	7.56	9.65	-38.93	-75.02	-61.92	-40.36	-20.70	11.00	29.70	60. Bénéfices après impôt
% of net income											**% du total du résultat net**
61. Provisions (net)	40.89	41.16	29.06	0.95	0.60	-0.22	4.10	4.46	-14.69	1.29	61. Provisions (nettes)
a. Provisions on loans	*39.38*	*54.46*	*38.52*	*8.20*	*0.48*	*-0.47*	*3.46*	..	..	..	*a. Provisions sur prêts*
b. Provisions on securities	*1.51*	*-13.30*	*-29.87*	*-7.24*	*0.12*	*0.25*	*0.64*	..	..	..	*b. Provisions sur titres*
c. Other	-	-	*20.41*	-	-	-	-	..	..	..	*c. Autres*
62. Profit before tax	59.11	58.84	70.94	99.05	99.40	100.22	95.90	95.54	114.69	98.71	62. Bénéfices avant impôt
63. Income tax	9.47	16.92	23.11	-4.79	-1.30	-0.42	-0.29	-3.58	12.65	9.03	63. Impôt sur le revenu
64. Profit after tax	49.64	41.92	47.83	103.84	100.69	100.64	96.20	99.12	102.04	89.68	64. Bénéfices après impôt

FINLAND / FINLANDE

Commercial banks / Banques commerciales

	1988	1989	1990	1991	1992	1993	1994	1995	1996	1997	
Per cent											*Pourcentage*
BALANCE SHEET ANALYSIS											**ANALYSE DU BILAN**
% of year-end balance sheet total											**% du total du bilan en fin d'exercice**
Assets											**Actif**
65. Cash & balance with Central bank	3.40	3.52	2.48	1.97	2.19	1.71	1.59	2.97	1.52	2.21	65. Caisse & solde auprès de la Banque centrale
66. Interbank deposits	1.92	1.74	1.28	0.61	1.58	0.84	0.84	0.36	0.68	1.48	66. Dépôts interbancaires
67. Loans	59.45	62.81	63.74	61.46	59.08	53.82	49.19	48.37	49.04	55.59	67. Prêts
68. Securities	16.28	15.67	15.46	20.92	20.96	25.23	28.75	29.07	26.58	25.44	68. Valeurs mobilières
69. Other assets	18.95	16.25	17.04	15.04	16.19	18.41	19.63	19.24	22.19	15.27	69. Autres actifs
Liabilities											**Passif**
70. Capital & reserves	7.09	7.00	7.19	7.35	5.22	4.85	4.89	4.58	5.00	5.23	70. Capital et réserves
71. Borrowing from Central bank	0.83	0.43	0.45	0.75	1.04	0.99	0.12	1.22	2.72	0.60	71. Emprunts auprès de la Banque centrale
72. Interbank deposits	4.08	3.73	3.40	3.51	4.22	3.02	3.93	4.55	4.51	5.19	72. Dépôts interbancaires
73. Non-bank deposits	51.64	46.10	47.99	46.09	47.98	48.96	50.11	53.64	54.17	55.09	73. Dépôts non bancaires
74. Bonds	6.45	8.18	10.80	11.93	11.08	8.88	9.98	8.20	6.19	6.85	74. Obligations
75. Other liabilities	29.91	34.56	30.17	30.36	30.46	33.29	30.96	27.81	27.41	27.05	75. Autres engagements
Memorandum items											***Pour mémoire***
76. Short-term securities	*6.11*	*5.57*	*6.34*	*8.09*	*7.50*	*10.61*	*14.75*	*9.68*	*8.12*	*8.65*	*76. Titres à court terme*
77. Bonds	*8.30*	*8.01*	*7.12*	*9.45*	*11.40*	*12.64*	*11.66*	*14.16*	*12.99*	*12.03*	*77. Obligations*
78. Shares and participations	*1.88*	*2.09*	*2.00*	*3.38*	*2.06*	*1.98*	*2.33*	*5.23*	*5.46*	*4.76*	*78. Actions et participations*
79. Claims on non-residents	*22.01*	*20.10*	*20.18*	*19.30*	*21.90*	*23.38*	*20.86*	*20.78*	*24.73*	*27.67*	*79. Créances sur des non-résidents*
80. Liabilities to non-residents	*39.05*	*37.34*	*42.77*	*41.03*	*39.40*	*33.56*	*28.53*	*25.28*	*24.83*	*26.06*	*80. Engagements envers des non-résidents*

* See notes on previous pages.

* Voir les notes en pages précédentes.

FINLAND — FINLANDE

Foreign commercial banks — Banques commerciales étrangères

	1988	1989	1990	1991	1992	1993	1994	1995	1996	1997	
Million markkaa											*Millions de markkas*
INCOME STATEMENT											**COMPTE DE RESULTATS**
1. Interest income	744	1121	984	1526	1554	1190	718	2247	1956	1951	1. Produits financiers
2. Interest expenses	715	1086	923	1507	1506	1137	666	2196	1669	1839	2. Frais financiers
3. Net interest income	29	35	61	19	48	53	52	51	287	112	3. Produits financiers nets
4. Non-interest income (net)	37	40	38	36	83	74	38	252	129	149	4. Produits non financiers (nets)
a. Fees and commissions receivable	..	..	..	..	..	..	..	..	..	..	*a. Frais et commissions à recevoir*
b. Fees and commissions payable	..	..	..	..	..	..	..	..	..	..	*b. Frais et commissions à payer*
c. Net profits or loss on financial operations	..	..	..	..	..	..	..	..	..	..	*c. Profits ou pertes nets sur opérations financières*
d. Other	..	..	..	..	..	..	..	..	..	..	*d. Autres*
5. Gross income	66	75	99	55	131	127	90	303	416	261	5. Résultat brut
6. Operating expenses	70	126	95	133	149	92	110	248	309	398	6. Frais d'exploitation
a. Staff costs	*39*	*37*	*37*	*47*	*38*	*39*	*40*	*123*	*165*	*193*	*a. Dépenses en personnel*
b. Property costs	*10*	*11*	*13*	*14*	*8*	*6*	*5*	*14*	*14*	*21*	*b. Dépenses en immobilier*
c. Other	*21*	*78*	*45*	*72*	*103*	*47*	*65*	*111*	*130*	*184*	*c. Autres*
7. Net income	-4	-51	4	-78	-18	35	-20	55	107	-137	7. Résultat net
8. Provisions (net)	-3	3	-	5	41	-5	-11	-10	20	-27	8. Provisions (nettes)
a. Provisions on loans	-	*1*	*2*	*5*	*3*	*-5*	*1*	..	..	..	*a. Provisions sur prêts*
b. Provisions on securities	*-3*	*2*	*-2*	-	*38*	-	*-12*	..	..	..	*b. Provisions sur titres*
c. Other	-	-	-	-	-	-	-	..	..	..	*c. Autres*
9. Profit before tax	-1	-54	4	-83	-59	40	-9	65	87	-110	9. Bénéfices avant impôt
10. Income tax	3	2	4	1	3	9	4	16	18	2	10. Impôt sur le revenu
11. Profit after tax	-4	-56	-	-84	-62	31	-13	49	69	-112	11. Bénéfices après impôt
12. Distributed profit	-	-	-	-	-	-	-	-	-	-	12. Bénéfices distribués
13. Retained profit	-4	-56	-	-84	-62	31	-13	49	69	-112	13. Bénéfices mis en réserve
BALANCE SHEET											**BILAN**
Assets											**Actif**
14. Cash & balance with Central bank	176	154	36	108	108	43	86	161	355	312	14. Caisse & solde auprès de la Banque centrale
15. Interbank deposits	323	81	297	314	33	4	104	81	122	192	15. Dépôts interbancaires
16. Loans	447	1458	792	1771	1899	380	354	5471	4242	6668	16. Prêts
17. Securities	3315	2637	2896	4528	4787	4430	6682	24783	15793	10404	17. Valeurs mobilières
18. Other assets	950	488	356	463	871	1331	5161	12771	20444	31034	18. Autres actifs
Liabilities											**Passif**
19. Capital & reserves	243	240	186	254	120	150	13	65	53	-145	19. Capital et réserves
20. Borrowing from Central bank	1	-	-	99	1	-	103	2147	497	-	20. Emprunts auprès de la Banque centrale
21. Interbank deposits	244	608	51	50	-	506	10	189	12	35	21. Dépôts interbancaires
22. Non-bank deposits	2910	1966	2267	2642	287	1458	3216	5193	2850	2615	22. Dépôts non bancaires
23. Bonds	-	-	-	-	-	-	-	-	-	-	23. Obligations
24. Other liabilities	1813	2004	1873	4139	7290	4074	9045	35673	37544	46105	24. Autres engagements
Balance sheet total											**Total du bilan**
25. End-year total	5211	4818	4377	7184	7698	6188	12387	43267	40956	48610	25. En fin d'exercice
26. Average total	5095	5015	4598	5781	7441	6943	9288	27827	42112	44783	26. Moyen

FINLAND / FINLANDE

Foreign commercial banks / Banques commerciales étrangères

	1988	1989	1990	1991	1992	1993	1994	1995	1996	1997	
Million markkaa											*Millions de markkas*
Memorandum items											***Pour mémoire***
27. Short-term securities	*3152*	*2304*	*2747*	*4298*	*4300*	*3556*	*6680*	*17195*	*11505*	*8784*	*27. Titres à court terme*
28. Bonds	*150*	*319*	*136*	*216*	*479*	*866*	-	*7577*	*4219*	*1732*	*28. Obligations*
29. Shares and participations	*13*	*14*	*13*	*14*	*8*	*8*	*2*	*11*	*159*	*95*	*29. Actions et participations*
30. Claims on non-residents	*745*	*714*	*237*	*918*	*1940*	*1331*	*3722*	*10440*	*14794*	*24495*	*30. Créances sur des non-résidents*
31. Liabilities to non-residents	*2860*	*1917*	*2229*	*2517*	*4875*	*1458*	*3333*	*12559*	*9461*	*14633*	*31. Engagements envers des non-résidents*
Capital adequacy											***Solvabilité***
32. Tier 1 Capital	..	..	..	..	..	..	..	..	..	..	*32. Fonds propres de base*
33. Tier 2 Capital	..	..	..	..	..	..	..	..	..	..	*33. Fonds propres complémentaires*
34. Supervisory deductions	..	..	..	..	..	..	..	..	..	..	*34. Eléments à déduire des fonds propres*
35. Total net capital resources	..	..	..	..	..	..	..	..	..	..	*35. Total net des ressources en capital*
36. Risk-weighted assets	..	..	..	..	..	..	..	..	..	..	*36. Actifs pondérés des risques*
SUPPLEMENTARY INFORMATION											**RENSEIGNEMENTS COMPLEMENTAIRES**
37. Number of institutions	4	4	4	5	4	4	4	4	4	5	37. Nombre d'institutions
38. Number of branches	-	-	-	-	-	-	-	5	9	12	38. Nombre de succursales
39. Number of employees (x 1000)	0.2	0.2	0.1	0.1	0.1	0.1	0.2	0.4	0.4	0.5	39. Nombre de salariés (x 1000)

FINLAND
Foreign commercial banks

FINLANDE
Banques commerciales étrangères

	1988	1989	1990	1991	1992	1993	1994	1995	1996	1997	
Per cent											*Pourcentage*
INCOME STATEMENT ANALYSIS											**ANALYSE DU COMPTE DE RESULTATS**
% of average balance sheet total											**% du total moyen du bilan**
40. Interest income	14.60	22.35	21.40	26.40	20.88	17.14	7.73	8.07	4.64	4.36	40. Produits financiers
41. Interest expenses	14.03	21.66	20.07	26.07	20.24	16.38	7.17	7.89	3.96	4.11	41. Frais financiers
42. Net interest income	0.57	0.70	1.33	0.33	0.65	0.76	0.56	0.18	0.68	0.25	42. Produits financiers nets
43. Non-interest income (net)	0.73	0.80	0.83	0.62	1.12	1.07	0.41	0.91	0.31	0.33	43. Produits non financiers (nets)
a. Fees and commissions receivable	..	..	..	..	..	..	..	..	..	..	*a. Frais et commissions à recevoir*
b. Fees and commissions payable	..	..	..	..	..	..	..	..	..	..	*b. Frais et commissions à payer*
c. Net profits or loss on financial operations	..	..	..	..	..	..	..	..	..	..	*c. Profits ou pertes nets sur opérations financières*
d. Other	..	..	..	..	..	..	..	..	..	..	*d. Autres*
44. Gross income	1.30	1.50	2.15	0.95	1.76	1.83	0.97	1.09	0.99	0.58	44. Résultat brut
45. Operating expenses	1.37	2.51	2.07	2.30	2.00	1.33	1.18	0.89	0.73	0.89	45. Frais d'exploitation
a. Staff costs	*0.77*	*0.74*	*0.80*	*0.81*	*0.51*	*0.56*	*0.43*	*0.44*	*0.39*	*0.43*	*a. Dépenses en personnel*
b. Property costs	*0.20*	*0.22*	*0.28*	*0.24*	*0.11*	*0.09*	*0.05*	*0.05*	*0.03*	*0.05*	*b. Dépenses en immobilier*
c. Other	*0.41*	*1.56*	*0.98*	*1.25*	*1.38*	*0.68*	*0.70*	*0.40*	*0.31*	*0.41*	*c. Autres*
46. Net income	-0.08	-1.02	0.09	-1.35	-0.24	0.50	-0.22	0.20	0.25	-0.31	46. Résultat net
47. Provisions (net)	-0.06	0.06	-	0.09	0.55	-0.07	-0.12	-0.04	0.05	-0.06	47. Provisions (nettes)
a. Provisions on loans	-	*0.02*	*0.04*	*0.09*	*0.04*	*-0.07*	*0.01*	..	..	..	*a. Provisions sur prêts*
b. Provisions on securities	*-0.06*	*0.04*	*-0.04*	-	*0.51*	-	*-0.13*	..	..	..	*b. Provisions sur titres*
c. Other	-	-	-	-	-	-	-	..	..	..	*c. Autres*
48. Profit before tax	-0.02	-1.08	0.09	-1.44	-0.79	0.58	-0.10	0.23	0.21	-0.25	48. Bénéfices avant impôt
49. Income tax	0.06	0.04	0.09	0.02	0.04	0.13	0.04	0.06	0.04	-	49. Impôt sur le revenu
50. Profit after tax	-0.08	-1.12	-	-1.45	-0.83	0.45	-0.14	0.18	0.16	-0.25	50. Bénéfices après impôt
51. Distributed profit	-	-	-	-	-	-	-	-	-	-	51. Bénéfices distribués
52. Retained profit	-0.08	-1.12	-	-1.45	-0.83	0.45	-0.14	0.18	0.16	-0.25	52. Bénéfices mis en réserve
% of gross income											**% du total du résultat brut**
53. Net interest income	43.94	46.67	61.62	34.55	36.64	41.73	57.78	16.83	68.99	42.91	53. Produits financiers nets
54. Non-interest income (net)	56.06	53.33	38.38	65.45	63.36	58.27	42.22	83.17	31.01	57.09	54. Produits non financiers (nets)
a. Fees and commissions receivable	..	..	..	..	..	..	..	..	..	..	*a. Frais et commissions à recevoir*
b. Fees and commissions payable	..	..	..	..	..	..	..	..	..	..	*b. Frais et commissions à payer*
c. Net profits or loss on financial operations	..	..	..	..	..	..	..	..	..	..	*c. Profits ou pertes nets sur opérations financières*
d. Other	..	..	..	..	..	..	..	..	..	..	*d. Autres*
55. Operating expenses	106.06	168.00	95.96	241.82	113.74	72.44	122.22	81.85	74.28	152.49	55. Frais d'exploitation
a. Staff costs	*59.09*	*49.33*	*37.37*	*85.45*	*29.01*	*30.71*	*44.44*	*40.59*	*39.66*	*73.95*	*a. Dépenses en personnel*
b. Property costs	*15.15*	*14.67*	*13.13*	*25.45*	*6.11*	*4.72*	*5.56*	*4.62*	*3.37*	*8.05*	*b. Dépenses en immobilier*
c. Other	*31.82*	*104.00*	*45.45*	*130.91*	*78.63*	*37.01*	*72.22*	*36.63*	*31.25*	*70.50*	*c. Autres*
56. Net income	-6.06	-68.00	4.04	-141.82	-13.74	27.56	-22.22	18.15	25.72	-52.49	56. Résultat net
57. Provisions (net)	-4.55	4.00	-	9.09	31.30	-3.94	-12.22	-3.30	4.81	-10.34	57. Provisions (nettes)
a. Provisions on loans	-	*1.33*	*2.02*	*9.09*	*2.29*	*-3.94*	*1.11*	..	..	..	*a. Provisions sur prêts*
b. Provisions on securities	*-4.55*	*2.67*	*-2.02*	-	*29.01*	-	*-13.33*	..	..	..	*b. Provisions sur titres*
c. Other	-	-	-	-	-	-	-	..	..	..	*c. Autres*
58. Profit before tax	-1.52	-72.00	4.04	-150.91	-45.04	31.50	-10.00	21.45	20.91	-42.15	58. Bénéfices avant impôt
59. Income tax	4.55	2.67	4.04	1.82	2.29	7.09	4.44	5.28	4.33	0.77	59. Impôt sur le revenu
60. Profit after tax	-6.06	-74.67	-	-152.73	-47.33	24.41	-14.44	16.17	16.59	-42.91	60. Bénéfices après impôt
% of net income											**% du total du résultat net**
61. Provisions (net)	75.00	-5.88	-	-6.41	..	-14.29	55.00	-18.18	18.69	19.71	61. Provisions (nettes)
a. Provisions on loans	-	*-1.96*	*50.00*	*-6.41*	..	*-14.29*	*-5.00*	..	..	..	*a. Provisions sur prêts*
b. Provisions on securities	*75.00*	*-3.92*	*-50.00*	-	..	-	*60.00*	..	..	..	*b. Provisions sur titres*
c. Other	-	-	-	-	..	-	-	..	..	..	*c. Autres*
62. Profit before tax	25.00	105.88	100.00	106.41	..	114.29	45.00	118.18	81.31	80.29	62. Bénéfices avant impôt
63. Income tax	-75.00	-3.92	100.00	-1.28	..	25.71	-20.00	29.09	16.82	-1.46	63. Impôt sur le revenu
64. Profit after tax	100.00	109.80	-	107.69	..	88.57	65.00	89.09	64.49	81.75	64. Bénéfices après impôt

FINLAND | FINLANDE

Foreign commercial banks | Banques commerciales étrangères

	1988	1989	1990	1991	1992	1993	1994	1995	1996	1997	
Per cent											*Pourcentage*
BALANCE SHEET ANALYSIS											**ANALYSE DU BILAN**
% of year-end balance sheet total											**% du total du bilan en fin d'exercice**
Assets											**Actif**
65. Cash & balance with Central bank	3.38	3.20	0.82	1.50	1.40	0.69	0.69	0.37	0.87	0.64	65. Caisse & solde auprès de la Banque centrale
66. Interbank deposits	6.20	1.68	6.79	4.37	0.43	0.06	0.84	0.19	0.30	0.39	66. Dépôts interbancaires
67. Loans	8.58	30.26	18.09	24.65	24.67	6.14	2.86	12.64	10.36	13.72	67. Prêts
68. Securities	63.62	54.73	66.16	63.03	62.18	71.59	53.94	57.28	38.56	21.40	68. Valeurs mobilières
69. Other assets	18.23	10.13	8.13	6.44	11.31	21.51	41.66	29.52	49.92	63.84	69. Autres actifs
Liabilities											**Passif**
70. Capital & reserves	4.66	4.98	4.25	3.54	1.56	2.42	0.10	0.15	0.13	-0.30	70. Capital et réserves
71. Borrowing from Central bank	0.02	-	-	1.38	0.01	-	0.83	4.96	1.21	-	71. Emprunts auprès de la Banque centrale
72. Interbank deposits	4.68	12.62	1.17	0.70	-	8.18	0.08	0.44	0.03	0.07	72. Dépôts interbancaires
73. Non-bank deposits	55.84	40.81	51.79	36.78	3.73	23.56	25.96	12.00	6.96	5.38	73. Dépôts non bancaires
74. Bonds	-	-	-	-	-	-	-	-	-	-	74. Obligations
75. Other liabilities	34.79	41.59	42.79	57.61	94.70	65.84	73.02	82.45	91.67	94.85	75. Autres engagements
Memorandum items											***Pour mémoire***
76. Short-term securities	*60.49*	*47.82*	*62.76*	*59.83*	*55.86*	*57.47*	*53.93*	*39.74*	*28.09*	*18.07*	*76. Titres à court terme*
77. Bonds	*2.88*	*6.62*	*3.11*	*3.01*	*6.22*	*13.99*	-	*17.51*	*10.30*	*3.56*	*77. Obligations*
78. Shares and participations	*0.25*	*0.29*	*0.30*	*0.19*	*0.10*	*0.13*	*0.02*	*0.03*	*0.39*	*0.20*	*78. Actions et participations*
79. Claims on non-residents	*14.30*	*14.82*	*5.41*	*12.78*	*25.20*	*21.51*	*30.05*	*24.13*	*36.12*	*50.39*	*79. Créances sur des non-résidents*
80. Liabilities to non-residents	*54.88*	*39.79*	*50.93*	*35.04*	*63.33*	*23.56*	*26.91*	*29.03*	*23.10*	*30.10*	*80. Engagements envers des non-résidents*

FINLAND / FINLANDE

Savings banks / Caisses d'épargne

	1988	1989	1990	1991	1992	1993	1994(1)	1995	1996	1997	
Million markkaa											*Millions de markkas*
INCOME STATEMENT											**COMPTE DE RESULTATS**
1. Interest income	7171	9967	12042	12413	10426	7610	2672	1405	1308	1306	1. Produits financiers
2. Interest expenses	4572	7041	9119	9888	10008	6198	2397	649	511	441	2. Frais financiers
3. Net interest income	2599	2926	2923	2525	418	1412	275	756	797	865	3. Produits financiers nets
4. Non-interest income (net)	3051	1865	2128	2401	3188	7416	757	315	362	362	4. Produits non financiers (nets)
a. Fees and commissions receivable	..	..	..	..	..	..	..	..	..	..	*a. Frais et commissions à recevoir*
b. Fees and commissions payable	..	..	..	..	..	..	..	..	..	..	*b. Frais et commissions à payer*
c. Net profits or loss on financial operations	..	..	..	..	..	..	..	..	..	..	*c. Profits ou pertes nets sur opérations financières*
d. Other	..	..	..	..	..	..	..	..	..	..	*d. Autres*
5. Gross income	5650	4791	5051	4926	3606	8828	1032	1071	1159	1227	5. Résultat brut
6. Operating expenses	3777	4337	4298	5760	14489	8391	2235	916	937	929	6. Frais d'exploitation
a. Staff costs	*1873*	*1830*	*1830*	*1714*	*1644*	*1456*	*672*	*313*	*314*	*340*	*a. Dépenses en personnel*
b. Property costs	*525*	*805*	*897*	*972*	*1127*	*1013*	*438*	*167*	*152*	*140*	*b. Dépenses en immobilier*
c. Other	*1379*	*1702*	*1571*	*3074*	*11718*	*5922*	*1125*	*436*	*471*	*449*	*c. Autres*
7. Net income	1873	454	753	-834	-10883	437	-1203	155	222	298	7. Résultat net
8. Provisions (net)	1028	234	508	-319	-370	17	9	20	24	24	8. Provisions (nettes)
a. Provisions on loans	*399*	*494*	*523*	*94*	*-262*	*15*	*16*	..	..	..	*a. Provisions sur prêts*
b. Provisions on securities	*425*	*-263*	*-23*	*-413*	*-108*	*2*	*-7*	..	..	..	*b. Provisions sur titres*
c. Other	*204*	*3*	*8*	-	-	-	-	..	..	..	*c. Autres*
9. Profit before tax	845	220	245	-515	-10513	420	-1212	135	198	274	9. Bénéfices avant impôt
10. Income tax	68	100	97	50	16	7	13	29	44	55	10. Impôt sur le revenu
11. Profit after tax	777	120	148	-565	-10529	413	-1225	106	154	219	11. Bénéfices après impôt
12. Distributed profit	-	-	-	-	-	-	-	-	-	-	12. Bénéfices distribués
13. Retained profit	777	120	148	-565	-10529	413	-1225	106	154	219	13. Bénéfices mis en réserve
BALANCE SHEET											**BILAN**
Assets											**Actif**
14. Cash & balance with Central bank	5960	9169	6279	4459	9577	838	818	776	764	807	14. Caisse & solde auprès de la Banque centrale
15. Interbank deposits	8182	8564	9134	9109	7771	32505	1692	1407	1077	1382	15. Dépôts interbancaires
16. Loans	69181	83957	85554	82047	73871	17398	18110	12374	13934	16005	16. Prêts
17. Securities	5603	9777	8780	8228	4910	6692	5163	4179	5686	6134	17. Valeurs mobilières
18. Other assets	10031	9786	12072	16181	17890	16571	18487	2275	2481	2299	18. Autres actifs
Liabilities											**Passif**
19. Capital & reserves	6317	8144	7891	7227	6178	3085	1487	1350	1694	1912	19. Capital et réserves
20. Borrowing from Central bank	1028	1178	1107	1150	2108	316	173	-	-	-	20. Emprunts auprès de la Banque centrale
21. Interbank deposits	84	250	173	72	96	84	14	-	-	-	21. Dépôts interbancaires
22. Non-bank deposits	65717	71340	68107	70422	66714	14568	16173	17561	19266	21608	22. Dépôts non bancaires
23. Bonds	1891	3238	2229	5516	7912	7240	5181	448	415	533	23. Obligations
24. Other liabilities	23920	37103	42312	35637	31011	48711	21242	1652	2567	2574	24. Autres engagements
Balance sheet total											**Total du bilan**
25. End-year total	98957	121253	121819	120024	114019	74004	44270	21011	23942	26627	25. En fin d'exercice
26. Average total	85171	110105	121536	120922	117022	94012	59137	32641	22477	25285	26. Moyen

FINLAND / FINLANDE

Savings banks / Caisses d'épargne

	1988	1989	1990	1991	1992	1993	1994(1)	1995	1996	1997	
Million markkaa											*Millions de markkas*
Memorandum items											***Pour mémoire***
27. Short-term securities	*953*	*1946*	*1329*	*1810*	*2236*	*3915*	*4140*	*2059*	*2550*	*2325*	*27. Titres à court terme*
28. Bonds	*2861*	*2611*	*2420*	*1742*	*1291*	*1458*	-	*1911*	*2900*	*3626*	*28. Obligations*
29. Shares and participations	*1789*	*5220*	*5031*	*4676*	*1383*	*1319*	*1023*	*209*	*236*	*183*	*29. Actions et participations*
30. Claims on non-residents	*394*	*742*	*54*	*28*	*39*	*98*	*19*	*69*	*104*	*238*	*30. Créances sur des non-résidents*
31. Liabilities to non-residents	*911*	*2318*	*321*	*4*	*1334*	*181*	*14*	*11*	*23*	*69*	*31. Engagements envers des non-résidents*
Capital adequacy											***Solvabilité***
32. Tier 1 Capital	..	..	..	..	..	..	..	..	..	..	*32. Fonds propres de base*
33. Tier 2 Capital	..	..	..	..	..	..	..	..	..	..	*33. Fonds propres complémentaires*
34. Supervisory deductions	..	..	..	..	..	..	..	..	..	..	*34. Eléments à déduire des fonds propres*
35. Total net capital resources	..	..	..	..	..	..	..	..	..	..	*35. Total net des ressources en capital*
36. Risk-weighted assets	..	..	..	..	..	..	..	..	..	..	*36. Actifs pondérés des risques*
SUPPLEMENTARY INFORMATION											**RENSEIGNEMENTS COMPLEMENTAIRES**
37. Number of institutions	211	178	150	86	39	41	41	40	40	40	37. Nombre d'institutions
38. Number of branches	1102	1130	984	967	845	173	233	211	207	211	38. Nombre de succursales
39. Number of employees (x 1000)	11.7	11.9	10.1	9.5	7.8	7.2	1.7	1.4	1.6	1.7	39. Nombre de salariés (x 1000)

1. Break in series. Beginning 1994, change in the composition of Savings banks.

1. Rupture dans les séries. A partir de 1994, changement dans la composition des Caisses d'épargne.

FINLAND
Savings banks

FINLANDE
Caisses d'épargne

	1988	1989	1990	1991	1992	1993	1994(1)	1995	1996	1997	
Per cent											*Pourcentage*
INCOME STATEMENT ANALYSIS											**ANALYSE DU COMPTE DE RESULTATS**
% of average balance sheet total											**% du total moyen du bilan**
40. Interest income	8.42	9.05	9.91	10.27	8.91	8.09	4.52	4.30	5.82	5.17	40. Produits financiers
41. Interest expenses	5.37	6.39	7.50	8.18	8.55	6.59	4.05	1.99	2.27	1.74	41. Frais financiers
42. Net interest income	3.05	2.66	2.41	2.09	0.36	1.50	0.47	2.32	3.55	3.42	42. Produits financiers nets
43. Non-interest income (net)	3.58	1.69	1.75	1.99	2.72	7.89	1.28	0.97	1.61	1.43	43. Produits non financiers (nets)
a. Fees and commissions receivable	..	..	..	..	..	..	..	..	..	..	*a. Frais et commissions à recevoir*
b. Fees and commissions payable	..	..	..	..	..	..	..	..	..	..	*b. Frais et commissions à payer*
c. Net profits or loss on financial operations	..	..	..	..	..	..	..	..	..	..	*c. Profits ou pertes nets sur opérations financières*
d. Other	..	..	..	..	..	..	..	..	..	..	*d. Autres*
44. Gross income	6.63	4.35	4.16	4.07	3.08	9.39	1.75	3.28	5.16	4.85	44. Résultat brut
45. Operating expenses	4.43	3.94	3.54	4.76	12.38	8.93	3.78	2.81	4.17	3.67	45. Frais d'exploitation
a. Staff costs	*2.20*	*1.66*	*1.51*	*1.42*	*1.40*	*1.55*	*1.14*	*0.96*	*1.40*	*1.34*	*a. Dépenses en personnel*
b. Property costs	*0.62*	*0.73*	*0.74*	*0.80*	*0.96*	*1.08*	*0.74*	*0.51*	*0.68*	*0.55*	*b. Dépenses en immobilier*
c. Other	*1.62*	*1.55*	*1.29*	*2.54*	*10.01*	*6.30*	*1.90*	*1.34*	*2.10*	*1.78*	*c. Autres*
46. Net income	2.20	0.41	0.62	-0.69	-9.30	0.46	-2.03	0.47	0.99	1.18	46. Résultat net
47. Provisions (net)	1.21	0.21	0.42	-0.26	-0.32	0.02	0.02	0.06	0.11	0.09	47. Provisions (nettes)
a. Provisions on loans	*0.47*	*0.45*	*0.43*	*0.08*	*-0.22*	*0.02*	*0.03*	..	..	..	*a. Provisions sur prêts*
b. Provisions on securities	*0.50*	*-0.24*	*-0.02*	*-0.34*	*-0.09*	-	*-0.01*	..	..	..	*b. Provisions sur titres*
c. Other	*0.24*	-	*0.01*	-	-	-	-	..	..	..	*c. Autres*
48. Profit before tax	0.99	0.20	0.20	-0.43	-8.98	0.45	-2.05	0.41	0.88	1.08	48. Bénéfices avant impôt
49. Income tax	0.08	0.09	0.08	0.04	0.01	0.01	0.02	0.09	0.20	0.22	49. Impôt sur le revenu
50. Profit after tax	0.91	0.11	0.12	-0.47	-9.00	0.44	-2.07	0.32	0.69	0.87	50. Bénéfices après impôt
51. Distributed profit	-	-	-	-	-	-	-	-	-	-	51. Bénéfices distribués
52. Retained profit	0.91	0.11	0.12	-0.47	-9.00	0.44	-2.07	0.32	0.69	0.87	52. Bénéfices mis en réserve
% of gross income											**% du total du résultat brut**
53. Net interest income	46.00	61.07	57.87	51.26	11.59	15.99	26.65	70.59	68.77	70.50	53. Produits financiers nets
54. Non-interest income (net)	54.00	38.93	42.13	48.74	88.41	84.01	73.35	29.41	31.23	29.50	54. Produits non financiers (nets)
a. Fees and commissions receivable	..	..	..	..	..	..	..	..	..	..	*a. Frais et commissions à recevoir*
b. Fees and commissions payable	..	..	..	..	..	..	..	..	..	..	*b. Frais et commissions à payer*
c. Net profits or loss on financial operations	..	..	..	..	..	..	..	..	..	..	*c. Profits ou pertes nets sur opérations financières*
d. Other	..	..	..	..	..	..	..	..	..	..	*d. Autres*
55. Operating expenses	66.85	90.52	85.09	116.93	..	95.05	..	85.53	80.85	75.71	55. Frais d'exploitation
a. Staff costs	*33.15*	*38.20*	*36.23*	*34.79*	..	*16.49*	..	*29.23*	*27.09*	*27.71*	*a. Dépenses en personnel*
b. Property costs	*9.29*	*16.80*	*17.76*	*19.73*	..	*11.47*	..	*15.59*	*13.11*	*11.41*	*b. Dépenses en immobilier*
c. Other	*24.41*	*35.52*	*31.10*	*62.40*	..	*67.08*	..	*40.71*	*40.64*	*36.59*	*c. Autres*
56. Net income	33.15	9.48	14.91	-16.93	..	4.95	..	14.47	19.15	24.29	56. Résultat net
57. Provisions (net)	18.19	4.88	10.06	-6.48	-10.26	0.19	0.87	1.87	2.07	1.96	57. Provisions (nettes)
a. Provisions on loans	*7.06*	*10.31*	*10.35*	*1.91*	*-7.27*	*0.17*	*1.55*	..	..	..	*a. Provisions sur prêts*
b. Provisions on securities	*7.52*	*-5.49*	*-0.46*	*-8.38*	*-3.00*	*0.02*	*-0.68*	..	..	..	*b. Provisions sur titres*
c. Other	*3.61*	*0.06*	*0.16*	-	-	-	-	..	..	..	*c. Autres*
58. Profit before tax	14.96	4.59	4.85	-10.45	..	4.76	..	12.61	17.08	22.33	58. Bénéfices avant impôt
59. Income tax	1.20	2.09	1.92	1.02	0.44	0.08	1.26	2.71	3.80	4.48	59. Impôt sur le revenu
60. Profit after tax	13.75	2.50	2.93	-11.47	..	4.68	..	9.90	13.29	17.85	60. Bénéfices après impôt
% of net income											**% du total du résultat net**
61. Provisions (net)	54.89	51.54	67.46	38.25	3.40	3.89	-0.75	12.90	10.81	8.05	61. Provisions (nettes)
a. Provisions on loans	*21.30*	*108.81*	*69.46*	*-11.27*	*2.41*	*3.43*	*-1.33*	..	..	..	*a. Provisions sur prêts*
b. Provisions on securities	*22.69*	*-57.93*	*-3.05*	*49.52*	*0.99*	*0.46*	*0.58*	..	..	..	*b. Provisions sur titres*
c. Other	*10.89*	*0.66*	*1.06*	-	-	-	-	..	..	..	*c. Autres*
62. Profit before tax	45.11	48.46	32.54	61.75	96.60	96.11	100.75	87.10	89.19	91.95	62. Bénéfices avant impôt
63. Income tax	3.63	22.03	12.88	-6.00	-0.15	1.60	-1.08	18.71	19.82	18.46	63. Impôt sur le revenu
64. Profit after tax	41.48	26.43	19.65	67.75	96.75	94.51	101.83	68.39	69.37	73.49	64. Bénéfices après impôt

FINLAND

Savings banks

FINLANDE

Caisses d'épargne

	1988	1989	1990	1991	1992	1993	1994(1)	1995	1996	1997	
Per cent											*Pourcentage*
BALANCE SHEET ANALYSIS											**ANALYSE DU BILAN**
% of year-end balance sheet total											**% du total du bilan en fin d'exercice**
Assets											**Actif**
65. Cash & balance with Central bank	6.02	7.56	5.15	3.72	8.40	1.13	1.85	3.69	3.19	3.03	65. Caisse & solde auprès de la Banque centrale
66. Interbank deposits	8.27	7.06	7.50	7.59	6.82	43.92	3.82	6.70	4.50	5.19	66. Dépôts interbancaires
67. Loans	69.91	69.24	70.23	68.36	64.79	23.51	40.91	58.89	58.20	60.11	67. Prêts
68. Securities	5.66	8.06	7.21	6.86	4.31	9.04	11.66	19.89	23.75	23.04	68. Valeurs mobilières
69. Other assets	10.14	8.07	9.91	13.48	15.69	22.39	41.76	10.83	10.36	8.63	69. Autres actifs
Liabilities											**Passif**
70. Capital & reserves	6.38	6.72	6.48	6.02	5.42	4.17	3.36	6.43	7.08	7.18	70. Capital et réserves
71. Borrowing from Central bank	1.04	0.97	0.91	0.96	1.85	0.43	0.39	-	-	-	71. Emprunts auprès de la Banque centrale
72. Interbank deposits	0.08	0.21	0.14	0.06	0.08	0.11	0.03	-	-	-	72. Dépôts interbancaires
73. Non-bank deposits	66.41	58.84	55.91	58.67	58.51	19.69	36.53	83.58	80.47	81.15	73. Dépôts non bancaires
74. Bonds	1.91	2.67	1.83	4.60	6.94	9.78	11.70	2.13	1.73	2.00	74. Obligations
75. Other liabilities	24.17	30.60	34.73	29.69	27.20	65.82	47.98	7.86	10.72	9.67	75. Autres engagements
Memorandum items											***Pour mémoire***
76. Short-term securities	*0.96*	*1.60*	*1.09*	*1.51*	*1.96*	*5.29*	*9.35*	*9.80*	*10.65*	*8.73*	*76. Titres à court terme*
77. Bonds	*2.89*	*2.15*	*1.99*	*1.45*	*1.13*	*1.97*	-	*9.10*	*12.11*	*13.62*	*77. Obligations*
78. Shares and participations	*1.81*	*4.31*	*4.13*	*3.90*	*1.21*	*1.78*	*2.31*	*0.99*	*0.99*	*0.69*	*78. Actions et participations*
79. Claims on non-residents	*0.40*	*0.61*	*0.04*	*0.02*	*0.03*	*0.13*	*0.04*	*0.33*	*0.43*	*0.89*	*79. Créances sur des non-résidents*
80. Liabilities to non-residents	*0.92*	*1.91*	*0.26*	-	*1.17*	*0.24*	*0.03*	*0.05*	*0.10*	*0.26*	*80. Engagements envers des non-résidents*

* See notes on previous pages.

* Voir les notes en pages précédentes.

FINLAND / FINLANDE

Co-operative banks / Banques mutualistes

	1988	1989	1990	1991	1992	1993	1994	1995	1996	1997	
Million markkaa											*Millions de markkas*
INCOME STATEMENT											**COMPTE DE RESULTATS**
1. Interest income	6337	8306	10342	11120	11397	9859	8602	8162	6644	5747	1. Produits financiers
2. Interest expenses	3953	5707	7252	7914	8590	6181	4255	4038	2947	2088	2. Frais financiers
3. Net interest income	2384	2599	3090	3206	2807	3678	4347	4124	3697	3659	3. Produits financiers nets
4. Non-interest income (net)	1321	1393	1524	2146	3097	2005	2067	2187	2883	2948	4. Produits non financiers (nets)
a. Fees and commissions receivable	..	..	..	..	..	..	..	..	..	..	*a. Frais et commissions à recevoir*
b. Fees and commissions payable	..	..	..	..	..	..	..	..	..	..	*b. Frais et commissions à payer*
c. Net profits or loss on financial operations	..	..	..	..	..	..	..	..	..	..	*c. Profits ou pertes nets sur opérations financières*
d. Other	..	..	..	..	..	..	..	..	..	..	*d. Autres*
5. Gross income	3705	3992	4614	5352	5904	5683	6414	6311	6580	6607	5. Résultat brut
6. Operating expenses	2992	3436	3825	4675	5817	7727	7897	6322	5895	5463	6. Frais d'exploitation
a. Staff costs	*1448*	*1647*	*1647*	*1664*	*1706*	*1514*	*1635*	*1504*	*1447*	*1329*	*a. Dépenses en personnel*
b. Property costs	*270*	*392*	*512*	*569*	*608*	*608*	*597*	*608*	*571*	*557*	*b. Dépenses en immobilier*
c. Other	*1274*	*1397*	*1666*	*2442*	*3503*	*5605*	*5665*	*4210*	*3877*	*3577*	*c. Autres*
7. Net income	713	556	789	677	87	-2044	-1483	-11	685	1144	7. Résultat net
8. Provisions (net)	548	357	458	315	-54	-74	12	15	16	6	8. Provisions (nettes)
a. Provisions on loans	*330*	*381*	*442*	*356*	*46*	*39*	*-9*	..	..	..	*a. Provisions sur prêts*
b. Provisions on securities	*195*	*-32*	*2*	*-41*	*-100*	*-113*	*21*	..	..	..	*b. Provisions sur titres*
c. Other	*23*	*8*	*14*	-	-	-	-	..	..	..	*c. Autres*
9. Profit before tax	165	199	331	362	141	-1970	-1495	-26	669	1138	9. Bénéfices avant impôt
10. Income tax	60	79	125	152	117	124	128	199	240	325	10. Impôt sur le revenu
11. Profit after tax	105	120	206	210	24	-2094	-1623	-225	429	813	11. Bénéfices après impôt
12. Distributed profit	61	66	62	50	28	20	2	27	37	59	12. Bénéfices distribués
13. Retained profit	44	54	144	160	-4	-2114	-1625	-252	392	754	13. Bénéfices mis en réserve
BALANCE SHEET											**BILAN**
Assets											**Actif**
14. Cash & balance with Central bank	4872	6534	5691	4034	4882	3239	2963	2831	2811	2722	14. Caisse & solde auprès de la Banque centrale
15. Interbank deposits	6658	7855	8177	9356	9871	13994	14078	15902	13233	15159	15. Dépôts interbancaires
16. Loans	62404	69874	75639	79594	79662	88924	84542	82940	78851	78932	16. Prêts
17. Securities	4441	4577	5577	6621	6721	6521	8370	9620	9926	9219	17. Valeurs mobilières
18. Other assets	5645	6650	8885	11282	15396	16704	15836	14537	13240	11824	18. Autres actifs
Liabilities											**Passif**
19. Capital & reserves	4473	5038	6280	6729	7719	8228	8125	8480	9118	10022	19. Capital et réserves
20. Borrowing from Central bank	501	692	519	542	474	-	-	-	-	-	20. Emprunts auprès de la Banque centrale
21. Interbank deposits	10	10	-	-	2	-	-	-	-	32	21. Dépôts interbancaires
22. Non-bank deposits	55318	61268	66679	71848	75846	89513	91244	95709	91067	91766	22. Dépôts non bancaires
23. Bonds	2502	3652	6022	9425	9838	9540	8259	7640	5902	4715	23. Obligations
24. Other liabilities	21216	24830	24469	22343	22653	22101	18161	14001	11974	11321	24. Autres engagements
Balance sheet total											**Total du bilan**
25. End-year total	84020	95490	103969	110887	116532	129382	125789	125830	118061	117856	25. En fin d'exercice
26. Average total	74231	89755	99730	107428	113710	122957	127586	125810	121946	117959	26. Moyen

FINLAND / FINLANDE

Co-operative banks / Banques mutualistes

	1988	1989	1990	1991	1992	1993	1994	1995	1996	1997	
Million markkaa											*Millions de markkas*
Memorandum items											***Pour mémoire***
27. Short-term securities	*293*	*129*	*161*	*1438*	*1525*	*1336*	*1286*	*1582*	*842*	*426*	*27. Titres à court terme*
28. Bonds	*2691*	*2905*	*4007*	*3543*	*3543*	*3387*	*5179*	*6274*	*7375*	*6864*	*28. Obligations*
29. Shares and participations	*1457*	*1543*	*1409*	*1640*	*1653*	*1798*	*1905*	*1764*	*1709*	*1929*	*29. Actions et participations*
30. Claims on non-residents	*55*	*59*	*78*	*7*	*8*	*5*	*5*	*6*	*1*	*5*	*30. Créances sur des non-résidents*
31. Liabilities to non-residents	-	-	-	*995*	*18*	*1173*	*3*	*4*	*2*	-	*31. Engagements envers des non-résidents*
Capital adequacy											***Solvabilité***
32. Tier 1 Capital	..	..	..	..	..	..	..	..	..	..	*32. Fonds propres de base*
33. Tier 2 Capital	..	..	..	..	..	..	..	..	..	..	*33. Fonds propres complémentaires*
34. Supervisory deductions	..	..	..	..	..	..	..	..	..	..	*34. Eléments à déduire des fonds propres*
35. Total net capital resources	..	..	..	..	..	..	..	..	..	..	*35. Total net des ressources en capital*
36. Risk-weighted assets	..	..	..	..	..	..	..	..	..	..	*36. Actifs pondérés des risques*
SUPPLEMENTARY INFORMATION											**RENSEIGNEMENTS COMPLEMENTAIRES**
37. Number of institutions	367	361	359	335	317	303	302	300	298	294	37. Nombre d'institutions
38. Number of branches	850	837	800	747	688	913	686	667	573	536	38. Nombre de succursales
39. Number of employees (x 1000)	9.4	9.6	9.3	9.0	8.7	8.6	9.1	8.6	7.4	7.0	39. Nombre de salariés (x 1000)

	1988	1989	1990	1991	1992	1993	1994	1995	1996	1997	
Per cent											*Pourcentage*
INCOME STATEMENT ANALYSIS											**ANALYSE DU COMPTE DE RESULTATS**
% of average balance sheet total											**% du total moyen du bilan**
40. Interest income	8.54	9.25	10.37	10.35	10.02	8.02	6.74	6.49	5.45	4.87	40. Produits financiers
41. Interest expenses	5.33	6.36	7.27	7.37	7.55	5.03	3.34	3.21	2.42	1.77	41. Frais financiers
42. Net interest income	3.21	2.90	3.10	2.98	2.47	2.99	3.41	3.28	3.03	3.10	42. Produits financiers nets
43. Non-interest income (net)	1.78	1.55	1.53	2.00	2.72	1.63	1.62	1.74	2.36	2.50	43. Produits non financiers (nets)
a. Fees and commissions receivable	..	..	..	..	..	..	..	..	..	..	*a. Frais et commissions à recevoir*
b. Fees and commissions payable	..	..	..	..	..	..	..	..	..	..	*b. Frais et commissions à payer*
c. Net profits or loss on financial operations	..	..	..	..	..	..	..	..	..	..	*c. Profits ou pertes nets sur opérations financières*
d. Other	..	..	..	..	..	..	..	..	..	..	*d. Autres*
44. Gross income	4.99	4.45	4.63	4.98	5.19	4.62	5.03	5.02	5.40	5.60	44. Résultat brut
45. Operating expenses	4.03	3.83	3.84	4.35	5.12	6.28	6.19	5.03	4.83	4.63	45. Frais d'exploitation
a. Staff costs	*1.95*	*1.83*	*1.65*	*1.55*	*1.50*	*1.23*	*1.28*	*1.20*	*1.19*	*1.13*	*a. Dépenses en personnel*
b. Property costs	*0.36*	*0.44*	*0.51*	*0.53*	*0.53*	*0.49*	*0.47*	*0.48*	*0.47*	*0.47*	*b. Dépenses en immobilier*
c. Other	*1.72*	*1.56*	*1.67*	*2.27*	*3.08*	*4.56*	*4.44*	*3.35*	*3.18*	*3.03*	*c. Autres*
46. Net income	0.96	0.62	0.79	0.63	0.08	-1.66	-1.16	-0.01	0.56	0.97	46. Résultat net
47. Provisions (net)	0.74	0.40	0.46	0.29	-0.05	-0.06	0.01	0.01	0.01	0.01	47. Provisions (nettes)
a. Provisions on loans	*0.44*	*0.42*	*0.44*	*0.33*	*0.04*	*0.03*	*-0.01*	..	..	..	*a. Provisions sur prêts*
b. Provisions on securities	*0.26*	*-0.04*	-	*-0.04*	*-0.09*	*-0.09*	*0.02*	..	..	..	*b. Provisions sur titres*
c. Other	*0.03*	*0.01*	*0.01*	-	-	-	-	..	..	..	*c. Autres*
48. Profit before tax	0.22	0.22	0.33	0.34	0.12	-1.60	-1.17	-0.02	0.55	0.96	48. Bénéfices avant impôt
49. Income tax	0.08	0.09	0.13	0.14	0.10	0.10	0.10	0.16	0.20	0.28	49. Impôt sur le revenu
50. Profit after tax	0.14	0.13	0.21	0.20	0.02	-1.70	-1.27	-0.18	0.35	0.69	50. Bénéfices après impôt
51. Distributed profit	0.08	0.07	0.06	0.05	0.02	0.02	-	0.02	0.03	0.05	51. Bénéfices distribués
52. Retained profit	0.06	0.06	0.14	0.15	-	-1.72	-1.27	-0.20	0.32	0.64	52. Bénéfices mis en réserve
% of gross income											**% du total du résultat brut**
53. Net interest income	64.35	65.11	66.97	59.90	47.54	64.72	67.77	65.35	56.19	55.38	53. Produits financiers nets
54. Non-interest income (net)	35.65	34.89	33.03	40.10	52.46	35.28	32.23	34.65	43.81	44.62	54. Produits non financiers (nets)
a. Fees and commissions receivable	..	..	..	..	..	..	..	..	..	..	*a. Frais et commissions à recevoir*
b. Fees and commissions payable	..	..	..	..	..	..	..	..	..	..	*b. Frais et commissions à payer*
c. Net profits or loss on financial operations	..	..	..	..	..	..	..	..	..	..	*c. Profits ou pertes nets sur opérations financières*
d. Other	..	..	..	..	..	..	..	..	..	..	*d. Autres*
55. Operating expenses	80.76	86.07	82.90	87.35	98.53	135.97	123.12	100.17	89.59	82.69	55. Frais d'exploitation
a. Staff costs	*39.08*	*41.26*	*35.70*	*31.09*	*28.90*	*26.64*	*25.49*	*23.83*	*21.99*	*20.12*	*a. Dépenses en personnel*
b. Property costs	*7.29*	*9.82*	*11.10*	*10.63*	*10.30*	*10.70*	*9.31*	*9.63*	*8.68*	*8.43*	*b. Dépenses en immobilier*
c. Other	*34.39*	*34.99*	*36.11*	*45.63*	*59.33*	*98.63*	*88.32*	*66.71*	*58.92*	*54.14*	*c. Autres*
56. Net income	19.24	13.93	17.10	12.65	1.47	-35.97	-23.12	-0.17	10.41	17.31	56. Résultat net
57. Provisions (net)	14.79	8.94	9.93	5.89	-0.91	-1.30	0.19	0.24	0.24	0.09	57. Provisions (nettes)
a. Provisions on loans	*8.91*	*9.54*	*9.58*	*6.65*	*0.78*	*0.69*	*-0.14*	..	..	..	*a. Provisions sur prêts*
b. Provisions on securities	*5.26*	*-0.80*	*0.04*	*-0.77*	*-1.69*	*-1.99*	*0.33*	..	..	..	*b. Provisions sur titres*
c. Other	*0.62*	*0.20*	*0.30*	-	-	-	-	..	..	..	*c. Autres*
58. Profit before tax	4.45	4.98	7.17	6.76	2.39	-34.66	-23.31	-0.41	10.17	17.22	58. Bénéfices avant impôt
59. Income tax	1.62	1.98	2.71	2.84	1.98	2.18	2.00	3.15	3.65	4.92	59. Impôt sur le revenu
60. Profit after tax	2.83	3.01	4.46	3.92	0.41	-36.85	-25.30	-3.57	6.52	12.31	60. Bénéfices après impôt
% of net income											**% du total du résultat net**
61. Provisions (net)	76.86	64.21	58.05	46.53	-62.07	3.62	-0.81	-136.36	2.34	0.52	61. Provisions (nettes)
a. Provisions on loans	*46.28*	*68.53*	*56.02*	*52.58*	*52.87*	*-1.91*	*0.61*	..	..	..	*a. Provisions sur prêts*
b. Provisions on securities	*27.35*	*-5.76*	*0.25*	*-6.06*	*-114.94*	*5.53*	*-1.42*	..	..	..	*b. Provisions sur titres*
c. Other	*3.23*	*1.44*	*1.77*	-	-	-	-	..	..	..	*c. Autres*
62. Profit before tax	23.14	35.79	41.95	53.47	162.07	96.38	100.81	..	97.66	99.48	62. Bénéfices avant impôt
63. Income tax	8.42	14.21	15.84	22.45	134.48	-6.07	-8.63	..	35.04	28.41	63. Impôt sur le revenu
64. Profit after tax	14.73	21.58	26.11	31.02	27.59	102.45	109.44	..	62.63	71.07	64. Bénéfices après impôt

	1988	1989	1990	1991	1992	1993	1994	1995	1996	1997	
Per cent											*Pourcentage*
BALANCE SHEET ANALYSIS											**ANALYSE DU BILAN**
% of year-end balance sheet total											**% du total du bilan en fin d'exercice**
Assets											**Actif**
65. Cash & balance with Central bank	5.80	6.84	5.47	3.64	4.19	2.50	2.36	2.25	2.38	2.31	65. Caisse & solde auprès de la Banque centrale
66. Interbank deposits	7.92	8.23	7.86	8.44	8.47	10.82	11.19	12.64	11.21	12.86	66. Dépôts interbancaires
67. Loans	74.27	73.17	72.75	71.78	68.36	68.73	67.21	65.91	66.79	66.97	67. Prêts
68. Securities	5.29	4.79	5.36	5.97	5.77	5.04	6.65	7.65	8.41	7.82	68. Valeurs mobilières
69. Other assets	6.72	6.96	8.55	10.17	13.21	12.91	12.59	11.55	11.21	10.03	69. Autres actifs
Liabilities											**Passif**
70. Capital & reserves	5.32	5.28	6.04	6.07	6.62	6.36	6.46	6.74	7.72	8.50	70. Capital et réserves
71. Borrowing from Central bank	0.60	0.72	0.50	0.49	0.41	-	-	-	-	-	71. Emprunts auprès de la Banque centrale
72. Interbank deposits	0.01	0.01	-	-	-	-	-	-	-	0.03	72. Dépôts interbancaires
73. Non-bank deposits	65.84	64.16	64.13	64.79	65.09	69.19	72.54	76.06	77.14	77.86	73. Dépôts non bancaires
74. Bonds	2.98	3.82	5.79	8.50	8.44	7.37	6.57	6.07	5.00	4.00	74. Obligations
75. Other liabilities	25.25	26.00	23.53	20.15	19.44	17.08	14.44	11.13	10.14	9.61	75. Autres engagements
Memorandum items											***Pour mémoire***
76. Short-term securities	*0.35*	*0.14*	*0.15*	*1.30*	*1.31*	*1.03*	*1.02*	*1.26*	*0.71*	*0.36*	*76. Titres à court terme*
77. Bonds	*3.20*	*3.04*	*3.85*	*3.20*	*3.04*	*2.62*	*4.12*	*4.99*	*6.25*	*5.82*	*77. Obligations*
78. Shares and participations	*1.73*	*1.62*	*1.36*	*1.48*	*1.42*	*1.39*	*1.51*	*1.40*	*1.45*	*1.64*	*78. Actions et participations*
79. Claims on non-residents	*0.07*	*0.06*	*0.08*	*0.01*	*0.01*	-	-	-	-	-	*79. Créances sur des non-résidents*
80. Liabilities to non-residents	-	-	-	*0.90*	*0.02*	*0.91*	-	-	-	-	*80. Engagements envers des non-résidents*

FRANCE
All banks

FRANCE
Ensemble des banques

Million French francs	1988	1989	1990	1991	1992	1993	1994	1995	1996	1997	Millions de francs français
INCOME STATEMENT											**COMPTE DE RESULTATS**
1. Interest income	1009694	1190278	1340977	1385954	1354409	1425991	1206736	1331567	1228201	1252663	1. Produits financiers
2. Interest expenses	774949	948273	1091208	1126018	1102977	1193519	979403	1113778	1024914	1065130	2. Frais financiers
3. Net interest income	234745	242005	249769	259936	251432	232472	227333	217789	203287	187534	3. Produits financiers nets
4. Non-interest income (net)	55968	60557	72790	91697	130043	165679	137282	182151	180634	212809	4. Produits non financiers (nets)
a. Fees and commissions receivable	..	..	..	..	..	*92642*	*98877*	*90361*	*102548*	*114324*	*a. Frais et commissions à recevoir*
b. Fees and commissions payable	..	..	..	..	..	*30092*	*30848*	*27017*	*31339*	*32701*	*b. Frais et commissions à payer*
c. Net profits or loss on financial operations	*709*	*383*	*1065*	*6583*	*7837*	*57990*	*29704*	*50239*	*64179*	*74205*	*c. Profits ou pertes nets sur opérations financières*
d. Other	*55259*	*60174*	*71725*	*85115*	*122206*	*45139*	*39549*	*68567*	*45246*	*56981*	*d. Autres*
5. Gross income	290713	302562	322559	351633	381475	398151	364615	399940	383921	400342	5. Résultat brut
6. Operating expenses	204334	218527	233474	244454	254918	257801	259889	262518	268374	275363	6. Frais d'exploitation
a. Staff costs	*113058*	*119257*	*125812*	*130362*	*135394*	*141658*	*140645*	*142290*	*145948*	*150738*	*a. Dépenses en personnel*
b. Property costs	*12425*	*13529*	*14944*	*15457*	*15337*	*14467*	*14159*	*14665*	*14466*	*13107*	*b. Dépenses en immobilier*
c. Other	*78852*	*85741*	*92718*	*98635*	*104187*	*101676*	*105085*	*105563*	*107960*	*111517*	*c. Autres*
7. Net income	86379	84035	89085	107179	126557	140350	104726	137422	115547	124980	7. Résultat net
8. Provisions (net)	29867	28837	37425	45023	81170	118883	100944	108912	78557	63194	8. Provisions (nettes)
a. Provisions on loans	*21240*	*17936*	*16635*	*31836*	*48512*	*103766*	*91470*	*84897*	*67485*	*61954*	*a. Provisions sur prêts*
b. Provisions on securities	*-4286*	*3446*	*8583*	*1476*	*14626*	*10919*	*10950*	*19967*	*9747*	*-1976*	*b. Provisions sur titres*
c. Other	*12913*	*7455*	*12207*	*11711*	*18032*	*4198*	*-1476*	*4047*	*1325*	*3216*	*c. Autres*
9. Profit before tax	56512	55198	51660	62156	45387	21467	3782	28510	36990	61786	9. Bénéfices avant impôt
10. Income tax	14680	14230	12240	14804	17451	17940	13782	18647	18241	18989	10. Impôt sur le revenu
11. Profit after tax	41832	40968	39420	47352	27936	3527	-10000	9863	18749	42798	11. Bénéfices après impôt
12. Distributed profit	17772	19059	20215	21499	20296	22493	20886	23170	25811	30961	12. Bénéfices distribués
13. Retained profit	24060	21909	19205	25853	7640	-18966	-30886	-13307	-7061	11836	13. Bénéfices mis en réserve
BALANCE SHEET											**BILAN**
Assets											**Actif**
14. Cash & balance with Central bank	172920	169185	126305	112979	68015	37566	34847	37851	59320	58279	14. Caisse & solde auprès de la Banque centrale
15. Interbank deposits	5269601	5742202	6077862	5945363	6144978	6582695	6597848	6913621	7232711	7541325	15. Dépôts interbancaires
16. Loans	4924195	5534081	6063585	6374522	6605304	6677026	6681385	6839377	6812684	7263672	16. Prêts
17. Securities	954343	1081494	1195292	1729495	2034701	2426133	2645804	2900922	3556060	3998106	17. Valeurs mobilières
18. Other assets	1154354	1358106	1606675	1339189	1428041	940892	960814	1067816	1117760	1332116	18. Autres actifs
Liabilities											**Passif**
19. Capital & reserves	367452	433817	508976	595549	655102	748312	774819	785523	773791	806959	19. Capital et réserves
20. Borrowing from Central bank	188379	199912	246453	203427	201535	35555	22665	14724	21336	32000	20. Emprunts auprès de la Banque centrale
21. Interbank deposits	5628342	6208164	6278748	6219400	6093769	6460470	6635411	6849676	7485504	7840720	21. Dépôts interbancaires
22. Non-bank deposits	2960740	3200707	3415472	3708179	3862696	4267827	4581565	5003888	5333507	6011739	22. Dépôts non bancaires
23. Bonds	2073982	2399780	2922003	3256746	3765388	3991842	3781463	3779205	3467526	3478960	23. Obligations
24. Other liabilities	1256518	1442688	1698067	1518246	1702548	1160305	1124777	1326571	1696871	2023120	24. Autres engagements
Balance sheet total											**Total du bilan**
25. End-year total	12475413	13885068	15069719	15501548	16281038	16664311	16920699	17759588	18778536	20193498	25. En fin d'exercice
26. Average total	11759263	13331073	14340336	15809633	16138135	17525343	17836966	18603549	20090123	22199029	26. Moyen

FRANCE
All banks

FRANCE
Ensemble des banques

	1988	1989	1990	1991	1992	1993	1994	1995	1996	1997	
Million French francs											*Millions de francs français*
Memorandum items											***Pour mémoire***
27. Short-term securities	..	..	..	..	..	..	..	..	..	..	*27. Titres à court terme*
28. Bonds	..	..	..	..	..	*1245397*	*1295152*	*1348649*	*1722090*	*1879216*	*28. Obligations*
29. Shares and participations	..	..	..	..	..	*502362*	*526389*	*540391*	*516660*	*548118*	*29. Actions et participations*
30. Claims on non-residents	*2922453*	*3234899*	*3717170*	*3727448*	*4216633*	*3253328*	*3128923*	*3335124*	*3558898*	*4378527*	*30. Créances sur des non-résidents*
31. Liabilities to non-residents	*2879663*	*3261710*	*3794796*	*3902550*	*4196000*	*2933944*	*3063172*	*3129866*	*3461604*	*4063994*	*31. Engagements envers des non-résidents*
Capital adequacy											***Solvabilité***
32. Tier 1 Capital	..	..	..	..	..	..	..	..	..	..	*32. Fonds propres de base*
33. Tier 2 Capital	..	..	..	..	..	..	..	..	..	..	*33. Fonds propres complémentaires*
34. Supervisory deductions	..	..	..	..	..	..	..	..	..	..	*34. Eléments à déduire des fonds propres*
35. Total net capital resources	..	..	..	..	..	..	..	..	..	..	*35. Total net des ressources en capital*
36. Risk-weighted assets	..	..	..	..	..	..	..	..	..	..	*36. Actifs pondérés des risques*
SUPPLEMENTARY INFORMATION											**RENSEIGNEMENTS COMPLEMENTAIRES**
37. Number of institutions	2050	2021	1981	1823	1701	1635	1618	1453	1404	1288	37. Nombre d'institutions
38. Number of branches	26010	26333	26124	25431	25357	26291	26200	26606	26303	26386	38. Nombre de succursales
39. Number of employees (x 1000)	444.6	443.1	440.0	433.6	425.0	406.1	409.2	407.7	404.2	397.3	39. Nombre de salariés (x 1000)

Notes

- The corporate data -- presented for all financial institutions and for each of the main categories of banks -- cover the activities and results of the foreign branches of banks with headquarters in France but exclude subsidiaries outside France.
- Foreign-controlled banks operating in France, in the form of branches or subsidiaries, are dealt with in the same way as banks under French control. However, branches of banks with headquarters in another European Union country are excluded.
- Average balance sheet totals (item 26) are based on the average of quarterly totals.

Notes

- Les données établies sur une base sociale -- ensemble des établissements de crédit et principales catégories juridiques -- incluent l'activité et les résultats des succursales à l'étranger dont le siège est en France. L'activité et les résultats des filiales étrangères sont exclus.
- Les établissements sous contrôle étranger opérant en France, sous la forme de succursales ou de filiales, sont traités dans les mêmes conditions que les banques sous contrôle français. Toutefois, sont exclues de cette présentation les succursales d'établissements dont le siège est implanté dans un autre pays de l'Union européenne.
- La moyenne du total des actifs/passifs (poste 26) est basée sur la moyenne des totaux des situations trimestrielles.

	1988	1989	1990	1991	1992	1993	1994	1995	1996	1997	
Per cent											*Pourcentage*
INCOME STATEMENT ANALYSIS											**ANALYSE DU COMPTE DE RESULTATS**
% of average balance sheet total											**% du total moyen du bilan**
40. Interest income	8.59	8.93	9.35	8.77	8.39	8.14	6.77	7.16	6.11	5.64	40. Produits financiers
41. Interest expenses	6.59	7.11	7.61	7.12	6.83	6.81	5.49	5.99	5.10	4.80	41. Frais financiers
42. Net interest income	2.00	1.82	1.74	1.64	1.56	1.33	1.27	1.17	1.01	0.84	42. Produits financiers nets
43. Non-interest income (net)	0.48	0.45	0.51	0.58	0.81	0.95	0.77	0.98	0.90	0.96	43. Produits non financiers (nets)
a. Fees and commissions receivable	..	..	..	..	..	*0.53*	*0.55*	*0.49*	*0.51*	*0.51*	*a. Frais et commissions à recevoir*
b. Fees and commissions payable	..	..	..	..	..	*0.17*	*0.17*	*0.15*	*0.16*	*0.15*	*b. Frais et commissions à payer*
c. Net profits or loss on financial operations	*0.01*	-	*0.01*	*0.04*	*0.05*	*0.33*	*0.17*	*0.27*	*0.32*	*0.33*	*c. Profits ou pertes nets sur opérations financières*
d. Other	*0.47*	*0.45*	*0.50*	*0.54*	*0.76*	*0.26*	*0.22*	*0.37*	*0.23*	*0.26*	*d. Autres*
44. Gross income	2.47	2.27	2.25	2.22	2.36	2.27	2.04	2.15	1.91	1.80	44. Résultat brut
45. Operating expenses	1.74	1.64	1.63	1.55	1.58	1.47	1.46	1.41	1.34	1.24	45. Frais d'exploitation
a. Staff costs	*0.96*	*0.89*	*0.88*	*0.82*	*0.84*	*0.81*	*0.79*	*0.76*	*0.73*	*0.68*	*a. Dépenses en personnel*
b. Property costs	*0.11*	*0.10*	*0.10*	*0.10*	*0.10*	*0.08*	*0.08*	*0.08*	*0.07*	*0.06*	*b. Dépenses en immobilier*
c. Other	*0.67*	*0.64*	*0.65*	*0.62*	*0.65*	*0.58*	*0.59*	*0.57*	*0.54*	*0.50*	*c. Autres*
46. Net income	0.73	0.63	0.62	0.68	0.78	0.80	0.59	0.74	0.58	0.56	46. Résultat net
47. Provisions (net)	0.25	0.22	0.26	0.28	0.50	0.68	0.57	0.59	0.39	0.28	47. Provisions (nettes)
a. Provisions on loans	*0.18*	*0.13*	*0.12*	*0.20*	*0.30*	*0.59*	*0.51*	*0.46*	*0.34*	*0.28*	*a. Provisions sur prêts*
b. Provisions on securities	*-0.04*	*0.03*	*0.06*	*0.01*	*0.09*	*0.06*	*0.06*	*0.11*	*0.05*	*-0.01*	*b. Provisions sur titres*
c. Other	*0.11*	*0.06*	*0.09*	*0.07*	*0.11*	*0.02*	*-0.01*	*0.02*	*0.01*	*0.01*	*c. Autres*
48. Profit before tax	0.48	0.41	0.36	0.39	0.28	0.12	0.02	0.15	0.18	0.28	48. Bénéfices avant impôt
49. Income tax	0.12	0.11	0.09	0.09	0.11	0.10	0.08	0.10	0.09	0.09	49. Impôt sur le revenu
50. Profit after tax	0.36	0.31	0.27	0.30	0.17	0.02	-0.06	0.05	0.09	0.19	50. Bénéfices après impôt
51. Distributed profit	0.15	0.14	0.14	0.14	0.13	0.13	0.12	0.12	0.13	0.14	51. Bénéfices distribués
52. Retained profit	0.20	0.16	0.13	0.16	0.05	-0.11	-0.17	-0.07	-0.04	0.05	52. Bénéfices mis en réserve
% of gross income											**% du total du résultat brut**
53. Net interest income	80.75	79.99	77.43	73.92	65.91	58.39	62.35	54.46	52.95	46.84	53. Produits financiers nets
54. Non-interest income (net)	19.25	20.01	22.57	26.08	34.09	41.61	37.65	45.54	47.05	53.16	54. Produits non financiers (nets)
a. Fees and commissions receivable	..	..	..	..	..	*23.27*	*27.12*	*22.59*	*26.71*	*28.56*	*a. Frais et commissions à recevoir*
b. Fees and commissions payable	..	..	..	..	..	*7.56*	*8.46*	*6.76*	*8.16*	*8.17*	*b. Frais et commissions à payer*
c. Net profits or loss on financial operations	*0.24*	*0.13*	*0.33*	*1.87*	*2.05*	*14.56*	*8.15*	*12.56*	*16.72*	*18.54*	*c. Profits ou pertes nets sur opérations financières*
d. Other	*19.01*	*19.89*	*22.24*	*24.21*	*32.04*	*11.34*	*10.85*	*17.14*	*11.79*	*14.23*	*d. Autres*
55. Operating expenses	70.29	72.23	72.38	69.52	66.82	64.75	71.28	65.64	69.90	68.78	55. Frais d'exploitation
a. Staff costs	*38.89*	*39.42*	*39.00*	*37.07*	*35.49*	*35.58*	*38.57*	*35.58*	*38.02*	*37.65*	*a. Dépenses en personnel*
b. Property costs	*4.27*	*4.47*	*4.63*	*4.40*	*4.02*	*3.63*	*3.88*	*3.67*	*3.77*	*3.27*	*b. Dépenses en immobilier*
c. Other	*27.12*	*28.34*	*28.74*	*28.05*	*27.31*	*25.54*	*28.82*	*26.39*	*28.12*	*27.86*	*c. Autres*
56. Net income	29.71	27.77	27.62	30.48	33.18	35.25	28.72	34.36	30.10	31.22	56. Résultat net
57. Provisions (net)	10.27	9.53	11.60	12.80	21.28	29.86	27.69	27.23	20.46	15.79	57. Provisions (nettes)
a. Provisions on loans	*7.31*	*5.93*	*5.16*	*9.05*	*12.72*	*26.06*	*25.09*	*21.23*	*17.58*	*15.48*	*a. Provisions sur prêts*
b. Provisions on securities	*-1.47*	*1.14*	*2.66*	*0.42*	*3.83*	*2.74*	*3.00*	*4.99*	*2.54*	*-0.49*	*b. Provisions sur titres*
c. Other	*4.44*	*2.46*	*3.78*	*3.33*	*4.73*	*1.05*	*-0.40*	*1.01*	*0.35*	*0.80*	*c. Autres*
58. Profit before tax	19.44	18.24	16.02	17.68	11.90	5.39	1.04	7.13	9.63	15.43	58. Bénéfices avant impôt
59. Income tax	5.05	4.70	3.79	4.21	4.57	4.51	3.78	4.66	4.75	4.74	59. Impôt sur le revenu
60. Profit after tax	14.39	13.54	12.22	13.47	7.32	0.89	-2.74	2.47	4.88	10.69	60. Bénéfices après impôt
% of net income											**% du total du résultat net**
61. Provisions (net)	34.58	34.32	42.01	42.01	64.14	84.70	96.39	79.25	67.99	50.56	61. Provisions (nettes)
a. Provisions on loans	*24.59*	*21.34*	*18.67*	*29.70*	*38.33*	*73.93*	*87.34*	*61.78*	*58.40*	*49.57*	*a. Provisions sur prêts*
b. Provisions on securities	*-4.96*	*4.10*	*9.63*	*1.38*	*11.56*	*7.78*	*10.46*	*14.53*	*8.44*	*-1.58*	*b. Provisions sur titres*
c. Other	*14.95*	*8.87*	*13.70*	*10.93*	*14.25*	*2.99*	*-1.41*	*2.94*	*1.15*	*2.57*	*c. Autres*
62. Profit before tax	65.42	65.68	57.99	57.99	35.86	15.30	3.61	20.75	32.01	49.44	62. Bénéfices avant impôt
63. Income tax	16.99	16.93	13.74	13.81	13.79	12.78	13.16	13.57	15.79	15.19	63. Impôt sur le revenu
64. Profit after tax	48.43	48.75	44.25	44.18	22.07	2.51	-9.55	7.18	16.23	34.24	64. Bénéfices après impôt

FRANCE
All banks

FRANCE
Ensemble des banques

	1988	1989	1990	1991	1992	1993	1994	1995	1996	1997	
Per cent											*Pourcentage*
BALANCE SHEET ANALYSIS											**ANALYSE DU BILAN**
% of year-end balance sheet total											**% du total du bilan en fin d'exercice**
Assets											**Actif**
65. Cash & balance with Central bank	1.39	1.22	0.84	0.73	0.42	0.23	0.21	0.21	0.32	0.29	65. Caisse & solde auprès de la Banque centrale
66. Interbank deposits	42.24	41.36	40.33	38.35	37.74	39.50	38.99	38.93	38.52	37.35	66. Dépôts interbancaires
67. Loans	39.47	39.86	40.24	41.12	40.57	40.07	39.49	38.51	36.28	35.97	67. Prêts
68. Securities	7.65	7.79	7.93	11.16	12.50	14.56	15.64	16.33	18.94	19.80	68. Valeurs mobilières
69. Other assets	9.25	9.78	10.66	8.64	8.77	5.65	5.68	6.01	5.95	6.60	69. Autres actifs
Liabilities											**Passif**
70. Capital & reserves	2.95	3.12	3.38	3.84	4.02	4.49	4.58	4.42	4.12	4.00	70. Capital et réserves
71. Borrowing from Central bank	1.51	1.44	1.64	1.31	1.24	0.21	0.13	0.08	0.11	0.16	71. Emprunts auprès de la Banque centrale
72. Interbank deposits	45.12	44.71	41.66	40.12	37.43	38.77	39.21	38.57	39.86	38.83	72. Dépôts interbancaires
73. Non-bank deposits	23.73	23.05	22.66	23.92	23.73	25.61	27.08	28.18	28.40	29.77	73. Dépôts non bancaires
74. Bonds	16.62	17.28	19.39	21.01	23.13	23.95	22.35	21.28	18.47	17.23	74. Obligations
75. Other liabilities	10.07	10.39	11.27	9.79	10.46	6.96	6.65	7.47	9.04	10.02	75. Autres engagements
Memorandum items											***Pour mémoire***
76. Short-term securities	..	..	..	..	..	..	..	..	..	..	*76. Titres à court terme*
77. Bonds	..	..	..	..	..	*7.47*	*7.65*	*7.59*	*9.17*	*9.31*	*77. Obligations*
78. Shares and participations	..	..	..	..	..	*3.01*	*3.11*	*3.04*	*2.75*	*2.71*	*78. Actions et participations*
79. Claims on non-residents	*23.43*	*23.30*	*24.67*	*24.05*	*25.90*	*19.52*	*18.49*	*18.78*	*18.95*	*21.68*	*79. Créances sur des non-résidents*
80. Liabilities to non-residents	*23.08*	*23.49*	*25.18*	*25.18*	*25.77*	*17.61*	*18.10*	*17.62*	*18.43*	*20.13*	*80. Engagements envers des non-résidents*

* See notes on previous pages.

* Voir les notes en pages précédentes.

FRANCE

Commercial banks / Banques commerciales

Million French francs	1988	1989	1990	1991	1992	1993	1994	1995	1996	1997	Millions de francs français
INCOME STATEMENT											**COMPTE DE RESULTATS**
1. Interest income	477009	605390	689870	687860	667739	714849	557809	669426	611975	662217	1. Produits financiers
2. Interest expenses	357886	488878	572077	570991	567793	620942	467038	585783	532872	586533	2. Frais financiers
3. Net interest income	119123	116512	117793	116869	99946	93907	90771	83643	79103	75684	3. Produits financiers nets
4. Non-interest income (net)	30662	32774	39615	50609	85902	105921	83668	103202	99417	127696	4. Produits non financiers (nets)
a. Fees and commissions receivable	..	..	..	..	..	*51392*	*54934*	*48803*	*56049*	*65332*	*a. Frais et commissions à recevoir*
b. Fees and commissions payable	..	..	..	..	..	*13203*	*14783*	*11934*	*14371*	*16087*	*b. Frais et commissions à payer*
c. Net profits or loss on financial operations	*-1017*	*474*	*338*	*2945*	*3728*	*42679*	*25443*	*36399*	*44146*	*52194*	*c. Profits ou pertes nets sur opérations financières*
d. Other	*31680*	*32300*	*39277*	*47664*	*82174*	*25052*	*18075*	*29933*	*13593*	*26257*	*d. Autres*
5. Gross income	149785	149286	157408	167478	185848	199828	174439	186845	178520	203380	5. Résultat brut
6. Operating expenses	109377	115758	122591	128415	134663	139320	139302	139021	143044	152037	6. Frais d'exploitation
a. Staff costs	*66066*	*69408*	*72646*	*74780*	*77282*	*80859*	*79496*	*79488*	*81860*	*87775*	*a. Dépenses en personnel*
b. Property costs	*6062*	*6481*	*7359*	*7932*	*8031*	*7714*	*7673*	*7508*	*8082*	*7404*	*b. Dépenses en immobilier*
c. Other	*37249*	*39869*	*42586*	*45703*	*49350*	*50747*	*52133*	*52024*	*53102*	*56858*	*c. Autres*
7. Net income	40408	33528	34817	39063	51185	60508	35137	47824	35476	51343	7. Résultat net
8. Provisions (net)	18244	15527	18778	18980	45667	63522	53956	38023	31669	35870	8. Provisions (nettes)
a. Provisions on loans	*14101*	*10438*	*4391*	*15016*	*25872*	*55413*	*46072*	*25538*	*28122*	*39527*	*a. Provisions sur prêts*
b. Provisions on securities	*-2993*	*1938*	*5791*	*-192*	*8488*	*7315*	*10823*	*11778*	*5784*	*-3160*	*b. Provisions sur titres*
c. Other	*7136*	*3151*	*8596*	*4156*	*11307*	*794*	*-2940*	*706*	*-2237*	*-498*	*c. Autres*
9. Profit before tax	22164	18001	16039	20083	5518	-3014	-18819	9801	3807	15473	9. Bénéfices avant impôt
10. Income tax	6792	5612	4285	5290	6587	4548	4149	4653	4195	3265	10. Impôt sur le revenu
11. Profit after tax	15372	12389	11754	14793	-1069	-7562	-22968	5148	-389	12208	11. Bénéfices après impôt
12. Distributed profit	6900	7707	7801	8520	7135	7763	6992	8694	12317	16414	12. Bénéfices distribués
13. Retained profit	8472	4682	3953	6273	-8204	-15325	-29960	-3546	-12705	-4206	13. Bénéfices mis en réserve
BALANCE SHEET											**BILAN**
Assets											**Actif**
14. Cash & balance with Central bank	131182	125075	79476	73546	42517	23418	21441	22848	43294	41099	14. Caisse & solde auprès de la Banque centrale
15. Interbank deposits	2713282	2959361	3199937	3038222	3552598	3711820	3628643	3736038	4015985	4279642	15. Dépôts interbancaires
16. Loans	2322752	2624220	2939519	3092549	3197034	3172440	3097118	3206055	3250665	3709733	16. Prêts
17. Securities	554633	635974	718197	1072814	1348412	1655767	1696752	1769680	2120119	2618455	17. Valeurs mobilières
18. Other assets	681057	803147	956134	776378	863368	628818	640605	697955	726154	944835	18. Autres actifs
Liabilities											**Passif**
19. Capital & reserves	143022	169327	203738	235273	276205	303881	308249	307659	315239	340051	19. Capital et réserves
20. Borrowing from Central bank	166882	174301	199632	182233	178987	27041	19097	12181	19424	30658	20. Emprunts auprès de la Banque centrale
21. Interbank deposits	3082312	3344754	3389267	3217563	3623724	3956838	3991247	4082402	4424898	4837351	21. Dépôts interbancaires
22. Non-bank deposits	1420381	1563196	1656666	1766012	1837436	1998841	2059574	2237969	2419128	2858572	22. Dépôts non bancaires
23. Bonds	911603	1108308	1499625	1807004	2095380	2099763	1946834	1891539	1841152	2018289	23. Obligations
24. Other liabilities	678706	787891	944335	845423	992199	805900	759559	900825	1136375	1508843	24. Autres engagements
Balance sheet total											**Total du bilan**
25. End-year total	6402906	7147777	7893263	8053509	9003930	9192264	9084560	9432576	10156216	11593763	25. En fin d'exercice
26. Average total	5969210	6993134	7494651	8185218	8579526	10065924	10191644	10397613	11265578	13419447	26. Moyen

FRANCE

Commercial banks

FRANCE

Banques commerciales

	1988	1989	1990	1991	1992	1993	1994	1995	1996	1997	
Million French francs											*Millions de francs français*
Memorandum items											***Pour mémoire***
27. Short-term securities	..	..	..	..	..	..	..	..	..	..	*27. Titres à court terme*
28. Bonds	..	..	..	..	..	*837888*	*817920*	*820832*	*1064813*	*1253636*	*28. Obligations*
29. Shares and participations	..	..	..	..	..	*292936*	*309940*	*259721*	*266940*	*276047*	*29. Actions et participations*
30. Claims on non-residents	*2793077*	*2935016*	*3381089*	*3349161*	*3775335*	*2720709*	*2626942*	*2766749*	*2864166*	*3565301*	*30. Créances sur des non-résidents*
31. Liabilities to non-residents	*2743653*	*2982889*	*3489028*	*3552549*	*3868305*	*2388398*	*2478113*	*2533944*	*2749485*	*3301241*	*31. Engagements envers des non-résidents*
Capital adequacy											***Solvabilité***
32. Tier 1 Capital	..	..	..	..	..	..	..	..	..	..	*32. Fonds propres de base*
33. Tier 2 Capital	..	..	..	..	..	..	..	..	..	..	*33. Fonds propres complémentaires*
34. Supervisory deductions	..	..	..	..	..	..	..	..	..	..	*34. Eléments à déduire des fonds propres*
35. Total net capital resources	..	..	..	..	..	..	..	..	..	..	*35. Total net des ressources en capital*
36. Risk-weighted assets	..	..	..	..	..	..	..	..	..	..	*36. Actifs pondérés des risques*
SUPPLEMENTARY INFORMATION											**RENSEIGNEMENTS COMPLEMENTAIRES**
37. Number of institutions	395	407	408	414	409	415	421	413	400	398	37. Nombre d'institutions
38. Number of branches	10293	10367	10166	10177	10081	10451	10131	10320	10240	9983	38. Nombre de succursales
39. Number of employees (x 1000)	248.3	246.9	243.1	238.7	232.3	219.2	218.0	213.6	208.7	207.9	39. Nombre de salariés (x 1000)

Notes

- Average balance sheet totals (item 26) are based on the average of quarterly totals.

Notes

- La moyenne du total des actifs/passifs (poste 26) est basée sur la moyenne des totaux des situations trimestrielles.

FRANCE
Commercial banks

FRANCE
Banques commerciales

	1988	1989	1990	1991	1992	1993	1994	1995	1996	1997	
Per cent											*Pourcentage*
INCOME STATEMENT ANALYSIS											**ANALYSE DU COMPTE DE RESULTATS**
% of average balance sheet total											**% du total moyen du bilan**
40. Interest income	7.99	8.66	9.20	8.40	7.78	7.10	5.47	6.44	5.43	4.93	40. Produits financiers
41. Interest expenses	6.00	6.99	7.63	6.98	6.62	6.17	4.58	5.63	4.73	4.37	41. Frais financiers
42. Net interest income	2.00	1.67	1.57	1.43	1.16	0.93	0.89	0.80	0.70	0.56	42. Produits financiers nets
43. Non-interest income (net)	0.51	0.47	0.53	0.62	1.00	1.05	0.82	0.99	0.88	0.95	43. Produits non financiers (nets)
a. Fees and commissions receivable	..	..	..	..	..	*0.51*	*0.54*	*0.47*	*0.50*	*0.49*	*a. Frais et commissions à recevoir*
b. Fees and commissions payable	..	..	..	..	..	*0.13*	*0.15*	*0.11*	*0.13*	*0.12*	*b. Frais et commissions à payer*
c. Net profits or loss on financial operations	*-0.02*	*0.01*	-	*0.04*	*0.04*	*0.42*	*0.25*	*0.35*	*0.39*	*0.39*	*c. Profits ou pertes nets sur opérations financières*
d. Other	*0.53*	*0.46*	*0.52*	*0.58*	*0.96*	*0.25*	*0.18*	*0.29*	*0.12*	*0.20*	*d. Autres*
44. Gross income	2.51	2.13	2.10	2.05	2.17	1.99	1.71	1.80	1.58	1.52	44. Résultat brut
45. Operating expenses	1.83	1.66	1.64	1.57	1.57	1.38	1.37	1.34	1.27	1.13	45. Frais d'exploitation
a. Staff costs	*1.11*	*0.99*	*0.97*	*0.91*	*0.90*	*0.80*	*0.78*	*0.76*	*0.73*	*0.65*	*a. Dépenses en personnel*
b. Property costs	*0.10*	*0.09*	*0.10*	*0.10*	*0.09*	*0.08*	*0.08*	*0.07*	*0.07*	*0.06*	*b. Dépenses en immobilier*
c. Other	*0.62*	*0.57*	*0.57*	*0.56*	*0.58*	*0.50*	*0.51*	*0.50*	*0.47*	*0.42*	*c. Autres*
46. Net income	0.68	0.48	0.46	0.48	0.60	0.60	0.34	0.46	0.31	0.38	46. Résultat net
47. Provisions (net)	0.31	0.22	0.25	0.23	0.53	0.63	0.53	0.37	0.28	0.27	47. Provisions (nettes)
a. Provisions on loans	*0.24*	*0.15*	*0.06*	*0.18*	*0.30*	*0.55*	*0.45*	*0.25*	*0.25*	*0.29*	*a. Provisions sur prêts*
b. Provisions on securities	*-0.05*	*0.03*	*0.08*	-	*0.10*	*0.07*	*0.11*	*0.11*	*0.05*	*-0.02*	*b. Provisions sur titres*
c. Other	*0.12*	*0.05*	*0.11*	*0.05*	*0.13*	*0.01*	*-0.03*	*0.01*	*-0.02*	-	*c. Autres*
48. Profit before tax	0.37	0.26	0.21	0.25	0.06	-0.03	-0.18	0.09	0.03	0.12	48. Bénéfices avant impôt
49. Income tax	0.11	0.08	0.06	0.06	0.08	0.05	0.04	0.04	0.04	0.02	49. Impôt sur le revenu
50. Profit after tax	0.26	0.18	0.16	0.18	-0.01	-0.08	-0.23	0.05	-	0.09	50. Bénéfices après impôt
51. Distributed profit	0.12	0.11	0.10	0.10	0.08	0.08	0.07	0.08	0.11	0.12	51. Bénéfices distribués
52. Retained profit	0.14	0.07	0.05	0.08	-0.10	-0.15	-0.29	-0.03	-0.11	-0.03	52. Bénéfices mis en réserve
% of gross income											**% du total du résultat brut**
53. Net interest income	79.53	78.05	74.83	69.78	53.78	46.99	52.04	44.77	44.31	37.21	53. Produits financiers nets
54. Non-interest income (net)	20.47	21.95	25.17	30.22	46.22	53.01	47.96	55.23	55.69	62.79	54. Produits non financiers (nets)
a. Fees and commissions receivable	..	..	..	..	..	*25.72*	*31.49*	*26.12*	*31.40*	*32.12*	*a. Frais et commissions à recevoir*
b. Fees and commissions payable	..	..	..	..	..	*6.61*	*8.47*	*6.39*	*8.05*	*7.91*	*b. Frais et commissions à payer*
c. Net profits or loss on financial operations	*-0.68*	*0.32*	*0.21*	*1.76*	*2.01*	*21.36*	*14.59*	*19.48*	*24.73*	*25.66*	*c. Profits ou pertes nets sur opérations financières*
d. Other	*21.15*	*21.64*	*24.95*	*28.46*	*44.22*	*12.54*	*10.36*	*16.02*	*7.61*	*12.91*	*d. Autres*
55. Operating expenses	73.02	77.54	77.88	76.68	72.46	69.72	79.86	74.40	80.13	74.76	55. Frais d'exploitation
a. Staff costs	*44.11*	*46.49*	*46.15*	*44.65*	*41.58*	*40.46*	*45.57*	*42.54*	*45.85*	*43.16*	*a. Dépenses en personnel*
b. Property costs	*4.05*	*4.34*	*4.68*	*4.74*	*4.32*	*3.86*	*4.40*	*4.02*	*4.53*	*3.64*	*b. Dépenses en immobilier*
c. Other	*24.87*	*26.71*	*27.05*	*27.29*	*26.55*	*25.40*	*29.89*	*27.84*	*29.75*	*27.96*	*c. Autres*
56. Net income	26.98	22.46	22.12	23.32	27.54	30.28	20.14	25.60	19.87	25.24	56. Résultat net
57. Provisions (net)	12.18	10.40	11.93	11.33	24.57	31.79	30.93	20.35	17.74	17.64	57. Provisions (nettes)
a. Provisions on loans	*9.41*	*6.99*	*2.79*	*8.97*	*13.92*	*27.73*	*26.41*	*13.67*	*15.75*	*19.44*	*a. Provisions sur prêts*
b. Provisions on securities	*-2.00*	*1.30*	*3.68*	*-0.11*	*4.57*	*3.66*	*6.20*	*6.30*	*3.24*	*-1.55*	*b. Provisions sur titres*
c. Other	*4.76*	*2.11*	*5.46*	*2.48*	*6.08*	*0.40*	*-1.69*	*0.38*	*-1.25*	*-0.24*	*c. Autres*
58. Profit before tax	14.80	12.06	10.19	11.99	2.97	-1.51	-10.79	5.25	2.13	7.61	58. Bénéfices avant impôt
59. Income tax	4.53	3.76	2.72	3.16	3.54	2.28	2.38	2.49	2.35	1.61	59. Impôt sur le revenu
60. Profit after tax	10.26	8.30	7.47	8.83	-0.58	-3.78	-13.17	2.76	-0.22	6.00	60. Bénéfices après impôt
% of net income											**% du total du résultat net**
61. Provisions (net)	45.15	46.31	53.93	48.59	89.22	104.98	153.56	79.51	89.27	69.86	61. Provisions (nettes)
a. Provisions on loans	*34.90*	*31.13*	*12.61*	*38.44*	*50.55*	*91.58*	*131.12*	*53.40*	*79.27*	*76.99*	*a. Provisions sur prêts*
b. Provisions on securities	*-7.41*	*5.78*	*16.63*	*-0.49*	*16.58*	*12.09*	*30.80*	*24.63*	*16.30*	*-6.15*	*b. Provisions sur titres*
c. Other	*17.66*	*9.40*	*24.69*	*10.64*	*22.09*	*1.31*	*-8.37*	*1.48*	*-6.31*	*-0.97*	*c. Autres*
62. Profit before tax	54.85	53.69	46.07	51.41	10.78	-4.98	-53.56	20.49	10.73	30.14	62. Bénéfices avant impôt
63. Income tax	16.81	16.74	12.31	13.54	12.87	7.52	11.81	9.73	11.82	6.36	63. Impôt sur le revenu
64. Profit after tax	38.04	36.95	33.76	37.87	-2.09	-12.50	-65.37	10.76	-1.10	23.78	64. Bénéfices après impôt

	1988	1989	1990	1991	1992	1993	1994	1995	1996	1997	
Per cent											*Pourcentage*
BALANCE SHEET ANALYSIS											**ANALYSE DU BILAN**
% of year-end balance sheet total											**% du total du bilan en fin d'exercice**
Assets											**Actif**
65. Cash & balance with Central bank	2.05	1.75	1.01	0.91	0.47	0.25	0.24	0.24	0.43	0.35	65. Caisse & solde auprès de la Banque centrale
66. Interbank deposits	42.38	41.40	40.54	37.73	39.46	40.38	39.94	39.61	39.54	36.91	66. Dépôts interbancaires
67. Loans	36.28	36.71	37.24	38.40	35.51	34.51	34.09	33.99	32.01	32.00	67. Prêts
68. Securities	8.66	8.90	9.10	13.32	14.98	18.01	18.68	18.76	20.88	22.59	68. Valeurs mobilières
69. Other assets	10.64	11.24	12.11	9.64	9.59	6.84	7.05	7.40	7.15	8.15	69. Autres actifs
Liabilities											**Passif**
70. Capital & reserves	2.23	2.37	2.58	2.92	3.07	3.31	3.39	3.26	3.10	2.93	70. Capital et réserves
71. Borrowing from Central bank	2.61	2.44	2.53	2.26	1.99	0.29	0.21	0.13	0.19	0.26	71. Emprunts auprès de la Banque centrale
72. Interbank deposits	48.14	46.79	42.94	39.95	40.25	43.05	43.93	43.28	43.57	41.72	72. Dépôts interbancaires
73. Non-bank deposits	22.18	21.87	20.99	21.93	20.41	21.74	22.67	23.73	23.82	24.66	73. Dépôts non bancaires
74. Bonds	14.24	15.51	19.00	22.44	23.27	22.84	21.43	20.05	18.13	17.41	74. Obligations
75. Other liabilities	10.60	11.02	11.96	10.50	11.02	8.77	8.36	9.55	11.19	13.01	75. Autres engagements
Memorandum items											***Pour mémoire***
76. Short-term securities	..	..	..	..	..	..	..	..	..	..	*76. Titres à court terme*
77. Bonds	..	..	..	..	..	*9.12*	*9.00*	*8.70*	*10.48*	*10.81*	*77. Obligations*
78. Shares and participations	..	..	..	..	..	*3.19*	*3.41*	*2.75*	*2.63*	*2.38*	*78. Actions et participations*
79. Claims on non-residents	*43.62*	*41.06*	*42.84*	*41.59*	*41.93*	*29.60*	*28.92*	*29.33*	*28.20*	*30.75*	*79. Créances sur des non-résidents*
80. Liabilities to non-residents	*42.85*	*41.73*	*44.20*	*44.11*	*42.96*	*25.98*	*27.28*	*26.86*	*27.07*	*28.47*	*80. Engagements envers des non-résidents*

* See notes on previous pages.

* Voir les notes en pages précédentes.

FRANCE
Large commercial banks

FRANCE
Grandes banques commerciales

	1988	1989	1990	1991	1992	1993	1994	1995	1996	1997	
Million French francs											*Millions de francs français*
INCOME STATEMENT											**COMPTE DE RESULTATS**
1. Interest income	371737	453953	523423	557294	582094	564010	460234	480334	456648	500232	1. Produits financiers
2. Interest expenses	274877	356680	421992	446751	460796	473054	368949	394961	380037	428193	2. Frais financiers
3. Net interest income	96860	97273	101431	110543	121298	90956	91285	85373	76611	72040	3. Produits financiers nets
4. Non-interest income (net)	32189	44557	50478	55055	50636	86095	69855	71489	88571	115559	4. Produits non financiers (nets)
a. Fees and commissions receivable	..	..	..	..	..	*45164*	*53880*	*46525*	*53445*	*63551*	*a. Frais et commissions à recevoir*
b. Fees and commissions payable	..	..	..	..	..	*9905*	*12782*	*9748*	*11943*	*16289*	*b. Frais et commissions à payer*
c. Net profits or loss on financial operations	..	..	..	..	..	*40799*	*19838*	*25083*	*38738*	*53044*	*c. Profits ou pertes nets sur opérations financières*
d. Other	..	..	..	..	..	*10038*	*8919*	*9628*	*8332*	*15253*	*d. Autres*
5. Gross income	129049	141830	151909	165598	171934	177051	161140	156862	165183	187599	5. Résultat brut
6. Operating expenses	87329	93729	105555	113711	118922	125080	125359	123903	127269	136834	6. Frais d'exploitation
a. Staff costs	*51267*	*54436*	*60595*	*64553*	*67446*	*73593*	*72209*	*71293*	*73817*	*80264*	*a. Dépenses en personnel*
b. Property costs	*5412*	*6066*	*7315*	*8457*	*8884*	*8318*	*8333*	*8901*	*8779*	*9268*	*b. Dépenses en immobilier*
c. Other	*30649*	*33228*	*37645*	*40701*	*42593*	*43169*	*44817*	*43709*	*44673*	*47302*	*c. Autres*
7. Net income	41720	48101	46354	51887	53012	51971	35781	32959	37914	50764	7. Résultat net
8. Provisions (net)	20420	23906	26990	32702	40500	43297	32198	21667	13945	19233	8. Provisions (nettes)
a. Provisions on loans	..	..	..	..	..	*46486*	*39395*	*22463*	*21882*	*29663*	*a. Provisions sur prêts*
b. Provisions on securities	..	..	..	..	..	*-3171*	*-4542*	*-895*	*-5884*	*-10566*	*b. Provisions sur titres*
c. Other	..	..	..	..	..	*-18*	*-2654*	*99*	*-2052*	*136*	*c. Autres*
9. Profit before tax	21300	24195	19364	19185	12512	8674	3583	11292	23969	31531	9. Bénéfices avant impôt
10. Income tax	6593	6232	4464	5827	4677	6236	6487	6158	7135	7276	10. Impôt sur le revenu
11. Profit after tax	14707	17963	14900	13358	7835	2438	-2904	5134	16834	24255	11. Bénéfices après impôt
12. Distributed profit	11813	14588	11473	10088	4489	-157	-5973	1723	13314	19629	12. Bénéfices distribués
13. Retained profit	2894	3375	3427	3270	3346	2595	3069	3411	3520	4627	13. Bénéfices mis en réserve
BALANCE SHEET											**BILAN**
Assets											**Actif**
14. Cash & balance with Central bank	88618	80328	60999	62944	42770	34745	29234	26047	39658	39971	14. Caisse & solde auprès de la Banque centrale
15. Interbank deposits	1319089	1359943	1422493	1311688	1625298	1821703	1672483	1692784	1772233	1980728	15. Dépôts interbancaires
16. Loans	1915070	2195698	2520626	2694960	2947556	2972956	2865339	2874004	3026883	3295571	16. Prêts
17. Securities	321767	361489	554970	898305	1061499	1344023	1305815	1423342	1776120	2053153	17. Valeurs mobilières
18. Other assets	604544	720477	804448	669719	742539	577052	533069	602789	634826	836412	18. Autres actifs
Liabilities											**Passif**
19. Capital & reserves	107290	103927	128280	144610	156316	248696	242577	231245	234047	250032	19. Capital et réserves
20. Borrowing from Central bank	130125	141485	169301	149765	138011	42100	25821	16005	22188	30517	20. Emprunts auprès de la Banque centrale
21. Interbank deposits	1689863	1750115	1795833	1749765	1972138	2373656	2298899	2379981	2595090	2888702	21. Dépôts interbancaires
22. Non-bank deposits	1535665	1738573	2162728	1699324	1889242	2012156	2004032	2067658	2249384	2484292	22. Dépôts non bancaires
23. Bonds	288957	322228	367725	1128139	1393178	1405376	1232961	1163275	1136314	1247458	23. Obligations
24. Other liabilities	497189	661607	739669	766015	870778	668493	601649	760802	1012696	1304833	24. Autres engagements
Balance sheet total											**Total du bilan**
25. End-year total	4249088	4717935	5363536	5637617	6419663	6750478	6405939	6618965	7249719	8205835	25. En fin d'exercice
26. Average total	..	4483512	5040736	5500577	6028640	6585071	6578209	6512452	6934342	7727777	26. Moyen

FRANCE
Large commercial banks

FRANCE
Grandes banques commerciales

	1988	1989	1990	1991	1992	1993	1994	1995	1996	1997	
Million French francs											*Millions de francs français*
Memorandum items											***Pour mémoire***
27. Short-term securities	..	..	..	..	..	..	..	..	..	..	*27. Titres à court terme*
28. Bonds	..	..	..	..	..	*793522*	*724175*	*782978*	*932149*	*972765*	*28. Obligations*
29. Shares and participations	*44824*	*64294*	*118523*	*152262*	*169317*	*182215*	*179527*	*127934*	*126140*	*123214*	*29. Actions et participations*
30. Claims on non-residents	..	..	..	..	..	..	..	..	..	..	*30. Créances sur des non-résidents*
31. Liabilities to non-residents	..	..	..	..	..	..	..	..	..	..	*31. Engagements envers des non-résidents*
Capital adequacy											***Solvabilité***
32. Tier 1 Capital	..	..	..	..	..	..	..	..	..	..	*32. Fonds propres de base*
33. Tier 2 Capital	..	..	..	..	..	..	..	..	..	..	*33. Fonds propres complémentaires*
34. Supervisory deductions	..	..	..	..	..	..	..	..	..	..	*34. Eléments à déduire des fonds propres*
35. Total net capital resources	..	..	..	..	..	..	..	..	..	..	*35. Total net des ressources en capital*
36. Risk-weighted assets	..	..	..	..	..	..	..	..	..	..	*36. Actifs pondérés des risques*
SUPPLEMENTARY INFORMATION											**RENSEIGNEMENTS COMPLEMENTAIRES**
37. Number of institutions	5	5	5	5	5	5	5	5	5	5	37. Nombre d'institutions
38. Number of branches	..	..	..	..	..	..	..	..	..	..	38. Nombre de succursales
39. Number of employees (x 1000)	..	..	..	..	..	..	..	..	..	..	39. Nombre de salariés (x 1000)

Notes

- The consolidated data for Large commercial banks cover all subsidiaries and branches, including non-financial agencies, in France and abroad. Accordingly, they are not comparable with the corporate data for Commercial banks.

Notes

- Les données consolidées des Grandes banques commerciales incluent l'ensemble des succursales et filiales, y compris les établissements non financiers installées en France et à l'étranger. Ces données ne sont donc pas comparables aux données de la catégorie des Banques commerciales.

FRANCE
Large commercial banks

FRANCE
Grandes banques commerciales

	1988	1989	1990	1991	1992	1993	1994	1995	1996	1997	
Per cent											*Pourcentage*
INCOME STATEMENT ANALYSIS											**ANALYSE DU COMPTE DE RESULTATS**
% of average balance sheet total											**% du total moyen du bilan**
40. Interest income	..	10.12	10.38	10.13	9.66	8.56	7.00	7.38	6.59	6.47	40. Produits financiers
41. Interest expenses	..	7.96	8.37	8.12	7.64	7.18	5.61	6.06	5.48	5.54	41. Frais financiers
42. Net interest income	..	2.17	2.01	2.01	2.01	1.38	1.39	1.31	1.10	0.93	42. Produits financiers nets
43. Non-interest income (net)	..	0.99	1.00	1.00	0.84	1.31	1.06	1.10	1.28	1.50	43. Produits non financiers (nets)
a. Fees and commissions receivable	..	..	..	..	..	*0.69*	*0.82*	*0.71*	*0.77*	*0.82*	*a. Frais et commissions à recevoir*
b. Fees and commissions payable	..	..	..	..	..	*0.15*	*0.19*	*0.15*	*0.17*	*0.21*	*b. Frais et commissions à payer*
c. Net profits or loss on financial operations	..	..	..	..	..	*0.62*	*0.30*	*0.39*	*0.56*	*0.69*	*c. Profits ou pertes nets sur opérations financières*
d. Other	..	..	..	..	..	*0.15*	*0.14*	*0.15*	*0.12*	*0.20*	*d. Autres*
44. Gross income	..	3.16	3.01	3.01	2.85	2.69	2.45	2.41	2.38	2.43	44. Résultat brut
45. Operating expenses	..	2.09	2.09	2.07	1.97	1.90	1.91	1.90	1.84	1.77	45. Frais d'exploitation
a. Staff costs	..	*1.21*	*1.20*	*1.17*	*1.12*	*1.12*	*1.10*	*1.09*	*1.06*	*1.04*	*a. Dépenses en personnel*
b. Property costs	..	*0.14*	*0.15*	*0.15*	*0.15*	*0.13*	*0.13*	*0.14*	*0.13*	*0.12*	*b. Dépenses en immobilier*
c. Other	..	*0.74*	*0.75*	*0.74*	*0.71*	*0.66*	*0.68*	*0.67*	*0.64*	*0.61*	*c. Autres*
46. Net income	..	1.07	0.92	0.94	0.88	0.79	0.54	0.51	0.55	0.66	46. Résultat net
47. Provisions (net)	..	0.53	0.54	0.59	0.67	0.66	0.49	0.33	0.20	0.25	47. Provisions (nettes)
a. Provisions on loans	..	..	..	..	..	*0.71*	*0.60*	*0.34*	*0.32*	*0.38*	*a. Provisions sur prêts*
b. Provisions on securities	..	..	..	..	..	*-0.05*	*-0.07*	*-0.01*	*-0.08*	*-0.14*	*b. Provisions sur titres*
c. Other	..	..	..	..	..	-	*-0.04*	-	*-0.03*	-	*c. Autres*
48. Profit before tax	..	0.54	0.38	0.35	0.21	0.13	0.05	0.17	0.35	0.41	48. Bénéfices avant impôt
49. Income tax	..	0.14	0.09	0.11	0.08	0.09	0.10	0.09	0.10	0.09	49. Impôt sur le revenu
50. Profit after tax	..	0.40	0.30	0.24	0.13	0.04	-0.04	0.08	0.24	0.31	50. Bénéfices après impôt
51. Distributed profit	..	0.33	0.23	0.18	0.07	-	-0.09	0.03	0.19	0.25	51. Bénéfices distribués
52. Retained profit	..	0.08	0.07	0.06	0.06	0.04	0.05	0.05	0.05	0.06	52. Bénéfices mis en réserve
% of gross income											**% du total du résultat brut**
53. Net interest income	75.06	68.58	66.77	66.75	70.55	51.37	56.65	54.43	46.38	38.40	53. Produits financiers nets
54. Non-interest income (net)	24.94	31.42	33.23	33.25	29.45	48.63	43.35	45.57	53.62	61.60	54. Produits non financiers (nets)
a. Fees and commissions receivable	..	..	..	..	..	*25.51*	*33.44*	*29.66*	*32.36*	*33.88*	*a. Frais et commissions à recevoir*
b. Fees and commissions payable	..	..	..	..	..	*5.59*	*7.93*	*6.21*	*7.23*	*8.68*	*b. Frais et commissions à payer*
c. Net profits or loss on financial operations	..	..	..	..	..	*23.04*	*12.31*	*15.99*	*23.45*	*28.28*	*c. Profits ou pertes nets sur opérations financières*
d. Other	..	..	..	..	..	*5.67*	*5.53*	*6.14*	*5.04*	*8.13*	*d. Autres*
55. Operating expenses	67.67	66.09	69.49	68.67	69.17	70.65	77.80	78.99	77.05	72.94	55. Frais d'exploitation
a. Staff costs	*39.73*	*38.38*	*39.89*	*38.98*	*39.23*	*41.57*	*44.81*	*45.45*	*44.69*	*42.78*	*a. Dépenses en personnel*
b. Property costs	*4.19*	*4.28*	*4.82*	*5.11*	*5.17*	*4.70*	*5.17*	*5.67*	*5.31*	*4.94*	*b. Dépenses en immobilier*
c. Other	*23.75*	*23.43*	*24.78*	*24.58*	*24.77*	*24.38*	*27.81*	*27.86*	*27.04*	*25.21*	*c. Autres*
56. Net income	32.33	33.91	30.51	31.33	30.83	29.35	22.20	21.01	22.95	27.06	56. Résultat net
57. Provisions (net)	15.82	16.86	17.77	19.75	23.56	24.45	19.98	13.81	8.44	10.25	57. Provisions (nettes)
a. Provisions on loans	..	..	..	..	..	*26.26*	*24.45*	*14.32*	*13.25*	*15.81*	*a. Provisions sur prêts*
b. Provisions on securities	..	..	..	..	..	*-1.79*	*-2.82*	*-0.57*	*-3.56*	*-5.63*	*b. Provisions sur titres*
c. Other	..	..	..	..	..	*-0.01*	*-1.65*	*0.06*	*-1.24*	*0.07*	*c. Autres*
58. Profit before tax	16.51	17.06	12.75	11.59	7.28	4.90	2.22	7.20	14.51	16.81	58. Bénéfices avant impôt
59. Income tax	5.11	4.39	2.94	3.52	2.72	3.52	4.03	3.93	4.32	3.88	59. Impôt sur le revenu
60. Profit after tax	11.40	12.67	9.81	8.07	4.56	1.38	-1.80	3.27	10.19	12.93	60. Bénéfices après impôt
% of net income											**% du total du résultat net**
61. Provisions (net)	48.95	49.70	58.23	63.03	76.40	83.31	89.99	65.74	36.78	37.89	61. Provisions (nettes)
a. Provisions on loans	..	..	..	..	..	*89.45*	*110.10*	*68.15*	*57.71*	*58.43*	*a. Provisions sur prêts*
b. Provisions on securities	..	..	..	..	..	*-6.10*	*-12.69*	*-2.72*	*-15.52*	*-20.81*	*b. Provisions sur titres*
c. Other	..	..	..	..	..	*-0.03*	*-7.42*	*0.30*	*-5.41*	*0.27*	*c. Autres*
62. Profit before tax	51.05	50.30	41.77	36.97	23.60	16.69	10.01	34.26	63.22	62.11	62. Bénéfices avant impôt
63. Income tax	15.80	12.96	9.63	11.23	8.82	12.00	18.13	18.68	18.82	14.33	63. Impôt sur le revenu
64. Profit after tax	35.25	37.34	32.14	25.74	14.78	4.69	-8.12	15.58	44.40	47.78	64. Bénéfices après impôt

FRANCE
Large commercial banks

FRANCE
Grandes banques commerciales

	1988	1989	1990	1991	1992	1993	1994	1995	1996	1997	
Per cent											*Pourcentage*
BALANCE SHEET ANALYSIS											**ANALYSE DU BILAN**
% of year-end balance sheet total											**% du total du bilan en fin d'exercice**
Assets											**Actif**
65. Cash & balance with Central bank	2.09	1.70	1.14	1.12	0.67	0.51	0.46	0.39	0.55	0.49	65. Caisse & solde auprès de la Banque centrale
66. Interbank deposits	31.04	28.82	26.52	23.27	25.32	26.99	26.11	25.57	24.45	24.14	66. Dépôts interbancaires
67. Loans	45.07	46.54	47.00	47.80	45.91	44.04	44.73	43.42	41.75	40.16	67. Prêts
68. Securities	7.57	7.66	10.35	15.93	16.54	19.91	20.38	21.50	24.50	25.02	68. Valeurs mobilières
69. Other assets	14.23	15.27	15.00	11.88	11.57	8.55	8.32	9.11	8.76	10.19	69. Autres actifs
Liabilities											**Passif**
70. Capital & reserves	2.53	2.20	2.39	2.57	2.43	3.68	3.79	3.49	3.23	3.05	70. Capital et réserves
71. Borrowing from Central bank	3.06	3.00	3.16	2.66	2.15	0.62	0.40	0.24	0.31	0.37	71. Emprunts auprès de la Banque centrale
72. Interbank deposits	39.77	37.09	33.48	31.04	30.72	35.16	35.89	35.96	35.80	35.20	72. Dépôts interbancaires
73. Non-bank deposits	36.14	36.85	40.32	30.14	29.43	29.81	31.28	31.24	31.03	30.27	73. Dépôts non bancaires
74. Bonds	6.80	6.83	6.86	20.01	21.70	20.82	19.25	17.57	15.67	15.20	74. Obligations
75. Other liabilities	11.70	14.02	13.79	13.59	13.56	9.90	9.39	11.49	13.97	15.90	75. Autres engagements
Memorandum items											***Pour mémoire***
76. Short-term securities	..	..	..	..	..	..	..	..	..	..	*76. Titres à court terme*
77. Bonds	..	..	..	..	..	*11.76*	*11.30*	*11.83*	*12.86*	*11.85*	*77. Obligations*
78. Shares and participations	*1.05*	*1.36*	*2.21*	*2.70*	*2.64*	*2.70*	*2.80*	*1.93*	*1.74*	*1.50*	*78. Actions et participations*
79. Claims on non-residents	..	..	..	..	..	..	..	..	..	..	*79. Créances sur des non-résidents*
80. Liabilities to non-residents	..	..	..	..	..	..	..	..	..	..	*80. Engagements envers des non-résidents*

* See notes on previous pages.

* Voir les notes en pages précédentes.

FRANCE
Savings banks

FRANCE
Caisses d'épargne

	1988	1989	1990	1991	1992	1993	1994	1995	1996	1997	
Million French francs											*Millions de francs français*
INCOME STATEMENT											**COMPTE DE RESULTATS**
1. Interest income	55208	60276	64192	70086	62369	61834	61680	67457	65056	66017	1. Produits financiers
2. Interest expenses	43623	45869	48896	52253	41136	41552	43122	47334	45258	47012	2. Frais financiers
3. Net interest income	11585	14407	15296	17833	21233	20282	18558	20123	19798	19004	3. Produits financiers nets
4. Non-interest income (net)	3528	2071	2491	3072	3826	6197	4581	6814	6554	7534	4. Produits non financiers (nets)
a. Fees and commissions receivable	..	..	..	..	..	*4809*	*5539*	*4499*	*5277*	*6404*	*a. Frais et commissions à recevoir*
b. Fees and commissions payable	..	..	..	..	..	*1164*	*1211*	*1304*	*1397*	*1450*	*b. Frais et commissions à payer*
c. Net profits or loss on financial operations	*36*	*-18*	*-20*	*101*	*543*	*1316*	*-1058*	*2565*	*1946*	*1854*	*c. Profits ou pertes nets sur opérations financières*
d. Other	*3492*	*2089*	*2511*	*2971*	*3284*	*1236*	*1310*	*1055*	*729*	*726*	*d. Autres*
5. Gross income	15113	16478	17787	20905	25059	26479	23139	26937	26352	26538	5. Résultat brut
6. Operating expenses	11970	13120	14622	16346	19312	20091	20486	21317	21631	21957	6. Frais d'exploitation
a. Staff costs	*7189*	*7791*	*8481*	*9244*	*10772*	*11438*	*11564*	*12174*	*12360*	*12539*	*a. Dépenses en personnel*
b. Property costs	*745*	*856*	*929*	*1050*	*1335*	*1472*	*1504*	*1556*	*1510*	*1519*	*b. Dépenses en immobilier*
c. Other	*4036*	*4474*	*5212*	*6052*	*7205*	*7180*	*7418*	*7587*	*7761*	*7899*	*c. Autres*
7. Net income	3143	3358	3165	4559	5747	6388	2653	5620	4721	4582	7. Résultat net
8. Provisions (net)	919	928	686	2121	2221	2620	1142	2337	1391	1584	8. Provisions (nettes)
a. Provisions on loans	*298*	*544*	*648*	*1360*	*1627*	*1640*	*1037*	*795*	*765*	*831*	*a. Provisions sur prêts*
b. Provisions on securities	*77*	*59*	*-87*	*-13*	*-29*	*-73*	*-42*	*-14*	*-168*	*-52*	*b. Provisions sur titres*
c. Other	*544*	*325*	*125*	*774*	*624*	*1052*	*147*	*1556*	*794*	*806*	*c. Autres*
9. Profit before tax	2224	2430	2479	2438	3526	3768	1511	3283	3330	2997	9. Bénéfices avant impôt
10. Income tax	139	378	523	855	1433	1994	194	1833	1665	1373	10. Impôt sur le revenu
11. Profit after tax	2085	2052	1956	1583	2093	1774	1317	1450	1665	1625	11. Bénéfices après impôt
12. Distributed profit	-	-	-	48	-	-	-	-	-	-	12. Bénéfices distribués
13. Retained profit	2085	2052	1956	1535	2093	1774	1317	1450	1665	1625	13. Bénéfices mis en réserve
BALANCE SHEET											**BILAN**
Assets											**Actif**
14. Cash & balance with Central bank	5272	2648	2691	2947	3078	2615	2749	2913	3017	3443	14. Caisse & solde auprès de la Banque centrale
15. Interbank deposits	733349	772524	689041	679144	483626	468192	493442	556490	543275	600103	15. Dépôts interbancaires
16. Loans	196214	218861	245482	252711	283909	298700	320726	334948	360736	388538	16. Prêts
17. Securities	3469	4852	6086	7753	77318	116768	139982	150458	191199	206185	17. Valeurs mobilières
18. Other assets	33309	36072	36698	39550	54981	42452	47476	56291	58295	63687	18. Autres actifs
Liabilities											**Passif**
19. Capital & reserves	20835	23342	25669	27836	37421	41243	43194	45917	48127	48886	19. Capital et réserves
20. Borrowing from Central bank	1080	436	18	24	638	358	116	80	64	65	20. Emprunts auprès de la Banque centrale
21. Interbank deposits	290605	342472	284132	305108	47725	33757	95627	100714	117888	161339	21. Dépôts interbancaires
22. Non-bank deposits	644903	648488	652587	631823	723659	774885	839042	923504	960889	1022591	22. Dépôts non bancaires
23. Bonds	1202	1528	2577	1790	44653	61437	9063	9427	5326	3522	23. Obligations
24. Other liabilities	12989	18691	15015	15525	48815	17047	17334	21459	24227	25553	24. Autres engagements
Balance sheet total											**Total du bilan**
25. End-year total	971613	1034957	979998	982106	902912	928727	1004376	1101100	1156521	1261955	25. En fin d'exercice
26. Average total	946352	1011108	978288	1228899	912780	914899	955025	1041831	1120411	1199618	26. Moyen

FRANCE
Savings banks

FRANCE
Caisses d'épargne

	1988	1989	1990	1991	1992	1993	1994	1995	1996	1997	
Million French francs											*Millions de francs français*
Memorandum items											**Pour mémoire**
27. Short-term securities	..	..	..	..	..	..	..	..	..	..	*27. Titres à court terme*
28. Bonds	..	..	..	..	..	*78763*	*99077*	*103535*	*133280*	*149411*	*28. Obligations*
29. Shares and participations	..	..	..	..	..	*3914*	*4467*	*4347*	*5448*	*6202*	*29. Actions et participations*
30. Claims on non-residents	*1*	*1*	*2*	*8*	*17*	*2526*	*5488*	*9433*	*18425*	*31497*	*30. Créances sur des non-résidents*
31. Liabilities to non-residents	*3*	*2*	*7*	*221*	*14*	*307*	*301*	*314*	*499*	*947*	*31. Engagements envers des non-résidents*
Capital adequacy											**Solvabilité**
32. Tier 1 Capital	..	..	..	..	..	..	..	..	..	..	*32. Fonds propres de base*
33. Tier 2 Capital	..	..	..	..	..	..	..	..	..	..	*33. Fonds propres complémentaires*
34. Supervisory deductions	..	..	..	..	..	..	..	..	..	..	*34. Eléments à déduire des fonds propres*
35. Total net capital resources	..	..	..	..	..	..	..	..	..	..	*35. Total net des ressources en capital*
36. Risk-weighted assets	..	..	..	..	..	..	..	..	..	..	*36. Actifs pondérés des risques*
SUPPLEMENTARY INFORMATION											**RENSEIGNEMENTS COMPLEMENTAIRES**
37. Number of institutions	280	212	186	36	36	35	35	35	34	34	37. Nombre d'institutions
38. Number of branches	4269	4432	4623	4030	4411	4308	4200	4226	4214	4270	38. Nombre de succursales
39. Number of employees (x 1000)	32.8	31.0	32.2	33.6	35.8	35.8	35.7	36.2	36.0	36.0	39. Nombre de salariés (x 1000)

Notes

- Average balance sheet totals (item 26) are based on the average of quarterly totals.

Notes

- La moyenne du total des actifs/passifs (poste 26) est basée sur la moyenne des totaux des situations trimestrielles.

FRANCE
Savings banks

FRANCE
Caisses d'épargne

	1988	1989	1990	1991	1992	1993	1994	1995	1996	1997	
Per cent											*Pourcentage*
INCOME STATEMENT ANALYSIS											**ANALYSE DU COMPTE DE RESULTATS**
% of average balance sheet total											**% du total moyen du bilan**
40. Interest income	5.83	5.96	6.56	5.70	6.83	6.76	6.46	6.47	5.81	5.50	40. Produits financiers
41. Interest expenses	4.61	4.54	5.00	4.25	4.51	4.54	4.52	4.54	4.04	3.92	41. Frais financiers
42. Net interest income	1.22	1.42	1.56	1.45	2.33	2.22	1.94	1.93	1.77	1.58	42. Produits financiers nets
43. Non-interest income (net)	0.37	0.20	0.25	0.25	0.42	0.68	0.48	0.65	0.58	0.63	43. Produits non financiers (nets)
a. Fees and commissions receivable	..	..	..	..	..	*0.53*	*0.58*	*0.43*	*0.47*	*0.53*	*a. Frais et commissions à recevoir*
b. Fees and commissions payable	..	..	..	..	..	*0.13*	*0.13*	*0.13*	*0.12*	*0.12*	*b. Frais et commissions à payer*
c. Net profits or loss on financial operations	-	-	-	*0.01*	*0.06*	*0.14*	*-0.11*	*0.25*	*0.17*	*0.15*	*c. Profits ou pertes nets sur opérations financières*
d. Other	*0.37*	*0.21*	*0.26*	*0.24*	*0.36*	*0.14*	*0.14*	*0.10*	*0.07*	*0.06*	*d. Autres*
44. Gross income	1.60	1.63	1.82	1.70	2.75	2.89	2.42	2.59	2.35	2.21	44. Résultat brut
45. Operating expenses	1.26	1.30	1.49	1.33	2.12	2.20	2.15	2.05	1.93	1.83	45. Frais d'exploitation
a. Staff costs	*0.76*	*0.77*	*0.87*	*0.75*	*1.18*	*1.25*	*1.21*	*1.17*	*1.10*	*1.05*	*a. Dépenses en personnel*
b. Property costs	*0.08*	*0.08*	*0.09*	*0.09*	*0.15*	*0.16*	*0.16*	*0.15*	*0.13*	*0.13*	*b. Dépenses en immobilier*
c. Other	*0.43*	*0.44*	*0.53*	*0.49*	*0.79*	*0.78*	*0.78*	*0.73*	*0.69*	*0.66*	*c. Autres*
46. Net income	0.33	0.33	0.32	0.37	0.63	0.70	0.28	0.54	0.42	0.38	46. Résultat net
47. Provisions (net)	0.10	0.09	0.07	0.17	0.24	0.29	0.12	0.22	0.12	0.13	47. Provisions (nettes)
a. Provisions on loans	*0.03*	*0.05*	*0.07*	*0.11*	*0.18*	*0.18*	*0.11*	*0.08*	*0.07*	*0.07*	*a. Provisions sur prêts*
b. Provisions on securities	*0.01*	*0.01*	*-0.01*	-	-	*-0.01*	-	-	*-0.01*	-	*b. Provisions sur titres*
c. Other	*0.06*	*0.03*	*0.01*	*0.06*	*0.07*	*0.11*	*0.02*	*0.15*	*0.07*	*0.07*	*c. Autres*
48. Profit before tax	0.24	0.24	0.25	0.20	0.39	0.41	0.16	0.32	0.30	0.25	48. Bénéfices avant impôt
49. Income tax	0.01	0.04	0.05	0.07	0.16	0.22	0.02	0.18	0.15	0.11	49. Impôt sur le revenu
50. Profit after tax	0.22	0.20	0.20	0.13	0.23	0.19	0.14	0.14	0.15	0.14	50. Bénéfices après impôt
51. Distributed profit	-	-	-	-	-	-	-	-	-	-	51. Bénéfices distribués
52. Retained profit	0.22	0.20	0.20	0.12	0.23	0.19	0.14	0.14	0.15	0.14	52. Bénéfices mis en réserve
% of gross income											**% du total du résultat brut**
53. Net interest income	76.66	87.43	86.00	85.30	84.73	76.60	80.20	74.70	75.13	71.61	53. Produits financiers nets
54. Non-interest income (net)	23.34	12.57	14.00	14.70	15.27	23.40	19.80	25.30	24.87	28.39	54. Produits non financiers (nets)
a. Fees and commissions receivable	..	..	..	..	..	*18.16*	*23.94*	*16.70*	*20.03*	*24.13*	*a. Frais et commissions à recevoir*
b. Fees and commissions payable	..	..	..	..	..	*4.40*	*5.23*	*4.84*	*5.30*	*5.46*	*b. Frais et commissions à payer*
c. Net profits or loss on financial operations	*0.24*	*-0.11*	*-0.11*	*0.48*	*2.17*	*4.97*	*-4.57*	*9.52*	*7.38*	*6.99*	*c. Profits ou pertes nets sur opérations financières*
d. Other	*23.11*	*12.68*	*14.12*	*14.21*	*13.11*	*4.67*	*5.66*	*3.92*	*2.77*	*2.74*	*d. Autres*
55. Operating expenses	79.20	79.62	82.21	78.19	77.07	75.88	88.53	79.14	82.08	82.74	55. Frais d'exploitation
a. Staff costs	*47.57*	*47.28*	*47.68*	*44.22*	*42.99*	*43.20*	*49.98*	*45.19*	*46.90*	*47.25*	*a. Dépenses en personnel*
b. Property costs	*4.93*	*5.19*	*5.22*	*5.02*	*5.33*	*5.56*	*6.50*	*5.78*	*5.73*	*5.72*	*b. Dépenses en immobilier*
c. Other	*26.71*	*27.15*	*29.30*	*28.95*	*28.75*	*27.12*	*32.06*	*28.17*	*29.45*	*29.76*	*c. Autres*
56. Net income	20.80	20.38	17.79	21.81	22.93	24.12	11.47	20.86	17.92	17.27	56. Résultat net
57. Provisions (net)	6.08	5.63	3.86	10.15	8.86	9.89	4.94	8.68	5.28	5.97	57. Provisions (nettes)
a. Provisions on loans	*1.97*	*3.30*	*3.64*	*6.51*	*6.49*	*6.19*	*4.48*	*2.95*	*2.90*	*3.13*	*a. Provisions sur prêts*
b. Provisions on securities	*0.51*	*0.36*	*-0.49*	*-0.06*	*-0.12*	*-0.28*	*-0.18*	*-0.05*	*-0.64*	*-0.20*	*b. Provisions sur titres*
c. Other	*3.60*	*1.97*	*0.70*	*3.70*	*2.49*	*3.97*	*0.64*	*5.78*	*3.01*	*3.04*	*c. Autres*
58. Profit before tax	14.72	14.75	13.94	11.66	14.07	14.23	6.53	12.19	12.64	11.29	58. Bénéfices avant impôt
59. Income tax	0.92	2.29	2.94	4.09	5.72	7.53	0.84	6.80	6.32	5.17	59. Impôt sur le revenu
60. Profit after tax	13.80	12.45	11.00	7.57	8.35	6.70	5.69	5.38	6.32	6.12	60. Bénéfices après impôt
% of net income											**% du total du résultat net**
61. Provisions (net)	29.24	27.64	21.67	46.52	38.65	41.01	43.05	41.58	29.46	34.57	61. Provisions (nettes)
a. Provisions on loans	*9.48*	*16.20*	*20.47*	*29.83*	*28.31*	*25.67*	*39.09*	*14.15*	*16.20*	*18.14*	*a. Provisions sur prêts*
b. Provisions on securities	*2.45*	*1.76*	*-2.75*	*-0.29*	*-0.50*	*-1.14*	*-1.58*	*-0.25*	*-3.56*	*-1.13*	*b. Provisions sur titres*
c. Other	*17.31*	*9.68*	*3.95*	*16.98*	*10.86*	*16.47*	*5.54*	*27.69*	*16.82*	*17.59*	*c. Autres*
62. Profit before tax	70.76	72.36	78.33	53.48	61.35	58.99	56.95	58.42	70.54	65.41	62. Bénéfices avant impôt
63. Income tax	4.42	11.26	16.52	18.75	24.93	31.21	7.31	32.62	35.27	29.97	63. Impôt sur le revenu
64. Profit after tax	66.34	61.11	61.80	34.72	36.42	27.77	49.64	25.80	35.27	35.46	64. Bénéfices après impôt

FRANCE
Savings banks

FRANCE
Caisses d'épargne

	1988	1989	1990	1991	1992	1993	1994	1995	1996	1997	
Per cent											*Pourcentage*
BALANCE SHEET ANALYSIS											**ANALYSE DU BILAN**
% of year-end balance sheet total											**% du total du bilan en fin d'exercice**
Assets											**Actif**
65. Cash & balance with Central bank	0.54	0.26	0.27	0.30	0.34	0.28	0.27	0.26	0.26	0.27	65. Caisse & solde auprès de la Banque centrale
66. Interbank deposits	75.48	74.64	70.31	69.15	53.56	50.41	49.13	50.54	46.97	47.55	66. Dépôts interbancaires
67. Loans	20.19	21.15	25.05	25.73	31.44	32.16	31.93	30.42	31.19	30.79	67. Prêts
68. Securities	0.36	0.47	0.62	0.79	8.56	12.57	13.94	13.66	16.53	16.34	68. Valeurs mobilières
69. Other assets	3.43	3.49	3.74	4.03	6.09	4.57	4.73	5.11	5.04	5.05	69. Autres actifs
Liabilities											**Passif**
70. Capital & reserves	2.14	2.26	2.62	2.83	4.14	4.44	4.30	4.17	4.16	3.87	70. Capital et réserves
71. Borrowing from Central bank	0.11	0.04	-	-	0.07	0.04	0.01	0.01	0.01	0.01	71. Emprunts auprès de la Banque centrale
72. Interbank deposits	29.91	33.09	28.99	31.07	5.29	3.63	9.52	9.15	10.19	12.78	72. Dépôts interbancaires
73. Non-bank deposits	66.37	62.66	66.59	64.33	80.15	83.44	83.54	83.87	83.08	81.03	73. Dépôts non bancaires
74. Bonds	0.12	0.15	0.26	0.18	4.95	6.62	0.90	0.86	0.46	0.28	74. Obligations
75. Other liabilities	1.34	1.81	1.53	1.58	5.41	1.84	1.73	1.95	2.09	2.02	75. Autres engagements
Memorandum items											***Pour mémoire***
76. Short-term securities	..	..	..	..	..	..	..	..	..	..	*76. Titres à court terme*
77. Bonds	..	..	..	..	..	*8.48*	*9.86*	*9.40*	*11.52*	*11.84*	*77. Obligations*
78. Shares and participations	..	..	..	..	..	*0.42*	*0.44*	*0.39*	*0.47*	*0.49*	*78. Actions et participations*
79. Claims on non-residents	-	-	-	-	-	*0.27*	*0.55*	*0.86*	*1.59*	*2.50*	*79. Créances sur des non-résidents*
80. Liabilities to non-residents	-	-	-	*0.02*	-	*0.03*	*0.03*	*0.03*	*0.04*	*0.08*	*80. Engagements envers des non-résidents*

* See notes on previous pages.

* Voir les notes en pages précédentes.

FRANCE — FRANCE

Co-operative banks — Banques mutualistes

	1988	1989	1990	1991	1992	1993	1994	1995	1996	1997	
Million French francs											*Millions de francs français*
INCOME STATEMENT											**COMPTE DE RESULTATS**
1. Interest income	215422	245341	273266	284814	290180	302760	270776	288713	269728	252854	1. Produits financiers
2. Interest expenses	151408	175858	200247	208426	207707	226057	200337	218237	206014	194253	2. Frais financiers
3. Net interest income	64014	69483	73019	76388	82473	76703	70439	70476	63715	58601	3. Produits financiers nets
4. Non-interest income (net)	6473	5869	9538	14136	13617	27078	28124	32957	40333	46957	4. Produits non financiers (nets)
a. Fees and commissions receivable	..	..	..	..	..	*25481*	*27198*	*27311*	*30306*	*33352*	*a. Frais et commissions à recevoir*
b. Fees and commissions payable	..	..	..	..	..	*10808*	*10336*	*10192*	*11829*	*12503*	*b. Frais et commissions à payer*
c. Net profits or loss on financial operations	*217*	*-420*	*-290*	*1380*	*1440*	*5331*	*2996*	*7805*	*14790*	*15230*	*c. Profits ou pertes nets sur opérations financières*
d. Other	*6255*	*6289*	*9829*	*12756*	*12177*	*7073*	*8266*	*8033*	*7066*	*10879*	*d. Autres*
5. Gross income	70487	75352	82557	90524	96090	103781	98563	103433	104047	105559	5. Résultat brut
6. Operating expenses	53545	57202	60931	63443	66091	65654	66752	68203	69484	69786	6. Frais d'exploitation
a. Staff costs	*28957*	*30622*	*32237*	*33296*	*34670*	*35510*	*36093*	*37107*	*37797*	*38035*	*a. Dépenses en personnel*
b. Property costs	*3186*	*3270*	*3338*	*3394*	*3530*	*3485*	*3506*	*3412*	*3478*	*3612*	*b. Dépenses en immobilier*
c. Other	*21402*	*23310*	*25356*	*26753*	*27890*	*26659*	*27154*	*27685*	*28209*	*28140*	*c. Autres*
7. Net income	16942	18150	21626	27081	29999	38127	31811	35230	34564	35772	7. Résultat net
8. Provisions (net)	7479	8123	11478	13727	15696	23421	18391	17460	15906	13318	8. Provisions (nettes)
a. Provisions on loans	*5069*	*4326*	*7548*	*9491*	*8841*	*20980*	*16542*	*14015*	*12246*	*9882*	*a. Provisions sur prêts*
b. Provisions on securities	*146*	*385*	*919*	*445*	*758*	*573*	*57*	*853*	*1046*	*883*	*b. Provisions sur titres*
c. Other	*2265*	*3411*	*3011*	*3791*	*6098*	*1868*	*1791*	*2591*	*2614*	*2553*	*c. Autres*
9. Profit before tax	9463	10027	10148	13354	14303	14706	13420	17770	18658	22454	9. Bénéfices avant impôt
10. Income tax	3569	3820	3393	4409	5267	6351	5165	8207	8063	9689	10. Impôt sur le revenu
11. Profit after tax	5894	6207	6755	8945	9036	8355	8255	9563	10595	12765	11. Bénéfices après impôt
12. Distributed profit	1462	1790	1807	2176	2555	2420	2647	2735	2959	3880	12. Bénéfices distribués
13. Retained profit	4432	4417	4948	6769	6481	5935	5608	6828	7637	8885	13. Bénéfices mis en réserve
BALANCE SHEET											**BILAN**
Assets											**Actif**
14. Cash & balance with Central bank	27461	34522	37322	30147	14991	8812	8896	9488	10933	12208	14. Caisse & solde auprès de la Banque centrale
15. Interbank deposits	1229501	1349433	1474238	1504305	1535896	1752636	1821189	2000307	1975176	1923467	15. Dépôts interbancaires
16. Loans	975434	1151635	1285240	1352492	1393626	1396465	1410596	1448514	1538655	1596289	16. Prêts
17. Securities	145002	173034	184344	268052	268265	286928	394792	496981	639842	645499	17. Valeurs mobilières
18. Other assets	247202	321078	392196	291350	298445	162458	171208	190783	211917	194513	18. Autres actifs
Liabilities											**Passif**
19. Capital & reserves	63684	72676	87452	116469	131350	136050	146722	160677	178538	194271	19. Capital et réserves
20. Borrowing from Central bank	9763	14908	22257	17604	20192	741	626	933	997	463	20. Emprunts auprès de la Banque centrale
21. Interbank deposits	1053864	1261548	1339453	1405356	1378176	1452842	1524101	1642709	1730264	1642626	21. Dépôts interbancaires
22. Non-bank deposits	830289	925072	1048224	1183186	1245533	1430879	1566252	1761324	1862719	1977319	22. Dépôts non bancaires
23. Bonds	428625	462660	502812	447746	450986	467123	451641	438463	415217	396430	23. Obligations
24. Other liabilities	238374	292837	373143	275985	284987	119664	117340	141966	188788	160867	24. Autres engagements
Balance sheet total											**Total du bilan**
25. End-year total	2624599	3029702	3373340	3446346	3511224	3607299	3806681	4146073	4376524	4371975	25. En fin d'exercice
26. Average total	2478794	2741006	3110641	3416549	3490033	3628285	3780283	4123728	4393091	4482697	26. Moyen

FRANCE
Co-operative banks

FRANCE
Banques mutualistes

	1988	1989	1990	1991	1992	1993	1994	1995	1996	1997	
Million French francs											*Millions de francs français*
Memorandum items											**Pour mémoire**
27. Short-term securities	..	..	..	..	..	..	..	..	..	..	*27. Titres à court terme*
28. Bonds	..	..	..	..	..	*150689*	*181706*	*199888*	*242572*	*206520*	*28. Obligations*
29. Shares and participations	..	..	..	..	..	*57532*	*63641*	*73096*	*97930*	*111174*	*29. Actions et participations*
30. Claims on non-residents	*85798*	*245068*	*264271*	*283446*	*327946*	*303492*	*274762*	*326745*	*342025*	*362318*	*30. Créances sur des non-résidents*
31. Liabilities to non-residents	*84674*	*230398*	*251231*	*266061*	*241536*	*167922*	*174386*	*176472*	*222839*	*215090*	*31. Engagements envers des non-résidents*
Capital adequacy											***Solvabilité***
32. Tier 1 Capital	..	..	..	..	..	..	..	..	..	..	*32. Fonds propres de base*
33. Tier 2 Capital	..	..	..	..	..	..	..	..	..	..	*33. Fonds propres complémentaires*
34. Supervisory deductions	..	..	..	..	..	..	..	..	..	..	*34. Eléments à déduire des fonds propres*
35. Total net capital resources	..	..	..	..	..	..	..	..	..	..	*35. Total net des ressources en capital*
36. Risk-weighted assets	..	..	..	..	..	..	..	..	..	..	*36. Actifs pondérés des risques*
SUPPLEMENTARY INFORMATION											**RENSEIGNEMENTS COMPLEMENTAIRES**
37. Number of institutions	182	178	176	168	158	150	144	136	133	131	37. Nombre d'institutions
38. Number of branches	11241	11311	11151	11048	10704	9903	10082	10113	10242	10365	38. Nombre de succursales
39. Number of employees (x 1000)	126.2	126.8	126.1	123.4	121.9	115.1	119.9	122.2	122.8	123.0	39. Nombre de salariés (x 1000)

Notes

- Average balance sheet totals (item 26) are based on the average of quarterly totals.

Notes

- La moyenne du total des actifs/passifs (poste 26) est basée sur la moyenne des totaux des situations trimestrielles.

	1988	1989	1990	1991	1992	1993	1994	1995	1996	1997	
Per cent											*Pourcentage*
INCOME STATEMENT ANALYSIS											**ANALYSE DU COMPTE DE RESULTATS**
% of average balance sheet total											**% du total moyen du bilan**
40. Interest income	8.69	8.95	8.78	8.34	8.31	8.34	7.16	7.00	6.14	5.64	40. Produits financiers
41. Interest expenses	6.11	6.42	6.44	6.10	5.95	6.23	5.30	5.29	4.69	4.33	41. Frais financiers
42. Net interest income	2.58	2.53	2.35	2.24	2.36	2.11	1.86	1.71	1.45	1.31	42. Produits financiers nets
43. Non-interest income (net)	0.26	0.21	0.31	0.41	0.39	0.75	0.74	0.80	0.92	1.05	43. Produits non financiers (nets)
a. Fees and commissions receivable	..	..	..	..	..	*0.70*	*0.72*	*0.66*	*0.69*	*0.74*	*a. Frais et commissions à recevoir*
b. Fees and commissions payable	..	..	..	..	..	*0.30*	*0.27*	*0.25*	*0.27*	*0.28*	*b. Frais et commissions à payer*
c. Net profits or loss on financial operations	*0.01*	*-0.02*	*-0.01*	*0.04*	*0.04*	*0.15*	*0.08*	*0.19*	*0.34*	*0.34*	*c. Profits ou pertes nets sur opérations financières*
d. Other	*0.25*	*0.23*	*0.32*	*0.37*	*0.35*	*0.19*	*0.22*	*0.19*	*0.16*	*0.24*	*d. Autres*
44. Gross income	2.84	2.75	2.65	2.65	2.75	2.86	2.61	2.51	2.37	2.35	44. Résultat brut
45. Operating expenses	2.16	2.09	1.96	1.86	1.89	1.81	1.77	1.65	1.58	1.56	45. Frais d'exploitation
a. Staff costs	*1.17*	*1.12*	*1.04*	*0.97*	*0.99*	*0.98*	*0.95*	*0.90*	*0.86*	*0.85*	*a. Dépenses en personnel*
b. Property costs	*0.13*	*0.12*	*0.11*	*0.10*	*0.10*	*0.10*	*0.09*	*0.08*	*0.08*	*0.08*	*b. Dépenses en immobilier*
c. Other	*0.86*	*0.85*	*0.82*	*0.78*	*0.80*	*0.73*	*0.72*	*0.67*	*0.64*	*0.63*	*c. Autres*
46. Net income	0.68	0.66	0.70	0.79	0.86	1.05	0.84	0.85	0.79	0.80	46. Résultat net
47. Provisions (net)	0.30	0.30	0.37	0.40	0.45	0.65	0.49	0.42	0.36	0.30	47. Provisions (nettes)
a. Provisions on loans	*0.20*	*0.16*	*0.24*	*0.28*	*0.25*	*0.58*	*0.44*	*0.34*	*0.28*	*0.22*	*a. Provisions sur prêts*
b. Provisions on securities	*0.01*	*0.01*	*0.03*	*0.01*	*0.02*	*0.02*	-	*0.02*	*0.02*	*0.02*	*b. Provisions sur titres*
c. Other	*0.09*	*0.12*	*0.10*	*0.11*	*0.17*	*0.05*	*0.05*	*0.06*	*0.06*	*0.06*	*c. Autres*
48. Profit before tax	0.38	0.37	0.33	0.39	0.41	0.41	0.35	0.43	0.42	0.50	48. Bénéfices avant impôt
49. Income tax	0.14	0.14	0.11	0.13	0.15	0.18	0.14	0.20	0.18	0.22	49. Impôt sur le revenu
50. Profit after tax	0.24	0.23	0.22	0.26	0.26	0.23	0.22	0.23	0.24	0.28	50. Bénéfices après impôt
51. Distributed profit	0.06	0.07	0.06	0.06	0.07	0.07	0.07	0.07	0.07	0.09	51. Bénéfices distribués
52. Retained profit	0.18	0.16	0.16	0.20	0.19	0.16	0.15	0.17	0.17	0.20	52. Bénéfices mis en réserve
% of gross income											**% du total du résultat brut**
53. Net interest income	90.82	92.21	88.45	84.38	85.83	73.91	71.47	68.14	61.24	55.51	53. Produits financiers nets
54. Non-interest income (net)	9.18	7.79	11.55	15.62	14.17	26.09	28.53	31.86	38.76	44.48	54. Produits non financiers (nets)
a. Fees and commissions receivable	..	..	..	..	..	*24.55*	*27.59*	*26.40*	*29.13*	*31.60*	*a. Frais et commissions à recevoir*
b. Fees and commissions payable	..	..	..	..	..	*10.41*	*10.49*	*9.85*	*11.37*	*11.84*	*b. Frais et commissions à payer*
c. Net profits or loss on financial operations	*0.31*	*-0.56*	*-0.35*	*1.52*	*1.50*	*5.14*	*3.04*	*7.55*	*14.21*	*14.43*	*c. Profits ou pertes nets sur opérations financières*
d. Other	*8.87*	*8.35*	*11.91*	*14.09*	*12.67*	*6.82*	*8.39*	*7.77*	*6.79*	*10.31*	*d. Autres*
55. Operating expenses	75.96	75.91	73.80	70.08	68.78	63.26	67.73	65.94	66.78	66.11	55. Frais d'exploitation
a. Staff costs	*41.08*	*40.64*	*39.05*	*36.78*	*36.08*	*34.22*	*36.62*	*35.88*	*36.33*	*36.03*	*a. Dépenses en personnel*
b. Property costs	*4.52*	*4.34*	*4.04*	*3.75*	*3.67*	*3.36*	*3.56*	*3.30*	*3.34*	*3.42*	*b. Dépenses en immobilier*
c. Other	*30.36*	*30.93*	*30.71*	*29.55*	*29.02*	*25.69*	*27.55*	*26.77*	*27.11*	*26.66*	*c. Autres*
56. Net income	24.04	24.09	26.20	29.92	31.22	36.74	32.27	34.06	33.22	33.89	56. Résultat net
57. Provisions (net)	10.61	10.78	13.90	15.16	16.33	22.57	18.66	16.88	15.29	12.62	57. Provisions (nettes)
a. Provisions on loans	*7.19*	*5.74*	*9.14*	*10.48*	*9.20*	*20.22*	*16.78*	*13.55*	*11.77*	*9.36*	*a. Provisions sur prêts*
b. Provisions on securities	*0.21*	*0.51*	*1.11*	*0.49*	*0.79*	*0.55*	*0.06*	*0.82*	*1.01*	*0.84*	*b. Provisions sur titres*
c. Other	*3.21*	*4.53*	*3.65*	*4.19*	*6.35*	*1.80*	*1.82*	*2.51*	*2.51*	*2.42*	*c. Autres*
58. Profit before tax	13.43	13.31	12.29	14.75	14.89	14.17	13.62	17.18	17.93	21.27	58. Bénéfices avant impôt
59. Income tax	5.06	5.07	4.11	4.87	5.48	6.12	5.24	7.93	7.75	9.18	59. Impôt sur le revenu
60. Profit after tax	8.36	8.24	8.18	9.88	9.40	8.05	8.38	9.25	10.18	12.09	60. Bénéfices après impôt
% of net income											**% du total du résultat net**
61. Provisions (net)	44.14	44.75	53.08	50.69	52.32	61.43	57.81	49.56	46.02	37.23	61. Provisions (nettes)
a. Provisions on loans	*29.92*	*23.83*	*34.90*	*35.05*	*29.47*	*55.03*	*52.00*	*39.78*	*35.43*	*27.62*	*a. Provisions sur prêts*
b. Provisions on securities	*0.86*	*2.12*	*4.25*	*1.64*	*2.53*	*1.50*	*0.18*	*2.42*	*3.03*	*2.47*	*b. Provisions sur titres*
c. Other	*13.37*	*18.79*	*13.92*	*14.00*	*20.33*	*4.90*	*5.63*	*7.35*	*7.56*	*7.14*	*c. Autres*
62. Profit before tax	55.86	55.25	46.92	49.31	47.68	38.57	42.19	50.44	53.98	62.77	62. Bénéfices avant impôt
63. Income tax	21.07	21.05	15.69	16.28	17.56	16.66	16.24	23.30	23.33	27.09	63. Impôt sur le revenu
64. Profit after tax	34.79	34.20	31.24	33.03	30.12	21.91	25.95	27.14	30.65	35.68	64. Bénéfices après impôt

FRANCE / FRANCE

Co-operative banks / Banques mutualistes

	1988	1989	1990	1991	1992	1993	1994	1995	1996	1997	
Per cent											*Pourcentage*
BALANCE SHEET ANALYSIS											**ANALYSE DU BILAN**
% of year-end balance sheet total											**% du total du bilan en fin d'exercice**
Assets											**Actif**
65. Cash & balance with Central bank	1.05	1.14	1.11	0.87	0.43	0.24	0.23	0.23	0.25	0.28	65. Caisse & solde auprès de la Banque centrale
66. Interbank deposits	46.85	44.54	43.70	43.65	43.74	48.59	47.84	48.25	45.13	44.00	66. Dépôts interbancaires
67. Loans	37.17	38.01	38.10	39.24	39.69	38.71	37.06	34.94	35.16	36.51	67. Prêts
68. Securities	5.52	5.71	5.46	7.78	7.64	7.95	10.37	11.99	14.62	14.76	68. Valeurs mobilières
69. Other assets	9.42	10.60	11.63	8.45	8.50	4.50	4.50	4.60	4.84	4.45	69. Autres actifs
Liabilities											**Passif**
70. Capital & reserves	2.43	2.40	2.59	3.38	3.74	3.77	3.85	3.88	4.08	4.44	70. Capital et réserves
71. Borrowing from Central bank	0.37	0.49	0.66	0.51	0.58	0.02	0.02	0.02	0.02	0.01	71. Emprunts auprès de la Banque centrale
72. Interbank deposits	40.15	41.64	39.71	40.78	39.25	40.28	40.04	39.62	39.54	37.57	72. Dépôts interbancaires
73. Non-bank deposits	31.63	30.53	31.07	34.33	35.47	39.67	41.14	42.48	42.56	45.23	73. Dépôts non bancaires
74. Bonds	16.33	15.27	14.91	12.99	12.84	12.95	11.86	10.58	9.49	9.07	74. Obligations
75. Other liabilities	9.08	9.67	11.06	8.01	8.12	3.32	3.08	3.42	4.31	3.68	75. Autres engagements
Memorandum items											***Pour mémoire***
76. Short-term securities	..	..	..	..	..	..	..	..	..	..	*76. Titres à court terme*
77. Bonds	..	..	..	..	..	*4.18*	*4.77*	*4.82*	*5.54*	*4.72*	*77. Obligations*
78. Shares and participations	..	..	..	..	..	*1.59*	*1.67*	*1.76*	*2.24*	*2.54*	*78. Actions et participations*
79. Claims on non-residents	*3.27*	*8.09*	*7.83*	*8.22*	*9.34*	*8.41*	*7.22*	*7.88*	*7.81*	*8.29*	*79. Créances sur des non-résidents*
80. Liabilities to non-residents	*3.23*	*7.60*	*7.45*	*7.72*	*6.88*	*4.66*	*4.58*	*4.26*	*5.09*	*4.92*	*80. Engagements envers des non-résidents*

* See notes on previous pages.

* Voir les notes en pages précédentes.

FRANCE
Other banks

FRANCE
Autres banques

	1988	1989	1990	1991	1992	1993	1994	1995	1996	1997	
Million French francs											*Millions de francs français*
INCOME STATEMENT											**COMPTE DE RESULTATS**
1. Interest income	262054	279271	313650	343194	334121	346548	316471	305970	281441	271576	1. Produits financiers
2. Interest expenses	222032	237668	269988	294348	286340	304968	268906	262423	240770	237332	2. Frais financiers
3. Net interest income	40022	41603	43662	48846	47781	41580	47565	43547	40672	34244	3. Produits financiers nets
4. Non-interest income (net)	15304	19843	21145	23880	26698	26484	20909	39178	34330	30621	4. Produits non financiers (nets)
a. Fees and commissions receivable	..	..	..	..	..	*10960*	*11207*	*9748*	*10916*	*9236*	*a. Frais et commissions à recevoir*
b. Fees and commissions payable	..	..	..	..	..	*4917*	*4519*	*3587*	*3741*	*2661*	*b. Frais et commissions à payer*
c. Net profits or loss on financial operations	*1472*	*347*	*1037*	*2156*	*2127*	*8664*	*2322*	*3470*	*3297*	*4928*	*c. Profits ou pertes nets sur opérations financières*
d. Other	*13832*	*19496*	*20108*	*21724*	*24571*	*11777*	*11899*	*29546*	*23857*	*19119*	*d. Autres*
5. Gross income	55326	61446	64807	72726	74479	68064	68474	82725	75002	64866	5. Résultat brut
6. Operating expenses	29443	32446	35330	36250	34852	32736	33349	33977	34215	31582	6. Frais d'exploitation
a. Staff costs	*10846*	*11435*	*12448*	*13042*	*12669*	*13851*	*13493*	*13521*	*13931*	*12389*	*a. Dépenses en personnel*
b. Property costs	*2432*	*2922*	*3317*	*3082*	*2441*	*1795*	*1476*	*2189*	*1396*	*573*	*b. Dépenses en immobilier*
c. Other	*16164*	*18089*	*19565*	*20126*	*19742*	*17090*	*18380*	*18268*	*18888*	*18620*	*c. Autres*
7. Net income	25883	29000	29477	36476	39627	35328	35125	48748	40787	33283	7. Résultat net
8. Provisions (net)	3225	4258	6483	10195	17586	29320	27455	51092	29591	12422	8. Provisions (nettes)
a. Provisions on loans	*1773*	*2627*	*4048*	*5969*	*12172*	*25733*	*27819*	*44548*	*26351*	*11713*	*a. Provisions sur prêts*
b. Provisions on securities	*-1516*	*1063*	*1960*	*1236*	*5410*	*3104*	*111*	*7350*	*3085*	*353*	*b. Provisions sur titres*
c. Other	*2968*	*569*	*475*	*2989*	*4*	*483*	*-475*	*-806*	*155*	*355*	*c. Autres*
9. Profit before tax	22658	24742	22994	26281	22041	6008	7670	-2344	11196	20862	9. Bénéfices avant impôt
10. Income tax	4181	4421	4039	4251	4163	5047	4273	3955	4318	4662	10. Impôt sur le revenu
11. Profit after tax	18477	20321	18955	22030	17878	961	3397	-6299	6878	16200	11. Bénéfices après impôt
12. Distributed profit	9410	9563	10607	10754	10606	12311	11248	11741	10535	10668	12. Bénéfices distribués
13. Retained profit	9067	10758	8348	11276	7272	-11350	-7851	-18040	-3657	5532	13. Bénéfices mis en réserve
BALANCE SHEET											**BILAN**
Assets											**Actif**
14. Cash & balance with Central bank	9006	6940	6815	6339	7429	2720	1760	2602	2076	1530	14. Caisse & solde auprès de la Banque centrale
15. Interbank deposits	593469	660884	714646	723692	572857	650046	654574	620786	698276	738113	15. Dépôts interbancaires
16. Loans	1429795	1539365	1593345	1676770	1730736	1809420	1852945	1849861	1662628	1569113	16. Prêts
17. Securities	251240	267634	286665	380876	340706	366670	414278	483803	604900	527967	17. Valeurs mobilières
18. Other assets	192786	197809	221647	231911	211246	107165	101525	122787	121395	129080	18. Autres actifs
Liabilities											**Passif**
19. Capital & reserves	139911	168472	192117	215972	210126	267139	276654	271271	231886	223752	19. Capital et réserves
20. Borrowing from Central bank	10654	10268	24546	3566	1718	7416	2826	1530	852	814	20. Emprunts auprès de la Banque centrale
21. Interbank deposits	1201562	1259390	1265896	1291373	1044144	1017032	1024436	1023851	1212454	1199404	21. Dépôts interbancaires
22. Non-bank deposits	65168	63950	57995	127158	56068	63223	116696	81091	90771	153257	22. Dépôts non bancaires
23. Bonds	732552	827283	916988	1000206	1174369	1363518	1373945	1439776	1205831	1060720	23. Obligations
24. Other liabilities	326449	343268	365574	381313	376547	217693	230525	262321	347480	327857	24. Autres engagements
Balance sheet total											**Total du bilan**
25. End-year total	2476295	2672631	2823118	3019588	2862973	2936022	3025082	3079839	3089275	2965804	25. En fin d'exercice
26. Average total	2364906	2585825	2756756	2978968	3155796	2914267	2190013	3040377	3311042	3097268	26. Moyen

FRANCE
Other banks

FRANCE
Autres banques

	1988	1989	1990	1991	1992	1993	1994	1995	1996	1997	
Million French francs											*Millions de francs français*
Memorandum items											***Pour mémoire***
27. Short-term securities	..	..	..	..	..	..	..	..	..	..	*27. Titres à court terme*
28. Bonds	..	..	..	..	..	*178057*	*196449*	*224394*	*281425*	*269649*	*28. Obligations*
29. Shares and participations	..	..	..	..	..	*147980*	*148340*	*203226*	*146342*	*154695*	*29. Actions et participations*
30. Claims on non-residents	*43576*	*54814*	*71808*	*94834*	*113334*	*226601*	*221731*	*232198*	*334281*	*419411*	*30. Créances sur des non-résidents*
31. Liabilities to non-residents	*51333*	*48420*	*54531*	*83720*	*86146*	*377318*	*410373*	*419136*	*488781*	*546716*	*31. Engagements envers des non-résidents*
Capital adequacy											***Solvabilité***
32. Tier 1 Capital	..	..	..	..	..	..	..	..	..	..	*32. Fonds propres de base*
33. Tier 2 Capital	..	..	..	..	..	..	..	..	..	..	*33. Fonds propres complémentaires*
34. Supervisory deductions	..	..	..	..	..	..	..	..	..	..	*34. Eléments à déduire des fonds propres*
35. Total net capital resources	..	..	..	..	..	..	..	..	..	..	*35. Total net des ressources en capital*
36. Risk-weighted assets	..	..	..	..	..	..	..	..	..	..	*36. Actifs pondérés des risques*
SUPPLEMENTARY INFORMATION											**RENSEIGNEMENTS COMPLEMENTAIRES**
37. Number of institutions	1193	1224	1211	1205	1098	1035	1018	869	837	725	37. Nombre d'institutions
38. Number of branches	207	223	184	176	161	1629	1768	1947	1607	1768	38. Nombre de succursales
39. Number of employees (x 1000)	37.3	38.3	38.6	37.8	35.0	36.0	35.6	36.2	36.7	30.4	39. Nombre de salariés (x 1000)

Notes

- Other banks include municipal credit institutions, finance companies and specialised financial institutions.
- Average balance sheet totals (item 26) are based on the average of quarterly totals.

Notes

- Autres banques comprennent les caisses de crédit municipal, les sociétés financières et les institutions financières spécialisées.
- La moyenne du total des actifs/passifs (poste 26) est basée sur la moyenne des totaux des situations trimestrielles.

FRANCE

Other banks

FRANCE

Autres banques

	1988	1989	1990	1991	1992	1993	1994	1995	1996	1997	
Per cent											*Pourcentage*
INCOME STATEMENT ANALYSIS											**ANALYSE DU COMPTE DE RESULTATS**
% of average balance sheet total											**% du total moyen du bilan**
40. Interest income	11.08	10.80	11.38	11.52	10.59	11.89	14.45	10.06	8.50	8.77	40. Produits financiers
41. Interest expenses	9.39	9.19	9.79	9.88	9.07	10.46	12.28	8.63	7.27	7.66	41. Frais financiers
42. Net interest income	1.69	1.61	1.58	1.64	1.51	1.43	2.17	1.43	1.23	1.11	42. Produits financiers nets
43. Non-interest income (net)	0.65	0.77	0.77	0.80	0.85	0.91	0.95	1.29	1.04	0.99	43. Produits non financiers (nets)
a. Fees and commissions receivable	..	..	..	..	..	*0.38*	*0.51*	*0.32*	*0.33*	*0.30*	*a. Frais et commissions à recevoir*
b. Fees and commissions payable	..	..	..	..	..	*0.17*	*0.21*	*0.12*	*0.11*	*0.09*	*b. Frais et commissions à payer*
c. Net profits or loss on financial operations	*0.06*	*0.01*	*0.04*	*0.07*	*0.07*	*0.30*	*0.11*	*0.11*	*0.10*	*0.16*	*c. Profits ou pertes nets sur opérations financières*
d. Other	*0.58*	*0.75*	*0.73*	*0.73*	*0.78*	*0.40*	*0.54*	*0.97*	*0.72*	*0.62*	*d. Autres*
44. Gross income	2.34	2.38	2.35	2.44	2.36	2.34	3.13	2.72	2.27	2.09	44. Résultat brut
45. Operating expenses	1.24	1.25	1.28	1.22	1.10	1.12	1.52	1.12	1.03	1.02	45. Frais d'exploitation
a. Staff costs	*0.46*	*0.44*	*0.45*	*0.44*	*0.40*	*0.48*	*0.62*	*0.44*	*0.42*	*0.40*	*a. Dépenses en personnel*
b. Property costs	*0.10*	*0.11*	*0.12*	*0.10*	*0.08*	*0.06*	*0.07*	*0.07*	*0.04*	*0.02*	*b. Dépenses en immobilier*
c. Other	*0.68*	*0.70*	*0.71*	*0.68*	*0.63*	*0.59*	*0.84*	*0.60*	*0.57*	*0.60*	*c. Autres*
46. Net income	1.09	1.12	1.07	1.22	1.26	1.21	1.60	1.60	1.23	1.07	46. Résultat net
47. Provisions (net)	0.14	0.16	0.24	0.34	0.56	1.01	1.25	1.68	0.89	0.40	47. Provisions (nettes)
a. Provisions on loans	*0.07*	*0.10*	*0.15*	*0.20*	*0.39*	*0.88*	*1.27*	*1.47*	*0.80*	*0.38*	*a. Provisions sur prêts*
b. Provisions on securities	*-0.06*	*0.04*	*0.07*	*0.04*	*0.17*	*0.11*	*0.01*	*0.24*	*0.09*	*0.01*	*b. Provisions sur titres*
c. Other	*0.13*	*0.02*	*0.02*	*0.10*	-	*0.02*	*-0.02*	*-0.03*	-	*0.01*	*c. Autres*
48. Profit before tax	0.96	0.96	0.83	0.88	0.70	0.21	0.35	-0.08	0.34	0.67	48. Bénéfices avant impôt
49. Income tax	0.18	0.17	0.15	0.14	0.13	0.17	0.20	0.13	0.13	0.15	49. Impôt sur le revenu
50. Profit after tax	0.78	0.79	0.69	0.74	0.57	0.03	0.16	-0.21	0.21	0.52	50. Bénéfices après impôt
51. Distributed profit	0.40	0.37	0.38	0.36	0.34	0.42	0.51	0.39	0.32	0.34	51. Bénéfices distribués
52. Retained profit	0.38	0.42	0.30	0.38	0.23	-0.39	-0.36	-0.59	-0.11	0.18	52. Bénéfices mis en réserve
% of gross income											**% du total du résultat brut**
53. Net interest income	72.34	67.71	67.37	67.16	64.15	61.09	69.46	52.64	54.23	52.79	53. Produits financiers nets
54. Non-interest income (net)	27.66	32.29	32.63	32.84	35.85	38.91	30.54	47.36	45.77	47.21	54. Produits non financiers (nets)
a. Fees and commissions receivable	..	..	..	..	..	*16.10*	*16.37*	*11.78*	*14.55*	*14.24*	*a. Frais et commissions à recevoir*
b. Fees and commissions payable	..	..	..	..	..	*7.22*	*6.60*	*4.34*	*4.99*	*4.10*	*b. Frais et commissions à payer*
c. Net profits or loss on financial operations	*2.66*	*0.56*	*1.60*	*2.96*	*2.86*	*12.73*	*3.39*	*4.19*	*4.40*	*7.60*	*c. Profits ou pertes nets sur opérations financières*
d. Other	*25.00*	*31.73*	*31.03*	*29.87*	*32.99*	*17.30*	*17.38*	*35.72*	*31.81*	*29.47*	*d. Autres*
55. Operating expenses	53.22	52.80	54.52	49.84	46.79	48.10	48.70	41.07	45.62	48.69	55. Frais d'exploitation
a. Staff costs	*19.60*	*18.61*	*19.21*	*17.93*	*17.01*	*20.35*	*19.71*	*16.34*	*18.57*	*19.10*	*a. Dépenses en personnel*
b. Property costs	*4.40*	*4.76*	*5.12*	*4.24*	*3.28*	*2.64*	*2.16*	*2.65*	*1.86*	*0.88*	*b. Dépenses en immobilier*
c. Other	*29.22*	*29.44*	*30.19*	*27.67*	*26.51*	*25.11*	*26.84*	*22.08*	*25.18*	*28.71*	*c. Autres*
56. Net income	46.78	47.20	45.48	50.16	53.21	51.90	51.30	58.93	54.38	51.31	56. Résultat net
57. Provisions (net)	5.83	6.93	10.00	14.02	23.61	43.08	40.10	61.76	39.45	19.15	57. Provisions (nettes)
a. Provisions on loans	*3.20*	*4.28*	*6.25*	*8.21*	*16.34*	*37.81*	*40.63*	*53.85*	*35.13*	*18.06*	*a. Provisions sur prêts*
b. Provisions on securities	*-2.74*	*1.73*	*3.02*	*1.70*	*7.26*	*4.56*	*0.16*	*8.88*	*4.11*	*0.54*	*b. Provisions sur titres*
c. Other	*5.36*	*0.93*	*0.73*	*4.11*	*0.01*	*0.71*	*-0.69*	*-0.97*	*0.21*	*0.55*	*c. Autres*
58. Profit before tax	40.95	40.27	35.48	36.14	29.59	8.83	11.20	-2.83	14.93	32.16	58. Bénéfices avant impôt
59. Income tax	7.56	7.19	6.23	5.85	5.59	7.42	6.24	4.78	5.76	7.19	59. Impôt sur le revenu
60. Profit after tax	33.40	33.07	29.25	30.29	24.00	1.41	4.96	-7.61	9.17	24.97	60. Bénéfices après impôt
% of net income											**% du total du résultat net**
61. Provisions (net)	12.46	14.68	21.99	27.95	44.38	82.99	78.16	104.81	72.55	37.32	61. Provisions (nettes)
a. Provisions on loans	*6.85*	*9.06*	*13.73*	*16.36*	*30.72*	*72.84*	*79.20*	*91.38*	*64.61*	*35.19*	*a. Provisions sur prêts*
b. Provisions on securities	*-5.86*	*3.67*	*6.65*	*3.39*	*13.65*	*8.79*	*0.32*	*15.08*	*7.56*	*1.06*	*b. Provisions sur titres*
c. Other	*11.47*	*1.96*	*1.61*	*8.19*	*0.01*	*1.37*	*-1.35*	*-1.65*	*0.38*	*1.07*	*c. Autres*
62. Profit before tax	87.54	85.32	78.01	72.05	55.62	17.01	21.84	-4.81	27.45	62.68	62. Bénéfices avant impôt
63. Income tax	16.15	15.24	13.70	11.65	10.51	14.29	12.17	8.11	10.59	14.01	63. Impôt sur le revenu
64. Profit after tax	71.39	70.07	64.30	60.40	45.12	2.72	9.67	-12.92	16.86	48.67	64. Bénéfices après impôt

FRANCE
Other banks

FRANCE
Autres banques

	1988	1989	1990	1991	1992	1993	1994	1995	1996	1997	
Per cent											*Pourcentage*
BALANCE SHEET ANALYSIS											**ANALYSE DU BILAN**
% of year-end balance sheet total											**% du total du bilan en fin d'exercice**
Assets											**Actif**
65. Cash & balance with Central bank	0.36	0.26	0.24	0.21	0.26	0.09	0.06	0.08	0.07	0.05	65. Caisse & solde auprès de la Banque centrale
66. Interbank deposits	23.97	24.73	25.31	23.97	20.01	22.14	21.64	20.16	22.60	24.89	66. Dépôts interbancaires
67. Loans	57.74	57.60	56.44	55.53	60.45	61.63	61.25	60.06	53.82	52.91	67. Prêts
68. Securities	10.15	10.01	10.15	12.61	11.90	12.49	13.69	15.71	19.58	17.80	68. Valeurs mobilières
69. Other assets	7.79	7.40	7.85	7.68	7.38	3.65	3.36	3.99	3.93	4.35	69. Autres actifs
Liabilities											**Passif**
70. Capital & reserves	5.65	6.30	6.81	7.15	7.34	9.10	9.15	8.81	7.51	7.54	70. Capital et réserves
71. Borrowing from Central bank	0.43	0.38	0.87	0.12	0.06	0.25	0.09	0.05	0.03	0.03	71. Emprunts auprès de la Banque centrale
72. Interbank deposits	48.52	47.12	44.84	42.77	36.47	34.64	33.86	33.24	39.25	40.44	72. Dépôts interbancaires
73. Non-bank deposits	2.63	2.39	2.05	4.21	1.96	2.15	3.86	2.63	2.94	5.17	73. Dépôts non bancaires
74. Bonds	29.58	30.95	32.48	33.12	41.02	46.44	45.42	46.75	39.03	35.77	74. Obligations
75. Other liabilities	13.18	12.84	12.95	12.63	13.15	7.41	7.62	8.52	11.25	11.05	75. Autres engagements
Memorandum items											***Pour mémoire***
76. Short-term securities	..	..	..	..	..	..	..	..	..	..	*76. Titres à court terme*
77. Bonds	..	..	..	..	..	*6.06*	*6.49*	*7.29*	*9.11*	*9.09*	*77. Obligations*
78. Shares and participations	..	..	..	..	..	*5.04*	*4.90*	*6.60*	*4.74*	*5.22*	*78. Actions et participations*
79. Claims on non-residents	*1.76*	*2.05*	*2.54*	*3.14*	*3.96*	*7.72*	*7.33*	*7.54*	*10.82*	*14.14*	*79. Créances sur des non-résidents*
80. Liabilities to non-residents	*2.07*	*1.81*	*1.93*	*2.77*	*3.01*	*12.85*	*13.57*	*13.61*	*15.82*	*18.43*	*80. Engagements envers des non-résidents*

* See notes on previous pages.

* Voir les notes en pages précédentes.

GERMANY
All banks

ALLEMAGNE
Ensemble des banques

	1989	1990	1991	1992	1993(1)	1994	1995	1996	1997	1998 p	
Million DM											*Millions de DM*
INCOME STATEMENT											**COMPTE DE RESULTATS**
1. Interest income	224774	272413	317946	356962	384049	382111	393155	404646	429702	..	1. Produits financiers
2. Interest expenses	157915	201200	236652	266815	276603	260637	272724	277931	300153	..	2. Frais financiers
3. Net interest income	66859	71213	81294	90147	107446	121474	120431	126715	129549	..	3. Produits financiers nets
4. Non-interest income (net) (2)	22957	26055	25789	28250	33327	28912	31951	33647	39745	..	4. Produits non financiers (nets) (2)
a. Fees and commissions receivable	..	..	..	..	*27771*	*28475*	*28351*	*31294*	*36887*	..	*a. Frais et commissions à recevoir*
b. Fees and commissions payable	..	..	..	..	*2655*	*2746*	*2866*	*3452*	*4180*	..	*b. Frais et commissions à payer*
c. Net profits or loss on financial operations	..	..	..	..	*6652*	*431*	*4297*	*3919*	*5079*	..	*c. Profits ou pertes nets sur opérations financières*
d. Other	..	..	..	..	*1559*	*2752*	*2169*	*1886*	*1959*	..	*d. Autres*
5. Gross income	89816	97268	107083	118397	140773	150386	152382	160362	169294	..	5. Résultat brut
6. Operating expenses	57993	62987	69779	76406	87828	91436	97289	102235	108623	..	6. Frais d'exploitation
a. Staff costs	*36971*	*40178*	*44264*	*48301*	*53949*	*55670*	*58783*	*60689*	*62858*	..	*a. Dépenses en personnel*
b. Property costs (3)	..	..	..	..	..	..	..	..	..	..	*b. Dépenses en immobilier (3)*
c. Other	..	..	..	..	*33879*	*35766*	*38506*	*41546*	*45765*	..	*c. Autres*
7. Net income	31823	34281	37304	41991	52945	58950	55093	58127	60671	..	7. Résultat net
8. Provisions (net)	15294	16807	14008	17325	23363	29908	21459	22696	25506	..	8. Provisions (nettes)
a. Provisions on loans	*15093*	*16295*	*13680*	*16900*	*23042*	*28389*	*20962*	*22165*	*24946*	..	*a. Provisions sur prêts*
b. Provisions on securities (4)	..	..	..	..	..	..	..	..	..	..	*b. Provisions sur titres (4)*
c. Other	..	..	..	..	*321*	*1519*	*497*	*531*	*560*	..	*c. Autres*
9. Profit before tax	16529	17474	23296	24666	29582	29042	33634	35431	35165	..	9. Bénéfices avant impôt
10. Income tax	9275	9408	13585	15266	16313	14116	17578	18670	18114	..	10. Impôt sur le revenu
11. Profit after tax	7254	8066	9711	9400	13269	14926	16056	16761	17051	..	11. Bénéfices après impôt
12. Distributed profit	5506	5828	6192	6522	8712	9403	10386	10795	11143	..	12. Bénéfices distribués
13. Retained profit	1748	2238	3519	2878	4557	5523	5670	5966	5908	..	13. Bénéfices mis en réserve
BALANCE SHEET											**BILAN**
Assets											**Actif**
14. Cash & balance with Central bank	85858	92447	93057	101914	95002	77324	79866	83492	83977	91047	14. Caisse & solde auprès de la Banque centrale
15. Interbank deposits	855091	942832	957079	1008667	1205859	1239952	1398490	1587652	1788605	1988370	15. Dépôts interbancaires
16. Loans	1923523	2103045	2369096	2594859	2988906	3197909	3484013	3791309	4124950	4418393	16. Prêts
17. Securities	535369	627941	667974	753966	1023748	1158357	1255950	1447453	1700509	1971844	17. Valeurs mobilières
18. Other assets	90902	95027	114479	113267	137687	138124	161661	173477	210817	264825	18. Autres actifs
Liabilities											**Passif**
19. Capital & reserves	133480	146444	161709	187401	217654	246503	267647	287905	321655	340717	19. Capital et réserves
20. Borrowing from Central bank	153961	164043	186258	152691	231356	198440	189710	197512	201250	195367	20. Emprunts auprès de la Banque centrale
21. Interbank deposits	798405	914820	964155	1100162	1245884	1428941	1673078	1881722	2206959	2577323	21. Dépôts interbancaires
22. Non-bank deposits	1843035	2010213	2197726	2354476	2783864	2850359	3002490	3285972	3567111	3820130	22. Dépôts non bancaires
23. Bonds	434797	480036	526178	586482	720182	838650	953289	1086703	1172240	1282163	23. Obligations
24. Other liabilities	127065	145736	165659	191461	252262	248773	293766	343569	439643	518779	24. Autres engagements
Balance sheet total											**Total du bilan**
25. End-year total	3490743	3861292	4201685	4572673	5451202	5811666	6379980	7083383	7908858	8734479	25. En fin d'exercice
26. Average total	3318573	3625716	3993446	4359930	5061788	5560841	5951023	6692623	7506990	8388365	26. Moyen

GERMANY / ALLEMAGNE

All banks / Ensemble des banques

	1989	1990	1991	1992	1993(1)	1994	1995	1996	1997	1998 p	
Million DM											*Millions de DM*
Memorandum items											***Pour mémoire***
27. Short-term securities	*51859*	*104948*	*132600*	*134122*	*171279*	*148225*	*157226*	*199059*	*261590*	*283587*	*27. Titres à court terme*
28. Bonds	*412249*	*431455*	*432463*	*497933*	*696572*	*831214*	*881546*	*1000282*	*1147278*	*1301125*	*28. Obligations*
29. Shares and participations	*71261*	*91538*	*102911*	*121911*	*155897*	*178918*	*217178*	*248112*	*291641*	*387132*	*29. Actions et participations*
30. Claims on non-residents	*572825*	*745902*	*687172*	*730577*	*934094*	*928465*	*1085478*	*1373997*	*1810048*	*2146348*	*30. Créances sur des non-résidents*
31. Liabilities to non-residents	*337417*	*440078*	*423857*	*530575*	*576967*	*693487*	*853966*	*1048418*	*1474223*	*1792870*	*31. Engagements envers des non-résidents*
Capital adequacy											***Solvabilité***
32. Tier 1 Capital	..	..	..	..	..	..	..	..	..	..	*32. Fonds propres de base*
33. Tier 2 Capital	..	..	..	..	..	..	..	..	..	..	*33. Fonds propres complémentaires*
34. Supervisory deductions	..	..	..	..	..	..	..	..	..	..	*34. Eléments à déduire des fonds propres*
35. Total net capital resources	..	..	..	..	..	..	..	..	..	..	*35. Total net des ressources en capital*
36. Risk-weighted assets	..	..	..	..	..	..	..	..	..	..	*36. Actifs pondérés des risques*
SUPPLEMENTARY INFORMATION											**RENSEIGNEMENTS COMPLEMENTAIRES**
37. Number of institutions	4089	3913	3716	3517	3769	3613	3500	3392	3284	3111	37. Nombre d'institutions
38. Number of branches	39651	39576	39228	39295	44922	44436	44012	43585	43013	..	38. Nombre de succursales
39. Number of employees (x 1000)	578	664	689	709	717	724	724	716	718	..	39. Nombre de salariés (x 1000)

1. Break in series due to change in methodology.

2. Non-interest income (item 4), in the national definition, excluding items 4.c and 4.d.

3. Property costs (item 6.b.) included under Other operating expenses (item 6.c.)

4. Provisions on securities (item 8.b.) included under Provisions on loans (item 8.a)

Notes

- All banks include Commercial banks, Regional giro institutions, Savings banks, Regional institutions of co-operative banks and Co-operative banks.

- Average balance sheet totals (item 26) are based on twelve end-month data.

Change in methodology

- As from 1993, data include eastern German credit institutions and are in accordance with the new accounting regulations.

1. Rupture dans les séries suite aux changements méthodologiques.

2. Produits non financiers (nets) (poste 4), suivant la définition nationale, non compris les rubriques 4.c et 4.d.

3. Les Dépenses en immobilier (poste 6.b.) sont incluses sous Autres frais d'exploitation (poste 6.c).

4. Les Provisions sur titres (poste 8.b.) sont incluses sous Provisions sur prêts (poste 8.a).

Notes

- L'Ensemble des banques comprend les Banques commerciales, les Organismes régionaux de compensation, les Caisses d'épargne, les Institutions régionales des banques mutualistes et les Banques mutualistes.

- La moyenne du total des actifs/passifs (poste 26) est basée sur douze données de fin de mois.

Changement méthodologique

- Depuis 1993, les données comprennent les organismes de crédit d'Allemagne orientale et sont conformes aux nouvelles règles de comptabilité.

GERMANY — ALLEMAGNE

All banks — Ensemble des banques

	1989	1990	1991	1992	1993(1)	1994	1995	1996	1997	1998 p	
Per cent											*Pourcentage*
INCOME STATEMENT ANALYSIS											**ANALYSE DU COMPTE DE RESULTATS**
% of average balance sheet total											**% du total moyen du bilan**
40. Interest income	6.77	7.51	7.96	8.19	7.59	6.87	6.61	6.05	5.72	..	40. Produits financiers
41. Interest expenses	4.76	5.55	5.93	6.12	5.46	4.69	4.58	4.15	4.00	..	41. Frais financiers
42. Net interest income	2.01	1.96	2.04	2.07	2.12	2.18	2.02	1.89	1.73	..	42. Produits financiers nets
43. Non-interest income (net)	0.69	0.72	0.65	0.65	0.66	0.52	0.54	0.50	0.53	..	43. Produits non financiers (nets)
a. Fees and commissions receivable	..	..	..	..	*0.55*	*0.51*	*0.48*	*0.47*	*0.49*	..	*a. Frais et commissions à recevoir*
b. Fees and commissions payable	..	..	..	..	*0.05*	*0.05*	*0.05*	*0.05*	*0.06*	..	*b. Frais et commissions à payer*
c. Net profits or loss on financial operations	..	..	..	..	*0.13*	*0.01*	*0.07*	*0.06*	*0.07*	..	*c. Profits ou pertes nets sur opérations financières*
d. Other	..	..	..	..	*0.03*	*0.05*	*0.04*	*0.03*	*0.03*	..	*d. Autres*
44. Gross income	2.71	2.68	2.68	2.72	2.78	2.70	2.56	2.40	2.26	..	44. Résultat brut
45. Operating expenses	1.75	1.74	1.75	1.75	1.74	1.64	1.63	1.53	1.45	..	45. Frais d'exploitation
a. Staff costs	*1.11*	*1.11*	*1.11*	*1.11*	*1.07*	*1.00*	*0.99*	*0.91*	*0.84*	..	*a. Dépenses en personnel*
b. Property costs	..	..	..	..	..	..	..	..	..	..	*b. Dépenses en immobilier*
c. Other	..	..	..	..	*0.67*	*0.64*	*0.65*	*0.62*	*0.61*	..	*c. Autres*
46. Net income	0.96	0.95	0.93	0.96	1.05	1.06	0.93	0.87	0.81	..	46. Résultat net
47. Provisions (net)	0.46	0.46	0.35	0.40	0.46	0.54	0.36	0.34	0.34	..	47. Provisions (nettes)
a. Provisions on loans	*0.45*	*0.45*	*0.34*	*0.39*	*0.46*	*0.51*	*0.35*	*0.33*	*0.33*	..	*a. Provisions sur prêts*
b. Provisions on securities	..	..	..	..	..	..	..	..	..	..	*b. Provisions sur titres*
c. Other	..	..	..	..	*0.01*	*0.03*	*0.01*	*0.01*	*0.01*	..	*c. Autres*
48. Profit before tax	0.50	0.48	0.58	0.57	0.58	0.52	0.57	0.53	0.47	..	48. Bénéfices avant impôt
49. Income tax	0.28	0.26	0.34	0.35	0.32	0.25	0.30	0.28	0.24	..	49. Impôt sur le revenu
50. Profit after tax	0.22	0.22	0.24	0.22	0.26	0.27	0.27	0.25	0.23	..	50. Bénéfices après impôt
51. Distributed profit	0.17	0.16	0.16	0.15	0.17	0.17	0.17	0.16	0.15	..	51. Bénéfices distribués
52. Retained profit	0.05	0.06	0.09	0.07	0.09	0.10	0.10	0.09	0.08	..	52. Bénéfices mis en réserve
% of gross income											**% du total du résultat brut**
53. Net interest income	74.44	73.21	75.92	76.14	76.33	80.77	79.03	79.02	76.52	..	53. Produits financiers nets
54. Non-interest income (net)	25.56	26.79	24.08	23.86	23.67	19.23	20.97	20.98	23.48	..	54. Produits non financiers (nets)
a. Fees and commissions receivable	..	..	..	..	*19.73*	*18.93*	*18.61*	*19.51*	*21.79*	..	*a. Frais et commissions à recevoir*
b. Fees and commissions payable	..	..	..	..	*1.89*	*1.83*	*1.88*	*2.15*	*2.47*	..	*b. Frais et commissions à payer*
c. Net profits or loss on financial operations	..	..	..	..	*4.73*	*0.29*	*2.82*	*2.44*	*3.00*	..	*c. Profits ou pertes nets sur opérations financières*
d. Other	..	..	..	..	*1.11*	*1.83*	*1.42*	*1.18*	*1.16*	..	*d. Autres*
55. Operating expenses	64.57	64.76	65.16	64.53	62.39	60.80	63.85	63.75	64.16	..	55. Frais d'exploitation
a. Staff costs	*41.16*	*41.31*	*41.34*	*40.80*	*38.32*	*37.02*	*38.58*	*37.85*	*37.13*	..	*a. Dépenses en personnel*
b. Property costs	..	..	..	..	..	..	..	..	..	..	*b. Dépenses en immobilier*
c. Other	..	..	..	..	*24.07*	*23.78*	*25.27*	*25.91*	*27.03*	..	*c. Autres*
56. Net income	35.43	35.24	34.84	35.47	37.61	39.20	36.15	36.25	35.84	..	56. Résultat net
57. Provisions (net)	17.03	17.28	13.08	14.63	16.60	19.89	14.08	14.15	15.07	..	57. Provisions (nettes)
a. Provisions on loans	*16.80*	*16.75*	*12.78*	*14.27*	*16.37*	*18.88*	*13.76*	*13.82*	*14.74*	..	*a. Provisions sur prêts*
b. Provisions on securities	..	..	..	..	..	..	..	..	..	..	*b. Provisions sur titres*
c. Other	..	..	..	..	*0.23*	*1.01*	*0.33*	*0.33*	*0.33*	..	*c. Autres*
58. Profit before tax	18.40	17.96	21.76	20.83	21.01	19.31	22.07	22.09	20.77	..	58. Bénéfices avant impôt
59. Income tax	10.33	9.67	12.69	12.89	11.59	9.39	11.54	11.64	10.70	..	59. Impôt sur le revenu
60. Profit after tax	8.08	8.29	9.07	7.94	9.43	9.93	10.54	10.45	10.07	..	60. Bénéfices après impôt
% of net income											**% du total du résultat net**
61. Provisions (net)	48.06	49.03	37.55	41.26	44.13	50.73	38.95	39.05	42.04	..	61. Provisions (nettes)
a. Provisions on loans	*47.43*	*47.53*	*36.67*	*40.25*	*43.52*	*48.16*	*38.05*	*38.13*	*41.12*	..	*a. Provisions sur prêts*
b. Provisions on securities	..	..	..	..	..	..	..	..	..	..	*b. Provisions sur titres*
c. Other	..	..	..	..	*0.61*	*2.58*	*0.90*	*0.91*	*0.92*	..	*c. Autres*
62. Profit before tax	51.94	50.97	62.45	58.74	55.87	49.27	61.05	60.95	57.96	..	62. Bénéfices avant impôt
63. Income tax	29.15	27.44	36.42	36.36	30.81	23.95	31.91	32.12	29.86	..	63. Impôt sur le revenu
64. Profit after tax	22.79	23.53	26.03	22.39	25.06	25.32	29.14	28.84	28.10	..	64. Bénéfices après impôt

GERMANY

All banks

ALLEMAGNE

Ensemble des banques

	1989	1990	1991	1992	1993(1)	1994	1995	1996	1997	1998 p	
Per cent											*Pourcentage*
BALANCE SHEET ANALYSIS											**ANALYSE DU BILAN**
% of year-end balance sheet total											**% du total du bilan en fin d'exercice**
Assets											**Actif**
65. Cash & balance with Central bank	2.46	2.39	2.21	2.23	1.74	1.33	1.25	1.18	1.06	1.04	65. Caisse & solde auprès de la Banque centrale
66. Interbank deposits	24.50	24.42	22.78	22.06	22.12	21.34	21.92	22.41	22.62	22.76	66. Dépôts interbancaires
67. Loans	55.10	54.46	56.38	56.75	54.83	55.03	54.61	53.52	52.16	50.59	67. Prêts
68. Securities	15.34	16.26	15.90	16.49	18.78	19.93	19.69	20.43	21.50	22.58	68. Valeurs mobilières
69. Other assets	2.60	2.46	2.72	2.48	2.53	2.38	2.53	2.45	2.67	3.03	69. Autres actifs
Liabilities											**Passif**
70. Capital & reserves	3.82	3.79	3.85	4.10	3.99	4.24	4.20	4.06	4.07	3.90	70. Capital et réserves
71. Borrowing from Central bank	4.41	4.25	4.43	3.34	4.24	3.41	2.97	2.79	2.54	2.24	71. Emprunts auprès de la Banque centrale
72. Interbank deposits	22.87	23.69	22.95	24.06	22.86	24.59	26.22	26.57	27.90	29.51	72. Dépôts interbancaires
73. Non-bank deposits	52.80	52.06	52.31	51.49	51.07	49.05	47.06	46.39	45.10	43.74	73. Dépôts non bancaires
74. Bonds	12.46	12.43	12.52	12.83	13.21	14.43	14.94	15.34	14.82	14.68	74. Obligations
75. Other liabilities	3.64	3.77	3.94	4.19	4.63	4.28	4.60	4.85	5.56	5.94	75. Autres engagements
Memorandum items											***Pour mémoire***
76. Short-term securities	*1.49*	*2.72*	*3.16*	*2.93*	*3.14*	*2.55*	*2.46*	*2.81*	*3.31*	*3.25*	*76. Titres à court terme*
77. Bonds	*11.81*	*11.17*	*10.29*	*10.89*	*12.78*	*14.30*	*13.82*	*14.12*	*14.51*	*14.90*	*77. Obligations*
78. Shares and participations	*2.04*	*2.37*	*2.45*	*2.67*	*2.86*	*3.08*	*3.40*	*3.50*	*3.69*	*4.43*	*78. Actions et participations*
79. Claims on non-residents	*16.41*	*19.32*	*16.35*	*15.98*	*17.14*	*15.98*	*17.01*	*19.40*	*22.89*	*24.57*	*79. Créances sur des non-résidents*
80. Liabilities to non-residents	*9.67*	*11.40*	*10.09*	*11.60*	*10.58*	*11.93*	*13.39*	*14.80*	*18.64*	*20.53*	*80. Engagements envers des non-résidents*

* See notes on previous pages.

* Voir les notes en pages précédentes.

GERMANY

Commercial banks

ALLEMAGNE

Banques commerciales

	1989	1990	1991	1992	1993(1)	1994	1995	1996	1997	1998 p	
Million DM											*Millions de DM*
INCOME STATEMENT											**COMPTE DE RESULTATS**
1. Interest income	75952	93502	109785	125197	128218	123287	126577	131853	143210	..	1. Produits financiers
2. Interest expenses	54081	68910	80576	92094	91170	82807	87298	89910	99112	..	2. Frais financiers
3. Net interest income	21871	24592	29209	33103	37048	40480	39279	41943	44098	..	3. Produits financiers nets
4. Non-interest income (net) (2)	12315	13742	12825	14735	16981	13809	15395	17278	19841	..	4. Produits non financiers (nets) (2)
a. Fees and commissions receivable	..	..	..	..	*14407*	*13936*	*13659*	*15627*	*19680*	..	*a. Frais et commissions à recevoir*
b. Fees and commissions payable	..	..	..	..	*1466*	*1559*	*1622*	*2042*	*2525*	..	*b. Frais et commissions à payer*
c. Net profits or loss on financial operations	..	..	..	..	*3932*	*137*	*2208*	*2012*	*2520*	..	*c. Profits ou pertes nets sur opérations financières*
d. Other	..	..	..	..	*108*	*1295*	*1150*	*1681*	*166*	..	*d. Autres*
5. Gross income	34186	38334	42034	47838	54029	54289	54674	59221	63939	..	5. Résultat brut
6. Operating expenses	22245	24427	27834	30451	33026	34627	36491	38859	42610	..	6. Frais d'exploitation
a. Staff costs	*14259*	*15555*	*17477*	*18961*	*20452*	*20947*	*21938*	*22758*	*24010*	..	*a. Dépenses en personnel*
b. Property costs (3)	..	..	..	..	-	-	-	-	-	..	*b. Dépenses en immobilier (3)*
c. Other	..	..	..	..	*12574*	*13680*	*14553*	*16101*	*18600*	..	*c. Autres*
7. Net income	11941	13907	14200	17387	21003	19662	18183	20362	21329	..	7. Résultat net
8. Provisions (net)	4467	6328	6317	10313	11746	9577	8062	9056	10505	..	8. Provisions (nettes)
a. Provisions on loans	*4314*	*5983*	*6157*	*10046*	*11539*	*9473*	*7692*	*8727*	*10234*	..	*a. Provisions sur prêts*
b. Provisions on securities (4)	..	..	..	..	..	..	..	..	..	..	*b. Provisions sur titres (4)*
c. Other	..	..	..	..	*207*	*104*	*370*	*329*	*271*	..	*c. Autres*
9. Profit before tax	7474	7579	7883	7074	9257	10085	10121	11306	10824	..	9. Bénéfices avant impôt
10. Income tax	3994	3434	3883	3821	3705	3682	3327	4297	3353	..	10. Impôt sur le revenu
11. Profit after tax	3480	4145	4000	3253	5552	6403	6794	7009	7471	..	11. Bénéfices après impôt
12. Distributed profit	2584	3041	2840	2894	4224	4576	5075	5431	5853	..	12. Bénéfices distribués
13. Retained profit	896	1104	1160	359	1328	1827	1719	1578	1618	..	13. Bénéfices mis en réserve
BALANCE SHEET											**BILAN**
Assets											**Actif**
14. Cash & balance with Central bank	32043	35665	37627	38792	35404	25057	26476	29958	31324	37305	14. Caisse & solde auprès de la Banque centrale
15. Interbank deposits	283241	311569	314517	345687	392646	429534	471495	542767	620917	693041	15. Dépôts interbancaires
16. Loans	664124	757560	865040	938289	1055138	1105296	1227395	1371940	1530940	1659316	16. Prêts
17. Securities	132739	156499	177994	205865	296656	315399	363410	438288	558701	677751	17. Valeurs mobilières
18. Other assets	26549	25353	26308	34854	42200	38270	50628	53768	66966	99619	18. Autres actifs
Liabilities											**Passif**
19. Capital & reserves	55417	64922	72356	82228	91355	106070	114427	120546	135893	137601	19. Capital et réserves
20. Borrowing from Central bank	60371	57210	60178	56101	99026	74264	73111	70098	65922	66651	20. Emprunts auprès de la Banque centrale
21. Interbank deposits	314931	348978	362609	415905	441897	545674	647220	715257	824782	979127	21. Dépôts interbancaires
22. Non-bank deposits	551267	634532	727226	784343	885548	849713	892057	1032605	1181099	1260234	22. Dépôts non bancaires
23. Bonds	101409	115170	125832	141938	196115	236239	279251	333503	369113	433085	23. Obligations
24. Other liabilities	55301	65834	73285	82972	108103	101596	133338	164712	232039	290334	24. Autres engagements
Balance sheet total											**Total du bilan**
25. End-year total	1138696	1286646	1421486	1563487	1822044	1913556	2139404	2436721	2808848	3167032	25. En fin d'exercice
26. Average total	1072589	1203377	1350934	1495870	1697098	1852710	1981009	2297747	2666504	3107516	26. Moyen

GERMANY
Commercial banks

ALLEMAGNE
Banques commerciales

	1989	1990	1991	1992	1993(1)	1994	1995	1996	1997	1998 p	
Million DM											*Millions de DM*
Memorandum items											***Pour mémoire***
27. Short-term securities	*13915*	*23196*	*38346*	*39895*	*62240*	*48808*	*57430*	*76507*	*121399*	*132336*	*27. Titres à court terme*
28. Bonds	*75707*	*76814*	*79780*	*98773*	*152047*	*178096*	*202767*	*242527*	*303125*	*358225*	*28. Obligations*
29. Shares and participations	*43117*	*56489*	*59868*	*67197*	*82369*	*88495*	*103213*	*119254*	*134177*	*187190*	*29. Actions et participations*
30. Claims on non-residents	*330289*	*397119*	*405332*	*437475*	*552554*	*596035*	*685536*	*848286*	*1121842*	*1304661*	*30. Créances sur des non-résidents*
31. Liabilities to non-residents	*260075*	*306926*	*319405*	*373253*	*410965*	*480595*	*588330*	*709012*	*955706*	*1113539*	*31. Engagements envers des non-résidents*
Capital adequacy											***Solvabilité***
32. Tier 1 Capital	..	..	..	..	..	..	..	..	..	..	*32. Fonds propres de base*
33. Tier 2 Capital	..	..	..	..	..	..	..	..	..	..	*33. Fonds propres complémentaires*
34. Supervisory deductions	..	..	..	..	..	..	..	..	..	..	*34. Eléments à déduire des fonds propres*
35. Total net capital resources	..	..	..	..	..	..	..	..	..	..	*35. Total net des ressources en capital*
36. Risk-weighted assets	..	..	..	..	..	..	..	..	..	..	*36. Actifs pondérés des risques*
SUPPLEMENTARY INFORMATION											**RENSEIGNEMENTS COMPLEMENTAIRES**
37. Number of institutions	264	274	281	276	270	273	266	258	249	244	37. Nombre d'institutions
38. Number of branches	6252	6255	6044	6394	7331	7303	7260	7235	7030	..	38. Nombre de succursales
39. Number of employees (x 1000)	193	215	218	223	221	220	218	213	216	..	39. Nombre de salariés (x 1000)

1. Break in series due to change in methodology.
2. Non-interest income (item 4), in the national definition, excluding items 4.c and 4.d.
3. Property costs (item 6.b.) included under Other operating expenses (item 6.c.).
4. Provisions on securities (item 8.b.) included under Provisions on loans (item 8.a).

Notes

- Average balance sheet totals (item 26) are based on twelve end-month data.

Change in methodology

- As from 1993, data include eastern German credit institutions and are in accordance with the new accounting regulations.

1. Rupture dans les séries suite aux changements méthodologiques.
2. Produits non financiers (nets) (poste 4), suivant la définition nationale, non compris les rubriques 4.c et 4.d.
3. Les Dépenses en immobilier (poste 6.b.) sont incluses sous Autres frais d'exploitation (poste 6.c).
4. Les Provisions sur titres (poste 8.b.) sont incluses sous Provisions sur prêts (poste 8.a).

Notes

- La moyenne du total des actifs/passifs (poste 26) est basée sur douze données de fin de mois.

Changement méthodologique

- Depuis 1993, les données comprennent les organismes de crédit d'Allemagne orientale et sont conformes aux nouvelles règles de comptabilité.

Per cent	1989	1990	1991	1992	1993(1)	1994	1995	1996	1997	1998 p	Pourcentage
INCOME STATEMENT ANALYSIS											**ANALYSE DU COMPTE DE RESULTATS**
% of average balance sheet total											**% du total moyen du bilan**
40. Interest income	7.08	7.77	8.13	8.37	7.56	6.65	6.39	5.74	5.37	..	40. Produits financiers
41. Interest expenses	5.04	5.73	5.96	6.16	5.37	4.47	4.41	3.91	3.72	..	41. Frais financiers
42. Net interest income	2.04	2.04	2.16	2.21	2.18	2.18	1.98	1.83	1.65	..	42. Produits financiers nets
43. Non-interest income (net)	1.15	1.14	0.95	0.99	1.00	0.75	0.78	0.75	0.74	..	43. Produits non financiers (nets)
a. Fees and commissions receivable	..	..	..	..	*0.85*	*0.75*	*0.69*	*0.68*	*0.74*	..	*a. Frais et commissions à recevoir*
b. Fees and commissions payable	..	..	..	..	*0.09*	*0.08*	*0.08*	*0.09*	*0.09*	..	*b. Frais et commissions à payer*
c. Net profits or loss on financial operations	..	..	..	..	*0.23*	*0.01*	*0.11*	*0.09*	*0.09*	..	*c. Profits ou pertes nets sur opérations financières*
d. Other	..	..	..	..	*0.01*	*0.07*	*0.06*	*0.07*	*0.01*	..	*d. Autres*
44. Gross income	3.19	3.19	3.11	3.20	3.18	2.93	2.76	2.58	2.40	..	44. Résultat brut
45. Operating expenses	2.07	2.03	2.06	2.04	1.95	1.87	1.84	1.69	1.60	..	45. Frais d'exploitation
a. Staff costs	*1.33*	*1.29*	*1.29*	*1.27*	*1.21*	*1.13*	*1.11*	*0.99*	*0.90*	..	*a. Dépenses en personnel*
b. Property costs	..	..	..	..	-	-	-	-	-	..	*b. Dépenses en immobilier*
c. Other	..	..	..	..	*0.74*	*0.74*	*0.73*	*0.70*	*0.70*	..	*c. Autres*
46. Net income	1.11	1.16	1.05	1.16	1.24	1.06	0.92	0.89	0.80	..	46. Résultat net
47. Provisions (net)	0.42	0.53	0.47	0.69	0.69	0.52	0.41	0.39	0.39	..	47. Provisions (nettes)
a. Provisions on loans	*0.40*	*0.50*	*0.46*	*0.67*	*0.68*	*0.51*	*0.39*	*0.38*	*0.38*	..	*a. Provisions sur prêts*
b. Provisions on securities	..	..	..	..	..	..	..	..	..	..	*b. Provisions sur titres*
c. Other	..	..	..	..	*0.01*	*0.01*	*0.02*	*0.01*	*0.01*	..	*c. Autres*
48. Profit before tax	0.70	0.63	0.58	0.47	0.55	0.54	0.51	0.49	0.41	..	48. Bénéfices avant impôt
49. Income tax	0.37	0.29	0.29	0.26	0.22	0.20	0.17	0.19	0.13	..	49. Impôt sur le revenu
50. Profit after tax	0.32	0.34	0.30	0.22	0.33	0.35	0.34	0.31	0.28	..	50. Bénéfices après impôt
51. Distributed profit	0.24	0.25	0.21	0.19	0.25	0.25	0.26	0.24	0.22	..	51. Bénéfices distribués
52. Retained profit	0.08	0.09	0.09	0.02	0.08	0.10	0.09	0.07	0.06	..	52. Bénéfices mis en réserve
% of gross income											**% du total du résultat brut**
53. Net interest income	63.98	64.15	69.49	69.20	68.57	74.56	71.84	70.82	68.97	..	53. Produits financiers nets
54. Non-interest income (net)	36.02	35.85	30.51	30.80	31.43	25.44	28.16	29.18	31.03	..	54. Produits non financiers (nets)
a. Fees and commissions receivable	..	..	..	..	*26.67*	*25.67*	*24.98*	*26.39*	*30.78*	..	*a. Frais et commissions à recevoir*
b. Fees and commissions payable	..	..	..	..	*2.71*	*2.87*	*2.97*	*3.45*	*3.95*	..	*b. Frais et commissions à payer*
c. Net profits or loss on financial operations	..	..	..	..	*7.28*	*0.25*	*4.04*	*3.40*	*3.94*	..	*c. Profits ou pertes nets sur opérations financières*
d. Other	..	..	..	..	*0.20*	*2.39*	*2.10*	*2.84*	*0.26*	..	*d. Autres*
55. Operating expenses	65.07	63.72	66.22	63.65	61.13	63.78	66.74	65.62	66.64	..	55. Frais d'exploitation
a. Staff costs	*41.71*	*40.58*	*41.58*	*39.64*	*37.85*	*38.58*	*40.13*	*38.43*	*37.55*	..	*a. Dépenses en personnel*
b. Property costs	..	..	..	..	-	-	-	-	-	..	*b. Dépenses en immobilier*
c. Other	..	..	..	..	*23.27*	*25.20*	*26.62*	*27.19*	*29.09*	..	*c. Autres*
56. Net income	34.93	36.28	33.78	36.35	38.87	36.22	33.26	34.38	33.36	..	56. Résultat net
57. Provisions (net)	13.07	16.51	15.03	21.56	21.74	17.64	14.75	15.29	16.43	..	57. Provisions (nettes)
a. Provisions on loans	*12.62*	*15.61*	*14.65*	*21.00*	*21.36*	*17.45*	*14.07*	*14.74*	*16.01*	..	*a. Provisions sur prêts*
b. Provisions on securities	..	..	..	..	..	..	..	..	..	..	*b. Provisions sur titres*
c. Other	..	..	..	..	*0.38*	*0.19*	*0.68*	*0.56*	*0.42*	..	*c. Autres*
58. Profit before tax	21.86	19.77	18.75	14.79	17.13	18.58	18.51	19.09	16.93	..	58. Bénéfices avant impôt
59. Income tax	11.68	8.96	9.24	7.99	6.86	6.78	6.09	7.26	5.24	..	59. Impôt sur le revenu
60. Profit after tax	10.18	10.81	9.52	6.80	10.28	11.79	12.43	11.84	11.68	..	60. Bénéfices après impôt
% of net income											**% du total du résultat net**
61. Provisions (net)	37.41	45.50	44.49	59.31	55.93	48.71	44.34	44.48	49.25	..	61. Provisions (nettes)
a. Provisions on loans	*36.13*	*43.02*	*43.36*	*57.78*	*54.94*	*48.18*	*42.30*	*42.86*	*47.98*	..	*a. Provisions sur prêts*
b. Provisions on securities	..	..	..	..	..	..	..	..	..	..	*b. Provisions sur titres*
c. Other	..	..	..	..	*0.99*	*0.53*	*2.03*	*1.62*	*1.27*	..	*c. Autres*
62. Profit before tax	62.59	54.50	55.51	40.69	44.07	51.29	55.66	55.52	50.75	..	62. Bénéfices avant impôt
63. Income tax	33.45	24.69	27.35	21.98	17.64	18.73	18.30	21.10	15.72	..	63. Impôt sur le revenu
64. Profit after tax	29.14	29.81	28.17	18.71	26.43	32.57	37.36	34.42	35.03	..	64. Bénéfices après impôt

GERMANY
Commercial banks

ALLEMAGNE
Banques commerciales

	1989	1990	1991	1992	1993(1)	1994	1995	1996	1997	1998 p	
Per cent											*Pourcentage*
BALANCE SHEET ANALYSIS											**ANALYSE DU BILAN**
% of year-end balance sheet total											**% du total du bilan en fin d'exercice**
Assets											**Actif**
65. Cash & balance with Central bank	2.81	2.77	2.65	2.48	1.94	1.31	1.24	1.23	1.12	1.18	65. Caisse & solde auprès de la Banque centrale
66. Interbank deposits	24.87	24.22	22.13	22.11	21.55	22.45	22.04	22.27	22.11	21.88	66. Dépôts interbancaires
67. Loans	58.32	58.88	60.85	60.01	57.91	57.76	57.37	56.30	54.50	52.39	67. Prêts
68. Securities	11.66	12.16	12.52	13.17	16.28	16.48	16.99	17.99	19.89	21.40	68. Valeurs mobilières
69. Other assets	2.33	1.97	1.85	2.23	2.32	2.00	2.37	2.21	2.38	3.15	69. Autres actifs
Liabilities											**Passif**
70. Capital & reserves	4.87	5.05	5.09	5.26	5.01	5.54	5.35	4.95	4.84	4.34	70. Capital et réserves
71. Borrowing from Central bank	5.30	4.45	4.23	3.59	5.43	3.88	3.42	2.88	2.35	2.10	71. Emprunts auprès de la Banque centrale
72. Interbank deposits	27.66	27.12	25.51	26.60	24.25	28.52	30.25	29.35	29.36	30.92	72. Dépôts interbancaires
73. Non-bank deposits	48.41	49.32	51.16	50.17	48.60	44.40	41.70	42.38	42.05	39.79	73. Dépôts non bancaires
74. Bonds	8.91	8.95	8.85	9.08	10.76	12.35	13.05	13.69	13.14	13.67	74. Obligations
75. Other liabilities	4.86	5.12	5.16	5.31	5.93	5.31	6.23	6.76	8.26	9.17	75. Autres engagements
Memorandum items											***Pour mémoire***
76. Short-term securities	*1.22*	*1.80*	*2.70*	*2.55*	*3.42*	*2.55*	*2.68*	*3.14*	*4.32*	*4.18*	*76. Titres à court terme*
77. Bonds	*6.65*	*5.97*	*5.61*	*6.32*	*8.34*	*9.31*	*9.48*	*9.95*	*10.79*	*11.31*	*77. Obligations*
78. Shares and participations	*3.79*	*4.39*	*4.21*	*4.30*	*4.52*	*4.62*	*4.82*	*4.89*	*4.78*	*5.91*	*78. Actions et participations*
79. Claims on non-residents	*29.01*	*30.86*	*28.51*	*27.98*	*30.33*	*31.15*	*32.04*	*34.81*	*39.94*	*41.20*	*79. Créances sur des non-résidents*
80. Liabilities to non-residents	*22.84*	*23.85*	*22.47*	*23.87*	*22.56*	*25.12*	*27.50*	*29.10*	*34.02*	*35.16*	*80. Engagements envers des non-résidents*

* See notes on previous pages.

* Voir les notes en pages précédentes.

GERMANY — ALLEMAGNE

Large commercial banks — Grandes banques commerciales

Million DM	1989	1990	1991	1992	1993(1)	1994	1995	1996	1997	1998 p	Millions de DM
INCOME STATEMENT											**COMPTE DE RESULTATS**
1. Interest income	35221	43650	50489	55719	56093	51849	55378	59348	66201	..	1. Produits financiers
2. Interest expenses	23823	30612	34827	38594	37872	33191	37813	40566	46164	..	2. Frais financiers
3. Net interest income	11398	13038	15662	17125	18221	18658	17565	18782	20037	..	3. Produits financiers nets
4. Non-interest income (net) (2)	5773	6997	6315	8204	9625	7805	9052	10083	11744	..	4. Produits non financiers (nets) (2)
a. Fees and commissions receivable	..	..	..	..	*8258*	*7683*	*7517*	*8732*	*11092*	..	*a. Frais et commissions à recevoir*
b. Fees and commissions payable	..	..	..	..	*368*	*431*	*526*	*728*	*868*	..	*b. Frais et commissions à payer*
c. Net profits or loss on financial operations	..	..	..	..	*1978*	*-51*	*1071*	*1154*	*1713*	..	*c. Profits ou pertes nets sur opérations financières*
d. Other	..	..	..	..	*-243*	*604*	*990*	*925*	*-193*	..	*d. Autres*
5. Gross income	17171	20035	21977	25329	27846	26463	26617	28865	31781	..	5. Résultat brut
6. Operating expenses	11571	12657	14795	16027	17075	17780	18657	20187	22773	..	6. Frais d'exploitation
a. Staff costs	*7702*	*8348*	*9671*	*10378*	*11105*	*11314*	*11827*	*12437*	*13357*	..	*a. Dépenses en personnel*
b. Property costs (3)	..	..	..	..	..	..	..	..	..	..	*b. Dépenses en immobilier (3)*
c. Other	..	..	..	..	*5970*	*6466*	*6830*	*7750*	*9416*	..	*c. Autres*
7. Net income	5600	7378	7182	9302	10771	8683	7960	8678	9008	..	7. Résultat net
8. Provisions (net)	1053	2708	2395	4423	6372	3877	3717	3207	5204	..	8. Provisions (nettes)
a. Provisions on loans	*1035*	*2491*	*2327*	*4217*	*6259*	*3877*	*3498*	*3028*	*5134*	..	*a. Provisions sur prêts*
b. Provisions on securities (4)	..	..	..	..	..	..	..	..	..	..	*b. Provisions sur titres (4)*
c. Other	..	..	..	..	*113*	-	*219*	*179*	*70*	..	*c. Autres*
9. Profit before tax	4547	4670	4787	4879	4399	4806	4243	5471	3804	..	9. Bénéfices avant impôt
10. Income tax	2493	1915	2320	1999	1706	1680	835	1857	998	..	10. Impôt sur le revenu
11. Profit after tax	2054	2755	2467	2880	2693	3126	3408	3614	2806	..	11. Bénéfices après impôt
12. Distributed profit	1304	1962	1543	1586	1668	1976	2018	2164	2406	..	12. Bénéfices distribués
13. Retained profit	750	793	924	1294	1025	1150	1390	1450	400	..	13. Bénéfices mis en réserve
BALANCE SHEET											**BILAN**
Assets											**Actif**
14. Cash & balance with Central bank	17006	20034	22041	21456	20936	14594	15449	18918	21730	20375	14. Caisse & solde auprès de la Banque centrale
15. Interbank deposits	135759	155820	151688	173501	185179	220925	242643	272937	318798	400093	15. Dépôts interbancaires
16. Loans	296500	345721	405306	418642	447449	457923	534991	623718	745507	843278	16. Prêts
17. Securities	63955	74472	83023	92907	140141	146082	183127	220013	302825	420472	17. Valeurs mobilières
18. Other assets	8385	8254	8240	10760	14481	12093	12343	14289	24049	54730	18. Autres actifs
Liabilities											**Passif**
19. Capital & reserves	26944	31303	34258	38059	42120	46446	50519	55270	65152	67362	19. Capital et réserves
20. Borrowing from Central bank	23045	17203	24044	18426	20868	26561	25374	20884	21624	33536	20. Emprunts auprès de la Banque centrale
21. Interbank deposits	127905	151037	148965	175391	181824	247249	313561	347893	431935	587514	21. Dépôts interbancaires
22. Non-bank deposits	291839	343846	402067	423614	473267	431910	473091	570850	682269	719941	22. Dépôts non bancaires
23. Bonds	23021	26870	26312	28232	48934	58833	75889	89649	98723	149594	23. Obligations
24. Other liabilities	28851	34042	34652	33544	41173	40618	50119	65329	113206	181001	24. Autres engagements
Balance sheet total											**Total du bilan**
25. End-year total	521605	604301	670298	717266	808186	851617	988553	1149875	1412909	1738948	25. En fin d'exercice
26. Average total	494426	563239	641255	694382	768766	829919	911755	1099382	1340110	1665557	26. Moyen

GERMANY
Large commercial banks

ALLEMAGNE
Grandes banques commerciales

	1989	1990	1991	1992	1993(1)	1994	1995	1996	1997	1998 p	
Million DM											*Millions de DM*
Memorandum items											***Pour mémoire***
27. Short-term securities	*8291*	*10071*	*14800*	*15548*	*28641*	*26708*	*35730*	*46110*	*82918*	*96082*	*27. Titres à court terme*
28. Bonds	*26290*	*25355*	*28915*	*33627*	*59251*	*66615*	*85061*	*106889*	*143297*	*201755*	*28. Obligations*
29. Shares and participations	*29374*	*39046*	*39308*	*43732*	*52249*	*52759*	*62336*	*67014*	*76610*	*122635*	*29. Actions et participations*
30. Claims on non-residents	*194585*	*233940*	*235265*	*257909*	*311555*	*351591*	*440135*	*552125*	*758031*	*954532*	*30. Créances sur des non-résidents*
31. Liabilities to non-residents	*166807*	*197384*	*202878*	*232226*	*252796*	*305451*	*398003*	*495553*	*692806*	*846666*	*31. Engagements envers des non-résidents*
Capital adequacy											***Solvabilité***
32. Tier 1 Capital	..	..	..	..	..	..	..	..	..	..	*32. Fonds propres de base*
33. Tier 2 Capital	..	..	..	..	..	..	..	..	..	..	*33. Fonds propres complémentaires*
34. Supervisory deductions	..	..	..	..	..	..	..	..	..	..	*34. Eléments à déduire des fonds propres*
35. Total net capital resources	..	..	..	..	..	..	..	..	..	..	*35. Total net des ressources en capital*
36. Risk-weighted assets	..	..	..	..	..	..	..	..	..	..	*36. Actifs pondérés des risques*
SUPPLEMENTARY INFORMATION											**RENSEIGNEMENTS COMPLEMENTAIRES**
37. Number of institutions	6	6	4	4	3	3	3	3	3	3	37. Nombre d'institutions
38. Number of branches	3110	3105	3043	3036	3598	3621	3624	3579	3553	..	38. Nombre de succursales
39. Number of employees (x 1000)	..	..	..	..	..	..	..	..	..	..	39. Nombre de salariés (x 1000)

1. Break in series due to change in methodology.
2. Non-interest income (item 4), in the national definition, excluding items 4.c and 4.d.
3. Property costs (item 6.b.) included under Other operating expenses (item 6.c.).
4. Provisions on securities (item 8.b.) included under Provisions on loans (item 8.a).

Notes

- Large commercial banks are a sub-group of Commercial banks.
- Average balance sheet totals (item 26) are based on twelve end-month data.

Change in methodology

- As from 1993, data include eastern German credit institutions and are in accordance with the new accounting regulations.

1. Rupture dans les séries suite aux changements méthodologiques.
2. Produits non financiers (nets) (poste 4), suivant la définition nationale, non compris les rubriques 4.c et 4.d.
3. Les Dépenses en immobilier (poste 6.b.) sont incluses sous Autres frais d'exploitation (poste 6.c).
4. Les Provisions sur titres (poste 8.b.) sont incluses sous Provisions sur prêts (poste 8.a).

Notes

- Les Grandes banques commerciales sont un sous-groupe des Banques commerciales.
- La moyenne du total des actifs/passifs (poste 26) est basée sur douze données de fin de mois.

Changement méthodologique

- Depuis 1993, les données comprennent les organismes de crédit d'Allemagne orientale et sont conformes aux nouvelles règles de comptabilité.

GERMANY — ALLEMAGNE

Large commercial banks — Grandes banques commerciales

	1989	1990	1991	1992	1993(1)	1994	1995	1996	1997	1998 p	
Per cent											*Pourcentage*
INCOME STATEMENT ANALYSIS											**ANALYSE DU COMPTE DE RESULTATS**
% of average balance sheet total											**% du total moyen du bilan**
40. Interest income	7.12	7.75	7.87	8.02	7.30	6.25	6.07	5.40	4.94	..	40. Produits financiers
41. Interest expenses	4.82	5.43	5.43	5.56	4.93	4.00	4.15	3.69	3.44	..	41. Frais financiers
42. Net interest income	2.31	2.31	2.44	2.47	2.37	2.25	1.93	1.71	1.50	..	42. Produits financiers nets
43. Non-interest income (net)	1.17	1.24	0.98	1.18	1.25	0.94	0.99	0.92	0.88	..	43. Produits non financiers (nets)
a. Fees and commissions receivable	..	..	..	..	*1.07*	*0.93*	*0.82*	*0.79*	*0.83*	..	*a. Frais et commissions à recevoir*
b. Fees and commissions payable	..	..	..	..	*0.05*	*0.05*	*0.06*	*0.07*	*0.06*	..	*b. Frais et commissions à payer*
c. Net profits or loss on financial operations	..	..	..	..	*0.26*	*-0.01*	*0.12*	*0.10*	*0.13*	..	*c. Profits ou pertes nets sur opérations financières*
d. Other	..	..	..	..	*-0.03*	*0.07*	*0.11*	*0.08*	*-0.01*	..	*d. Autres*
44. Gross income	3.47	3.56	3.43	3.65	3.62	3.19	2.92	2.63	2.37	..	44. Résultat brut
45. Operating expenses	2.34	2.25	2.31	2.31	2.22	2.14	2.05	1.84	1.70	..	45. Frais d'exploitation
a. Staff costs	*1.56*	*1.48*	*1.51*	*1.49*	*1.44*	*1.36*	*1.30*	*1.13*	*1.00*	..	*a. Dépenses en personnel*
b. Property costs	..	..	..	..	..	..	..	..	..	..	*b. Dépenses en immobilier*
c. Other	..	..	..	..	*0.78*	*0.78*	*0.75*	*0.70*	*0.70*	..	*c. Autres*
46. Net income	1.13	1.31	1.12	1.34	1.40	1.05	0.87	0.79	0.67	..	46. Résultat net
47. Provisions (net)	0.21	0.48	0.37	0.64	0.83	0.47	0.41	0.29	0.39	..	47. Provisions (nettes)
a. Provisions on loans	*0.21*	*0.44*	*0.36*	*0.61*	*0.81*	*0.47*	*0.38*	*0.28*	*0.38*	..	*a. Provisions sur prêts*
b. Provisions on securities	..	..	..	..	..	..	..	..	..	..	*b. Provisions sur titres*
c. Other	..	..	..	..	*0.01*	-	*0.02*	*0.02*	*0.01*	..	*c. Autres*
48. Profit before tax	0.92	0.83	0.75	0.70	0.57	0.58	0.47	0.50	0.28	..	48. Bénéfices avant impôt
49. Income tax	0.50	0.34	0.36	0.29	0.22	0.20	0.09	0.17	0.07	..	49. Impôt sur le revenu
50. Profit after tax	0.42	0.49	0.38	0.41	0.35	0.38	0.37	0.33	0.21	..	50. Bénéfices après impôt
51. Distributed profit	0.26	0.35	0.24	0.23	0.22	0.24	0.22	0.20	0.18	..	51. Bénéfices distribués
52. Retained profit	0.15	0.14	0.14	0.19	0.13	0.14	0.15	0.13	0.03	..	52. Bénéfices mis en réserve
% of gross income											**% du total du résultat brut**
53. Net interest income	66.38	65.08	71.27	67.61	65.43	70.51	65.99	65.07	63.05	..	53. Produits financiers nets
54. Non-interest income (net)	33.62	34.92	28.73	32.39	34.57	29.49	34.01	34.93	36.95	..	54. Produits non financiers (nets)
a. Fees and commissions receivable	..	..	..	..	*29.66*	*29.03*	*28.24*	*30.25*	*34.90*	..	*a. Frais et commissions à recevoir*
b. Fees and commissions payable	..	..	..	..	*1.32*	*1.63*	*1.98*	*2.52*	*2.73*	..	*b. Frais et commissions à payer*
c. Net profits or loss on financial operations	..	..	..	..	*7.10*	*-0.19*	*4.02*	*4.00*	*5.39*	..	*c. Profits ou pertes nets sur opérations financières*
d. Other	..	..	..	..	*-0.87*	*2.28*	*3.72*	*3.20*	*-0.61*	..	*d. Autres*
55. Operating expenses	67.39	63.17	67.32	63.28	61.32	67.19	70.09	69.94	71.66	..	55. Frais d'exploitation
a. Staff costs	*44.85*	*41.67*	*44.01*	*40.97*	*39.88*	*42.75*	*44.43*	*43.09*	*42.03*	..	*a. Dépenses en personnel*
b. Property costs	..	..	..	..	..	..	..	..	..	..	*b. Dépenses en immobilier*
c. Other	..	..	..	..	*21.44*	*24.43*	*25.66*	*26.85*	*29.63*	..	*c. Autres*
56. Net income	32.61	36.83	32.68	36.72	38.68	32.81	29.91	30.06	28.34	..	56. Résultat net
57. Provisions (net)	6.13	13.52	10.90	17.46	22.88	14.65	13.96	11.11	16.37	..	57. Provisions (nettes)
a. Provisions on loans	*6.03*	*12.43*	*10.59*	*16.65*	*22.48*	*14.65*	*13.14*	*10.49*	*16.15*	..	*a. Provisions sur prêts*
b. Provisions on securities	..	..	..	..	..	..	..	..	..	..	*b. Provisions sur titres*
c. Other	..	..	..	..	*0.41*	-	*0.82*	*0.62*	*0.22*	..	*c. Autres*
58. Profit before tax	26.48	23.31	21.78	19.26	15.80	18.16	15.94	18.95	11.97	..	58. Bénéfices avant impôt
59. Income tax	14.52	9.56	10.56	7.89	6.13	6.35	3.14	6.43	3.14	..	59. Impôt sur le revenu
60. Profit after tax	11.96	13.75	11.23	11.37	9.67	11.81	12.80	12.52	8.83	..	60. Bénéfices après impôt
% of net income											**% du total du résultat net**
61. Provisions (net)	18.80	36.70	33.35	47.55	59.16	44.65	46.70	36.96	57.77	..	61. Provisions (nettes)
a. Provisions on loans	*18.48*	*33.76*	*32.40*	*45.33*	*58.11*	*44.65*	*43.94*	*34.89*	*56.99*	..	*a. Provisions sur prêts*
b. Provisions on securities	..	..	..	..	..	..	..	..	..	..	*b. Provisions sur titres*
c. Other	..	..	..	..	*1.05*	-	*2.75*	*2.06*	*0.78*	..	*c. Autres*
62. Profit before tax	81.20	63.30	66.65	52.45	40.84	55.35	53.30	63.04	42.23	..	62. Bénéfices avant impôt
63. Income tax	44.52	25.96	32.30	21.49	15.84	19.35	10.49	21.40	11.08	..	63. Impôt sur le revenu
64. Profit after tax	36.68	37.34	34.35	30.96	25.00	36.00	42.81	41.65	31.15	..	64. Bénéfices après impôt

GERMANY
Large commercial banks

ALLEMAGNE
Grandes banques commerciales

	1989	1990	1991	1992	1993(1)	1994	1995	1996	1997	1998 p	
Per cent											*Pourcentage*
BALANCE SHEET ANALYSIS											**ANALYSE DU BILAN**
% of year-end balance sheet total											**% du total du bilan en fin d'exercice**
Assets											**Actif**
65. Cash & balance with Central bank	3.26	3.32	3.29	2.99	2.59	1.71	1.56	1.65	1.54	1.17	65. Caisse & solde auprès de la Banque centrale
66. Interbank deposits	26.03	25.79	22.63	24.19	22.91	25.94	24.55	23.74	22.56	23.01	66. Dépôts interbancaires
67. Loans	56.84	57.21	60.47	58.37	55.36	53.77	54.12	54.24	52.76	48.49	67. Prêts
68. Securities	12.26	12.32	12.39	12.95	17.34	17.15	18.52	19.13	21.43	24.18	68. Valeurs mobilières
69. Other assets	1.61	1.37	1.23	1.50	1.79	1.42	1.25	1.24	1.70	3.15	69. Autres actifs
Liabilities											**Passif**
70. Capital & reserves	5.17	5.18	5.11	5.31	5.21	5.45	5.11	4.81	4.61	3.87	70. Capital et réserves
71. Borrowing from Central bank	4.42	2.85	3.59	2.57	2.58	3.12	2.57	1.82	1.53	1.93	71. Emprunts auprès de la Banque centrale
72. Interbank deposits	24.52	24.99	22.22	24.45	22.50	29.03	31.72	30.25	30.57	33.79	72. Dépôts interbancaires
73. Non-bank deposits	55.95	56.90	59.98	59.06	58.56	50.72	47.86	49.64	48.29	41.40	73. Dépôts non bancaires
74. Bonds	4.41	4.45	3.93	3.94	6.05	6.91	7.68	7.80	6.99	8.60	74. Obligations
75. Other liabilities	5.53	5.63	5.17	4.68	5.09	4.77	5.07	5.68	8.01	10.41	75. Autres engagements
Memorandum items											***Pour mémoire***
76. Short-term securities	*1.59*	*1.67*	*2.21*	*2.17*	*3.54*	*3.14*	*3.61*	*4.01*	*5.87*	*5.53*	*76. Titres à court terme*
77. Bonds	*5.04*	*4.20*	*4.31*	*4.69*	*7.33*	*7.82*	*8.60*	*9.30*	*10.14*	*11.60*	*77. Obligations*
78. Shares and participations	*5.63*	*6.46*	*5.86*	*6.10*	*6.46*	*6.20*	*6.31*	*5.83*	*5.42*	*7.05*	*78. Actions et participations*
79. Claims on non-residents	*37.31*	*38.71*	*35.10*	*35.96*	*38.55*	*41.29*	*44.52*	*48.02*	*53.65*	*54.89*	*79. Créances sur des non-résidents*
80. Liabilities to non-residents	*31.98*	*32.66*	*30.27*	*32.38*	*31.28*	*35.87*	*40.26*	*43.10*	*49.03*	*48.69*	*80. Engagements envers des non-résidents*

* See notes on previous pages.

* Voir les notes en pages précédentes.

GERMANY / ALLEMAGNE

Regional giro institutions / Organismes régionaux de compensation

	1989	1990	1991	1992	1993(1)	1994	1995	1996	1997	1998 p	
Million DM											*Millions de DM*
INCOME STATEMENT											**COMPTE DE RESULTATS**
1. Interest income	46856	56817	67101	76780	82029	85756	91024	98124	109605	..	1. Produits financiers
2. Interest expenses	42153	52078	61750	70142	74208	75737	81164	86676	97176	..	2. Frais financiers
3. Net interest income	4703	4739	5351	6638	7821	10019	9860	11448	12429	..	3. Produits financiers nets
4. Non-interest income (net) (2)	1473	1349	1857	2006	2701	1388	2249	1834	3424	..	4. Produits non financiers (nets) (2)
a. Fees and commissions receivable	..	..	..	..	*1650*	*1823*	*1840*	*2089*	*2617*	..	*a. Frais et commissions à recevoir*
b. Fees and commissions payable	..	..	..	..	*416*	*399*	*409*	*499*	*632*	..	*b. Frais et commissions à payer*
c. Net profits or loss on financial operations	..	..	..	..	*1022*	*-64*	*780*	*640*	*1051*	..	*c. Profits ou pertes nets sur opérations financières*
d. Other	..	..	..	..	*445*	*28*	*38*	*-396*	*388*	..	*d. Autres*
5. Gross income	6176	6088	7208	8644	10522	11407	12109	13282	15853	..	5. Résultat brut
6. Operating expenses	3308	3604	3873	5063	5524	5970	6583	7227	8057	..	6. Frais d'exploitation
a. Staff costs	*2171*	*2393*	*2468*	*3220*	*3401*	*3486*	*3888*	*4172*	*4434*	..	*a. Dépenses en personnel*
b. Property costs (3)	..	..	..	..	..	..	..	..	..	..	*b. Dépenses en immobilier (3)*
c. Other	..	..	..	..	*2123*	*2484*	*2695*	*3055*	*3623*	..	*c. Autres*
7. Net income	2868	2484	3335	3581	4998	5437	5526	6055	7796	..	7. Résultat net
8. Provisions (net)	1122	1579	1899	1771	2399	2823	2203	2560	3052	..	8. Provisions (nettes)
a. Provisions on loans	*1090*	*1551*	*1825*	*1697*	*2398*	*2656*	*2177*	*2450*	*3023*	..	*a. Provisions sur prêts*
b. Provisions on securities (4)	..	..	..	..	..	..	..	..	..	..	*b. Provisions sur titres (4)*
c. Other	..	..	..	..	*1*	*167*	*26*	*110*	*29*	..	*c. Autres*
9. Profit before tax	1746	905	1436	1810	2599	2614	3323	3495	4744	..	9. Bénéfices avant impôt
10. Income tax	1016	433	766	889	1328	1115	1542	1299	2180	..	10. Impôt sur le revenu
11. Profit after tax	730	472	670	921	1271	1499	1781	2196	2564	..	11. Bénéfices après impôt
12. Distributed profit	374	336	327	434	503	550	631	866	861	..	12. Bénéfices distribués
13. Retained profit	356	136	343	487	768	949	1150	1330	1703	..	13. Bénéfices mis en réserve
BALANCE SHEET											**BILAN**
Assets											**Actif**
14. Cash & balance with Central bank	5325	7106	4334	5357	5550	3240	3954	4650	3847	4364	14. Caisse & solde auprès de la Banque centrale
15. Interbank deposits	286439	317729	329932	368961	433992	460760	533677	639661	743920	828696	15. Dépôts interbancaires
16. Loans	354110	382774	444196	523715	628712	672947	724321	787508	877670	946999	16. Prêts
17. Securities	69504	116932	124858	158334	201622	224794	259753	307565	377690	467761	17. Valeurs mobilières
18. Other assets	13529	14559	16378	20179	30832	33454	41507	45332	64609	81820	18. Autres actifs
Liabilities											**Passif**
19. Capital & reserves	16331	17442	20265	29846	36348	40788	44628	49724	58258	67518	19. Capital et réserves
20. Borrowing from Central bank	25183	32448	43979	31831	67281	46009	44485	48442	48359	42394	20. Emprunts auprès de la Banque centrale
21. Interbank deposits	213735	280076	305577	371072	419636	446589	527200	616342	762388	892128	21. Dépôts interbancaires
22. Non-bank deposits	178316	191566	211546	260784	309832	346858	381272	436775	504120	578360	22. Dépôts non bancaires
23. Bonds	277285	295797	312236	344492	411510	461832	508403	562519	597593	635767	23. Obligations
24. Other liabilities	18057	21771	26095	38521	56101	53119	57224	70914	97018	113473	24. Autres engagements
Balance sheet total											**Total du bilan**
25. End-year total	728907	839100	919698	1076546	1300708	1395195	1563212	1784716	2067736	2329640	25. En fin d'exercice
26. Average total	699495	774961	872439	1021846	1194272	1321304	1440883	1662667	1923358	2180454	26. Moyen

GERMANY
Regional giro institutions

ALLEMAGNE
Organismes régionaux de compensation

	1989	1990	1991	1992	1993(1)	1994	1995	1996	1997	1998 p	
Million DM											*Millions de DM*
Memorandum items											***Pour mémoire***
27. Short-term securities	*7514*	*40637*	*44877*	*42029*	*39899*	*29343*	*26131*	*38931*	*52631*	*73883*	*27. Titres à court terme*
28. Bonds	*52600*	*63689*	*65843*	*97520*	*138342*	*167236*	*195498*	*225979*	*279638*	*338671*	*28. Obligations*
29. Shares and participations	*9390*	*12606*	*14138*	*18785*	*23381*	*28215*	*38124*	*42655*	*45421*	*55207*	*29. Actions et participations*
30. Claims on non-residents	*184436*	*272157*	*222613*	*247934*	*304288*	*284607*	*324240*	*438668*	*596709*	*724204*	*30. Créances sur des non-résidents*
31. Liabilities to non-residents	*61469*	*104877*	*87723*	*134346*	*134531*	*175500*	*223601*	*290166*	*447685*	*575024*	*31. Engagements envers des non-résidents*
Capital adequacy											***Solvabilité***
32. Tier 1 Capital	..	..	..	..	..	..	..	..	..	..	*32. Fonds propres de base*
33. Tier 2 Capital	..	..	..	..	..	..	..	..	..	..	*33. Fonds propres complémentaires*
34. Supervisory deductions	..	..	..	..	..	..	..	..	..	..	*34. Eléments à déduire des fonds propres*
35. Total net capital resources	..	..	..	..	..	..	..	..	..	..	*35. Total net des ressources en capital*
36. Risk-weighted assets	..	..	..	..	..	..	..	..	..	..	*36. Actifs pondérés des risques*
SUPPLEMENTARY INFORMATION											**RENSEIGNEMENTS COMPLEMENTAIRES**
37. Number of institutions	11	11	11	12	13	13	13	13	13	13	37. Nombre d'institutions
38. Number of branches	219	309	290	329	436	433	433	436	428	..	38. Nombre de succursales
39. Number of employees (x 1000)	24	24	25	32	34	33	33	34	34	..	39. Nombre de salariés (x 1000)

1. Break in series due to change in methodology.
2. Non-interest income (item 4), in the national definition, excluding items 4.c and 4.d.
3. Property costs (item 6.b.) included under Other operating expenses (item 6.c.).
4. Provisions on securities (item 8.b.) included under Provisions on loans (item 8.a).

Notes

- Average balance sheet totals (item 26) are based on twelve end-month data.

Change in methodology

- As from 1993, data include eastern German credit institutions and are in accordance with the new accounting regulations.

1. Rupture dans les séries suite aux changements méthodologiques.
2. Produits non financiers (nets) (poste 4), suivant la définition nationale, non compris les rubriques 4.c et 4.d.
3. Les Dépenses en immobilier (poste 6.b.) sont incluses sous Autres frais d'exploitation (poste 6.c).
4. Les Provisions sur titres (poste 8.b.) sont incluses sous Provisions sur prêts (poste 8.a).

Notes

- La moyenne du total des actifs/passifs (poste 26) est basée sur douze données de fin de mois.

Changement méthodologique

- Depuis 1993, les données comprennent les organismes de crédit d'Allemagne orientale et sont conformes aux nouvelles règles de comptabilité.

GERMANY — ALLEMAGNE

Regional giro institutions — Organismes régionaux de compensation

	1989	1990	1991	1992	1993(1)	1994	1995	1996	1997	1998 p	
Per cent											*Pourcentage*
INCOME STATEMENT ANALYSIS											**ANALYSE DU COMPTE DE RESULTATS**
% of average balance sheet total											**% du total moyen du bilan**
40. Interest income	6.70	7.33	7.69	7.51	6.87	6.49	6.32	5.90	5.70	..	40. Produits financiers
41. Interest expenses	6.03	6.72	7.08	6.86	6.21	5.73	5.63	5.21	5.05	..	41. Frais financiers
42. Net interest income	0.67	0.61	0.61	0.65	0.65	0.76	0.68	0.69	0.65	..	42. Produits financiers nets
43. Non-interest income (net)	0.21	0.17	0.21	0.20	0.23	0.11	0.16	0.11	0.18	..	43. Produits non financiers (nets)
a. Fees and commissions receivable	..	..	..	..	*0.14*	*0.14*	*0.13*	*0.13*	*0.14*	..	*a. Frais et commissions à recevoir*
b. Fees and commissions payable	..	..	..	..	*0.03*	*0.03*	*0.03*	*0.03*	*0.03*	..	*b. Frais et commissions à payer*
c. Net profits or loss on financial operations	..	..	..	..	*0.09*	-	*0.05*	*0.04*	*0.05*	..	*c. Profits ou pertes nets sur opérations financières*
d. Other	..	..	..	..	*0.04*	-	-	*-0.02*	*0.02*	..	*d. Autres*
44. Gross income	0.88	0.79	0.83	0.85	0.88	0.86	0.84	0.80	0.82	..	44. Résultat brut
45. Operating expenses	0.47	0.47	0.44	0.50	0.46	0.45	0.46	0.43	0.42	..	45. Frais d'exploitation
a. Staff costs	*0.31*	*0.31*	*0.28*	*0.32*	*0.28*	*0.26*	*0.27*	*0.25*	*0.23*	..	*a. Dépenses en personnel*
b. Property costs	..	..	..	..	..	..	..	..	..	..	*b. Dépenses en immobilier*
c. Other	..	..	..	..	*0.18*	*0.19*	*0.19*	*0.18*	*0.19*	..	*c. Autres*
46. Net income	0.41	0.32	0.38	0.35	0.42	0.41	0.38	0.36	0.41	..	46. Résultat net
47. Provisions (net)	0.16	0.20	0.22	0.17	0.20	0.21	0.15	0.15	0.16	..	47. Provisions (nettes)
a. Provisions on loans	*0.16*	*0.20*	*0.21*	*0.17*	*0.20*	*0.20*	*0.15*	*0.15*	*0.16*	..	*a. Provisions sur prêts*
b. Provisions on securities	..	..	..	..	..	..	..	..	..	..	*b. Provisions sur titres*
c. Other	..	..	..	..	-	*0.01*	-	*0.01*	-	..	*c. Autres*
48. Profit before tax	0.25	0.12	0.16	0.18	0.22	0.20	0.23	0.21	0.25	..	48. Bénéfices avant impôt
49. Income tax	0.15	0.06	0.09	0.09	0.11	0.08	0.11	0.08	0.11	..	49. Impôt sur le revenu
50. Profit after tax	0.10	0.06	0.08	0.09	0.11	0.11	0.12	0.13	0.13	..	50. Bénéfices après impôt
51. Distributed profit	0.05	0.04	0.04	0.04	0.04	0.04	0.04	0.05	0.04	..	51. Bénéfices distribués
52. Retained profit	0.05	0.02	0.04	0.05	0.06	0.07	0.08	0.08	0.09	..	52. Bénéfices mis en réserve
% of gross income											**% du total du résultat brut**
53. Net interest income	76.15	77.84	74.24	76.79	74.33	87.83	81.43	86.19	78.40	..	53. Produits financiers nets
54. Non-interest income (net)	23.85	22.16	25.76	23.21	25.67	12.17	18.57	13.81	21.60	..	54. Produits non financiers (nets)
a. Fees and commissions receivable	..	..	..	..	*15.68*	*15.98*	*15.20*	*15.73*	*16.51*	..	*a. Frais et commissions à recevoir*
b. Fees and commissions payable	..	..	..	..	*3.95*	*3.50*	*3.38*	*3.76*	*3.99*	..	*b. Frais et commissions à payer*
c. Net profits or loss on financial operations	..	..	..	..	*9.71*	*-0.56*	*6.44*	*4.82*	*6.63*	..	*c. Profits ou pertes nets sur opérations financières*
d. Other	..	..	..	..	*4.23*	*0.25*	*0.31*	*-2.98*	*2.45*	..	*d. Autres*
55. Operating expenses	53.56	59.20	53.73	58.57	52.50	52.34	54.36	54.41	50.82	..	55. Frais d'exploitation
a. Staff costs	*35.15*	*39.31*	*34.24*	*37.25*	*32.32*	*30.56*	*32.11*	*31.41*	*27.97*	..	*a. Dépenses en personnel*
b. Property costs	..	..	..	..	..	..	..	..	..	..	*b. Dépenses en immobilier*
c. Other	..	..	..	..	*20.18*	*21.78*	*22.26*	*23.00*	*22.85*	..	*c. Autres*
56. Net income	46.44	40.80	46.27	41.43	47.50	47.66	45.64	45.59	49.18	..	56. Résultat net
57. Provisions (net)	18.17	25.94	26.35	20.49	22.80	24.75	18.19	19.27	19.25	..	57. Provisions (nettes)
a. Provisions on loans	*17.65*	*25.48*	*25.32*	*19.63*	*22.79*	*23.28*	*17.98*	*18.45*	*19.07*	..	*a. Provisions sur prêts*
b. Provisions on securities	..	..	..	..	..	..	..	..	..	..	*b. Provisions sur titres*
c. Other	..	..	..	..	*0.01*	*1.46*	*0.21*	*0.83*	*0.18*	..	*c. Autres*
58. Profit before tax	28.27	14.87	19.92	20.94	24.70	22.92	27.44	26.31	29.92	..	58. Bénéfices avant impôt
59. Income tax	16.45	7.11	10.63	10.28	12.62	9.77	12.73	9.78	13.75	..	59. Impôt sur le revenu
60. Profit after tax	11.82	7.75	9.30	10.65	12.08	13.14	14.71	16.53	16.17	..	60. Bénéfices après impôt
% of net income											**% du total du résultat net**
61. Provisions (net)	39.12	63.57	56.94	49.46	48.00	51.92	39.87	42.28	39.15	..	61. Provisions (nettes)
a. Provisions on loans	*38.01*	*62.44*	*54.72*	*47.39*	*47.98*	*48.85*	*39.40*	*40.46*	*38.78*	..	*a. Provisions sur prêts*
b. Provisions on securities	..	..	..	..	..	..	..	..	..	..	*b. Provisions sur titres*
c. Other	..	..	..	..	*0.02*	*3.07*	*0.47*	*1.82*	*0.37*	..	*c. Autres*
62. Profit before tax	60.88	36.43	43.06	50.54	52.00	48.08	60.13	57.72	60.85	..	62. Bénéfices avant impôt
63. Income tax	35.43	17.43	22.97	24.83	26.57	20.51	27.90	21.45	27.96	..	63. Impôt sur le revenu
64. Profit after tax	25.45	19.00	20.09	25.72	25.43	27.57	32.23	36.27	32.89	..	64. Bénéfices après impôt

GERMANY
Regional giro institutions

ALLEMAGNE
Organismes régionaux de compensation

	1989	1990	1991	1992	1993(1)	1994	1995	1996	1997	1998 p	
Per cent											*Pourcentage*
BALANCE SHEET ANALYSIS											**ANALYSE DU BILAN**
% of year-end balance sheet total											**% du total du bilan en fin d'exercice**
Assets											**Actif**
65. Cash & balance with Central bank	0.73	0.85	0.47	0.50	0.43	0.23	0.25	0.26	0.19	0.19	65. Caisse & solde auprès de la Banque centrale
66. Interbank deposits	39.30	37.87	35.87	34.27	33.37	33.02	34.14	35.84	35.98	35.57	66. Dépôts interbancaires
67. Loans	48.58	45.62	48.30	48.65	48.34	48.23	46.34	44.13	42.45	40.65	67. Prêts
68. Securities	9.54	13.94	13.58	14.71	15.50	16.11	16.62	17.23	18.27	20.08	68. Valeurs mobilières
69. Other assets	1.86	1.74	1.78	1.87	2.37	2.40	2.66	2.54	3.12	3.51	69. Autres actifs
Liabilities											**Passif**
70. Capital & reserves	2.24	2.08	2.20	2.77	2.79	2.92	2.85	2.79	2.82	2.90	70. Capital et réserves
71. Borrowing from Central bank	3.45	3.87	4.78	2.96	5.17	3.30	2.85	2.71	2.34	1.82	71. Emprunts auprès de la Banque centrale
72. Interbank deposits	29.32	33.38	33.23	34.47	32.26	32.01	33.73	34.53	36.87	38.29	72. Dépôts interbancaires
73. Non-bank deposits	24.46	22.83	23.00	24.22	23.82	24.86	24.39	24.47	24.38	24.83	73. Dépôts non bancaires
74. Bonds	38.04	35.25	33.95	32.00	31.64	33.10	32.52	31.52	28.90	27.29	74. Obligations
75. Other liabilities	2.48	2.59	2.84	3.58	4.31	3.81	3.66	3.97	4.69	4.87	75. Autres engagements
Memorandum items											***Pour mémoire***
76. Short-term securities	*1.03*	*4.84*	*4.88*	*3.90*	*3.07*	*2.10*	*1.67*	*2.18*	*2.55*	*3.17*	*76. Titres à court terme*
77. Bonds	*7.22*	*7.59*	*7.16*	*9.06*	*10.64*	*11.99*	*12.51*	*12.66*	*13.52*	*14.54*	*77. Obligations*
78. Shares and participations	*1.29*	*1.50*	*1.54*	*1.74*	*1.80*	*2.02*	*2.44*	*2.39*	*2.20*	*2.37*	*78. Actions et participations*
79. Claims on non-residents	*25.30*	*32.43*	*24.21*	*23.03*	*23.39*	*20.40*	*20.74*	*24.58*	*28.86*	*31.09*	*79. Créances sur des non-résidents*
80. Liabilities to non-residents	*8.43*	*12.50*	*9.54*	*12.48*	*10.34*	*12.58*	*14.30*	*16.26*	*21.65*	*24.68*	*80. Engagements envers des non-résidents*

* See notes on previous pages.

* Voir les notes en pages précédentes.

GERMANY
Savings banks

ALLEMAGNE
Caisses d'épargne

Million DM	1989	1990	1991	1992	1993(1)	1994	1995	1996	1997	1998 p	Millions de DM
INCOME STATEMENT											**COMPTE DE RESULTATS**
1. Interest income	57466	67561	78362	85138	99669	100277	101815	101810	102628	..	1. Produits financiers
2. Interest expenses	33152	42593	50204	55437	61591	57175	58316	56951	58213	..	2. Frais financiers
3. Net interest income	24314	24968	28158	29701	38078	43102	43499	44859	44415	..	3. Produits financiers nets
4. Non-interest income (net) (2)	4097	5387	5633	6164	7374	6823	7681	7354	8837	..	4. Produits non financiers (nets) (2)
a. Fees and commissions receivable	..	..	..	..	*6468*	*7086*	*7219*	*7543*	*8027*	..	*a. Frais et commissions à recevoir*
b. Fees and commissions payable	..	..	..	..	*207*	*208*	*224*	*255*	*331*	..	*b. Frais et commissions à payer*
c. Net profits or loss on financial operations	..	..	..	..	*1071*	*205*	*716*	*703*	*957*	..	*c. Profits ou pertes nets sur opérations financières*
d. Other	..	..	..	..	*42*	*-260*	*-30*	*-637*	*184*	..	*d. Autres*
5. Gross income	28411	30355	33791	35865	45452	49925	51180	52213	53252	..	5. Résultat brut
6. Operating expenses	18409	19731	21782	22991	28638	29237	31280	32435	33496	..	6. Frais d'exploitation
a. Staff costs	*11864*	*12776*	*14231*	*15040*	*17728*	*18287*	*19291*	*19788*	*20110*	..	*a. Dépenses en personnel*
b. Property costs (3)	..	..	..	..	..	..	..	..	..	..	*b. Dépenses en immobilier (3)*
c. Other	..	..	..	..	*10910*	*10950*	*11989*	*12647*	*13386*	..	*c. Autres*
7. Net income	10002	10624	12009	12874	16814	20688	19900	19778	19756	..	7. Résultat net
8. Provisions (net)	5859	5681	3573	3467	5977	10981	7587	7230	7459	..	8. Provisions (nettes)
a. Provisions on loans	*5850*	*5671*	*3550*	*3446*	*5878*	*10093*	*7547*	*7210*	*7393*	..	*a. Provisions sur prêts*
b. Provisions on securities (4)	..	..	..	..	..	..	..	..	..	..	*b. Provisions sur titres (4)*
c. Other	..	..	..	..	*99*	*888*	*40*	*20*	*66*	..	*c. Autres*
9. Profit before tax	4143	4943	8436	9407	10837	9707	12313	12548	12297	..	9. Bénéfices avant impôt
10. Income tax	2466	3133	5612	6475	7006	5661	7953	8193	8096	..	10. Impôt sur le revenu
11. Profit after tax	1677	1810	2824	2932	3831	4046	4360	4355	4201	..	11. Bénéfices après impôt
12. Distributed profit	1159	1240	1614	1726	2269	2425	2571	2493	2413	..	12. Bénéfices distribués
13. Retained profit	518	570	1210	1206	1562	1621	1789	1862	1788	..	13. Bénéfices mis en réserve
BALANCE SHEET											**BILAN**
Assets											**Actif**
14. Cash & balance with Central bank	29921	30259	29855	33908	33658	28734	29234	27885	27903	27917	14. Caisse & solde auprès de la Banque centrale
15. Interbank deposits	95999	107769	112200	92305	135787	109603	127556	132383	143205	152101	15. Dépôts interbancaires
16. Loans	561165	595639	652187	685475	800910	869221	930949	987728	1035081	1088493	16. Prêts
17. Securities	200023	213906	220649	230666	322312	382643	386469	416275	443322	476316	17. Valeurs mobilières
18. Other assets	28700	31408	36680	32972	38344	37917	39245	41148	42642	44084	18. Autres actifs
Liabilities											**Passif**
19. Capital & reserves	34655	36411	38900	40977	49544	54119	58479	63119	67839	72213	19. Capital et réserves
20. Borrowing from Central bank	38355	42747	48466	38075	42726	47242	44449	48128	55073	56903	20. Emprunts auprès de la Banque centrale
21. Interbank deposits	94993	100577	110026	118366	158962	198913	228396	253984	286118	320615	21. Dépôts interbancaires
22. Non-bank deposits	684637	721904	760428	775360	961866	993253	1034851	1083811	1121875	1174213	22. Dépôts non bancaires
23. Bonds	28102	40537	52476	58781	63860	77037	87447	94110	97695	98397	23. Obligations
24. Other liabilities	35066	36805	41275	43767	54053	57554	59831	62267	63553	66570	24. Autres engagements
Balance sheet total											**Total du bilan**
25. End-year total	915808	978981	1051571	1075326	1331011	1428118	1513453	1605419	1692153	1788911	25. En fin d'exercice
26. Average total	875042	934259	999930	1029488	1253312	1367636	1438297	1539310	1634968	1724574	26. Moyen

GERMANY — ALLEMAGNE

Savings banks — Caisses d'épargne

	1989	1990	1991	1992	1993(1)	1994	1995	1996	1997	1998 p	
Million DM											*Millions de DM*
Memorandum items											***Pour mémoire***
27. Short-term securities	16671	20248	23108	22241	29184	33717	36753	42075	39842	36692	*27. Titres à court terme*
28. Bonds	174336	181083	180251	185685	260719	306844	299628	315905	326790	340645	*28. Obligations*
29. Shares and participations	9016	12575	17290	22740	32409	42082	50088	58295	76690	98979	*29. Actions et participations*
30. Claims on non-residents	21563	27051	24154	17581	26976	24001	25017	27676	28268	33290	*30. Créances sur des non-résidents*
31. Liabilities to non-residents	7637	12385	7891	11002	14234	14684	15685	16718	21247	25236	*31. Engagements envers des non-résidents*
Capital adequacy											***Solvabilité***
32. Tier 1 Capital	..	..	..	..	..	..	..	..	..	..	*32. Fonds propres de base*
33. Tier 2 Capital	..	..	..	..	..	..	..	..	..	..	*33. Fonds propres complémentaires*
34. Supervisory deductions	..	..	..	..	..	..	..	..	..	..	*34. Eléments à déduire des fonds propres*
35. Total net capital resources	..	..	..	..	..	..	..	..	..	..	*35. Total net des ressources en capital*
36. Risk-weighted assets	..	..	..	..	..	..	..	..	..	..	*36. Actifs pondérés des risques*
SUPPLEMENTARY INFORMATION											**RENSEIGNEMENTS COMPLEMENTAIRES**
37. Number of institutions	583	575	558	542	704	657	626	607	598	594	37. Nombre d'institutions
38. Number of branches	17359	17212	17033	16923	19510	19271	19071	18895	18751	..	38. Nombre de succursales
39. Number of employees (x 1000)	234	267	281	284	288	291	290	288	289	..	39. Nombre de salariés (x 1000)

1. Break in series due to change in methodology.
2. Non-interest income (item 4), in the national definition, excluding items 4.c and 4.d.
3. Property costs (item 6.b.) included under Other operating expenses (item 6.c.).
4. Provisions on securities (item 8.b.) included under Provisions on loans (item 8.a).

Notes

- Average balance sheet totals (item 26) are based on twelve end-month data.

Change in methodology

- As from 1993, data include eastern German credit institutions and are in accordance with the new accounting regulations.

1. Rupture dans les séries suite aux changements méthodologiques.
2. Produits non financiers (nets) (poste 4), suivant la définition nationale, non compris les rubriques 4.c et 4.d.
3. Les Dépenses en immobilier (poste 6.b.) sont incluses sous Autres frais d'exploitation (poste 6.c).
4. Les Provisions sur titres (poste 8.b.) sont incluses sous Provisions sur prêts (poste 8.a).

Notes

- La moyenne du total des actifs/passifs (poste 26) est basée sur douze données de fin de mois.

Changement méthodologique

- Depuis 1993, les données comprennent les organismes de crédit d'Allemagne orientale et sont conformes aux nouvelles règles de comptabilité.

GERMANY — ALLEMAGNE

Savings banks — Caisses d'épargne

	1989	1990	1991	1992	1993(1)	1994	1995	1996	1997	1998 p	
Per cent											*Pourcentage*
INCOME STATEMENT ANALYSIS											**ANALYSE DU COMPTE DE RESULTATS**
% of average balance sheet total											**% du total moyen du bilan**
40. Interest income	6.57	7.23	7.84	8.27	7.95	7.33	7.08	6.61	6.28	..	40. Produits financiers
41. Interest expenses	3.79	4.56	5.02	5.38	4.91	4.18	4.05	3.70	3.56	..	41. Frais financiers
42. Net interest income	2.78	2.67	2.82	2.89	3.04	3.15	3.02	2.91	2.72	..	42. Produits financiers nets
43. Non-interest income (net)	0.47	0.58	0.56	0.60	0.59	0.50	0.53	0.48	0.54	..	43. Produits non financiers (nets)
a. Fees and commissions receivable	..	..	..	..	*0.52*	*0.52*	*0.50*	*0.49*	*0.49*	..	*a. Frais et commissions à recevoir*
b. Fees and commissions payable	..	..	..	..	*0.02*	*0.02*	*0.02*	*0.02*	*0.02*	..	*b. Frais et commissions à payer*
c. Net profits or loss on financial operations	..	..	..	..	*0.09*	*0.01*	*0.05*	*0.05*	*0.06*	..	*c. Profits ou pertes nets sur opérations financières*
d. Other	..	..	..	..	-	*-0.02*	-	*-0.04*	*0.01*	..	*d. Autres*
44. Gross income	3.25	3.25	3.38	3.48	3.63	3.65	3.56	3.39	3.26	..	44. Résultat brut
45. Operating expenses	2.10	2.11	2.18	2.23	2.28	2.14	2.17	2.11	2.05	..	45. Frais d'exploitation
a. Staff costs	*1.36*	*1.37*	*1.42*	*1.46*	*1.41*	*1.34*	*1.34*	*1.29*	*1.23*	..	*a. Dépenses en personnel*
b. Property costs	..	..	..	..	..	..	..	..	..	..	*b. Dépenses en immobilier*
c. Other	..	..	..	..	*0.87*	*0.80*	*0.83*	*0.82*	*0.82*	..	*c. Autres*
46. Net income	1.14	1.14	1.20	1.25	1.34	1.51	1.38	1.28	1.21	..	46. Résultat net
47. Provisions (net)	0.67	0.61	0.36	0.34	0.48	0.80	0.53	0.47	0.46	..	47. Provisions (nettes)
a. Provisions on loans	*0.67*	*0.61*	*0.36*	*0.33*	*0.47*	*0.74*	*0.52*	*0.47*	*0.45*	..	*a. Provisions sur prêts*
b. Provisions on securities	..	..	..	..	..	..	..	..	..	..	*b. Provisions sur titres*
c. Other	..	..	..	..	*0.01*	*0.06*	-	-	-	..	*c. Autres*
48. Profit before tax	0.47	0.53	0.84	0.91	0.86	0.71	0.86	0.82	0.75	..	48. Bénéfices avant impôt
49. Income tax	0.28	0.34	0.56	0.63	0.56	0.41	0.55	0.53	0.50	..	49. Impôt sur le revenu
50. Profit after tax	0.19	0.19	0.28	0.28	0.31	0.30	0.30	0.28	0.26	..	50. Bénéfices après impôt
51. Distributed profit	0.13	0.13	0.16	0.17	0.18	0.18	0.18	0.16	0.15	..	51. Bénéfices distribués
52. Retained profit	0.06	0.06	0.12	0.12	0.12	0.12	0.12	0.12	0.11	..	52. Bénéfices mis en réserve
% of gross income											**% du total du résultat brut**
53. Net interest income	85.58	82.25	83.33	82.81	83.78	86.33	84.99	85.92	83.41	..	53. Produits financiers nets
54. Non-interest income (net)	14.42	17.75	16.67	17.19	16.22	13.67	15.01	14.08	16.59	..	54. Produits non financiers (nets)
a. Fees and commissions receivable	..	..	..	..	*14.23*	*14.19*	*14.11*	*14.45*	*15.07*	..	*a. Frais et commissions à recevoir*
b. Fees and commissions payable	..	..	..	..	*0.46*	*0.42*	*0.44*	*0.49*	*0.62*	..	*b. Frais et commissions à payer*
c. Net profits or loss on financial operations	..	..	..	..	*2.36*	*0.41*	*1.40*	*1.35*	*1.80*	..	*c. Profits ou pertes nets sur opérations financières*
d. Other	..	..	..	..	*0.09*	*-0.52*	*-0.06*	*-1.22*	*0.35*	..	*d. Autres*
55. Operating expenses	64.80	65.00	64.46	64.10	63.01	58.56	61.12	62.12	62.90	..	55. Frais d'exploitation
a. Staff costs	*41.76*	*42.09*	*42.11*	*41.94*	*39.00*	*36.63*	*37.69*	*37.90*	*37.76*	..	*a. Dépenses en personnel*
b. Property costs	..	..	..	..	..	..	..	..	..	..	*b. Dépenses en immobilier*
c. Other	..	..	..	..	*24.00*	*21.93*	*23.43*	*24.22*	*25.14*	..	*c. Autres*
56. Net income	35.20	35.00	35.54	35.90	36.99	41.44	38.88	37.88	37.10	..	56. Résultat net
57. Provisions (net)	20.62	18.72	10.57	9.67	13.15	21.99	14.82	13.85	14.01	..	57. Provisions (nettes)
a. Provisions on loans	*20.59*	*18.68*	*10.51*	*9.61*	*12.93*	*20.22*	*14.75*	*13.81*	*13.88*	..	*a. Provisions sur prêts*
b. Provisions on securities	..	..	..	..	..	..	..	..	..	..	*b. Provisions sur titres*
c. Other	..	..	..	..	*0.22*	*1.78*	*0.08*	*0.04*	*0.12*	..	*c. Autres*
58. Profit before tax	14.58	16.28	24.97	26.23	23.84	19.44	24.06	24.03	23.09	..	58. Bénéfices avant impôt
59. Income tax	8.68	10.32	16.61	18.05	15.41	11.34	15.54	15.69	15.20	..	59. Impôt sur le revenu
60. Profit after tax	5.90	5.96	8.36	8.18	8.43	8.10	8.52	8.34	7.89	..	60. Bénéfices après impôt
% of net income											**% du total du résultat net**
61. Provisions (net)	58.58	53.47	29.75	26.93	35.55	53.08	38.13	36.56	37.76	..	61. Provisions (nettes)
a. Provisions on loans	*58.49*	*53.38*	*29.56*	*26.77*	*34.96*	*48.79*	*37.92*	*36.45*	*37.42*	..	*a. Provisions sur prêts*
b. Provisions on securities	..	..	..	..	..	..	..	..	..	..	*b. Provisions sur titres*
c. Other	..	..	..	..	*0.59*	*4.29*	*0.20*	*0.10*	*0.33*	..	*c. Autres*
62. Profit before tax	41.42	46.53	70.25	73.07	64.45	46.92	61.87	63.44	62.24	..	62. Bénéfices avant impôt
63. Income tax	24.66	29.49	46.73	50.30	41.67	27.36	39.96	41.42	40.98	..	63. Impôt sur le revenu
64. Profit after tax	16.77	17.04	23.52	22.77	22.78	19.56	21.91	22.02	21.26	..	64. Bénéfices après impôt

	1989	1990	1991	1992	1993(1)	1994	1995	1996	1997	1998 p	
Per cent											*Pourcentage*
BALANCE SHEET ANALYSIS											**ANALYSE DU BILAN**
% of year-end balance sheet total											**% du total du bilan en fin d'exercice**
Assets											**Actif**
65. Cash & balance with Central bank	3.27	3.09	2.84	3.15	2.53	2.01	1.93	1.74	1.65	1.56	65. Caisse & solde auprès de la Banque centrale
66. Interbank deposits	10.48	11.01	10.67	8.58	10.20	7.67	8.43	8.25	8.46	8.50	66. Dépôts interbancaires
67. Loans	61.28	60.84	62.02	63.75	60.17	60.86	61.51	61.52	61.17	60.85	67. Prêts
68. Securities	21.84	21.85	20.98	21.45	24.22	26.79	25.54	25.93	26.20	26.63	68. Valeurs mobilières
69. Other assets	3.13	3.21	3.49	3.07	2.88	2.66	2.59	2.56	2.52	2.46	69. Autres actifs
Liabilities											**Passif**
70. Capital & reserves	3.78	3.72	3.70	3.81	3.72	3.79	3.86	3.93	4.01	4.04	70. Capital et réserves
71. Borrowing from Central bank	4.19	4.37	4.61	3.54	3.21	3.31	2.94	3.00	3.25	3.18	71. Emprunts auprès de la Banque centrale
72. Interbank deposits	10.37	10.27	10.46	11.01	11.94	13.93	15.09	15.82	16.91	17.92	72. Dépôts interbancaires
73. Non-bank deposits	74.76	73.74	72.31	72.10	72.27	69.55	68.38	67.51	66.30	65.64	73. Dépôts non bancaires
74. Bonds	3.07	4.14	4.99	5.47	4.80	5.39	5.78	5.86	5.77	5.50	74. Obligations
75. Other liabilities	3.83	3.76	3.93	4.07	4.06	4.03	3.95	3.88	3.76	3.72	75. Autres engagements
Memorandum items											***Pour mémoire***
76. Short-term securities	*1.82*	*2.07*	*2.20*	*2.07*	*2.19*	*2.36*	*2.43*	*2.62*	*2.35*	*2.05*	*76. Titres à court terme*
77. Bonds	*19.04*	*18.50*	*17.14*	*17.27*	*19.59*	*21.49*	*19.80*	*19.68*	*19.31*	*19.04*	*77. Obligations*
78. Shares and participations	*0.98*	*1.28*	*1.64*	*2.11*	*2.43*	*2.95*	*3.31*	*3.63*	*4.53*	*5.53*	*78. Actions et participations*
79. Claims on non-residents	*2.35*	*2.76*	*2.30*	*1.63*	*2.03*	*1.68*	*1.65*	*1.72*	*1.67*	*1.86*	*79. Créances sur des non-résidents*
80. Liabilities to non-residents	*0.83*	*1.27*	*0.75*	*1.02*	*1.07*	*1.03*	*1.04*	*1.04*	*1.26*	*1.41*	*80. Engagements envers des non-résidents*

* See notes on previous pages.

* Voir les notes en pages précédentes.

GERMANY

Regional institutions of co-operative banks

ALLEMAGNE

Institutions régionales des banques mutualistes

	1989	1990	1991	1992	1993(1)	1994	1995	1996	1997	1998 p	
Million DM											*Millions de DM*
INCOME STATEMENT											**COMPTE DE RESULTATS**
1. Interest income	11113	14172	15773	16099	15530	14851	13950	13913	15556	..	1. Produits financiers
2. Interest expenses	9891	12999	14684	14635	13693	11867	11745	11695	13150	..	2. Frais financiers
3. Net interest income	1222	1173	1089	1464	1837	2984	2205	2218	2406	..	3. Produits financiers nets
4. Non-interest income (net) (2)	938	1307	1271	585	756	1329	802	1035	1079	..	4. Produits non financiers (nets) (2)
a. Fees and commissions receivable	..	..	..	..	*804*	*778*	*810*	*906*	*1012*	..	*a. Frais et commissions à recevoir*
b. Fees and commissions payable	..	..	..	..	*269*	*252*	*256*	*262*	*252*	..	*b. Frais et commissions à payer*
c. Net profits or loss on financial operations	..	..	..	..	*301*	*182*	*299*	*298*	*344*	..	*c. Profits ou pertes nets sur opérations financières*
d. Other	..	..	..	..	*-80*	*621*	*-51*	*93*	*-25*	..	*d. Autres*
5. Gross income	2160	2480	2360	2049	2593	4313	3007	3253	3485	..	5. Résultat brut
6. Operating expenses	1055	1175	1222	1344	1457	1527	1633	1734	1931	..	6. Frais d'exploitation
a. Staff costs	*577*	*647*	*660*	*723*	*769*	*801*	*847*	*859*	*958*	..	*a. Dépenses en personnel*
b. Property costs (3)	..	..	..	..	..	..	..	..	..	..	*b. Dépenses en immobilier (3)*
c. Other	..	..	..	..	*688*	*726*	*786*	*875*	*973*	..	*c. Autres*
7. Net income	1105	1305	1138	705	1136	2786	1374	1519	1554	..	7. Résultat net
8. Provisions (net)	623	844	728	244	700	1692	338	258	456	..	8. Provisions (nettes)
a. Provisions on loans	*623*	*725*	*670*	*189*	*698*	*1691*	*335*	*232*	*359*	..	*a. Provisions sur prêts*
b. Provisions on securities (4)	..	..	..	..	..	..	..	..	..	..	*b. Provisions sur titres (4)*
c. Other	..	..	..	..	*2*	*1*	*3*	*26*	*97*	..	*c. Autres*
9. Profit before tax	482	461	410	461	436	1094	1036	1261	1098	..	9. Bénéfices avant impôt
10. Income tax	93	177	228	261	260	543	519	572	601	..	10. Impôt sur le revenu
11. Profit after tax	389	284	182	200	176	551	517	689	497	..	11. Bénéfices après impôt
12. Distributed profit	559	219	119	78	91	185	315	183	310	..	12. Bénéfices distribués
13. Retained profit	-170	65	63	122	85	366	202	506	187	..	13. Bénéfices mis en réserve
BALANCE SHEET											**BILAN**
Assets											**Actif**
14. Cash & balance with Central bank	2739	2247	2925	2102	1195	998	1723	1113	1367	3341	14. Caisse & solde auprès de la Banque centrale
15. Interbank deposits	102158	107746	102957	106576	117859	128297	140904	146671	151423	178022	15. Dépôts interbancaires
16. Loans	36028	38412	51773	58011	57046	58457	67168	78450	87006	100137	16. Prêts
17. Securities	38995	40883	38670	39914	49568	52943	62997	86501	112027	129336	17. Valeurs mobilières
18. Other assets	4217	4258	14284	3980	3887	4565	5012	6835	9766	11038	18. Autres actifs
Liabilities											**Passif**
19. Capital & reserves	6725	6446	7180	7890	8513	9349	10094	10844	12742	14042	19. Capital et réserves
20. Borrowing from Central bank	11529	11993	15690	10254	8228	14600	11517	13767	13481	13717	20. Emprunts auprès de la Banque centrale
21. Interbank deposits	130758	139772	145210	148468	160210	156250	177575	193278	219971	257041	21. Dépôts interbancaires
22. Non-bank deposits	12563	14712	17599	19028	21946	25462	27961	34983	40957	57262	22. Dépôts non bancaires
23. Bonds	18525	15454	18346	19042	21349	28982	35323	50672	57060	61707	23. Obligations
24. Other liabilities	4037	5169	6584	5901	9309	10617	15334	16026	17378	18105	24. Autres engagements
Balance sheet total											**Total du bilan**
25. End-year total	184137	193546	210609	210583	229555	245260	277804	319570	361589	421874	25. En fin d'exercice
26. Average total	173658	178846	194435	188434	200135	230507	248733	291098	335243	386145	26. Moyen

GERMANY — ALLEMAGNE

Regional institutions of co-operative banks — Institutions régionales des banques mutualistes

	1989	1990	1991	1992	1993(1)	1994	1995	1996	1997	1998 p	
Million DM											*Millions de DM*
Memorandum items											***Pour mémoire***
27. Short-term securities	*2446*	*7982*	*10499*	*11801*	*14428*	*10899*	*10141*	*14533*	*19376*	*18674*	*27. Titres à court terme*
28. Bonds	*30436*	*27049*	*21166*	*20777*	*26538*	*32886*	*38869*	*57525*	*75326*	*89818*	*28. Obligations*
29. Shares and participations	*6113*	*5852*	*7005*	*7336*	*8602*	*9158*	*13987*	*14443*	*17325*	*20844*	*29. Actions et participations*
30. Claims on non-residents	*31136*	*42780*	*34701*	*27719*	*34757*	*35554*	*35347*	*44286*	*47358*	*68010*	*30. Créances sur des non-résidents*
31. Liabilities to non-residents	*3745*	*10054*	*7674*	*7998*	*8091*	*11830*	*13621*	*17549*	*32508*	*58891*	*31. Engagements envers des non-résidents*
Capital adequacy											***Solvabilité***
32. Tier 1 Capital	..	..	..	..	..	..	..	..	..	..	*32. Fonds propres de base*
33. Tier 2 Capital	..	..	..	..	..	..	..	..	..	..	*33. Fonds propres complémentaires*
34. Supervisory deductions	..	..	..	..	..	..	..	..	..	..	*34. Eléments à déduire des fonds propres*
35. Total net capital resources	..	..	..	..	..	..	..	..	..	..	*35. Total net des ressources en capital*
36. Risk-weighted assets	..	..	..	..	..	..	..	..	..	..	*36. Actifs pondérés des risques*
SUPPLEMENTARY INFORMATION											**RENSEIGNEMENTS COMPLEMENTAIRES**
37. Number of institutions	6	4	4	4	4	4	4	4	4	4	37. Nombre d'institutions
38. Number of branches	32	31	29	31	46	46	43	42	42	..	38. Nombre de succursales
39. Number of employees (x 1000)	7	7	7	7	7	7	7	7	7	..	39. Nombre de salariés (x 1000)

1. Break in series due to change in methodology.
2. Non-interest income (item 4), in the national definition, excluding items 4.c and 4.d.
3. Property costs (item 6.b.) included under Other operating expenses (item 6.c.).
4. Provisions on securities (item 8.b.) included under Provisions on loans (item 8.a).

Notes

- Average balance sheet totals (item 26) are based on twelve end-month data.

Change in methodology

- As from 1993, data include eastern German credit institutions and are in accordance with the new accounting regulations.

1. Rupture dans les séries suite aux changements méthodologiques.
2. Produits non financiers (nets) (poste 4), suivant la définition nationale, non compris les rubriques 4.c et 4.d.
3. Les Dépenses en immobilier (poste 6.b.) sont incluses sous Autres frais d'exploitation (poste 6.c).
4. Les Provisions sur titres (poste 8.b.) sont incluses sous Provisions sur prêts (poste 8.a).

Notes

- La moyenne du total des actifs/passifs (poste 26) est basée sur douze données de fin de mois.

Changement méthodologique

- Depuis 1993, les données comprennent les organismes de crédit d'Allemagne orientale et sont conformes aux nouvelles règles de comptabilité.

GERMANY — ALLEMAGNE

Regional institutions of co-operative banks — Institutions régionales des banques mutualistes

Per cent	1989	1990	1991	1992	1993(1)	1994	1995	1996	1997	1998 p	Pourcentage
INCOME STATEMENT ANALYSIS											**ANALYSE DU COMPTE DE RESULTATS**
% of average balance sheet total											**% du total moyen du bilan**
40. Interest income	6.40	7.92	8.11	8.54	7.76	6.44	5.61	4.78	4.64	..	40. Produits financiers
41. Interest expenses	5.70	7.27	7.55	7.77	6.84	5.15	4.72	4.02	3.92	..	41. Frais financiers
42. Net interest income	0.70	0.66	0.56	0.78	0.92	1.29	0.89	0.76	0.72	..	42. Produits financiers nets
43. Non-interest income (net)	0.54	0.73	0.65	0.31	0.38	0.58	0.32	0.36	0.32	..	43. Produits non financiers (nets)
a. Fees and commissions receivable	..	..	..	..	*0.40*	*0.34*	*0.33*	*0.31*	*0.30*	..	*a. Frais et commissions à recevoir*
b. Fees and commissions payable	..	..	..	..	*0.13*	*0.11*	*0.10*	*0.09*	*0.08*	..	*b. Frais et commissions à payer*
c. Net profits or loss on financial operations	..	..	..	..	*0.15*	*0.08*	*0.12*	*0.10*	*0.10*	..	*c. Profits ou pertes nets sur opérations financières*
d. Other	..	..	..	..	*-0.04*	*0.27*	*-0.02*	*0.03*	*-0.01*	..	*d. Autres*
44. Gross income	1.24	1.39	1.21	1.09	1.30	1.87	1.21	1.12	1.04	..	44. Résultat brut
45. Operating expenses	0.61	0.66	0.63	0.71	0.73	0.66	0.66	0.60	0.58	..	45. Frais d'exploitation
a. Staff costs	*0.33*	*0.36*	*0.34*	*0.38*	*0.38*	*0.35*	*0.34*	*0.30*	*0.29*	..	*a. Dépenses en personnel*
b. Property costs	..	..	..	..	..	..	..	..	..	..	*b. Dépenses en immobilier*
c. Other	..	..	..	..	*0.34*	*0.31*	*0.32*	*0.30*	*0.29*	..	*c. Autres*
46. Net income	0.64	0.73	0.59	0.37	0.57	1.21	0.55	0.52	0.46	..	46. Résultat net
47. Provisions (net)	0.36	0.47	0.37	0.13	0.35	0.73	0.14	0.09	0.14	..	47. Provisions (nettes)
a. Provisions on loans	*0.36*	*0.41*	*0.34*	*0.10*	*0.35*	*0.73*	*0.13*	*0.08*	*0.11*	..	*a. Provisions sur prêts*
b. Provisions on securities	..	..	..	..	..	..	..	..	..	..	*b. Provisions sur titres*
c. Other	..	..	..	..	-	-	-	*0.01*	*0.03*	..	*c. Autres*
48. Profit before tax	0.28	0.26	0.21	0.24	0.22	0.47	0.42	0.43	0.33	..	48. Bénéfices avant impôt
49. Income tax	0.05	0.10	0.12	0.14	0.13	0.24	0.21	0.20	0.18	..	49. Impôt sur le revenu
50. Profit after tax	0.22	0.16	0.09	0.11	0.09	0.24	0.21	0.24	0.15	..	50. Bénéfices après impôt
51. Distributed profit	0.32	0.12	0.06	0.04	0.05	0.08	0.13	0.06	0.09	..	51. Bénéfices distribués
52. Retained profit	-0.10	0.04	0.03	0.06	0.04	0.16	0.08	0.17	0.06	..	52. Bénéfices mis en réserve
% of gross income											**% du total du résultat brut**
53. Net interest income	56.57	47.30	46.14	71.45	70.84	69.19	73.33	68.18	69.04	..	53. Produits financiers nets
54. Non-interest income (net)	43.43	52.70	53.86	28.55	29.16	30.81	26.67	31.82	30.96	..	54. Produits non financiers (nets)
a. Fees and commissions receivable	..	..	..	..	*31.01*	*18.04*	*26.94*	*27.85*	*29.04*	..	*a. Frais et commissions à recevoir*
b. Fees and commissions payable	..	..	..	..	*10.37*	*5.84*	*8.51*	*8.05*	*7.23*	..	*b. Frais et commissions à payer*
c. Net profits or loss on financial operations	..	..	..	..	*11.61*	*4.22*	*9.94*	*9.16*	*9.87*	..	*c. Profits ou pertes nets sur opérations financières*
d. Other	..	..	..	..	*-3.09*	*14.40*	*-1.70*	*2.86*	*-0.72*	..	*d. Autres*
55. Operating expenses	48.84	47.38	51.78	65.59	56.19	35.40	54.31	53.30	55.41	..	55. Frais d'exploitation
a. Staff costs	*26.71*	*26.09*	*27.97*	*35.29*	*29.66*	*18.57*	*28.17*	*26.41*	*27.49*	..	*a. Dépenses en personnel*
b. Property costs	..	..	..	..	..	..	..	..	..	..	*b. Dépenses en immobilier*
c. Other	..	..	..	..	*26.53*	*16.83*	*26.14*	*26.90*	*27.92*	..	*c. Autres*
56. Net income	51.16	52.62	48.22	34.41	43.81	64.60	45.69	46.70	44.59	..	56. Résultat net
57. Provisions (net)	28.84	34.03	30.85	11.91	27.00	39.23	11.24	7.93	13.08	..	57. Provisions (nettes)
a. Provisions on loans	*28.84*	*29.23*	*28.39*	*9.22*	*26.92*	*39.21*	*11.14*	*7.13*	*10.30*	..	*a. Provisions sur prêts*
b. Provisions on securities	..	..	..	..	..	..	..	..	..	..	*b. Provisions sur titres*
c. Other	..	..	..	..	*0.08*	*0.02*	*0.10*	*0.80*	*2.78*	..	*c. Autres*
58. Profit before tax	22.31	18.59	17.37	22.50	16.81	25.37	34.45	38.76	31.51	..	58. Bénéfices avant impôt
59. Income tax	4.31	7.14	9.66	12.74	10.03	12.59	17.26	17.58	17.25	..	59. Impôt sur le revenu
60. Profit after tax	18.01	11.45	7.71	9.76	6.79	12.78	17.19	21.18	14.26	..	60. Bénéfices après impôt
% of net income											**% du total du résultat net**
61. Provisions (net)	56.38	64.67	63.97	34.61	61.62	60.73	24.60	16.98	29.34	..	61. Provisions (nettes)
a. Provisions on loans	*56.38*	*55.56*	*58.88*	*26.81*	*61.44*	*60.70*	*24.38*	*15.27*	*23.10*	..	*a. Provisions sur prêts*
b. Provisions on securities	..	..	..	..	..	..	..	..	..	..	*b. Provisions sur titres*
c. Other	..	..	..	..	*0.18*	*0.04*	*0.22*	*1.71*	*6.24*	..	*c. Autres*
62. Profit before tax	43.62	35.33	36.03	65.39	38.38	39.27	75.40	83.02	70.66	..	62. Bénéfices avant impôt
63. Income tax	8.42	13.56	20.04	37.02	22.89	19.49	37.77	37.66	38.67	..	63. Impôt sur le revenu
64. Profit after tax	35.20	21.76	15.99	28.37	15.49	19.78	37.63	45.36	31.98	..	64. Bénéfices après impôt

GERMANY

Regional institutions of co-operative banks

ALLEMAGNE

Institutions régionales des banques mutualistes

	1989	1990	1991	1992	1993(1)	1994	1995	1996	1997	1998 p	
Per cent											*Pourcentage*
BALANCE SHEET ANALYSIS											**ANALYSE DU BILAN**
% of year-end balance sheet total											**% du total du bilan en fin d'exercice**
Assets											**Actif**
65. Cash & balance with Central bank	1.49	1.16	1.39	1.00	0.52	0.41	0.62	0.35	0.38	0.79	65. Caisse & solde auprès de la Banque centrale
66. Interbank deposits	55.48	55.67	48.89	50.61	51.34	52.31	50.72	45.90	41.88	42.20	66. Dépôts interbancaires
67. Loans	19.57	19.85	24.58	27.55	24.85	23.83	24.18	24.55	24.06	23.74	67. Prêts
68. Securities	21.18	21.12	18.36	18.95	21.59	21.59	22.68	27.07	30.98	30.66	68. Valeurs mobilières
69. Other assets	2.29	2.20	6.78	1.89	1.69	1.86	1.80	2.14	2.70	2.62	69. Autres actifs
Liabilities											**Passif**
70. Capital & reserves	3.65	3.33	3.41	3.75	3.71	3.81	3.63	3.39	3.52	3.33	70. Capital et réserves
71. Borrowing from Central bank	6.26	6.20	7.45	4.87	3.58	5.95	4.15	4.31	3.73	3.25	71. Emprunts auprès de la Banque centrale
72. Interbank deposits	71.01	72.22	68.95	70.50	69.79	63.71	63.92	60.48	60.83	60.93	72. Dépôts interbancaires
73. Non-bank deposits	6.82	7.60	8.36	9.04	9.56	10.38	10.07	10.95	11.33	13.57	73. Dépôts non bancaires
74. Bonds	10.06	7.98	8.71	9.04	9.30	11.82	12.72	15.86	15.78	14.63	74. Obligations
75. Other liabilities	2.19	2.67	3.13	2.80	4.06	4.33	5.52	5.01	4.81	4.29	75. Autres engagements
Memorandum items											***Pour mémoire***
76. Short-term securities	*1.33*	*4.12*	*4.99*	*5.60*	*6.29*	*4.44*	*3.65*	*4.55*	*5.36*	*4.43*	*76. Titres à court terme*
77. Bonds	*16.53*	*13.98*	*10.05*	*9.87*	*11.56*	*13.41*	*13.99*	*18.00*	*20.83*	*21.29*	*77. Obligations*
78. Shares and participations	*3.32*	*3.02*	*3.33*	*3.48*	*3.75*	*3.73*	*5.03*	*4.52*	*4.79*	*4.94*	*78. Actions et participations*
79. Claims on non-residents	*16.91*	*22.10*	*16.48*	*13.16*	*15.14*	*14.50*	*12.72*	*13.86*	*13.10*	*16.12*	*79. Créances sur des non-résidents*
80. Liabilities to non-residents	*2.03*	*5.19*	*3.64*	*3.80*	*3.52*	*4.82*	*4.90*	*5.49*	*8.99*	*13.96*	*80. Engagements envers des non-résidents*

* See notes on previous pages.

* Voir les notes en pages précédentes.

GERMANY — ALLEMAGNE

Co-operative banks — Banques mutualistes

	1989	1990	1991	1992	1993(1)	1994	1995	1996	1997	1998 p	
Million DM											*Millions de DM*
INCOME STATEMENT											**COMPTE DE RESULTATS**
1. Interest income	33387	40361	46925	53748	58603	57940	59789	58946	58703	..	1. Produits financiers
2. Interest expenses	18638	24620	29438	34507	35941	33051	34201	32699	32502	..	2. Frais financiers
3. Net interest income	14749	15741	17487	19241	22662	24889	25588	26247	26201	..	3. Produits financiers nets
4. Non-interest income (net) (2)	4134	4270	4203	4760	5515	5563	5824	6146	6564	..	4. Produits non financiers (nets) (2)
a. Fees and commissions receivable	..	..	..	..	*4442*	*4852*	*4823*	*5129*	*5551*	..	*a. Frais et commissions à recevoir*
b. Fees and commissions payable	..	..	..	..	*297*	*328*	*355*	*394*	*440*	..	*b. Frais et commissions à payer*
c. Net profits or loss on financial operations	..	..	..	..	*326*	*-29*	*294*	*266*	*207*	..	*c. Profits ou pertes nets sur opérations financières*
d. Other	..	..	..	..	*1044*	*1068*	*1062*	*1145*	*1246*	..	*d. Autres*
5. Gross income	18883	20011	21690	24001	28177	30452	31412	32393	32765	..	5. Résultat brut
6. Operating expenses	12976	14050	15068	16557	19183	20075	21302	21980	22529	..	6. Frais d'exploitation
a. Staff costs	*8100*	*8807*	*9428*	*10357*	*11599*	*12149*	*12819*	*13112*	*13346*	..	*a. Dépenses en personnel*
b. Property costs (3)	..	..	..	..	..	..	..	..	..	..	*b. Dépenses en immobilier (3)*
c. Other	..	..	..	..	*7584*	*7926*	*8483*	*8868*	*9183*	..	*c. Autres*
7. Net income	5907	5961	6622	7444	8994	10377	10110	10413	10236	..	7. Résultat net
8. Provisions (net)	3223	2375	1491	1530	2541	4835	3269	3592	4034	..	8. Provisions (nettes)
a. Provisions on loans	*3216*	*2365*	*1478*	*1522*	*2529*	*4476*	*3211*	*3546*	*3937*	..	*a. Provisions sur prêts*
b. Provisions on securities (4)	..	..	..	..	..	..	..	..	..	..	*b. Provisions sur titres (4)*
c. Other	..	..	..	..	*12*	*359*	*58*	*46*	*97*	..	*c. Autres*
9. Profit before tax	2684	3586	5131	5914	6453	5542	6841	6821	6202	..	9. Bénéfices avant impôt
10. Income tax	1706	2231	3096	3820	4014	3115	4237	4309	3884	..	10. Impôt sur le revenu
11. Profit after tax	978	1355	2035	2094	2439	2427	2604	2512	2318	..	11. Bénéfices après impôt
12. Distributed profit	830	992	1292	1390	1625	1667	1794	1822	1706	..	12. Bénéfices distribués
13. Retained profit	148	363	743	704	814	760	810	690	612	..	13. Bénéfices mis en réserve
BALANCE SHEET											**BILAN**
Assets											**Actif**
14. Cash & balance with Central bank	15830	17170	18317	21756	19195	19295	18479	19886	19536	18120	14. Caisse & solde auprès de la Banque centrale
15. Interbank deposits	87254	98019	101699	99288	125575	111758	124858	126170	129140	136510	15. Dépôts interbancaires
16. Loans	308096	328660	360749	395299	447100	491988	534180	565683	594253	623448	16. Prêts
17. Securities	94108	99721	105973	119457	153590	182578	183321	198824	208769	220680	17. Valeurs mobilières
18. Other assets	17907	19449	20833	21221	22424	23918	25269	26394	26834	28264	18. Autres actifs
Liabilities											**Passif**
19. Capital & reserves	20352	21223	23008	26460	31894	36177	40019	43672	46923	49343	19. Capital et réserves
20. Borrowing from Central bank	18523	19645	17945	16430	14095	16325	16148	17077	18415	15702	20. Emprunts auprès de la Banque centrale
21. Interbank deposits	43988	45417	45706	49800	65179	81515	92687	102861	113700	128412	21. Dépôts interbancaires
22. Non-bank deposits	416252	447499	485201	521466	604672	635073	666349	697798	719060	750061	22. Dépôts non bancaires
23. Bonds	9476	13078	17288	22229	27348	34560	42865	45899	50779	53207	23. Obligations
24. Other liabilities	14604	16157	18423	20636	24696	25887	28039	29650	29655	30297	24. Autres engagements
Balance sheet total											**Total du bilan**
25. End-year total	523195	563019	607571	657021	767884	829537	886107	936957	978532	1027022	25. En fin d'exercice
26. Average total	497789	534273	575708	624292	716971	788684	842101	901801	946917	989676	26. Moyen

GERMANY | ALLEMAGNE

Co-operative banks | Banques mutualistes

	1989	1990	1991	1992	1993(1)	1994	1995	1996	1997	1998 p	
Million DM											*Millions de DM*
Memorandum items											***Pour mémoire***
27. Short-term securities	*11313*	*12885*	*15821*	*18236*	*25528*	*25458*	*26771*	*27013*	*28342*	*22002*	*27. Titres à court terme*
28. Bonds	*79170*	*82820*	*85535*	*95354*	*118926*	*146152*	*144784*	*158346*	*162399*	*173766*	*28. Obligations*
29. Shares and participations	*3625*	*4016*	*4617*	*5867*	*9136*	*10968*	*11766*	*13465*	*18028*	*24912*	*29. Actions et participations*
30. Claims on non-residents	*5401*	*6795*	*8269*	*7585*	*15519*	*15268*	*15338*	*15081*	*15871*	*16183*	*30. Créances sur des non-résidents*
31. Liabilities to non-residents	*4491*	*5836*	*4973*	*6989*	*9146*	*10878*	*12729*	*14973*	*17077*	*20180*	*31. Engagements envers des non-résidents*
Capital adequacy											***Solvabilité***
32. Tier 1 Capital	..	..	..	..	..	..	..	..	..	..	*32. Fonds propres de base*
33. Tier 2 Capital	..	..	..	..	..	..	..	..	..	..	*33. Fonds propres complémentaires*
34. Supervisory deductions	..	..	..	..	..	..	..	..	..	..	*34. Eléments à déduire des fonds propres*
35. Total net capital resources	..	..	..	..	..	..	..	..	..	..	*35. Total net des ressources en capital*
36. Risk-weighted assets	..	..	..	..	..	..	..	..	..	..	*36. Actifs pondérés des risques*
SUPPLEMENTARY INFORMATION											**RENSEIGNEMENTS COMPLEMENTAIRES**
37. Number of institutions	3225	3049	2862	2683	2778	2666	2591	2510	2420	2256	37. Nombre d'institutions
38. Number of branches	15789	15769	15815	15618	17599	17383	17205	16977	16762	..	38. Nombre de succursales
39. Number of employees (x 1000)	120	151	158	163	167	173	176	174	172	..	39. Nombre de salariés (x 1000)

1. Break in series due to change in methodology.
2. Non-interest income (item 4), in the national definition, excluding items 4.c and 4.d.
3. Property costs (item 6.b.) included under Other operating expenses (item 6.c.).
4. Provisions on securities (item 8.b.) included under Provisions on loans (item 8.a).

Notes

- Average balance sheet totals (item 26) are based on twelve end-month data.

Change in methodology

- As from 1993, data include eastern German credit institutions and are in accordance with the new accounting regulations.

1. Rupture dans les séries suite aux changements méthodologiques.
2. Produits non financiers (nets) (poste 4), suivant la définition nationale, non compris les rubriques 4.c et 4.d.
3. Les Dépenses en immobilier (poste 6.b.) sont incluses sous Autres frais d'exploitation (poste 6.c).
4. Les Provisions sur titres (poste 8.b.) sont incluses sous Provisions sur prêts (poste 8.a).

Notes

- La moyenne du total des actifs/passifs (poste 26) est basée sur douze données de fin de mois.

Changement méthodologique

- Depuis 1993, les données comprennent les organismes de crédit d'Allemagne orientale et sont conformes aux nouvelles règles de comptabilité.

GERMANY
Co-operative banks

ALLEMAGNE
Banques mutualistes

	1989	1990	1991	1992	1993(1)	1994	1995	1996	1997	1998 p	
Per cent											*Pourcentage*
INCOME STATEMENT ANALYSIS											**ANALYSE DU COMPTE DE RESULTATS**
% of average balance sheet total											**% du total moyen du bilan**
40. Interest income	6.71	7.55	8.15	8.61	8.17	7.35	7.10	6.54	6.20	..	40. Produits financiers
41. Interest expenses	3.74	4.61	5.11	5.53	5.01	4.19	4.06	3.63	3.43	..	41. Frais financiers
42. Net interest income	2.96	2.95	3.04	3.08	3.16	3.16	3.04	2.91	2.77	..	42. Produits financiers nets
43. Non-interest income (net)	0.83	0.80	0.73	0.76	0.77	0.71	0.69	0.68	0.69	..	43. Produits non financiers (nets)
a. Fees and commissions receivable	..	..	..	..	*0.62*	*0.62*	*0.57*	*0.57*	*0.59*	..	*a. Frais et commissions à recevoir*
b. Fees and commissions payable	..	..	..	..	*0.04*	*0.04*	*0.04*	*0.04*	*0.05*	..	*b. Frais et commissions à payer*
c. Net profits or loss on financial operations	..	..	..	..	*0.05*	-	*0.03*	*0.03*	*0.02*	..	*c. Profits ou pertes nets sur opérations financières*
d. Other	..	..	..	..	*0.15*	*0.14*	*0.13*	*0.13*	*0.13*	..	*d. Autres*
44. Gross income	3.79	3.75	3.77	3.84	3.93	3.86	3.73	3.59	3.46	..	44. Résultat brut
45. Operating expenses	2.61	2.63	2.62	2.65	2.68	2.55	2.53	2.44	2.38	..	45. Frais d'exploitation
a. Staff costs	*1.63*	*1.65*	*1.64*	*1.66*	*1.62*	*1.54*	*1.52*	*1.45*	*1.41*	..	*a. Dépenses en personnel*
b. Property costs	..	..	..	..	..	..	..	..	..	..	*b. Dépenses en immobilier*
c. Other	..	..	..	..	*1.06*	*1.00*	*1.01*	*0.98*	*0.97*	..	*c. Autres*
46. Net income	1.19	1.12	1.15	1.19	1.25	1.32	1.20	1.15	1.08	..	46. Résultat net
47. Provisions (net)	0.65	0.44	0.26	0.25	0.35	0.61	0.39	0.40	0.43	..	47. Provisions (nettes)
a. Provisions on loans	*0.65*	*0.44*	*0.26*	*0.24*	*0.35*	*0.57*	*0.38*	*0.39*	*0.42*	..	*a. Provisions sur prêts*
b. Provisions on securities	..	..	..	..	..	..	..	..	..	..	*b. Provisions sur titres*
c. Other	..	..	..	..	-	*0.05*	*0.01*	*0.01*	*0.01*	..	*c. Autres*
48. Profit before tax	0.54	0.67	0.89	0.95	0.90	0.70	0.81	0.76	0.65	..	48. Bénéfices avant impôt
49. Income tax	0.34	0.42	0.54	0.61	0.56	0.39	0.50	0.48	0.41	..	49. Impôt sur le revenu
50. Profit after tax	0.20	0.25	0.35	0.34	0.34	0.31	0.31	0.28	0.24	..	50. Bénéfices après impôt
51. Distributed profit	0.17	0.19	0.22	0.22	0.23	0.21	0.21	0.20	0.18	..	51. Bénéfices distribués
52. Retained profit	0.03	0.07	0.13	0.11	0.11	0.10	0.10	0.08	0.06	..	52. Bénéfices mis en réserve
% of gross income											**% du total du résultat brut**
53. Net interest income	78.11	78.66	80.62	80.17	80.43	81.73	81.46	81.03	79.97	..	53. Produits financiers nets
54. Non-interest income (net)	21.89	21.34	19.38	19.83	19.57	18.27	18.54	18.97	20.03	..	54. Produits non financiers (nets)
a. Fees and commissions receivable	..	..	..	..	*15.76*	*15.93*	*15.35*	*15.83*	*16.94*	..	*a. Frais et commissions à recevoir*
b. Fees and commissions payable	..	..	..	..	*1.05*	*1.08*	*1.13*	*1.22*	*1.34*	..	*b. Frais et commissions à payer*
c. Net profits or loss on financial operations	..	..	..	..	*1.16*	*-0.10*	*0.94*	*0.82*	*0.63*	..	*c. Profits ou pertes nets sur opérations financières*
d. Other	..	..	..	..	*3.71*	*3.51*	*3.38*	*3.53*	*3.80*	..	*d. Autres*
55. Operating expenses	68.72	70.21	69.47	68.98	68.08	65.92	67.81	67.85	68.76	..	55. Frais d'exploitation
a. Staff costs	*42.90*	*44.01*	*43.47*	*43.15*	*41.16*	*39.90*	*40.81*	*40.48*	*40.73*	..	*a. Dépenses en personnel*
b. Property costs	..	..	..	..	..	..	..	..	..	..	*b. Dépenses en immobilier*
c. Other	..	..	..	..	*26.92*	*26.03*	*27.01*	*27.38*	*28.03*	..	*c. Autres*
56. Net income	31.28	29.79	30.53	31.02	31.92	34.08	32.19	32.15	31.24	..	56. Résultat net
57. Provisions (net)	17.07	11.87	6.87	6.37	9.02	15.88	10.41	11.09	12.31	..	57. Provisions (nettes)
a. Provisions on loans	*17.03*	*11.82*	*6.81*	*6.34*	*8.98*	*14.70*	*10.22*	*10.95*	*12.02*	..	*a. Provisions sur prêts*
b. Provisions on securities	..	..	..	..	..	..	..	..	..	..	*b. Provisions sur titres*
c. Other	..	..	..	..	*0.04*	*1.18*	*0.18*	*0.14*	*0.30*	..	*c. Autres*
58. Profit before tax	14.21	17.92	23.66	24.64	22.90	18.20	21.78	21.06	18.93	..	58. Bénéfices avant impôt
59. Income tax	9.03	11.15	14.27	15.92	14.25	10.23	13.49	13.30	11.85	..	59. Impôt sur le revenu
60. Profit after tax	5.18	6.77	9.38	8.72	8.66	7.97	8.29	7.75	7.07	..	60. Bénéfices après impôt
% of net income											**% du total du résultat net**
61. Provisions (net)	54.56	39.84	22.52	20.55	28.25	46.59	32.33	34.50	39.41	..	61. Provisions (nettes)
a. Provisions on loans	*54.44*	*39.67*	*22.32*	*20.45*	*28.12*	*43.13*	*31.76*	*34.05*	*38.46*	..	*a. Provisions sur prêts*
b. Provisions on securities	..	..	..	..	..	..	..	..	..	..	*b. Provisions sur titres*
c. Other	..	..	..	..	*0.13*	*3.46*	*0.57*	*0.44*	*0.95*	..	*c. Autres*
62. Profit before tax	45.44	60.16	77.48	79.45	71.75	53.41	67.67	65.50	60.59	..	62. Bénéfices avant impôt
63. Income tax	28.88	37.43	46.75	51.32	44.63	30.02	41.91	41.38	37.94	..	63. Impôt sur le revenu
64. Profit after tax	16.56	22.73	30.73	28.13	27.12	23.39	25.76	24.12	22.65	..	64. Bénéfices après impôt

GERMANY
Co-operative banks

ALLEMAGNE
Banques mutualistes

	1989	1990	1991	1992	1993(1)	1994	1995	1996	1997	1998 p	
Per cent											*Pourcentage*
BALANCE SHEET ANALYSIS											**ANALYSE DU BILAN**
% of year-end balance sheet total											**% du total du bilan en fin d'exercice**
Assets											**Actif**
65. Cash & balance with Central bank	3.03	3.05	3.01	3.31	2.50	2.33	2.09	2.12	2.00	1.76	65. Caisse & solde auprès de la Banque centrale
66. Interbank deposits	16.68	17.41	16.74	15.11	16.35	13.47	14.09	13.47	13.20	13.29	66. Dépôts interbancaires
67. Loans	58.89	58.37	59.38	60.17	58.22	59.31	60.28	60.37	60.73	60.70	67. Prêts
68. Securities	17.99	17.71	17.44	18.18	20.00	22.01	20.69	21.22	21.33	21.49	68. Valeurs mobilières
69. Other assets	3.42	3.45	3.43	3.23	2.92	2.88	2.85	2.82	2.74	2.75	69. Autres actifs
Liabilities											**Passif**
70. Capital & reserves	3.89	3.77	3.79	4.03	4.15	4.36	4.52	4.66	4.80	4.80	70. Capital et réserves
71. Borrowing from Central bank	3.54	3.49	2.95	2.50	1.84	1.97	1.82	1.82	1.88	1.53	71. Emprunts auprès de la Banque centrale
72. Interbank deposits	8.41	8.07	7.52	7.58	8.49	9.83	10.46	10.98	11.62	12.50	72. Dépôts interbancaires
73. Non-bank deposits	79.56	79.48	79.86	79.37	78.75	76.56	75.20	74.47	73.48	73.03	73. Dépôts non bancaires
74. Bonds	1.81	2.32	2.85	3.38	3.56	4.17	4.84	4.90	5.19	5.18	74. Obligations
75. Other liabilities	2.79	2.87	3.03	3.14	3.22	3.12	3.16	3.16	3.03	2.95	75. Autres engagements
Memorandum items											***Pour mémoire***
76. Short-term securities	*2.16*	*2.29*	*2.60*	*2.78*	*3.32*	*3.07*	*3.02*	*2.88*	*2.90*	*2.14*	*76. Titres à court terme*
77. Bonds	*15.13*	*14.71*	*14.08*	*14.51*	*15.49*	*17.62*	*16.34*	*16.90*	*16.60*	*16.92*	*77. Obligations*
78. Shares and participations	*0.69*	*0.71*	*0.76*	*0.89*	*1.19*	*1.32*	*1.33*	*1.44*	*1.84*	*2.43*	*78. Actions et participations*
79. Claims on non-residents	*1.03*	*1.21*	*1.36*	*1.15*	*2.02*	*1.84*	*1.73*	*1.61*	*1.62*	*1.58*	*79. Créances sur des non-résidents*
80. Liabilities to non-residents	*0.86*	*1.04*	*0.82*	*1.06*	*1.19*	*1.31*	*1.44*	*1.60*	*1.75*	*1.96*	*80. Engagements envers des non-résidents*

* See notes on previous pages.

* Voir les notes en pages précédentes.

GREECE
Commercial banks

GRECE
Banques commerciales

	1989	1990	1991	1992	1993	1994	1995	1996	1997	
Million drachmas										*Millions de drachmes*
INCOME STATEMENT										**COMPTE DE RESULTATS**
1. Interest income	810801	1036099	1262406	1433138	1589503	1822130	1761664	1925357	2051887	1. Produits financiers
2. Interest expenses	726260	906804	1058188	1254678	1383660	1621449	1425600	1555322	1560952	2. Frais financiers
3. Net interest income	84541	129295	204218	178460	205843	200681	336064	370035	490935	3. Produits financiers nets
4. Non-interest income (net)	124699	162721	233967	244891	286193	420286	344776	413590	480431	4. Produits non financiers (nets)
a. Fees and commissions receivable	..	..	..	*132372*	*155459*	*225300*	*202100*	*230186*	*243916*	*a. Frais et commissions à recevoir*
b. Fees and commissions payable	..	..	..	*1324*	*4935*	*7093*	*11351*	*12403*	*20893*	*b. Frais et commissions à payer*
c. Net profits or loss on financial operations	..	..	..	*80408*	*92222*	*122663*	*75665*	*138709*	*168285*	*c. Profits ou pertes nets sur opérations financières*
d. Other (1)	..	..	..	*33435*	*43447*	*79416*	*78362*	*57098*	*89123*	*d. Autres (1)*
5. Gross income	209240	292016	438185	423351	492036	620967	680840	783625	971366	5. Résultat brut
6. Operating expenses	156387	187198	224921	258439	308571	369367	437593	534763	613856	6. Frais d'exploitation
a. Staff costs	*119771*	*143740*	*170408*	*184861*	*214426*	*259686*	*304346*	*368584*	*406884*	*a. Dépenses en personnel*
b. Property costs	*8302*	*9349*	*13163*	*18546*	*20979*	*25341*	*34282*	*40880*	*49018*	*b. Dépenses en immobilier*
c. Other	*28314*	*34109*	*41350*	*55032*	*73166*	*84340*	*98965*	*125299*	*157954*	*c. Autres*
7. Net income	52853	104818	213264	164912	183465	251600	243247	248862	357510	7. Résultat net
8. Provisions (net)	22034	35758	63983	35905	44700	57981	41537	102027	141067	8. Provisions (nettes)
a. Provisions on loans	*18589*	*32052*	*60506*	*32988*	*44261*	*55643*	*37534*	*97497*	*134595*	*a. Provisions sur prêts*
b. Provisions on securities	..	..	..	*547*	-	*254*	*110*	*328*	*2173*	*b. Provisions sur titres*
c. Other	..	..	..	*2370*	*439*	*2084*	*3893*	*4202*	*4299*	*c. Autres*
9. Profit before tax	30819	69060	149281	129007	138765	193619	201710	146835	216443	9. Bénéfices avant impôt
10. Income tax	3847	14306	24108	42032	46105	54599	57444	55574	64293	10. Impôt sur le revenu
11. Profit after tax	26972	54754	125173	86975	92660	139020	144266	91261	152150	11. Bénéfices après impôt
12. Distributed profit	15572	32859	59333	42248	54204	73996	81389	50649	87492	12. Bénéfices distribués
13. Retained profit	11400	21895	65840	44727	38456	65024	62877	40612	64658	13. Bénéfices mis en réserve
BALANCE SHEET										**BILAN**
Assets										**Actif**
14. Cash & balance with Central bank	1320877	1491539	1767795	2155478	2490771	2837652	3725158	3522883	4188914	14. Caisse & solde auprès de la Banque centrale
15. Interbank deposits	398722	449363	571899	796507	1101032	1706498	1940254	2109612	3191877	15. Dépôts interbancaires
16. Loans	2297698	2424713	2610509	2939091	3358861	3858319	4787221	6262746	7561125	16. Prêts
17. Securities	2694366	3287455	3869357	4441205	5156437	5489608	5943486	6502602	7730960	17. Valeurs mobilières
18. Other assets	632496	847931	1280489	1782388	2018707	1438616	663144	1467686	1030301	18. Autres actifs
Liabilities										**Passif**
19. Capital & reserves	230484	331782	473424	558540	642884	746500	826338	888234	1208981	19. Capital et réserves
20. Borrowing from Central bank	29734	37482	30198	25045	26399	22354	248032	140586	697526	20. Emprunts auprès de la Banque centrale
21. Interbank deposits	138630	114612	210746	265597	395454	940169	1516995	1224518	1651046	21. Dépôts interbancaires
22. Non-bank deposits	6035693	6884165	7993838	9432922	11093788	11519309	12534764	14942536	18688768	22. Dépôts non bancaires
23. Bonds	-	-	119125	119125	120122	120096	120077	103217	86205	23. Obligations
24. Other liabilities	909618	1132960	1272718	1713440	1847161	1982265	1813057	2566438	1370651	24. Autres engagements
Balance sheet total										**Total du bilan**
25. End-year total	7344159	8501001	10100049	12114669	14125808	15330693	17059263	19865529	23703177	25. En fin d'exercice
26. Average total	6740317	7929385	9321100	11180991	13124486	14726912	16050121	18663828	21784353	26. Moyen

GREECE / GRECE

Commercial banks / Banques commerciales

	1989	1990	1991	1992	1993	1994	1995	1996	1997	
Million drachmas										*Millions de drachmes*
Memorandum items										***Pour mémoire***
27. Short-term securities	*2287331*	*2609230*	*1331164*	*766113*	*234529*	*339189*	*418056*	*120035*	*258817*	*27. Titres à court terme*
28. Bonds	*156967*	*380370*	*2166431*	*3194076*	*4356727*	*4380005*	*4768553*	*5408790*	*6722599*	*28. Obligations*
29. Shares and participations	*250068*	*297855*	*371762*	*481016*	*565221*	*770414*	*756877*	*973777*	*749544*	*29. Actions et participations*
30. Claims on non-residents	..	..	..	..	..	..	..	..	..	*30. Créances sur des non-résidents*
31. Liabilities to non-residents	..	..	..	..	..	..	..	..	..	*31. Engagements envers des non-résidents*
Capital adequacy										***Solvabilité***
32. Tier 1 Capital	..	..	..	..	..	..	..	..	..	*32. Fonds propres de base*
33. Tier 2 Capital	..	..	..	..	..	..	..	..	..	*33. Fonds propres complémentaires*
34. Supervisory deductions	..	..	..	..	..	..	..	..	..	*34. Eléments à déduire des fonds propres*
35. Total net capital resources	..	..	..	..	..	..	*798907*	*914548*	*1252224*	*35. Total net des ressources en capital*
36. Risk-weighted assets	..	..	..	..	..	..	*6047752*	*8767728*	*11313738*	*36. Actifs pondérés des risques*
SUPPLEMENTARY INFORMATION										**RENSEIGNEMENTS COMPLEMENTAIRES**
37. Number of institutions	15	15	19	19	20	19	18	20	19	37. Nombre d'institutions
38. Number of branches	1065	1079	1117	1154	1200	1244	1469	1599	1775	38. Nombre de succursales
39. Number of employees (x 1000)	37.2	36.4	37.2	37.1	37.5	39.6	40.3	43.1	43.6	39. Nombre de salariés (x 1000)

1. Other non-interest income (item 4.d) includes dividend income on shares and participations.

Notes

- Commercial banks incorporated in Greece.

1. Les Autres produits non financier (poste 4.d.) incluent les revenus de dividendes d'actions et de participations.

Notes

- Banques commerciales de droit grècque.

GREECE / GRECE

Commercial banks / Banques commerciales

	1989	1990	1991	1992	1993	1994	1995	1996	1997	
Per cent										*Pourcentage*
INCOME STATEMENT ANALYSIS										**ANALYSE DU COMPTE DE RESULTATS**
% of average balance sheet total										**% du total moyen du bilan**
40. Interest income	12.03	13.07	13.54	12.82	12.11	12.37	10.98	10.32	9.42	40. Produits financiers
41. Interest expenses	10.77	11.44	11.35	11.22	10.54	11.01	8.88	8.33	7.17	41. Frais financiers
42. Net interest income	1.25	1.63	2.19	1.60	1.57	1.36	2.09	1.98	2.25	42. Produits financiers nets
43. Non-interest income (net)	1.85	2.05	2.51	2.19	2.18	2.85	2.15	2.22	2.21	43. Produits non financiers (nets)
a. Fees and commissions receivable	..	..	..	*1.18*	*1.18*	*1.53*	*1.26*	*1.23*	*1.12*	*a. Frais et commissions à recevoir*
b. Fees and commissions payable	..	..	..	*0.01*	*0.04*	*0.05*	*0.07*	*0.07*	*0.10*	*b. Frais et commissions à payer*
c. Net profits or loss on financial operations	..	..	..	*0.72*	*0.70*	*0.83*	*0.47*	*0.74*	*0.77*	*c. Profits ou pertes nets sur opérations financières*
d. Other	..	..	..	*0.30*	*0.33*	*0.54*	*0.49*	*0.31*	*0.41*	*d. Autres*
44. Gross income	3.10	3.68	4.70	3.79	3.75	4.22	4.24	4.20	4.46	44. Résultat brut
45. Operating expenses	2.32	2.36	2.41	2.31	2.35	2.51	2.73	2.87	2.82	45. Frais d'exploitation
a. Staff costs	*1.78*	*1.81*	*1.83*	*1.65*	*1.63*	*1.76*	*1.90*	*1.97*	*1.87*	*a. Dépenses en personnel*
b. Property costs	*0.12*	*0.12*	*0.14*	*0.17*	*0.16*	*0.17*	*0.21*	*0.22*	*0.23*	*b. Dépenses en immobilier*
c. Other	*0.42*	*0.43*	*0.44*	*0.49*	*0.56*	*0.57*	*0.62*	*0.67*	*0.73*	*c. Autres*
46. Net income	0.78	1.32	2.29	1.47	1.40	1.71	1.52	1.33	1.64	46. Résultat net
47. Provisions (net)	0.33	0.45	0.69	0.32	0.34	0.39	0.26	0.55	0.65	47. Provisions (nettes)
a. Provisions on loans	*0.28*	*0.40*	*0.65*	*0.30*	*0.34*	*0.38*	*0.23*	*0.52*	*0.62*	*a. Provisions sur prêts*
b. Provisions on securities	..	..	..	-	-	-	-	-	*0.01*	*b. Provisions sur titres*
c. Other	..	..	..	*0.02*	-	*0.01*	*0.02*	*0.02*	*0.02*	*c. Autres*
48. Profit before tax	0.46	0.87	1.60	1.15	1.06	1.31	1.26	0.79	0.99	48. Bénéfices avant impôt
49. Income tax	0.06	0.18	0.26	0.38	0.35	0.37	0.36	0.30	0.30	49. Impôt sur le revenu
50. Profit after tax	0.40	0.69	1.34	0.78	0.71	0.94	0.90	0.49	0.70	50. Bénéfices après impôt
51. Distributed profit	0.23	0.41	0.64	0.38	0.41	0.50	0.51	0.27	0.40	51. Bénéfices distribués
52. Retained profit	0.17	0.28	0.71	0.40	0.29	0.44	0.39	0.22	0.30	52. Bénéfices mis en réserve
% of gross income										**% du total du résultat brut**
53. Net interest income	40.40	44.28	46.61	42.15	41.83	32.32	49.36	47.22	50.54	53. Produits financiers nets
54. Non-interest income (net)	59.60	55.72	53.39	57.85	58.17	67.68	50.64	52.78	49.46	54. Produits non financiers (nets)
a. Fees and commissions receivable	..	..	..	*31.27*	*31.60*	*36.28*	*29.68*	*29.37*	*25.11*	*a. Frais et commissions à recevoir*
b. Fees and commissions payable	..	..	..	*0.31*	*1.00*	*1.14*	*1.67*	*1.58*	*2.15*	*b. Frais et commissions à payer*
c. Net profits or loss on financial operations	..	..	..	*18.99*	*18.74*	*19.75*	*11.11*	*17.70*	*17.32*	*c. Profits ou pertes nets sur opérations financières*
d. Other	..	..	..	*7.90*	*8.83*	*12.79*	*11.51*	*7.29*	*9.18*	*d. Autres*
55. Operating expenses	74.74	64.11	51.33	61.05	62.71	59.48	64.27	68.24	63.20	55. Frais d'exploitation
a. Staff costs	*57.24*	*49.22*	*38.89*	*43.67*	*43.58*	*41.82*	*44.70*	*47.04*	*41.89*	*a. Dépenses en personnel*
b. Property costs	*3.97*	*3.20*	*3.00*	*4.38*	*4.26*	*4.08*	*5.04*	*5.22*	*5.05*	*b. Dépenses en immobilier*
c. Other	*13.53*	*11.68*	*9.44*	*13.00*	*14.87*	*13.58*	*14.54*	*15.99*	*16.26*	*c. Autres*
56. Net income	25.26	35.89	48.67	38.95	37.29	40.52	35.73	31.76	36.80	56. Résultat net
57. Provisions (net)	10.53	12.25	14.60	8.48	9.08	9.34	6.10	13.02	14.52	57. Provisions (nettes)
a. Provisions on loans	*8.88*	*10.98*	*13.81*	*7.79*	*9.00*	*8.96*	*5.51*	*12.44*	*13.86*	*a. Provisions sur prêts*
b. Provisions on securities	..	..	..	*0.13*	-	*0.04*	*0.02*	*0.04*	*0.22*	*b. Provisions sur titres*
c. Other	..	..	..	*0.56*	*0.09*	*0.34*	*0.57*	*0.54*	*0.44*	*c. Autres*
58. Profit before tax	14.73	23.65	34.07	30.47	28.20	31.18	29.63	18.74	22.28	58. Bénéfices avant impôt
59. Income tax	1.84	4.90	5.50	9.93	9.37	8.79	8.44	7.09	6.62	59. Impôt sur le revenu
60. Profit after tax	12.89	18.75	28.57	20.54	18.83	22.39	21.19	11.65	15.66	60. Bénéfices après impôt
% of net income										**% du total du résultat net**
61. Provisions (net)	41.69	34.11	30.00	21.77	24.36	23.04	17.08	41.00	39.46	61. Provisions (nettes)
a. Provisions on loans	*35.17*	*30.58*	*28.37*	*20.00*	*24.13*	*22.12*	*15.43*	*39.18*	*37.65*	*a. Provisions sur prêts*
b. Provisions on securities	..	..	..	*0.33*	-	*0.10*	*0.05*	*0.13*	*0.61*	*b. Provisions sur titres*
c. Other	..	..	..	*1.44*	*0.24*	*0.83*	*1.60*	*1.69*	*1.20*	*c. Autres*
62. Profit before tax	58.31	65.89	70.00	78.23	75.64	76.96	82.92	59.00	60.54	62. Bénéfices avant impôt
63. Income tax	7.28	13.65	11.30	25.49	25.13	21.70	23.62	22.33	17.98	63. Impôt sur le revenu
64. Profit after tax	51.03	52.24	58.69	52.74	50.51	55.25	59.31	36.67	42.56	64. Bénéfices après impôt

GREECE
Commercial banks

GRECE
Banques commerciales

Per cent	1989	1990	1991	1992	1993	1994	1995	1996	1997	Pourcentage
BALANCE SHEET ANALYSIS										**ANALYSE DU BILAN**
% of year-end balance sheet total										**% du total du bilan en fin d'exercice**
Assets										**Actif**
65. Cash & balance with Central bank	17.99	17.55	17.50	17.79	17.63	18.51	21.84	17.73	17.67	65. Caisse & solde auprès de la Banque centrale
66. Interbank deposits	5.43	5.29	5.66	6.57	7.79	11.13	11.37	10.62	13.47	66. Dépôts interbancaires
67. Loans	31.29	28.52	25.85	24.26	23.78	25.17	28.06	31.53	31.90	67. Prêts
68. Securities	36.69	38.67	38.31	36.66	36.50	35.81	34.84	32.73	32.62	68. Valeurs mobilières
69. Other assets	8.61	9.97	12.68	14.71	14.29	9.38	3.89	7.39	4.35	69. Autres actifs
Liabilities										**Passif**
70. Capital & reserves	3.14	3.90	4.69	4.61	4.55	4.87	4.84	4.47	5.10	70. Capital et réserves
71. Borrowing from Central bank	0.40	0.44	0.30	0.21	0.19	0.15	1.45	0.71	2.94	71. Emprunts auprès de la Banque centrale
72. Interbank deposits	1.89	1.35	2.09	2.19	2.80	6.13	8.89	6.16	6.97	72. Dépôts interbancaires
73. Non-bank deposits	82.18	80.98	79.15	77.86	78.54	75.14	73.48	75.22	78.84	73. Dépôts non bancaires
74. Bonds	-	-	1.18	0.98	0.85	0.78	0.70	0.52	0.36	74. Obligations
75. Other liabilities	12.39	13.33	12.60	14.14	13.08	12.93	10.63	12.92	5.78	75. Autres engagements
Memorandum items										***Pour mémoire***
76. Short-term securities	*31.14*	*30.69*	*13.18*	*6.32*	*1.66*	*2.21*	*2.45*	*0.60*	*1.09*	*76. Titres à court terme*
77. Bonds	*2.14*	*4.47*	*21.45*	*26.37*	*30.84*	*28.57*	*27.95*	*27.23*	*28.36*	*77. Obligations*
78. Shares and participations	*3.40*	*3.50*	*3.68*	*3.97*	*4.00*	*5.03*	*4.44*	*4.90*	*3.16*	*78. Actions et participations*
79. Claims on non-residents	..	..	..	..	..	..	..	..	..	*79. Créances sur des non-résidents*
80. Liabilities to non-residents	..	..	..	..	..	..	..	..	..	*80. Engagements envers des non-résidents*

* See notes on previous pages.

* Voir les notes en pages précédentes.

GREECE
Large commercial banks

GRECE
Grandes banques commerciales

	1988	1989	1990	1991	1992	1993	1994	1995	1996	1997	
Million drachmas											*Millions de drachmes*
INCOME STATEMENT											**COMPTE DE RESULTATS**
1. Interest income	575166	708956	890880	1068795	1203677	1300006	1440979	1413564	1508121	1600134	1. Produits financiers
2. Interest expenses	538274	644999	798348	912049	1085177	1159732	1321417	1178216	1254187	1272124	2. Frais financiers
3. Net interest income	36892	63957	92532	156746	118500	140274	119562	235348	253934	328010	3. Produits financiers nets
4. Non-interest income (net)	96544	103671	135770	196760	196542	223679	349770	266967	301673	363289	4. Produits non financiers (nets)
a. Fees and commissions receivable	..	..	..	..	*103896*	*116152*	*181317*	*157709*	*166344*	*168857*	*a. Frais et commissions à recevoir*
b. Fees and commissions payable	..	..	..	..	*1307*	*4575*	*6131*	*9478*	*10079*	*18728*	*b. Frais et commissions à payer*
c. Net profits or loss on financial operations	..	..	..	..	*62210*	*72652*	*103013*	*50007*	*86248*	*149859*	*c. Profits ou pertes nets sur opérations financières*
d. Other (1)	..	..	..	..	*31743*	*39450*	*71571*	*68729*	*59160*	*63301*	*d. Autres (1)*
5. Gross income	133436	167628	228302	353506	315042	363953	469332	502315	555607	691299	5. Résultat brut
6. Operating expenses	108286	128358	151969	178455	198993	233028	275646	333031	389895	442489	6. Frais d'exploitation
a. Staff costs	*83952*	*100241*	*118929*	*138279*	*147857*	*168130*	*202185*	*241168*	*280323*	*305121*	*a. Dépenses en personnel*
b. Property costs	*4581*	*6271*	*6597*	*9073*	*11662*	*13313*	*16520*	*24243*	*26758*	*32184*	*b. Dépenses en immobilier*
c. Other	*19753*	*21846*	*26443*	*31103*	*39474*	*51585*	*56941*	*67620*	*82814*	*105184*	*c. Autres*
7. Net income	25150	39270	76333	175051	116049	130925	193686	169284	165712	248810	7. Résultat net
8. Provisions (net)	10760	19350	31240	59044	24506	30252	44356	27730	81065	119420	8. Provisions (nettes)
a. Provisions on loans	*9920*	*16178*	*29200*	*56171*	*24112*	*29882*	*44241*	*27205*	*80350*	*114628*	*a. Provisions sur prêts*
b. Provisions on securities	..	..	..	..	*17*	*-*	*81*	*78*	*86*	*2173*	*b. Provisions sur titres*
c. Other	..	..	..	..	*377*	*370*	*34*	*447*	*629*	*2619*	*c. Autres*
9. Profit before tax	14390	19920	45093	116007	91543	100673	149330	141554	84647	129390	9. Bénéfices avant impôt
10. Income tax	2244	2714	9498	17547	26789	30387	38534	39336	31923	36100	10. Impôt sur le revenu
11. Profit after tax	12146	17206	35595	98460	64754	70286	110796	102218	52724	93290	11. Bénéfices après impôt
12. Distributed profit	9723	8768	19583	41679	29745	39918	56433	60698	30947	60948	12. Bénéfices distribués
13. Retained profit	2423	8438	16012	56781	35009	30368	54363	41520	21777	32344	13. Bénéfices mis en réserve
BALANCE SHEET											**BILAN**
Assets											**Actif**
14. Cash & balance with Central bank	1165163	1153461	1373922	1604560	1913734	2207539	2378388	3079319	2874325	3487044	14. Caisse & solde auprès de la Banque centrale
15. Interbank deposits	281820	296536	320288	388178	582607	807989	1058011	1340191	1599616	2216426	15. Dépôts interbancaires
16. Loans	1647158	1948042	1996282	2120142	2293430	2590358	2917673	3662437	4503138	5460560	16. Prêts
17. Securities	1949543	2527840	2968372	3453143	3823378	4575126	4922240	5385805	5715084	6730159	17. Valeurs mobilières
18. Other assets	338723	513998	721156	1082620	1612072	1622812	1239852	561871	1164955	863156	18. Autres actifs
Liabilities											**Passif**
19. Capital & reserves	149671	167870	247835	351624	408236	477322	586903	628072	605976	835215	19. Capital et réserves
20. Borrowing from Central bank	41278	5523	12086	5896	1385	1370	666	221807	86125	353502	20. Emprunts auprès de la Banque centrale
21. Interbank deposits	66746	74608	78980	154198	179240	289281	805002	1266173	867304	1131645	21. Dépôts interbancaires
22. Non-bank deposits	4453687	5395410	6035308	6848311	8017463	9322416	9432971	10481954	11868587	14892178	22. Dépôts non bancaires
23. Bonds	-	-	-	119125	119125	119125	119125	119125	103217	86205	23. Obligations
24. Other liabilities	671025	796466	1005811	1169489	1499772	1594310	1571497	1312492	2325909	1458600	24. Autres engagements
Balance sheet total											**Total du bilan**
25. End-year total	5382407	6439877	7380020	8648643	10225221	11803824	12516164	14029623	15857118	18757345	25. En fin d'exercice
26. Average total	4919463	5911142	6909949	8014201	9474283	11015235	12159995	13272895	14943371	17307232	26. Moyen

GREECE
Large commercial banks

GRECE
Grandes banques commerciales

	1988	1989	1990	1991	1992	1993	1994	1995	1996	1997	
Million drachmas											*Millions de drachmes*
Memorandum items											***Pour mémoire***
27. Short-term securities	*1607086*	*2133756*	*2317709*	*969054*	*506022*	*160917*	*282618*	*305449*	*73201*	*229677*	*27. Titres à court terme*
28. Bonds	*115355*	*149571*	*366025*	*2135623*	*2916980*	*3884467*	*3924375*	*4368009*	*4780075*	*5819737*	*28. Obligations*
29. Shares and participations	*227102*	*244513*	*284638*	*348466*	*400376*	*529742*	*715247*	*712347*	*861808*	*680745*	*29. Actions et participations*
30. Claims on non-residents	..	..	..	..	..	..	..	..	..	..	*30. Créances sur des non-résidents*
31. Liabilities to non-residents	..	..	..	..	..	..	..	..	..	..	*31. Engagements envers des non-résidents*
Capital adequacy											***Solvabilité***
32. Tier 1 Capital	..	..	..	..	..	..	..	..	..	..	*32. Fonds propres de base*
33. Tier 2 Capital	..	..	..	..	..	..	..	..	..	..	*33. Fonds propres complémentaires*
34. Supervisory deductions	..	..	..	..	..	..	..	..	..	..	*34. Eléments à déduire des fonds propres*
35. Total net capital resources	..	..	..	..	..	..	*564498*	*590392*	*667674*	*922126*	*35. Total net des ressources en capital*
36. Risk-weighted assets	..	..	..	..	..	..	*3871720*	*4639271*	*6709905*	*8426088*	*36. Actifs pondérés des risques*
SUPPLEMENTARY INFORMATION											**RENSEIGNEMENTS COMPLEMENTAIRES**
37. Number of institutions	4	4	4	4	4	4	4	4	4	4	37. Nombre d'institutions
38. Number of branches	797	799	802	812	824	843	856	1100	1128	1268	38. Nombre de succursales
39. Number of employees (x 1000)	29.4	29.7	28.7	28.7	28.3	28.2	29.4	30.9	31.3	31.1	39. Nombre de salariés (x 1000)

1. Other non-interest income (item 4.d) includes dividend income on shares and participations.

Notes

- Large commercial banks are a sub-group of Commercial banks.

1. Les Autres produits non financier (poste 4.d.) incluent les revenus de dividendes d'actions et de participations.

Notes

- Les Grandes banques commerciales sont un sous-groupe des Banques commerciales.

GREECE / GRECE

Large commercial banks / Grandes banques commerciales

	1988	1989	1990	1991	1992	1993	1994	1995	1996	1997	
Per cent											*Pourcentage*
INCOME STATEMENT ANALYSIS											**ANALYSE DU COMPTE DE RESULTATS**
% of average balance sheet total											**% du total moyen du bilan**
40. Interest income	11.69	11.99	12.89	13.34	12.70	11.80	11.85	10.65	10.09	9.25	40. Produits financiers
41. Interest expenses	10.94	10.91	11.55	11.38	11.45	10.53	10.87	8.88	8.39	7.35	41. Frais financiers
42. Net interest income	0.75	1.08	1.34	1.96	1.25	1.27	0.98	1.77	1.70	1.90	42. Produits financiers nets
43. Non-interest income (net)	1.96	1.75	1.96	2.46	2.07	2.03	2.88	2.01	2.02	2.10	43. Produits non financiers (nets)
a. Fees and commissions receivable	..	..	..	..	*1.10*	*1.05*	*1.49*	*1.19*	*1.11*	*0.98*	*a. Frais et commissions à recevoir*
b. Fees and commissions payable	..	..	..	..	*0.01*	*0.04*	*0.05*	*0.07*	*0.07*	*0.11*	*b. Frais et commissions à payer*
c. Net profits or loss on financial operations	..	..	..	..	*0.66*	*0.66*	*0.85*	*0.38*	*0.58*	*0.87*	*c. Profits ou pertes nets sur opérations financières*
d. Other	..	..	..	..	*0.34*	*0.36*	*0.59*	*0.52*	*0.40*	*0.37*	*d. Autres*
44. Gross income	2.71	2.84	3.30	4.41	3.33	3.30	3.86	3.78	3.72	3.99	44. Résultat brut
45. Operating expenses	2.20	2.17	2.20	2.23	2.10	2.12	2.27	2.51	2.61	2.56	45. Frais d'exploitation
a. Staff costs	*1.71*	*1.70*	*1.72*	*1.73*	*1.56*	*1.53*	*1.66*	*1.82*	*1.88*	*1.76*	*a. Dépenses en personnel*
b. Property costs	*0.09*	*0.11*	*0.10*	*0.11*	*0.12*	*0.12*	*0.14*	*0.18*	*0.18*	*0.19*	*b. Dépenses en immobilier*
c. Other	*0.40*	*0.37*	*0.38*	*0.39*	*0.42*	*0.47*	*0.47*	*0.51*	*0.55*	*0.61*	*c. Autres*
46. Net income	0.51	0.66	1.10	2.18	1.22	1.19	1.59	1.28	1.11	1.44	46. Résultat net
47. Provisions (net)	0.22	0.33	0.45	0.74	0.26	0.27	0.36	0.21	0.54	0.69	47. Provisions (nettes)
a. Provisions on loans	*0.20*	*0.27*	*0.42*	*0.70*	*0.25*	*0.27*	*0.36*	*0.20*	*0.54*	*0.66*	*a. Provisions sur prêts*
b. Provisions on securities	..	..	..	..	-	-	-	-	-	*0.01*	*b. Provisions sur titres*
c. Other	..	..	..	..	-	-	-	-	-	*0.02*	*c. Autres*
48. Profit before tax	0.29	0.34	0.65	1.45	0.97	0.91	1.23	1.07	0.57	0.75	48. Bénéfices avant impôt
49. Income tax	0.05	0.05	0.14	0.22	0.28	0.28	0.32	0.30	0.21	0.21	49. Impôt sur le revenu
50. Profit after tax	0.25	0.29	0.52	1.23	0.68	0.64	0.91	0.77	0.35	0.54	50. Bénéfices après impôt
51. Distributed profit	0.20	0.15	0.28	0.52	0.31	0.36	0.46	0.46	0.21	0.35	51. Bénéfices distribués
52. Retained profit	0.05	0.14	0.23	0.71	0.37	0.28	0.45	0.31	0.15	0.19	52. Bénéfices mis en réserve
% of gross income											**% du total du résultat brut**
53. Net interest income	27.65	38.15	40.53	44.34	37.61	38.54	25.47	46.85	45.70	47.45	53. Produits financiers nets
54. Non-interest income (net)	72.35	61.85	59.47	55.66	62.39	61.46	74.53	53.15	54.30	52.55	54. Produits non financiers (nets)
a. Fees and commissions receivable	..	..	..	..	*32.98*	*31.91*	*38.63*	*31.40*	*29.94*	*24.43*	*a. Frais et commissions à recevoir*
b. Fees and commissions payable	..	..	..	..	*0.41*	*1.26*	*1.31*	*1.89*	*1.81*	*2.71*	*b. Frais et commissions à payer*
c. Net profits or loss on financial operations	..	..	..	..	*19.75*	*19.96*	*21.95*	*9.96*	*15.52*	*21.68*	*c. Profits ou pertes nets sur opérations financières*
d. Other	..	..	..	..	*10.08*	*10.84*	*15.25*	*13.68*	*10.65*	*9.16*	*d. Autres*
55. Operating expenses	81.15	76.57	66.56	50.48	63.16	64.03	58.73	66.30	70.17	64.01	55. Frais d'exploitation
a. Staff costs	*62.92*	*59.80*	*52.09*	*39.12*	*46.93*	*46.20*	*43.08*	*48.01*	*50.45*	*44.14*	*a. Dépenses en personnel*
b. Property costs	*3.43*	*3.74*	*2.89*	*2.57*	*3.70*	*3.66*	*3.52*	*4.83*	*4.82*	*4.66*	*b. Dépenses en immobilier*
c. Other	*14.80*	*13.03*	*11.58*	*8.80*	*12.53*	*14.17*	*12.13*	*13.46*	*14.91*	*15.22*	*c. Autres*
56. Net income	18.85	23.43	33.44	49.52	36.84	35.97	41.27	33.70	29.83	35.99	56. Résultat net
57. Provisions (net)	8.06	11.54	13.68	16.70	7.78	8.31	9.45	5.52	14.59	17.27	57. Provisions (nettes)
a. Provisions on loans	*7.43*	*9.65*	*12.79*	*15.89*	*7.65*	*8.21*	*9.43*	*5.42*	*14.46*	*16.58*	*a. Provisions sur prêts*
b. Provisions on securities	..	..	..	..	*0.01*	-	*0.02*	*0.02*	*0.02*	*0.31*	*b. Provisions sur titres*
c. Other	..	..	..	..	*0.12*	*0.10*	*0.01*	*0.09*	*0.11*	*0.38*	*c. Autres*
58. Profit before tax	10.78	11.88	19.75	32.82	29.06	27.66	31.82	28.18	15.24	18.72	58. Bénéfices avant impôt
59. Income tax	1.68	1.62	4.16	4.96	8.50	8.35	8.21	7.83	5.75	5.22	59. Impôt sur le revenu
60. Profit after tax	9.10	10.26	15.59	27.85	20.55	19.31	23.61	20.35	9.49	13.49	60. Bénéfices après impôt
% of net income											**% du total du résultat net**
61. Provisions (net)	42.78	49.27	40.93	33.73	21.12	23.11	22.90	16.38	48.92	48.00	61. Provisions (nettes)
a. Provisions on loans	*39.44*	*41.20*	*38.25*	*32.09*	*20.78*	*22.82*	*22.84*	*16.07*	*48.49*	*46.07*	*a. Provisions sur prêts*
b. Provisions on securities	..	..	..	..	*0.01*	-	*0.04*	*0.05*	*0.05*	*0.87*	*b. Provisions sur titres*
c. Other	..	..	..	..	*0.32*	*0.28*	*0.02*	*0.26*	*0.38*	*1.05*	*c. Autres*
62. Profit before tax	57.22	50.73	59.07	66.27	78.88	76.89	77.10	83.62	51.08	52.00	62. Bénéfices avant impôt
63. Income tax	8.92	6.91	12.44	10.02	23.08	23.21	19.90	23.24	19.26	14.51	63. Impôt sur le revenu
64. Profit after tax	48.29	43.81	46.63	56.25	55.80	53.68	57.20	60.38	31.82	37.49	64. Bénéfices après impôt

GREECE / GRECE

Large commercial banks / Grandes banques commerciales

	1988	1989	1990	1991	1992	1993	1994	1995	1996	1997	
Per cent											*Pourcentage*
BALANCE SHEET ANALYSIS											**ANALYSE DU BILAN**
% of year-end balance sheet total											**% du total du bilan en fin d'exercice**
Assets											**Actif**
65. Cash & balance with Central bank	21.65	17.91	18.62	18.55	18.72	18.70	19.00	21.95	18.13	18.59	65. Caisse & solde auprès de la Banque centrale
66. Interbank deposits	5.24	4.60	4.34	4.49	5.70	6.85	8.45	9.55	10.09	11.82	66. Dépôts interbancaires
67. Loans	30.60	30.25	27.05	24.51	22.43	21.95	23.31	26.11	28.40	29.11	67. Prêts
68. Securities	36.22	39.25	40.22	39.93	37.39	38.76	39.33	38.39	36.04	35.88	68. Valeurs mobilières
69. Other assets	6.29	7.98	9.77	12.52	15.77	13.75	9.91	4.00	7.35	4.60	69. Autres actifs
Liabilities											**Passif**
70. Capital & reserves	2.78	2.61	3.36	4.07	3.99	4.04	4.69	4.48	3.82	4.45	70. Capital et réserves
71. Borrowing from Central bank	0.77	0.09	0.16	0.07	0.01	0.01	0.01	1.58	0.54	1.88	71. Emprunts auprès de la Banque centrale
72. Interbank deposits	1.24	1.16	1.07	1.78	1.75	2.45	6.43	9.02	5.47	6.03	72. Dépôts interbancaires
73. Non-bank deposits	82.75	83.78	81.78	79.18	78.41	78.98	75.37	74.71	74.85	79.39	73. Dépôts non bancaires
74. Bonds	-	-	-	1.38	1.17	1.01	0.95	0.85	0.65	0.46	74. Obligations
75. Other liabilities	12.47	12.37	13.63	13.52	14.67	13.51	12.56	9.36	14.67	7.78	75. Autres engagements
Memorandum items											***Pour mémoire***
76. Short-term securities	*29.86*	*33.13*	*31.41*	*11.20*	*4.95*	*1.36*	*2.26*	*2.18*	*0.46*	*1.22*	*76. Titres à court terme*
77. Bonds	*2.14*	*2.32*	*4.96*	*24.69*	*28.53*	*32.91*	*31.35*	*31.13*	*30.14*	*31.03*	*77. Obligations*
78. Shares and participations	*4.22*	*3.80*	*3.86*	*4.03*	*3.92*	*4.49*	*5.71*	*5.08*	*5.43*	*3.63*	*78. Actions et participations*
79. Claims on non-residents	..	..	..	..	..	..	..	..	..	..	*79. Créances sur des non-résidents*
80. Liabilities to non-residents	..	..	..	..	..	..	..	..	..	..	*80. Engagements envers des non-résidents*

* See notes on previous pages.

* Voir les notes en pages précédentes.

HUNGARY
Commercial banks

HONGRIE
Banques commerciales

	1994	1995	1996	1997	
Million forints					*Millions de forints*
INCOME STATEMENT					**COMPTE DE RESULTATS**
1. Interest income	449003	607492	665689	779222	1. Produits financiers
2. Interest expenses	299590	424421	470004	559568	2. Frais financiers
3. Net interest income	149413	183071	195685	219654	3. Produits financiers nets
4. Non-interest income (net)	-20581	-45938	11882	16289	4. Produits non financiers (nets)
a. Fees and commissions receivable	*45256*	*52954*	*50747*	*61260*	*a. Frais et commissions à recevoir*
b. Fees and commissions payable	*16831*	*20871*	*13760*	*18962*	*b. Frais et commissions à payer*
c. Net profits or loss on financial operations	*23219*	*19759*	*39283*	*31573*	*c. Profits ou pertes nets sur opérations financières*
d. Other	*-72225*	*-97780*	*-64388*	*-57582*	*d. Autres*
5. Gross income	128832	137133	207567	235943	5. Résultat brut
6. Operating expenses	98573	124072	148171	192460	6. Frais d'exploitation
a. Staff costs	*47507*	*56625*	*67008*	*80817*	*a. Dépenses en personnel*
b. Property costs	*15398*	*19500*	*26258*	*35381*	*b. Dépenses en immobilier*
c. Other	*35668*	*47947*	*54905*	*76262*	*c. Autres*
7. Net income	30259	13061	59396	43483	7. Résultat net
8. Provisions (net)	-30814	-68094	-24214	-33131	8. Provisions (nettes)
a. Provisions on loans	..	..	..	..	*a. Provisions sur prêts*
b. Provisions on securities	..	..	..	..	*b. Provisions sur titres*
c. Other	..	..	..	..	*c. Autres*
9. Profit before tax (1)	25558	53910	77556	77662	9. Bénéfices avant impôt (1)
10. Income tax	9752	11944	16142	16679	10. Impôt sur le revenu
11. Profit after tax	15806	41966	61414	60983	11. Bénéfices après impôt
12. Distributed profit (2)	9939	13296	18366	2144	12. Bénéfices distribués (2)
13. Retained profit	5867	28670	43048	58839	13. Bénéfices mis en réserve
BALANCE SHEET					**BILAN**
Assets					**Actif**
14. Cash & balance with Central bank	565570	769040	710801	1031517	14. Caisse & solde auprès de la Banque centrale
15. Interbank deposits	331649	449656	822164	874116	15. Dépôts interbancaires
16. Loans	1368767	1501397	1649608	2150639	16. Prêts
17. Securities	684411	704005	965913	1191413	17. Valeurs mobilières
18. Other assets (3)	121463	269540	339830	433381	18. Autres actifs (3)
Liabilities					**Passif**
19. Capital & reserves (4)	243187	347747	450555	642909	19. Capital et réserves (4)
20. Borrowing from Central bank	400541	300564	226516	181786	20. Emprunts auprès de la Banque centrale
21. Interbank deposits	260270	380224	622814	1015639	21. Dépôts interbancaires
22. Non-bank deposits	1775491	2143811	2583907	3184694	22. Dépôts non bancaires
23. Bonds	204608	286890	361024	327841	23. Obligations
24. Other liabilities	187763	234402	243500	328197	24. Autres engagements
Balance sheet total					**Total du bilan**
25. End-year total	3071860	3693638	4488316	5681066	25. En fin d'exercice
26. Average total	..	3382749	4090977	5084691	26. Moyen

HUNGARY
Commercial banks

HONGRIE
Banques commerciales

Million forints	1994	1995	1996	1997	Millions de forints
Memorandum items					**Pour mémoire**
27. Short-term securities	..	..	..	..	*27. Titres à court terme*
28. Bonds	..	..	..	..	*28. Obligations*
29. Shares and participations	..	..	..	..	*29. Actions et participations*
30. Claims on non-residents	..	..	..	..	*30. Créances sur des non-résidents*
31. Liabilities to non-residents	..	..	..	..	*31. Engagements envers des non-résidents*
Capital adequacy					**Solvabilité**
32. Tier 1 Capital	*209474*	*295794*	*377188*	*539555*	*32. Fonds propres de base*
33. Tier 2 Capital	*33665*	*51567*	*72029*	*97184*	*33. Fonds propres complémentaires*
34. Supervisory deductions	*42764*	*53984*	*69128*	*177470*	*34. Eléments à déduire des fonds propres*
35. Total net capital resources	*200375*	*293377*	*380089*	*459269*	*35. Total net des ressources en capital*
36. Risk-weighted assets	*1316460*	*1654935*	*2147003*	*2881625*	*36. Actifs pondérés des risques*
SUPPLEMENTARY INFORMATION					**RENSEIGNEMENTS COMPLEMENTAIRES**
37. Number of institutions	44	43	42	43	37. Nombre d'institutions
38. Number of branches	..	..	..	..	38. Nombre de succursales
39. Number of employees (x 1000)	36	36	33	32	39. Nombre de salariés (x 1000)

1. Profit before tax (item 9) includes extraordinary profits/losses in the amount of million Ft -35515 in 1994, million Ft -27245 in 1995, million Ft -6054 in 1996, and million Ft 1047 in 1997.

2. Distributed profit (item 12) also includes the distributed profit paid from retained profit.

3. Other assets (item 18) includes the provisions on loans, on interest, and on investments.

4. Capital and reserves (item 19) does not include provisions generated on future and contingent liabilities, on exchange rate risk and on exchange rate loss.

1. Les "Bénéfices avant impôt" (poste 9) comprennent des bénéfices/pertes extraordinaires d'un montant de -35515 millions de Ft en 1994, -27245 millions de Ft en 1995, -6054 millions de Ft en 1996, et 1047 millions de Ft en 1997.

2. Les "Bénéfices distribués" (poste 12) prennent également en compte les bénéfices distribués payés à partir des bénéfices mis en réserve.

3. Autres actifs (poste 18) incluent les provisions sur les prêts, sur l'intérêt, et sur les investissements.

4. Capital et réserves (poste 19) ne comprend pas les provisions sur les dettes futures et imprévues, sur le risque de change et sur les pertes de change.

HUNGARY
Commercial banks

HONGRIE
Banques commerciales

	1994	1995	1996	1997	
Per cent					*Pourcentage*
INCOME STATEMENT ANALYSIS					**ANALYSE DU COMPTE DE RESULTATS**
% of average balance sheet total					**% du total moyen du bilan**
40. Interest income	..	17.96	16.27	15.32	40. Produits financiers
41. Interest expenses	..	12.55	11.49	11.00	41. Frais financiers
42. Net interest income	..	5.41	4.78	4.32	42. Produits financiers nets
43. Non-interest income (net)	..	-1.36	0.29	0.32	43. Produits non financiers (nets)
a. Fees and commissions receivable	..	*1.57*	*1.24*	*1.20*	*a. Frais et commissions à recevoir*
b. Fees and commissions payable	..	*0.62*	*0.34*	*0.37*	*b. Frais et commissions à payer*
c. Net profits or loss on financial operations	..	*0.58*	*0.96*	*0.62*	*c. Profits ou pertes nets sur opérations financières*
d. Other	..	*-2.89*	*-1.57*	*-1.13*	*d. Autres*
44. Gross income	..	4.05	5.07	4.64	44. Résultat brut
45. Operating expenses	..	3.67	3.62	3.79	45. Frais d'exploitation
a. Staff costs	..	*1.67*	*1.64*	*1.59*	*a. Dépenses en personnel*
b. Property costs	..	*0.58*	*0.64*	*0.70*	*b. Dépenses en immobilier*
c. Other	..	*1.42*	*1.34*	*1.50*	*c. Autres*
46. Net income	..	0.39	1.45	0.86	46. Résultat net
47. Provisions (net)	..	-2.01	-0.59	-0.65	47. Provisions (nettes)
a. Provisions on loans	..	..	..	..	*a. Provisions sur prêts*
b. Provisions on securities	..	..	..	..	*b. Provisions sur titres*
c. Other	..	..	..	..	*c. Autres*
48. Profit before tax	..	1.59	1.90	1.53	48. Bénéfices avant impôt
49. Income tax	..	0.35	0.39	0.33	49. Impôt sur le revenu
50. Profit after tax	..	1.24	1.50	1.20	50. Bénéfices après impôt
51. Distributed profit	..	0.39	0.45	0.04	51. Bénéfices distribués
52. Retained profit	..	0.85	1.05	1.16	52. Bénéfices mis en réserve
% of gross income					**% du total du résultat brut**
53. Net interest income	115.98	133.50	94.28	93.10	53. Produits financiers nets
54. Non-interest income (net)	-15.98	-33.50	5.72	6.90	54. Produits non financiers (nets)
a. Fees and commissions receivable	*35.13*	*38.62*	*24.45*	*25.96*	*a. Frais et commissions à recevoir*
b. Fees and commissions payable	*13.06*	*15.22*	*6.63*	*8.04*	*b. Frais et commissions à payer*
c. Net profits or loss on financial operations	*18.02*	*14.41*	*18.93*	*13.38*	*c. Profits ou pertes nets sur opérations financières*
d. Other	*-56.06*	*-71.30*	*-31.02*	*-24.41*	*d. Autres*
55. Operating expenses	76.51	90.48	71.38	81.57	55. Frais d'exploitation
a. Staff costs	*36.88*	*41.29*	*32.28*	*34.25*	*a. Dépenses en personnel*
b. Property costs	*11.95*	*14.22*	*12.65*	*15.00*	*b. Dépenses en immobilier*
c. Other	*27.69*	*34.96*	*26.45*	*32.32*	*c. Autres*
56. Net income	23.49	9.52	28.62	18.43	56. Résultat net
57. Provisions (net)	-23.92	-49.66	-11.67	-14.04	57. Provisions (nettes)
a. Provisions on loans	..	..	..	..	*a. Provisions sur prêts*
b. Provisions on securities	..	..	..	..	*b. Provisions sur titres*
c. Other	..	..	..	..	*c. Autres*
58. Profit before tax	19.84	39.31	37.36	32.92	58. Bénéfices avant impôt
59. Income tax	7.57	8.71	7.78	7.07	59. Impôt sur le revenu
60. Profit after tax	12.27	30.60	29.59	25.85	60. Bénéfices après impôt
% of net income					**% du total du résultat net**
61. Provisions (net)	-101.83	-521.35	-40.77	-76.19	61. Provisions (nettes)
a. Provisions on loans	..	..	..	..	*a. Provisions sur prêts*
b. Provisions on securities	..	..	..	..	*b. Provisions sur titres*
c. Other	..	..	..	..	*c. Autres*
62. Profit before tax	84.46	412.76	130.57	178.60	62. Bénéfices avant impôt
63. Income tax	32.23	91.45	27.18	38.36	63. Impôt sur le revenu
64. Profit after tax	52.24	321.31	103.40	140.25	64. Bénéfices après impôt

HUNGARY
Commercial banks

HONGRIE
Banques commerciales

	1994	1995	1996	1997	
Per cent					*Pourcentage*
BALANCE SHEET ANALYSIS					**ANALYSE DU BILAN**
% of year-end balance sheet total					**% du total du bilan en fin d'exercice**
Assets					**Actif**
65. Cash & balance with Central bank	18.41	20.82	15.84	18.16	65. Caisse & solde auprès de la Banque centrale
66. Interbank deposits	10.80	12.17	18.32	15.39	66. Dépôts interbancaires
67. Loans	44.56	40.65	36.75	37.86	67. Prêts
68. Securities	22.28	19.06	21.52	20.97	68. Valeurs mobilières
69. Other assets	3.95	7.30	7.57	7.63	69. Autres actifs
Liabilities					**Passif**
70. Capital & reserves	7.92	9.41	10.04	11.32	70. Capital et réserves
71. Borrowing from Central bank	13.04	8.14	5.05	3.20	71. Emprunts auprès de la Banque centrale
72. Interbank deposits	8.47	10.29	13.88	17.88	72. Dépôts interbancaires
73. Non-bank deposits	57.80	58.04	57.57	56.06	73. Dépôts non bancaires
74. Bonds	6.66	7.77	8.04	5.77	74. Obligations
75. Other liabilities	6.11	6.35	5.43	5.78	75. Autres engagements
Memorandum items					***Pour mémoire***
76. Short-term securities	..	..	..	..	*76. Titres à court terme*
77. Bonds	..	..	..	..	*77. Obligations*
78. Shares and participations	..	..	..	..	*78. Actions et participations*
79. Claims on non-residents	..	..	..	..	*79. Créances sur des non-résidents*
80. Liabilities to non-residents	..	..	..	..	*80. Engagements envers des non-résidents*

* See notes on previous pages.

* Voir les notes en pages précédentes.

ICELAND — ISLANDE

Commercial banks and savings banks — Banques commerciales et caisses d'épargne

Million Icelandic krónur	1988	1989	1990	1991	1992	1993	1994	1995(1)	1996	1997	Millions de couronnes islandaises
INCOME STATEMENT											**COMPTE DE RESULTATS**
1. Interest income	31450	37854	29516	33827	26546	27916	22455	23772	25956	29901	1. Produits financiers
2. Interest expenses	22647	28694	18830	22429	14572	15366	10490	12024	13747	16674	2. Frais financiers
3. Net interest income	8803	9160	10686	11398	11974	12550	11965	11748	12209	13227	3. Produits financiers nets
4. Non-interest income (net)	2665	4300	4273	4475	4583	5334	6147	5449	6344	7328	4. Produits non financiers (nets)
a. Fees and commissions receivable	*2303*	*3154*	*3538*	*3837*	*4235*	*4591*	*5004*	*4490*	*4805*	*5297*	*a. Frais et commissions à recevoir*
b. Fees and commissions payable	-	-	-	-	-	-	-	*225*	*407*	*474*	*b. Frais et commissions à payer*
c. Net profits or loss on financial operations	*184*	*575*	*175*	*224*	*-134*	*474*	*435*	*392*	*795*	*1188*	*c. Profits ou pertes nets sur opérations financières*
d. Other	*178*	*571*	*560*	*414*	*482*	*269*	*708*	*792*	*1151*	*1317*	*d. Autres*
5. Gross income	11468	13460	14959	15873	16557	17884	18112	17197	18553	20555	5. Résultat brut
6. Operating expenses	8963	9937	11080	12440	12425	11584	12169	12483	13178	14232	6. Frais d'exploitation
a. Staff costs	*4936*	*5433*	*5472*	*5994*	*6021*	*5727*	*5907*	*6506*	*6822*	*7331*	*a. Dépenses en personnel*
b. Property costs (2)	*1329*	*1485*	*1608*	*1817*	*1793*	*1692*	*1871*	*1910*	*1740*	*5922*	*b. Dépenses en immobilier (2)*
c. Other (2)	*2698*	*3019*	*4000*	*4629*	*4611*	*4165*	*4391*	*4067*	*4616*	*979*	*c. Autres (2)*
7. Net income	2505	3523	3879	3433	4132	6300	5943	4714	5375	6323	7. Résultat net
8. Provisions (net)	976	1530	2585	2530	6802	6047	4715	2918	2959	2429	8. Provisions (nettes)
a. Provisions on loans	*976*	*1530*	*2585*	*2530*	*6802*	*6047*	*4715*	*2918*	*2959*	*2429*	*a. Provisions sur prêts*
b. Provisions on securities	-	-	-	-	-	-	-	-	-	-	*b. Provisions sur titres*
c. Other	-	-	-	-	-	-	-	-	-	-	*c. Autres*
9. Profit before tax	1529	1993	1294	903	-2670	253	1228	1796	2416	3894	9. Bénéfices avant impôt
10. Income tax	597	744	297	395	97	421	480	527	542	939	10. Impôt sur le revenu
11. Profit after tax	932	1249	997	508	-2767	-168	748	1269	1874	2955	11. Bénéfices après impôt
12. Distributed profit	109	169	50	288	189	97	159	184	287	352	12. Bénéfices distribués
13. Retained profit	823	1080	947	220	-2956	-265	589	1085	1587	2603	13. Bénéfices mis en réserve
BALANCE SHEET											**BILAN**
Assets											**Actif**
14. Cash & balance with Central bank	14453	19633	15188	16873	14642	11901	11740	10570	13720	15634	14. Caisse & solde auprès de la Banque centrale
15. Interbank deposits	5199	6058	6339	6898	6211	10799	11511	14947	20818	37134	15. Dépôts interbancaires
16. Loans	123547	152548	158736	178640	185216	191021	194164	197695	219624	246502	16. Prêts
17. Securities	4215	9514	22522	23910	27861	31678	23456	26804	34090	47631	17. Valeurs mobilières
18. Other assets	7922	9757	10583	11180	11135	11462	10520	13243	13418	12254	18. Autres actifs
Liabilities											**Passif**
19. Capital & reserves	11943	15975	16163	19536	16718	19025	19885	20982	23094	25127	19. Capital et réserves
20. Borrowing from Central bank	4587	4737	3625	3378	2520	1599	3107	4841	1945	6475	20. Emprunts auprès de la Banque centrale
21. Interbank deposits	2332	2582	2192	2475	2404	1812	2147	8077	14288	16374	21. Dépôts interbancaires
22. Non-bank deposits	84774	108543	124645	142809	147998	157888	160736	164356	175402	191521	22. Dépôts non bancaires
23. Bonds	8817	13792	17453	19181	20666	22549	22273	23537	31027	42430	23. Obligations
24. Other liabilities	42883	51881	49290	50122	54759	53988	43243	41466	55914	77228	24. Autres engagements
Balance sheet total											**Total du bilan**
25. End-year total	155336	197510	213368	237501	245065	256861	251391	263258	301670	359155	25. En fin d'exercice
26. Average total	135678	176423	205439	225435	241283	250963	254126	257325	282464	330413	26. Moyen

ICELAND

Commercial banks and savings banks

ISLANDE

Banques commerciales et caisses d'épargne

	1988	1989	1990	1991	1992	1993	1994	1995(1)	1996	1997	
Million Icelandic krónur											*Millions de couronnes islandaises*
Memorandum items											**Pour mémoire**
27. Short-term securities	*168*	*2833*	*5870*	*5226*	*8361*	*7202*	*2191*	*6324*	*9057*	*5549*	*27. Titres à court terme*
28. Bonds	*3299*	*5202*	*14626*	*15006*	*15500*	*20453*	*17127*	*15695*	*19354*	*31831*	*28. Obligations*
29. Shares and participations	*748*	*1479*	*2026*	*3678*	*4000*	*4023*	*4138*	*4785*	*6742*	*10251*	*29. Actions et participations*
30. Claims on non-residents	*2942*	*3766*	*4488*	*4645*	*4524*	*6812*	*8105*	*5213*	*6951*	*13110*	*30. Créances sur des non-résidents*
31. Liabilities to non-residents	*35109*	*42728*	*39071*	*39900*	*43769*	*43126*	*31843*	*27938*	*27845*	*37475*	*31. Engagements envers des non-résidents*
Capital adequacy											**Solvabilité**
32. Tier 1 Capital	..	..	..	..	*16718*	*19025*	*19885*	*20982*	*23094*	*25127*	*32. Fonds propres de base*
33. Tier 2 Capital	..	..	..	..	*1291*	*2680*	*2497*	*2120*	*3459*	*4374*	*33. Fonds propres complémentaires*
34. Supervisory deductions	..	..	..	..	*2327*	*2271*	*2313*	*2020*	*2627*	*3463*	*34. Eléments à déduire des fonds propres*
35. Total net capital resources	..	..	..	..	*15682*	*19434*	*20069*	*21082*	*23927*	*26038*	*35. Total net des ressources en capital*
36. Risk-weighted assets	..	..	..	..	*175718*	*182206*	*177710*	*183292*	*214417*	*251767*	*36. Actifs pondérés des risques*
SUPPLEMENTARY INFORMATION											**RENSEIGNEMENTS COMPLEMENTAIRES**
37. Number of institutions	41	41	35	36	36	34	33	33	33	31	37. Nombre d'institutions
38. Number of branches	183	183	176	177	178	174	176	179	179	182	38. Nombre de succursales
39. Number of employees (x 1000)	3.1	2.9	2.8	2.8	2.7	2.6	2.5	2.6	2.6	2.6	39. Nombre de salariés (x 1000)

1. Break in series in 1995 due to new accounting regulations.
2. The breakdown of "Property costs" and "Other operating expenses" (items 6.b. and 6.c.) is estimated for the year 1995 and 1996.

Notes

- Includes all commercial banks and savings banks operating in Iceland. The figures are based on non-consolidated accounts.

1. Rupture dans les séries en 1995 suite aux nouvelles règles de comptabilité.
2. La ventilation des rubriques "Dépenses en immobilier" et "Autres frais d'exploitation" (poste 6.b. et poste 6.c.) est une estimation pour les années 1995 et 1996

Notes

- Comprend toutes les banques commerciales et les caisses d'épargne en activité en Islande. Les chiffres sont basées sur des comptes non consolidés.

Commercial banks and savings banks — Banques commerciales et caisses d'épargne

Per cent	1988	1989	1990	1991	1992	1993	1994	1995(1)	1996	1997	Pourcentage
INCOME STATEMENT ANALYSIS											**ANALYSE DU COMPTE DE RESULTATS**
% of average balance sheet total											**% du total moyen du bilan**
40. Interest income	23.18	21.46	14.37	15.01	11.00	11.12	8.84	9.24	9.19	9.05	40. Produits financiers
41. Interest expenses	16.69	16.26	9.17	9.95	6.04	6.12	4.13	4.67	4.87	5.05	41. Frais financiers
42. Net interest income	6.49	5.19	5.20	5.06	4.96	5.00	4.71	4.57	4.32	4.00	42. Produits financiers nets
43. Non-interest income (net)	1.96	2.44	2.08	1.99	1.90	2.13	2.42	2.12	2.25	2.22	43. Produits non financiers (nets)
a. Fees and commissions receivable	*1.70*	*1.79*	*1.72*	*1.70*	*1.76*	*1.83*	*1.97*	*1.74*	*1.70*	*1.60*	*a. Frais et commissions à recevoir*
b. Fees and commissions payable	-	-	-	-	-	-	-	*0.09*	*0.14*	*0.14*	*b. Frais et commissions à payer*
c. Net profits or loss on financial operations	*0.14*	*0.33*	*0.09*	*0.10*	*-0.06*	*0.19*	*0.17*	*0.15*	*0.28*	*0.36*	*c. Profits ou pertes nets sur opérations financières*
d. Other	*0.13*	*0.32*	*0.27*	*0.18*	*0.20*	*0.11*	*0.28*	*0.31*	*0.41*	*0.40*	*d. Autres*
44. Gross income	8.45	7.63	7.28	7.04	6.86	7.13	7.13	6.68	6.57	6.22	44. Résultat brut
45. Operating expenses	6.61	5.63	5.39	5.52	5.15	4.62	4.79	4.85	4.67	4.31	45. Frais d'exploitation
a. Staff costs	*3.64*	*3.08*	*2.66*	*2.66*	*2.50*	*2.28*	*2.32*	*2.53*	*2.42*	*2.22*	*a. Dépenses en personnel*
b. Property costs	*0.98*	*0.84*	*0.78*	*0.81*	*0.74*	*0.67*	*0.74*	*0.74*	*0.62*	*1.79*	*b. Dépenses en immobilier*
c. Other	*1.99*	*1.71*	*1.95*	*2.05*	*1.91*	*1.66*	*1.73*	*1.58*	*1.63*	*0.30*	*c. Autres*
46. Net income	1.85	2.00	1.89	1.52	1.71	2.51	2.34	1.83	1.90	1.91	46. Résultat net
47. Provisions (net)	0.72	0.87	1.26	1.12	2.82	2.41	1.86	1.13	1.05	0.74	47. Provisions (nettes)
a. Provisions on loans	*0.72*	*0.87*	*1.26*	*1.12*	*2.82*	*2.41*	*1.86*	*1.13*	*1.05*	*0.74*	*a. Provisions sur prêts*
b. Provisions on securities	-	-	-	-	-	-	-	-	-	-	*b. Provisions sur titres*
c. Other	-	-	-	-	-	-	-	-	-	-	*c. Autres*
48. Profit before tax	1.13	1.13	0.63	0.40	-1.11	0.10	0.48	0.70	0.86	1.18	48. Bénéfices avant impôt
49. Income tax	0.44	0.42	0.14	0.18	0.04	0.17	0.19	0.20	0.19	0.28	49. Impôt sur le revenu
50. Profit after tax	0.69	0.71	0.49	0.23	-1.15	-0.07	0.29	0.49	0.66	0.89	50. Bénéfices après impôt
51. Distributed profit	0.08	0.10	0.02	0.13	0.08	0.04	0.06	0.07	0.10	0.11	51. Bénéfices distribués
52. Retained profit	0.61	0.61	0.46	0.10	-1.23	-0.11	0.23	0.42	0.56	0.79	52. Bénéfices mis en réserve
% of gross income											**% du total du résultat brut**
53. Net interest income	76.76	68.05	71.44	71.81	72.32	70.17	66.06	68.31	65.81	64.35	53. Produits financiers nets
54. Non-interest income (net)	23.24	31.95	28.56	28.19	27.68	29.83	33.94	31.69	34.19	35.65	54. Produits non financiers (nets)
a. Fees and commissions receivable	*20.08*	*23.43*	*23.65*	*24.17*	*25.58*	*25.67*	*27.63*	*26.11*	*25.90*	*25.77*	*a. Frais et commissions à recevoir*
b. Fees and commissions payable	-	-	-	-	-	-	-	*1.31*	*2.19*	*2.31*	*b. Frais et commissions à payer*
c. Net profits or loss on financial operations	*1.60*	*4.27*	*1.17*	*1.41*	*-0.81*	*2.65*	*2.40*	*2.28*	*4.29*	*5.78*	*c. Profits ou pertes nets sur opérations financières*
d. Other	*1.55*	*4.24*	*3.74*	*2.61*	*2.91*	*1.50*	*3.91*	*4.61*	*6.20*	*6.41*	*d. Autres*
55. Operating expenses	78.16	73.83	74.07	78.37	75.04	64.77	67.19	72.59	71.03	69.24	55. Frais d'exploitation
a. Staff costs	*43.04*	*40.36*	*36.58*	*37.76*	*36.37*	*32.02*	*32.61*	*37.83*	*36.77*	*35.67*	*a. Dépenses en personnel*
b. Property costs	*11.59*	*11.03*	*10.75*	*11.45*	*10.83*	*9.46*	*10.33*	*11.11*	*9.38*	*28.81*	*b. Dépenses en immobilier*
c. Other	*23.53*	*22.43*	*26.74*	*29.16*	*27.85*	*23.29*	*24.24*	*23.65*	*24.88*	*4.76*	*c. Autres*
56. Net income	21.84	26.17	25.93	21.63	24.96	35.23	32.81	27.41	28.97	30.76	56. Résultat net
57. Provisions (net)	8.51	11.37	17.28	15.94	41.08	33.81	26.03	16.97	15.95	11.82	57. Provisions (nettes)
a. Provisions on loans	*8.51*	*11.37*	*17.28*	*15.94*	*41.08*	*33.81*	*26.03*	*16.97*	*15.95*	*11.82*	*a. Provisions sur prêts*
b. Provisions on securities	-	-	-	-	-	-	-	-	-	-	*b. Provisions sur titres*
c. Other	-	-	-	-	-	-	-	-	-	-	*c. Autres*
58. Profit before tax	13.33	14.81	8.65	5.69	-16.13	1.41	6.78	10.44	13.02	18.94	58. Bénéfices avant impôt
59. Income tax	5.21	5.53	1.99	2.49	0.59	2.35	2.65	3.06	2.92	4.57	59. Impôt sur le revenu
60. Profit after tax	8.13	9.28	6.66	3.20	-16.71	-0.94	4.13	7.38	10.10	14.38	60. Bénéfices après impôt
% of net income											**% du total du résultat net**
61. Provisions (net)	38.96	43.43	66.64	73.70	164.62	95.98	79.34	61.90	55.05	38.42	61. Provisions (nettes)
a. Provisions on loans	*38.96*	*43.43*	*66.64*	*73.70*	*164.62*	*95.98*	*79.34*	*61.90*	*55.05*	*38.42*	*a. Provisions sur prêts*
b. Provisions on securities	-	-	-	-	-	-	-	-	-	-	*b. Provisions sur titres*
c. Other	-	-	-	-	-	-	-	-	-	-	*c. Autres*
62. Profit before tax	61.04	56.57	33.36	26.30	-64.62	4.02	20.66	38.10	44.95	61.58	62. Bénéfices avant impôt
63. Income tax	23.83	21.12	7.66	11.51	2.35	6.68	8.08	11.18	10.08	14.85	63. Impôt sur le revenu
64. Profit after tax	37.21	35.45	25.70	14.80	-66.97	-2.67	12.59	26.92	34.87	46.73	64. Bénéfices après impôt

ICELAND / ISLANDE

Commercial banks and savings banks / Banques commerciales et caisses d'épargne

	1988	1989	1990	1991	1992	1993	1994	1995(1)	1996	1997	
Per cent											*Pourcentage*
BALANCE SHEET ANALYSIS											**ANALYSE DU BILAN**
% of year-end balance sheet total											**% du total du bilan en fin d'exercice**
Assets											**Actif**
65. Cash & balance with Central bank	9.30	9.94	7.12	7.10	5.97	4.63	4.67	4.02	4.55	4.35	65. Caisse & solde auprès de la Banque centrale
66. Interbank deposits	3.35	3.07	2.97	2.90	2.53	4.20	4.58	5.68	6.90	10.34	66. Dépôts interbancaires
67. Loans	79.54	77.24	74.40	75.22	75.58	74.37	77.24	75.10	72.80	68.63	67. Prêts
68. Securities	2.71	4.82	10.56	10.07	11.37	12.33	9.33	10.18	11.30	13.26	68. Valeurs mobilières
69. Other assets	5.10	4.94	4.96	4.71	4.54	4.46	4.18	5.03	4.45	3.41	69. Autres actifs
Liabilities											**Passif**
70. Capital & reserves	7.69	8.09	7.58	8.23	6.82	7.41	7.91	7.97	7.66	7.00	70. Capital et réserves
71. Borrowing from Central bank	2.95	2.40	1.70	1.42	1.03	0.62	1.24	1.84	0.64	1.80	71. Emprunts auprès de la Banque centrale
72. Interbank deposits	1.50	1.31	1.03	1.04	0.98	0.71	0.85	3.07	4.74	4.56	72. Dépôts interbancaires
73. Non-bank deposits	54.57	54.96	58.42	60.13	60.39	61.47	63.94	62.43	58.14	53.33	73. Dépôts non bancaires
74. Bonds	5.68	6.98	8.18	8.08	8.43	8.78	8.86	8.94	10.29	11.81	74. Obligations
75. Other liabilities	27.61	26.27	23.10	21.10	22.34	21.02	17.20	15.75	18.53	21.50	75. Autres engagements
Memorandum items											***Pour mémoire***
76. Short-term securities	*0.11*	*1.43*	*2.75*	*2.20*	*3.41*	*2.80*	*0.87*	*2.40*	*3.00*	*1.55*	*76. Titres à court terme*
77. Bonds	*2.12*	*2.63*	*6.85*	*6.32*	*6.32*	*7.96*	*6.81*	*5.96*	*6.42*	*8.86*	*77. Obligations*
78. Shares and participations	*0.48*	*0.75*	*0.95*	*1.55*	*1.63*	*1.57*	*1.65*	*1.82*	*2.23*	*2.85*	*78. Actions et participations*
79. Claims on non-residents	*1.89*	*1.91*	*2.10*	*1.96*	*1.85*	*2.65*	*3.22*	*1.98*	*2.30*	*3.65*	*79. Créances sur des non-résidents*
80. Liabilities to non-residents	*22.60*	*21.63*	*18.31*	*16.80*	*17.86*	*16.79*	*12.67*	*10.61*	*9.23*	*10.43*	*80. Engagements envers des non-résidents*

* See notes on previous pages.

* Voir les notes en pages précédentes.

IRELAND
All banks

IRLANDE
Ensemble des banques

	1995	1996	1997	
Million Irish pounds				*Millions de livres irlandaises*
INCOME STATEMENT				**COMPTE DE RESULTATS**
1. Interest income	5508.5	6084.9	9182.9	1. Produits financiers
2. Interest expenses	3364.1	3879.8	6457.1	2. Frais financiers
3. Net interest income	2144.4	2205.1	2725.8	3. Produits financiers nets
4. Non-interest income (net)	910.8	1043.7	1393.3	4. Produits non financiers (nets)
a. Fees and commissions receivable	*733.3*	*800.0*	*1062.4*	*a. Frais et commissions à recevoir*
b. Fees and commissions payable	*69.0*	*80.3*	*113.0*	*b. Frais et commissions à payer*
c. Net profits or loss on financial operations	*113.5*	*120.0*	*165.2*	*c. Profits ou pertes nets sur opérations financières*
d. Other	*133.1*	*203.9*	*278.7*	*d. Autres*
5. Gross income	3055.2	3248.8	4119.2	5. Résultat brut
6. Operating expenses	1810.9	1871.2	2401.7	6. Frais d'exploitation
a. Staff costs	*1064.9*	*1090.2*	*1327.6*	*a. Dépenses en personnel*
b. Property costs	*128.0*	*142.3*	*174.1*	*b. Dépenses en immobilier*
c. Other	*617.9*	*638.7*	*900.0*	*c. Autres*
7. Net income	1244.4	1377.6	1717.5	7. Résultat net
8. Provisions (net)	116.7	115.2	157.0	8. Provisions (nettes)
a. Provisions on loans	*115.0*	*113.6*	*154.7*	*a. Provisions sur prêts*
b. Provisions on securities	*1.7*	*0.2*	*1.5*	*b. Provisions sur titres*
c. Other	-	*1.4*	*0.8*	*c. Autres*
9. Profit before tax (1)	1082.3	1268.8	1684.3	9. Bénéfices avant impôt (1)
10. Income tax	309.0	364.3	449.5	10. Impôt sur le revenu
11. Profit after tax	773.2	904.5	1234.8	11. Bénéfices après impôt
12. Distributed profit	296.3	330.9	415.1	12. Bénéfices distribués
13. Retained profit (2)	430.9	552.6	708.5	13. Bénéfices mis en réserve (2)
BALANCE SHEET				**BILAN**
Assets				**Actif**
14. Cash & balance with Central bank	472.2	530.0	681.5	14. Caisse & solde auprès de la Banque centrale
15. Interbank deposits	14951.2	17585.1	27722.0	15. Dépôts interbancaires
16. Loans	43953.9	51878.1	85871.9	16. Prêts
17. Securities	14944.3	18148.8	30034.7	17. Valeurs mobilières
18. Other assets (3)	5487.0	6437.9	11073.0	18. Autres actifs (3)
Liabilities				**Passif**
19. Capital & reserves	5346.6	6318.6	8841.5	19. Capital et réserves
20. Borrowing from Central bank	-	-	-	20. Emprunts auprès de la Banque centrale
21. Interbank deposits	17999.2	22855.1	41344.0	21. Dépôts interbancaires
22. Non-bank deposits	44876.0	49061.3	75622.1	22. Dépôts non bancaires
23. Bonds	6071.1	9294.8	17875.6	23. Obligations
24. Other liabilities (3)	5515.8	7050.1	11699.9	24. Autres engagements (3)
Balance sheet total				**Total du bilan**
25. End-year total	79808.7	94580.0	155383.1	25. En fin d'exercice
26. Average total	72153.8	87194.3	124981.5	26. Moyen

IRELAND / IRLANDE

All banks / Ensemble des banques

	1995	1996	1997	
Million Irish pounds				*Millions de livres irlandaises*
Memorandum items				***Pour mémoire***
27. Short-term securities	*3793.8*	*1392.4*	*4146.5*	*27. Titres à court terme*
28. Bonds	*10973.2*	*16322.9*	*24770.3*	*28. Obligations*
29. Shares and participations	*177.3*	*433.5*	*1118.0*	*29. Actions et participations*
30. Claims on non-residents	*40922.0*	*53253.5*	*92371.7*	*30. Créances sur des non-résidents*
31. Liabilities to non-residents	*42269.5*	*53617.7*	*81934.1*	*31. Engagements envers des non-résidents*
Capital adequacy				***Solvabilité***
32. Tier 1 Capital	*5141.4*	*6211.0*	*8085.7*	*32. Fonds propres de base*
33. Tier 2 Capital	*1713.5*	*2226.1*	*3231.9*	*33. Fonds propres complémentaires*
34. Supervisory deductions	*200.7*	*348.9*	*673.3*	*34. Eléments à déduire des fonds propres*
35. Total net capital resources	*6654.3*	*8088.1*	*10644.3*	*35. Total net des ressources en capital*
36. Risk-weighted assets	*47908.7*	*58221.6*	*81601.1*	*36. Actifs pondérés des risques*
SUPPLEMENTARY INFORMATION				**RENSEIGNEMENTS COMPLEMENTAIRES**
37. Number of institutions	44	48	52	37. Nombre d'institutions
38. Number of branches	1300	1517	1492	38. Nombre de succursales
39. Number of employees (x 1000)	33.3	32.3	44.0	39. Nombre de salariés (x 1000)

1. Profit before tax (item 9) is adjusted by (+) Income from Associate and (-) Exceptional items.

2. Retained profit (item 13) has been adjusted to include (+) Transfer from reserves and (-) Minority interest/Transfers to reserves/Non-equity dividends.

3. Other assets (item 18) and Other liabilities (item 24) include long-term assurance assets/liabilities attributable to policyholders.

Notes

- All banks comprises the following categories of credit institutions:
  - Branches and subsidiaries of Irish-authorised credit institutions
  - Irish branches of non-EEA credit institutions
  - Irish subsidiaries of international banks
  - Building societies
  - 2 State-owned credit institutions
  - 1 savings bank

1. La rubrique Bénéfices avant impôt (poste 9) est corrigé par (+) Revenu d'entreprises associées et (-) Eléments exceptionnels.

2. Les Bénéfices mis en réserve (poste 13) a été ajusté pour prendre en compte (+) les Transferts provenant des réserves et (-) Intérêts minoritaires/Dotations aux réserves, Rémunération de titres hors actions.

3. Les Autres actifs (poste 18) et Autres engagements (poste 24) comprennent les actifs/engagements d'assurance à long terme attribuables aux porteurs de police.

Notes

- Par "Ensemble des banques", on entend les catégories suivantes d'établissements de crédit :
  - Succursales et filiales d'établissements de crédit irlandais agréés
  - Succursales irlandaises d'établissements de crédit de pays non membres de l'EEE
  - Filiales irlandaises de banques internationales
  - Caisses de crédit hypothécaire
  - 2 établissements de crédit publics
  - 1 caisse d'épargne

IRELAND
All banks

IRLANDE
Ensemble des banques

	1995	1996	1997	
Per cent				*Pourcentage*
INCOME STATEMENT ANALYSIS				**ANALYSE DU COMPTE DE RESULTATS**
% of average balance sheet total				**% du total moyen du bilan**
40. Interest income	7.63	6.98	7.35	40. Produits financiers
41. Interest expenses	4.66	4.45	5.17	41. Frais financiers
42. Net interest income	2.97	2.53	2.18	42. Produits financiers nets
43. Non-interest income (net)	1.26	1.20	1.11	43. Produits non financiers (nets)
a. Fees and commissions receivable	*1.02*	*0.92*	*0.85*	*a. Frais et commissions à recevoir*
b. Fees and commissions payable	*0.10*	*0.09*	*0.09*	*b. Frais et commissions à payer*
c. Net profits or loss on financial operations	*0.16*	*0.14*	*0.13*	*c. Profits ou pertes nets sur opérations financières*
d. Other	*0.18*	*0.23*	*0.22*	*d. Autres*
44. Gross income	4.23	3.73	3.30	44. Résultat brut
45. Operating expenses	2.51	2.15	1.92	45. Frais d'exploitation
a. Staff costs	*1.48*	*1.25*	*1.06*	*a. Dépenses en personnel*
b. Property costs	*0.18*	*0.16*	*0.14*	*b. Dépenses en immobilier*
c. Other	*0.86*	*0.73*	*0.72*	*c. Autres*
46. Net income	1.72	1.58	1.37	46. Résultat net
47. Provisions (net)	0.16	0.13	0.13	47. Provisions (nettes)
a. Provisions on loans	*0.16*	*0.13*	*0.12*	*a. Provisions sur prêts*
b. Provisions on securities	-	-	-	*b. Provisions sur titres*
c. Other	-	-	-	*c. Autres*
48. Profit before tax	1.50	1.46	1.35	48. Bénéfices avant impôt
49. Income tax	0.43	0.42	0.36	49. Impôt sur le revenu
50. Profit after tax	1.07	1.04	0.99	50. Bénéfices après impôt
51. Distributed profit	0.41	0.38	0.33	51. Bénéfices distribués
52. Retained profit	0.60	0.63	0.57	52. Bénéfices mis en réserve
% of gross income				**% du total du résultat brut**
53. Net interest income	70.19	67.87	66.17	53. Produits financiers nets
54. Non-interest income (net)	29.81	32.13	33.82	54. Produits non financiers (nets)
a. Fees and commissions receivable	*24.00*	*24.62*	*25.79*	*a. Frais et commissions à recevoir*
b. Fees and commissions payable	*2.26*	*2.47*	*2.74*	*b. Frais et commissions à payer*
c. Net profits or loss on financial operations	*3.71*	*3.69*	*4.01*	*c. Profits ou pertes nets sur opérations financières*
d. Other	*4.36*	*6.28*	*6.77*	*d. Autres*
55. Operating expenses	59.27	57.60	58.31	55. Frais d'exploitation
a. Staff costs	*34.86*	*33.56*	*32.23*	*a. Dépenses en personnel*
b. Property costs	*4.19*	*4.38*	*4.23*	*b. Dépenses en immobilier*
c. Other	*20.22*	*19.66*	*21.85*	*c. Autres*
56. Net income	40.73	42.40	41.69	56. Résultat net
57. Provisions (net)	3.82	3.55	3.81	57. Provisions (nettes)
a. Provisions on loans	*3.76*	*3.50*	*3.76*	*a. Provisions sur prêts*
b. Provisions on securities	*0.06*	*0.01*	*0.04*	*b. Provisions sur titres*
c. Other	-	*0.04*	*0.02*	*c. Autres*
58. Profit before tax	35.42	39.05	40.89	58. Bénéfices avant impôt
59. Income tax	10.11	11.21	10.91	59. Impôt sur le revenu
60. Profit after tax	25.31	27.84	29.98	60. Bénéfices après impôt
% of net income				**% du total du résultat net**
61. Provisions (net)	9.38	8.36	9.14	61. Provisions (nettes)
a. Provisions on loans	*9.24*	*8.25*	*9.01*	*a. Provisions sur prêts*
b. Provisions on securities	*0.14*	*0.01*	*0.09*	*b. Provisions sur titres*
c. Other	-	*0.10*	*0.05*	*c. Autres*
62. Profit before tax	86.97	92.10	98.07	62. Bénéfices avant impôt
63. Income tax	24.83	26.44	26.17	63. Impôt sur le revenu
64. Profit after tax	62.13	65.66	71.90	64. Bénéfices après impôt

IRELAND / IRLANDE

All banks / Ensemble des banques

	1995	1996	1997	
Per cent				*Pourcentage*
BALANCE SHEET ANALYSIS				**ANALYSE DU BILAN**
% of year-end balance sheet total				**% du total du bilan en fin d'exercice**
Assets				**Actif**
65. Cash & balance with Central bank	0.59	0.56	0.44	65. Caisse & solde auprès de la Banque centrale
66. Interbank deposits	18.73	18.59	17.84	66. Dépôts interbancaires
67. Loans	55.07	54.85	55.26	67. Prêts
68. Securities	18.73	19.19	19.33	68. Valeurs mobilières
69. Other assets	6.88	6.81	7.13	69. Autres actifs
Liabilities				**Passif**
70. Capital & reserves	6.70	6.68	5.69	70. Capital et réserves
71. Borrowing from Central bank	-	-	-	71. Emprunts auprès de la Banque centrale
72. Interbank deposits	22.55	24.16	26.61	72. Dépôts interbancaires
73. Non-bank deposits	56.23	51.87	48.67	73. Dépôts non bancaires
74. Bonds	7.61	9.83	11.50	74. Obligations
75. Other liabilities	6.91	7.45	7.53	75. Autres engagements
Memorandum items				***Pour mémoire***
76. Short-term securities	*4.75*	*1.47*	*2.67*	*76. Titres à court terme*
77. Bonds	*13.75*	*17.26*	*15.94*	*77. Obligations*
78. Shares and participations	*0.22*	*0.46*	*0.72*	*78. Actions et participations*
79. Claims on non-residents	*51.28*	*56.31*	*59.45*	*79. Créances sur des non-résidents*
80. Liabilities to non-residents	*52.96*	*56.69*	*52.73*	*80. Engagements envers des non-résidents*

* See notes on previous pages. Voir les notes en pages précédentes.

ITALY
All banks

ITALIE
Ensemble des banques

	1988	1989	1990	1991	1992	1993	1994	1995	1996	1997	
Billion lire											*Milliards de lires*
INCOME STATEMENT											**COMPTE DE RESULTATS**
1. Interest income	114815	132845	149666	161368	193086	207621	182831	203631	200680	177553	1. Produits financiers
2. Interest expenses	73378	86595	97592	105253	126996	140339	119755	134939	132928	113929	2. Frais financiers
3. Net interest income	41437	46250	52074	56115	66090	67282	63076	68692	67752	63623	3. Produits financiers nets
4. Non-interest income (net)	12896	12830	15113	16280	13745	24646	18689	17355	22437	26029	4. Produits non financiers (nets)
a. Fees and commissions receivable	*5747*	*6106*	*6554*	*7155*	*9024*	*9741*	*10057*	*9424*	*10682*	*14506*	*a. Frais et commissions à recevoir*
b. Fees and commissions payable	*1459*	*1982*	*3292*	*4249*	*6480*	*3984*	*2203*	*2358*	*2625*	*2841*	*b. Frais et commissions à payer*
c. Net profits or loss on financial operations	*1803*	*2000*	*2527*	*2669*	*3109*	*1538*	*1193*	*874*	*1171*	*3374*	*c. Profits ou pertes nets sur opérations financières*
d. Other	*6805*	*6706*	*9324*	*10705*	*8092*	*17351*	*9642*	*9414*	*13210*	*10991*	*d. Autres*
5. Gross income	54333	59080	67187	72395	79835	91928	81764	86047	90189	89653	5. Résultat brut
6. Operating expenses	34253	37009	41720	47016	52608	56217	56222	58695	60503	61919	6. Frais d'exploitation
a. Staff costs	*22609*	*24701*	*27469*	*30774*	*33836*	*35623*	*36650*	*37553*	*39144*	*38911*	*a. Dépenses en personnel*
b. Property costs	*9440*	*10385*	*11735*	*13371*	*15163*	*16205*	*15886*	*16754*	*16996*	*18517*	*b. Dépenses en immobilier*
c. Other	*2204*	*1923*	*2516*	*2871*	*3609*	*4389*	*3686*	*4389*	*4364*	*4492*	*c. Autres*
7. Net income	20080	22071	25467	25379	27227	35711	25542	27352	29686	27733	7. Résultat net
8. Provisions (net)	7798	8817	10010	9391	12937	17512	18955	18728	17202	19001	8. Provisions (nettes)
a. Provisions on loans	*2334*	*7265*	*8444*	*8770*	*10009*	*16441*	*11935*	*16386*	*12228*	*15775*	*a. Provisions sur prêts*
b. Provisions on securities	*1120*	*1394*	*675*	*412*	*3160*	*60*	*6040*	*-208*	*-683*	*-675*	*b. Provisions sur titres*
c. Other	*4344*	*158*	*891*	*209*	*-232*	*1011*	*980*	*2550*	*5657*	*3901*	*c. Autres*
9. Profit before tax	12282	13254	15457	15988	14290	18199	6587	8624	12485	8732	9. Bénéfices avant impôt
10. Income tax	5345	6161	6490	7198	7540	12638	5399	7992	7957	7583	10. Impôt sur le revenu
11. Profit after tax	6937	7093	8967	8790	6750	5561	1188	631	4528	1149	11. Bénéfices après impôt
12. Distributed profit	2096	2235	2690	2943	3524	3339	2727	3327	3980	4375	12. Bénéfices distribués
13. Retained profit	4841	4858	6277	5847	3226	2222	-1540	-2696	548	-3226	13. Bénéfices mis en réserve
BALANCE SHEET											**BILAN**
Assets											**Actif**
14. Cash & balance with Central bank	105833	116793	128632	132872	131947	108514	92683	78984	80792	86795	14. Caisse & solde auprès de la Banque centrale
15. Interbank deposits	99439	116797	95018	97380	157731	171104	165105	151689	180349	184485	15. Dépôts interbancaires
16. Loans	552421	667177	775334	885151	988281	1028446	1039247	1073005	1077372	1157992	16. Prêts
17. Securities	231854	224628	221493	274021	327281	349770	385660	351959	381534	343139	17. Valeurs mobilières
18. Other assets	357497	451087	478550	548687	648868	754412	782197	874349	960585	1038170	18. Autres actifs
Liabilities											**Passif**
19. Capital & reserves	71643	84402	92686	122069	147918	155355	165646	164302	168848	174789	19. Capital et réserves
20. Borrowing from Central bank	5749	6334	7600	8858	8936	2722	2834	7989	1897	2854	20. Emprunts auprès de la Banque centrale
21. Interbank deposits	110274	133963	105370	103221	159231	179086	166644	166029	190655	199088	21. Dépôts interbancaires
22. Non-bank deposits	610840	678142	751263	819278	851220	919115	922392	934382	949687	880490	22. Dépôts non bancaires
23. Bonds	120577	129641	135872	153174	166407	194113	217028	216626	276202	377376	23. Obligations
24. Other liabilities	427962	544001	606237	731513	920394	961856	990349	1040657	1093344	1175984	24. Autres engagements
Balance sheet total											**Total du bilan**
25. End-year total	1347045	1576483	1699027	1938112	2254107	2412247	2464892	2529985	2680633	2810581	25. En fin d'exercice
26. Average total	1234140	1397449	1547585	1705251	2033386	2249923	2363863	2408554	2504135	2658212	26. Moyen

ITALY
All banks

ITALIE
Ensemble des banques

	1988	1989	1990	1991	1992	1993	1994	1995	1996	1997	
Billion lire											*Milliards de lires*
Memorandum items											***Pour mémoire***
27. Short-term securities	*22442*	*24706*	*29388*	*31634*	*31210*	*74863*	*68453*	*44628*	*52664*	*32069*	*27. Titres à court terme*
28. Bonds	*209412*	*199922*	*192104*	*242387*	*296072*	*274908*	*317207*	*307331*	*328871*	*311070*	*28. Obligations*
29. Shares and participations	*18530*	*24029*	*26348*	*37438*	*41643*	*43427*	*50065*	*51203*	*57210*	*62558*	*29. Actions et participations*
30. Claims on non-residents	*86561*	*110370*	*116102*	*124897*	*165178*	*229057*	*201917*	*231097*	*293861*	*310563*	*30. Créances sur des non-résidents*
31. Liabilities to non-residents	*159526*	*205534*	*232106*	*279740*	*367477*	*369979*	*375505*	*343459*	*357361*	*390454*	*31. Engagements envers des non-résidents*
Capital adequacy											***Solvabilité***
32. Tier 1 Capital	..	..	..	*113611*	*131471*	*141709*	*146279*	*147364*	*151794*	*158374*	*32. Fonds propres de base*
33. Tier 2 Capital	..	..	..	*36839*	*31541*	*31222*	*29566*	*35947*	*36007*	*37747*	*33. Fonds propres complémentaires*
34. Supervisory deductions	..	..	..	*6055*	*6545*	*5823*	*6130*	*7082*	*6054*	*6324*	*34. Eléments à déduire des fonds propres*
35. Total net capital resources	..	..	..	*144395*	*156467*	*167108*	*169715*	*176229*	*181747*	*189797*	*35. Total net des ressources en capital*
36. Risk-weighted assets	..	..	..	..	*1359188*	*1364512*	*1389998*	*1434125*	*1409444*	*1504290*	*36. Actifs pondérés des risques*
SUPPLEMENTARY INFORMATION											**RENSEIGNEMENTS COMPLEMENTAIRES**
37. Number of institutions	403	391	379	368	351	335	284	271	264	255	37. Nombre d'institutions
38. Number of branches	13316	13677	14711	16309	17582	18926	19925	20840	21438	22323	38. Nombre de succursales
39. Number of employees (x 1000)	325.3	325.7	330.9	336.6	337.3	340.0	338.5	337.5	327.1	322.2	39. Nombre de salariés (x 1000)

Notes

- All banks comprises the following categories of banks:
  - Limited company banks
  - Co-operative banks
  - Main mutual banks
  - Central credit institutions
  - Branches of foreign banks
- Average balance sheet totals (item 26) are a weighted average of monthly data.

Notes

- "L'Ensemble des banques" regroupe les catégories suivantes:
  - Banques société anonyme
  - Banques mutualistes
  - Mutuelles principales
  - Institutions centrales de crédit
  - Succursales de banques étrangères
- La moyenne du total des actifs/passifs (poste 26) est une moyenne pondérée des données mensuelles.

ITALY — ITALIE

All banks — Ensemble des banques

	1988	1989	1990	1991	1992	1993	1994	1995	1996	1997	
Per cent											*Pourcentage*
INCOME STATEMENT ANALYSIS											**ANALYSE DU COMPTE DE RESULTATS**
% of average balance sheet total											**% du total moyen du bilan**
40. Interest income	9.30	9.51	9.67	9.46	9.50	9.23	7.73	8.45	8.01	6.68	40. Produits financiers
41. Interest expenses	5.95	6.20	6.31	6.17	6.25	6.24	5.07	5.60	5.31	4.29	41. Frais financiers
42. Net interest income	3.36	3.31	3.36	3.29	3.25	2.99	2.67	2.85	2.71	2.39	42. Produits financiers nets
43. Non-interest income (net)	1.04	0.92	0.98	0.95	0.68	1.10	0.79	0.72	0.90	0.98	43. Produits non financiers (nets)
a. Fees and commissions receivable	*0.47*	*0.44*	*0.42*	*0.42*	*0.44*	*0.43*	*0.43*	*0.39*	*0.43*	*0.55*	*a. Frais et commissions à recevoir*
b. Fees and commissions payable	*0.12*	*0.14*	*0.21*	*0.25*	*0.32*	*0.18*	*0.09*	*0.10*	*0.10*	*0.11*	*b. Frais et commissions à payer*
c. Net profits or loss on financial operations	*0.15*	*0.14*	*0.16*	*0.16*	*0.15*	*0.07*	*0.05*	*0.04*	*0.05*	*0.13*	*c. Profits ou pertes nets sur opérations financières*
d. Other	*0.55*	*0.48*	*0.60*	*0.63*	*0.40*	*0.77*	*0.41*	*0.39*	*0.53*	*0.41*	*d. Autres*
44. Gross income	4.40	4.23	4.34	4.25	3.93	4.09	3.46	3.57	3.60	3.37	44. Résultat brut
45. Operating expenses	2.78	2.65	2.70	2.76	2.59	2.50	2.38	2.44	2.42	2.33	45. Frais d'exploitation
a. Staff costs	*1.83*	*1.77*	*1.77*	*1.80*	*1.66*	*1.58*	*1.55*	*1.56*	*1.56*	*1.46*	*a. Dépenses en personnel*
b. Property costs	*0.76*	*0.74*	*0.76*	*0.78*	*0.75*	*0.72*	*0.67*	*0.70*	*0.68*	*0.70*	*b. Dépenses en immobilier*
c. Other	*0.18*	*0.14*	*0.16*	*0.17*	*0.18*	*0.20*	*0.16*	*0.18*	*0.17*	*0.17*	*c. Autres*
46. Net income	1.63	1.58	1.65	1.49	1.34	1.59	1.08	1.14	1.19	1.04	46. Résultat net
47. Provisions (net)	0.63	0.63	0.65	0.55	0.64	0.78	0.80	0.78	0.69	0.71	47. Provisions (nettes)
a. Provisions on loans	*0.19*	*0.52*	*0.55*	*0.51*	*0.49*	*0.73*	*0.50*	*0.68*	*0.49*	*0.59*	*a. Provisions sur prêts*
b. Provisions on securities	*0.09*	*0.10*	*0.04*	*0.02*	*0.16*	-	*0.26*	*-0.01*	*-0.03*	*-0.03*	*b. Provisions sur titres*
c. Other	*0.35*	*0.01*	*0.06*	*0.01*	*-0.01*	*0.04*	*0.04*	*0.11*	*0.23*	*0.15*	*c. Autres*
48. Profit before tax	1.00	0.95	1.00	0.94	0.70	0.81	0.28	0.36	0.50	0.33	48. Bénéfices avant impôt
49. Income tax	0.43	0.44	0.42	0.42	0.37	0.56	0.23	0.33	0.32	0.29	49. Impôt sur le revenu
50. Profit after tax	0.56	0.51	0.58	0.52	0.33	0.25	0.05	0.03	0.18	0.04	50. Bénéfices après impôt
51. Distributed profit	0.17	0.16	0.17	0.17	0.17	0.15	0.12	0.14	0.16	0.16	51. Bénéfices distribués
52. Retained profit	0.39	0.35	0.41	0.34	0.16	0.10	-0.07	-0.11	0.02	-0.12	52. Bénéfices mis en réserve
% of gross income											**% du total du résultat brut**
53. Net interest income	76.26	78.28	77.51	77.51	82.78	73.19	77.14	79.83	75.12	70.97	53. Produits financiers nets
54. Non-interest income (net)	23.74	21.72	22.49	22.49	17.22	26.81	22.86	20.17	24.88	29.03	54. Produits non financiers (nets)
a. Fees and commissions receivable	*10.58*	*10.34*	*9.75*	*9.88*	*11.30*	*10.60*	*12.30*	*10.95*	*11.84*	*16.18*	*a. Frais et commissions à recevoir*
b. Fees and commissions payable	*2.69*	*3.35*	*4.90*	*5.87*	*8.12*	*4.33*	*2.69*	*2.74*	*2.91*	*3.17*	*b. Frais et commissions à payer*
c. Net profits or loss on financial operations	*3.32*	*3.39*	*3.76*	*3.69*	*3.89*	*1.67*	*1.46*	*1.02*	*1.30*	*3.76*	*c. Profits ou pertes nets sur opérations financières*
d. Other	*12.52*	*11.35*	*13.88*	*14.79*	*10.14*	*18.87*	*11.79*	*10.94*	*14.65*	*12.26*	*d. Autres*
55. Operating expenses	63.04	62.64	62.10	64.94	65.90	61.15	68.76	68.21	67.08	69.07	55. Frais d'exploitation
a. Staff costs	*41.61*	*41.81*	*40.88*	*42.51*	*42.38*	*38.75*	*44.82*	*43.64*	*43.40*	*43.40*	*a. Dépenses en personnel*
b. Property costs	*17.37*	*17.58*	*17.47*	*18.47*	*18.99*	*17.63*	*19.43*	*19.47*	*18.84*	*20.65*	*b. Dépenses en immobilier*
c. Other	*4.06*	*3.25*	*3.74*	*3.97*	*4.52*	*4.77*	*4.51*	*5.10*	*4.84*	*5.01*	*c. Autres*
56. Net income	36.96	37.36	37.90	35.06	34.10	38.85	31.24	31.79	32.92	30.93	56. Résultat net
57. Provisions (net)	14.35	14.92	14.90	12.97	16.20	19.05	23.18	21.76	19.07	21.19	57. Provisions (nettes)
a. Provisions on loans	*4.30*	*12.30*	*12.57*	*12.11*	*12.54*	*17.88*	*14.60*	*19.04*	*13.56*	*17.60*	*a. Provisions sur prêts*
b. Provisions on securities	*2.06*	*2.36*	*1.00*	*0.57*	*3.96*	*0.07*	*7.39*	*-0.24*	*-0.76*	*-0.75*	*b. Provisions sur titres*
c. Other	*8.00*	*0.27*	*1.33*	*0.29*	*-0.29*	*1.10*	*1.20*	*2.96*	*6.27*	*4.35*	*c. Autres*
58. Profit before tax	22.61	22.43	23.01	22.08	17.90	19.80	8.06	10.02	13.84	9.74	58. Bénéfices avant impôt
59. Income tax	9.84	10.43	9.66	9.94	9.44	13.75	6.60	9.29	8.82	8.46	59. Impôt sur le revenu
60. Profit after tax	12.77	12.01	13.35	12.14	8.45	6.05	1.45	0.73	5.02	1.28	60. Bénéfices après impôt
% of net income											**% du total du résultat net**
61. Provisions (net)	38.83	39.95	39.31	37.00	47.52	49.04	74.21	68.47	57.95	68.51	61. Provisions (nettes)
a. Provisions on loans	*11.62*	*32.92*	*33.16*	*34.56*	*36.76*	*46.04*	*46.73*	*59.91*	*41.19*	*56.88*	*a. Provisions sur prêts*
b. Provisions on securities	*5.58*	*6.32*	*2.65*	*1.62*	*11.61*	*0.17*	*23.65*	*-0.76*	*-2.30*	*-2.43*	*b. Provisions sur titres*
c. Other	*21.63*	*0.72*	*3.50*	*0.82*	*-0.85*	*2.83*	*3.84*	*9.32*	*19.06*	*14.07*	*c. Autres*
62. Profit before tax	61.17	60.05	60.69	63.00	52.48	50.96	25.79	31.53	42.06	31.49	62. Bénéfices avant impôt
63. Income tax	26.62	27.91	25.48	28.36	27.69	35.39	21.14	29.22	26.80	27.34	63. Impôt sur le revenu
64. Profit after tax	34.55	32.14	35.21	34.63	24.79	15.57	4.65	2.31	15.25	4.14	64. Bénéfices après impôt

ITALY
All banks

ITALIE
Ensemble des banques

	1988	1989	1990	1991	1992	1993	1994	1995	1996	1997	
Per cent											*Pourcentage*
BALANCE SHEET ANALYSIS											**ANALYSE DU BILAN**
% of year-end balance sheet total											**% du total du bilan en fin d'exercice**
Assets											**Actif**
65. Cash & balance with Central bank	7.86	7.41	7.57	6.86	5.85	4.50	3.76	3.12	3.01	3.09	65. Caisse & solde auprès de la Banque centrale
66. Interbank deposits	7.38	7.41	5.59	5.02	7.00	7.09	6.70	6.00	6.73	6.56	66. Dépôts interbancaires
67. Loans	41.01	42.32	45.63	45.67	43.84	42.63	42.16	42.41	40.19	41.20	67. Prêts
68. Securities	17.21	14.25	13.04	14.14	14.52	14.50	15.65	13.91	14.23	12.21	68. Valeurs mobilières
69. Other assets	26.54	28.61	28.17	28.31	28.79	31.27	31.73	34.56	35.83	36.94	69. Autres actifs
Liabilities											**Passif**
70. Capital & reserves	5.32	5.35	5.46	6.30	6.56	6.44	6.72	6.49	6.30	6.22	70. Capital et réserves
71. Borrowing from Central bank	0.43	0.40	0.45	0.46	0.40	0.11	0.11	0.32	0.07	0.10	71. Emprunts auprès de la Banque centrale
72. Interbank deposits	8.19	8.50	6.20	5.33	7.06	7.42	6.76	6.56	7.11	7.08	72. Dépôts interbancaires
73. Non-bank deposits	45.35	43.02	44.22	42.27	37.76	38.10	37.42	36.93	35.43	31.33	73. Dépôts non bancaires
74. Bonds	8.95	8.22	8.00	7.90	7.38	8.05	8.80	8.56	10.30	13.43	74. Obligations
75. Other liabilities	31.77	34.51	35.68	37.74	40.83	39.87	40.18	41.13	40.79	41.84	75. Autres engagements
Memorandum items											***Pour mémoire***
76. Short-term securities	*1.67*	*1.57*	*1.73*	*1.63*	*1.38*	*3.10*	*2.78*	*1.76*	*1.96*	*1.14*	*76. Titres à court terme*
77. Bonds	*15.55*	*12.68*	*11.31*	*12.51*	*13.13*	*11.40*	*12.87*	*12.15*	*12.27*	*11.07*	*77. Obligations*
78. Shares and participations	*1.38*	*1.52*	*1.55*	*1.93*	*1.85*	*1.80*	*2.03*	*2.02*	*2.13*	*2.23*	*78. Actions et participations*
79. Claims on non-residents	*6.43*	*7.00*	*6.83*	*6.44*	*7.33*	*9.50*	*8.19*	*9.13*	*10.96*	*11.05*	*79. Créances sur des non-résidents*
80. Liabilities to non-residents	*11.84*	*13.04*	*13.66*	*14.43*	*16.30*	*15.34*	*15.23*	*13.58*	*13.33*	*13.89*	*80. Engagements envers des non-résidents*

* See notes on previous pages.

* Voir les notes en pages précédentes.

JAPAN

Commercial banks

JAPON

Banques commerciales

	1988	1989	1990	1991	1992	1993	1994	1995	1996	1997	
100 million yen											*100 millions de yen*
INCOME STATEMENT											**COMPTE DE RESULTATS**
1. Interest income	281848	388258	481476	462453	360912	301478	281579	278801	245896	210308	1. Produits financiers
2. Interest expenses	211888	318008	413323	379443	269818	214466	189919	178634	148361	118791	2. Frais financiers
3. Net interest income	69960	70250	68153	83010	91094	87012	91660	100168	97535	91517	3. Produits financiers nets
4. Non-interest income (net)	24369	21992	21663	10197	3489	2702	-2945	1992	-5229	5865	4. Produits non financiers (nets)
a. Fees and commissions receivable	..	..	..	..	..	..	..	*14968*	*14989*	*15083*	*a. Frais et commissions à recevoir*
b. Fees and commissions payable	..	..	..	..	..	..	..	*5489*	*5550*	*5657*	*b. Frais et commissions à payer*
c. Net profits or loss on financial operations	..	..	..	..	..	..	..	*-7316*	*-15143*	*-8111*	*c. Profits ou pertes nets sur opérations financières*
d. Other	..	..	..	..	..	..	..	*-170*	*475*	*4550*	*d. Autres*
5. Gross income	94329	92242	89816	93207	94583	89714	88716	102160	92305	97382	5. Résultat brut
6. Operating expenses	52811	56619	60639	64193	66294	67111	67730	67977	70006	69376	6. Frais d'exploitation
a. Staff costs	*29558*	*30796*	*32255*	*33713*	*34624*	*35312*	*35507*	*35628*	*35146*	*34888*	*a. Dépenses en personnel*
b. Property costs	..	..	..	..	..	..	..	*28478*	*31172*	*30471*	*b. Dépenses en immobilier*
c. Other	..	..	..	..	..	..	..	*3869*	*3686*	*4014*	*c. Autres*
7. Net income	41518	35623	29177	29014	28289	22603	20986	34183	22299	28006	7. Résultat net
8. Provisions (net)	3147	3101	2125	5335	9612	9739	13054	45842	19931	62804	8. Provisions (nettes)
a. Provisions on loans	*2851*	*2937*	*2009*	*5480*	*9329*	*9550*	*13019*	*45760*	*19753*	*65317*	*a. Provisions sur prêts*
b. Provisions on securities (1)	*296*	*164*	*116*	*-145*	*283*	*189*	*35*	*82*	*177*	*-2513*	*b. Provisions sur titres (1)*
c. Other	-	-	-	-	-	-	-	-	-	-	*c. Autres*
9. Profit before tax	38371	32522	27052	23679	18677	12864	7932	-11659	2367	-34798	9. Bénéfices avant impôt
10. Income tax	20235	15521	12743	12628	11084	6137	5849	10980	2303	5391	10. Impôt sur le revenu
11. Profit after tax	18136	17001	14309	11051	7593	6727	2083	-22639	64	-40189	11. Bénéfices après impôt
12. Distributed profit	1493	1638	1694	1697	1706	1685	1756	1446	1727	1903	12. Bénéfices distribués
13. Retained profit	16643	15363	12615	9354	5887	5042	327	-24085	-1663	-42092	13. Bénéfices mis en réserve
BALANCE SHEET											**BILAN**
Assets											**Actif**
14. Cash & balance with Central bank (2)	..	..	..	..	..	..	..	..	..	..	14. Caisse & solde auprès de la Banque centrale (2)
15. Interbank deposits	994636	1232259	1010134	845110	710380	737768	679009	596516	520874	413237	15. Dépôts interbancaires
16. Loans	3537651	4098926	4330109	4484647	4538361	4520965	4520184	4653040	4714569	4564309	16. Prêts
17. Securities	835621	1014487	1022177	978035	960568	952841	983659	998309	1012661	994871	17. Valeurs mobilières
18. Other assets	1037496	1287869	1170455	1138940	786390	711979	705356	713139	772029	992493	18. Autres actifs
Liabilities											**Passif**
19. Capital & reserves	175958	226715	239712	249044	253907	258587	258042	233091	238884	196544	19. Capital et réserves
20. Borrowing from Central bank	46336	33141	35555	30535	39738	39515	28183	8244	6231	47702	20. Emprunts auprès de la Banque centrale
21. Interbank deposits (3)	..	..	..	..	..	..	..	..	..	..	21. Dépôts interbancaires (3)
22. Non-bank deposits	4906164	5808225	5736884	5554169	5357468	5363045	5394567	5412819	5421534	5221281	22. Dépôts non bancaires
23. Bonds	57657	58214	55069	56237	56566	54374	58466	70157	70111	64559	23. Obligations
24. Other liabilities	1219289	1507246	1465655	1556746	1288020	1208032	1148950	1236692	1283375	1434824	24. Autres engagements
Balance sheet total											**Total du bilan**
25. End-year total	6405404	7633541	7532875	7446732	6995699	6923553	6888208	6961003	7020135	6964910	25. En fin d'exercice
26. Average total	5971836	7019472	7583208	7489804	7221216	6959626	6905881	6924606	6990569	6992522	26. Moyen

JAPAN
Commercial banks

JAPON
Banques commerciales

	1988	1989	1990	1991	1992	1993	1994	1995	1996	1997	
100 million yen											*100 millions de yen*
Memorandum items											***Pour mémoire***
27. Short-term securities	..	..	..	..	..	..	..	..	..	..	*27. Titres à court terme*
28. Bonds	..	..	..	..	..	..	..	..	..	..	*28. Obligations*
29. Shares and participations	*173678*	*219140*	*247808*	*258658*	*258058*	*271948*	*300249*	*323250*	*329416*	*332399*	*29. Actions et participations*
30. Claims on non-residents	..	..	..	..	..	..	..	..	..	..	*30. Créances sur des non-résidents*
31. Liabilities to non-residents	..	..	..	..	..	..	..	..	..	..	*31. Engagements envers des non-résidents*
Capital adequacy											***Solvabilité***
32. Tier 1 Capital	..	..	..	..	..	..	..	*238614*	*245248*	*255955*	*32. Fonds propres de base*
33. Tier 2 Capital	..	..	..	..	..	..	..	*195991*	*187011*	*211711*	*33. Fonds propres complémentaires*
34. Supervisory deductions	..	..	..	..	..	..	..	-	-	*130*	*34. Eléments à déduire des fonds propres*
35. Total net capital resources	..	..	..	..	..	..	..	*434605*	*432260*	*467537*	*35. Total net des ressources en capital*
36. Risk-weighted assets	..	..	..	..	..	..	..	*4699002*	*4710222*	*4853411*	*36. Actifs pondérés des risques*
SUPPLEMENTARY INFORMATION											**RENSEIGNEMENTS COMPLEMENTAIRES**
37. Number of institutions	145	145	144	143	141	140	140	139	136	136	37. Nombre d'institutions
38. Number of branches	13727	14045	14325	14632	14782	14804	14823	14693	14567	14395	38. Nombre de succursales
39. Number of employees (x 1000)	397.0	397.0	399.0	406.0	412.0	417.0	414.0	399.6	383.0	367.1	39. Nombre de salariés (x 1000)

1. In 1997, the main components of Provisions on securities (item 8.b) were abolished in the Japanese accounting system. The 1997 figure represents the outflow of the assets of this item. Thereafter, the amount for this item will be negligible.

2. Cash and balance with Central bank (item 14) is included under Interbank deposits (item 15).

3. Interbank deposits (item 21) are included under Non-bank deposits (item 22).

Notes

- The term Commercial banks corresponds to the term Ordinary banks used in Japanese publications.
- Data relate to fiscal years ending 31st March.

1. En 1997, les principales composantes des Provisions sur titres (poste 8.b) ont été supprimées du système de comptabilité japonais. Le montant publié pour l'année 1997 correspond à la sortie des actifs de ce poste. Par la suite, ce montant sera négligeable.

2. Caisse et solde auprès de la Banque centrale (poste 14) est inclus sous Dépôts interbancaires (poste 15).

3. Les Dépôts interbancaires (poste 21) sont inclus sous Dépôts non bancaires (poste 22).

Notes

- Le terme, Banques commerciales correspond au terme Ordinary banks utilisé dans les publications japonaises.
- Les données portent sur l'exercice financier qui se termine le 31 mars

JAPAN / JAPON
Commercial banks / Banques commerciales

	1988	1989	1990	1991	1992	1993	1994	1995	1996	1997	
Per cent											*Pourcentage*
INCOME STATEMENT ANALYSIS											**ANALYSE DU COMPTE DE RESULTATS**
% of average balance sheet total											**% du total moyen du bilan**
40. Interest income	4.72	5.53	6.35	6.17	5.00	4.33	4.08	4.03	3.52	3.01	40. Produits financiers
41. Interest expenses	3.55	4.53	5.45	5.07	3.74	3.08	2.75	2.58	2.12	1.70	41. Frais financiers
42. Net interest income	1.17	1.00	0.90	1.11	1.26	1.25	1.33	1.45	1.40	1.31	42. Produits financiers nets
43. Non-interest income (net)	0.41	0.31	0.29	0.14	0.05	0.04	-0.04	0.03	-0.07	0.08	43. Produits non financiers (nets)
a. Fees and commissions receivable	..	..	..	..	..	..	..	*0.22*	*0.21*	*0.22*	*a. Frais et commissions à recevoir*
b. Fees and commissions payable	..	..	..	..	..	..	..	*0.08*	*0.08*	*0.08*	*b. Frais et commissions à payer*
c. Net profits or loss on financial operations	..	..	..	..	..	..	..	*-0.11*	*-0.22*	*-0.12*	*c. Profits ou pertes nets sur opérations financières*
d. Other	..	..	..	..	..	..	..	-	*0.01*	*0.07*	*d. Autres*
44. Gross income	1.58	1.31	1.18	1.24	1.31	1.29	1.28	1.48	1.32	1.39	44. Résultat brut
45. Operating expenses	0.88	0.81	0.80	0.86	0.92	0.96	0.98	0.98	1.00	0.99	45. Frais d'exploitation
a. Staff costs	*0.49*	*0.44*	*0.43*	*0.45*	*0.48*	*0.51*	*0.51*	*0.51*	*0.50*	*0.50*	*a. Dépenses en personnel*
b. Property costs	..	..	..	..	..	..	..	*0.41*	*0.45*	*0.44*	*b. Dépenses en immobilier*
c. Other	..	..	..	..	..	..	..	*0.06*	*0.05*	*0.06*	*c. Autres*
46. Net income	0.70	0.51	0.38	0.39	0.39	0.32	0.30	0.49	0.32	0.40	46. Résultat net
47. Provisions (net)	0.05	0.04	0.03	0.07	0.13	0.14	0.19	0.66	0.29	0.90	47. Provisions (nettes)
a. Provisions on loans	*0.05*	*0.04*	*0.03*	*0.07*	*0.13*	*0.14*	*0.19*	*0.66*	*0.28*	*0.93*	*a. Provisions sur prêts*
b. Provisions on securities	-	-	-	-	-	-	-	-	-	*-0.04*	*b. Provisions sur titres*
c. Other	-	-	-	-	-	-	-	-	-	-	*c. Autres*
48. Profit before tax	0.64	0.46	0.36	0.32	0.26	0.18	0.11	-0.17	0.03	-0.50	48. Bénéfices avant impôt
49. Income tax	0.34	0.22	0.17	0.17	0.15	0.09	0.08	0.16	0.03	0.08	49. Impôt sur le revenu
50. Profit after tax	0.30	0.24	0.19	0.15	0.11	0.10	0.03	-0.33	-	-0.57	50. Bénéfices après impôt
51. Distributed profit	0.03	0.02	0.02	0.02	0.02	0.02	0.03	0.02	0.02	0.03	51. Bénéfices distribués
52. Retained profit	0.28	0.22	0.17	0.12	0.08	0.07	-	-0.35	-0.02	-0.60	52. Bénéfices mis en réserve
% of gross income											**% du total du résultat brut**
53. Net interest income	74.17	76.16	75.88	89.06	96.31	96.99	103.32	98.05	105.67	93.98	53. Produits financiers nets
54. Non-interest income (net)	25.83	23.84	24.12	10.94	3.69	3.01	-3.32	1.95	-5.66	6.02	54. Produits non financiers (nets)
a. Fees and commissions receivable	..	..	..	..	..	..	..	*14.65*	*16.24*	*15.49*	*a. Frais et commissions à recevoir*
b. Fees and commissions payable	..	..	..	..	..	..	..	*5.37*	*6.01*	*5.81*	*b. Frais et commissions à payer*
c. Net profits or loss on financial operations	..	..	..	..	..	..	..	*-7.16*	*-16.41*	*-8.33*	*c. Profits ou pertes nets sur opérations financières*
d. Other	..	..	..	..	..	..	..	*-0.17*	*0.51*	*4.67*	*d. Autres*
55. Operating expenses	55.99	61.38	67.51	68.87	70.09	74.81	76.34	66.54	75.84	71.24	55. Frais d'exploitation
a. Staff costs	*31.34*	*33.39*	*35.91*	*36.17*	*36.61*	*39.36*	*40.02*	*34.87*	*38.08*	*35.83*	*a. Dépenses en personnel*
b. Property costs	..	..	..	..	..	..	..	*27.88*	*33.77*	*31.29*	*b. Dépenses en immobilier*
c. Other	..	..	..	..	..	..	..	*3.79*	*3.99*	*4.12*	*c. Autres*
56. Net income	44.01	38.62	32.49	31.13	29.91	25.19	23.66	33.46	24.16	28.76	56. Résultat net
57. Provisions (net)	3.34	3.36	2.37	5.72	10.16	10.86	14.71	44.87	21.59	64.49	57. Provisions (nettes)
a. Provisions on loans	*3.02*	*3.18*	*2.24*	*5.88*	*9.86*	*10.64*	*14.67*	*44.79*	*21.40*	*67.07*	*a. Provisions sur prêts*
b. Provisions on securities	*0.31*	*0.18*	*0.13*	*-0.16*	*0.30*	*0.21*	*0.04*	*0.08*	*0.19*	*-2.58*	*b. Provisions sur titres*
c. Other	-	-	-	-	-	-	-	-	-	-	*c. Autres*
58. Profit before tax	40.68	35.26	30.12	25.40	19.75	14.34	8.94	-11.41	2.56	-35.73	58. Bénéfices avant impôt
59. Income tax	21.45	16.83	14.19	13.55	11.72	6.84	6.59	10.75	2.49	5.54	59. Impôt sur le revenu
60. Profit after tax	19.23	18.43	15.93	11.86	8.03	7.50	2.35	-22.16	0.07	-41.27	60. Bénéfices après impôt
% of net income											**% du total du résultat net**
61. Provisions (net)	7.58	8.71	7.28	18.39	33.98	43.09	62.20	134.11	89.38	224.25	61. Provisions (nettes)
a. Provisions on loans	*6.87*	*8.24*	*6.89*	*18.89*	*32.98*	*42.25*	*62.04*	*133.87*	*88.58*	*233.23*	*a. Provisions sur prêts*
b. Provisions on securities	*0.71*	*0.46*	*0.40*	*-0.50*	*1.00*	*0.84*	*0.17*	*0.24*	*0.79*	*-8.97*	*b. Provisions sur titres*
c. Other	-	-	-	-	-	-	-	-	-	-	*c. Autres*
62. Profit before tax	92.42	91.29	92.72	81.61	66.02	56.91	37.80	-34.11	10.61	-124.25	62. Bénéfices avant impôt
63. Income tax	48.74	43.57	43.67	43.52	39.18	27.15	27.87	32.12	10.33	19.25	63. Impôt sur le revenu
64. Profit after tax	43.68	47.72	49.04	38.09	26.84	29.76	9.93	-66.23	0.29	-143.50	64. Bénéfices après impôt

JAPAN
Commercial banks

JAPON
Banques commerciales

	1988	1989	1990	1991	1992	1993	1994	1995	1996	1997	
Per cent											*Pourcentage*
BALANCE SHEET ANALYSIS											**ANALYSE DU BILAN**
% of year-end balance sheet total											**% du total du bilan en fin d'exercice**
Assets											**Actif**
65. Cash & balance with Central bank	..	..	..	..	..	..	..	..	..	..	65. Caisse & solde auprès de la Banque centrale
66. Interbank deposits	15.53	16.14	13.41	11.35	10.15	10.66	9.86	8.57	7.42	5.93	66. Dépôts interbancaires
67. Loans	55.23	53.70	57.48	60.22	64.87	65.30	65.62	66.84	67.16	65.53	67. Prêts
68. Securities	13.05	13.29	13.57	13.13	13.73	13.76	14.28	14.34	14.43	14.28	68. Valeurs mobilières
69. Other assets	16.20	16.87	15.54	15.29	11.24	10.28	10.24	10.24	11.00	14.25	69. Autres actifs
Liabilities											**Passif**
70. Capital & reserves	2.75	2.97	3.18	3.34	3.63	3.73	3.75	3.35	3.40	2.82	70. Capital et réserves
71. Borrowing from Central bank	0.72	0.43	0.47	0.41	0.57	0.57	0.41	0.12	0.09	0.68	71. Emprunts auprès de la Banque centrale
72. Interbank deposits	..	..	..	..	..	..	..	..	..	..	72. Dépôts interbancaires
73. Non-bank deposits	76.59	76.09	76.16	74.59	76.58	77.46	78.32	77.76	77.23	74.97	73. Dépôts non bancaires
74. Bonds	0.90	0.76	0.73	0.76	0.81	0.79	0.85	1.01	1.00	0.93	74. Obligations
75. Other liabilities	19.04	19.75	19.46	20.91	18.41	17.45	16.68	17.77	18.28	20.60	75. Autres engagements
Memorandum items											***Pour mémoire***
76. Short-term securities	..	..	..	..	..	..	..	..	..	..	*76. Titres à court terme*
77. Bonds	..	..	..	..	..	..	..	..	..	..	*77. Obligations*
78. Shares and participations	*2.71*	*2.87*	*3.29*	*3.47*	*3.69*	*3.93*	*4.36*	*4.64*	*4.69*	*4.77*	*78. Actions et participations*
79. Claims on non-residents	..	..	..	..	..	..	..	..	..	..	*79. Créances sur des non-résidents*
80. Liabilities to non-residents	..	..	..	..	..	..	..	..	..	..	*80. Engagements envers des non-résidents*

* See notes on previous pages.

* Voir les notes en pages précédentes.

JAPAN
Large commercial banks

JAPON
Grandes banques commerciales

100 million yen	1988	1989	1990	1991	1992	1993	1994	1995	1996	1997	100 millions de yen
INCOME STATEMENT											**COMPTE DE RESULTATS**
1. Interest income	204088	270559	323647	298368	226675	188626	177263	187678	167869	136417	1. Produits financiers
2. Interest expenses	167313	238474	293346	257605	180932	145110	135250	136670	119912	94233	2. Frais financiers
3. Net interest income	36775	32085	30301	40763	45743	43516	42013	51009	47956	42184	3. Produits financiers nets
4. Non-interest income (net)	24566	19003	17000	9026	2807	548	-241	-1394	-3559	4926	4. Produits non financiers (nets)
a. Fees and commissions receivable	..	..	..	..	..	..	..	*9471*	*9369*	*9322*	*a. Frais et commissions à recevoir*
b. Fees and commissions payable	..	..	..	..	..	..	..	*3068*	*3089*	*3251*	*b. Frais et commissions à payer*
c. Net profits or loss on financial operations	..	..	..	..	..	..	..	*-9205*	*-10210*	*-6090*	*c. Profits ou pertes nets sur opérations financières*
d. Other	..	..	..	..	..	..	..	*1408*	*369*	*4945*	*d. Autres*
5. Gross income	61341	51088	47301	49789	48550	44064	41772	49614	44396	47110	5. Résultat brut
6. Operating expenses	28559	27233	29367	31018	31779	32023	32239	32336	33380	32450	6. Frais d'exploitation
a. Staff costs	*12772*	*13378*	*14079*	*14658*	*14970*	*15140*	*15135*	*15161*	*15000*	*14601*	*a. Dépenses en personnel*
b. Property costs	..	..	..	..	..	..	..	*15099*	*16407*	*15752*	*b. Dépenses en immobilier*
c. Other	..	..	..	..	..	..	..	*2076*	*1973*	*2096*	*c. Autres*
7. Net income	32782	23855	17934	18771	16771	12041	9533	17278	11015	14660	7. Résultat net
8. Provisions (net)	6361	2354	1503	4330	7368	6438	8884	30706	10774	42957	8. Provisions (nettes)
a. Provisions on loans	*2080*	*2224*	*1425*	*4354*	*7114*	*6316*	*8809*	*30645*	*10622*	*44538*	*a. Provisions sur prêts*
b. Provisions on securities (1)	*4281*	*130*	*78*	*-24*	*254*	*122*	*75*	*61*	*151*	*-1581*	*b. Provisions sur titres (1)*
c. Other	-	-	-	-	-	-	-	-	-	-	*c. Autres*
9. Profit before tax	26421	21501	16431	14441	9403	5603	649	-13428	240	-28297	9. Bénéfices avant impôt
10. Income tax	13940	10470	7577	7965	5727	2418	1343	4091	718	1503	10. Impôt sur le revenu
11. Profit after tax	12481	11031	8854	6476	3676	3185	-693	-17518	-477	-29800	11. Bénéfices après impôt
12. Distributed profit	1838	1069	1115	1113	1113	1105	1130	887	1128	1323	12. Bénéfices distribués
13. Retained profit	10643	9962	7739	5363	2563	2080	-1823	-18405	-1606	-31123	13. Bénéfices mis en réserve
BALANCE SHEET											**BILAN**
Assets											**Actif**
14. Cash & balance with Central bank (2)	..	..	..	..	..	..	..	..	..	..	14. Caisse & solde auprès de la Banque centrale (2)
15. Interbank deposits	883583	1046119	858603	694322	556503	568884	517242	450130	396230	309679	15. Dépôts interbancaires
16. Loans	2159315	2520336	2660295	2736541	2743890	2703186	2670535	2771343	2834197	2656555	16. Prêts
17. Securities	449216	560295	538856	513847	513673	504841	531647	537436	542816	556199	17. Valeurs mobilières
18. Other assets	720189	956143	858749	804944	546982	481154	473919	504433	566710	749765	18. Autres actifs
Liabilities											**Passif**
19. Capital & reserves	104939	137039	144097	148493	149928	152224	149560	131435	134346	103308	19. Capital et réserves
20. Borrowing from Central bank	43204	27135	28024	26353	34859	34790	23605	1011	1013	43994	20. Emprunts auprès de la Banque centrale
21. Interbank deposits (3)	..	..	..	..	..	..	..	..	..	..	21. Dépôts interbancaires (3)
22. Non-bank deposits	3045140	3644553	3535869	3292328	3087810	3060102	3034603	3069487	3073519	2888778	22. Dépôts non bancaires
23. Bonds	52623	53948	51568	53546	54181	52944	57213	69287	68974	63033	23. Obligations
24. Other liabilities	966397	1220218	1156945	1228934	1034270	958005	928363	992122	1062102	1173085	24. Autres engagements
Balance sheet total											**Total du bilan**
25. End-year total	4212303	5082893	4916503	4749654	4361048	4258065	4193343	4263342	4339954	4272198	25. En fin d'exercice
26. Average total	3910362	4647598	4999698	4833079	4555351	4309557	4225704	4228342	4301648	4306076	26. Moyen

JAPAN
Large commercial banks

JAPON
Grandes banques commerciales

	1988	1989	1990	1991	1992	1993	1994	1995	1996	1997	
100 million yen											*100 millions de yen*
Memorandum items											***Pour mémoire***
27. Short-term securities	..	..	..	..	..	..	..	..	..	..	*27. Titres à court terme*
28. Bonds	..	..	..	..	..	..	..	..	..	..	*28. Obligations*
29. Shares and participations	*132497*	*169114*	*192011*	*201849*	*200637*	*211988*	*238626*	*256135*	*262972*	*267007*	*29. Actions et participations*
30. Claims on non-residents	..	..	..	..	..	..	..	..	..	..	*30. Créances sur des non-résidents*
31. Liabilities to non-residents	..	..	..	..	..	..	..	..	..	..	*31. Engagements envers des non-résidents*
Capital adequacy											***Solvabilité***
32. Tier 1 Capital	..	..	..	..	..	..	..	*150245*	*155033*	*143886*	*32. Fonds propres de base*
33. Tier 2 Capital	..	..	..	..	..	..	..	*146837*	*147093*	*139724*	*33. Fonds propres complémentaires*
34. Supervisory deductions	..	..	..	..	..	..	..	-	-	*100*	*34. Eléments à déduire des fonds propres*
35. Total net capital resources	..	..	..	..	..	..	..	*297081*	*302127*	*283510*	*35. Total net des ressources en capital*
36. Risk-weighted assets	..	..	..	..	..	..	..	*3286754*	*3351642*	*3061973*	*36. Actifs pondérés des risques*
SUPPLEMENTARY INFORMATION											**RENSEIGNEMENTS COMPLEMENTAIRES**
37. Number of institutions	13	13	12	11	11	11	11	11	10	9	37. Nombre d'institutions
38. Number of branches	3099	3182	3249	3280	3293	3238	3224	3199	3174	2955	38. Nombre de succursales
39. Number of employees (x 1000)	152.0	152.0	152.0	154.0	157.0	158.0	155.0	149.0	139.4	128.6	39. Nombre de salariés (x 1000)

1. In 1997, the main components of Provisions on securities (item 8.b) were abolished in the Japanese accounting system. The 1997 figure represents the outflow of the assets of this item. Thereafter, the amount for this item will be negligible.

2. Cash and balance with Central bank (item 14) is included under Interbank deposits (item 15).

3. Interbank deposits (item 21) are included under Non-bank deposits (item 22).

Notes

- The term Large commercial banks corresponds to the term City banks used in Japanese publications. Data are based on the annual publication of the Federation of Bankers Associations of Japan *Analysis of Financial Statements of All Banks.*
- Data relate to fiscal years ending 31st March.

1. En 1997, les principales composantes des Provisions sur titres (poste 8.b) ont été supprimées du système de comptabilité japonais. Le montant publié pour l'année 1997 correspond à la sortie des actifs de ce poste. Par la suite, ce montant sera négligeable.

2. Caisse et solde auprès de la Banque centrale (poste 14) est inclus sous Dépôts interbancaires (poste 15).

3. Les Dépôts interbancaires (poste 21) sont inclus sous Dépôts non bancaires (poste 22).

Notes

- Le terme, Grande banques commerciales correspond au terme City banks utilisé dans les publications japonaises. Ces données sont extraites d'une publication annuelle de la Fédération des associations de banquiers du Japon *Analysis of Financial Statements of All Banks.*
- Les données portent sur l'exercice financier qui se termine le 31 mars.

JAPAN
Large commercial banks

JAPON
Grandes banques commerciales

	1988	1989	1990	1991	1992	1993	1994	1995	1996	1997	
Per cent											*Pourcentage*
INCOME STATEMENT ANALYSIS											**ANALYSE DU COMPTE DE RESULTATS**
% of average balance sheet total											**% du total moyen du bilan**
40. Interest income	5.22	5.82	6.47	6.17	4.98	4.38	4.19	4.44	3.90	3.17	40. Produits financiers
41. Interest expenses	4.28	5.13	5.87	5.33	3.97	3.37	3.20	3.23	2.79	2.19	41. Frais financiers
42. Net interest income	0.94	0.69	0.61	0.84	1.00	1.01	0.99	1.21	1.11	0.98	42. Produits financiers nets
43. Non-interest income (net)	0.63	0.41	0.34	0.19	0.06	0.01	-0.01	-0.03	-0.08	0.11	43. Produits non financiers (nets)
a. Fees and commissions receivable	..	..	..	..	..	..	..	*0.22*	*0.22*	*0.22*	*a. Frais et commissions à recevoir*
b. Fees and commissions payable	..	..	..	..	..	..	..	*0.07*	*0.07*	*0.08*	*b. Frais et commissions à payer*
c. Net profits or loss on financial operations	..	..	..	..	..	..	..	*-0.22*	*-0.24*	*-0.14*	*c. Profits ou pertes nets sur opérations financières*
d. Other	..	..	..	..	..	..	..	*0.03*	*0.01*	*0.11*	*d. Autres*
44. Gross income	1.57	1.10	0.95	1.03	1.07	1.02	0.99	1.17	1.03	1.09	44. Résultat brut
45. Operating expenses	0.73	0.59	0.59	0.64	0.70	0.74	0.76	0.76	0.78	0.75	45. Frais d'exploitation
a. Staff costs	*0.33*	*0.29*	*0.28*	*0.30*	*0.33*	*0.35*	*0.36*	*0.36*	*0.35*	*0.34*	*a. Dépenses en personnel*
b. Property costs	..	..	..	..	..	..	..	*0.36*	*0.38*	*0.37*	*b. Dépenses en immobilier*
c. Other	..	..	..	..	..	..	..	*0.05*	*0.05*	*0.05*	*c. Autres*
46. Net income	0.84	0.51	0.36	0.39	0.37	0.28	0.23	0.41	0.26	0.34	46. Résultat net
47. Provisions (net)	0.16	0.05	0.03	0.09	0.16	0.15	0.21	0.73	0.25	1.00	47. Provisions (nettes)
a. Provisions on loans	*0.05*	*0.05*	*0.03*	*0.09*	*0.16*	*0.15*	*0.21*	*0.72*	*0.25*	*1.03*	*a. Provisions sur prêts*
b. Provisions on securities	*0.11*	-	-	-	*0.01*	-	-	-	-	*-0.04*	*b. Provisions sur titres*
c. Other	-	-	-	-	-	-	-	-	-	-	*c. Autres*
48. Profit before tax	0.68	0.46	0.33	0.30	0.21	0.13	0.02	-0.32	0.01	-0.66	48. Bénéfices avant impôt
49. Income tax	0.36	0.23	0.15	0.16	0.13	0.06	0.03	0.10	0.02	0.03	49. Impôt sur le revenu
50. Profit after tax	0.32	0.24	0.18	0.13	0.08	0.07	-0.02	-0.41	-0.01	-0.69	50. Bénéfices après impôt
51. Distributed profit	0.05	0.02	0.02	0.02	0.02	0.03	0.03	0.02	0.03	0.03	51. Bénéfices distribués
52. Retained profit	0.27	0.21	0.15	0.11	0.06	0.05	-0.04	-0.44	-0.04	-0.72	52. Bénéfices mis en réserve
% of gross income											**% du total du résultat brut**
53. Net interest income	59.95	62.80	64.06	81.87	94.22	98.76	100.58	102.81	108.02	89.54	53. Produits financiers nets
54. Non-interest income (net)	40.05	37.20	35.94	18.13	5.78	1.24	-0.58	-2.81	-8.02	10.46	54. Produits non financiers (nets)
a. Fees and commissions receivable	..	..	..	..	..	..	..	*19.09*	*21.10*	*19.79*	*a. Frais et commissions à recevoir*
b. Fees and commissions payable	..	..	..	..	..	..	..	*6.18*	*6.96*	*6.90*	*b. Frais et commissions à payer*
c. Net profits or loss on financial operations	..	..	..	..	..	..	..	*-18.55*	*-23.00*	*-12.93*	*c. Profits ou pertes nets sur opérations financières*
d. Other	..	..	..	..	..	..	..	*2.84*	*0.83*	*10.50*	*d. Autres*
55. Operating expenses	46.56	53.31	62.09	62.30	65.46	72.67	77.18	65.18	75.19	68.88	55. Frais d'exploitation
a. Staff costs	*20.82*	*26.19*	*29.76*	*29.44*	*30.83*	*34.36*	*36.23*	*30.56*	*33.79*	*30.99*	*a. Dépenses en personnel*
b. Property costs	..	..	..	..	..	..	..	*30.43*	*36.96*	*33.44*	*b. Dépenses en immobilier*
c. Other	..	..	..	..	..	..	..	*4.18*	*4.44*	*4.45*	*c. Autres*
56. Net income	53.44	46.69	37.91	37.70	34.54	27.33	22.82	34.82	24.81	31.12	56. Résultat net
57. Provisions (net)	10.37	4.61	3.18	8.70	15.18	14.61	21.27	61.89	24.27	91.18	57. Provisions (nettes)
a. Provisions on loans	*3.39*	*4.35*	*3.01*	*8.74*	*14.65*	*14.33*	*21.09*	*61.77*	*23.93*	*94.54*	*a. Provisions sur prêts*
b. Provisions on securities	*6.98*	*0.25*	*0.16*	*-0.05*	*0.52*	*0.28*	*0.18*	*0.12*	*0.34*	*-3.36*	*b. Provisions sur titres*
c. Other	-	-	-	-	-	-	-	-	-	-	*c. Autres*
58. Profit before tax	43.07	42.09	34.74	29.00	19.37	12.72	1.55	-27.06	0.54	-60.07	58. Bénéfices avant impôt
59. Income tax	22.73	20.49	16.02	16.00	11.80	5.49	3.22	8.25	1.62	3.19	59. Impôt sur le revenu
60. Profit after tax	20.35	21.59	18.72	13.01	7.57	7.23	-1.66	-35.31	-1.07	-63.26	60. Bénéfices après impôt
% of net income											**% du total du résultat net**
61. Provisions (net)	19.40	9.87	8.38	23.07	43.93	53.47	93.19	177.72	97.81	293.02	61. Provisions (nettes)
a. Provisions on loans	*6.34*	*9.32*	*7.95*	*23.20*	*42.42*	*52.45*	*92.41*	*177.36*	*96.43*	*303.81*	*a. Provisions sur prêts*
b. Provisions on securities	*13.06*	*0.54*	*0.43*	*-0.13*	*1.51*	*1.01*	*0.79*	*0.35*	*1.37*	*-10.78*	*b. Provisions sur titres*
c. Other	-	-	-	-	-	-	-	-	-	-	*c. Autres*
62. Profit before tax	80.60	90.13	91.62	76.93	56.07	46.53	6.81	-77.72	2.18	-193.02	62. Bénéfices avant impôt
63. Income tax	42.52	43.89	42.25	42.43	34.15	20.08	14.09	23.68	6.52	10.25	63. Impôt sur le revenu
64. Profit after tax	38.07	46.24	49.37	34.50	21.92	26.45	-7.27	-101.39	-4.33	-203.27	64. Bénéfices après impôt

JAPAN
Large commercial banks

JAPON
Grandes banques commerciales

	1988	1989	1990	1991	1992	1993	1994	1995	1996	1997	
Per cent											*Pourcentage*
BALANCE SHEET ANALYSIS											**ANALYSE DU BILAN**
% of year-end balance sheet total											**% du total du bilan en fin d'exercice**
Assets											**Actif**
65. Cash & balance with Central bank	..	..	..	..	..	..	..	..	..	..	65. Caisse & solde auprès de la Banque centrale
66. Interbank deposits	20.98	20.58	17.46	14.62	12.76	13.36	12.33	10.56	9.13	7.25	66. Dépôts interbancaires
67. Loans	51.26	49.58	54.11	57.62	62.92	63.48	63.69	65.00	65.30	62.18	67. Prêts
68. Securities	10.66	11.02	10.96	10.82	11.78	11.86	12.68	12.61	12.51	13.02	68. Valeurs mobilières
69. Other assets	17.10	18.81	17.47	16.95	12.54	11.30	11.30	11.83	13.06	17.55	69. Autres actifs
Liabilities											**Passif**
70. Capital & reserves	2.49	2.70	2.93	3.13	3.44	3.57	3.57	3.08	3.10	2.42	70. Capital et réserves
71. Borrowing from Central bank	1.03	0.53	0.57	0.55	0.80	0.82	0.56	0.02	0.02	1.03	71. Emprunts auprès de la Banque centrale
72. Interbank deposits	..	..	..	..	..	..	..	..	..	..	72. Dépôts interbancaires
73. Non-bank deposits	72.29	71.70	71.92	69.32	70.80	71.87	72.37	72.00	70.82	67.62	73. Dépôts non bancaires
74. Bonds	1.25	1.06	1.05	1.13	1.24	1.24	1.36	1.63	1.59	1.48	74. Obligations
75. Other liabilities	22.94	24.01	23.53	25.87	23.72	22.50	22.14	23.27	24.47	27.46	75. Autres engagements
Memorandum items											***Pour mémoire***
76. Short-term securities	..	..	..	..	..	..	..	..	..	..	*76. Titres à court terme*
77. Bonds	..	..	..	..	..	..	..	..	..	..	*77. Obligations*
78. Shares and participations	*3.15*	*3.33*	*3.91*	*4.25*	*4.60*	*4.98*	*5.69*	*6.01*	*6.06*	*6.25*	*78. Actions et participations*
79. Claims on non-residents	..	..	..	..	..	..	..	..	..	..	*79. Créances sur des non-résidents*
80. Liabilities to non-residents	..	..	..	..	..	..	..	..	..	..	*80. Engagements envers des non-résidents*

* See notes on previous pages.

* Voir les notes en pages précédentes.

KOREA — COREE

Commercial banks — Banques commerciales

	1990	1991	1992	1993	1994	1995	1996	1997	
Billion won									*Milliards de won*
INCOME STATEMENT									**COMPTE DE RESULTATS**
1. Interest income	7365.3	9254.6	10471.3	10109.9	12308.6	18321.7	21755.8	31892.0	1. Produits financiers
2. Interest expenses	5471.5	6735.4	7383.2	6983.0	8882.0	13401.6	15696.3	24074.8	2. Frais financiers
3. Net interest income	1893.8	2519.1	3088.1	3127.0	3426.7	4920.2	6059.5	7817.2	3. Produits financiers nets
4. Non-interest income (net)	1336.0	1595.6	2247.9	2868.9	4906.1	4419.5	4358.6	2688.7	4. Produits non financiers (nets)
a. Fees and commissions receivable	*806.3*	*929.2*	*1250.5*	*1551.8*	*2480.8*	*2249.4*	*2281.0*	*10299.2*	*a. Frais et commissions à recevoir*
b. Fees and commissions payable	*113.0*	*113.7*	*184.1*	*175.9*	*237.9*	*372.8*	*650.1*	*8039.4*	*b. Frais et commissions à payer*
c. Net profits or loss on financial operations	*576.2*	*728.6*	*1139.7*	*1453.1*	*2407.9*	*2353.9*	*2569.1*	*2696.9*	*c. Profits ou pertes nets sur opérations financières*
d. Other	*66.4*	*51.6*	*41.8*	*39.9*	*255.3*	*189.1*	*158.6*	*-2268.1*	*d. Autres*
5. Gross income	3229.8	4114.7	5336.0	5995.8	8332.7	9339.7	10418.0	10505.9	5. Résultat brut
6. Operating expenses	1999.9	2582.1	3176.5	3649.8	4362.6	6033.0	6982.0	8093.9	6. Frais d'exploitation
a. Staff costs	*1080.2*	*1817.6*	*2221.3*	*2595.4*	*3187.4*	*4228.8*	*4964.4*	*5609.0*	*a. Dépenses en personnel*
b. Property costs	*919.7*	*764.5*	*955.2*	*1054.4*	*1175.1*	*1804.1*	*2017.6*	*2484.8*	*b. Dépenses en immobilier*
c. Other	-	-	-	-	-	-	-	-	*c. Autres*
7. Net income	1229.9	1532.7	2159.5	2346.0	3970.1	3306.7	3436.0	2412.0	7. Résultat net
8. Provisions (net)	409.3	528.5	942.5	1023.4	2371.8	2319.7	2342.0	6192.7	8. Provisions (nettes)
a. Provisions on loans	*381.8*	*484.3*	*787.6*	*995.5*	*2127.3*	*1758.0*	*1547.7*	*3511.3*	*a. Provisions sur prêts*
b. Provisions on securities	*27.5*	*44.2*	*95.7*	*-33.1*	*183.6*	*543.5*	*895.0*	*2759.4*	*b. Provisions sur titres*
c. Other	-	-	*59.2*	*61.0*	*60.9*	*18.2*	*-100.7*	*-78.0*	*c. Autres*
9. Profit before tax	820.6	1004.1	1217.0	1322.6	1598.3	987.0	1094.1	-3780.7	9. Bénéfices avant impôt
10. Income tax	115.8	179.3	285.5	433.6	550.1	119.2	247.2	139.2	10. Impôt sur le revenu
11. Profit after tax	705.3	824.8	931.5	889.0	1048.2	867.8	846.9	-3919.9	11. Bénéfices après impôt
12. Distributed profit	340.5	373.7	371.2	301.4	345.6	296.4	367.1	96.2	12. Bénéfices distribués
13. Retained profit	364.8	451.1	560.3	587.6	702.6	571.4	479.8	-4016.1	13. Bénéfices mis en réserve
BALANCE SHEET									**BILAN**
Assets									**Actif**
14. Cash & balance with Central bank	23503.1	24553.7	21872.2	18804.4	19757.7	23126.1	24179.6	18539.9	14. Caisse & solde auprès de la Banque centrale
15. Interbank deposits	4025.1	4256.0	5669.3	7082.9	8904.5	12295.6	15342.9	18084.3	15. Dépôts interbancaires
16. Loans	57280.1	70704.5	80870.5	88380.9	106470.1	136722.4	163458.4	225690.0	16. Prêts
17. Securities	14610.5	17163.0	19065.9	23407.6	30931.3	42294.2	52291.0	73769.2	17. Valeurs mobilières
18. Other assets	17257.2	20721.9	24544.3	28288.8	34487.0	45553.2	56888.6	84854.5	18. Autres actifs
Liabilities									**Passif**
19. Capital & reserves	10927.7	12182.8	13014.3	13977.6	16416.1	18618.3	20106.0	18046.4	19. Capital et réserves
20. Borrowing from Central bank	9143.9	10462.2	13636.1	12719.1	10524.5	8768.6	5273.7	9838.1	20. Emprunts auprès de la Banque centrale
21. Interbank deposits	234.4	192.2	119.9	967.1	1870.9	3112.3	2747.1	2842.7	21. Dépôts interbancaires
22. Non-bank deposits	69128.3	80795.6	88246.6	98933.6	118869.2	157821.8	184124.5	252100.0	22. Dépôts non bancaires
23. Bonds	1091.3	812.6	793.0	679.4	1034.8	3226.7	8816.7	21912.6	23. Obligations
24. Other liabilities	26150.4	32953.6	36212.3	38687.9	51835.1	68443.8	91092.5	116198.1	24. Autres engagements
Balance sheet total									**Total du bilan**
25. End-year total	116676.1	137399.1	152022.1	165964.6	200550.6	259991.5	312160.5	420937.9	25. En fin d'exercice
26. Average total	91055.2	112296.4	130383.4	144079.8	169498.5	225579.0	269206.5	370844.1	26. Moyen

KOREA
Commercial banks

COREE
Banques commerciales

	1990	1991	1992	1993	1994	1995	1996	1997	
Billion won									*Milliards de won*
Memorandum items									***Pour mémoire***
27. Short-term securities	..	..	..	..	..	..	..	..	*27. Titres à court terme*
28. Bonds	..	..	..	..	..	..	..	..	*28. Obligations*
29. Shares and participations	*1910.8*	*2211.1*	*2733.5*	*3605.5*	*6267.8*	*8530.6*	*9136.3*	*10187.0*	*29. Actions et participations*
30. Claims on non-residents	..	..	..	..	..	..	..	..	*30. Créances sur des non-résidents*
31. Liabilities to non-residents	..	..	..	..	..	..	..	..	*31. Engagements envers des non-résidents*
Capital adequacy									***Solvabilité***
32. Tier 1 Capital	..	..	..	*14912.0*	*17063.1*	*19338.7*	*20632.3*	*13892.8*	*32. Fonds propres de base*
33. Tier 2 Capital	..	..	..	*2747.4*	*3161.9*	*3340.4*	*5237.8*	*11177.2*	*33. Fonds propres complémentaires*
34. Supervisory deductions	..	..	..	*39.1*	*45.8*	*116.5*	*129.2*	*164.6*	*34. Eléments à déduire des fonds propres*
35. Total net capital resources	..	..	..	*17620.3*	*20179.2*	*22562.6*	*25740.9*	*24905.4*	*35. Total net des ressources en capital*
36. Risk-weighted assets	..	..	..	*160166.5*	*190033.0*	*241932.0*	*281496.2*	*353749.7*	*36. Actifs pondérés des risques*
SUPPLEMENTARY INFORMATION									**RENSEIGNEMENTS COMPLEMENTAIRES**
37. Number of institutions	21	23	24	24	24	25	25	26	37. Nombre d'institutions
38. Number of branches	2390	2737	3029	3381	3750	4632	5185	6077	38. Nombre de succursales
39. Number of employees (x 1000)	82.2	86.6	88.0	87.7	87.2	103.2	103.9	114.0	39. Nombre de salariés (x 1000)

Notes

- Commercial banks: nation-wide commercial banks and regional banks.

- Average balance sheet totals (item 26) are based on daily data.

Notes

- Les Banques commerciales : les banques commerciales nationales et les banques régionales.

- La moyenne du total des actifs/passifs (poste 26) est basée sur des données journalières.

KOREA — COREE

Commercial banks — Banques commerciales

	1990	1991	1992	1993	1994	1995	1996	1997	
Per cent									*Pourcentage*
INCOME STATEMENT ANALYSIS									**ANALYSE DU COMPTE DE RESULTATS**
% of average balance sheet total									**% du total moyen du bilan**
40. Interest income	8.09	8.24	8.03	7.02	7.26	8.12	8.08	8.60	40. Produits financiers
41. Interest expenses	6.01	6.00	5.66	4.85	5.24	5.94	5.83	6.49	41. Frais financiers
42. Net interest income	2.08	2.24	2.37	2.17	2.02	2.18	2.25	2.11	42. Produits financiers nets
43. Non-interest income (net)	1.47	1.42	1.72	1.99	2.89	1.96	1.62	0.73	43. Produits non financiers (nets)
a. Fees and commissions receivable	*0.89*	*0.83*	*0.96*	*1.08*	*1.46*	*1.00*	*0.85*	*2.78*	*a. Frais et commissions à recevoir*
b. Fees and commissions payable	*0.12*	*0.10*	*0.14*	*0.12*	*0.14*	*0.17*	*0.24*	*2.17*	*b. Frais et commissions à payer*
c. Net profits or loss on financial operations	*0.63*	*0.65*	*0.87*	*1.01*	*1.42*	*1.04*	*0.95*	*0.73*	*c. Profits ou pertes nets sur opérations financières*
d. Other	*0.07*	*0.05*	*0.03*	*0.03*	*0.15*	*0.08*	*0.06*	*-0.61*	*d. Autres*
44. Gross income	3.55	3.66	4.09	4.16	4.92	4.14	3.87	2.83	44. Résultat brut
45. Operating expenses	2.20	2.30	2.44	2.53	2.57	2.67	2.59	2.18	45. Frais d'exploitation
a. Staff costs	*1.19*	*1.62*	*1.70*	*1.80*	*1.88*	*1.87*	*1.84*	*1.51*	*a. Dépenses en personnel*
b. Property costs	*1.01*	*0.68*	*0.73*	*0.73*	*0.69*	*0.80*	*0.75*	*0.67*	*b. Dépenses en immobilier*
c. Other	-	-	-	-	-	-	-	-	*c. Autres*
46. Net income	1.35	1.36	1.66	1.63	2.34	1.47	1.28	0.65	46. Résultat net
47. Provisions (net)	0.45	0.47	0.72	0.71	1.40	1.03	0.87	1.67	47. Provisions (nettes)
a. Provisions on loans	*0.42*	*0.43*	*0.60*	*0.69*	*1.26*	*0.78*	*0.57*	*0.95*	*a. Provisions sur prêts*
b. Provisions on securities	*0.03*	*0.04*	*0.07*	*-0.02*	*0.11*	*0.24*	*0.33*	*0.74*	*b. Provisions sur titres*
c. Other	-	-	*0.05*	*0.04*	*0.04*	*0.01*	*-0.04*	*-0.02*	*c. Autres*
48. Profit before tax	0.90	0.89	0.93	0.92	0.94	0.44	0.41	-1.02	48. Bénéfices avant impôt
49. Income tax	0.13	0.16	0.22	0.30	0.32	0.05	0.09	0.04	49. Impôt sur le revenu
50. Profit after tax	0.77	0.73	0.71	0.62	0.62	0.38	0.31	-1.06	50. Bénéfices après impôt
51. Distributed profit	0.37	0.33	0.28	0.21	0.20	0.13	0.14	0.03	51. Bénéfices distribués
52. Retained profit	0.40	0.40	0.43	0.41	0.41	0.25	0.18	-1.08	52. Bénéfices mis en réserve
% of gross income									**% du total du résultat brut**
53. Net interest income	58.64	61.22	57.87	52.15	41.12	52.68	58.16	74.41	53. Produits financiers nets
54. Non-interest income (net)	41.36	38.78	42.13	47.85	58.88	47.32	41.84	25.59	54. Produits non financiers (nets)
a. Fees and commissions receivable	*24.96*	*22.58*	*23.44*	*25.88*	*29.77*	*24.08*	*21.89*	*98.03*	*a. Frais et commissions à recevoir*
b. Fees and commissions payable	*3.50*	*2.76*	*3.45*	*2.93*	*2.86*	*3.99*	*6.24*	*76.52*	*b. Frais et commissions à payer*
c. Net profits or loss on financial operations	*17.84*	*17.71*	*21.36*	*24.24*	*28.90*	*25.20*	*24.66*	*25.67*	*c. Profits ou pertes nets sur opérations financières*
d. Other	*2.06*	*1.25*	*0.78*	*0.67*	*3.06*	*2.02*	*1.52*	*-21.59*	*d. Autres*
55. Operating expenses	61.92	62.75	59.53	60.87	52.36	64.60	67.02	77.04	55. Frais d'exploitation
a. Staff costs	*33.44*	*44.17*	*41.63*	*43.29*	*38.25*	*45.28*	*47.65*	*53.39*	*a. Dépenses en personnel*
b. Property costs	*28.48*	*18.58*	*17.90*	*17.59*	*14.10*	*19.32*	*19.37*	*23.65*	*b. Dépenses en immobilier*
c. Other	-	-	-	-	-	-	-	-	*c. Autres*
56. Net income	38.08	37.25	40.47	39.13	47.64	35.40	32.98	22.96	56. Résultat net
57. Provisions (net)	12.67	12.84	17.66	17.07	28.46	24.84	22.48	58.94	57. Provisions (nettes)
a. Provisions on loans	*11.82*	*11.77*	*14.76*	*16.60*	*25.53*	*18.82*	*14.86*	*33.42*	*a. Provisions sur prêts*
b. Provisions on securities	*0.85*	*1.07*	*1.79*	*-0.55*	*2.20*	*5.82*	*8.59*	*26.27*	*b. Provisions sur titres*
c. Other	-	-	*1.11*	*1.02*	*0.73*	*0.19*	*-0.97*	*-0.74*	*c. Autres*
58. Profit before tax	25.41	24.40	22.81	22.06	19.18	10.57	10.50	-35.99	58. Bénéfices avant impôt
59. Income tax	3.59	4.36	5.35	7.23	6.60	1.28	2.37	1.32	59. Impôt sur le revenu
60. Profit after tax	21.84	20.05	17.46	14.83	12.58	9.29	8.13	-37.31	60. Bénéfices après impôt
% of net income									**% du total du résultat net**
61. Provisions (net)	33.28	34.48	43.64	43.62	59.74	70.15	68.16	256.75	61. Provisions (nettes)
a. Provisions on loans	*31.04*	*31.60*	*36.47*	*42.43*	*53.58*	*53.16*	*45.04*	*145.58*	*a. Provisions sur prêts*
b. Provisions on securities	*2.24*	*2.88*	*4.43*	*-1.41*	*4.62*	*16.44*	*26.05*	*114.40*	*b. Provisions sur titres*
c. Other	-	-	*2.74*	*2.60*	*1.53*	*0.55*	*-2.93*	*-3.23*	*c. Autres*
62. Profit before tax	66.72	65.51	56.36	56.38	40.26	29.85	31.84	-156.75	62. Bénéfices avant impôt
63. Income tax	9.42	11.70	13.22	18.48	13.86	3.60	7.19	5.77	63. Impôt sur le revenu
64. Profit after tax	57.35	53.81	43.13	37.89	26.40	26.24	24.65	-162.52	64. Bénéfices après impôt

KOREA
Commercial banks

COREE
Banques commerciales

	1990	1991	1992	1993	1994	1995	1996	1997	
Per cent									*Pourcentage*
BALANCE SHEET ANALYSIS									**ANALYSE DU BILAN**
% of year-end balance sheet total									**% du total du bilan en fin d'exercice**
Assets									**Actif**
65. Cash & balance with Central bank	20.14	17.87	14.39	11.33	9.85	8.89	7.75	4.40	65. Caisse & solde auprès de la Banque centrale
66. Interbank deposits	3.45	3.10	3.73	4.27	4.44	4.73	4.92	4.30	66. Dépôts interbancaires
67. Loans	49.09	51.46	53.20	53.25	53.09	52.59	52.36	53.62	67. Prêts
68. Securities	12.52	12.49	12.54	14.10	15.42	16.27	16.75	17.52	68. Valeurs mobilières
69. Other assets	14.79	15.08	16.15	17.05	17.20	17.52	18.22	20.16	69. Autres actifs
Liabilities									**Passif**
70. Capital & reserves	9.37	8.87	8.56	8.42	8.19	7.16	6.44	4.29	70. Capital et réserves
71. Borrowing from Central bank	7.84	7.61	8.97	7.66	5.25	3.37	1.69	2.34	71. Emprunts auprès de la Banque centrale
72. Interbank deposits	0.20	0.14	0.08	0.58	0.93	1.20	0.88	0.68	72. Dépôts interbancaires
73. Non-bank deposits	59.25	58.80	58.05	59.61	59.27	60.70	58.98	59.89	73. Dépôts non bancaires
74. Bonds	0.94	0.59	0.52	0.41	0.52	1.24	2.82	5.21	74. Obligations
75. Other liabilities	22.41	23.98	23.82	23.31	25.85	26.33	29.18	27.60	75. Autres engagements
Memorandum items									***Pour mémoire***
76. Short-term securities	..	..	..	..	..	..	..	..	*76. Titres à court terme*
77. Bonds	..	..	..	..	..	..	..	..	*77. Obligations*
78. Shares and participations	*1.64*	*1.61*	*1.80*	*2.17*	*3.13*	*3.28*	*2.93*	*2.42*	*78. Actions et participations*
79. Claims on non-residents	..	..	..	..	..	..	..	..	*79. Créances sur des non-résidents*
80. Liabilities to non-residents	..	..	..	..	..	..	..	..	*80. Engagements envers des non-résidents*

* See notes on previous pages.

* Voir les notes en pages précédentes.

KOREA / COREE

Foreign commercial banks / Banques commerciales étrangères

	1990	1991	1992	1993	1994	1995	1996	1997	
Billion won									*Milliards de won*
INCOME STATEMENT									**COMPTE DE RESULTATS**
1. Interest income	945.7	1015.5	1084.1	994.5	1170.7	1567.7	1716.9	2386.1	1. Produits financiers
2. Interest expenses	736.1	744.9	749.0	696.9	810.2	1162.3	1186.5	1752.6	2. Frais financiers
3. Net interest income	209.6	270.6	335.2	297.6	360.6	405.4	530.4	633.5	3. Produits financiers nets
4. Non-interest income (net)	171.7	203.3	204.5	195.9	182.9	201.7	310.9	1672.1	4. Produits non financiers (nets)
a. Fees and commissions receivable	*290.9*	*191.1*	*196.4*	*184.7*	*192.9*	*235.2*	*908.0*	*4391.3*	*a. Frais et commissions à recevoir*
b. Fees and commissions payable	*136.2*	*5.5*	*4.5*	*5.1*	*35.7*	*67.3*	*637.1*	*2737.4*	*b. Frais et commissions à payer*
c. Net profits or loss on financial operations	*7.3*	*14.4*	*10.4*	*15.2*	*21.9*	*36.8*	*37.4*	*26.6*	*c. Profits ou pertes nets sur opérations financières*
d. Other	*9.8*	*3.2*	*2.2*	*1.1*	*3.8*	*-3.0*	*2.6*	*-8.4*	*d. Autres*
5. Gross income	381.3	473.8	539.6	493.5	543.5	607.1	841.3	2305.7	5. Résultat brut
6. Operating expenses	165.5	169.5	191.6	210.8	221.0	245.3	290.9	321.4	6. Frais d'exploitation
a. Staff costs	..	..	..	..	..	..	..	..	*a. Dépenses en personnel*
b. Property costs	..	..	..	..	..	..	..	..	*b. Dépenses en immobilier*
c. Other	..	..	..	..	..	..	..	..	*c. Autres*
7. Net income	215.9	304.3	348.0	282.6	322.5	361.8	550.4	1984.3	7. Résultat net
8. Provisions (net)	14.8	44.0	44.3	32.5	18.4	62.4	72.4	211.8	8. Provisions (nettes)
a. Provisions on loans	*14.8*	*44.0*	*44.3*	*32.5*	*18.4*	*53.4*	*69.6*	*145.6*	*a. Provisions sur prêts*
b. Provisions on securities	-	-	-	-	-	*-0.1*	*0.3*	*66.2*	*b. Provisions sur titres*
c. Other	-	-	-	-	-	*9.0*	*2.4*	-	*c. Autres*
9. Profit before tax	201.1	260.3	303.7	250.1	304.1	299.5	478.0	1772.5	9. Bénéfices avant impôt
10. Income tax	68.5	88.3	108.1	86.2	98.1	64.4	111.8	550.8	10. Impôt sur le revenu
11. Profit after tax	132.6	171.9	195.6	164.0	206.0	235.0	366.2	1221.7	11. Bénéfices après impôt
12. Distributed profit	..	..	..	..	..	..	..	..	12. Bénéfices distribués
13. Retained profit	..	..	..	..	..	..	..	..	13. Bénéfices mis en réserve
BALANCE SHEET									**BILAN**
Assets									**Actif**
14. Cash & balance with Central bank	125.6	85.0	45.4	42.9	22.5	42.7	70.2	161.3	14. Caisse & solde auprès de la Banque centrale
15. Interbank deposits	383.5	356.0	576.9	560.7	655.2	1563.0	2018.1	3476.7	15. Dépôts interbancaires
16. Loans	4930.4	6439.5	6279.4	5213.0	5971.5	11156.4	15400.2	24484.2	16. Prêts
17. Securities	238.0	225.0	481.7	893.0	930.5	2044.6	2601.5	6904.4	17. Valeurs mobilières
18. Other assets	2517.8	3834.8	4161.9	4626.7	5690.9	4583.7	3902.3	11110.3	18. Autres actifs
Liabilities									**Passif**
19. Capital & reserves	1109.3	1301.8	1559.9	1750.3	1956.6	2609.6	3251.2	4272.2	19. Capital et réserves
20. Borrowing from Central bank	11.6	14.0	26.7	33.8	3.3	1.6	1.5	-	20. Emprunts auprès de la Banque centrale
21. Interbank deposits	3.0	3.1	0.1	0.1	0.1	606.2	352.5	979.1	21. Dépôts interbancaires
22. Non-bank deposits	1679.6	2306.5	1712.3	1583.4	1757.0	1587.0	1651.6	3218.1	22. Dépôts non bancaires
23. Bonds	-	-	-	-	-	-	-	-	23. Obligations
24. Other liabilities	5391.8	7314.9	8246.3	7968.7	9553.6	14586.0	18735.6	37667.5	24. Autres engagements
Balance sheet total									**Total du bilan**
25. End-year total	8195.3	10940.3	11545.3	11336.3	13270.6	19390.3	23992.3	46136.9	25. En fin d'exercice
26. Average total	9325.7	10890.2	12737.4	13550.9	14806.7	19025.5	22721.5	33140.7	26. Moyen

KOREA
Foreign commercial banks

COREE
Banques commerciales étrangères

	1990	1991	1992	1993	1994	1995	1996	1997	
Billion won									*Milliards de won*
Memorandum items									***Pour mémoire***
27. Short-term securities	..	..	..	..	..	..	..	..	*27. Titres à court terme*
28. Bonds	..	..	..	..	..	..	..	..	*28. Obligations*
29. Shares and participations	*3.2*	*8.8*	*3.7*	*4.8*	*71.6*	*9.4*	*2.7*	*18.2*	*29. Actions et participations*
30. Claims on non-residents	..	..	..	..	..	..	..	..	*30. Créances sur des non-résidents*
31. Liabilities to non-residents	..	..	..	..	..	..	..	..	*31. Engagements envers des non-résidents*
Capital adequacy									***Solvabilité***
32. Tier 1 Capital	..	..	..	*1726.9*	*1900.3*	*2584.1*	*3179.9*	*4262.5*	*32. Fonds propres de base*
33. Tier 2 Capital	..	..	..	*148.5*	*148.5*	*143.7*	*188.8*	*1803.9*	*33. Fonds propres complémentaires*
34. Supervisory deductions	..	..	..	-	-	-	-	-	*34. Eléments à déduire des fonds propres*
35. Total net capital resources	..	..	..	*1875.5*	*2048.8*	*2727.8*	*3368.7*	*6066.4*	*35. Total net des ressources en capital*
36. Risk-weighted assets	..	..	..	*10668.5*	*12322.0*	*14966.0*	*19270.7*	*30560.8*	*36. Actifs pondérés des risques*
SUPPLEMENTARY INFORMATION									**RENSEIGNEMENTS COMPLEMENTAIRES**
37. Number of institutions	52	52	51	52	52	52	48	53	37. Nombre d'institutions
38. Number of branches	69	70	73	74	72	71	67	68	38. Nombre de succursales
39. Number of employees (x 1000)	2.8	2.7	2.6	2.6	2.7	2.7	2.5	2.6	39. Nombre de salariés (x 1000)

Notes

- Foreign commercial banks: domestic branches of foreign commercial banks.
- Average balance sheet totals (item 26) are based on daily data.

Notes

- Les Banques commerciales étrangères : les succursales nationales des banques commerciales étrangères.
- La moyenne du total des actifs/passifs (poste 26) est basée sur des données journalières.

KOREA — COREE

Foreign commercial banks — Banques commerciales étrangères

	1990	1991	1992	1993	1994	1995	1996	1997	
Per cent									*Pourcentage*
INCOME STATEMENT ANALYSIS									**ANALYSE DU COMPTE DE RESULTATS**
% of average balance sheet total									**% du total moyen du bilan**
40. Interest income	10.14	9.32	8.51	7.34	7.91	8.24	7.56	7.20	40. Produits financiers
41. Interest expenses	7.89	6.84	5.88	5.14	5.47	6.11	5.22	5.29	41. Frais financiers
42. Net interest income	2.25	2.48	2.63	2.20	2.44	2.13	2.33	1.91	42. Produits financiers nets
43. Non-interest income (net)	1.84	1.87	1.61	1.45	1.24	1.06	1.37	5.05	43. Produits non financiers (nets)
a. Fees and commissions receivable	*3.12*	*1.75*	*1.54*	*1.36*	*1.30*	*1.24*	*4.00*	*13.25*	*a. Frais et commissions à recevoir*
b. Fees and commissions payable	*1.46*	*0.05*	*0.04*	*0.04*	*0.24*	*0.35*	*2.80*	*8.26*	*b. Frais et commissions à payer*
c. Net profits or loss on financial operations	*0.08*	*0.13*	*0.08*	*0.11*	*0.15*	*0.19*	*0.16*	*0.08*	*c. Profits ou pertes nets sur opérations financières*
d. Other	*0.11*	*0.03*	*0.02*	*0.01*	*0.03*	*-0.02*	*0.01*	*-0.03*	*d. Autres*
44. Gross income	4.09	4.35	4.24	3.64	3.67	3.19	3.70	6.96	44. Résultat brut
45. Operating expenses	1.77	1.56	1.50	1.56	1.49	1.29	1.28	0.97	45. Frais d'exploitation
a. Staff costs	..	..	..	..	..	..	..	..	*a. Dépenses en personnel*
b. Property costs	..	..	..	..	..	..	..	..	*b. Dépenses en immobilier*
c. Other	..	..	..	..	..	..	..	..	*c. Autres*
46. Net income	2.32	2.79	2.73	2.09	2.18	1.90	2.42	5.99	46. Résultat net
47. Provisions (net)	0.16	0.40	0.35	0.24	0.12	0.33	0.32	0.64	47. Provisions (nettes)
a. Provisions on loans	*0.16*	*0.40*	*0.35*	*0.24*	*0.12*	*0.28*	*0.31*	*0.44*	*a. Provisions sur prêts*
b. Provisions on securities	-	-	-	-	-	-	-	*0.20*	*b. Provisions sur titres*
c. Other	-	-	-	-	-	*0.05*	*0.01*	-	*c. Autres*
48. Profit before tax	2.16	2.39	2.38	1.85	2.05	1.57	2.10	5.35	48. Bénéfices avant impôt
49. Income tax	0.73	0.81	0.85	0.64	0.66	0.34	0.49	1.66	49. Impôt sur le revenu
50. Profit after tax	1.42	1.58	1.54	1.21	1.39	1.24	1.61	3.69	50. Bénéfices après impôt
51. Distributed profit	..	..	..	..	..	..	..	..	51. Bénéfices distribués
52. Retained profit	..	..	..	..	..	..	..	..	52. Bénéfices mis en réserve
% of gross income									**% du total du résultat brut**
53. Net interest income	54.97	57.11	62.12	60.30	66.35	66.78	63.05	27.48	53. Produits financiers nets
54. Non-interest income (net)	45.03	42.91	37.90	39.70	33.65	33.22	36.95	72.52	54. Produits non financiers (nets)
a. Fees and commissions receivable	*76.29*	*40.33*	*36.40*	*37.43*	*35.49*	*38.74*	*107.93*	*190.45*	*a. Frais et commissions à recevoir*
b. Fees and commissions payable	*35.72*	*1.16*	*0.83*	*1.03*	*6.57*	*11.09*	*75.73*	*118.72*	*b. Frais et commissions à payer*
c. Net profits or loss on financial operations	*1.91*	*3.04*	*1.93*	*3.08*	*4.03*	*6.06*	*4.45*	*1.15*	*c. Profits ou pertes nets sur opérations financières*
d. Other	*2.57*	*0.68*	*0.41*	*0.22*	*0.70*	*-0.49*	*0.31*	*-0.36*	*d. Autres*
55. Operating expenses	43.40	35.77	35.51	42.72	40.66	40.41	34.58	13.94	55. Frais d'exploitation
a. Staff costs	..	..	..	..	..	..	..	..	*a. Dépenses en personnel*
b. Property costs	..	..	..	..	..	..	..	..	*b. Dépenses en immobilier*
c. Other	..	..	..	..	..	..	..	..	*c. Autres*
56. Net income	56.62	64.23	64.49	57.26	59.34	59.59	65.42	86.06	56. Résultat net
57. Provisions (net)	3.88	9.29	8.21	6.59	3.39	10.28	8.61	9.19	57. Provisions (nettes)
a. Provisions on loans	*3.88*	*9.29*	*8.21*	*6.59*	*3.39*	*8.80*	*8.27*	*6.31*	*a. Provisions sur prêts*
b. Provisions on securities	-	-	-	-	-	*-0.02*	*0.04*	*2.87*	*b. Provisions sur titres*
c. Other	-	-	-	-	-	*1.48*	*0.29*	-	*c. Autres*
58. Profit before tax	52.74	54.94	56.28	50.68	55.95	49.33	56.82	76.87	58. Bénéfices avant impôt
59. Income tax	17.96	18.64	20.03	17.47	18.05	10.61	13.29	23.89	59. Impôt sur le revenu
60. Profit after tax	34.78	36.28	36.25	33.23	37.90	38.71	43.53	52.99	60. Bénéfices après impôt
% of net income									**% du total du résultat net**
61. Provisions (net)	6.86	14.46	12.73	11.50	5.71	17.25	13.15	10.67	61. Provisions (nettes)
a. Provisions on loans	*6.86*	*14.46*	*12.73*	*11.50*	*5.71*	*14.76*	*12.65*	*7.34*	*a. Provisions sur prêts*
b. Provisions on securities	-	-	-	-	-	*-0.03*	*0.05*	*3.34*	*b. Provisions sur titres*
c. Other	-	-	-	-	-	*2.49*	*0.44*	-	*c. Autres*
62. Profit before tax	93.14	85.54	87.27	88.50	94.29	82.78	86.85	89.33	62. Bénéfices avant impôt
63. Income tax	31.73	29.02	31.06	30.50	30.42	17.80	20.31	27.76	63. Impôt sur le revenu
64. Profit after tax	61.42	56.49	56.21	58.03	63.88	64.95	66.53	61.57	64. Bénéfices après impôt

KOREA — COREE

Foreign commercial banks — Banques commerciales étrangères

	1990	1991	1992	1993	1994	1995	1996	1997	
Per cent									*Pourcentage*
BALANCE SHEET ANALYSIS									**ANALYSE DU BILAN**
% of year-end balance sheet total									**% du total du bilan en fin d'exercice**
Assets									**Actif**
65. Cash & balance with Central bank	1.53	0.78	0.39	0.38	0.17	0.22	0.29	0.35	65. Caisse & solde auprès de la Banque centrale
66. Interbank deposits	4.68	3.25	5.00	4.95	4.94	8.06	8.41	7.54	66. Dépôts interbancaires
67. Loans	60.16	58.86	54.39	45.99	45.00	57.54	64.19	53.07	67. Prêts
68. Securities	2.90	2.06	4.17	7.88	7.01	10.54	10.84	14.97	68. Valeurs mobilières
69. Other assets	30.72	35.05	36.05	40.81	42.88	23.64	16.26	24.08	69. Autres actifs
Liabilities									**Passif**
70. Capital & reserves	13.54	11.90	13.51	15.44	14.74	13.46	13.55	9.26	70. Capital et réserves
71. Borrowing from Central bank	0.14	0.13	0.23	0.30	0.02	0.01	0.01	-	71. Emprunts auprès de la Banque centrale
72. Interbank deposits	0.04	0.03	-	-	-	3.13	1.47	2.12	72. Dépôts interbancaires
73. Non-bank deposits	20.49	21.08	14.83	13.97	13.24	8.18	6.88	6.98	73. Dépôts non bancaires
74. Bonds	-	-	-	-	-	-	-	-	74. Obligations
75. Other liabilities	65.79	66.86	71.43	70.29	71.99	75.22	78.09	81.64	75. Autres engagements
Memorandum items									***Pour mémoire***
76. Short-term securities	..	..	..	..	..	..	..	..	*76. Titres à court terme*
77. Bonds	..	..	..	..	..	..	..	..	*77. Obligations*
78. Shares and participations	*0.04*	*0.08*	*0.03*	*0.04*	*0.54*	*0.05*	*0.01*	*0.04*	*78. Actions et participations*
79. Claims on non-residents	..	..	..	..	..	..	..	..	*79. Créances sur des non-résidents*
80. Liabilities to non-residents	..	..	..	..	..	..	..	..	*80. Engagements envers des non-résidents*

* See notes on previous pages.

* Voir les notes en pages précédentes.

LUXEMBOURG

Commercial banks

LUXEMBOURG

Banques commerciales

Million Luxembourg francs	1989	1990	1991	1992	1993	1994	1995	1996	1997	1998 p	Millions de francs luxembourgeois
INCOME STATEMENT											**COMPTE DE RESULTATS**
1. Interest income	970360	1185123	1251957	1375962	1306736	1169830	1353652	1249952	1368937	1580371	1. Produits financiers
2. Interest expenses	883077	1090911	1143722	1259077	1188477	1044867	1226676	1121810	1241477	1450574	2. Frais financiers
3. Net interest income	87283	94212	108235	116885	118259	124963	126976	128142	127460	129797	3. Produits financiers nets
4. Non-interest income (net)	32137	50738	39044	48172	77335	61830	66935	79461	104055	159208	4. Produits non financiers (nets)
a. Fees and commissions receivable	..	..	..	..	..	..	..	..	..	..	*a. Frais et commissions à recevoir*
b. Fees and commissions payable	..	..	..	..	..	..	..	..	..	..	*b. Frais et commissions à payer*
c. Net profits or loss on financial operations	..	..	..	..	..	..	..	..	..	..	*c. Profits ou pertes nets sur opérations financières*
d. Other	..	..	..	..	..	..	..	..	..	..	*d. Autres*
5. Gross income	119420	144950	147279	165057	195594	186793	193911	207603	231515	289005	5. Résultat brut
6. Operating expenses	46244	54089	59720	65000	74261	83989	90246	96548	101552	111983	6. Frais d'exploitation
a. Staff costs	*27326*	*28291*	*31205*	*33820*	*38155*	*44102*	*46374*	*48591*	*51048*	*53823*	*a. Dépenses en personnel*
b. Property costs	..	..	..	..	..	..	..	..	..	..	*b. Dépenses en immobilier*
c. Other	..	..	..	..	..	..	..	..	..	..	*c. Autres*
7. Net income	73176	90861	87559	100057	121333	102804	103665	111055	129963	177022	7. Résultat net
8. Provisions (net)	38723	63860	54302	55180	41160	14069	11976	5299	21663	37122	8. Provisions (nettes)
a. Provisions on loans	..	..	..	..	..	..	..	..	..	..	*a. Provisions sur prêts*
b. Provisions on securities	..	..	..	..	..	..	..	..	..	..	*b. Provisions sur titres*
c. Other	..	..	..	..	..	..	..	..	..	..	*c. Autres*
9. Profit before tax	34453	27001	33257	44877	80173	88735	91689	105756	108300	139900	9. Bénéfices avant impôt
10. Income tax	10566	7919	9539	16498	25635	26230	30714	36572	36415	28025	10. Impôt sur le revenu
11. Profit after tax	23887	19082	23718	28379	54538	62505	60975	69184	71885	111875	11. Bénéfices après impôt
12. Distributed profit	..	..	..	..	..	..	..	..	..	..	12. Bénéfices distribués
13. Retained profit	..	..	..	..	..	..	..	..	..	..	13. Bénéfices mis en réserve
BALANCE SHEET											**BILAN**
Assets											**Actif**
14. Cash & balance with Central bank	22550	21999	23912	25247	138581	59853	33626	41348	37757	30084	14. Caisse & solde auprès de la Banque centrale
15. Interbank deposits	6827903	7542436	7595436	8514637	9359103	10610714	10710146	10724519	11342404	11588846	15. Dépôts interbancaires
16. Loans	2705253	2991164	3111790	3560101	3570761	3257258	3469054	3554890	3903829	3966557	16. Prêts
17. Securities	825196	947786	1030649	1366487	2379016	3078582	3473901	4216772	4698088	5206269	17. Valeurs mobilières
18. Other assets	955869	976829	989324	957609	573503	662785	687019	718811	856374	1022281	18. Autres actifs
Liabilities											**Passif**
19. Capital & reserves	400727	437490	509944	402292	424215	424215	459686	474720	474419	525081	19. Capital et réserves
20. Borrowing from Central bank	-	-	-	-	-	-	-	-	-	-	20. Emprunts auprès de la Banque centrale
21. Interbank deposits	5664861	5862019	5781106	6308312	7029508	7992635	8620676	8876709	9716801	10365931	21. Dépôts interbancaires
22. Non-bank deposits	4362287	5018640	5233632	6122701	7074785	7486709	7226160	7579426	7833431	7730101	22. Dépôts non bancaires
23. Bonds	361339	557124	643922	683190	684930	864671	1131912	1401735	1726997	1645526	23. Obligations
24. Other liabilities	547557	604941	582507	907586	807526	900962	935312	923750	1086804	1547398	24. Autres engagements
Balance sheet total											**Total du bilan**
25. End-year total	11336771	12480214	12751111	14424081	16020964	17669192	18373746	19256340	20838452	21814037	25. En fin d'exercice
26. Average total	11126632	12212272	13003686	13841317	15450298	16710459	18027275	18828510	20319246	22186822	26. Moyen

LUXEMBOURG
Commercial banks

LUXEMBOURG
Banques commerciales

	1989	1990	1991	1992	1993	1994	1995	1996	1997	1998 p	
Million Luxembourg francs											*Millions de francs luxembourgeois*
Memorandum items											***Pour mémoire***
27. Short-term securities	..	..	..	..	..	..	..	..	..	..	*27. Titres à court terme*
28. Bonds	*324005*	*380893*	*480731*	*700081*	*767318*	*1046597*	..	..	..	..	*28. Obligations*
29. Shares and participations	*86293*	*121414*	*86639*	*89378*	*79085*	*97430*	*54809*	*62875*	*98497*	*171982*	*29. Actions et participations*
30. Claims on non-residents	*10020284*	*11050104*	*11263515*	*12563961*	*13329213*	*14455445*	*14849237*	*16003439*	*17420284*	*18570404*	*30. Créances sur des non-résidents*
31. Liabilities to non-residents	*9226691*	*10258551*	*10446855*	*11558901*	*11981772*	*12896224*	*13294824*	*13957263*	*14947354*	*16280556*	*31. Engagements envers des non-résidents*
Capital adequacy											***Solvabilité***
32. Tier 1 Capital	..	..	..	..	..	..	..	..	..	..	*32. Fonds propres de base*
33. Tier 2 Capital	..	..	..	..	..	..	..	..	..	..	*33. Fonds propres complémentaires*
34. Supervisory deductions	..	..	..	..	..	..	..	..	..	..	*34. Eléments à déduire des fonds propres*
35. Total net capital resources	..	..	..	..	..	..	..	..	..	..	*35. Total net des ressources en capital*
36. Risk-weighted assets	..	..	..	..	..	..	..	..	..	..	*36. Actifs pondérés des risques*
SUPPLEMENTARY INFORMATION											**RENSEIGNEMENTS COMPLEMENTAIRES**
37. Number of institutions	166	177	187	213	218	222	220	221	215	209	37. Nombre d'institutions
38. Number of branches	295	297	308	303	306	367	395	386	365	289	38. Nombre de succursales
39. Number of employees (x 1000)	15.2	16.3	17.1	17.6	18.5	19.7	18.3	18.6	19.1	19.8	39. Nombre de salariés (x 1000)

Notes

- Average balance sheet totals (item 26) are based on thirteen end-month data.

Notes

- La moyenne du total des actifs/passifs (poste 26) est basée sur treize données de fin de mois.

LUXEMBOURG

Commercial banks

LUXEMBOURG

Banques commerciales

Per cent	1989	1990	1991	1992	1993	1994	1995	1996	1997	1998 p	Pourcentage
INCOME STATEMENT ANALYSIS											**ANALYSE DU COMPTE DE RESULTATS**
% of average balance sheet total											**% du total moyen du bilan**
40. Interest income	8.72	9.70	9.63	9.94	8.46	7.00	7.51	6.64	6.74	7.12	40. Produits financiers
41. Interest expenses	7.94	8.93	8.80	9.10	7.69	6.25	6.80	5.96	6.11	6.54	41. Frais financiers
42. Net interest income	0.78	0.77	0.83	0.84	0.77	0.75	0.70	0.68	0.63	0.59	42. Produits financiers nets
43. Non-interest income (net)	0.29	0.42	0.30	0.35	0.50	0.37	0.37	0.42	0.51	0.72	43. Produits non financiers (nets)
a. Fees and commissions receivable	..	..	..	..	..	..	..	..	..	..	*a. Frais et commissions à recevoir*
b. Fees and commissions payable	..	..	..	..	..	..	..	..	..	..	*b. Frais et commissions à payer*
c. Net profits or loss on financial operations	..	..	..	..	..	..	..	..	..	..	*c. Profits ou pertes nets sur opérations financières*
d. Other	..	..	..	..	..	..	..	..	..	..	*d. Autres*
44. Gross income	1.07	1.19	1.13	1.19	1.27	1.12	1.08	1.10	1.14	1.30	44. Résultat brut
45. Operating expenses	0.42	0.44	0.46	0.47	0.48	0.50	0.50	0.51	0.50	0.50	45. Frais d'exploitation
a. Staff costs	*0.25*	*0.23*	*0.24*	*0.24*	*0.25*	*0.26*	*0.26*	*0.26*	*0.25*	*0.24*	*a. Dépenses en personnel*
b. Property costs	..	..	..	..	..	..	..	..	..	..	*b. Dépenses en immobilier*
c. Other	..	..	..	..	..	..	..	..	..	..	*c. Autres*
46. Net income	0.66	0.74	0.67	0.72	0.79	0.62	0.58	0.59	0.64	0.80	46. Résultat net
47. Provisions (net)	0.35	0.52	0.42	0.40	0.27	0.08	0.07	0.03	0.11	0.17	47. Provisions (nettes)
a. Provisions on loans	..	..	..	..	..	..	..	..	..	..	*a. Provisions sur prêts*
b. Provisions on securities	..	..	..	..	..	..	..	..	..	..	*b. Provisions sur titres*
c. Other	..	..	..	..	..	..	..	..	..	..	*c. Autres*
48. Profit before tax	0.31	0.22	0.26	0.32	0.52	0.53	0.51	0.56	0.53	0.63	48. Bénéfices avant impôt
49. Income tax	0.09	0.06	0.07	0.12	0.17	0.16	0.17	0.19	0.18	0.13	49. Impôt sur le revenu
50. Profit after tax	0.21	0.16	0.18	0.21	0.35	0.37	0.34	0.37	0.35	0.50	50. Bénéfices après impôt
51. Distributed profit	..	..	..	..	..	..	..	..	..	..	51. Bénéfices distribués
52. Retained profit	..	..	..	..	..	..	..	..	..	..	52. Bénéfices mis en réserve
% of gross income											**% du total du résultat brut**
53. Net interest income	73.09	65.00	73.49	70.81	60.46	66.90	65.48	61.72	55.05	44.91	53. Produits financiers nets
54. Non-interest income (net)	26.91	35.00	26.51	29.19	39.54	33.10	34.52	38.28	44.95	55.09	54. Produits non financiers (nets)
a. Fees and commissions receivable	..	..	..	..	..	..	..	..	..	..	*a. Frais et commissions à recevoir*
b. Fees and commissions payable	..	..	..	..	..	..	..	..	..	..	*b. Frais et commissions à payer*
c. Net profits or loss on financial operations	..	..	..	..	..	..	..	..	..	..	*c. Profits ou pertes nets sur opérations financières*
d. Other	..	..	..	..	..	..	..	..	..	..	*d. Autres*
55. Operating expenses	38.72	37.32	40.55	39.38	37.97	44.96	46.54	46.51	43.86	38.75	55. Frais d'exploitation
a. Staff costs	*22.88*	*19.52*	*21.19*	*20.49*	*19.51*	*23.61*	*23.92*	*23.41*	*22.05*	*18.62*	*a. Dépenses en personnel*
b. Property costs	..	..	..	..	..	..	..	..	..	..	*b. Dépenses en immobilier*
c. Other	..	..	..	..	..	..	..	..	..	..	*c. Autres*
56. Net income	61.28	62.68	59.45	60.62	62.03	55.04	53.46	53.49	56.14	61.25	56. Résultat net
57. Provisions (net)	32.43	44.06	36.87	33.43	21.04	7.53	6.18	2.55	9.36	12.84	57. Provisions (nettes)
a. Provisions on loans	..	..	..	..	..	..	..	..	..	..	*a. Provisions sur prêts*
b. Provisions on securities	..	..	..	..	..	..	..	..	..	..	*b. Provisions sur titres*
c. Other	..	..	..	..	..	..	..	..	..	..	*c. Autres*
58. Profit before tax	28.85	18.63	22.58	27.19	40.99	47.50	47.28	50.94	46.78	48.41	58. Bénéfices avant impôt
59. Income tax	8.85	5.46	6.48	10.00	13.11	14.04	15.84	17.62	15.73	9.70	59. Impôt sur le revenu
60. Profit after tax	20.00	13.16	16.10	17.19	27.88	33.46	31.44	33.33	31.05	38.71	60. Bénéfices après impôt
% of net income											**% du total du résultat net**
61. Provisions (net)	52.92	70.28	62.02	55.15	33.92	13.69	11.55	4.77	16.67	20.97	61. Provisions (nettes)
a. Provisions on loans	..	..	..	..	..	..	..	..	..	..	*a. Provisions sur prêts*
b. Provisions on securities	..	..	..	..	..	..	..	..	..	..	*b. Provisions sur titres*
c. Other	..	..	..	..	..	..	..	..	..	..	*c. Autres*
62. Profit before tax	47.08	29.72	37.98	44.85	66.08	86.31	88.45	95.23	83.33	79.03	62. Bénéfices avant impôt
63. Income tax	14.44	8.72	10.89	16.49	21.13	25.51	29.63	32.93	28.02	15.83	63. Impôt sur le revenu
64. Profit after tax	32.64	21.00	27.09	28.36	44.95	60.80	58.82	62.30	55.31	63.20	64. Bénéfices après impôt

	1989	1990	1991	1992	1993	1994	1995	1996	1997	1998 p	
Per cent											*Pourcentage*
BALANCE SHEET ANALYSIS											**ANALYSE DU BILAN**
% of year-end balance sheet total											**% du total du bilan en fin d'exercice**
Assets											**Actif**
65. Cash & balance with Central bank	0.20	0.18	0.19	0.18	0.86	0.34	0.18	0.21	0.18	0.14	65. Caisse & solde auprès de la Banque centrale
66. Interbank deposits	60.23	60.44	59.57	59.03	58.42	60.05	58.29	55.69	54.43	53.13	66. Dépôts interbancaires
67. Loans	23.86	23.97	24.40	24.68	22.29	18.43	18.88	18.46	18.73	18.18	67. Prêts
68. Securities	7.28	7.59	8.08	9.47	14.85	17.42	18.91	21.90	22.55	23.87	68. Valeurs mobilières
69. Other assets	8.43	7.83	7.76	6.64	3.58	3.75	3.74	3.73	4.11	4.69	69. Autres actifs
Liabilities											**Passif**
70. Capital & reserves	3.53	3.51	4.00	2.79	2.65	2.40	2.50	2.47	2.28	2.41	70. Capital et réserves
71. Borrowing from Central bank	-	-	-	-	-	-	-	-	-	-	71. Emprunts auprès de la Banque centrale
72. Interbank deposits	49.97	46.97	45.34	43.73	43.88	45.23	46.92	46.10	46.63	47.52	72. Dépôts interbancaires
73. Non-bank deposits	38.48	40.21	41.04	42.45	44.16	42.37	39.33	39.36	37.59	35.44	73. Dépôts non bancaires
74. Bonds	3.19	4.46	5.05	4.74	4.28	4.89	6.16	7.28	8.29	7.54	74. Obligations
75. Other liabilities	4.83	4.85	4.57	6.29	5.04	5.10	5.09	4.80	5.22	7.09	75. Autres engagements
Memorandum items											***Pour mémoire***
76. Short-term securities	..	..	..	..	..	..	..	..	..	..	*76. Titres à court terme*
77. Bonds	*2.86*	*3.05*	*3.77*	*4.85*	*4.79*	*5.92*	..	..	..	..	*77. Obligations*
78. Shares and participations	*0.76*	*0.97*	*0.68*	*0.62*	*0.49*	*0.55*	*0.30*	*0.33*	*0.47*	*0.79*	*78. Actions et participations*
79. Claims on non-residents	*88.39*	*88.54*	*88.33*	*87.10*	*83.20*	*81.81*	*80.82*	*83.11*	*83.60*	*85.13*	*79. Créances sur des non-résidents*
80. Liabilities to non-residents	*81.39*	*82.20*	*81.93*	*80.14*	*74.79*	*72.99*	*72.36*	*72.48*	*71.73*	*74.63*	*80. Engagements envers des non-résidents*

* See notes on previous pages.

* Voir les notes en pages précédentes.

MEXICO / MEXIQUE

Commercial banks / Banques commerciales

	1989	1990	1991	1992	1993	1994	1995	1996	1997(1)	1998 p	
Million pesos											*Millions de pesos*
INCOME STATEMENT											**COMPTE DE RESULTATS**
1. Interest income (2)	31152	52738	61862	73980	92987	104325	311439	244677	207028	286819	1. Produits financiers (2)
2. Interest expenses (2)	24884	41966	46169	50532	63501	72931	266830	209147	165082	220757	2. Frais financiers (2)
3. Net interest income (2)	6268	10772	15694	23449	29486	31394	44609	35530	41946	66062	3. Produits financiers nets (2)
4. Non-interest income (net) (2)	2299	3361	5587	7031	9502	8673	17070	28593	25131	14374	4. Produits non financiers (nets) (2)
a. Fees and commissions receivable	..	..	*2604*	*2482*	*3183*	*4070*	*9856*	*6625*	*9836*	*13608*	*a. Frais et commissions à recevoir*
b. Fees and commissions payable	..	..	*384*	*538*	*742*	*893*	*1897*	*1677*	*1838*	*2445*	*b. Frais et commissions à payer*
c. Net profits or loss on financial operations	..	..	*3387*	*5879*	*6458*	*4786*	*9182*	*22542*	*11527*	*-2305*	*c. Profits ou pertes nets sur opérations financières*
d. Other	..	..	*-20*	*-792*	*604*	*709*	*-71*	*1103*	*5605*	*5517*	*d. Autres*
5. Gross income	8567	14133	21281	30480	38988	40067	61679	64123	67077	80436	5. Résultat brut
6. Operating expenses	5947	9753	14295	18045	21534	25720	32919	40828	49149	56509	6. Frais d'exploitation
a. Staff costs	*2663*	*4224*	*6002*	*8626*	*10661*	*12301*	*13330*	*15953*	*21452*	*23951*	*a. Dépenses en personnel*
b. Property costs	..	..	*7856*	*8816*	*10176*	*11859*	*17750*	*22595*	*25011*	*28317*	*b. Dépenses en immobilier*
c. Other	..	..	*436*	*603*	*697*	*1560*	*1838*	*2280*	*2686*	*4241*	*c. Autres*
7. Net income	2620	4380	6986	12435	17454	14347	28760	23295	17929	23927	7. Résultat net
8. Provisions (net)	-	279	1266	3502	6885	9619	24668	29998	16482	16563	8. Provisions (nettes)
a. Provisions on loans	-	*279*	*1266*	*3502*	*6885*	*9619*	*24668*	*29998*	*16482*	*16563*	*a. Provisions sur prêts*
b. Provisions on securities	-	-	-	-	-	-	-	-	-	-	*b. Provisions sur titres*
c. Other	-	-	-	-	-	-	-	-	-	-	*c. Autres*
9. Profit before tax	2620	4101	5719	8933	10569	4728	4092	-6704	1447	7364	9. Bénéfices avant impôt
10. Income tax	590	1100	1643	2414	2160	1048	781	615	665	630	10. Impôt sur le revenu
11. Profit after tax	2030	3001	4077	6519	8409	3680	3312	-7318	782	6734	11. Bénéfices après impôt
12. Distributed profit	232	402	565	691	624	254	187	180	100	127	12. Bénéfices distribués
13. Retained profit	1798	2599	3512	5828	7785	3427	3125	-7498	681	6608	13. Bénéfices mis en réserve
BALANCE SHEET											**BILAN**
Assets											**Actif**
14. Cash & balance with Central bank	8665	6204	7270	6945	5850	9529	11912	16186	21093	20150	14. Caisse & solde auprès de la Banque centrale
15. Interbank deposits (2) (3)	..	4112	5688	4056	5284	7646	24128	24169	71584	115395	15. Dépôts interbancaires (2) (3)
16. Loans	80628	126251	187833	263654	321495	444600	607548	699242	745549	872485	16. Prêts
17. Securities	28853	49882	103665	75691	93243	153306	187239	245179	148103	130871	17. Valeurs mobilières
18. Other assets	23387	43475	50022	64787	84933	112334	115830	190945	61635	78592	18. Autres actifs
Liabilities											**Passif**
19. Capital & reserves	9180	14340	19305	26028	33712	40035	64580	70743	84196	102433	19. Capital et réserves
20. Borrowing from Central bank	1172	1908	3059	4576	5294	6837	13051	19831	18659	18323	20. Emprunts auprès de la Banque centrale
21. Interbank deposits (4)	17363	25461	29146	33204	43843	104165	154807	122260	148848	181279	21. Dépôts interbancaires (4)
22. Non-bank deposits	87398	165845	268748	314100	386315	479618	593050	793182	730903	847833	22. Dépôts non bancaires
23. Bonds (5)	..	..	..	..	..	..	..	..	..	..	23. Obligations (5)
24. Other liabilities	26419	22370	34219	37224	41642	96761	121170	169706	65358	67624	24. Autres engagements
Balance sheet total											**Total du bilan**
25. End-year total	141533	229924	354477	415132	510805	727415	946657	1175722	1047963	1217492	25. En fin d'exercice
26. Average total	118543	185728	292200	384804	462968	619110	874177	1084768	1111842	1132728	26. Moyen

MEXICO
Commercial banks

MEXIQUE
Banques commerciales

Million pesos	1989	1990	1991	1992	1993	1994	1995	1996	1997(1)	1998 p	Millions de pesos
Memorandum items											**Pour mémoire**
27. Short-term securities	..	..	..	..	..	..	..	..	..	..	*27. Titres à court terme*
28. Bonds	..	..	..	..	..	..	..	..	..	..	*28. Obligations*
29. Shares and participations	..	*1930*	*4358*	*4164*	*5762*	*12815*	*21802*	*24788*	*21847*	*15741*	*29. Actions et participations*
30. Claims on non-residents	..	..	..	..	..	..	..	..	..	..	*30. Créances sur des non-résidents*
31. Liabilities to non-residents	..	..	..	..	..	..	..	..	..	..	*31. Engagements envers des non-résidents*
Capital adequacy											***Solvabilité***
32. Tier 1 Capital	..	..	..	..	..	*30613*	*48169*	*56660*	*66558*	*76255*	*32. Fonds propres de base*
33. Tier 2 Capital	..	..	..	..	..	*20707*	*32387*	*32745*	*34963*	*38949*	*33. Fonds propres complémentaires*
34. Supervisory deductions	..	..	..	..	..	..	-	-	-	-	*34. Eléments à déduire des fonds propres*
35. Total net capital resources	..	..	*16533*	*31008*	*39897*	*51320*	*80555*	*89405*	*101521*	*115204*	*35. Total net des ressources en capital*
36. Risk-weighted assets	..	..	*211776*	*337507*	*411476*	*523231*	*666146*	*684399*	*746944*	*799330*	*36. Actifs pondérés des risques*
SUPPLEMENTARY INFORMATION											**RENSEIGNEMENTS COMPLEMENTAIRES**
37. Number of institutions	13	13	13	13	14	26	42	41	39	39	37. Nombre d'institutions
38. Number of branches	3647	3624	3621	3535	3763	4338	4806	6264	6411	6563	38. Nombre de succursales
39. Number of employees (x 1000)	131.6	137.3	137.5	138.9	131.2	126.9	121.0	130.6	121.3	119.3	39. Nombre de salariés (x 1000)

1. Break in series in 1997 due to new accounting regulations.
2. Change in methodology.
3. Interbank deposits as assets (item 15) includes deposits in domestic and foreign banks.
4. Interbank deposits as liabilities (item 21) includes deposits and loans in domestic and foreign banks.
5. Bonds (item 23) are included under Capital and reserves (item 19).

Notes

- Due to their special situation as a result of mergers and acquisitions, the following banks are excluded from the coverage: Inverlat, Union, Cremi, Oriente, Obrero, and Interestatal. Banpais and Centro are excluded from the coverage until 1997. Beginning 1996, Sureste, Promotor del Norte and Anahuac are excluded.

Change in methodology

- Beginning 1991 the composition of Interest income, Interest expenses, Net interest income and Non-interest income(net) (items 1 to 4) is consistent with the country's methodology and shows the same financial margins as in national publications.
- Until 1991, the sub-items (a., b., c. and d.) of Non-interest income (item 4) are included under Interest income or Interest expenses (item 1 or 2).
- Until 1990, Interbank deposits (item 15) is included under Cash and balance with Central bank (item 14).

1. Rupture dans les séries en 1997 suite aux nouvelles règles de comptabilité.
2. Changement méthodologique.
3. Les Dépôts interbancaires sous la rubrique de l'actif (poste 15) incluent les dépôts dans les banques domestiques et étrangères.
4. Les Dépôts interbancaires sous la rubrique du passif (poste 21) incluent les dépôts et les prêts dans les banques domestiques et étrangères.
5. Les Obligations (poste 23) sont incluses sous Capital et réserves (poste 19).

Notes

- Compte tenu de leur situation spéciale à la suite de fusions et acquisitions, les banques suivantes sont exclues du champ de couverture : Inverlat, Union, Cremi, Oriente, Obrero et Interestatal. Banpais et Centro sont exclues jusqu'en 1997. A compter de 1996, Sureste, Capital, Promotor del Norte et Anahuac sont exclues.

Changement méthodologique

- A compter de 1991, la composition des Produits financiers, Frais financiers, Produits financiers (nets) et Produits non financiers (nets) (postes 1 à 4) sont conformes à la méthodologie du pays et font apparaître la même marge financière que les publications nationales.
- Jusqu'en 1991, les sous-catégories (a., b., c. et d.) des Produits non financiers (poste 4) sont incluses sous la rubrique Produits financiers ou la rubrique Frais financiers (poste 1 ou poste 2).
- Jusqu'en 1990, les Dépôts interbancaires (poste 15) sont inclus sous la rubrique Caisse et solde auprès de la Banque centrale (poste 14)

Commercial banks / Banques commerciales

	1989	1990	1991	1992	1993	1994	1995	1996	1997(1)	1998 p	
Per cent											*Pourcentage*
INCOME STATEMENT ANALYSIS											**ANALYSE DU COMPTE DE RESULTATS**
% of average balance sheet total											**% du total moyen du bilan**
40. Interest income	26.28	28.40	21.17	19.23	20.08	16.85	35.63	22.56	18.62	25.32	40. Produits financiers
41. Interest expenses	20.99	22.60	15.80	13.13	13.72	11.78	30.52	19.28	14.85	19.49	41. Frais financiers
42. Net interest income	5.29	5.80	5.37	6.09	6.37	5.07	5.10	3.28	3.77	5.83	42. Produits financiers nets
43. Non-interest income (net)	1.94	1.81	1.91	1.83	2.05	1.40	1.95	2.64	2.26	1.27	43. Produits non financiers (nets)
a. Fees and commissions receivable	..	..	*0.89*	*0.65*	*0.69*	*0.66*	*1.13*	*0.61*	*0.88*	*1.20*	*a. Frais et commissions à recevoir*
b. Fees and commissions payable	..	..	*0.13*	*0.14*	*0.16*	*0.14*	*0.22*	*0.15*	*0.17*	*0.22*	*b. Frais et commissions à payer*
c. Net profits or loss on financial operations	..	..	*1.16*	*1.53*	*1.39*	*0.77*	*1.05*	*2.08*	*1.04*	*-0.20*	*c. Profits ou pertes nets sur opérations financières*
d. Other	..	..	*-0.01*	*-0.21*	*0.13*	*0.11*	*-0.01*	*0.10*	*0.50*	*0.49*	*d. Autres*
44. Gross income	7.23	7.61	7.28	7.92	8.42	6.47	7.06	5.91	6.03	7.10	44. Résultat brut
45. Operating expenses	5.02	5.25	4.89	4.69	4.65	4.15	3.77	3.76	4.42	4.99	45. Frais d'exploitation
a. Staff costs	*2.25*	*2.27*	*2.05*	*2.24*	*2.30*	*1.99*	*1.52*	*1.47*	*1.93*	*2.11*	*a. Dépenses en personnel*
b. Property costs	..	..	*2.69*	*2.29*	*2.20*	*1.92*	*2.03*	*2.08*	*2.25*	*2.50*	*b. Dépenses en immobilier*
c. Other	..	..	*0.15*	*0.16*	*0.15*	*0.25*	*0.21*	*0.21*	*0.24*	*0.37*	*c. Autres*
46. Net income	2.21	2.36	2.39	3.23	3.77	2.32	3.29	2.15	1.61	2.11	46. Résultat net
47. Provisions (net)	-	0.15	0.43	0.91	1.49	1.55	2.82	2.77	1.48	1.46	47. Provisions (nettes)
a. Provisions on loans	-	*0.15*	*0.43*	*0.91*	*1.49*	*1.55*	*2.82*	*2.77*	*1.48*	*1.46*	*a. Provisions sur prêts*
b. Provisions on securities	-	-	-	-	-	-	-	-	-	-	*b. Provisions sur titres*
c. Other	-	-	-	-	-	-	-	-	-	-	*c. Autres*
48. Profit before tax	2.21	2.21	1.96	2.32	2.28	0.76	0.47	-0.62	0.13	0.65	48. Bénéfices avant impôt
49. Income tax	0.50	0.59	0.56	0.63	0.47	0.17	0.09	0.06	0.06	0.06	49. Impôt sur le revenu
50. Profit after tax	1.71	1.62	1.40	1.69	1.82	0.59	0.38	-0.67	0.07	0.59	50. Bénéfices après impôt
51. Distributed profit	0.20	0.22	0.19	0.18	0.13	0.04	0.02	0.02	0.01	0.01	51. Bénéfices distribués
52. Retained profit	1.52	1.40	1.20	1.51	1.68	0.55	0.36	-0.69	0.06	0.58	52. Bénéfices mis en réserve
% of gross income											**% du total du résultat brut**
53. Net interest income	73.16	76.22	73.75	76.93	75.63	78.35	72.32	55.41	62.53	82.13	53. Produits financiers nets
54. Non-interest income (net)	26.84	23.78	26.25	23.07	24.37	21.65	27.68	44.59	37.47	17.87	54. Produits non financiers (nets)
a. Fees and commissions receivable	..	..	*12.24*	*8.14*	*8.16*	*10.16*	*15.98*	*10.33*	*14.66*	*16.92*	*a. Frais et commissions à recevoir*
b. Fees and commissions payable	..	..	*1.80*	*1.77*	*1.90*	*2.23*	*3.08*	*2.62*	*2.74*	*3.04*	*b. Frais et commissions à payer*
c. Net profits or loss on financial operations	..	..	*15.92*	*19.29*	*16.56*	*11.94*	*14.89*	*35.15*	*17.18*	*-2.87*	*c. Profits ou pertes nets sur opérations financières*
d. Other	..	..	*-0.09*	*-2.60*	*1.55*	*1.77*	*-0.12*	*1.72*	*8.36*	*6.86*	*d. Autres*
55. Operating expenses	69.42	69.01	67.17	59.20	55.23	64.19	53.37	63.67	73.27	70.25	55. Frais d'exploitation
a. Staff costs	*31.08*	*29.89*	*28.20*	*28.30*	*27.34*	*30.70*	*21.61*	*24.88*	*31.98*	*29.78*	*a. Dépenses en personnel*
b. Property costs	..	..	*36.92*	*28.92*	*26.10*	*29.60*	*28.78*	*35.24*	*37.29*	*35.20*	*b. Dépenses en immobilier*
c. Other	..	..	*2.05*	*1.98*	*1.79*	*3.89*	*2.98*	*3.56*	*4.00*	*5.27*	*c. Autres*
56. Net income	30.58	30.99	32.83	40.80	44.77	35.81	46.63	36.33	26.73	29.75	56. Résultat net
57. Provisions (net)	-	1.97	5.95	11.49	17.66	24.01	39.99	46.78	24.57	20.59	57. Provisions (nettes)
a. Provisions on loans	-	*1.97*	*5.95*	*11.49*	*17.66*	*24.01*	*39.99*	*46.78*	*24.57*	*20.59*	*a. Provisions sur prêts*
b. Provisions on securities	-	-	-	-	-	-	-	-	-	-	*b. Provisions sur titres*
c. Other	-	-	-	-	-	-	-	-	-	-	*c. Autres*
58. Profit before tax	30.58	29.02	26.87	29.31	27.11	11.80	6.63	-10.45	2.16	9.16	58. Bénéfices avant impôt
59. Income tax	6.89	7.78	7.72	7.92	5.54	2.62	1.27	0.96	0.99	0.78	59. Impôt sur le revenu
60. Profit after tax	23.70	21.23	19.16	21.39	21.57	9.18	5.37	-11.41	1.17	8.37	60. Bénéfices après impôt
% of net income											**% du total du résultat net**
61. Provisions (net)	-	6.37	18.12	28.16	39.45	67.05	85.77	128.77	91.93	69.22	61. Provisions (nettes)
a. Provisions on loans	-	*6.37*	*18.12*	*28.16*	*39.45*	*67.05*	*85.77*	*128.77*	*91.93*	*69.22*	*a. Provisions sur prêts*
b. Provisions on securities	-	-	-	-	-	-	-	-	-	-	*b. Provisions sur titres*
c. Other	-	-	-	-	-	-	-	-	-	-	*c. Autres*
62. Profit before tax	100.00	93.63	81.86	71.84	60.55	32.95	14.23	-28.78	8.07	30.78	62. Bénéfices avant impôt
63. Income tax	22.52	25.11	23.52	19.41	12.38	7.30	2.72	2.64	3.71	2.63	63. Impôt sur le revenu
64. Profit after tax	77.48	68.52	58.36	52.42	48.18	25.65	11.52	-31.41	4.36	28.14	64. Bénéfices après impôt

MEXICO
Commercial banks

MEXIQUE
Banques commerciales

	1989	1990	1991	1992	1993	1994	1995	1996	1997(1)	1998 p	
Per cent											*Pourcentage*
BALANCE SHEET ANALYSIS											**ANALYSE DU BILAN**
% of year-end balance sheet total											**% du total du bilan en fin d'exercice**
Assets											**Actif**
65. Cash & balance with Central bank	6.12	2.70	2.05	1.67	1.15	1.31	1.26	1.38	2.01	1.66	65. Caisse & solde auprès de la Banque centrale
66. Interbank deposits	..	1.79	1.60	0.98	1.03	1.05	2.55	2.06	6.83	9.48	66. Dépôts interbancaires
67. Loans	56.97	54.91	52.99	63.51	62.94	61.12	64.18	59.47	71.14	71.66	67. Prêts
68. Securities	20.39	21.69	29.24	18.23	18.25	21.08	19.78	20.85	14.13	10.75	68. Valeurs mobilières
69. Other assets	16.52	18.91	14.11	15.61	16.63	15.44	12.24	16.24	5.88	6.46	69. Autres actifs
Liabilities											**Passif**
70. Capital & reserves	6.49	6.24	5.45	6.27	6.60	5.50	6.82	6.02	8.03	8.41	70. Capital et réserves
71. Borrowing from Central bank	0.83	0.83	0.86	1.10	1.04	0.94	1.38	1.69	1.78	1.50	71. Emprunts auprès de la Banque centrale
72. Interbank deposits	12.27	11.07	8.22	8.00	8.58	14.32	16.35	10.40	14.20	14.89	72. Dépôts interbancaires
73. Non-bank deposits	61.75	72.13	75.82	75.66	75.63	65.93	62.65	67.46	69.75	69.64	73. Dépôts non bancaires
74. Bonds	..	..	..	..	..	..	..	..	..	..	74. Obligations
75. Other liabilities	18.67	9.73	9.65	8.97	8.15	13.30	12.80	14.43	6.24	5.55	75. Autres engagements
Memorandum items											***Pour mémoire***
76. Short-term securities	..	..	..	..	..	..	..	..	..	..	*76. Titres à court terme*
77. Bonds	..	..	..	..	..	..	..	..	..	..	*77. Obligations*
78. Shares and participations	..	*0.84*	*1.23*	*1.00*	*1.13*	*1.76*	*2.30*	*2.11*	*2.08*	*1.29*	*78. Actions et participations*
79. Claims on non-residents	..	..	..	..	..	..	..	..	..	..	*79. Créances sur des non-résidents*
80. Liabilities to non-residents	..	..	..	..	..	..	..	..	..	..	*80. Engagements envers des non-résidents*

* See notes on previous pages.

* Voir les notes en pages précédentes.

NETHERLANDS — PAYS-BAS

All banks — Ensemble des banques

	1989	1990	1991	1992	1993	1994	1995	1996	1997	1998 p	
Million guilders											*Millions de florins*
INCOME STATEMENT (1)											**COMPTE DE RESULTATS (1)**
1. Interest income	..	..	..	..	99664	94750	100582	106318	126786	164236	1. Produits financiers
2. Interest expenses	..	..	..	..	75842	68617	73546	76031	91475	122271	2. Frais financiers
3. Net interest income	17270	18309	20331	22215	23822	26133	27036	30287	35311	41965	3. Produits financiers nets
4. Non-interest income (net)	7285	7256	8570	9132	12129	10517	13481	16985	23126	28312	4. Produits non financiers (nets)
a. Fees and commissions receivable	..	..	..	..	..	..	..	..	..	*20154*	*a. Frais et commissions à recevoir*
b. Fees and commissions payable	..	..	..	..	..	..	..	..	..	*2537*	*b. Frais et commissions à payer*
c. Net profits or loss on financial operations	..	..	..	..	*2744*	*1341*	*2815*	*3768*	*4900*	*4926*	*c. Profits ou pertes nets sur opérations financières*
d. Other	..	..	..	..	*2086*	*1239*	*1580*	*2113*	*2277*	*5769*	*d. Autres*
5. Gross income	24555	25565	28901	31347	35951	36650	40517	47272	58437	70277	5. Résultat brut
6. Operating expenses	16056	17612	19510	21074	23930	24576	27265	31806	40444	49402	6. Frais d'exploitation
a. Staff costs	*9265*	*10183*	*11242*	*12245*	*13274*	*13585*	*15053*	*17162*	*21534*	*27477*	*a. Dépenses en personnel*
b. Property costs	*1248*	*1357*	*1511*	*1564*	*2454*	*1999*	*2091*	*2330*	*2907*	*3828*	*b. Dépenses en immobilier*
c. Other	*5543*	*6072*	*6757*	*7265*	*8202*	*8992*	*10121*	*12314*	*16003*	*18097*	*c. Autres*
7. Net income	8499	7953	9391	10273	12021	12074	13252	15466	17993	20875	7. Résultat net
8. Provisions (net)	1542	2410	3328	3283	3125	2427	2371	2901	3660	5892	8. Provisions (nettes)
a. Provisions on loans	..	..	..	..	*2968*	*2423*	*2334*	*2937*	*2959*	*5481*	*a. Provisions sur prêts*
b. Provisions on securities	..	..	..	..	*153*	*3*	*35*	*-28*	*-39*	*250*	*b. Provisions sur titres*
c. Other	..	..	..	..	*4*	*1*	*2*	*-8*	*741*	*161*	*c. Autres*
9. Profit before tax	6957	5543	6063	6990	8896	9647	10881	12565	14333	14983	9. Bénéfices avant impôt
10. Income tax	1693	1443	1667	1985	2674	2819	3279	3351	3938	4489	10. Impôt sur le revenu
11. Profit after tax	5264	4100	4396	5005	6222	6828	7602	9214	10395	10494	11. Bénéfices après impôt
12. Distributed profit	..	..	..	..	..	..	..	..	..	..	12. Bénéfices distribués
13. Retained profit	..	..	..	..	..	..	..	..	..	..	13. Bénéfices mis en réserve
BALANCE SHEET											**BILAN**
Assets											**Actif**
14. Cash & balance with Central bank	22879	26110	22511	29446	36154	37349	23960	28899	39824	..	14. Caisse & solde auprès de la Banque centrale
15. Interbank deposits	223004	261984	259165	265622	280384	262497	281225	271492	311859	..	15. Dépôts interbancaires
16. Loans	501308	685356	731174	789757	856348	883475	976245	1117256	1355185	..	16. Prêts
17. Securities	77642	118789	122342	139692	158231	183931	217611	283649	412310	..	17. Valeurs mobilières
18. Other assets	62595	30251	32468	31019	32790	34742	39907	44619	52610	..	18. Autres actifs
Liabilities											**Passif**
19. Capital & reserves	38756	45047	47634	50459	56031	59681	64039	71526	93151	..	19. Capital et réserves
20. Borrowing from Central bank	4891	9328	3045	6647	4056	7921	10146	13096	14687	..	20. Emprunts auprès de la Banque centrale
21. Interbank deposits	197499	265314	285345	296965	329205	324057	348055	409265	543545	..	21. Dépôts interbancaires
22. Non-bank deposits	422644	510650	535246	580987	618785	623038	677208	735888	881431	..	22. Dépôts non bancaires
23. Bonds	138017	167192	167845	168702	185287	217687	248554	285510	325062	..	23. Obligations
24. Other liabilities	85621	124959	128545	151776	170543	169610	190946	230630	313912	..	24. Autres engagements
Balance sheet total											**Total du bilan**
25. End-year total	887428	1122490	1167660	1255536	1363907	1401994	1538948	1745915	2171788	..	25. En fin d'exercice
26. Average total	817041	1004959	1145075	1211598	1309722	1382951	1470471	1642432	1958852	..	26. Moyen

NETHERLANDS
All banks

PAYS-BAS
Ensemble des banques

	1989	1990	1991	1992	1993	1994	1995	1996	1997	1998 p	
Million guilders											*Millions de florins*
Memorandum items											***Pour mémoire***
27. Short-term securities (2)	..	27525	23333	24900	25350	34092	46576	45487	78565	..	*27. Titres à court terme (2)*
28. Bonds	74111	86122	93604	110535	126878	143462	159092	220826	301023	..	*28. Obligations*
29. Shares and participations	3531	6281	6708	6898	6890	7117	9783	12061	18583	..	*29. Actions et participations*
30. Claims on non-residents	280183	314206	321725	343747	379936	347670	375656	416243	531726	..	*30. Créances sur des non-résidents*
31. Liabilities to non-residents	232405	259304	267940	298789	328408	324423	354514	428483	586570	..	*31. Engagements envers des non-résidents*
Capital adequacy											***Solvabilité***
32. Tier 1 Capital	..	46709	48828	51558	56784	60617	66158	74708	97519	109085	*32. Fonds propres de base*
33. Tier 2 Capital	..	21111	22421	25001	27733	28967	31422	37525	35272	36923	*33. Fonds propres complémentaires*
34. Supervisory deductions	..	973	901	979	1016	1297	1507	1377	1486	1806	*34. Eléments à déduire des fonds propres*
35. Total net capital resources	..	66847	70348	75580	83501	88287	96073	110856	131305	144202	*35. Total net des ressources en capital*
36. Risk-weighted assets	..	573593	611899	655756	682024	721882	799928	972077	1139454	1301509	*36. Actifs pondérés des risques*
SUPPLEMENTARY INFORMATION											**RENSEIGNEMENTS COMPLEMENTAIRES**
37. Number of institutions	170	180	173	177	175	173	174	172	169	..	37. Nombre d'institutions
38. Number of branches	8006	7992	7827	7518	7167	7269	6729	6822	7032	..	38. Nombre de succursales
39. Number of employees (x 1000)	117.4	122.9	119.9	119.9	115.4	109.0	111.4	115.9	120.4	..	39. Nombre de salariés (x 1000)

1. Break in series in 1993 due to changes in methodology.
2. Up to 1990, Short-term securities (item 27) are included under Bonds (item 28).

Notes

- Data cover universal banks, banks organised on a co-operative basis, savings banks, the Postbank, mortgage banks, other capital market institutions and security credit institutions.

Change in methodology:

- As from 1993, the reporting system underlying the income statement has been adapted to legal changes.

1. En 1993, rupture dans les séries consécutive aux changements méthodologiques
2. Jusqu'en 1990, les Titres à court terme (poste 27) sont inclus sous Obligations (poste 28).

Notes

- Les données concernent les banques universelles, les banques organisées en mutuelles, les caisses d'épargne, la Banque postale, les banques hypothécaires, les autres institutions du marché financier et les institutions des titre de crédit.

Changement méthodologique :

- Depuis 1993, le règlement en vigueur sur lequel repose le compte de résultats a été adapté en fonction des modifications legislatives.

NETHERLANDS — PAYS-BAS

All banks — Ensemble des banques

	1989	1990	1991	1992	1993	1994	1995	1996	1997	1998 p	
Per cent											*Pourcentage*
INCOME STATEMENT ANALYSIS											**ANALYSE DU COMPTE DE RESULTATS**
% of average balance sheet total											**% du total moyen du bilan**
40. Interest income	..	..	..	..	7.61	6.85	6.84	6.47	6.47	..	40. Produits financiers
41. Interest expenses	..	..	..	..	5.79	4.96	5.00	4.63	4.67	..	41. Frais financiers
42. Net interest income	2.11	1.82	1.78	1.83	1.82	1.89	1.84	1.84	1.80	..	42. Produits financiers nets
43. Non-interest income (net)	0.89	0.72	0.75	0.75	0.93	0.76	0.92	1.03	1.18	..	43. Produits non financiers (nets)
a. Fees and commissions receivable	..	..	..	..	..	..	..	..	..	..	*a. Frais et commissions à recevoir*
b. Fees and commissions payable	..	..	..	..	..	..	..	..	..	..	*b. Frais et commissions à payer*
c. Net profits or loss on financial operations	..	..	..	..	*0.21*	*0.10*	*0.19*	*0.23*	*0.25*	..	*c. Profits ou pertes nets sur opérations financières*
d. Other	..	..	..	..	*0.16*	*0.09*	*0.11*	*0.13*	*0.12*	..	*d. Autres*
44. Gross income	3.01	2.54	2.52	2.59	2.74	2.65	2.76	2.88	2.98	..	44. Résultat brut
45. Operating expenses	1.97	1.75	1.70	1.74	1.83	1.78	1.85	1.94	2.06	..	45. Frais d'exploitation
a. Staff costs	*1.13*	*1.01*	*0.98*	*1.01*	*1.01*	*0.98*	*1.02*	*1.04*	*1.10*	..	*a. Dépenses en personnel*
b. Property costs	*0.15*	*0.14*	*0.13*	*0.13*	*0.19*	*0.14*	*0.14*	*0.14*	*0.15*	..	*b. Dépenses en immobilier*
c. Other	*0.68*	*0.60*	*0.59*	*0.60*	*0.63*	*0.65*	*0.69*	*0.75*	*0.82*	..	*c. Autres*
46. Net income	1.04	0.79	0.82	0.85	0.92	0.87	0.90	0.94	0.92	..	46. Résultat net
47. Provisions (net)	0.19	0.24	0.29	0.27	0.24	0.18	0.16	0.18	0.19	..	47. Provisions (nettes)
a. Provisions on loans	..	..	..	..	*0.23*	*0.18*	*0.16*	*0.18*	*0.15*	..	*a. Provisions sur prêts*
b. Provisions on securities	..	..	..	..	*0.01*	-	-	-	-	..	*b. Provisions sur titres*
c. Other	..	..	..	..	-	-	-	-	*0.04*	..	*c. Autres*
48. Profit before tax	0.85	0.55	0.53	0.58	0.68	0.70	0.74	0.77	0.73	..	48. Bénéfices avant impôt
49. Income tax	0.21	0.14	0.15	0.16	0.20	0.20	0.22	0.20	0.20	..	49. Impôt sur le revenu
50. Profit after tax	0.64	0.41	0.38	0.41	0.48	0.49	0.52	0.56	0.53	..	50. Bénéfices après impôt
51. Distributed profit	..	..	..	..	..	..	..	..	..	..	51. Bénéfices distribués
52. Retained profit	..	..	..	..	..	..	..	..	..	..	52. Bénéfices mis en réserve
% of gross income											**% du total du résultat brut**
53. Net interest income	70.33	71.62	70.35	70.87	66.26	71.30	66.73	64.07	60.43	59.71	53. Produits financiers nets
54. Non-interest income (net)	29.67	28.38	29.65	29.13	33.74	28.70	33.27	35.93	39.57	40.29	54. Produits non financiers (nets)
a. Fees and commissions receivable	..	..	..	..	..	..	..	..	..	*28.68*	*a. Frais et commissions à recevoir*
b. Fees and commissions payable	..	..	..	..	..	..	..	..	..	*3.61*	*b. Frais et commissions à payer*
c. Net profits or loss on financial operations	..	..	..	..	*7.63*	*3.66*	*6.95*	*7.97*	*8.39*	*7.01*	*c. Profits ou pertes nets sur opérations financières*
d. Other	..	..	..	..	*5.80*	*3.38*	*3.90*	*4.47*	*3.90*	*8.21*	*d. Autres*
55. Operating expenses	65.39	68.89	67.51	67.23	66.56	67.06	67.29	67.28	69.21	70.30	55. Frais d'exploitation
a. Staff costs	*37.73*	*39.83*	*38.90*	*39.06*	*36.92*	*37.07*	*37.15*	*36.30*	*36.85*	*39.10*	*a. Dépenses en personnel*
b. Property costs	*5.08*	*5.31*	*5.23*	*4.99*	*6.83*	*5.45*	*5.16*	*4.93*	*4.97*	*5.45*	*b. Dépenses en immobilier*
c. Other	*22.57*	*23.75*	*23.38*	*23.18*	*22.81*	*24.53*	*24.98*	*26.05*	*27.39*	*25.75*	*c. Autres*
56. Net income	34.61	31.11	32.49	32.77	33.44	32.94	32.71	32.72	30.79	29.70	56. Résultat net
57. Provisions (net)	6.28	9.43	11.52	10.47	8.69	6.62	5.85	6.14	6.26	8.38	57. Provisions (nettes)
a. Provisions on loans	..	..	..	..	*8.26*	*6.61*	*5.76*	*6.21*	*5.06*	*7.80*	*a. Provisions sur prêts*
b. Provisions on securities	..	..	..	..	*0.43*	*0.01*	*0.09*	*-0.06*	*-0.07*	*0.36*	*b. Provisions sur titres*
c. Other	..	..	..	..	*0.01*	-	-	*-0.02*	*1.27*	*0.23*	*c. Autres*
58. Profit before tax	28.33	21.68	20.98	22.30	24.74	26.32	26.86	26.58	24.53	21.32	58. Bénéfices avant impôt
59. Income tax	6.89	5.64	5.77	6.33	7.44	7.69	8.09	7.09	6.74	6.39	59. Impôt sur le revenu
60. Profit after tax	21.44	16.04	15.21	15.97	17.31	18.63	18.76	19.49	17.79	14.93	60. Bénéfices après impôt
% of net income											**% du total du résultat net**
61. Provisions (net)	18.14	30.30	35.44	31.96	26.00	20.10	17.89	18.76	20.34	28.23	61. Provisions (nettes)
a. Provisions on loans	..	..	..	..	*24.69*	*20.07*	*17.61*	*18.99*	*16.45*	*26.26*	*a. Provisions sur prêts*
b. Provisions on securities	..	..	..	..	*1.27*	*0.02*	*0.26*	*-0.18*	*-0.22*	*1.20*	*b. Provisions sur titres*
c. Other	..	..	..	..	*0.03*	*0.01*	*0.02*	*-0.05*	*4.12*	*0.77*	*c. Autres*
62. Profit before tax	81.86	69.70	64.56	68.04	74.00	79.90	82.11	81.24	79.66	71.77	62. Bénéfices avant impôt
63. Income tax	19.92	18.14	17.75	19.32	22.24	23.35	24.74	21.67	21.89	21.50	63. Impôt sur le revenu
64. Profit after tax	61.94	51.55	46.81	48.72	51.76	56.55	57.36	59.58	57.77	50.27	64. Bénéfices après impôt

NETHERLANDS / PAYS-BAS

All banks / Ensemble des banques

	1989	1990	1991	1992	1993	1994	1995	1996	1997	1998 p	
Per cent											*Pourcentage*
BALANCE SHEET ANALYSIS											**ANALYSE DU BILAN**
% of year-end balance sheet total											**% du total du bilan en fin d'exercice**
Assets											**Actif**
65. Cash & balance with Central bank	2.58	2.33	1.93	2.35	2.65	2.66	1.56	1.66	1.83	..	65. Caisse & solde auprès de la Banque centrale
66. Interbank deposits	25.13	23.34	22.20	21.16	20.56	18.72	18.27	15.55	14.36	..	66. Dépôts interbancaires
67. Loans	56.49	61.06	62.62	62.90	62.79	63.02	63.44	63.99	62.40	..	67. Prêts
68. Securities	8.75	10.58	10.48	11.13	11.60	13.12	14.14	16.25	18.98	..	68. Valeurs mobilières
69. Other assets	7.05	2.69	2.78	2.47	2.40	2.48	2.59	2.56	2.42	..	69. Autres actifs
Liabilities											**Passif**
70. Capital & reserves	4.37	4.01	4.08	4.02	4.11	4.26	4.16	4.10	4.29	..	70. Capital et réserves
71. Borrowing from Central bank	0.55	0.83	0.26	0.53	0.30	0.56	0.66	0.75	0.68	..	71. Emprunts auprès de la Banque centrale
72. Interbank deposits	22.26	23.64	24.44	23.65	24.14	23.11	22.62	23.44	25.03	..	72. Dépôts interbancaires
73. Non-bank deposits	47.63	45.49	45.84	46.27	45.37	44.44	44.00	42.15	40.59	..	73. Dépôts non bancaires
74. Bonds	15.55	14.89	14.37	13.44	13.59	15.53	16.15	16.35	14.97	..	74. Obligations
75. Other liabilities	9.65	11.13	11.01	12.09	12.50	12.10	12.41	13.21	14.45	..	75. Autres engagements
Memorandum items											***Pour mémoire***
76. Short-term securities	..	*2.45*	*2.00*	*1.98*	*1.86*	*2.43*	*3.03*	*2.61*	*3.62*	..	*76. Titres à court terme*
77. Bonds	*8.35*	*7.67*	*8.02*	*8.80*	*9.30*	*10.23*	*10.34*	*12.65*	*13.86*	..	*77. Obligations*
78. Shares and participations	*0.40*	*0.56*	*0.57*	*0.55*	*0.51*	*0.51*	*0.64*	*0.69*	*0.86*	..	*78. Actions et participations*
79. Claims on non-residents	*31.57*	*27.99*	*27.55*	*27.38*	*27.86*	*24.80*	*24.41*	*23.84*	*24.48*	..	*79. Créances sur des non-résidents*
80. Liabilities to non-residents	*26.19*	*23.10*	*22.95*	*23.80*	*24.08*	*23.14*	*23.04*	*24.54*	*27.01*	..	*80. Engagements envers des non-résidents*

* See notes on previous pages.

* Voir les notes en pages précédentes.

NEW ZEALAND
All banks

NOUVELLE-ZELANDE
Ensemble des banques

	1990	1991	1992	1993	1994	1995	1996	1997	
Million New Zealand dollars									*Millions de dollars de Nouvelle-Zélande*
INCOME STATEMENT									**COMPTE DE RESULTATS**
1. Interest income	8950	8783	7276	6625	6845	9365	10697	10466	1. Produits financiers
2. Interest expenses	6680	6422	4810	4289	4383	6579	7870	7375	2. Frais financiers
3. Net interest income	2270	2361	2466	2336	2462	2786	2827	3090	3. Produits financiers nets
4. Non-interest income (net)	1299	1583	1331	1496	1406	1592	1682	1778	4. Produits non financiers (nets)
a. Fees and commissions receivable	..	..	..	..	..	..	..	..	*a. Frais et commissions à recevoir*
b. Fees and commissions payable	..	..	..	..	..	..	..	..	*b. Frais et commissions à payer*
c. Net profits or loss on financial operations	..	..	..	..	..	..	..	..	*c. Profits ou pertes nets sur opérations financières*
d. Other	..	..	..	..	..	..	..	..	*d. Autres*
5. Gross income	3569	3944	3797	3832	3868	4378	4509	4868	5. Résultat brut
6. Operating expenses	2618	2876	2701	2739	2716	2910	3091	3157	6. Frais d'exploitation
a. Staff costs	..	..	..	..	..	..	..	..	*a. Dépenses en personnel*
b. Property costs	..	..	..	..	..	..	..	..	*b. Dépenses en immobilier*
c. Other	..	..	..	..	..	..	..	..	*c. Autres*
7. Net income	951	1068	1096	1093	1152	1468	1418	1711	7. Résultat net
8. Provisions (net)	393	521	523	53	-97	-9	-43	88	8. Provisions (nettes)
a. Provisions on loans	..	..	..	..	..	..	..	..	*a. Provisions sur prêts*
b. Provisions on securities	..	..	..	..	..	..	..	..	*b. Provisions sur titres*
c. Other	..	..	..	..	..	..	..	..	*c. Autres*
9. Profit before tax	558	547	573	1040	1249	1477	1461	1623	9. Bénéfices avant impôt
10. Income tax	152	232	260	339	410	462	445	505	10. Impôt sur le revenu
11. Profit after tax	406	315	313	701	839	1015	1016	1118	11. Bénéfices après impôt
12. Distributed profit	222	342	357	199	627	528	1010	399	12. Bénéfices distribués
13. Retained profit	184	-27	-44	502	212	487	6	719	13. Bénéfices mis en réserve
BALANCE SHEET (1)									**BILAN (1)**
Assets									**Actif**
14. Cash & balance with Central bank	296	428	459	462	474	529	1154	1488	14. Caisse & solde auprès de la Banque centrale
15. Interbank deposits	9482	9028	8916	7872	7431	8846	4957	3563	15. Dépôts interbancaires
16. Loans	49376	50001	54730	59393	68898	79793	89660	98916	16. Prêts
17. Securities	15131	16355	16229	14704	11046	10059	12394	13838	17. Valeurs mobilières
18. Other assets	3719	4543	2945	2862	4134	4065	10436	12359	18. Autres actifs
Liabilities									**Passif**
19. Capital & reserves	4870	4606	3571	4093	4420	4887	4364	6289	19. Capital et réserves
20. Borrowing from Central bank (2)	..	..	..	..	..	..	..	..	20. Emprunts auprès de la Banque centrale (2)
21. Interbank deposits (2)	..	..	..	..	..	..	..	..	21. Dépôts interbancaires (2)
22. Non-bank deposits	71171	73752	77514	78997	84183	94017	93915	100641	22. Dépôts non bancaires
23. Bonds (2)	..	..	..	..	..	..	..	..	23. Obligations (2)
24. Other liabilities	1964	1995	2194	2204	3380	4388	20321	23234	24. Autres engagements
Balance sheet total									**Total du bilan**
25. End-year total	78005	80353	83279	85293	91984	103292	118601	130164	25. En fin d'exercice
26. Average total	71344	79179	84404	84286	88513	97660	112040	121548	26. Moyen

NEW ZEALAND
All banks

NOUVELLE-ZELANDE
Ensemble des banques

	1990	1991	1992	1993	1994	1995	1996	1997	
Million New Zealand dollars									*Millions de dollars de Nouvelle-Zélande*
Memorandum items									***Pour mémoire***
27. Short-term securities	..	..	..	..	..	..	..	..	*27. Titres à court terme*
28. Bonds	..	..	..	..	..	..	..	..	*28. Obligations*
29. Shares and participations	*700*	*402*	*1409*	*1484*	*450*	*592*	*729*	*415*	*29. Actions et participations*
30. Claims on non-residents	*1882*	*1307*	*1014*	*3513*	*1669*	*2224*	*3982*	*2324*	*30. Créances sur des non-résidents*
31. Liabilities to non-residents	*10762*	*11712*	*16443*	*16442*	*18486*	*21912*	*23640*	*29054*	*31. Engagements envers des non-résidents*
Capital adequacy									***Solvabilité***
32. Tier 1 Capital	*3842*	*3891*	*2965*	*3473*	*3855*	*4379*	*3838*	*4282*	*32. Fonds propres de base*
33. Tier 2 Capital	..	..	..	..	..	..	..	..	*33. Fonds propres complémentaires*
34. Supervisory deductions	..	..	..	..	..	..	..	..	*34. Eléments à déduire des fonds propres*
35. Total net capital resources	*5204*	*5156*	*4319*	*4841*	*5222*	*5962*	*5951*	*6502*	*35. Total net des ressources en capital*
36. Risk-weighted assets	*47449*	*46380*	*43646*	*45005*	*49757*	*56929*	*56649*	*61728*	*36. Actifs pondérés des risques*
SUPPLEMENTARY INFORMATION									**RENSEIGNEMENTS COMPLEMENTAIRES**
37. Number of institutions	20	21	20	18	15	15	17	18	37. Nombre d'institutions
38. Number of branches	..	..	..	..	..	..	..	..	38. Nombre de succursales
39. Number of employees (x 1000)	..	..	..	..	..	..	..	..	39. Nombre de salariés (x 1000)

1. Change in methodology.

2. Borrowing from Central bank (item 20), Interbank deposits (item 21), and Bonds (item 23) are included under Non-bank deposits (item 22).

Change in methodology

As from 1996, due to new reporting requirements, balance-sheet data are not directly comparable with earlier figures.

1. Changement méthodologique.

2. Les Emprunts auprès de la Banque centrale (poste 20), les Dépôts interbancaires (poste 21), et les Obligations (poste 23) sont inclus sous Dépôts non bancaires (poste 22).

Changement méthodologique

A partir de 1996, suite aux révisions du règlement en vigueur, les données du bilan ne sont pas directement comparables avec celles des années précédentes.

NEW ZEALAND
All banks

NOUVELLE-ZELANDE
Ensemble des banques

	1990	1991	1992	1993	1994	1995	1996	1997	
Per cent									*Pourcentage*
INCOME STATEMENT ANALYSIS									**ANALYSE DU COMPTE DE RESULTATS**
% of average balance sheet total									**% du total moyen du bilan**
40. Interest income	12.54	11.09	8.62	7.86	7.73	9.59	9.55	8.61	40. Produits financiers
41. Interest expenses	9.36	8.11	5.70	5.09	4.95	6.74	7.02	6.07	41. Frais financiers
42. Net interest income	3.18	2.98	2.92	2.77	2.78	2.85	2.52	2.54	42. Produits financiers nets
43. Non-interest income (net)	1.82	2.00	1.58	1.77	1.59	1.63	1.50	1.46	43. Produits non financiers (nets)
a. Fees and commissions receivable	..	..	..	..	..	..	..	..	*a. Frais et commissions à recevoir*
b. Fees and commissions payable	..	..	..	..	..	..	..	..	*b. Frais et commissions à payer*
c. Net profits or loss on financial operations	..	..	..	..	..	..	..	..	*c. Profits ou pertes nets sur opérations financières*
d. Other	..	..	..	..	..	..	..	..	*d. Autres*
44. Gross income	5.00	4.98	4.50	4.55	4.37	4.48	4.02	4.01	44. Résultat brut
45. Operating expenses	3.67	3.63	3.20	3.25	3.07	2.98	2.76	2.60	45. Frais d'exploitation
a. Staff costs	..	..	..	..	..	..	..	..	*a. Dépenses en personnel*
b. Property costs	..	..	..	..	..	..	..	..	*b. Dépenses en immobilier*
c. Other	..	..	..	..	..	..	..	..	*c. Autres*
46. Net income	1.33	1.35	1.30	1.30	1.30	1.50	1.27	1.41	46. Résultat net
47. Provisions (net)	0.55	0.66	0.62	0.06	-0.11	-0.01	-0.04	0.07	47. Provisions (nettes)
a. Provisions on loans	..	..	..	..	..	..	..	..	*a. Provisions sur prêts*
b. Provisions on securities	..	..	..	..	..	..	..	..	*b. Provisions sur titres*
c. Other	..	..	..	..	..	..	..	..	*c. Autres*
48. Profit before tax	0.78	0.69	0.68	1.23	1.41	1.51	1.30	1.34	48. Bénéfices avant impôt
49. Income tax	0.21	0.29	0.31	0.40	0.46	0.47	0.40	0.42	49. Impôt sur le revenu
50. Profit after tax	0.57	0.40	0.37	0.83	0.95	1.04	0.91	0.92	50. Bénéfices après impôt
51. Distributed profit	0.31	0.43	0.42	0.24	0.71	0.54	0.90	0.33	51. Bénéfices distribués
52. Retained profit	0.26	-0.03	-0.05	0.60	0.24	0.50	0.01	0.59	52. Bénéfices mis en réserve
% of gross income									**% du total du résultat brut**
53. Net interest income	63.60	59.86	64.95	60.96	63.65	63.64	62.70	63.48	53. Produits financiers nets
54. Non-interest income (net)	36.40	40.14	35.05	39.04	36.35	36.36	37.30	36.52	54. Produits non financiers (nets)
a. Fees and commissions receivable	..	..	..	..	..	..	..	..	*a. Frais et commissions à recevoir*
b. Fees and commissions payable	..	..	..	..	..	..	..	..	*b. Frais et commissions à payer*
c. Net profits or loss on financial operations	..	..	..	..	..	..	..	..	*c. Profits ou pertes nets sur opérations financières*
d. Other	..	..	..	..	..	..	..	..	*d. Autres*
55. Operating expenses	73.35	72.92	71.14	71.48	70.22	66.47	68.55	64.85	55. Frais d'exploitation
a. Staff costs	..	..	..	..	..	..	..	..	*a. Dépenses en personnel*
b. Property costs	..	..	..	..	..	..	..	..	*b. Dépenses en immobilier*
c. Other	..	..	..	..	..	..	..	..	*c. Autres*
56. Net income	26.65	27.08	28.86	28.52	29.78	33.53	31.45	35.15	56. Résultat net
57. Provisions (net)	11.01	13.21	13.77	1.38	-2.51	-0.21	-0.95	1.81	57. Provisions (nettes)
a. Provisions on loans	..	..	..	..	..	..	..	..	*a. Provisions sur prêts*
b. Provisions on securities	..	..	..	..	..	..	..	..	*b. Provisions sur titres*
c. Other	..	..	..	..	..	..	..	..	*c. Autres*
58. Profit before tax	15.63	13.87	15.09	27.14	32.29	33.74	32.40	33.34	58. Bénéfices avant impôt
59. Income tax	4.26	5.88	6.85	8.85	10.60	10.55	9.87	10.37	59. Impôt sur le revenu
60. Profit after tax	11.38	7.99	8.24	18.29	21.69	23.18	22.53	22.97	60. Bénéfices après impôt
% of net income									**% du total du résultat net**
61. Provisions (net)	41.32	48.78	47.72	4.85	-8.42	-0.61	-3.03	5.14	61. Provisions (nettes)
a. Provisions on loans	..	..	..	..	..	..	..	..	*a. Provisions sur prêts*
b. Provisions on securities	..	..	..	..	..	..	..	..	*b. Provisions sur titres*
c. Other	..	..	..	..	..	..	..	..	*c. Autres*
62. Profit before tax	58.68	51.22	52.28	95.15	108.42	100.61	103.03	94.86	62. Bénéfices avant impôt
63. Income tax	15.98	21.72	23.72	31.02	35.59	31.47	31.38	29.51	63. Impôt sur le revenu
64. Profit after tax	42.69	29.49	28.56	64.14	72.83	69.14	71.65	65.34	64. Bénéfices après impôt

NEW ZEALAND
All banks

NOUVELLE-ZELANDE
Ensemble des banques

	1990	1991	1992	1993	1994	1995	1996	1997	
Per cent									*Pourcentage*
BALANCE SHEET ANALYSIS									**ANALYSE DU BILAN**
% of year-end balance sheet total									**% du total du bilan en fin d'exercice**
Assets									**Actif**
65. Cash & balance with Central bank	0.38	0.53	0.55	0.54	0.52	0.51	0.97	1.14	65. Caisse & solde auprès de la Banque centrale
66. Interbank deposits	12.16	11.24	10.71	9.23	8.08	8.56	4.18	2.74	66. Dépôts interbancaires
67. Loans	63.30	62.23	65.72	69.63	74.90	77.25	75.60	75.99	67. Prêts
68. Securities	19.40	20.35	19.49	17.24	12.01	9.74	10.45	10.63	68. Valeurs mobilières
69. Other assets	4.77	5.65	3.54	3.36	4.49	3.94	8.80	9.49	69. Autres actifs
Liabilities									**Passif**
70. Capital & reserves	6.24	5.73	4.29	4.80	4.81	4.73	3.68	4.83	70. Capital et réserves
71. Borrowing from Central bank	..	..	..	..	..	..	..	..	71. Emprunts auprès de la Banque centrale
72. Interbank deposits	..	..	..	..	..	..	..	..	72. Dépôts interbancaires
73. Non-bank deposits	91.24	91.78	93.08	92.62	91.52	91.02	79.19	77.32	73. Dépôts non bancaires
74. Bonds	..	..	..	..	..	..	..	..	74. Obligations
75. Other liabilities	2.52	2.48	2.63	2.58	3.67	4.25	17.13	17.85	75. Autres engagements
Memorandum items									***Pour mémoire***
76. Short-term securities	..	..	..	..	..	..	..	..	*76. Titres à court terme*
77. Bonds	..	..	..	..	..	..	..	..	*77. Obligations*
78. Shares and participations	*0.90*	*0.50*	*1.69*	*1.74*	*0.49*	*0.57*	*0.61*	*0.32*	*78. Actions et participations*
79. Claims on non-residents	*2.41*	*1.63*	*1.22*	*4.12*	*1.81*	*2.15*	*3.36*	*1.79*	*79. Créances sur des non-résidents*
80. Liabilities to non-residents	*13.80*	*14.58*	*19.74*	*19.28*	*20.10*	*21.21*	*19.93*	*22.32*	*80. Engagements envers des non-résidents*

* See notes on previous pages.

* Voir les notes en pages précédentes.

NORWAY — NORVEGE
All banks — Ensemble des banques

Million Norwegian kroner	1989	1990	1991	1992	1993	1994	1995	1996	1997	1998 p	Millions de couronnes norvégiennes
INCOME STATEMENT											**COMPTE DE RESULTATS**
1. Interest income	76422	75022	70070	67670	58660	51286	52543	53452	52608	69199	1. Produits financiers
2. Interest expenses	55286	54807	50888	46937	35813	27693	30079	30524	29612	44074	2. Frais financiers
3. Net interest income	21136	20215	19182	20733	22847	23593	22464	22929	22995	25125	3. Produits financiers nets
4. Non-interest income (net)	7455	5155	3604	5555	8776	5522	7936	8069	8985	8035	4. Produits non financiers (nets)
a. Fees and commissions receivable	*3852*	*3223*	*3294*	*3411*	*3613*	*4848*	*5310*	*6150*	*7047*	*7287*	*a. Frais et commissions à recevoir*
b. Fees and commissions payable	-	-	*36*	*23*	*30*	*37*	*93*	*791*	*1057*	*1183*	*b. Frais et commissions à payer*
c. Net profits or loss on financial operations	*2805*	*1172*	*-321*	*1354*	*4278*	*-200*	*1851*	*1774*	*2192*	*1064*	*c. Profits ou pertes nets sur opérations financières*
d. Other	*797*	*760*	*668*	*813*	*916*	*912*	*870*	*937*	*803*	*867*	*d. Autres*
5. Gross income	28591	25370	22786	26288	31623	29115	30400	30998	31981	33160	5. Résultat brut
6. Operating expenses (1)	17250	17933	20051	15859	15942	19149	21047	21539	21996	22986	6. Frais d'exploitation (1)
a. Staff costs	*8262*	*8557*	*8416*	*7868*	*7762*	*8386*	*9128*	*9794*	*10738*	*11526*	*a. Dépenses en personnel*
b. Property costs	*1784*	*1764*	*3965*	*1669*	*1471*	*1440*	*1449*	*1574*	*1579*	*1681*	*b. Dépenses en immobilier*
c. Other	*7214*	*7612*	*7670*	*6322*	*6707*	*9322*	*10469*	*10172*	*9679*	*9779*	*c. Autres*
7. Net income	11341	7437	2735	10429	15681	9966	9353	9459	9985	10174	7. Résultat net
8. Provisions (net) (1)	9891	11655	21632	11670	8822	1124	-795	-1015	-100	1071	8. Provisions (nettes) (1)
a. Provisions on loans	*10481*	*10926*	*21371*	*11691*	*7336*	*674*	*-911*	*-593*	*-153*	*1441*	*a. Provisions sur prêts*
b. Provisions on securities	..	..	..	..	..	..	..	*4*	-	*32*	*b. Provisions sur titres*
c. Other	..	..	..	..	..	..	..	*-425*	*53*	*-403*	*c. Autres*
9. Profit before tax	1450	-4218	-18897	-1241	6859	8842	10148	10473	10085	9103	9. Bénéfices avant impôt
10. Income tax	570	273	200	404	917	1168	1263	1598	1670	1151	10. Impôt sur le revenu
11. Profit after tax	880	-4491	-19097	-1645	5942	7674	8885	8875	8415	7952	11. Bénéfices après impôt
12. Distributed profit	775	36	24	122	619	2392	2898	3280	3061	-	12. Bénéfices distribués
13. Retained profit	105	-4527	-19121	-1767	5323	5282	5987	5595	5354	7952	13. Bénéfices mis en réserve
BALANCE SHEET											**BILAN**
Assets											**Actif**
14. Cash & balance with Central bank	3083	3136	3634	4890	3151	4738	5489	28658	17707	12700	14. Caisse & solde auprès de la Banque centrale
15. Interbank deposits	17799	20753	28470	41658	24142	27165	21658	27536	28759	39262	15. Dépôts interbancaires
16. Loans	459632	474753	451560	468575	461766	540180	581006	663828	777211	866636	16. Prêts
17. Securities	91045	84430	65803	67493	69792	91316	97289	118406	118595	120831	17. Valeurs mobilières
18. Other assets	33147	31573	28613	28094	27578	31781	30934	36429	37113	46966	18. Autres actifs
Liabilities											**Passif**
19. Capital & reserves	26204	23768	16785	21512	33909	45089	51675	58593	65196	68647	19. Capital et réserves
20. Borrowing from Central bank	58562	55880	44492	39111	16973	5207	10348	474	7835	16845	20. Emprunts auprès de la Banque centrale
21. Interbank deposits	76315	74980	66364	48480	38323	37937	37237	98250	127142	115912	21. Dépôts interbancaires
22. Non-bank deposits	355087	372338	376059	409667	402294	506342	526381	566193	568461	601575	22. Dépôts non bancaires
23. Bonds	48038	50601	43859	64784	64575	61379	60542	78881	121131	168651	23. Obligations
24. Other liabilities	40499	37077	30522	27155	30356	39224	50192	72466	89620	114765	24. Autres engagements
Balance sheet total											**Total du bilan**
25. End-year total	604707	614645	578080	610710	586431	695179	736376	874858	979385	1086396	25. En fin d'exercice
26. Average total	612183	639189	621660	591255	611885	710384	746940	854304	954765	1068048	26. Moyen

NORWAY
All banks

NORVEGE
Ensemble des banques

	1989	1990	1991	1992	1993	1994	1995	1996	1997	1998 p	
Million Norwegian kroner											*Millions de couronnes norvégiennes*
Memorandum items											***Pour mémoire***
27. Short-term securities	*9813*	*13128*	*8549*	*5420*	*10216*	*28603*	*32996*	*42873*	*41270*	*28786*	*27. Titres à court terme*
28. Bonds	*69770*	*58262*	*47245*	*52360*	*48806*	*50183*	*50417*	*57260*	*54401*	*69710*	*28. Obligations*
29. Shares and participations	*11462*	*13037*	*10009*	*9713*	*10770*	*12529*	*13875*	*18273*	*23103*	*24270*	*29. Actions et participations*
30. Claims on non-residents	*43500*	*47335*	*54139*	*79515*	*50114*	*49911*	*47724*	*60458*	*69617*	*91758*	*30. Créances sur des non-résidents*
31. Liabilities to non-residents	*134193*	*129315*	*96143*	*75435*	*70414*	*60255*	*57556*	*123234*	*183545*	*219592*	*31. Engagements envers des non-résidents*
Capital adequacy											***Solvabilité***
32. Tier 1 Capital	..	..	*21658*	*28908*	*39831*	*44833*	*51559*	*58426*	*64389*	*71249*	*32. Fonds propres de base*
33. Tier 2 Capital	..	..	*16037*	*18221*	*23277*	*21553*	*17487*	*18854*	*21754*	*22972*	*33. Fonds propres complémentaires*
34. Supervisory deductions	..	..	*518*	*321*	*122*	*181*	*640*	*639*	*2044*	*1399*	*34. Eléments à déduire des fonds propres*
35. Total net capital resources	..	..	*37177*	*46808*	*62986*	*66206*	*68408*	*76645*	*84100*	*92823*	*35. Total net des ressources en capital*
36. Risk-weighted assets	..	..	*471028*	*475552*	*469712*	*472039*	*509119*	*592319*	*692261*	*762318*	*36. Actifs pondérés des risques*
SUPPLEMENTARY INFORMATION											**RENSEIGNEMENTS COMPLEMENTAIRES**
37. Number of institutions	179	164	156	155	153	152	153	153	154	154	37. Nombre d'institutions
38. Number of branches	1796	1796	1661	1593	1561	1570	1556	1622	1584	1541	38. Nombre de succursales
39. Number of employees (x 1000)	31.9	31.2	27.8	26.7	25.9	27.4	27.5	24.5	24.0	23.0	39. Nombre de salariés (x 1000)

1. Change in methodology.

Notes

- All banks include Commercial banks and Savings banks.
- Average balance sheet totals (item 26) are based on thirteen end-month data.

Change in methodology

- Due to methodological changes, write-downs are included under Operating expenses (item 6) and not under Provisions (net) (item 8) in the 1991 data.

1. Changement méthodologique.

Notes

- L'Ensemble des banques comprend les Banques commerciales et les Caisses d'épargne.
- La moyenne du total des actifs/passifs (poste 26) est basée sur treize données de fin de mois.

Changement méthodologique

- Suite aux changements méthodologiques, les dévaluations sont incluses sous la rubrique Frais d'exploitation (poste 6) et non sous la rubrique Provisions (nettes) (poste 8) pour les données de 1991.

NORWAY
All banks

NORVEGE
Ensemble des banques

	1989	1990	1991	1992	1993	1994	1995	1996	1997	1998 p	
Per cent											*Pourcentage*
INCOME STATEMENT ANALYSIS											**ANALYSE DU COMPTE DE RESULTATS**
% of average balance sheet total											**% du total moyen du bilan**
40. Interest income	12.48	11.74	11.27	11.45	9.59	7.22	7.03	6.26	5.51	6.48	40. Produits financiers
41. Interest expenses	9.03	8.57	8.19	7.94	5.85	3.90	4.03	3.57	3.10	4.13	41. Frais financiers
42. Net interest income	3.45	3.16	3.09	3.51	3.73	3.32	3.01	2.68	2.41	2.35	42. Produits financiers nets
43. Non-interest income (net)	1.22	0.81	0.58	0.94	1.43	0.78	1.06	0.94	0.94	0.75	43. Produits non financiers (nets)
a. Fees and commissions receivable	*0.63*	*0.50*	*0.53*	*0.58*	*0.59*	*0.68*	*0.71*	*0.72*	*0.74*	*0.68*	*a. Frais et commissions à recevoir*
b. Fees and commissions payable	-	-	*0.01*	-	-	*0.01*	*0.01*	*0.09*	*0.11*	*0.11*	*b. Frais et commissions à payer*
c. Net profits or loss on financial operations	*0.46*	*0.18*	*-0.05*	*0.23*	*0.70*	*-0.03*	*0.25*	*0.21*	*0.23*	*0.10*	*c. Profits ou pertes nets sur opérations financières*
d. Other	*0.13*	*0.12*	*0.11*	*0.14*	*0.15*	*0.13*	*0.12*	*0.11*	*0.08*	*0.08*	*d. Autres*
44. Gross income	4.67	3.97	3.67	4.45	5.17	4.10	4.07	3.63	3.35	3.10	44. Résultat brut
45. Operating expenses	2.82	2.81	3.23	2.68	2.61	2.70	2.82	2.52	2.30	2.15	45. Frais d'exploitation
a. Staff costs	*1.35*	*1.34*	*1.35*	*1.33*	*1.27*	*1.18*	*1.22*	*1.15*	*1.12*	*1.08*	*a. Dépenses en personnel*
b. Property costs	*0.29*	*0.28*	*0.64*	*0.28*	*0.24*	*0.20*	*0.19*	*0.18*	*0.17*	*0.16*	*b. Dépenses en immobilier*
c. Other	*1.18*	*1.19*	*1.23*	*1.07*	*1.10*	*1.31*	*1.40*	*1.19*	*1.01*	*0.92*	*c. Autres*
46. Net income	1.85	1.16	0.44	1.76	2.56	1.40	1.25	1.11	1.05	0.95	46. Résultat net
47. Provisions (net)	1.62	1.82	3.48	1.97	1.44	0.16	-0.11	-0.12	-0.01	0.10	47. Provisions (nettes)
a. Provisions on loans	*1.71*	*1.71*	*3.44*	*1.98*	*1.20*	*0.09*	*-0.12*	*-0.07*	*-0.02*	*0.13*	*a. Provisions sur prêts*
b. Provisions on securities	..	..	..	..	..	..	..	-	-	-	*b. Provisions sur titres*
c. Other	..	..	..	..	..	..	..	*-0.05*	*0.01*	*-0.04*	*c. Autres*
48. Profit before tax	0.24	-0.66	-3.04	-0.21	1.12	1.24	1.36	1.23	1.06	0.85	48. Bénéfices avant impôt
49. Income tax	0.09	0.04	0.03	0.07	0.15	0.16	0.17	0.19	0.17	0.11	49. Impôt sur le revenu
50. Profit after tax	0.14	-0.70	-3.07	-0.28	0.97	1.08	1.19	1.04	0.88	0.74	50. Bénéfices après impôt
51. Distributed profit	0.13	0.01	-	0.02	0.10	0.34	0.39	0.38	0.32	-	51. Bénéfices distribués
52. Retained profit	0.02	-0.71	-3.08	-0.30	0.87	0.74	0.80	0.65	0.56	0.74	52. Bénéfices mis en réserve
% of gross income											**% du total du résultat brut**
53. Net interest income	73.93	79.68	84.18	78.87	72.25	81.03	73.89	73.97	71.90	75.77	53. Produits financiers nets
54. Non-interest income (net)	26.07	20.32	15.82	21.13	27.75	18.97	26.11	26.03	28.09	24.23	54. Produits non financiers (nets)
a. Fees and commissions receivable	*13.47*	*12.70*	*14.46*	*12.98*	*11.43*	*16.65*	*17.47*	*19.84*	*22.03*	*21.98*	*a. Frais et commissions à recevoir*
b. Fees and commissions payable	-	-	*0.16*	*0.09*	*0.09*	*0.13*	*0.31*	*2.55*	*3.31*	*3.57*	*b. Frais et commissions à payer*
c. Net profits or loss on financial operations	*9.81*	*4.62*	*-1.41*	*5.15*	*13.53*	*-0.69*	*6.09*	*5.72*	*6.85*	*3.21*	*c. Profits ou pertes nets sur opérations financières*
d. Other	*2.79*	*3.00*	*2.93*	*3.09*	*2.90*	*3.13*	*2.86*	*3.02*	*2.51*	*2.61*	*d. Autres*
55. Operating expenses	60.33	70.69	88.00	60.33	50.41	65.77	69.23	69.49	68.78	69.32	55. Frais d'exploitation
a. Staff costs	*28.90*	*33.73*	*36.93*	*29.93*	*24.55*	*28.80*	*30.03*	*31.60*	*33.58*	*34.76*	*a. Dépenses en personnel*
b. Property costs	*6.24*	*6.95*	*17.40*	*6.35*	*4.65*	*4.95*	*4.77*	*5.08*	*4.94*	*5.07*	*b. Dépenses en immobilier*
c. Other	*25.23*	*30.00*	*33.66*	*24.05*	*21.21*	*32.02*	*34.44*	*32.82*	*30.26*	*29.49*	*c. Autres*
56. Net income	39.67	29.31	12.00	39.67	49.59	34.23	30.77	30.51	31.22	30.68	56. Résultat net
57. Provisions (net)	34.59	45.94	94.94	44.39	27.90	3.86	-2.62	-3.27	-0.31	3.23	57. Provisions (nettes)
a. Provisions on loans	*36.66*	*43.07*	*93.79*	*44.47*	*23.20*	*2.31*	*-3.00*	*-1.91*	*-0.48*	*4.35*	*a. Provisions sur prêts*
b. Provisions on securities	..	..	..	..	..	..	..	*0.01*	-	*0.10*	*b. Provisions sur titres*
c. Other	..	..	..	..	..	..	..	*-1.37*	*0.17*	*-1.22*	*c. Autres*
58. Profit before tax	5.07	-16.63	-82.93	-4.72	21.69	30.37	33.38	33.79	31.53	27.45	58. Bénéfices avant impôt
59. Income tax	1.99	1.08	0.88	1.54	2.90	4.01	4.15	5.16	5.22	3.47	59. Impôt sur le revenu
60. Profit after tax	3.08	-17.70	-83.81	-6.26	18.79	26.36	29.23	28.63	26.31	23.98	60. Bénéfices après impôt
% of net income											**% du total du résultat net**
61. Provisions (net)	87.21	156.72	790.93	111.90	56.26	11.28	-8.50	-10.73	-1.00	10.53	61. Provisions (nettes)
a. Provisions on loans	*92.42*	*146.91*	*781.39*	*112.10*	*46.78*	*6.76*	*-9.74*	*-6.27*	*-1.53*	*14.16*	*a. Provisions sur prêts*
b. Provisions on securities	..	..	..	..	..	..	..	*0.04*	-	*0.31*	*b. Provisions sur titres*
c. Other	..	..	..	..	..	..	..	*-4.49*	*0.53*	*-3.96*	*c. Autres*
62. Profit before tax	12.79	-56.72	-690.93	-11.90	43.74	88.72	108.50	110.72	101.00	89.47	62. Bénéfices avant impôt
63. Income tax	5.03	3.67	7.31	3.87	5.85	11.72	13.50	16.89	16.73	11.31	63. Impôt sur le revenu
64. Profit after tax	7.76	-60.39	-698.24	-15.77	37.89	77.00	95.00	93.83	84.28	78.16	64. Bénéfices après impôt

NORWAY — NORVEGE

All banks — Ensemble des banques

	1989	1990	1991	1992	1993	1994	1995	1996	1997	1998 p	
Per cent											*Pourcentage*
BALANCE SHEET ANALYSIS											**ANALYSE DU BILAN**
% of year-end balance sheet total											**% du total du bilan en fin d'exercice**
Assets											**Actif**
65. Cash & balance with Central bank	0.51	0.51	0.63	0.80	0.54	0.68	0.75	3.28	1.81	1.17	65. Caisse & solde auprès de la Banque centrale
66. Interbank deposits	2.94	3.38	4.92	6.82	4.12	3.91	2.94	3.15	2.94	3.61	66. Dépôts interbancaires
67. Loans	76.01	77.24	78.11	76.73	78.74	77.70	78.90	75.88	79.36	79.77	67. Prêts
68. Securities	15.06	13.74	11.38	11.05	11.90	13.14	13.21	13.53	12.11	11.12	68. Valeurs mobilières
69. Other assets	5.48	5.14	4.95	4.60	4.70	4.57	4.20	4.16	3.79	4.32	69. Autres actifs
Liabilities											**Passif**
70. Capital & reserves	4.33	3.87	2.90	3.52	5.78	6.49	7.02	6.70	6.66	6.32	70. Capital et réserves
71. Borrowing from Central bank	9.68	9.09	7.70	6.40	2.89	0.75	1.41	0.05	0.80	1.55	71. Emprunts auprès de la Banque centrale
72. Interbank deposits	12.62	12.20	11.48	7.94	6.53	5.46	5.06	11.23	12.98	10.67	72. Dépôts interbancaires
73. Non-bank deposits	58.72	60.58	65.05	67.08	68.60	72.84	71.48	64.72	58.04	55.37	73. Dépôts non bancaires
74. Bonds	7.94	8.23	7.59	10.61	11.01	8.83	8.22	9.02	12.37	15.52	74. Obligations
75. Other liabilities	6.70	6.03	5.28	4.45	5.18	5.64	6.82	8.28	9.15	10.56	75. Autres engagements
Memorandum items											***Pour mémoire***
76. Short-term securities	*1.62*	*2.14*	*1.48*	*0.89*	*1.74*	*4.11*	*4.48*	*4.90*	*4.21*	*2.65*	*76. Titres à court terme*
77. Bonds	*11.54*	*9.48*	*8.17*	*8.57*	*8.32*	*7.22*	*6.85*	*6.55*	*5.55*	*6.42*	*77. Obligations*
78. Shares and participations	*1.90*	*2.12*	*1.73*	*1.59*	*1.84*	*1.80*	*1.88*	*2.09*	*2.36*	*2.23*	*78. Actions et participations*
79. Claims on non-residents	*7.19*	*7.70*	*9.37*	*13.02*	*8.55*	*7.18*	*6.48*	*6.91*	*7.11*	*8.45*	*79. Créances sur des non-résidents*
80. Liabilities to non-residents	*22.19*	*21.04*	*16.63*	*12.35*	*12.01*	*8.67*	*7.82*	*14.09*	*18.74*	*20.21*	*80. Engagements envers des non-résidents*

* See notes on previous pages.

* Voir les notes en pages précédentes.

NORWAY — NORVEGE

Commercial banks — Banques commerciales

Million Norwegian kroner	1989	1990	1991	1992	1993	1994	1995	1996	1997	1998 p	Millions de couronnes norvégiennes
INCOME STATEMENT											**COMPTE DE RESULTATS**
1. Interest income	43709	43631	40234	38821	32757	30524	31116	31933	32061	42249	1. Produits financiers
2. Interest expenses	33093	33431	30930	28587	21644	17761	19291	19444	19671	28626	2. Frais financiers
3. Net interest income	10616	10200	9304	10234	11113	12763	11825	12490	12390	13623	3. Produits financiers nets
4. Non-interest income (net)	5229	3570	2188	3850	5433	4375	5415	5646	6246	5666	4. Produits non financiers (nets)
a. Fees and commissions receivable	*2609*	*2070*	*2155*	*2133*	*2204*	*3224*	*3530*	*4026*	*4491*	*4573*	*a. Frais et commissions à recevoir*
b. Fees and commissions payable	-	-	*6*	*1*	*4*	*1*	*50*	*334*	*501*	*595*	*b. Frais et commissions à payer*
c. Net profits or loss on financial operations	*2008*	*981*	*-395*	*1132*	*2559*	*468*	*1295*	*1278*	*1693*	*1055*	*c. Profits ou pertes nets sur opérations financières*
d. Other	*612*	*519*	*434*	*587*	*674*	*684*	*641*	*677*	*562*	*634*	*d. Autres*
5. Gross income	15845	13770	11492	14084	16546	17138	17240	18136	18635	19290	5. Résultat brut
6. Operating expenses (1)	9522	10151	11742	8659	8602	11556	12930	13210	13556	14335	6. Frais d'exploitation (1)
a. Staff costs	*4723*	*4928*	*4751*	*4348*	*4392*	*4822*	*5354*	*5975*	*6568*	*7209*	*a. Dépenses en personnel*
b. Property costs	*1021*	*1009*	*2863*	*1036*	*897*	*925*	*936*	*994*	*946*	*988*	*b. Dépenses en immobilier*
c. Other	*3788*	*4214*	*4128*	*3275*	*3312*	*5809*	*6640*	*6242*	*6043*	*6138*	*c. Autres*
7. Net income	6323	3619	-250	5425	7944	5582	4310	4926	5079	4955	7. Résultat net
8. Provisions (net) (1)	5710	7593	16780	9842	6082	328	-1186	-1111	-363	633	8. Provisions (nettes) (1)
a. Provisions on loans	*5308*	*7051*	*16663*	*7800*	*4836*	*-209*	*-1346*	*-837*	*-446*	*686*	*a. Provisions sur prêts*
b. Provisions on securities	..	..	..	..	..	..	..	*1*	-	*32*	*b. Provisions sur titres*
c. Other	..	..	..	..	..	..	..	*-274*	*83*	*-86*	*c. Autres*
9. Profit before tax	613	-3974	-17030	-4417	1862	5254	5496	6036	5442	4322	9. Bénéfices avant impôt
10. Income tax	287	61	8	77	262	387	267	412	385	229	10. Impôt sur le revenu
11. Profit after tax	326	-4035	-17038	-4494	1600	4867	5229	5624	5057	4093	11. Bénéfices après impôt
12. Distributed profit	699	15	13	105	199	1742	2107	2394	2074	-	12. Bénéfices distribués
13. Retained profit	-373	-4050	-17051	-4599	1401	3125	3122	3231	2983	4093	13. Bénéfices mis en réserve
BALANCE SHEET											**BILAN**
Assets											**Actif**
14. Cash & balance with Central bank	1404	1283	1797	2535	1079	2284	2819	23791	11595	7617	14. Caisse & solde auprès de la Banque centrale
15. Interbank deposits	13416	17261	23493	36086	20082	21321	18022	21960	21452	29476	15. Dépôts interbancaires
16. Loans	272208	281433	258981	273155	256624	320973	341793	392181	465533	521174	16. Prêts
17. Securities	50082	48439	33969	40519	39824	62728	66804	88281	89690	87035	17. Valeurs mobilières
18. Other assets	23933	22850	19944	19628	19644	23115	22649	29080	29099	37864	18. Autres actifs
Liabilities											**Passif**
19. Capital & reserves	15202	13153	7122	8167	15163	24365	28270	32593	36580	37138	19. Capital et réserves
20. Borrowing from Central bank	27636	32814	29881	28544	8261	2437	5478	327	6198	10442	20. Emprunts auprès de la Banque centrale
21. Interbank deposits	60590	62219	50655	38093	32779	31852	30596	80080	95613	82893	21. Dépôts interbancaires
22. Non-bank deposits	186508	193767	190741	219812	205032	297843	309298	336143	333594	350285	22. Dépôts non bancaires
23. Bonds	43067	44105	38446	56546	54837	47468	46149	58509	86380	120638	23. Obligations
24. Other liabilities	28038	25207	21339	20761	21183	26456	32296	47641	59005	81768	24. Autres engagements
Balance sheet total											**Total du bilan**
25. End-year total	361042	371266	338184	371923	337255	430421	452087	555293	617369	683165	25. En fin d'exercice
26. Average total	361350	387647	373090	349682	360924	448808	467886	551830	612142	682007	26. Moyen

NORWAY / NORVEGE

Commercial banks / Banques commerciales

	1989	1990	1991	1992	1993	1994	1995	1996	1997	1998 p	
Million Norwegian kroner											*Millions de couronnes norvégiennes*
Memorandum items											***Pour mémoire***
27. Short-term securities	*6941*	*10318*	*5327*	*3807*	*6933*	*23287*	*25106*	*32984*	*33575*	*20500*	*27. Titres à court terme*
28. Bonds	*34291*	*28024*	*21172*	*29839*	*26335*	*31517*	*33457*	*42806*	*40572*	*51825*	*28. Obligations*
29. Shares and participations	*8850*	*10095*	*7470*	*6872*	*6556*	*7924*	*8241*	*12491*	*15614*	*16513*	*29. Actions et participations*
30. Claims on non-residents	*37838*	*42318*	*48780*	*73447*	*45567*	*42583*	*42717*	*54218*	*61225*	*81202*	*30. Créances sur des non-résidents*
31. Liabilities to non-residents	*114870*	*112266*	*82903*	*66734*	*60748*	*50439*	*48909*	*107755*	*146927*	*174602*	*31. Engagements envers des non-résidents*
Capital adequacy											***Solvabilité***
32. Tier 1 Capital	..	..	*11510*	*13353*	*20080*	*24008*	*28139*	*32529*	*35917*	*38000*	*32. Fonds propres de base*
33. Tier 2 Capital	..	..	*10621*	*13706*	*17484*	*14461*	*11506*	*12293*	*14164*	*15052*	*33. Fonds propres complémentaires*
34. Supervisory deductions	..	..	*321*	*116*	*88*	*42*	*338*	*257*	*1113*	*815*	*34. Eléments à déduire des fonds propres*
35. Total net capital resources	..	..	*21810*	*26943*	*37476*	*38427*	*39308*	*44567*	*48968*	*52237*	*35. Total net des ressources en capital*
36. Risk-weighted assets	..	..	*306639*	*312264*	*302948*	*296395*	*319997*	*379733*	*447813*	*478386*	*36. Actifs pondérés des risques*
SUPPLEMENTARY INFORMATION											**RENSEIGNEMENTS COMPLEMENTAIRES**
37. Number of institutions	28	22	21	21	20	20	20	20	21	21	37. Nombre d'institutions
38. Number of branches	602	602	540	488	451	480	448	462	468	467	38. Nombre de succursales
39. Number of employees (x 1000)	17.0	16.6	14.5	13.3	13.1	14.7	15.0	13.8	13.0	13.0	39. Nombre de salariés (x 1000)

1. Change in methodology.

Notes

- As from 1994, data for the Postal saving bank (Postbanken) are included under Commercial banks.
- Average balance sheet totals (item 26) are based on thirteen end-month data.

Change in methodology

- Due to methodological changes, write-downs are included under Operating expenses (item 6) and not under Provisions (net) (item 8) in the 1991 data.

1. Changement méthodologique.

Notes

- Depuis 1994, les données de la Banque postale (Postbanken) sont comprises dans la catégorie Banques commerciales.
- La moyenne du total des actifs/passifs (poste 26) est basée sur treize données de fin de mois.

Changement méthodologique

- Suite aux changements méthodologiques, les dévaluations sont incluses sous la rubrique Frais d'exploitation (poste 6) et non sous la rubrique Provisions (nettes) (poste 8) pour les données de 1991.

Per cent	1989	1990	1991	1992	1993	1994	1995	1996	1997	1998 p	Pourcentage
INCOME STATEMENT ANALYSIS											**ANALYSE DU COMPTE DE RESULTATS**
% of average balance sheet total											**% du total moyen du bilan**
40. Interest income	12.10	11.26	10.78	11.10	9.08	6.80	6.65	5.79	5.24	6.19	40. Produits financiers
41. Interest expenses	9.16	8.62	8.29	8.18	6.00	3.96	4.12	3.52	3.21	4.20	41. Frais financiers
42. Net interest income	2.94	2.63	2.49	2.93	3.08	2.84	2.53	2.26	2.02	2.00	42. Produits financiers nets
43. Non-interest income (net)	1.45	0.92	0.59	1.10	1.51	0.97	1.16	1.02	1.02	0.83	43. Produits non financiers (nets)
a. Fees and commissions receivable	*0.72*	*0.53*	*0.58*	*0.61*	*0.61*	*0.72*	*0.75*	*0.73*	*0.73*	*0.67*	*a. Frais et commissions à recevoir*
b. Fees and commissions payable	-	-	-	-	-	-	*0.01*	*0.06*	*0.08*	*0.09*	*b. Frais et commissions à payer*
c. Net profits or loss on financial operations	*0.56*	*0.25*	*-0.11*	*0.32*	*0.71*	*0.10*	*0.28*	*0.23*	*0.28*	*0.15*	*c. Profits ou pertes nets sur opérations financières*
d. Other	*0.17*	*0.13*	*0.12*	*0.17*	*0.19*	*0.15*	*0.14*	*0.12*	*0.09*	*0.09*	*d. Autres*
44. Gross income	4.38	3.55	3.08	4.03	4.58	3.82	3.68	3.29	3.04	2.83	44. Résultat brut
45. Operating expenses	2.64	2.62	3.15	2.48	2.38	2.57	2.76	2.39	2.21	2.10	45. Frais d'exploitation
a. Staff costs	*1.31*	*1.27*	*1.27*	*1.24*	*1.22*	*1.07*	*1.14*	*1.08*	*1.07*	*1.06*	*a. Dépenses en personnel*
b. Property costs	*0.28*	*0.26*	*0.77*	*0.30*	*0.25*	*0.21*	*0.20*	*0.18*	*0.15*	*0.14*	*b. Dépenses en immobilier*
c. Other	*1.05*	*1.09*	*1.11*	*0.94*	*0.92*	*1.29*	*1.42*	*1.13*	*0.99*	*0.90*	*c. Autres*
46. Net income	1.75	0.93	-0.07	1.55	2.20	1.24	0.92	0.89	0.83	0.73	46. Résultat net
47. Provisions (net)	1.58	1.96	4.50	2.81	1.69	0.07	-0.25	-0.20	-0.06	0.09	47. Provisions (nettes)
a. Provisions on loans	*1.47*	*1.82*	*4.47*	*2.23*	*1.34*	*-0.05*	*-0.29*	*-0.15*	*-0.07*	*0.10*	*a. Provisions sur prêts*
b. Provisions on securities	..	..	..	..	..	..	..	-	-	-	*b. Provisions sur titres*
c. Other	..	..	..	..	..	..	..	*-0.05*	*0.01*	*-0.01*	*c. Autres*
48. Profit before tax	0.17	-1.03	-4.56	-1.26	0.52	1.17	1.17	1.09	0.89	0.63	48. Bénéfices avant impôt
49. Income tax	0.08	0.02	-	0.02	0.07	0.09	0.06	0.07	0.06	0.03	49. Impôt sur le revenu
50. Profit after tax	0.09	-1.04	-4.57	-1.29	0.44	1.08	1.12	1.02	0.83	0.60	50. Bénéfices après impôt
51. Distributed profit	0.19	-	-	0.03	0.06	0.39	0.45	0.43	0.34	-	51. Bénéfices distribués
52. Retained profit	-0.10	-1.04	-4.57	-1.32	0.39	0.70	0.67	0.59	0.49	0.60	52. Bénéfices mis en réserve
% of gross income											**% du total du résultat brut**
53. Net interest income	67.00	74.07	80.96	72.66	67.16	74.47	68.59	68.87	66.49	70.62	53. Produits financiers nets
54. Non-interest income (net)	33.00	25.93	19.04	27.34	32.84	25.53	31.41	31.13	33.52	29.37	54. Produits non financiers (nets)
a. Fees and commissions receivable	*16.47*	*15.03*	*18.75*	*15.14*	*13.32*	*18.81*	*20.48*	*22.20*	*24.10*	*23.71*	*a. Frais et commissions à recevoir*
b. Fees and commissions payable	-	-	*0.05*	*0.01*	*0.02*	*0.01*	*0.29*	*1.84*	*2.69*	*3.08*	*b. Frais et commissions à payer*
c. Net profits or loss on financial operations	*12.67*	*7.12*	*-3.44*	*8.04*	*15.47*	*2.73*	*7.51*	*7.05*	*9.09*	*5.47*	*c. Profits ou pertes nets sur opérations financières*
d. Other	*3.86*	*3.77*	*3.78*	*4.17*	*4.07*	*3.99*	*3.72*	*3.73*	*3.02*	*3.29*	*d. Autres*
55. Operating expenses	60.09	73.72	102.18	61.48	51.99	67.43	75.00	72.84	72.74	74.31	55. Frais d'exploitation
a. Staff costs	*29.81*	*35.79*	*41.34*	*30.87*	*26.54*	*28.14*	*31.06*	*32.95*	*35.25*	*37.37*	*a. Dépenses en personnel*
b. Property costs	*6.44*	*7.33*	*24.91*	*7.36*	*5.42*	*5.40*	*5.43*	*5.48*	*5.08*	*5.12*	*b. Dépenses en immobilier*
c. Other	*23.91*	*30.60*	*35.92*	*23.25*	*20.02*	*33.90*	*38.52*	*34.42*	*32.43*	*31.82*	*c. Autres*
56. Net income	39.91	26.28	-2.18	38.52	48.01	32.57	25.00	27.16	27.26	25.69	56. Résultat net
57. Provisions (net)	36.04	55.14	146.01	69.88	36.76	1.91	-6.88	-6.13	-1.95	3.28	57. Provisions (nettes)
a. Provisions on loans	*33.50*	*51.21*	*145.00*	*55.38*	*29.23*	*-1.22*	*-7.81*	*-4.62*	*-2.39*	*3.56*	*a. Provisions sur prêts*
b. Provisions on securities	..	..	..	..	..	..	..	*0.01*	-	*0.17*	*b. Provisions sur titres*
c. Other	..	..	..	..	..	..	..	*-1.51*	*0.45*	*-0.45*	*c. Autres*
58. Profit before tax	3.87	-28.86	-148.19	-31.36	11.25	30.66	31.88	33.28	29.20	22.41	58. Bénéfices avant impôt
59. Income tax	1.81	0.44	0.07	0.55	1.58	2.26	1.55	2.27	2.07	1.19	59. Impôt sur le revenu
60. Profit after tax	2.06	-29.30	-148.26	-31.91	9.67	28.40	30.33	31.01	27.14	21.22	60. Bénéfices après impôt
% of net income											**% du total du résultat net**
61. Provisions (net)	90.31	209.81	-6712.00	181.42	76.56	5.88	-27.52	-22.55	-7.15	12.77	61. Provisions (nettes)
a. Provisions on loans	*83.95*	*194.83*	*-6665.20*	*143.78*	*60.88*	*-3.74*	*-31.23*	*-16.99*	*-8.78*	*13.84*	*a. Provisions sur prêts*
b. Provisions on securities	..	..	..	..	..	..	..	*0.02*	-	*0.65*	*b. Provisions sur titres*
c. Other	..	..	..	..	..	..	..	*-5.56*	*1.63*	*-1.74*	*c. Autres*
62. Profit before tax	9.69	-109.81	6812.00	-81.42	23.44	94.12	127.52	122.53	107.15	87.23	62. Bénéfices avant impôt
63. Income tax	4.54	1.69	-3.20	1.42	3.30	6.93	6.19	8.36	7.58	4.62	63. Impôt sur le revenu
64. Profit after tax	5.16	-111.49	6815.20	-82.84	20.14	87.19	121.32	114.17	99.57	82.60	64. Bénéfices après impôt

NORWAY — NORVEGE
Commercial banks — Banques commerciales

	1989	1990	1991	1992	1993	1994	1995	1996	1997	1998 p	
Per cent											*Pourcentage*
BALANCE SHEET ANALYSIS											**ANALYSE DU BILAN**
% of year-end balance sheet total											**% du total du bilan en fin d'exercice**
Assets											**Actif**
65. Cash & balance with Central bank	0.39	0.35	0.53	0.68	0.32	0.53	0.62	4.28	1.88	1.11	65. Caisse & solde auprès de la Banque centrale
66. Interbank deposits	3.72	4.65	6.95	9.70	5.95	4.95	3.99	3.95	3.47	4.31	66. Dépôts interbancaires
67. Loans	75.40	75.80	76.58	73.44	76.09	74.57	75.60	70.63	75.41	76.29	67. Prêts
68. Securities	13.87	13.05	10.04	10.89	11.81	14.57	14.78	15.90	14.53	12.74	68. Valeurs mobilières
69. Other assets	6.63	6.15	5.90	5.28	5.82	5.37	5.01	5.24	4.71	5.54	69. Autres actifs
Liabilities											**Passif**
70. Capital & reserves	4.21	3.54	2.11	2.20	4.50	5.66	6.25	5.87	5.93	5.44	70. Capital et réserves
71. Borrowing from Central bank	7.65	8.84	8.84	7.67	2.45	0.57	1.21	0.06	1.00	1.53	71. Emprunts auprès de la Banque centrale
72. Interbank deposits	16.78	16.76	14.98	10.24	9.72	7.40	6.77	14.42	15.49	12.13	72. Dépôts interbancaires
73. Non-bank deposits	51.66	52.19	56.40	59.10	60.79	69.20	68.42	60.53	54.03	51.27	73. Dépôts non bancaires
74. Bonds	11.93	11.88	11.37	15.20	16.26	11.03	10.21	10.54	13.99	17.66	74. Obligations
75. Other liabilities	7.77	6.79	6.31	5.58	6.28	6.15	7.14	8.58	9.56	11.97	75. Autres engagements
Memorandum items											***Pour mémoire***
76. Short-term securities	*1.92*	*2.78*	*1.58*	*1.02*	*2.06*	*5.41*	*5.55*	*5.94*	*5.44*	*3.00*	*76. Titres à court terme*
77. Bonds	*9.50*	*7.55*	*6.26*	*8.02*	*7.81*	*7.32*	*7.40*	*7.71*	*6.57*	*7.59*	*77. Obligations*
78. Shares and participations	*2.45*	*2.72*	*2.21*	*1.85*	*1.94*	*1.84*	*1.82*	*2.25*	*2.53*	*2.42*	*78. Actions et participations*
79. Claims on non-residents	*10.48*	*11.40*	*14.42*	*19.75*	*13.51*	*9.89*	*9.45*	*9.76*	*9.92*	*11.89*	*79. Créances sur des non-résidents*
80. Liabilities to non-residents	*31.82*	*30.24*	*24.51*	*17.94*	*18.01*	*11.72*	*10.82*	*19.41*	*23.80*	*25.56*	*80. Engagements envers des non-résidents*

* See notes on previous pages.

* Voir les notes en pages précédentes.

NORWAY — NORVEGE

Savings banks — Caisses d'épargne

	1989	1990	1991	1992	1993	1994	1995	1996	1997	1998 p	
Million Norwegian kroner											*Millions de couronnes norvégiennes*
INCOME STATEMENT											**COMPTE DE RESULTATS**
1. Interest income	32713	31391	29836	28849	25903	20762	21427	21519	20547	26950	1. Produits financiers
2. Interest expenses	22193	21376	19958	18350	14169	9932	10788	11080	9941	15448	2. Frais financiers
3. Net interest income	10520	10015	9878	10499	11734	10830	10639	10439	10606	11501	3. Produits financiers nets
4. Non-interest income (net)	2226	1585	1416	1705	3343	1147	2521	2423	2740	2369	4. Produits non financiers (nets)
a. Fees and commissions receivable	*1243*	*1153*	*1139*	*1278*	*1409*	*1624*	*1780*	*2124*	*2556*	*2714*	*a. Frais et commissions à recevoir*
b. Fees and commissions payable	-	-	*30*	*22*	*26*	*36*	*43*	*457*	*556*	*587*	*b. Frais et commissions à payer*
c. Net profits or loss on financial operations	*797*	*191*	*74*	*222*	*1719*	*-668*	*556*	*496*	*498*	*9*	*c. Profits ou pertes nets sur opérations financières*
d. Other	*185*	*241*	*234*	*226*	*242*	*228*	*229*	*260*	*241*	*234*	*d. Autres*
5. Gross income	12746	11600	11294	12204	15077	11977	13160	12862	13345	13870	5. Résultat brut
6. Operating expenses (1)	7728	7782	8309	7200	7340	7593	8117	8329	8439	8651	6. Frais d'exploitation (1)
a. Staff costs	*3539*	*3629*	*3665*	*3520*	*3370*	*3564*	*3774*	*3819*	*4169*	*4318*	*a. Dépenses en personnel*
b. Property costs	*763*	*755*	*1102*	*633*	*574*	*515*	*513*	*580*	*634*	*693*	*b. Dépenses en immobilier*
c. Other	*3426*	*3398*	*3542*	*3047*	*3395*	*3513*	*3829*	*3930*	*3636*	*3641*	*c. Autres*
7. Net income	5018	3818	2985	5004	7737	4384	5043	4533	4906	5219	7. Résultat net
8. Provisions (net) (1)	4181	4062	4852	1828	2740	796	391	96	262	438	8. Provisions (nettes) (1)
a. Provisions on loans	*5173*	*3875*	*4708*	*3891*	*2500*	*883*	*435*	*244*	*293*	*755*	*a. Provisions sur prêts*
b. Provisions on securities	..	..	..	..	..	..	..	*3*	-	-	*b. Provisions sur titres*
c. Other	..	..	..	..	..	..	..	*-151*	*-30*	*-317*	*c. Autres*
9. Profit before tax	837	-244	-1867	3176	4997	3588	4652	4437	4643	4781	9. Bénéfices avant impôt
10. Income tax	283	212	192	327	655	781	996	1186	1285	922	10. Impôt sur le revenu
11. Profit after tax	554	-456	-2059	2849	4342	2807	3656	3251	3359	3859	11. Bénéfices après impôt
12. Distributed profit	76	21	11	17	420	650	791	886	987	-	12. Bénéfices distribués
13. Retained profit	478	-477	-2070	2832	3922	2157	2865	2364	2372	3859	13. Bénéfices mis en réserve
BALANCE SHEET											**BILAN**
Assets											**Actif**
14. Cash & balance with Central bank	1679	1853	1837	2355	2072	2454	2670	4867	6112	5084	14. Caisse & solde auprès de la Banque centrale
15. Interbank deposits	4383	3492	4977	5572	4060	5844	3636	5576	7307	9786	15. Dépôts interbancaires
16. Loans	187424	193320	192579	195420	205142	219207	239213	271647	311677	345463	16. Prêts
17. Securities	40963	35991	31834	26974	29968	28588	30485	30125	28905	33796	17. Valeurs mobilières
18. Other assets	9214	8723	8669	8466	7934	8666	8285	7349	8013	9103	18. Autres actifs
Liabilities											**Passif**
19. Capital & reserves	11002	10615	9663	13345	18746	20724	23405	26000	28617	31509	19. Capital et réserves
20. Borrowing from Central bank	30926	23066	14611	10567	8712	2770	4870	147	1637	6403	20. Emprunts auprès de la Banque centrale
21. Interbank deposits	15724	12761	15709	10387	5544	6085	6641	18170	31529	33018	21. Dépôts interbancaires
22. Non-bank deposits	168579	178570	185317	189855	197262	208499	217083	230050	234867	251290	22. Dépôts non bancaires
23. Bonds	4971	6496	5413	8238	9738	13911	14393	20372	34751	48013	23. Obligations
24. Other liabilities	12461	11870	9183	6394	9173	12768	17896	24825	30615	33001	24. Autres engagements
Balance sheet total											**Total du bilan**
25. End-year total	243665	243379	239896	238787	249176	264758	284289	319565	362015	403231	25. En fin d'exercice
26. Average total	250833	251542	248570	241573	250961	261576	279054	302474	342623	386041	26. Moyen

NORWAY
Savings banks

NORVEGE
Caisses d'épargne

	1989	1990	1991	1992	1993	1994	1995	1996	1997	1998 p	
Million Norwegian kroner											*Millions de couronnes norvégiennes*
Memorandum items											***Pour mémoire***
27. Short-term securities	*2872*	*2810*	*3222*	*1613*	*3283*	*5316*	*7890*	*9889*	*7695*	*8286*	*27. Titres à court terme*
28. Bonds	*35479*	*30238*	*26073*	*22521*	*22471*	*18666*	*16960*	*14454*	*13829*	*17884*	*28. Obligations*
29. Shares and participations	*2612*	*2942*	*2539*	*2841*	*4214*	*4605*	*5634*	*5782*	*7489*	*7757*	*29. Actions et participations*
30. Claims on non-residents	*5662*	*5017*	*5359*	*6069*	*4547*	*7328*	*5007*	*6240*	*8392*	*10556*	*30. Créances sur des non-résidents*
31. Liabilities to non-residents	*19323*	*17049*	*13240*	*8701*	*9666*	*9816*	*8647*	*15479*	*36618*	*44991*	*31. Engagements envers des non-résidents*
Capital adequacy											***Solvabilité***
32. Tier 1 Capital	..	..	*10148*	*15555*	*19751*	*20825*	*23420*	*25897*	*28472*	*33249*	*32. Fonds propres de base*
33. Tier 2 Capital	..	..	*5416*	*4515*	*5793*	*7092*	*5981*	*6561*	*7590*	*7920*	*33. Fonds propres complémentaires*
34. Supervisory deductions	..	..	*197*	*205*	*34*	*139*	*302*	*382*	*931*	*584*	*34. Eléments à déduire des fonds propres*
35. Total net capital resources	..	..	*15367*	*19865*	*25510*	*27779*	*29100*	*32078*	*35132*	*40586*	*35. Total net des ressources en capital*
36. Risk-weighted assets	..	..	*164389*	*163288*	*166764*	*175644*	*189122*	*212586*	*244448*	*283932*	*36. Actifs pondérés des risques*
SUPPLEMENTARY INFORMATION											**RENSEIGNEMENTS COMPLEMENTAIRES**
37. Number of institutions	151	142	135	134	133	132	133	133	133	133	37. Nombre d'institutions
38. Number of branches	1194	1194	1121	1105	1110	1090	1124	1160	1116	1074	38. Nombre de succursales
39. Number of employees (x 1000)	14.9	14.6	13.3	13.4	12.8	12.7	11.2	10.6	11.0	11.0	39. Nombre de salariés (x 1000)

1. Change in methodology.

Notes

- Average balance sheet totals (item 26) are based on thirteen end-month data.

Change in methodology

- Due to methodological changes, write-downs are included under Operating expenses (item 6) and not under Provisions (net) (item 8) in the 1991 data.

1. Changement méthodologique.

Notes

- La moyenne du total des actifs/passifs (poste 26) est basée sur treize données de fin de mois.

Changement méthodologique

- Suite aux changements méthodologiques, les dévaluations sont incluses sous la rubrique Frais d'exploitation (poste 6) et non sous la rubrique Provisions (nettes) (poste 8) pour les données de 1991.

NORWAY — NORVEGE

Savings banks — Caisses d'épargne

	1989	1990	1991	1992	1993	1994	1995	1996	1997	1998 p	
Per cent											*Pourcentage*
INCOME STATEMENT ANALYSIS											**ANALYSE DU COMPTE DE RESULTATS**
% of average balance sheet total											**% du total moyen du bilan**
40. Interest income	13.04	12.48	12.00	11.94	10.32	7.94	7.68	7.11	6.00	6.98	40. Produits financiers
41. Interest expenses	8.85	8.50	8.03	7.60	5.65	3.80	3.87	3.66	2.90	4.00	41. Frais financiers
42. Net interest income	4.19	3.98	3.97	4.35	4.68	4.14	3.81	3.45	3.10	2.98	42. Produits financiers nets
43. Non-interest income (net)	0.89	0.63	0.57	0.71	1.33	0.44	0.90	0.80	0.80	0.61	43. Produits non financiers (nets)
a. Fees and commissions receivable	*0.50*	*0.46*	*0.46*	*0.53*	*0.56*	*0.62*	*0.64*	*0.70*	*0.75*	*0.70*	*a. Frais et commissions à recevoir*
b. Fees and commissions payable	-	-	*0.01*	*0.01*	*0.01*	*0.01*	*0.02*	*0.15*	*0.16*	*0.15*	*b. Frais et commissions à payer*
c. Net profits or loss on financial operations	*0.32*	*0.08*	*0.03*	*0.09*	*0.68*	*-0.26*	*0.20*	*0.16*	*0.15*	-	*c. Profits ou pertes nets sur opérations financières*
d. Other	*0.07*	*0.10*	*0.09*	*0.09*	*0.10*	*0.09*	*0.08*	*0.09*	*0.07*	*0.06*	*d. Autres*
44. Gross income	5.08	4.61	4.54	5.05	6.01	4.58	4.72	4.25	3.89	3.59	44. Résultat brut
45. Operating expenses	3.08	3.09	3.34	2.98	2.92	2.90	2.91	2.75	2.46	2.24	45. Frais d'exploitation
a. Staff costs	*1.41*	*1.44*	*1.47*	*1.46*	*1.34*	*1.36*	*1.35*	*1.26*	*1.22*	*1.12*	*a. Dépenses en personnel*
b. Property costs	*0.30*	*0.30*	*0.44*	*0.26*	*0.23*	*0.20*	*0.18*	*0.19*	*0.19*	*0.18*	*b. Dépenses en immobilier*
c. Other	*1.37*	*1.35*	*1.42*	*1.26*	*1.35*	*1.34*	*1.37*	*1.30*	*1.06*	*0.94*	*c. Autres*
46. Net income	2.00	1.52	1.20	2.07	3.08	1.68	1.81	1.50	1.43	1.35	46. Résultat net
47. Provisions (net)	1.67	1.61	1.95	0.76	1.09	0.30	0.14	0.03	0.08	0.11	47. Provisions (nettes)
a. Provisions on loans	*2.06*	*1.54*	*1.89*	*1.61*	*1.00*	*0.34*	*0.16*	*0.08*	*0.09*	*0.20*	*a. Provisions sur prêts*
b. Provisions on securities	..	..	..	..	..	..	..	-	-	-	*b. Provisions sur titres*
c. Other	..	..	..	..	..	..	..	*-0.05*	*-0.01*	*-0.08*	*c. Autres*
48. Profit before tax	0.33	-0.10	-0.75	1.31	1.99	1.37	1.67	1.47	1.36	1.24	48. Bénéfices avant impôt
49. Income tax	0.11	0.08	0.08	0.14	0.26	0.30	0.36	0.39	0.38	0.24	49. Impôt sur le revenu
50. Profit after tax	0.22	-0.18	-0.83	1.18	1.73	1.07	1.31	1.07	0.98	1.00	50. Bénéfices après impôt
51. Distributed profit	0.03	0.01	-	0.01	0.17	0.25	0.28	0.29	0.29	-	51. Bénéfices distribués
52. Retained profit	0.19	-0.19	-0.83	1.17	1.56	0.82	1.03	0.78	0.69	1.00	52. Bénéfices mis en réserve
% of gross income											**% du total du résultat brut**
53. Net interest income	82.54	86.34	87.46	86.03	77.83	90.42	80.84	81.16	79.48	82.92	53. Produits financiers nets
54. Non-interest income (net)	17.46	13.66	12.54	13.97	22.17	9.58	19.16	18.84	20.53	17.08	54. Produits non financiers (nets)
a. Fees and commissions receivable	*9.75*	*9.94*	*10.09*	*10.47*	*9.35*	*13.56*	*13.53*	*16.51*	*19.15*	*19.57*	*a. Frais et commissions à recevoir*
b. Fees and commissions payable	-	-	*0.27*	*0.18*	*0.17*	*0.30*	*0.33*	*3.55*	*4.17*	*4.23*	*b. Frais et commissions à payer*
c. Net profits or loss on financial operations	*6.25*	*1.65*	*0.66*	*1.82*	*11.40*	*-5.58*	*4.22*	*3.86*	*3.73*	*0.06*	*c. Profits ou pertes nets sur opérations financières*
d. Other	*1.45*	*2.08*	*2.07*	*1.85*	*1.61*	*1.90*	*1.74*	*2.02*	*1.81*	*1.69*	*d. Autres*
55. Operating expenses	60.63	67.09	73.57	59.00	48.68	63.40	61.68	64.76	63.24	62.37	55. Frais d'exploitation
a. Staff costs	*27.77*	*31.28*	*32.45*	*28.84*	*22.35*	*29.76*	*28.68*	*29.69*	*31.24*	*31.13*	*a. Dépenses en personnel*
b. Property costs	*5.99*	*6.51*	*9.76*	*5.19*	*3.81*	*4.30*	*3.90*	*4.51*	*4.75*	*5.00*	*b. Dépenses en immobilier*
c. Other	*26.88*	*29.29*	*31.36*	*24.97*	*22.52*	*29.33*	*29.10*	*30.56*	*27.25*	*26.25*	*c. Autres*
56. Net income	39.37	32.91	26.43	41.00	51.32	36.60	38.32	35.24	36.76	37.63	56. Résultat net
57. Provisions (net)	32.80	35.02	42.96	14.98	18.17	6.65	2.97	0.75	1.96	3.16	57. Provisions (nettes)
a. Provisions on loans	*40.59*	*33.41*	*41.69*	*31.88*	*16.58*	*7.37*	*3.31*	*1.90*	*2.20*	*5.44*	*a. Provisions sur prêts*
b. Provisions on securities	..	..	..	..	..	..	..	*0.02*	-	-	*b. Provisions sur titres*
c. Other	..	..	..	..	..	..	..	*-1.17*	*-0.22*	*-2.29*	*c. Autres*
58. Profit before tax	6.57	-2.10	-16.53	26.02	33.14	29.96	35.35	34.50	34.79	34.47	58. Bénéfices avant impôt
59. Income tax	2.22	1.83	1.70	2.68	4.34	6.52	7.57	9.22	9.63	6.65	59. Impôt sur le revenu
60. Profit after tax	4.35	-3.93	-18.23	23.34	28.80	23.44	27.78	25.28	25.17	27.82	60. Bénéfices après impôt
% of net income											**% du total du résultat net**
61. Provisions (net)	83.32	106.39	162.55	36.53	35.41	18.16	7.75	2.12	5.34	8.39	61. Provisions (nettes)
a. Provisions on loans	*103.09*	*101.49*	*157.72*	*77.76*	*32.31*	*20.14*	*8.63*	*5.38*	*5.97*	*14.47*	*a. Provisions sur prêts*
b. Provisions on securities	..	..	..	..	..	..	..	*0.07*	-	-	*b. Provisions sur titres*
c. Other	..	..	..	..	..	..	..	*-3.33*	*-0.61*	*-6.07*	*c. Autres*
62. Profit before tax	16.68	-6.39	-62.55	63.47	64.59	81.84	92.25	97.88	94.64	91.61	62. Bénéfices avant impôt
63. Income tax	5.64	5.55	6.43	6.53	8.47	17.81	19.75	26.16	26.19	17.67	63. Impôt sur le revenu
64. Profit after tax	11.04	-11.94	-68.98	56.93	56.12	64.03	72.50	71.72	68.47	73.94	64. Bénéfices après impôt

NORWAY — NORVEGE

Savings banks — Caisses d'épargne

	1989	1990	1991	1992	1993	1994	1995	1996	1997	1998 p	
Per cent											*Pourcentage*
BALANCE SHEET ANALYSIS											**ANALYSE DU BILAN**
% of year-end balance sheet total											**% du total du bilan en fin d'exercice**
Assets											**Actif**
65. Cash & balance with Central bank	0.69	0.76	0.77	0.99	0.83	0.93	0.94	1.52	1.69	1.26	65. Caisse & solde auprès de la Banque centrale
66. Interbank deposits	1.80	1.43	2.07	2.33	1.63	2.21	1.28	1.74	2.02	2.43	66. Dépôts interbancaires
67. Loans	76.92	79.43	80.28	81.84	82.33	82.80	84.14	85.01	86.10	85.67	67. Prêts
68. Securities	16.81	14.79	13.27	11.30	12.03	10.80	10.72	9.43	7.98	8.38	68. Valeurs mobilières
69. Other assets	3.78	3.58	3.61	3.55	3.18	3.27	2.91	2.30	2.21	2.26	69. Autres actifs
Liabilities											**Passif**
70. Capital & reserves	4.52	4.36	4.03	5.59	7.52	7.83	8.23	8.14	7.90	7.81	70. Capital et réserves
71. Borrowing from Central bank	12.69	9.48	6.09	4.43	3.50	1.05	1.71	0.05	0.45	1.59	71. Emprunts auprès de la Banque centrale
72. Interbank deposits	6.45	5.24	6.55	4.35	2.22	2.30	2.34	5.69	8.71	8.19	72. Dépôts interbancaires
73. Non-bank deposits	69.18	73.37	77.25	79.51	79.17	78.75	76.36	71.99	64.88	62.32	73. Dépôts non bancaires
74. Bonds	2.04	2.67	2.26	3.45	3.91	5.25	5.06	6.37	9.60	11.91	74. Obligations
75. Other liabilities	5.11	4.88	3.83	2.68	3.68	4.82	6.30	7.77	8.46	8.18	75. Autres engagements
Memorandum items											***Pour mémoire***
76. Short-term securities	*1.18*	*1.15*	*1.34*	*0.68*	*1.32*	*2.01*	*2.78*	*3.09*	*2.13*	*2.05*	*76. Titres à court terme*
77. Bonds	*14.56*	*12.42*	*10.87*	*9.43*	*9.02*	*7.05*	*5.97*	*4.52*	*3.82*	*4.44*	*77. Obligations*
78. Shares and participations	*1.07*	*1.21*	*1.06*	*1.19*	*1.69*	*1.74*	*1.98*	*1.81*	*2.07*	*1.92*	*78. Actions et participations*
79. Claims on non-residents	*2.32*	*2.06*	*2.23*	*2.54*	*1.82*	*2.77*	*1.76*	*1.95*	*2.32*	*2.62*	*79. Créances sur des non-résidents*
80. Liabilities to non-residents	*7.93*	*7.01*	*5.52*	*3.64*	*3.88*	*3.71*	*3.04*	*4.84*	*10.12*	*11.16*	*80. Engagements envers des non-résidents*

* See notes on previous pages.

* Voir les notes en pages précédentes.

POLAND
All banks

POLOGNE
Ensemble des banques

	1993	1994	1995	1996	1997	1998 p	
Million zlotys							*Millions de zlotys*
INCOME STATEMENT							**COMPTE DE RESULTATS**
1. Interest income	13485	15990	21461	26182	32388	40073	1. Produits financiers
2. Interest expenses	9546	10955	13814	15861	20577	26935	2. Frais financiers
3. Net interest income	3939	5035	7647	10320	11812	13138	3. Produits financiers nets
4. Non-interest income (net)	1639	1770	2464	3261	4566	5755	4. Produits non financiers (nets)
a. Fees and commissions receivable	*935*	*1186*	*1531*	*2091*	*3159*	*3696*	*a. Frais et commissions à recevoir*
b. Fees and commissions payable	*231*	*146*	*222*	*212*	*347*	*457*	*b. Frais et commissions à payer*
c. Net profits or loss on financial operations	*885*	*939*	*1023*	*707*	*271*	*178*	*c. Profits ou pertes nets sur opérations financières*
d. Other (1)	*49*	*-209*	*132*	*674*	*1483*	*2338*	*d. Autres (1)*
5. Gross income	5578	6805	10111	13581	16378	18893	5. Résultat brut
6. Operating expenses	2677	3594	4962	6922	9012	11582	6. Frais d'exploitation
a. Staff costs	*1320*	*1841*	*2716*	*3756*	*4778*	*5992*	*a. Dépenses en personnel*
b. Property costs	*154*	*297*	*532*	*711*	*937*	*1256*	*b. Dépenses en immobilier*
c. Other	*1203*	*1456*	*1715*	*2454*	*3297*	*4334*	*c. Autres*
7. Net income	2901	3211	5149	6660	7366	7311	7. Résultat net
8. Provisions (net)	1974	2008	459	257	709	1842	8. Provisions (nettes)
a. Provisions on loans	*1819*	*1661*	*118*	*-12*	*675*	*1744*	*a. Provisions sur prêts*
b. Provisions on securities	*25*	*170*	*71*	*-23*	*34*	*98*	*b. Provisions sur titres*
c. Other	*129*	*177*	*270*	*291*	-	-	*c. Autres*
9. Profit before tax	927	1203	4690	6403	6657	5469	9. Bénéfices avant impôt
10. Income tax (2)	1328	1081	1843	1983	2161	2370	10. Impôt sur le revenu (2)
11. Profit after tax	-401	122	2847	4420	4496	3099	11. Bénéfices après impôt
12. Distributed profit	..	..	..	..	..	..	12. Bénéfices distribués
13. Retained profit	..	..	..	..	..	..	13. Bénéfices mis en réserve
BALANCE SHEET							**BILAN**
Assets							**Actif**
14. Cash & balance with Central bank	8266	9799	13941	14423	18141	24947	14. Caisse & solde auprès de la Banque centrale
15. Interbank deposits (3)	12708	19156	19997	25641	33689	42105	15. Dépôts interbancaires (3)
16. Loans (4)	27083	31302	45762	77025	105303	136321	16. Prêts (4)
17. Securities	19611	30978	46240	61942	65793	85854	17. Valeurs mobilières
18. Other assets	15333	18441	23402	18046	24743	31452	18. Autres actifs
Liabilities							**Passif**
19. Capital & reserves	7177	10194	13169	14142	20188	26827	19. Capital et réserves
20. Borrowing from Central bank (5)	5053	5505	6031	9397	7914	6291	20. Emprunts auprès de la Banque centrale (5)
21. Interbank deposits	5510	7541	11330	15666	16473	32244	21. Dépôts interbancaires
22. Non-bank deposits	49275	69801	90759	118894	152719	197973	22. Dépôts non bancaires
23. Bonds	326	627	1745	1156	2609	1666	23. Obligations
24. Other liabilities	15660	16007	26309	37822	47766	55678	24. Autres engagements
Balance sheet total							**Total du bilan**
25. End-year total	83001	109676	149342	197077	247669	320679	25. En fin d'exercice
26. Average total	..	96338	129509	173210	222373	284174	26. Moyen

POLAND
All banks

POLOGNE
Ensemble des banques

	1993	1994	1995	1996	1997	1998 p	
Million zlotys							*Millions de zlotys*
Memorandum items							***Pour mémoire***
27. Short-term securities	..	..	..	..	..	..	*27. Titres à court terme*
28. Bonds	..	..	..	..	..	..	*28. Obligations*
29. Shares and participations	..	..	..	..	..	..	*29. Actions et participations*
30. Claims on non-residents	..	..	..	..	*25593*	*18955*	*30. Créances sur des non-résidents*
31. Liabilities to non-residents	..	..	..	..	*15070*	*18667*	*31. Engagements envers des non-résidents*
Capital adequacy							***Solvabilité***
32. Tier 1 Capital (6)	*5604*	*8234*	*10183*	*13444*	*17175*	*25224*	*32. Fonds propres de base (6)*
33. Tier 2 Capital	*878*	*1304*	*2345*	*3082*	*4044*	*1817*	*33. Fonds propres complémentaires*
34. Supervisory deductions	*3088*	*4281*	*4867*	*3999*	*3358*	*3785*	*34. Eléments à déduire des fonds propres*
35. Total net capital resources	*3394*	*5257*	*7661*	*12526*	*17861*	*23256*	*35. Total net des ressources en capital*
36. Risk-weighted assets	*37285*	*48067*	*67457*	*102924*	*143465*	*193691*	*36. Actifs pondérés des risques*
SUPPLEMENTARY INFORMATION							**RENSEIGNEMENTS COMPLEMENTAIRES**
37. Number of institutions	1740	1694	1591	1475	1378	1272	37. Nombre d'institutions
38. Number of branches	1436	1454	1501	2082	2210	2532	38. Nombre de succursales
39. Number of employees (x 1000)	120	129	136	144	172	174	39. Nombre de salariés (x 1000)

1. Other non-interest income (item 4.d) includes investment income, foreign exchange gains or losses, other operating income and expense, and extraordinary items.
2. Income tax (item 10) includes corporate income tax and other taxes
3. Interbank deposits (item 15) cover operations with financial entities: term and demand due, and current accounts.
4. Loans (item 16) include due from non-financial and government entities.
5. Borrowing from the Central bank (item 20): operations with the Central bank.
6. Change in methodology.

Notes

- All banks include Commercial banks and Co-operative banks.
- Until 1996, the data for Number of branches and employees (items 38 and 39) does not include Co-operative banks.

Change in methodology

- Beginning 1997, data for Tier 1 Capital (item 32) are based on new banking regulations.

1. Les Autres produits non financier (poste 4.d.) incluent le revenu des investissements, les gains et pertes de change, les autres revenus et frais d'exploitation, ainsi que les éléments extraordinaires.
2. L'Impôt sur le revenu (poste 10) comprend l'impôt sur les bénéfices des sociétés et d'autres impôts.
3. Les Dépôts interbancaires (poste 15) comprennent les créances à vue et à terme et les comptes courants sur des entités financières.
4. Les Prêts (poste 16) comprennent les créances sur des entités non financières et sur des administrations publiques
5. Les Emprunts auprès de la Banque centrale (poste 20) : les opérations avec la Banque centrale.
6. Changement méthodologique.

Notes

- L'Ensemble des banques comprend les Banques commerciales et les Banques mutualistes.
- Jusqu'en 1996, les données pour Nombre de succursales (poste 38) et Nombre de salariés (poste 39) ne concernent pas les Banques mutualistes.

Changement méthodologique

- A partir de 1997, les données pour les Fonds propres de base (poste 32) sont établies en tenant compte de la nouvelle reglementation bancaire.

POLAND
All banks

POLOGNE
Ensemble des banques

Per cent	1993	1994	1995	1996	1997	1998 p	Pourcentage
INCOME STATEMENT ANALYSIS							**ANALYSE DU COMPTE DE RESULTATS**
% of average balance sheet total							**% du total moyen du bilan**
40. Interest income	..	16.60	16.57	15.12	14.56	14.10	40. Produits financiers
41. Interest expenses	..	11.37	10.67	9.16	9.25	9.48	41. Frais financiers
42. Net interest income	..	5.23	5.90	5.96	5.31	4.62	42. Produits financiers nets
43. Non-interest income (net)	..	1.84	1.90	1.88	2.05	2.03	43. Produits non financiers (nets)
a. Fees and commissions receivable	..	*1.23*	*1.18*	*1.21*	*1.42*	*1.30*	*a. Frais et commissions à recevoir*
b. Fees and commissions payable	..	*0.15*	*0.17*	*0.12*	*0.16*	*0.16*	*b. Frais et commissions à payer*
c. Net profits or loss on financial operations	..	*0.97*	*0.79*	*0.41*	*0.12*	*0.06*	*c. Profits ou pertes nets sur opérations financières*
d. Other	..	*-0.22*	*0.10*	*0.39*	*0.67*	*0.82*	*d. Autres*
44. Gross income	..	7.06	7.81	7.84	7.37	6.65	44. Résultat brut
45. Operating expenses	..	3.73	3.83	4.00	4.05	4.08	45. Frais d'exploitation
a. Staff costs	..	*1.91*	*2.10*	*2.17*	*2.15*	*2.11*	*a. Dépenses en personnel*
b. Property costs	..	*0.31*	*0.41*	*0.41*	*0.42*	*0.44*	*b. Dépenses en immobilier*
c. Other	..	*1.51*	*1.32*	*1.42*	*1.48*	*1.53*	*c. Autres*
46. Net income	..	3.33	3.98	3.85	3.31	2.57	46. Résultat net
47. Provisions (net)	..	2.08	0.35	0.15	0.32	0.65	47. Provisions (nettes)
a. Provisions on loans	..	*1.72*	*0.09*	*-0.01*	*0.30*	*0.61*	*a. Provisions sur prêts*
b. Provisions on securities	..	*0.18*	*0.05*	*-0.01*	*0.02*	*0.03*	*b. Provisions sur titres*
c. Other	..	*0.18*	*0.21*	*0.17*	-	-	*c. Autres*
48. Profit before tax	..	1.25	3.62	3.70	2.99	1.92	48. Bénéfices avant impôt
49. Income tax	..	1.12	1.42	1.14	0.97	0.83	49. Impôt sur le revenu
50. Profit after tax	..	0.13	2.20	2.55	2.02	1.09	50. Bénéfices après impôt
51. Distributed profit	..	..	..	..	..	..	51. Bénéfices distribués
52. Retained profit	..	..	..	..	..	..	52. Bénéfices mis en réserve
% of gross income							**% du total du résultat brut**
53. Net interest income	70.62	73.99	75.63	75.99	72.12	69.54	53. Produits financiers nets
54. Non-interest income (net)	29.38	26.01	24.37	24.01	27.88	30.46	54. Produits non financiers (nets)
a. Fees and commissions receivable	*16.76*	*17.43*	*15.14*	*15.40*	*19.29*	*19.56*	*a. Frais et commissions à recevoir*
b. Fees and commissions payable	*4.14*	*2.15*	*2.20*	*1.56*	*2.12*	*2.42*	*b. Frais et commissions à payer*
c. Net profits or loss on financial operations	*15.87*	*13.80*	*10.12*	*5.21*	*1.65*	*0.94*	*c. Profits ou pertes nets sur opérations financières*
d. Other	*0.88*	*-3.07*	*1.31*	*4.96*	*9.05*	*12.37*	*d. Autres*
55. Operating expenses	47.99	52.81	49.08	50.97	55.03	61.30	55. Frais d'exploitation
a. Staff costs	*23.66*	*27.05*	*26.86*	*27.66*	*29.17*	*31.72*	*a. Dépenses en personnel*
b. Property costs	*2.76*	*4.36*	*5.26*	*5.24*	*5.72*	*6.65*	*b. Dépenses en immobilier*
c. Other	*21.57*	*21.40*	*16.96*	*18.07*	*20.13*	*22.94*	*c. Autres*
56. Net income	52.01	47.19	50.92	49.04	44.97	38.70	56. Résultat net
57. Provisions (net)	35.39	29.51	4.54	1.89	4.33	9.75	57. Provisions (nettes)
a. Provisions on loans	*32.61*	*24.41*	*1.17*	*-0.09*	*4.12*	*9.23*	*a. Provisions sur prêts*
b. Provisions on securities	*0.45*	*2.50*	*0.70*	*-0.17*	*0.21*	*0.52*	*b. Provisions sur titres*
c. Other	*2.31*	*2.60*	*2.67*	*2.14*	-	-	*c. Autres*
58. Profit before tax	16.62	17.68	46.39	47.15	40.65	28.95	58. Bénéfices avant impôt
59. Income tax	23.81	15.89	18.23	14.60	13.19	12.54	59. Impôt sur le revenu
60. Profit after tax	-7.19	1.79	28.16	32.55	27.45	16.40	60. Bénéfices après impôt
% of net income							**% du total du résultat net**
61. Provisions (net)	68.05	62.54	8.91	3.86	9.63	25.19	61. Provisions (nettes)
a. Provisions on loans	*62.70*	*51.73*	*2.29*	*-0.18*	*9.16*	*23.85*	*a. Provisions sur prêts*
b. Provisions on securities	*0.86*	*5.29*	*1.38*	*-0.35*	*0.46*	*1.34*	*b. Provisions sur titres*
c. Other	*4.45*	*5.51*	*5.24*	*4.37*	-	-	*c. Autres*
62. Profit before tax	31.95	37.46	91.09	96.14	90.37	74.81	62. Bénéfices avant impôt
63. Income tax	45.78	33.67	35.79	29.77	29.34	32.42	63. Impôt sur le revenu
64. Profit after tax	-13.82	3.80	55.29	66.37	61.04	42.39	64. Bénéfices après impôt

POLAND
All banks

POLOGNE
Ensemble des banques

	1993	1994	1995	1996	1997	1998 p	
Per cent							*Pourcentage*
BALANCE SHEET ANALYSIS							**ANALYSE DU BILAN**
% of year-end balance sheet total							**% du total du bilan en fin d'exercice**
Assets							**Actif**
65. Cash & balance with Central bank	9.96	8.93	9.33	7.32	7.32	7.78	65. Caisse & solde auprès de la Banque centrale
66. Interbank deposits	15.31	17.47	13.39	13.01	13.60	13.13	66. Dépôts interbancaires
67. Loans	32.63	28.54	30.64	39.08	42.52	42.51	67. Prêts
68. Securities	23.63	28.25	30.96	31.43	26.56	26.77	68. Valeurs mobilières
69. Other assets	18.47	16.81	15.67	9.16	9.99	9.81	69. Autres actifs
Liabilities							**Passif**
70. Capital & reserves	8.65	9.29	8.82	7.18	8.15	8.37	70. Capital et réserves
71. Borrowing from Central bank	6.09	5.02	4.04	4.77	3.20	1.96	71. Emprunts auprès de la Banque centrale
72. Interbank deposits	6.64	6.88	7.59	7.95	6.65	10.05	72. Dépôts interbancaires
73. Non-bank deposits	59.37	63.64	60.77	60.33	61.66	61.74	73. Dépôts non bancaires
74. Bonds	0.39	0.57	1.17	0.59	1.05	0.52	74. Obligations
75. Other liabilities	18.87	14.59	17.62	19.19	19.29	17.36	75. Autres engagements
Memorandum items							***Pour mémoire***
76. Short-term securities	..	..	..	..	..	..	*76. Titres à court terme*
77. Bonds	..	..	..	..	..	..	*77. Obligations*
78. Shares and participations	..	..	..	..	..	..	*78. Actions et participations*
79. Claims on non-residents	..	..	..	..	*10.33*	*5.91*	*79. Créances sur des non-résidents*
80. Liabilities to non-residents	..	..	..	..	*6.08*	*5.82*	*80. Engagements envers des non-résidents*

* See notes on previous pages.

* Voir les notes en pages précédentes.

POLAND
Commercial banks

POLOGNE
Banques commerciales

	1993	1994	1995	1996	1997	1998 p	
Million zlotys							*Millions de zlotys*
INCOME STATEMENT							**COMPTE DE RESULTATS**
1. Interest income	12070	14680	20089	24615	30384	37833	1. Produits financiers
2. Interest expenses	8743	10023	12955	14999	19512	25650	2. Frais financiers
3. Net interest income	3327	4657	7134	9616	10872	12183	3. Produits financiers nets
4. Non-interest income (net)	1569	1679	2331	3075	4335	5485	4. Produits non financiers (nets)
a. Fees and commissions receivable	*850*	*1071*	*1395*	*1909*	*2928*	*3428*	*a. Frais et commissions à recevoir*
b. Fees and commissions payable	*212*	*126*	*209*	*199*	*337*	*447*	*b. Frais et commissions à payer*
c. Net profits or loss on financial operations	*884*	*938*	*1023*	*707*	*267*	*176*	*c. Profits ou pertes nets sur opérations financières*
d. Other (1)	*47*	*-205*	*122*	*658*	*1477*	*2328*	*d. Autres (1)*
5. Gross income	4896	6336	9465	12691	15207	17668	5. Résultat brut
6. Operating expenses	2099	3157	4434	6263	8173	10663	6. Frais d'exploitation
a. Staff costs	*1120*	*1689*	*2344*	*3296*	*4189*	*5339*	*a. Dépenses en personnel*
b. Property costs	*138*	*274*	*500*	*673*	*892*	*1203*	*b. Dépenses en immobilier*
c. Other	*842*	*1193*	*1590*	*2295*	*3092*	*4121*	*c. Autres*
7. Net income	2797	3179	5031	6428	7034	7005	7. Résultat net
8. Provisions (net)	1745	1824	480	290	726	1823	8. Provisions (nettes)
a. Provisions on loans	*1595*	*1479*	*144*	*26*	*693*	*1725*	*a. Provisions sur prêts*
b. Provisions on securities	*25*	*170*	*71*	*-23*	*33*	*98*	*b. Provisions sur titres*
c. Other	*126*	*175*	*265*	*286*	-	-	*c. Autres*
9. Profit before tax	1052	1355	4551	6138	6308	5182	9. Bénéfices avant impôt
10. Income tax (2)	1267	1038	1789	1909	2036	2261	10. Impôt sur le revenu (2)
11. Profit after tax	-215	317	2762	4229	4272	2921	11. Bénéfices après impôt
12. Distributed profit (3)	225	462	600	833	734	..	12. Bénéfices distribués (3)
13. Retained profit (4)	755	1355	2300	3396	3727	..	13. Bénéfices mis en réserve (4)
BALANCE SHEET							**BILAN**
Assets							**Actif**
14. Cash & balance with Central bank	7595	9333	13502	13926	17451	24566	14. Caisse & solde auprès de la Banque centrale
15. Interbank deposits (5)	11046	17200	17209	22797	30668	37275	15. Dépôts interbancaires (5)
16. Loans (6)	25285	29240	43285	72543	99777	129928	16. Prêts (6)
17. Securities	19430	30809	45879	61210	64631	84689	17. Valeurs mobilières
18. Other assets	14152	17289	22291	17483	23888	30519	18. Autres actifs
Liabilities							**Passif**
19. Capital & reserves	6657	9648	12491	13502	19295	25689	19. Capital et réserves
20. Borrowing from Central bank (7)	5052	5489	6011	9395	7909	6291	20. Emprunts auprès de la Banque centrale (7)
21. Interbank deposits	5288	7325	11213	15512	16411	32205	21. Dépôts interbancaires
22. Non-bank deposits	45218	65343	85203	111846	143807	187088	22. Dépôts non bancaires
23. Bonds	326	626	1741	1120	2538	1606	23. Obligations
24. Other liabilities	14968	15440	25507	36586	46455	54099	24. Autres engagements
Balance sheet total							**Total du bilan**
25. End-year total	77509	103870	142165	187960	236415	306977	25. En fin d'exercice
26. Average total	..	90689	123018	165063	212187	271696	26. Moyen

POLAND

Commercial banks

POLOGNE

Banques commerciales

	1993	1994	1995	1996	1997	1998 p	
Million zlotys							*Millions de zlotys*
Memorandum items							***Pour mémoire***
27. Short-term securities	..	..	..	..	..	..	*27. Titres à court terme*
28. Bonds	..	..	..	..	..	..	*28. Obligations*
29. Shares and participations	..	..	..	..	..	..	*29. Actions et participations*
30. Claims on non-residents	..	..	..	..	*25593*	*18955*	*30. Créances sur des non-résidents*
31. Liabilities to non-residents	..	..	..	..	*15070*	*18667*	*31. Engagements envers des non-résidents*
Capital adequacy							***Solvabilité***
32. Tier 1 Capital (8)	*5144*	*7758*	*9667*	*12794*	*16322*	*24145*	*32. Fonds propres de base (8)*
33. Tier 2 Capital	*823*	*1241*	*2191*	*2930*	*3885*	*1697*	*33. Fonds propres complémentaires*
34. Supervisory deductions	*2696*	*3805*	*4508*	*3699*	*3098*	*3554*	*34. Eléments à déduire des fonds propres*
35. Total net capital resources	*3271*	*5194*	*7350*	*12024*	*17109*	*22288*	*35. Total net des ressources en capital*
36. Risk-weighted assets	*34673*	*45119*	*63753*	*97469*	*136672*	*185504*	*36. Actifs pondérés des risques*
SUPPLEMENTARY INFORMATION							**RENSEIGNEMENTS COMPLEMENTAIRES**
37. Number of institutions	87	82	81	81	83	83	37. Nombre d'institutions
38. Number of branches	1436	1454	1501	1580	1629	1864	38. Nombre de succursales
39. Number of employees (x 1000)	119.8	128.7	136.1	144.2	147.0	149.0	39. Nombre de salariés (x 1000)

1. Other non-interest income (item 4.d) includes investment income, foreign exchange gains or losses, other operating income and expense, and extraordinary items.
2. Income tax (item 10) includes corporate income tax and other taxes
3. Distributed profit (item 12) includes deductions for social funds.
4. Retained profit (item 13) includes the part of profit allocated for banks' capital raising, and coverage of previous years' losses.
5. Interbank deposits (item 15) cover operations with financial entities: term and demand due, and current accounts.
6. Loans (item 16) include due from non-financial and government entities.
7. Borrowing from the Central bank (item 20): operations with the Central bank.
8. Change in methodology.

Notes

- Commercial banks include Polish commercial banks and Foreign commercial banks.

Change in methodology

- Beginning 1997, data for Tier 1 Capital (item 32) are based on new banking regulations.

1. Les Autres produits non financier (poste 4.d.) incluent le revenu des investissements, les gains et pertes de change, les autres revenus et frais d'exploitation, ainsi que les éléments extraordinaires.
2. L'Impôt sur le revenu (poste 10) comprend l'impôt sur les bénéfices des sociétés et d'autres impôts.
3. Les "Bénéfices distribués" (poste 12) incluent les déductions pour les fonds sociaux.
4. Les Bénéfices mis en réserve (poste 13) incluent la part des bénéfices affectée à la collecte de capitaux des banques et la couverture des pertes des années précédentes.
5. Les Dépôts interbancaires (poste 15) comprennent les créances à vue et à terme et les comptes courants sur des entités financières.
6. Les Prêts (poste 16) comprennent les créances sur des entités non financières et sur des administrations publiques
7. Les Emprunts auprès de la Banque centrale (poste 20) : les opérations avec la Banque centrale.
8. Changement méthodologique.

Notes

- Les Banques commerciales comprennent les Banques commerciales polonaises et les Banques commerciales étrangères.

Changement méthodologique

- A partir de 1997, les données pour les Fonds propres de base (poste 32) sont établies en tenant compte de la nouvelle reglementation bancaire.

POLAND
Commercial banks

POLOGNE
Banques commerciales

	1993	1994	1995	1996	1997	1998 p	
Per cent							*Pourcentage*
INCOME STATEMENT ANALYSIS							**ANALYSE DU COMPTE DE RESULTATS**
% of average balance sheet total							**% du total moyen du bilan**
40. Interest income	..	16.19	16.33	14.91	14.32	13.92	40. Produits financiers
41. Interest expenses	..	11.05	10.53	9.09	9.20	9.44	41. Frais financiers
42. Net interest income	..	5.14	5.80	5.83	5.12	4.48	42. Produits financiers nets
43. Non-interest income (net)	..	1.85	1.89	1.86	2.04	2.02	43. Produits non financiers (nets)
a. Fees and commissions receivable	..	*1.18*	*1.13*	*1.16*	*1.38*	*1.26*	*a. Frais et commissions à recevoir*
b. Fees and commissions payable	..	*0.14*	*0.17*	*0.12*	*0.16*	*0.16*	*b. Frais et commissions à payer*
c. Net profits or loss on financial operations	..	*1.03*	*0.83*	*0.43*	*0.13*	*0.06*	*c. Profits ou pertes nets sur opérations financières*
d. Other	..	*-0.23*	*0.10*	*0.40*	*0.70*	*0.86*	*d. Autres*
44. Gross income	..	6.99	7.69	7.69	7.17	6.50	44. Résultat brut
45. Operating expenses	..	3.48	3.60	3.79	3.85	3.92	45. Frais d'exploitation
a. Staff costs	..	*1.86*	*1.91*	*2.00*	*1.97*	*1.97*	*a. Dépenses en personnel*
b. Property costs	..	*0.30*	*0.41*	*0.41*	*0.42*	*0.44*	*b. Dépenses en immobilier*
c. Other	..	*1.32*	*1.29*	*1.39*	*1.46*	*1.52*	*c. Autres*
46. Net income	..	3.51	4.09	3.89	3.32	2.58	46. Résultat net
47. Provisions (net)	..	2.01	0.39	0.18	0.34	0.67	47. Provisions (nettes)
a. Provisions on loans	..	*1.63*	*0.12*	*0.02*	*0.33*	*0.63*	*a. Provisions sur prêts*
b. Provisions on securities	..	*0.19*	*0.06*	*-0.01*	*0.02*	*0.04*	*b. Provisions sur titres*
c. Other	..	*0.19*	*0.22*	*0.17*	-	-	*c. Autres*
48. Profit before tax	..	1.49	3.70	3.72	2.97	1.91	48. Bénéfices avant impôt
49. Income tax	..	1.14	1.45	1.16	0.96	0.83	49. Impôt sur le revenu
50. Profit after tax	..	0.35	2.25	2.56	2.01	1.08	50. Bénéfices après impôt
51. Distributed profit	..	0.51	0.49	0.50	0.35	..	51. Bénéfices distribués
52. Retained profit	..	1.49	1.87	2.06	1.76	..	52. Bénéfices mis en réserve
% of gross income							**% du total du résultat brut**
53. Net interest income	67.95	73.50	75.37	75.77	71.49	68.96	53. Produits financiers nets
54. Non-interest income (net)	32.05	26.50	24.63	24.23	28.51	31.04	54. Produits non financiers (nets)
a. Fees and commissions receivable	*17.36*	*16.90*	*14.74*	*15.04*	*19.25*	*19.40*	*a. Frais et commissions à recevoir*
b. Fees and commissions payable	*4.33*	*1.99*	*2.21*	*1.57*	*2.22*	*2.53*	*b. Frais et commissions à payer*
c. Net profits or loss on financial operations	*18.06*	*14.80*	*10.81*	*5.57*	*1.76*	*1.00*	*c. Profits ou pertes nets sur opérations financières*
d. Other	*0.96*	*-3.24*	*1.29*	*5.18*	*9.71*	*13.18*	*d. Autres*
55. Operating expenses	42.87	49.83	46.85	49.35	53.74	60.35	55. Frais d'exploitation
a. Staff costs	*22.88*	*26.66*	*24.76*	*25.97*	*27.55*	*30.22*	*a. Dépenses en personnel*
b. Property costs	*2.82*	*4.32*	*5.28*	*5.30*	*5.87*	*6.81*	*b. Dépenses en immobilier*
c. Other	*17.20*	*18.83*	*16.80*	*18.08*	*20.33*	*23.32*	*c. Autres*
56. Net income	57.13	50.17	53.15	50.65	46.26	39.65	56. Résultat net
57. Provisions (net)	35.64	28.79	5.07	2.29	4.77	10.32	57. Provisions (nettes)
a. Provisions on loans	*32.58*	*23.34*	*1.52*	*0.20*	*4.56*	*9.76*	*a. Provisions sur prêts*
b. Provisions on securities	*0.51*	*2.68*	*0.75*	*-0.18*	*0.22*	*0.55*	*b. Provisions sur titres*
c. Other	*2.57*	*2.76*	*2.80*	*2.25*	-	-	*c. Autres*
58. Profit before tax	21.49	21.39	48.08	48.36	41.48	29.33	58. Bénéfices avant impôt
59. Income tax	25.88	16.38	18.90	15.04	13.39	12.80	59. Impôt sur le revenu
60. Profit after tax	-4.39	5.00	29.18	33.32	28.09	16.53	60. Bénéfices après impôt
% of net income							**% du total du résultat net**
61. Provisions (net)	62.39	57.38	9.54	4.51	10.32	26.02	61. Provisions (nettes)
a. Provisions on loans	*57.03*	*46.52*	*2.86*	*0.40*	*9.85*	*24.63*	*a. Provisions sur prêts*
b. Provisions on securities	*0.89*	*5.35*	*1.41*	*-0.36*	*0.47*	*1.40*	*b. Provisions sur titres*
c. Other	*4.50*	*5.50*	*5.27*	*4.45*	-	-	*c. Autres*
62. Profit before tax	37.61	42.62	90.46	95.49	89.68	73.98	62. Bénéfices avant impôt
63. Income tax	45.30	32.65	35.56	29.70	28.95	32.28	63. Impôt sur le revenu
64. Profit after tax	-7.69	9.97	54.90	65.79	60.73	41.70	64. Bénéfices après impôt

POLAND
Commercial banks

POLOGNE
Banques commerciales

	1993	1994	1995	1996	1997	1998 p	
Per cent							*Pourcentage*
BALANCE SHEET ANALYSIS							**ANALYSE DU BILAN**
% of year-end balance sheet total							**% du total du bilan en fin d'exercice**
Assets							**Actif**
65. Cash & balance with Central bank	9.80	8.99	9.50	7.41	7.38	8.00	65. Caisse & solde auprès de la Banque centrale
66. Interbank deposits	14.25	16.56	12.10	12.13	12.97	12.14	66. Dépôts interbancaires
67. Loans	32.62	28.15	30.45	38.59	42.20	42.32	67. Prêts
68. Securities	25.07	29.66	32.27	32.57	27.34	27.59	68. Valeurs mobilières
69. Other assets	18.26	16.64	15.68	9.30	10.10	9.94	69. Autres actifs
Liabilities							**Passif**
70. Capital & reserves	8.59	9.29	8.79	7.18	8.16	8.37	70. Capital et réserves
71. Borrowing from Central bank	6.52	5.28	4.23	5.00	3.35	2.05	71. Emprunts auprès de la Banque centrale
72. Interbank deposits	6.82	7.05	7.89	8.25	6.94	10.49	72. Dépôts interbancaires
73. Non-bank deposits	58.34	62.91	59.93	59.51	60.83	60.95	73. Dépôts non bancaires
74. Bonds	0.42	0.60	1.22	0.60	1.07	0.52	74. Obligations
75. Other liabilities	19.31	14.86	17.94	19.46	19.65	17.62	75. Autres engagements
Memorandum items							***Pour mémoire***
76. Short-term securities	..	..	..	..	..	..	*76. Titres à court terme*
77. Bonds	..	..	..	..	..	..	*77. Obligations*
78. Shares and participations	..	..	..	..	..	..	*78. Actions et participations*
79. Claims on non-residents	..	..	..	..	*10.83*	*6.17*	*79. Créances sur des non-résidents*
80. Liabilities to non-residents	..	..	..	..	*6.37*	*6.08*	*80. Engagements envers des non-résidents*

* See notes on previous pages.

* Voir les notes en pages précédentes.

POLAND / POLOGNE

Polish commercial banks / Banques commerciales polonaises

Million zlotys	1993	1994	1995	1996	1997	1998 p	Millions de zlotys
INCOME STATEMENT							**COMPTE DE RESULTATS**
1. Interest income	11822	14167	19112	20934	24994	30622	1. Produits financiers
2. Interest expenses	8567	9687	12312	12812	16103	21061	2. Frais financiers
3. Net interest income	3255	4480	6800	8121	8891	9561	3. Produits financiers nets
4. Non-interest income (net)	1430	1500	2116	2479	3391	4123	4. Produits non financiers (nets)
a. Fees and commissions receivable	*820*	*1025*	*1313*	*1508*	*2345*	*2671*	*a. Frais et commissions à recevoir*
b. Fees and commissions payable	*206*	*115*	*175*	*157*	*253*	*329*	*b. Frais et commissions à payer*
c. Net profits or loss on financial operations	*770*	*791*	*868*	*516*	*245*	*123*	*c. Profits ou pertes nets sur opérations financières*
d. Other (1)	*46*	*-201*	*110*	*613*	*1054*	*1658*	*d. Autres (1)*
5. Gross income	4685	5980	8916	10600	12282	13684	5. Résultat brut
6. Operating expenses	2034	3039	4186	5195	6548	8450	6. Frais d'exploitation
a. Staff costs	*1097*	*1647*	*2257*	*2813*	*3485*	*4400*	*a. Dépenses en personnel*
b. Property costs	*132*	*265*	*471*	*546*	*711*	*958*	*b. Dépenses en immobilier*
c. Other	*805*	*1128*	*1456*	*1835*	*2352*	*3092*	*c. Autres*
7. Net income	2651	2941	4730	5405	5734	5234	7. Résultat net
8. Provisions (net)	1736	1801	446	207	488	1519	8. Provisions (nettes)
a. Provisions on loans	*1584*	*1465*	*126*	*4*	*467*	*1443*	*a. Provisions sur prêts*
b. Provisions on securities	*25*	*170*	*72*	*-15*	*21*	*76*	*b. Provisions sur titres*
c. Other	*126*	*165*	*249*	*219*	-	-	*c. Autres*
9. Profit before tax	915	1140	4284	5198	5246	3715	9. Bénéfices avant impôt
10. Income tax (2)	1243	961	1674	1556	1623	1722	10. Impôt sur le revenu (2)
11. Profit after tax	-328	179	2610	3643	3623	1993	11. Bénéfices après impôt
12. Distributed profit (3)	225	459	591	730	656	..	12. Bénéfices distribués (3)
13. Retained profit (4)	660	1224	2142	2914	3146	..	13. Bénéfices mis en réserve (4)
BALANCE SHEET							**BILAN**
Assets							**Actif**
14. Cash & balance with Central bank	7435	9047	13074	11973	14998	21552	14. Caisse & solde auprès de la Banque centrale
15. Interbank deposits (5)	10077	16043	15710	16611	22125	29203	15. Dépôts interbancaires (5)
16. Loans (6)	24608	27895	40737	61002	81767	101899	16. Prêts (6)
17. Securities	19218	30309	44652	55662	58767	75008	17. Valeurs mobilières
18. Other assets	14023	17077	21792	15646	20957	26310	18. Autres actifs
Liabilities							**Passif**
19. Capital & reserves	6439	9210	11451	9989	14156	18889	19. Capital et réserves
20. Borrowing from Central bank (7)	5051	5486	6001	9261	7835	6240	20. Emprunts auprès de la Banque centrale (7)
21. Interbank deposits	4659	6476	9496	10945	10155	21411	21. Dépôts interbancaires
22. Non-bank deposits	44219	63528	82575	97471	124595	160368	22. Dépôts non bancaires
23. Bonds	270	607	1636	1075	1830	1316	23. Obligations
24. Other liabilities	14725	15063	24806	32152	40044	45747	24. Autres engagements
Balance sheet total							**Total du bilan**
25. End-year total	75360	100370	135965	160892	198615	253972	25. En fin d'exercice
26. Average total	..	87866	118168	148429	179754	226294	26. Moyen

POLAND
Polish commercial banks

POLOGNE
Banques commerciales polonaises

	1993	1994	1995	1996	1997	1998 p	
Million zlotys							*Millions de zlotys*
Memorandum items							***Pour mémoire***
27. Short-term securities	..	..	..	..	..	..	*27. Titres à court terme*
28. Bonds	..	..	..	..	..	..	*28. Obligations*
29. Shares and participations	..	..	..	..	..	..	*29. Actions et participations*
30. Claims on non-residents	..	..	..	..	*19719*	*15010*	*30. Créances sur des non-résidents*
31. Liabilities to non-residents	..	..	..	..	*9212*	*10697*	*31. Engagements envers des non-résidents*
Capital adequacy							***Solvabilité***
32. Tier 1 Capital (8)	*5016*	*7468*	*8877*	*10095*	*12214*	*17937*	*32. Fonds propres de base (8)*
33. Tier 2 Capital	*806*	*1179*	*2022*	*2167*	*2901*	*1233*	*33. Fonds propres complémentaires*
34. Supervisory deductions	*2694*	*3795*	*4433*	*3508*	*2880*	*3355*	*34. Eléments à déduire des fonds propres*
35. Total net capital resources	*3128*	*4852*	*6466*	*8754*	*12235*	*15815*	*35. Total net des ressources en capital*
36. Risk-weighted assets	*33257*	*42356*	*59660*	*79185*	*106954*	*142068*	*36. Actifs pondérés des risques*
SUPPLEMENTARY INFORMATION							**RENSEIGNEMENTS COMPLEMENTAIRES**
37. Number of institutions	77	71	63	56	54	52	37. Nombre d'institutions
38. Number of branches	1426	1441	1472	1437	1460	1572	38. Nombre de succursales
39. Number of employees (x 1000)	119.0	127.7	134.0	129.1	131.0	131.0	39. Nombre de salariés (x 1000)

1. Other non-interest income (item 4.d) includes investment income, foreign exchange gains or losses, other operating income and expense, and extraordinary items.
2. Income tax (item 10) includes corporate income tax and other taxes
3. Distributed profit (item 12) includes deductions for social funds.
4. Retained profit (item 13) includes the part of profit allocated for banks' capital raising, and coverage of previous years' losses.
5. Interbank deposits (item 15) cover operations with financial entities: term and demand due, and current accounts.
6. Loans (item 16) include due from non-financial and government entities.
7. Borrowing from the Central bank (item 20): operations with the Central bank.
8. Change in methodology.

Notes

- Polish commercial banks: Banks with a majority of Polish capital.

Change in methodology

- Beginning 1997, data for Tier 1 Capital (item 32) are based on new banking regulations.

1. Les Autres produits non financier (poste 4.d.) incluent le revenu des investissements, les gains et pertes de change, les autres revenus et frais d'exploitation, ainsi que les éléments extraordinaires.
2. L'Impôt sur le revenu (poste 10) comprend l'impôt sur les bénéfices des sociétés et d'autres impôts.
3. Les "Bénéfices distribués" (poste 12) incluent les déductions pour les fonds sociaux.
4. Les Bénéfices mis en réserve (poste 13) incluent la part des bénéfices affectée à la collecte de capitaux des banques et la couverture des pertes des années précédentes.
5. Les Dépôts interbancaires (poste 15) comprennent les créances à vue et à terme et les comptes courants sur des entités financières.
6. Les Prêts (poste 16) comprennent les créances sur des entités non financières et sur des administrations publiques
7. Les Emprunts auprès de la Banque centrale (poste 20) : les opérations avec la Banque centrale.
8. Changement méthodologique.

Notes

- Banques commerciales polonaises : Banques ayant une majorité de capitaux polonais.

Changement méthodologique

- A partir de 1997, les données pour les Fonds propres de base (poste 32) sont établies en tenant compte de la nouvelle reglementation bancaire.

POLAND
Polish commercial banks

POLOGNE
Banques commerciales polonaises

	1993	1994	1995	1996	1997	1998 p	
Per cent							*Pourcentage*
INCOME STATEMENT ANALYSIS							**ANALYSE DU COMPTE DE RESULTATS**
% of average balance sheet total							**% du total moyen du bilan**
40. Interest income	..	16.12	16.17	14.10	13.90	13.53	40. Produits financiers
41. Interest expenses	..	11.02	10.42	8.63	8.96	9.31	41. Frais financiers
42. Net interest income	..	5.10	5.75	5.47	4.95	4.23	42. Produits financiers nets
43. Non-interest income (net)	..	1.71	1.79	1.67	1.89	1.82	43. Produits non financiers (nets)
a. Fees and commissions receivable	..	*1.17*	*1.11*	*1.02*	*1.30*	*1.18*	*a. Frais et commissions à recevoir*
b. Fees and commissions payable	..	*0.13*	*0.15*	*0.11*	*0.14*	*0.15*	*b. Frais et commissions à payer*
c. Net profits or loss on financial operations	..	*0.90*	*0.73*	*0.35*	*0.14*	*0.05*	*c. Profits ou pertes nets sur opérations financières*
d. Other	..	*-0.23*	*0.09*	*0.41*	*0.59*	*0.73*	*d. Autres*
44. Gross income	..	6.81	7.55	7.14	6.83	6.05	44. Résultat brut
45. Operating expenses	..	3.46	3.54	3.50	3.64	3.73	45. Frais d'exploitation
a. Staff costs	..	*1.87*	*1.91*	*1.90*	*1.94*	*1.94*	*a. Dépenses en personnel*
b. Property costs	..	*0.30*	*0.40*	*0.37*	*0.40*	*0.42*	*b. Dépenses en immobilier*
c. Other	..	*1.28*	*1.23*	*1.24*	*1.31*	*1.37*	*c. Autres*
46. Net income	..	3.35	4.00	3.64	3.19	2.31	46. Résultat net
47. Provisions (net)	..	2.05	0.38	0.14	0.27	0.67	47. Provisions (nettes)
a. Provisions on loans	..	*1.67*	*0.11*	-	*0.26*	*0.64*	*a. Provisions sur prêts*
b. Provisions on securities	..	*0.19*	*0.06*	*-0.01*	*0.01*	*0.03*	*b. Provisions sur titres*
c. Other	..	*0.19*	*0.21*	*0.15*	-	-	*c. Autres*
48. Profit before tax	..	1.30	3.63	3.50	2.92	1.64	48. Bénéfices avant impôt
49. Income tax	..	1.09	1.42	1.05	0.90	0.76	49. Impôt sur le revenu
50. Profit after tax	..	0.20	2.21	2.45	2.02	0.88	50. Bénéfices après impôt
51. Distributed profit	..	0.52	0.50	0.49	0.36	..	51. Bénéfices distribués
52. Retained profit	..	1.39	1.81	1.96	1.75	..	52. Bénéfices mis en réserve
% of gross income							**% du total du résultat brut**
53. Net interest income	69.48	74.92	76.27	76.61	72.39	69.87	53. Produits financiers nets
54. Non-interest income (net)	30.52	25.08	23.73	23.39	27.61	30.13	54. Produits non financiers (nets)
a. Fees and commissions receivable	*17.50*	*17.14*	*14.73*	*14.23*	*19.09*	*19.52*	*a. Frais et commissions à recevoir*
b. Fees and commissions payable	*4.40*	*1.92*	*1.96*	*1.48*	*2.06*	*2.40*	*b. Frais et commissions à payer*
c. Net profits or loss on financial operations	*16.44*	*13.23*	*9.74*	*4.87*	*1.99*	*0.90*	*c. Profits ou pertes nets sur opérations financières*
d. Other	*0.98*	*-3.36*	*1.23*	*5.78*	*8.58*	*12.12*	*d. Autres*
55. Operating expenses	43.42	50.82	46.95	49.01	53.31	61.75	55. Frais d'exploitation
a. Staff costs	*23.42*	*27.54*	*25.31*	*26.54*	*28.37*	*32.15*	*a. Dépenses en personnel*
b. Property costs	*2.82*	*4.43*	*5.28*	*5.15*	*5.79*	*7.00*	*b. Dépenses en immobilier*
c. Other	*17.18*	*18.86*	*16.33*	*17.31*	*19.15*	*22.60*	*c. Autres*
56. Net income	56.58	49.18	53.05	50.99	46.69	38.25	56. Résultat net
57. Provisions (net)	37.05	30.12	5.00	1.95	3.97	11.10	57. Provisions (nettes)
a. Provisions on loans	*33.81*	*24.50*	*1.41*	*0.04*	*3.80*	*10.55*	*a. Provisions sur prêts*
b. Provisions on securities	*0.53*	*2.84*	*0.81*	*-0.14*	*0.17*	*0.56*	*b. Provisions sur titres*
c. Other	*2.69*	*2.76*	*2.79*	*2.07*	-	-	*c. Autres*
58. Profit before tax	19.53	19.06	48.05	49.04	42.71	27.15	58. Bénéfices avant impôt
59. Income tax	26.53	16.07	18.78	14.68	13.21	12.58	59. Impôt sur le revenu
60. Profit after tax	-7.00	2.99	29.27	34.37	29.50	14.56	60. Bénéfices après impôt
% of net income							**% du total du résultat net**
61. Provisions (net)	65.48	61.24	9.43	3.83	8.51	29.02	61. Provisions (nettes)
a. Provisions on loans	*59.75*	*49.81*	*2.66*	*0.07*	*8.14*	*27.57*	*a. Provisions sur prêts*
b. Provisions on securities	*0.94*	*5.78*	*1.52*	*-0.28*	*0.37*	*1.45*	*b. Provisions sur titres*
c. Other	*4.75*	*5.61*	*5.26*	*4.05*	-	-	*c. Autres*
62. Profit before tax	34.52	38.76	90.57	96.17	91.49	70.98	62. Bénéfices avant impôt
63. Income tax	46.89	32.68	35.39	28.79	28.30	32.90	63. Impôt sur le revenu
64. Profit after tax	-12.37	6.09	55.18	67.40	63.18	38.08	64. Bénéfices après impôt

POLAND
Polish commercial banks

POLOGNE
Banques commerciales polonaises

	1993	1994	1995	1996	1997	1998 p	
Per cent							*Pourcentage*
BALANCE SHEET ANALYSIS							**ANALYSE DU BILAN**
% of year-end balance sheet total							**% du total du bilan en fin d'exercice**
Assets							**Actif**
65. Cash & balance with Central bank	9.87	9.01	9.62	7.44	7.55	8.49	65. Caisse & solde auprès de la Banque centrale
66. Interbank deposits	13.37	15.98	11.55	10.32	11.14	11.50	66. Dépôts interbancaires
67. Loans	32.65	27.79	29.96	37.91	41.17	40.12	67. Prêts
68. Securities	25.50	30.20	32.84	34.60	29.59	29.53	68. Valeurs mobilières
69. Other assets	18.61	17.01	16.03	9.72	10.55	10.36	69. Autres actifs
Liabilities							**Passif**
70. Capital & reserves	8.54	9.18	8.42	6.21	7.13	7.44	70. Capital et réserves
71. Borrowing from Central bank	6.70	5.47	4.41	5.76	3.94	2.46	71. Emprunts auprès de la Banque centrale
72. Interbank deposits	6.18	6.45	6.98	6.80	5.11	8.43	72. Dépôts interbancaires
73. Non-bank deposits	58.68	63.29	60.73	60.58	62.73	63.14	73. Dépôts non bancaires
74. Bonds	0.36	0.60	1.20	0.67	0.92	0.52	74. Obligations
75. Other liabilities	19.54	15.01	18.24	19.98	20.16	18.01	75. Autres engagements
Memorandum items							***Pour mémoire***
76. Short-term securities	..	..	..	..	..	..	*76. Titres à court terme*
77. Bonds	..	..	..	..	..	..	*77. Obligations*
78. Shares and participations	..	..	..	..	..	..	*78. Actions et participations*
79. Claims on non-residents	..	..	..	..	*9.93*	*5.91*	*79. Créances sur des non-résidents*
80. Liabilities to non-residents	..	..	..	..	*4.64*	*4.21*	*80. Engagements envers des non-résidents*

* See notes on previous pages.

* Voir les notes en pages précédentes.

POLAND
Foreign commercial banks

POLOGNE
Banques commerciales étrangères

	1993	1994	1995	1996	1997	1998 p	
Million zlotys							*Millions de zlotys*
INCOME STATEMENT							**COMPTE DE RESULTATS**
1. Interest income	248	513	977	3682	5390	7211	1. Produits financiers
2. Interest expenses	176	337	643	2187	3409	4589	2. Frais financiers
3. Net interest income	72	176	334	1495	1981	2622	3. Produits financiers nets
4. Non-interest income (net)	139	179	215	596	943	1364	4. Produits non financiers (nets)
a. Fees and commissions receivable	*30*	*46*	*83*	*401*	*583*	*757*	*a. Frais et commissions à recevoir*
b. Fees and commissions payable	*6*	*11*	*33*	*41*	*84*	*118*	*b. Frais et commissions à payer*
c. Net profits or loss on financial operations	*115*	*148*	*155*	*192*	*22*	*53*	*c. Profits ou pertes nets sur opérations financières*
d. Other (1)	*1*	*-4*	*11*	*45*	*422*	*672*	*d. Autres (1)*
5. Gross income	211	355	549	2091	2924	3986	5. Résultat brut
6. Operating expenses	66	117	249	1068	1628	2213	6. Frais d'exploitation
a. Staff costs	*23*	*43*	*86*	*483*	*706*	*940*	*a. Dépenses en personnel*
b. Property costs	*6*	*9*	*29*	*127*	*181*	*245*	*b. Dépenses en immobilier*
c. Other	*38*	*65*	*133*	*459*	*741*	*1028*	*c. Autres*
7. Net income	145	238	300	1023	1296	1773	7. Résultat net
8. Provisions (net)	10	23	34	83	238	303	8. Provisions (nettes)
a. Provisions on loans	*10*	*13*	*18*	*23*	*226*	*282*	*a. Provisions sur prêts*
b. Provisions on securities	-	-	-	*-7*	*12*	*21*	*b. Provisions sur titres*
c. Other	-	*10*	*16*	*68*	-	-	*c. Autres*
9. Profit before tax	135	215	266	940	1058	1470	9. Bénéfices avant impôt
10. Income tax (2)	23	78	115	354	413	539	10. Impôt sur le revenu (2)
11. Profit after tax	112	137	151	586	645	931	11. Bénéfices après impôt
12. Distributed profit (3)	-	4	10	103	78	..	12. Bénéfices distribués (3)
13. Retained profit (4)	95	131	158	483	581	..	13. Bénéfices mis en réserve (4)
BALANCE SHEET							**BILAN**
Assets							**Actif**
14. Cash & balance with Central bank	160	286	428	1953	2453	3014	14. Caisse & solde auprès de la Banque centrale
15. Interbank deposits (5)	969	1158	1499	6186	8543	8072	15. Dépôts interbancaires (5)
16. Loans (6)	678	1345	2549	11541	18009	28029	16. Prêts (6)
17. Securities	212	500	1226	5549	5864	9681	17. Valeurs mobilières
18. Other assets	130	212	498	1838	2931	4209	18. Autres actifs
Liabilities							**Passif**
19. Capital & reserves	218	438	1040	3513	5139	6799	19. Capital et réserves
20. Borrowing from Central bank (7)	2	3	10	133	73	51	20. Emprunts auprès de la Banque centrale (7)
21. Interbank deposits	630	850	1717	4567	6257	10794	21. Dépôts interbancaires
22. Non-bank deposits	1000	1814	2627	14376	19212	26720	22. Dépôts non bancaires
23. Bonds	56	20	106	45	707	290	23. Obligations
24. Other liabilities	243	377	701	4434	6411	8351	24. Autres engagements
Balance sheet total							**Total du bilan**
25. End-year total	2149	3500	6201	27067	37800	53005	25. En fin d'exercice
26. Average total	..	2824	4850	16634	32433	45402	26. Moyen

POLAND
Foreign commercial banks

POLOGNE
Banques commerciales étrangères

	1993	1994	1995	1996	1997	1998 p	
Million zlotys							*Millions de zlotys*
Memorandum items							***Pour mémoire***
27. Short-term securities	..	..	..	..	..	..	*27. Titres à court terme*
28. Bonds	..	..	..	..	..	..	*28. Obligations*
29. Shares and participations	..	..	..	..	..	..	*29. Actions et participations*
30. Claims on non-residents	..	..	..	..	*5874*	*3946*	*30. Créances sur des non-résidents*
31. Liabilities to non-residents	..	..	..	..	*5859*	*7970*	*31. Engagements envers des non-résidents*
Capital adequacy							***Solvabilité***
32. Tier 1 Capital (8)	*127*	*289*	*791*	*2700*	*4108*	*6208*	*32. Fonds propres de base (8)*
33. Tier 2 Capital	*16*	*62*	*169*	*763*	*984*	*463*	*33. Fonds propres complémentaires*
34. Supervisory deductions	*3*	*10*	*74*	*193*	*218*	*198*	*34. Eléments à déduire des fonds propres*
35. Total net capital resources	*140*	*341*	*886*	*3270*	*4874*	*6473*	*35. Total net des ressources en capital*
36. Risk-weighted assets	*1416*	*2764*	*4093*	*18284*	*29718*	*43436*	*36. Actifs pondérés des risques*
SUPPLEMENTARY INFORMATION							**RENSEIGNEMENTS COMPLEMENTAIRES**
37. Number of institutions	10	11	18	25	29	31	37. Nombre d'institutions
38. Number of branches	10	13	29	143	169	292	38. Nombre de succursales
39. Number of employees (x 1000)	0.7	1.0	2.0	15.1	16.0	18.0	39. Nombre de salariés (x 1000)

1. Other non-interest income (item 4.d) includes investment income, foreign exchange gains or losses, other operating income and expense, and extraordinary items.
2. Income tax (item 10) includes corporate income tax and other taxes
3. Distributed profit (item 12) includes deductions for social funds.
4. Retained profit (item 13) includes the part of profit allocated for banks' capital raising, and coverage of previous years' losses.
5. Interbank deposits (item 15) cover operations with financial entities: term and demand due, and current accounts.
6. Loans (item 16) include due from non-financial and government entities.
7. Borrowing from the Central bank (item 20): operations with the Central bank.
8. Change in methodology.

Notes

- Foreign commercial banks: Banks with a majority of foreign capital.

Change in methodology

- Beginning 1997, data for Tier 1 Capital (item 32) are based on new banking regulations.

1. Les Autres produits non financier (poste 4.d.) incluent le revenu des investissements, les gains et pertes de change, les autres revenus et frais d'exploitation, ainsi que les éléments extraordinaires.
2. L'Impôt sur le revenu (poste 10) comprend l'impôt sur les bénéfices des sociétés et d'autres impôts.
3. Les "Bénéfices distribués" (poste 12) incluent les déductions pour les fonds sociaux.
4. Les Bénéfices mis en réserve (poste 13) incluent la part des bénéfices affectée à la collecte de capitaux des banques et la couverture des pertes des années précédentes.
5. Les Dépôts interbancaires (poste 15) comprennent les créances à vue et à terme et les comptes courants sur des entités financières.
6. Les Prêts (poste 16) comprennent les créances sur des entités non financières et sur des administrations publiques
7. Les Emprunts auprès de la Banque centrale (poste 20) : les opérations avec la Banque centrale.
8. Changement méthodologique.

Notes

- Banques commerciales étrangères : Banques ayant une majorité de capitaux étrangers.

Changement méthodologique

- A partir de 1997, les données pour les Fonds propres de base (poste 32) sont établies en tenant compte de la nouvelle reglementation bancaire.

POLAND
Foreign commercial banks

POLOGNE
Banques commerciales étrangères

	1993	1994	1995	1996	1997	1998 p	
Per cent							*Pourcentage*
INCOME STATEMENT ANALYSIS							**ANALYSE DU COMPTE DE RESULTATS**
% of average balance sheet total							**% du total moyen du bilan**
40. Interest income	..	18.17	20.14	22.14	16.62	15.88	40. Produits financiers
41. Interest expenses	..	11.93	13.26	13.15	10.51	10.11	41. Frais financiers
42. Net interest income	..	6.23	6.89	8.99	6.11	5.78	42. Produits financiers nets
43. Non-interest income (net)	..	6.34	4.43	3.58	2.91	3.00	43. Produits non financiers (nets)
a. Fees and commissions receivable	..	*1.63*	*1.71*	*2.41*	*1.80*	*1.67*	*a. Frais et commissions à recevoir*
b. Fees and commissions payable	..	*0.39*	*0.68*	*0.25*	*0.26*	*0.26*	*b. Frais et commissions à payer*
c. Net profits or loss on financial operations	..	*5.24*	*3.20*	*1.15*	*0.07*	*0.12*	*c. Profits ou pertes nets sur opérations financières*
d. Other	..	*-0.14*	*0.23*	*0.27*	*1.30*	*1.48*	*d. Autres*
44. Gross income	..	12.57	11.32	12.57	9.02	8.78	44. Résultat brut
45. Operating expenses	..	4.14	5.13	6.42	5.02	4.87	45. Frais d'exploitation
a. Staff costs	..	*1.52*	*1.77*	*2.90*	*2.18*	*2.07*	*a. Dépenses en personnel*
b. Property costs	..	*0.32*	*0.60*	*0.76*	*0.56*	*0.54*	*b. Dépenses en immobilier*
c. Other	..	*2.30*	*2.74*	*2.76*	*2.28*	*2.26*	*c. Autres*
46. Net income	..	8.43	6.19	6.15	4.00	3.91	46. Résultat net
47. Provisions (net)	..	0.81	0.70	0.50	0.73	0.67	47. Provisions (nettes)
a. Provisions on loans	..	*0.46*	*0.37*	*0.14*	*0.70*	*0.62*	*a. Provisions sur prêts*
b. Provisions on securities	..	-	-	*-0.04*	*0.04*	*0.05*	*b. Provisions sur titres*
c. Other	..	*0.35*	*0.33*	*0.41*	-	-	*c. Autres*
48. Profit before tax	..	7.61	5.48	5.65	3.26	3.24	48. Bénéfices avant impôt
49. Income tax	..	2.76	2.37	2.13	1.27	1.19	49. Impôt sur le revenu
50. Profit after tax	..	4.85	3.11	3.52	1.99	2.05	50. Bénéfices après impôt
51. Distributed profit	..	0.14	0.21	0.62	0.24	..	51. Bénéfices distribués
52. Retained profit	..	4.64	3.26	2.90	1.79	..	52. Bénéfices mis en réserve
% of gross income							**% du total du résultat brut**
53. Net interest income	34.12	49.58	60.84	71.50	67.75	65.78	53. Produits financiers nets
54. Non-interest income (net)	65.88	50.42	39.16	28.50	32.25	34.22	54. Produits non financiers (nets)
a. Fees and commissions receivable	*14.22*	*12.96*	*15.12*	*19.18*	*19.94*	*18.99*	*a. Frais et commissions à recevoir*
b. Fees and commissions payable	*2.84*	*3.10*	*6.01*	*1.96*	*2.87*	*2.96*	*b. Frais et commissions à payer*
c. Net profits or loss on financial operations	*54.50*	*41.69*	*28.23*	*9.18*	*0.75*	*1.33*	*c. Profits ou pertes nets sur opérations financières*
d. Other	*0.47*	*-1.13*	*2.00*	*2.15*	*14.43*	*16.86*	*d. Autres*
55. Operating expenses	31.28	32.96	45.36	51.08	55.68	55.52	55. Frais d'exploitation
a. Staff costs	*10.90*	*12.11*	*15.66*	*23.10*	*24.15*	*23.58*	*a. Dépenses en personnel*
b. Property costs	*2.84*	*2.54*	*5.28*	*6.07*	*6.19*	*6.15*	*b. Dépenses en immobilier*
c. Other	*18.01*	*18.31*	*24.23*	*21.95*	*25.34*	*25.79*	*c. Autres*
56. Net income	68.72	67.04	54.64	48.92	44.32	44.48	56. Résultat net
57. Provisions (net)	4.74	6.48	6.19	3.97	8.14	7.60	57. Provisions (nettes)
a. Provisions on loans	*4.74*	*3.66*	*3.28*	*1.10*	*7.73*	*7.07*	*a. Provisions sur prêts*
b. Provisions on securities	-	-	-	*-0.33*	*0.41*	*0.53*	*b. Provisions sur titres*
c. Other	-	*2.82*	*2.91*	*3.25*	-	-	*c. Autres*
58. Profit before tax	63.98	60.56	48.45	44.95	36.18	36.88	58. Bénéfices avant impôt
59. Income tax	10.90	21.97	20.95	16.93	14.12	13.52	59. Impôt sur le revenu
60. Profit after tax	53.08	38.59	27.50	28.02	22.06	23.36	60. Bénéfices après impôt
% of net income							**% du total du résultat net**
61. Provisions (net)	6.90	9.66	11.33	8.11	18.36	17.09	61. Provisions (nettes)
a. Provisions on loans	*6.90*	*5.46*	*6.00*	*2.25*	*17.44*	*15.91*	*a. Provisions sur prêts*
b. Provisions on securities	-	-	-	*-0.68*	*0.93*	*1.18*	*b. Provisions sur titres*
c. Other	-	*4.20*	*5.33*	*6.65*	-	-	*c. Autres*
62. Profit before tax	93.10	90.34	88.67	91.89	81.64	82.91	62. Bénéfices avant impôt
63. Income tax	15.86	32.77	38.33	34.60	31.87	30.40	63. Impôt sur le revenu
64. Profit after tax	77.24	57.56	50.33	57.28	49.77	52.51	64. Bénéfices après impôt

POLAND
Foreign commercial banks

POLOGNE
Banques commerciales étrangères

	1993	1994	1995	1996	1997	1998 p	
Per cent							*Pourcentage*
BALANCE SHEET ANALYSIS							**ANALYSE DU BILAN**
% of year-end balance sheet total							**% du total du bilan en fin d'exercice**
Assets							**Actif**
65. Cash & balance with Central bank	7.45	8.17	6.90	7.22	6.49	5.69	65. Caisse & solde auprès de la Banque centrale
66. Interbank deposits	45.09	33.09	24.17	22.85	22.60	15.23	66. Dépôts interbancaires
67. Loans	31.55	38.43	41.11	42.64	47.64	52.88	67. Prêts
68. Securities	9.87	14.29	19.77	20.50	15.51	18.26	68. Valeurs mobilières
69. Other assets	6.05	6.06	8.03	6.79	7.75	7.94	69. Autres actifs
Liabilities							**Passif**
70. Capital & reserves	10.14	12.51	16.77	12.98	13.60	12.83	70. Capital et réserves
71. Borrowing from Central bank	0.09	0.09	0.16	0.49	0.19	0.10	71. Emprunts auprès de la Banque centrale
72. Interbank deposits	29.32	24.29	27.69	16.87	16.55	20.36	72. Dépôts interbancaires
73. Non-bank deposits	46.53	51.83	42.36	53.11	50.83	50.41	73. Dépôts non bancaires
74. Bonds	2.61	0.57	1.71	0.17	1.87	0.55	74. Obligations
75. Other liabilities	11.31	10.77	11.30	16.38	16.96	15.76	75. Autres engagements
Memorandum items							***Pour mémoire***
76. Short-term securities	..	..	..	..	..	..	*76. Titres à court terme*
77. Bonds	..	..	..	..	..	..	*77. Obligations*
78. Shares and participations	..	..	..	..	..	..	*78. Actions et participations*
79. Claims on non-residents	..	..	..	..	*15.54*	*7.44*	*79. Créances sur des non-résidents*
80. Liabilities to non-residents	..	..	..	..	*15.50*	*15.04*	*80. Engagements envers des non-résidents*

* See notes on previous pages.

* Voir les notes en pages précédentes.

POLAND — Co-operative banks

POLOGNE — Banques mutualistes

Million zlotys	1993	1994	1995	1996	1997	1998 p	*Millions de zlotys*
INCOME STATEMENT							**COMPTE DE RESULTATS**
1. Interest income	1415	1310	1373	1567	2004	2239	1. Produits financiers
2. Interest expenses	803	932	859	863	1065	1285	2. Frais financiers
3. Net interest income	612	378	514	705	939	954	3. Produits financiers nets
4. Non-interest income (net)	69	92	134	186	234	268	4. Produits non financiers (nets)
a. Fees and commissions receivable	*85*	*115*	*136*	*182*	*232*	*268*	*a. Frais et commissions à recevoir*
b. Fees and commissions payable	*19*	*21*	*13*	*13*	*10*	*10*	*b. Frais et commissions à payer*
c. Net profits or loss on financial operations	*1*	*1*	-	-	*5*	*2*	*c. Profits ou pertes nets sur opérations financières*
d. Other (1)	*2*	*-4*	*11*	*16*	*7*	*8*	*d. Autres (1)*
5. Gross income	681	470	648	891	1173	1222	5. Résultat brut
6. Operating expenses	577	437	528	659	838	918	6. Frais d'exploitation
a. Staff costs	*200*	*152*	*372*	*461*	*589*	*653*	*a. Dépenses en personnel*
b. Property costs	*16*	*23*	*32*	*39*	*45*	*52*	*b. Dépenses en immobilier*
c. Other	*361*	*263*	*125*	*160*	*204*	*213*	*c. Autres*
7. Net income	104	33	120	232	335	304	7. Résultat net
8. Provisions (net)	229	185	-21	-33	-17	18	8. Provisions (nettes)
a. Provisions on loans	*224*	*182*	*-26*	*-38*	*-18*	*18*	*a. Provisions sur prêts*
b. Provisions on securities	-	*1*	-	-	*1*	-	*b. Provisions sur titres*
c. Other	*4*	*2*	*5*	*5*	-	-	*c. Autres*
9. Profit before tax	-125	-152	141	265	352	286	9. Bénéfices avant impôt
10. Income tax (2)	61	43	54	73	125	109	10. Impôt sur le revenu (2)
11. Profit after tax	-186	-195	87	191	227	177	11. Bénéfices après impôt
12. Distributed profit	..	..	..	..	..	..	12. Bénéfices distribués
13. Retained profit	..	..	..	..	..	..	13. Bénéfices mis en réserve
BALANCE SHEET							**BILAN**
Assets							**Actif**
14. Cash & balance with Central bank	670	466	439	497	690	381	14. Caisse & solde auprès de la Banque centrale
15. Interbank deposits (3)	1662	1955	2788	2844	3021	4830	15. Dépôts interbancaires (3)
16. Loans (4)	1798	2063	2477	4483	5527	6392	16. Prêts (4)
17. Securities	181	170	361	731	1162	1165	17. Valeurs mobilières
18. Other assets	1181	1152	1111	562	855	933	18. Autres actifs
Liabilities							**Passif**
19. Capital & reserves	520	546	678	640	894	1138	19. Capital et réserves
20. Borrowing from Central bank (5)	1	16	20	2	5	-	20. Emprunts auprès de la Banque centrale (5)
21. Interbank deposits	222	216	117	154	62	39	21. Dépôts interbancaires
22. Non-bank deposits	4057	4459	5557	7048	8913	10886	22. Dépôts non bancaires
23. Bonds	-	1	4	37	71	60	23. Obligations
24. Other liabilities	692	567	802	1236	1311	1579	24. Autres engagements
Balance sheet total							**Total du bilan**
25. End-year total	5492	5805	7177	9117	11254	13702	25. En fin d'exercice
26. Average total	..	5649	6491	8147	10186	12478	26. Moyen

POLAND
Co-operative banks

POLOGNE
Banques mutualistes

	1993	1994	1995	1996	1997	1998 p	
Million zlotys							*Millions de zlotys*
Memorandum items							***Pour mémoire***
27. Short-term securities	..	..	..	..	..	..	*27. Titres à court terme*
28. Bonds	..	..	..	..	..	..	*28. Obligations*
29. Shares and participations	..	..	..	..	..	..	*29. Actions et participations*
30. Claims on non-residents	..	..	..	..	-	-	*30. Créances sur des non-résidents*
31. Liabilities to non-residents	..	..	..	..	-	-	*31. Engagements envers des non-résidents*
Capital adequacy							***Solvabilité***
32. Tier 1 Capital (6)	*460*	*476*	*516*	*650*	*853*	*1079*	*32. Fonds propres de base (6)*
33. Tier 2 Capital	*56*	*63*	*154*	*152*	*159*	*120*	*33. Fonds propres complémentaires*
34. Supervisory deductions	*392*	*476*	*359*	*300*	*260*	*231*	*34. Eléments à déduire des fonds propres*
35. Total net capital resources	*124*	*63*	*311*	*502*	*752*	*968*	*35. Total net des ressources en capital*
36. Risk-weighted assets	*2612*	*2948*	*3704*	*5455*	*6793*	*8187*	*36. Actifs pondérés des risques*
SUPPLEMENTARY INFORMATION							**RENSEIGNEMENTS COMPLEMENTAIRES**
37. Number of institutions	1653	1612	1510	1394	1295	1189	37. Nombre d'institutions
38. Number of branches	..	..	..	502	581	668	38. Nombre de succursales
39. Number of employees (x 1000)	..	..	..	25	25	25	39. Nombre de salariés (x 1000)

1. Other non-interest income (item 4.d) includes investment income, foreign exchange gains or losses, other operating income and expense, and extraordinary items.
2. Income tax (item 10) includes corporate income tax and other taxes
3. Interbank deposits (item 15) cover operations with financial entities: term and demand due, and current accounts.
4. Loans (item 16) include due from non-financial and government entities.
5. Borrowing from the Central bank (item 20): operations with the Central bank.
6. Change in methodology.

Change in methodology

- Beginning 1997, data for Tier 1 Capital (item 32) are based on new banking regulations.

1. Les Autres produits non financier (poste 4.d.) incluent le revenu des investissements, les gains et pertes de change, les autres revenus et frais d'exploitation, ainsi que les éléments extraordinaires.
2. L'Impôt sur le revenu (poste 10) comprend l'impôt sur les bénéfices des sociétés et d'autres impôts.
3. Les Dépôts interbancaires (poste 15) comprennent les créances à vue et à terme et les comptes courants sur des entités financières.
4. Les Prêts (poste 16) comprennent les créances sur des entités non financières et sur des administrations publiques
5. Les Emprunts auprès de la Banque centrale (poste 20) : les opérations avec la Banque centrale.
6. Changement méthodologique.

Changement méthodologique

- A partir de 1997, les données pour les Fonds propres de base (poste 32) sont établies en tenant compte de la nouvelle reglementation bancaire.

POLAND
Co-operative banks

POLOGNE
Banques mutualistes

	1993	1994	1995	1996	1997	1998 p	
Per cent							*Pourcentage*
INCOME STATEMENT ANALYSIS							**ANALYSE DU COMPTE DE RESULTATS**
% of average balance sheet total							**% du total moyen du bilan**
40. Interest income	..	23.19	21.15	19.23	19.67	17.94	40. Produits financiers
41. Interest expenses	..	16.50	13.23	10.59	10.46	10.30	41. Frais financiers
42. Net interest income	..	6.69	7.92	8.65	9.22	7.65	42. Produits financiers nets
43. Non-interest income (net)	..	1.63	2.06	2.28	2.30	2.15	43. Produits non financiers (nets)
a. Fees and commissions receivable	..	*2.04*	*2.10*	*2.23*	*2.28*	*2.15*	*a. Frais et commissions à recevoir*
b. Fees and commissions payable	..	*0.37*	*0.20*	*0.16*	*0.10*	*0.08*	*b. Frais et commissions à payer*
c. Net profits or loss on financial operations	..	*0.02*	-	-	*0.05*	*0.02*	*c. Profits ou pertes nets sur opérations financières*
d. Other	..	*-0.07*	*0.17*	*0.20*	*0.07*	*0.06*	*d. Autres*
44. Gross income	..	8.32	9.98	10.94	11.52	9.79	44. Résultat brut
45. Operating expenses	..	7.74	8.13	8.09	8.23	7.36	45. Frais d'exploitation
a. Staff costs	..	*2.69*	*5.73*	*5.66*	*5.78*	*5.23*	*a. Dépenses en personnel*
b. Property costs	..	*0.41*	*0.49*	*0.48*	*0.44*	*0.42*	*b. Dépenses en immobilier*
c. Other	..	*4.66*	*1.93*	*1.96*	*2.00*	*1.71*	*c. Autres*
46. Net income	..	0.58	1.85	2.85	3.29	2.44	46. Résultat net
47. Provisions (net)	..	3.27	-0.32	-0.41	-0.17	0.14	47. Provisions (nettes)
a. Provisions on loans	..	*3.22*	*-0.40*	*-0.47*	*-0.18*	*0.14*	*a. Provisions sur prêts*
b. Provisions on securities	..	*0.02*	-	-	*0.01*	-	*b. Provisions sur titres*
c. Other	..	*0.04*	*0.08*	*0.06*	-	-	*c. Autres*
48. Profit before tax	..	-2.69	2.17	3.25	3.46	2.29	48. Bénéfices avant impôt
49. Income tax	..	0.76	0.83	0.90	1.23	0.87	49. Impôt sur le revenu
50. Profit after tax	..	-3.45	1.34	2.34	2.23	1.42	50. Bénéfices après impôt
51. Distributed profit	..	..	..	..	..	..	51. Bénéfices distribués
52. Retained profit	..	..	..	..	..	..	52. Bénéfices mis en réserve
% of gross income							**% du total du résultat brut**
53. Net interest income	89.87	80.43	79.32	79.12	80.05	78.07	53. Produits financiers nets
54. Non-interest income (net)	10.13	19.57	20.68	20.88	19.95	21.93	54. Produits non financiers (nets)
a. Fees and commissions receivable	*12.48*	*24.47*	*20.99*	*20.43*	*19.78*	*21.93*	*a. Frais et commissions à recevoir*
b. Fees and commissions payable	*2.79*	*4.47*	*2.01*	*1.46*	*0.85*	*0.82*	*b. Frais et commissions à payer*
c. Net profits or loss on financial operations	*0.15*	*0.21*	-	-	*0.43*	*0.16*	*c. Profits ou pertes nets sur opérations financières*
d. Other	*0.29*	*-0.85*	*1.70*	*1.80*	*0.60*	*0.65*	*d. Autres*
55. Operating expenses	84.73	92.98	81.48	73.96	71.44	75.12	55. Frais d'exploitation
a. Staff costs	*29.37*	*32.34*	*57.41*	*51.74*	*50.21*	*53.44*	*a. Dépenses en personnel*
b. Property costs	*2.35*	*4.89*	*4.94*	*4.38*	*3.84*	*4.26*	*b. Dépenses en immobilier*
c. Other	*53.01*	*55.96*	*19.29*	*17.96*	*17.39*	*17.43*	*c. Autres*
56. Net income	15.27	7.02	18.52	26.04	28.56	24.88	56. Résultat net
57. Provisions (net)	33.63	39.36	-3.24	-3.70	-1.45	1.47	57. Provisions (nettes)
a. Provisions on loans	*32.89*	*38.72*	*-4.01*	*-4.26*	*-1.53*	*1.47*	*a. Provisions sur prêts*
b. Provisions on securities	-	*0.21*	-	-	*0.09*	-	*b. Provisions sur titres*
c. Other	*0.59*	*0.43*	*0.77*	*0.56*	-	-	*c. Autres*
58. Profit before tax	-18.36	-32.34	21.76	29.74	30.01	23.40	58. Bénéfices avant impôt
59. Income tax	8.96	9.15	8.33	8.19	10.66	8.92	59. Impôt sur le revenu
60. Profit after tax	-27.31	-41.49	13.43	21.44	19.35	14.48	60. Bénéfices après impôt
% of net income							**% du total du résultat net**
61. Provisions (net)	220.19	560.61	-17.50	-14.22	-5.07	5.92	61. Provisions (nettes)
a. Provisions on loans	*215.38*	*551.52*	*-21.67*	*-16.38*	*-5.37*	*5.92*	*a. Provisions sur prêts*
b. Provisions on securities	-	*3.03*	-	-	*0.30*	-	*b. Provisions sur titres*
c. Other	*3.85*	*6.06*	*4.17*	*2.16*	-	-	*c. Autres*
62. Profit before tax	-120.19	-460.61	117.50	114.22	105.07	94.08	62. Bénéfices avant impôt
63. Income tax	58.65	130.30	45.00	31.47	37.31	35.86	63. Impôt sur le revenu
64. Profit after tax	-178.85	-590.91	72.50	82.33	67.76	58.22	64. Bénéfices après impôt

POLAND
Co-operative banks

POLOGNE
Banques mutualistes

	1993	1994	1995	1996	1997	1998 p	
Per cent							*Pourcentage*
BALANCE SHEET ANALYSIS							**ANALYSE DU BILAN**
% of year-end balance sheet total							**% du total du bilan en fin d'exercice**
Assets							**Actif**
65. Cash & balance with Central bank	12.20	8.03	6.12	5.45	6.13	2.78	65. Caisse & solde auprès de la Banque centrale
66. Interbank deposits	30.26	33.68	38.85	31.19	26.84	35.25	66. Dépôts interbancaires
67. Loans	32.74	35.54	34.51	49.17	49.11	46.65	67. Prêts
68. Securities	3.30	2.93	5.03	8.02	10.33	8.50	68. Valeurs mobilières
69. Other assets	21.50	19.84	15.48	6.16	7.60	6.81	69. Autres actifs
Liabilities							**Passif**
70. Capital & reserves	9.47	9.41	9.45	7.02	7.94	8.31	70. Capital et réserves
71. Borrowing from Central bank	0.02	0.28	0.28	0.02	0.04	-	71. Emprunts auprès de la Banque centrale
72. Interbank deposits	4.04	3.72	1.63	1.69	0.55	0.28	72. Dépôts interbancaires
73. Non-bank deposits	73.87	76.81	77.43	77.31	79.20	79.45	73. Dépôts non bancaires
74. Bonds	-	0.02	0.06	0.41	0.63	0.44	74. Obligations
75. Other liabilities	12.60	9.77	11.17	13.56	11.65	11.52	75. Autres engagements
Memorandum items							***Pour mémoire***
76. Short-term securities	..	..	..	..	..	..	*76. Titres à court terme*
77. Bonds	..	..	..	..	..	..	*77. Obligations*
78. Shares and participations	..	..	..	..	..	..	*78. Actions et participations*
79. Claims on non-residents	..	..	..	..	-	-	*79. Créances sur des non-résidents*
80. Liabilities to non-residents	..	..	..	..	-	-	*80. Engagements envers des non-résidents*

* See notes on previous pages.

* Voir les notes en pages précédentes.

PORTUGAL

Commercial banks

PORTUGAL

Banques commerciales

	1988	1989	1990(1)	1991	1992(1)	1993	1994	1995	1996	1997	
Million escudos											*Millions d'escudos*
INCOME STATEMENT											**COMPTE DE RESULTATS**
1. Interest income	944041	1171919	1543263	1910743	2411085	2429412	2377520	2566732	2543853	2529744	1. Produits financiers
2. Interest expenses	649072	780109	995986	1246944	1714724	1726223	1689595	1880828	1859601	1751964	2. Frais financiers
3. Net interest income	294969	391810	547277	663799	696361	703189	687925	685904	684253	777780	3. Produits financiers nets
4. Non-interest income (net)	64212	76182	127345	154924	188507	222166	194929	216155	309239	363773	4. Produits non financiers (nets)
a. Fees and commissions receivable	..	..	..	..	*85060*	*101281*	*101843*	*105307*	*118467*	*164157*	*a. Frais et commissions à recevoir*
b. Fees and commissions payable	..	..	..	..	*9183*	*11721*	*13934*	*17585*	*20034*	*22531*	*b. Frais et commissions à payer*
c. Net profits or loss on financial operations	..	..	..	..	*77952*	*90884*	*55580*	*69352*	*131789*	*135455*	*c. Profits ou pertes nets sur opérations financières*
d. Other	..	..	..	..	*34677*	*41722*	*51439*	*59081*	*79017*	*86694*	*d. Autres*
5. Gross income	359181	467992	674622	818723	884868	925356	882854	902059	993491	1141553	5. Résultat brut
6. Operating expenses	183213	219080	280913	367679	473175	519945	545363	585791	639027	689155	6. Frais d'exploitation
a. Staff costs	*121684*	*141475*	*172842*	*216208*	*269005*	*291275*	*303070*	*326125*	*347656*	*378888*	*a. Dépenses en personnel*
b. Property costs	..	..	..	..	*66079*	*70673*	*72922*	*72176*	*72260*	*77444*	*b. Dépenses en immobilier*
c. Other	..	..	..	..	*138090*	*157998*	*169371*	*187490*	*219111*	*232823*	*c. Autres*
7. Net income	175968	248912	393709	451044	411693	405410	337491	316268	354465	452398	7. Résultat net
8. Provisions (net)	115176	151446	231939	236953	227372	188701	152127	120615	126694	149833	8. Provisions (nettes)
a. Provisions on loans	..	..	*220648*	*218120*	*204884*	*235527*	*179874*	*136818*	*155127*	*157764*	*a. Provisions sur prêts*
b. Provisions on securities	..	..	*11493*	*19225*	*49699*	*-7692*	*12862*	*11816*	*-3293*	*20450*	*b. Provisions sur titres*
c. Other	..	..	*-202*	*-392*	*-27211*	*-39133*	*-40609*	*-28019*	*-25140*	*-28383*	*c. Autres*
9. Profit before tax	60792	97466	161770	214091	184322	216709	185364	195653	227771	302566	9. Bénéfices avant impôt
10. Income tax	4053	23304	38814	55937	39842	45665	39747	39856	47521	62842	10. Impôt sur le revenu
11. Profit after tax	56739	74162	122956	158154	144480	171044	145616	155797	180250	239724	11. Bénéfices après impôt
12. Distributed profit	..	..	..	..	..	..	..	..	..	..	12. Bénéfices distribués
13. Retained profit	..	..	..	..	..	..	..	..	..	..	13. Bénéfices mis en réserve
BALANCE SHEET											**BILAN**
Assets											**Actif**
14. Cash & balance with Central bank	465639	1319298	1424899	1807694	2349918	2150887	2157980	2076872	1902491	1656862	14. Caisse & solde auprès de la Banque centrale
15. Interbank deposits	1263484	1242249	2334765	2102738	2634380	4673073	5998840	7356909	9438058	11341619	15. Dépôts interbancaires
16. Loans	3631461	3851876	4765890	5952732	8059651	8859756	9240971	10358136	11631400	13996425	16. Prêts
17. Securities	1407330	1545134	2221676	4089252	4879737	5655517	6563745	7220509	7807854	7910407	17. Valeurs mobilières
18. Other assets	1971423	2342169	1017021	1000235	1254658	3376438	4029162	4061431	4792517	6456760	18. Autres actifs
Liabilities											**Passif**
19. Capital & reserves	836160	1063216	1289880	1732169	2087256	2343014	2522409	2556361	2953656	3360935	19. Capital et réserves
20. Borrowing from Central bank	21686	30932	45412	196482	25193	236253	499342	601010	222730	110990	20. Emprunts auprès de la Banque centrale
21. Interbank deposits	333275	505209	1240662	1795270	3323410	4865871	5923982	7428486	10034919	11858298	21. Dépôts interbancaires
22. Non-bank deposits	6465273	7539688	8047619	9763854	12106953	13561334	14784308	16302717	17430248	19170682	22. Dépôts non bancaires
23. Bonds	91676	92159	134255	184859	237473	362013	323595	311825	547176	752300	23. Obligations
24. Other liabilities	991267	1069522	1006423	1280017	1398060	3347186	3937063	3873457	4383592	6108871	24. Autres engagements
Balance sheet total											**Total du bilan**
25. End-year total	8739337	10300726	11764251	14952651	19178345	24715672	27990698	31073857	35572320	41362075	25. En fin d'exercice
26. Average total	8059120	9520032	..	13358451	..	22061087	26195306	30044522	32833758	38845726	26. Moyen

PORTUGAL — PORTUGAL

Commercial banks — Banques commerciales

	1988	1989	1990(1)	1991	1992(1)	1993	1994	1995	1996	1997	
Million escudos											*Millions d'escudos*
Memorandum items											***Pour mémoire***
27. Short-term securities	302597	522655	708908	1375478	1009187	905412	1229682	861809	902358	741438	*27. Titres à court terme*
28. Bonds	845926	816299	1164697	2141720	2887669	3449158	3749058	4509935	4774768	5000634	*28. Obligations*
29. Shares and participations	131635	184629	280616	428802	674148	805945	1022256	1236676	1550402	1844131	*29. Actions et participations*
30. Claims on non-residents	611988	698218	810947	1168368	2870043	4890907	5840835	6585604	7525190	9212473	*30. Créances sur des non-résidents*
31. Liabilities to non-residents	301338	466196	772540	1305575	2956014	4085160	5145501	6044035	7635503	9239324	*31. Engagements envers des non-résidents*
Capital adequacy											***Solvabilité***
32. Tier 1 Capital	..	..	..	..	..	1440475	1622567	1697897	1854456	2049617	*32. Fonds propres de base*
33. Tier 2 Capital (1)	..	..	..	..	..	324137	356810	404473	640414	862154	*33. Fonds propres complémentaires (1)*
34. Supervisory deductions	..	..	..	..	..	365516	418113	556267	694199	852582	*34. Eléments à déduire des fonds propres*
35. Total net capital resources (1)	..	..	..	..	..	1399096	1561264	1546103	1800671	2059189	*35. Total net des ressources en capital (1)*
36. Risk-weighted assets	..	..	..	..	..	11152253	12157562	13732796	16157383	19477825	*36. Actifs pondérés des risques*
SUPPLEMENTARY INFORMATION											**RENSEIGNEMENTS COMPLEMENTAIRES**
37. Number of institutions	27	29	33	35	27	35	37	37	39	44	37. Nombre d'institutions
38. Number of branches	1607	1741	1999	2520	2657	2936	3155	3447	3766	4121	38. Nombre de succursales
39. Number of employees (x 1000)	58.4	58.1	59.2	61.1	63.0	61.0	61.0	60.0	60.0	60.0	39. Nombre de salariés (x 1000)

1. Break in series due to changes in methodology.

Change in methodology

- Until 1989, time deposits with the Central bank are included under Interbank deposits (item 15).
- As from 1990, data are based on the new accounting framework for the Portugese banking sector, introduced in January 1990. Also from 1990, data were revised taking into account the European Directives regarding capital funds and reserves. In addition, branches in off-shore centres of Madeira and Santa Maria Islands are also included.
- As from 1992, data are consolidated worldwide.
- As from 1993, average balance sheet totals (item 26) are based on quarterly data.
- As from 1997, Tier 2 Capital (item 33) includes Tier 3 Capital.
- As from 1997, Risk-weighted assets (item 36) are the global own funds requirements, i.e. own funds requirements x 12.5

1. Rupture dans les séries consécutive aux changements méthodologiques.

Changement méthodologique

- Jusqu'en 1989, les dépôts à terme auprès de la Banque centrale sont inclus sous "Dépôts interbancaires" (poste 15).
- A partir de 1990, les données sont établies à l'aide du nouveau cadre comptable pour le secteur bancaire portugais introduit en janvier 1990. Egalement à partir de 1990, les données ont été révisées en prenant en compte les directives européennes concernant les capitaux et réserves. De plus, les succursales des centres extraterritoriaux des îles de Madère et Santa Maria sont également inclues.
- A partir de 1992, les données sont regroupées sur une base mondiale.
- A partir de 1993, la moyenne du total des actifs/passifs (poste 26) est basée sur les données trimestrielles.
- A partir de 1997, les données de la rubrique Fonds propres complémentaires (poste 33) incluent les fonds propres surcomplémentaires.
- A partir de 1997, les Actifs pondérés des risques (poste 36) sont égaux au montant minimum du total des fonds propres, à savoir la norme de fonds propres, multiplié par 12.5.

PORTUGAL
Commercial banks

PORTUGAL
Banques commerciales

Per cent	1988	1989	1990(1)	1991	1992(1)	1993	1994	1995	1996	1997	Pourcentage
INCOME STATEMENT ANALYSIS											**ANALYSE DU COMPTE DE RESULTATS**
% of average balance sheet total											**% du total moyen du bilan**
40. Interest income	11.71	12.31	..	14.30	..	11.01	9.08	8.54	7.75	6.51	40. Produits financiers
41. Interest expenses	8.05	8.19	..	9.33	..	7.82	6.45	6.26	5.66	4.51	41. Frais financiers
42. Net interest income	3.66	4.12	..	4.97	..	3.19	2.63	2.28	2.08	2.00	42. Produits financiers nets
43. Non-interest income (net)	0.80	0.80	..	1.16	..	1.01	0.74	0.72	0.94	0.94	43. Produits non financiers (nets)
a. Fees and commissions receivable	..	..	..	..	..	*0.46*	*0.39*	*0.35*	*0.36*	*0.42*	*a. Frais et commissions à recevoir*
b. Fees and commissions payable	..	..	..	..	..	*0.05*	*0.05*	*0.06*	*0.06*	*0.06*	*b. Frais et commissions à payer*
c. Net profits or loss on financial operations	..	..	..	..	..	*0.41*	*0.21*	*0.23*	*0.40*	*0.35*	*c. Profits ou pertes nets sur opérations financières*
d. Other	..	..	..	..	..	*0.19*	*0.20*	*0.20*	*0.24*	*0.22*	*d. Autres*
44. Gross income	4.46	4.92	..	6.13	..	4.19	3.37	3.00	3.03	2.94	44. Résultat brut
45. Operating expenses	2.27	2.30	..	2.75	..	2.36	2.08	1.95	1.95	1.77	45. Frais d'exploitation
a. Staff costs	*1.51*	*1.49*	..	*1.62*	..	*1.32*	*1.16*	*1.09*	*1.06*	*0.98*	*a. Dépenses en personnel*
b. Property costs	..	..	..	..	..	*0.32*	*0.28*	*0.24*	*0.22*	*0.20*	*b. Dépenses en immobilier*
c. Other	..	..	..	..	..	*0.72*	*0.65*	*0.62*	*0.67*	*0.60*	*c. Autres*
46. Net income	2.18	2.61	..	3.38	..	1.84	1.29	1.05	1.08	1.16	46. Résultat net
47. Provisions (net)	1.43	1.59	..	1.77	..	0.86	0.58	0.40	0.39	0.39	47. Provisions (nettes)
a. Provisions on loans	..	..	..	*1.63*	..	*1.07*	*0.69*	*0.46*	*0.47*	*0.41*	*a. Provisions sur prêts*
b. Provisions on securities	..	..	..	*0.14*	..	*-0.03*	*0.05*	*0.04*	*-0.01*	*0.05*	*b. Provisions sur titres*
c. Other	..	..	..	-	..	*-0.18*	*-0.16*	*-0.09*	*-0.08*	*-0.07*	*c. Autres*
48. Profit before tax	0.75	1.02	..	1.60	..	0.98	0.71	0.65	0.69	0.78	48. Bénéfices avant impôt
49. Income tax	0.05	0.24	..	0.42	..	0.21	0.15	0.13	0.14	0.16	49. Impôt sur le revenu
50. Profit after tax	0.70	0.78	..	1.18	..	0.78	0.56	0.52	0.55	0.62	50. Bénéfices après impôt
51. Distributed profit	..	..	..	..	..	..	..	..	..	..	51. Bénéfices distribués
52. Retained profit	..	..	..	..	..	..	..	..	..	..	52. Bénéfices mis en réserve
% of gross income											**% du total du résultat brut**
53. Net interest income	82.12	83.72	81.12	81.08	78.70	75.99	77.92	76.04	68.87	68.13	53. Produits financiers nets
54. Non-interest income (net)	17.88	16.28	18.88	18.92	21.30	24.01	22.08	23.96	31.13	31.87	54. Produits non financiers (nets)
a. Fees and commissions receivable	..	..	..	..	*9.61*	*10.95*	*11.54*	*11.67*	*11.92*	*14.38*	*a. Frais et commissions à recevoir*
b. Fees and commissions payable	..	..	..	..	*1.04*	*1.27*	*1.58*	*1.95*	*2.02*	*1.97*	*b. Frais et commissions à payer*
c. Net profits or loss on financial operations	..	..	..	..	*8.81*	*9.82*	*6.30*	*7.69*	*13.27*	*11.87*	*c. Profits ou pertes nets sur opérations financières*
d. Other	..	..	..	..	*3.92*	*4.51*	*5.83*	*6.55*	*7.95*	*7.59*	*d. Autres*
55. Operating expenses	51.01	46.81	41.64	44.91	53.47	56.19	61.77	64.94	64.32	60.37	55. Frais d'exploitation
a. Staff costs	*33.88*	*30.23*	*25.62*	*26.41*	*30.40*	*31.48*	*34.33*	*36.15*	*34.99*	*33.19*	*a. Dépenses en personnel*
b. Property costs	..	..	..	..	*7.47*	*7.64*	*8.26*	*8.00*	*7.27*	*6.78*	*b. Dépenses en immobilier*
c. Other	..	..	..	..	*15.61*	*17.07*	*19.18*	*20.78*	*22.05*	*20.40*	*c. Autres*
56. Net income	48.99	53.19	58.36	55.09	46.53	43.81	38.23	35.06	35.68	39.63	56. Résultat net
57. Provisions (net)	32.07	32.36	34.38	28.94	25.70	20.39	17.23	13.37	12.75	13.13	57. Provisions (nettes)
a. Provisions on loans	..	..	*32.71*	*26.64*	*23.15*	*25.45*	*20.37*	*15.17*	*15.61*	*13.82*	*a. Provisions sur prêts*
b. Provisions on securities	..	..	*1.70*	*2.35*	*5.62*	*-0.83*	*1.46*	*1.31*	*-0.33*	*1.79*	*b. Provisions sur titres*
c. Other	..	..	*-0.03*	*-0.05*	*-3.08*	*-4.23*	*-4.60*	*-3.11*	*-2.53*	*-2.49*	*c. Autres*
58. Profit before tax	16.93	20.83	23.98	26.15	20.83	23.42	21.00	21.69	22.93	26.50	58. Bénéfices avant impôt
59. Income tax	1.13	4.98	5.75	6.83	4.50	4.93	4.50	4.42	4.78	5.50	59. Impôt sur le revenu
60. Profit after tax	15.80	15.85	18.23	19.32	16.33	18.48	16.49	17.27	18.14	21.00	60. Bénéfices après impôt
% of net income											**% du total du résultat net**
61. Provisions (net)	65.45	60.84	58.91	52.53	55.23	46.55	45.08	38.14	35.74	33.12	61. Provisions (nettes)
a. Provisions on loans	..	..	*56.04*	*48.36*	*49.77*	*58.10*	*53.30*	*43.26*	*43.76*	*34.87*	*a. Provisions sur prêts*
b. Provisions on securities	..	..	*2.92*	*4.26*	*12.07*	*-1.90*	*3.81*	*3.74*	*-0.93*	*4.52*	*b. Provisions sur titres*
c. Other	..	..	*-0.05*	*-0.09*	*-6.61*	*-9.65*	*-12.03*	*-8.86*	*-7.09*	*-6.27*	*c. Autres*
62. Profit before tax	34.55	39.16	41.09	47.47	44.77	53.45	54.92	61.86	64.26	66.88	62. Bénéfices avant impôt
63. Income tax	2.30	9.36	9.86	12.40	9.68	11.26	11.78	12.60	13.41	13.89	63. Impôt sur le revenu
64. Profit after tax	32.24	29.79	31.23	35.06	35.09	42.19	43.15	49.26	50.85	52.99	64. Bénéfices après impôt

	1988	1989	1990(1)	1991	1992(1)	1993	1994	1995	1996	1997	
Per cent											*Pourcentage*
BALANCE SHEET ANALYSIS											**ANALYSE DU BILAN**
% of year-end balance sheet total											**% du total du bilan en fin d'exercice**
Assets											**Actif**
65. Cash & balance with Central bank	5.33	12.81	12.11	12.09	12.25	8.70	7.71	6.68	5.35	4.01	65. Caisse & solde auprès de la Banque centrale
66. Interbank deposits	14.46	12.06	19.85	14.06	13.74	18.91	21.43	23.68	26.53	27.42	66. Dépôts interbancaires
67. Loans	41.55	37.39	40.51	39.81	42.02	35.85	33.01	33.33	32.70	33.84	67. Prêts
68. Securities	16.10	15.00	18.88	27.35	25.44	22.88	23.45	23.24	21.95	19.12	68. Valeurs mobilières
69. Other assets	22.56	22.74	8.65	6.69	6.54	13.66	14.39	13.07	13.47	15.61	69. Autres actifs
Liabilities											**Passif**
70. Capital & reserves	9.57	10.32	10.96	11.58	10.88	9.48	9.01	8.23	8.30	8.13	70. Capital et réserves
71. Borrowing from Central bank	0.25	0.30	0.39	1.31	0.13	0.96	1.78	1.93	0.63	0.27	71. Emprunts auprès de la Banque centrale
72. Interbank deposits	3.81	4.90	10.55	12.01	17.33	19.69	21.16	23.91	28.21	28.67	72. Dépôts interbancaires
73. Non-bank deposits	73.98	73.20	68.41	65.30	63.13	54.87	52.82	52.46	49.00	46.35	73. Dépôts non bancaires
74. Bonds	1.05	0.89	1.14	1.24	1.24	1.46	1.16	1.00	1.54	1.82	74. Obligations
75. Other liabilities	11.34	10.38	8.55	8.56	7.29	13.54	14.07	12.47	12.32	14.77	75. Autres engagements
Memorandum items											***Pour mémoire***
76. Short-term securities	*3.46*	*5.07*	*6.03*	*9.20*	*5.26*	*3.66*	*4.39*	*2.77*	*2.54*	*1.79*	*76. Titres à court terme*
77. Bonds	*9.68*	*7.92*	*9.90*	*14.32*	*15.06*	*13.96*	*13.39*	*14.51*	*13.42*	*12.09*	*77. Obligations*
78. Shares and participations	*1.51*	*1.79*	*2.39*	*2.87*	*3.52*	*3.26*	*3.65*	*3.98*	*4.36*	*4.46*	*78. Actions et participations*
79. Claims on non-residents	*7.00*	*6.78*	*6.89*	*7.81*	*14.97*	*19.79*	*20.87*	*21.19*	*21.15*	*22.27*	*79. Créances sur des non-résidents*
80. Liabilities to non-residents	*3.45*	*4.53*	*6.57*	*8.73*	*15.41*	*16.53*	*18.38*	*19.45*	*21.46*	*22.34*	*80. Engagements envers des non-résidents*

* See notes on previous pages.

* Voir les notes en pages précédentes.

SPAIN
All banks

ESPAGNE
Ensemble des banques

	1988	1989	1990	1991	1992	1993(1)	1994(1)	1995	1996	1997	
Billion pesetas											*Milliards de pesetas*
INCOME STATEMENT											**COMPTE DE RESULTATS**
1. Interest income	5237	6373	7676	8558	8972	10230	9251	10093	10137	8543	1. Produits financiers
2. Interest expenses	3054	3961	5039	5621	5961	7099	5972	6907	6922	5252	2. Frais financiers
3. Net interest income	2183	2412	2637	2937	3011	3131	3279	3186	3215	3291	3. Produits financiers nets
4. Non-interest income (net)	525	515	589	689	766	1090	896	959	1167	1361	4. Produits non financiers (nets)
a. Fees and commissions receivable	*315*	*365*	*468*	*570*	*628*	*680*	*747*	*766*	*832*	*993*	*a. Frais et commissions à recevoir*
b. Fees and commissions payable	*62*	*79*	*133*	*199*	*102*	*113*	*131*	*145*	*157*	*177*	*b. Frais et commissions à payer*
c. Net profits or loss on financial operations	*195*	*144*	*170*	*204*	*117*	*428*	*101*	*205*	*444*	*469*	*c. Profits ou pertes nets sur opérations financières*
d. Other	*76*	*85*	*84*	*114*	*124*	*95*	*179*	*133*	*48*	*75*	*d. Autres*
5. Gross income	2708	2927	3226	3626	3777	4221	4175	4145	4381	4652	5. Résultat brut
6. Operating expenses	1740	1784	1970	2122	2280	2518	2493	2621	2724	2858	6. Frais d'exploitation
a. Staff costs	*1200*	*1164*	*1229*	*1287*	*1385*	*1560*	*1517*	*1609*	*1672*	*1755*	*a. Dépenses en personnel*
b. Property costs	*510*	*593*	*709*	*804*	*864*	*925*	*945*	*977*	*1016*	*1064*	*b. Dépenses en immobilier*
c. Other	*30*	*27*	*31*	*30*	*31*	*34*	*30*	*35*	*36*	*39*	*c. Autres*
7. Net income	968	1144	1256	1504	1497	1703	1683	1525	1658	1793	7. Résultat net
8. Provisions (net)	363	312	380	477	599	1359	845	574	603	564	8. Provisions (nettes)
a. Provisions on loans	*285*	*181*	*192*	*389*	*524*	*1048*	*553*	*488*	*369*	*276*	*a. Provisions sur prêts*
b. Provisions on securities	*26*	*21*	*79*	*46*	*92*	*195*	*273*	*126*	*112*	*71*	*b. Provisions sur titres*
c. Other	*52*	*110*	*110*	*42*	*-17*	*117*	*19*	*-40*	*121*	*215*	*c. Autres*
9. Profit before tax	605	832	876	1028	898	344	838	951	1055	1229	9. Bénéfices avant impôt
10. Income tax (2)	158	231	239	249	222	234	198	215	227	254	10. Impôt sur le revenu (2)
11. Profit after tax	447	601	637	778	676	110	640	736	829	975	11. Bénéfices après impôt
12. Distributed profit	188	243	262	317	315	317	346	370	365	458	12. Bénéfices distribués
13. Retained profit	259	358	375	461	365	-201	295	366	463	517	13. Bénéfices mis en réserve
BALANCE SHEET											**BILAN**
Assets											**Actif**
14. Cash & balance with Central bank	5141	5930	5034	5788	4984	4305	4300	3703	3249	3084	14. Caisse & solde auprès de la Banque centrale
15. Interbank deposits	6773	8301	9721	11744	14307	19416	17501	19188	20520	23257	15. Dépôts interbancaires
16. Loans	23800	28055	31457	37341	40786	43125	48589	52357	56615	63851	16. Prêts
17. Securities	13042	14159	15469	14277	15116	17553	21542	23401	24789	24740	17. Valeurs mobilières
18. Other assets	6197	7049	8456	9720	11716	18947	18760	21572	21104	20023	18. Autres actifs
Liabilities											**Passif**
19. Capital & reserves	4907	5572	6451	8231	8428	9160	10219	10369	10857	11578	19. Capital et réserves
20. Borrowing from Central bank	957	2112	1590	1572	4282	6525	6063	6643	4447	2265	20. Emprunts auprès de la Banque centrale
21. Interbank deposits	6250	6804	7563	9863	11574	16930	17971	19500	20904	23437	21. Dépôts interbancaires
22. Non-bank deposits	35170	40280	44500	48383	51277	56329	60805	67665	71111	74608	22. Dépôts non bancaires
23. Bonds	1379	1107	1007	1210	1276	1757	3071	3291	3871	4504	23. Obligations
24. Other liabilities	6290	7618	9026	9611	10073	12646	12563	12753	15085	18562	24. Autres engagements
Balance sheet total											**Total du bilan**
25. End-year total	54953	63493	70137	78868	86910	103347	110692	120221	126276	134954	25. En fin d'exercice
26. Average total	52021	59223	66815	74503	82889	95128	109096	115456	123249	130614	26. Moyen

SPAIN
All banks

ESPAGNE
Ensemble des banques

	1988	1989	1990	1991	1992	1993(1)	1994(1)	1995	1996	1997	
Billion pesetas											*Milliards de pesetas*
Memorandum items											***Pour mémoire***
27. Short-term securities	*6204*	*7237*	*8142*	*6064*	*6456*	*5840*	*6371*	*6839*	*6423*	*4826*	*27. Titres à court terme*
28. Bonds	*5382*	*5194*	*5378*	*5480*	*5745*	*8299*	*11491*	*12340*	*13688*	*14298*	*28. Obligations*
29. Shares and participations	*1456*	*1728*	*1949*	*2732*	*2915*	*3415*	*3680*	*4222*	*4678*	*5617*	*29. Actions et participations*
30. Claims on non-residents	*2800*	*3019*	*3792*	*4511*	*7858*	*16518*	*14583*	*17734*	*17031*	*16866*	*30. Créances sur des non-résidents*
31. Liabilities to non-residents	*4246*	*4876*	*6447*	*7373*	*9342*	*12308*	*13261*	*13263*	*16194*	*20483*	*31. Engagements envers des non-résidents*
Capital adequacy (2)											***Solvabilité (2)***
32. Tier 1 Capital	*3265*	*3759*	*4481*	*5528*	*5915*	*5478*	*6113*	*6478*	*7022*	*8070*	*32. Fonds propres de base*
33. Tier 2 Capital	*292*	*388*	*507*	*595*	*693*	*945*	*1007*	*1283*	*1787*	*2167*	*33. Fonds propres complémentaires*
34. Supervisory deductions	-	-	-	-	-	*142*	*415*	*194*	*195*	*127*	*34. Eléments à déduire des fonds propres*
35. Total net capital resources	*3557*	*4146*	*4988*	*6123*	*6608*	*6281*	*6705*	*7567*	*8615*	*10109*	*35. Total net des ressources en capital*
36. Risk-weighted assets	*35537*	*41885*	*47931*	*58548*	*64671*	*59062*	*59138*	*63372*	*69845*	*82958*	*36. Actifs pondérés des risques*
SUPPLEMENTARY INFORMATION											**RENSEIGNEMENTS COMPLEMENTAIRES**
37. Number of institutions	334	333	327	323	319	316	316	318	313	307	37. Nombre d'institutions
38. Number of branches	33757	34511	35234	34873	35429	35193	35544	36251	37079	37634	38. Nombre de succursales
39. Number of employees (x 1000)	242	248	252	256	253	247	246	245	242	242	39. Nombre de salariés (x 1000)

1. Break in series in 1993 due to restructuring of a major bank.

   Break in series in 1994. Three official credit banks were classifiec as Commercial banks and no longer as Official credit institutions.

2. Change in methodology.

Notes

- All banks include Commercial banks, Savings banks and Co-operative banks.

Change in methodology

- As from 1992, Income tax (item 10) includes tax on domestic activities of resident entities rather than total tax.
- As from 1993, credit entities' branches from the European Union (EU) are not subject to capital requirements. As from 1994, credit entities' from non-EU members are also not subject to capital requirements if these countries have similar legislation.
- As from 1993, the means of calculating capital adequacy requirements has changed, as the gearing ratio and the additional surcharges relating to concentration have disappeared.
- As from 1994, trading portfolio price risk became subject to a different treatment than that of credit risk.

1. Rupture dans les séries en 1993 suite à la restructuration de l'une des principales banques.

   Rupture dans les séries en 1994. Trois banques publiques de crédit ont été classées dans les Banques commerciales et non plus dans les Institutions publiques de crédit.

2. Changement méthodologique.

Notes

- L'Ensemble des banques comprend les Banques commerciales, les Caisses d'épargne et les Banques mutualistes.

Changement méthodologique

- A partir de 1992, la rubrique Impôt sur le revenu (poste 10) inclut l'impôt sur les activités domestiques des entités résidentes plutôt que l'impôt total.
- A partir de 1993, les succursales des entités de crédit de l'Union Européenne (UE) ne sont pas soumises à des exigences de capital. A partir de 1994, les entités de crédit des pays non membres de l'UE ne sont pas non plus soumises à des exigences de capital si ces pays ont une législation semblable.
- A partir de 1993, les moyens de calcul pour la solvabilité exigée a changé, étant donné que le ratio d'effets de levier et les charges supplémentaires relatifs à la concentration ont disparus.
- A partir de 1994, le risque du prix du portefeuille de transactions a été sujet à une couverture différente que celle du risque de crédit.

SPAIN — ESPAGNE

All banks — Ensemble des banques

	1988	1989	1990	1991	1992	1993(1)	1994(1)	1995	1996	1997	
Per cent											*Pourcentage*
INCOME STATEMENT ANALYSIS											**ANALYSE DU COMPTE DE RESULTATS**
% of average balance sheet total											**% du total moyen du bilan**
40. Interest income	10.07	10.76	11.49	11.49	10.82	10.75	8.48	8.74	8.22	6.54	40. Produits financiers
41. Interest expenses	5.87	6.69	7.54	7.54	7.19	7.46	5.47	5.98	5.62	4.02	41. Frais financiers
42. Net interest income	4.20	4.07	3.95	3.94	3.63	3.29	3.01	2.76	2.61	2.52	42. Produits financiers nets
43. Non-interest income (net)	1.01	0.87	0.88	0.92	0.92	1.15	0.82	0.83	0.95	1.04	43. Produits non financiers (nets)
a. Fees and commissions receivable	*0.61*	*0.62*	*0.70*	*0.77*	*0.76*	*0.71*	*0.68*	*0.66*	*0.68*	*0.76*	*a. Frais et commissions à recevoir*
b. Fees and commissions payable	*0.12*	*0.13*	*0.20*	*0.27*	*0.12*	*0.12*	*0.12*	*0.13*	*0.13*	*0.14*	*b. Frais et commissions à payer*
c. Net profits or loss on financial operations	*0.37*	*0.24*	*0.25*	*0.27*	*0.14*	*0.45*	*0.09*	*0.18*	*0.36*	*0.36*	*c. Profits ou pertes nets sur opérations financières*
d. Other	*0.15*	*0.14*	*0.13*	*0.15*	*0.15*	*0.10*	*0.16*	*0.12*	*0.04*	*0.06*	*d. Autres*
44. Gross income	5.21	4.94	4.83	4.87	4.56	4.44	3.83	3.59	3.55	3.56	44. Résultat brut
45. Operating expenses	3.34	3.01	2.95	2.85	2.75	2.65	2.29	2.27	2.21	2.19	45. Frais d'exploitation
a. Staff costs	*2.31*	*1.97*	*1.84*	*1.73*	*1.67*	*1.64*	*1.39*	*1.39*	*1.36*	*1.34*	*a. Dépenses en personnel*
b. Property costs	*0.98*	*1.00*	*1.06*	*1.08*	*1.04*	*0.97*	*0.87*	*0.85*	*0.82*	*0.81*	*b. Dépenses en immobilier*
c. Other	*0.06*	*0.05*	*0.05*	*0.04*	*0.04*	*0.04*	*0.03*	*0.03*	*0.03*	*0.03*	*c. Autres*
46. Net income	1.86	1.93	1.88	2.02	1.81	1.79	1.54	1.32	1.35	1.37	46. Résultat net
47. Provisions (net)	0.70	0.53	0.57	0.64	0.72	1.43	0.77	0.50	0.49	0.43	47. Provisions (nettes)
a. Provisions on loans	*0.55*	*0.31*	*0.29*	*0.52*	*0.63*	*1.10*	*0.51*	*0.42*	*0.30*	*0.21*	*a. Provisions sur prêts*
b. Provisions on securities	*0.05*	*0.04*	*0.12*	*0.06*	*0.11*	*0.20*	*0.25*	*0.11*	*0.09*	*0.05*	*b. Provisions sur titres*
c. Other	*0.10*	*0.19*	*0.16*	*0.06*	*-0.02*	*0.12*	*0.02*	*-0.03*	*0.10*	*0.16*	*c. Autres*
48. Profit before tax	1.16	1.40	1.31	1.38	1.08	0.36	0.77	0.82	0.86	0.94	48. Bénéfices avant impôt
49. Income tax	0.30	0.39	0.36	0.33	0.27	0.25	0.18	0.19	0.18	0.19	49. Impôt sur le revenu
50. Profit after tax	0.86	1.01	0.95	1.04	0.82	0.12	0.59	0.64	0.67	0.75	50. Bénéfices après impôt
51. Distributed profit	0.36	0.41	0.39	0.43	0.38	0.33	0.32	0.32	0.30	0.35	51. Bénéfices distribués
52. Retained profit	0.50	0.60	0.56	0.62	0.44	-0.21	0.27	0.32	0.38	0.40	52. Bénéfices mis en réserve
% of gross income											**% du total du résultat brut**
53. Net interest income	80.61	82.41	81.74	81.00	79.72	74.18	78.54	76.86	73.39	70.74	53. Produits financiers nets
54. Non-interest income (net)	19.39	17.59	18.26	19.00	20.28	25.82	21.46	23.14	26.64	29.26	54. Produits non financiers (nets)
a. Fees and commissions receivable	*11.63*	*12.47*	*14.51*	*15.72*	*16.63*	*16.11*	*17.89*	*18.48*	*18.99*	*21.35*	*a. Frais et commissions à recevoir*
b. Fees and commissions payable	*2.29*	*2.70*	*4.12*	*5.49*	*2.70*	*2.68*	*3.14*	*3.50*	*3.58*	*3.80*	*b. Frais et commissions à payer*
c. Net profits or loss on financial operations	*7.20*	*4.92*	*5.27*	*5.63*	*3.10*	*10.14*	*2.42*	*4.95*	*10.13*	*10.08*	*c. Profits ou pertes nets sur opérations financières*
d. Other	*2.81*	*2.90*	*2.60*	*3.14*	*3.28*	*2.25*	*4.29*	*3.21*	*1.10*	*1.61*	*d. Autres*
55. Operating expenses	64.25	60.95	61.07	58.52	60.37	59.65	59.71	63.23	62.18	61.44	55. Frais d'exploitation
a. Staff costs	*44.31*	*39.77*	*38.10*	*35.49*	*36.67*	*36.96*	*36.34*	*38.82*	*38.16*	*37.73*	*a. Dépenses en personnel*
b. Property costs	*18.83*	*20.26*	*21.98*	*22.17*	*22.88*	*21.91*	*22.63*	*23.57*	*23.19*	*22.87*	*b. Dépenses en immobilier*
c. Other	*1.11*	*0.92*	*0.96*	*0.83*	*0.82*	*0.81*	*0.72*	*0.84*	*0.82*	*0.84*	*c. Autres*
56. Net income	35.75	39.08	38.93	41.48	39.63	40.35	40.31	36.79	37.85	38.54	56. Résultat net
57. Provisions (net)	13.40	10.66	11.78	13.15	15.86	32.20	20.24	13.85	13.76	12.12	57. Provisions (nettes)
a. Provisions on loans	*10.52*	*6.18*	*5.95*	*10.73*	*13.87*	*24.83*	*13.25*	*11.77*	*8.42*	*5.93*	*a. Provisions sur prêts*
b. Provisions on securities	*0.96*	*0.72*	*2.45*	*1.27*	*2.44*	*4.62*	*6.54*	*3.04*	*2.56*	*1.53*	*b. Provisions sur titres*
c. Other	*1.92*	*3.76*	*3.41*	*1.16*	*-0.45*	*2.77*	*0.46*	*-0.97*	*2.76*	*4.62*	*c. Autres*
58. Profit before tax	22.34	28.43	27.15	28.35	23.78	8.15	20.07	22.94	24.08	26.42	58. Bénéfices avant impôt
59. Income tax	5.83	7.89	7.41	6.87	5.88	5.54	4.74	5.19	5.18	5.46	59. Impôt sur le revenu
60. Profit after tax	16.51	20.53	19.75	21.46	17.90	2.61	15.33	17.76	18.92	20.96	60. Bénéfices après impôt
% of net income											**% du total du résultat net**
61. Provisions (net)	37.50	27.27	30.25	31.72	40.01	79.80	50.21	37.64	36.37	31.46	61. Provisions (nettes)
a. Provisions on loans	*29.44*	*15.82*	*15.29*	*25.86*	*35.00*	*61.54*	*32.86*	*32.00*	*22.26*	*15.39*	*a. Provisions sur prêts*
b. Provisions on securities	*2.69*	*1.84*	*6.29*	*3.06*	*6.15*	*11.45*	*16.22*	*8.26*	*6.76*	*3.96*	*b. Provisions sur titres*
c. Other	*5.37*	*9.62*	*8.76*	*2.79*	*-1.14*	*6.87*	*1.13*	*-2.62*	*7.30*	*11.99*	*c. Autres*
62. Profit before tax	62.50	72.73	69.75	68.35	59.99	20.20	49.79	62.36	63.63	68.54	62. Bénéfices avant impôt
63. Income tax	16.32	20.19	19.03	16.56	14.83	13.74	11.76	14.10	13.69	14.17	63. Impôt sur le revenu
64. Profit after tax	46.18	52.53	50.72	51.73	45.16	6.46	38.03	48.26	50.00	54.38	64. Bénéfices après impôt

SPAIN
All banks

ESPAGNE
Ensemble des banques

	1988	1989	1990	1991	1992	1993(1)	1994(1)	1995	1996	1997	
Per cent											*Pourcentage*
BALANCE SHEET ANALYSIS											**ANALYSE DU BILAN**
% of year-end balance sheet total											**% du total du bilan en fin d'exercice**
Assets											**Actif**
65. Cash & balance with Central bank	9.36	9.34	7.18	7.34	5.73	4.17	3.88	3.08	2.57	2.29	65. Caisse & solde auprès de la Banque centrale
66. Interbank deposits	12.33	13.07	13.86	14.89	16.46	18.79	15.81	15.96	16.25	17.23	66. Dépôts interbancaires
67. Loans	43.31	44.19	44.85	47.35	46.93	41.73	43.90	43.55	44.83	47.31	67. Prêts
68. Securities	23.73	22.30	22.06	18.10	17.39	16.98	19.46	19.46	19.63	18.33	68. Valeurs mobilières
69. Other assets	11.28	11.10	12.06	12.32	13.48	18.33	16.95	17.94	16.71	14.84	69. Autres actifs
Liabilities											**Passif**
70. Capital & reserves	8.93	8.78	9.20	10.44	9.70	8.86	9.23	8.62	8.60	8.58	70. Capital et réserves
71. Borrowing from Central bank	1.74	3.33	2.27	1.99	4.93	6.31	5.48	5.53	3.52	1.68	71. Emprunts auprès de la Banque centrale
72. Interbank deposits	11.37	10.72	10.78	12.51	13.32	16.38	16.24	16.22	16.55	17.37	72. Dépôts interbancaires
73. Non-bank deposits	64.00	63.44	63.45	61.35	59.00	54.50	54.93	56.28	56.31	55.28	73. Dépôts non bancaires
74. Bonds	2.51	1.74	1.44	1.53	1.47	1.70	2.77	2.74	3.07	3.34	74. Obligations
75. Other liabilities	11.45	12.00	12.87	12.19	11.59	12.24	11.35	10.61	11.95	13.75	75. Autres engagements
Memorandum items											***Pour mémoire***
76. Short-term securities	*11.29*	*11.40*	*11.61*	*7.69*	*7.43*	*5.65*	*5.76*	*5.69*	*5.09*	*3.58*	*76. Titres à court terme*
77. Bonds	*9.79*	*8.18*	*7.67*	*6.95*	*6.61*	*8.03*	*10.38*	*10.26*	*10.84*	*10.59*	*77. Obligations*
78. Shares and participations	*2.65*	*2.72*	*2.78*	*3.46*	*3.35*	*3.30*	*3.32*	*3.51*	*3.70*	*4.16*	*78. Actions et participations*
79. Claims on non-residents	*5.10*	*4.75*	*5.41*	*5.72*	*9.04*	*15.98*	*13.17*	*14.75*	*13.49*	*12.50*	*79. Créances sur des non-résidents*
80. Liabilities to non-residents	*7.73*	*7.68*	*9.19*	*9.35*	*10.75*	*11.91*	*11.98*	*11.03*	*12.82*	*15.18*	*80. Engagements envers des non-résidents*

* See notes on previous pages.

* Voir les notes en pages précédentes.

SPAIN
Commercial banks

ESPAGNE
Banques commerciales

	1988	1989	1990	1991	1992	1993(1)	1994(1)	1995	1996	1997	
Billion pesetas											*Milliards de pesetas*
INCOME STATEMENT											**COMPTE DE RESULTATS**
1. Interest income	3308	4036	4819	5520	5664	6445	5876	6381	6245	5101	1. Produits financiers
2. Interest expenses	1977	2566	3224	3690	3886	4668	4015	4669	4592	3432	2. Frais financiers
3. Net interest income	1331	1470	1595	1830	1778	1777	1861	1711	1653	1669	3. Produits financiers nets
4. Non-interest income (net)	373	362	433	535	547	820	626	677	795	906	4. Produits non financiers (nets)
a. Fees and commissions receivable	*261*	*296*	*380*	*464*	*475*	*497*	*526*	*527*	*555*	*653*	*a. Frais et commissions à recevoir*
b. Fees and commissions payable	*48*	*58*	*107*	*165*	*76*	*81*	*95*	*104*	*110*	*122*	*b. Frais et commissions à payer*
c. Net profits or loss on financial operations	*141*	*100*	*134*	*173*	*77*	*352*	*81*	*172*	*342*	*351*	*c. Profits ou pertes nets sur opérations financières*
d. Other	*20*	*24*	*25*	*62*	*71*	*52*	*114*	*82*	*8*	*24*	*d. Autres*
5. Gross income	1704	1832	2027	2365	2325	2597	2487	2389	2448	2575	5. Résultat brut
6. Operating expenses	1005	1049	1182	1326	1408	1546	1470	1530	1562	1629	6. Frais d'exploitation
a. Staff costs	*688*	*689*	*750*	*813*	*867*	*977*	*893*	*944*	*963*	*1024*	*a. Dépenses en personnel*
b. Property costs	*297*	*340*	*407*	*486*	*514*	*540*	*551*	*562*	*576*	*580*	*b. Dépenses en immobilier*
c. Other	*20*	*21*	*25*	*26*	*27*	*29*	*26*	*25*	*23*	*26*	*c. Autres*
7. Net income	699	783	845	1039	917	1052	1017	858	886	945	7. Résultat net
8. Provisions (net)	252	208	223	318	342	1046	538	327	325	307	8. Provisions (nettes)
a. Provisions on loans	*219*	*138*	*127*	*258*	*335*	*736*	*329*	*279*	*185*	*128*	*a. Provisions sur prêts*
b. Provisions on securities	*24*	*17*	*47*	*41*	*46*	*211*	*215*	*113*	*88*	*48*	*b. Provisions sur titres*
c. Other	*9*	*53*	*49*	*20*	*-39*	*98*	*-6*	*-64*	*52*	*130*	*c. Autres*
9. Profit before tax	447	575	622	721	576	6	480	531	561	638	9. Bénéfices avant impôt
10. Income tax (2)	134	179	189	185	149	153	120	117	109	119	10. Impôt sur le revenu (2)
11. Profit after tax	313	396	433	536	427	-147	359	414	452	519	11. Bénéfices après impôt
12. Distributed profit	141	186	207	262	255	245	276	290	267	342	12. Bénéfices distribués
13. Retained profit	173	210	226	275	175	-386	85	125	185	177	13. Bénéfices mis en réserve
BALANCE SHEET											**BILAN**
Assets											**Actif**
14. Cash & balance with Central bank	2751	2979	2516	3105	2513	2181	2151	1875	1582	1455	14. Caisse & solde auprès de la Banque centrale
15. Interbank deposits	4585	5504	6384	7636	8678	12521	11795	12733	13151	15882	15. Dépôts interbancaires
16. Loans	15359	17773	19723	23922	25006	25993	29254	31214	33044	36360	16. Prêts
17. Securities	7020	7697	8508	8385	8873	11568	13282	13976	14332	14049	17. Valeurs mobilières
18. Other assets	4343	4791	5508	6640	8466	14451	13916	16159	15942	15204	18. Autres actifs
Liabilities											**Passif**
19. Capital & reserves	3318	3728	4231	5719	5639	6002	6641	6560	6557	6738	19. Capital et réserves
20. Borrowing from Central bank	919	1553	1296	1243	2593	5417	4793	5222	3433	1383	20. Emprunts auprès de la Banque centrale
21. Interbank deposits	5512	5978	6241	8554	9881	14860	15425	16531	17464	19635	21. Dépôts interbancaires
22. Non-bank deposits	18975	21334	23800	26142	26649	28842	30472	34552	34924	36356	22. Dépôts non bancaires
23. Bonds	689	591	586	720	707	1026	2308	2351	2793	3078	23. Obligations
24. Other liabilities	4646	5558	6487	7311	8066	10566	10760	10740	12881	15760	24. Autres engagements
Balance sheet total											**Total du bilan**
25. End-year total	34059	38743	42639	49688	53535	66713	70399	75956	78052	82949	25. En fin d'exercice
26. Average total	32800	36401	40691	46164	51612	60124	70633	73177	77004	80500	26. Moyen

SPAIN

Commercial banks

ESPAGNE

Banques commerciales

	1988	1989	1990	1991	1992	1993(1)	1994(1)	1995	1996	1997	
Billion pesetas											*Milliards de pesetas*
Memorandum items											***Pour mémoire***
27. Short-term securities	*3733*	*4016*	*4445*	*3221*	*3396*	*3337*	*3483*	*3961*	*3443*	*2587*	*27. Titres à court terme*
28. Bonds	*2175*	*2395*	*2628*	*2979*	*3214*	*5599*	*6984*	*6885*	*7601*	*7851*	*28. Obligations*
29. Shares and participations	*1112*	*1285*	*1436*	*2185*	*2263*	*2633*	*2815*	*3130*	*3287*	*3612*	*29. Actions et participations*
30. Claims on non-residents	*2665*	*2821*	*3375*	*3983*	*6777*	*14204*	*12267*	*14906*	*14490*	*14281*	*30. Créances sur des non-résidents*
31. Liabilities to non-residents	*3841*	*4420*	*5739*	*6603*	*8523*	*11327*	*12202*	*12177*	*14794*	*18153*	*31. Engagements envers des non-résidents*
Capital adequacy (2)											***Solvabilité (2)***
32. Tier 1 Capital	*2233*	*2610*	*3007*	*3905*	*4037*	*3463*	*3874*	*3927*	*4118*	*4834*	*32. Fonds propres de base*
33. Tier 2 Capital	*123*	*194*	*276*	*326*	*394*	*509*	*565*	*888*	*1259*	*1524*	*33. Fonds propres complémentaires*
34. Supervisory deductions	-	-	-	-	-	*119*	*317*	*167*	*178*	*100*	*34. Eléments à déduire des fonds propres*
35. Total net capital resources	*2355*	*2804*	*3283*	*4231*	*4432*	*3852*	*4121*	*4648*	*5199*	*6257*	*35. Total net des ressources en capital*
36. Risk-weighted assets	*24352*	*29065*	*32288*	*41183*	*44414*	*40107*	*38701*	*40722*	*44621*	*53693*	*36. Actifs pondérés des risques*
SUPPLEMENTARY INFORMATION											**RENSEIGNEMENTS COMPLEMENTAIRES**
37. Number of institutions	138	145	154	160	164	164	165	170	165	159	37. Nombre d'institutions
38. Number of branches	16691	16677	16917	17824	18058	17636	17557	17842	17674	17530	38. Nombre de succursales
39. Number of employees (x 1000)	155	156	157	162	159	153	151	149	143	139	39. Nombre de salariés (x 1000)

1. Break in series in 1993 due to restructuring of a major bank.

   Break in series in 1994. Three official credit banks were classified as Commercial banks and no longer as Official credit institutions.

2. Change in methodology.

Change in methodology

- As from 1992, Income tax (item 10) includes tax on domestic activities of resident entities rather than total tax.
- As from 1993, credit entities' branches from the European Union (EU) are not subject to capital requirements. As from 1994, credit entities' from non-EU members are also not subject to capital requirements if these countries have similar legislation.
- As from 1993, the means of calculating capital adequacy requirements has changed, as the gearing ratio and the additional surcharges relating to concentration have disappeared.
- As from 1994, trading portfolio price risk became subject to a different treatment than that of credit risk.

1. Rupture dans les séries en 1993 suite à la restructuration de l'une des principales banques.

   Rupture dans les séries en 1994. Trois banques publiques de crédit ont été classées dans les Banques commerciales et non plus dans les Institutions publiques de crédit.

2. Changement méthodologique.

Changement méthodologique

- A partir de 1992, la rubrique Impôt sur le revenu (poste 10) inclut l'impôt sur les activités domestiques des entités résidentes plutôt que l'impôt total.
- A partir de 1993, les succursales des entités de crédit de l'Union Européenne (UE) ne sont pas soumises à des exigences de capital. A partir de 1994, les entités de crédit des pays non membres de l'UE ne sont pas non plus soumises à des exigences de capital si ces pays ont une législation semblable.
- A partir de 1993, les moyens de calcul pour la solvabilité exigée a changé, étant donné que le ratio d'effets de levier et les charges supplémentaires relatifs à la concentration ont disparus.
- A partir de 1994, le risque du prix du portefeuille de transactions a été sujet à une couverture différente que celle du risque de crédit.

SPAIN — ESPAGNE

Commercial banks — Banques commerciales

	1988	1989	1990	1991	1992	1993(1)	1994(1)	1995	1996	1997	
Per cent											*Pourcentage*
INCOME STATEMENT ANALYSIS											**ANALYSE DU COMPTE DE RESULTATS**
% of average balance sheet total											**% du total moyen du bilan**
40. Interest income	10.09	11.09	11.84	11.96	10.97	10.72	8.32	8.72	8.11	6.34	40. Produits financiers
41. Interest expenses	6.03	7.05	7.92	7.99	7.53	7.76	5.68	6.38	5.96	4.26	41. Frais financiers
42. Net interest income	4.06	4.04	3.92	3.96	3.44	2.96	2.63	2.34	2.15	2.07	42. Produits financiers nets
43. Non-interest income (net)	1.14	0.99	1.06	1.16	1.06	1.36	0.89	0.93	1.03	1.13	43. Produits non financiers (nets)
a. Fees and commissions receivable	*0.80*	*0.81*	*0.93*	*1.01*	*0.92*	*0.83*	*0.74*	*0.72*	*0.72*	*0.81*	*a. Frais et commissions à recevoir*
b. Fees and commissions payable	*0.15*	*0.16*	*0.26*	*0.36*	*0.15*	*0.13*	*0.13*	*0.14*	*0.14*	*0.15*	*b. Frais et commissions à payer*
c. Net profits or loss on financial operations	*0.43*	*0.27*	*0.33*	*0.37*	*0.15*	*0.59*	*0.11*	*0.24*	*0.44*	*0.44*	*c. Profits ou pertes nets sur opérations financières*
d. Other	*0.06*	*0.07*	*0.06*	*0.13*	*0.14*	*0.09*	*0.16*	*0.11*	*0.01*	*0.03*	*d. Autres*
44. Gross income	5.20	5.03	4.98	5.12	4.50	4.32	3.52	3.26	3.18	3.20	44. Résultat brut
45. Operating expenses	3.06	2.88	2.90	2.87	2.73	2.57	2.08	2.09	2.03	2.02	45. Frais d'exploitation
a. Staff costs	*2.10*	*1.89*	*1.84*	*1.76*	*1.68*	*1.62*	*1.26*	*1.29*	*1.25*	*1.27*	*a. Dépenses en personnel*
b. Property costs	*0.91*	*0.93*	*1.00*	*1.05*	*1.00*	*0.90*	*0.78*	*0.77*	*0.75*	*0.72*	*b. Dépenses en immobilier*
c. Other	*0.06*	*0.06*	*0.06*	*0.06*	*0.05*	*0.05*	*0.04*	*0.03*	*0.03*	*0.03*	*c. Autres*
46. Net income	2.13	2.15	2.08	2.25	1.78	1.75	1.44	1.17	1.15	1.17	46. Résultat net
47. Provisions (net)	0.77	0.57	0.55	0.69	0.66	1.74	0.76	0.45	0.42	0.38	47. Provisions (nettes)
a. Provisions on loans	*0.67*	*0.38*	*0.31*	*0.56*	*0.65*	*1.22*	*0.47*	*0.38*	*0.24*	*0.16*	*a. Provisions sur prêts*
b. Provisions on securities	*0.07*	*0.05*	*0.12*	*0.09*	*0.09*	*0.35*	*0.30*	*0.15*	*0.11*	*0.06*	*b. Provisions sur titres*
c. Other	*0.03*	*0.15*	*0.12*	*0.04*	*-0.08*	*0.16*	*-0.01*	*-0.09*	*0.07*	*0.16*	*c. Autres*
48. Profit before tax	1.36	1.58	1.53	1.56	1.12	0.01	0.68	0.73	0.73	0.79	48. Bénéfices avant impôt
49. Income tax	0.41	0.49	0.46	0.40	0.29	0.25	0.17	0.16	0.14	0.15	49. Impôt sur le revenu
50. Profit after tax	0.95	1.09	1.06	1.16	0.83	-0.24	0.51	0.57	0.59	0.64	50. Bénéfices après impôt
51. Distributed profit	0.43	0.51	0.51	0.57	0.49	0.41	0.39	0.40	0.35	0.42	51. Bénéfices distribués
52. Retained profit	0.53	0.58	0.56	0.60	0.34	-0.64	0.12	0.17	0.24	0.22	52. Bénéfices mis en réserve
% of gross income											**% du total du résultat brut**
53. Net interest income	78.11	80.24	78.69	77.38	76.47	68.43	74.83	71.62	67.52	64.82	53. Produits financiers nets
54. Non-interest income (net)	21.89	19.76	21.36	22.62	23.53	31.57	25.17	28.34	32.48	35.18	54. Produits non financiers (nets)
a. Fees and commissions receivable	*15.32*	*16.16*	*18.75*	*19.62*	*20.43*	*19.14*	*21.15*	*22.06*	*22.67*	*25.36*	*a. Frais et commissions à recevoir*
b. Fees and commissions payable	*2.82*	*3.17*	*5.28*	*6.98*	*3.27*	*3.12*	*3.82*	*4.35*	*4.49*	*4.74*	*b. Frais et commissions à payer*
c. Net profits or loss on financial operations	*8.27*	*5.46*	*6.61*	*7.32*	*3.31*	*13.55*	*3.26*	*7.20*	*13.97*	*13.63*	*c. Profits ou pertes nets sur opérations financières*
d. Other	*1.17*	*1.31*	*1.23*	*2.62*	*3.05*	*2.00*	*4.58*	*3.43*	*0.33*	*0.93*	*d. Autres*
55. Operating expenses	58.98	57.26	58.31	56.07	60.56	59.53	59.11	64.04	63.81	63.26	55. Frais d'exploitation
a. Staff costs	*40.38*	*37.61*	*37.00*	*34.38*	*37.29*	*37.62*	*35.91*	*39.51*	*39.34*	*39.77*	*a. Dépenses en personnel*
b. Property costs	*17.43*	*18.56*	*20.08*	*20.55*	*22.11*	*20.79*	*22.16*	*23.52*	*23.53*	*22.52*	*b. Dépenses en immobilier*
c. Other	*1.17*	*1.15*	*1.23*	*1.10*	*1.16*	*1.12*	*1.05*	*1.05*	*0.94*	*1.01*	*c. Autres*
56. Net income	41.02	42.74	41.69	43.93	39.44	40.51	40.89	35.91	36.19	36.70	56. Résultat net
57. Provisions (net)	14.79	11.35	11.00	13.45	14.71	40.28	21.63	13.69	13.28	11.92	57. Provisions (nettes)
a. Provisions on loans	*12.85*	*7.53*	*6.27*	*10.91*	*14.41*	*28.34*	*13.23*	*11.68*	*7.56*	*4.97*	*a. Provisions sur prêts*
b. Provisions on securities	*1.41*	*0.93*	*2.32*	*1.73*	*1.98*	*8.12*	*8.64*	*4.73*	*3.59*	*1.86*	*b. Provisions sur titres*
c. Other	*0.53*	*2.89*	*2.42*	*0.85*	*-1.68*	*3.77*	*-0.24*	*-2.68*	*2.12*	*5.05*	*c. Autres*
58. Profit before tax	26.23	31.39	30.69	30.49	24.77	0.23	19.30	22.23	22.92	24.78	58. Bénéfices avant impôt
59. Income tax	7.86	9.77	9.32	7.82	6.41	5.89	4.83	4.90	4.45	4.62	59. Impôt sur le revenu
60. Profit after tax	18.37	21.62	21.36	22.66	18.37	-5.66	14.44	17.33	18.46	20.16	60. Bénéfices après impôt
% of net income											**% du total du résultat net**
61. Provisions (net)	36.05	26.56	26.39	30.61	37.30	99.43	52.90	38.11	36.68	32.49	61. Provisions (nettes)
a. Provisions on loans	*31.33*	*17.62*	*15.03*	*24.83*	*36.53*	*69.96*	*32.35*	*32.52*	*20.88*	*13.54*	*a. Provisions sur prêts*
b. Provisions on securities	*3.43*	*2.17*	*5.56*	*3.95*	*5.02*	*20.06*	*21.14*	*13.17*	*9.93*	*5.08*	*b. Provisions sur titres*
c. Other	*1.29*	*6.77*	*5.80*	*1.92*	*-4.25*	*9.32*	*-0.59*	*-7.46*	*5.87*	*13.76*	*c. Autres*
62. Profit before tax	63.95	73.44	73.61	69.39	62.81	0.57	47.20	61.89	63.32	67.51	62. Bénéfices avant impôt
63. Income tax	19.17	22.86	22.37	17.81	16.25	14.54	11.80	13.64	12.30	12.59	63. Impôt sur le revenu
64. Profit after tax	44.78	50.57	51.24	51.59	46.56	-13.97	35.30	48.25	51.02	54.92	64. Bénéfices après impôt

SPAIN
Commercial banks

ESPAGNE
Banques commerciales

	1988	1989	1990	1991	1992	1993(1)	1994(1)	1995	1996	1997	
Per cent											*Pourcentage*
BALANCE SHEET ANALYSIS											**ANALYSE DU BILAN**
% of year-end balance sheet total											**% du total du bilan en fin d'exercice**
Assets											**Actif**
65. Cash & balance with Central bank	8.08	7.69	5.90	6.25	4.69	3.27	3.06	2.47	2.03	1.75	65. Caisse & solde auprès de la Banque centrale
66. Interbank deposits	13.46	14.21	14.97	15.37	16.21	18.77	16.75	16.76	16.85	19.15	66. Dépôts interbancaires
67. Loans	45.10	45.87	46.26	48.14	46.71	38.96	41.55	41.09	42.34	43.83	67. Prêts
68. Securities	20.61	19.87	19.95	16.88	16.57	17.34	18.87	18.40	18.36	16.94	68. Valeurs mobilières
69. Other assets	12.75	12.37	12.92	13.36	15.81	21.66	19.77	21.27	20.42	18.33	69. Autres actifs
Liabilities											**Passif**
70. Capital & reserves	9.74	9.62	9.92	11.51	10.53	9.00	9.43	8.64	8.40	8.12	70. Capital et réserves
71. Borrowing from Central bank	2.70	4.01	3.04	2.50	4.84	8.12	6.81	6.88	4.40	1.67	71. Emprunts auprès de la Banque centrale
72. Interbank deposits	16.18	15.43	14.64	17.22	18.46	22.27	21.91	21.76	22.37	23.67	72. Dépôts interbancaires
73. Non-bank deposits	55.71	55.07	55.82	52.61	49.78	43.23	43.28	45.49	44.74	43.83	73. Dépôts non bancaires
74. Bonds	2.02	1.53	1.37	1.45	1.32	1.54	3.28	3.10	3.58	3.71	74. Obligations
75. Other liabilities	13.64	14.35	15.21	14.71	15.07	15.84	15.28	14.14	16.50	19.00	75. Autres engagements
Memorandum items											***Pour mémoire***
76. Short-term securities	*10.96*	*10.37*	*10.42*	*6.48*	*6.34*	*5.00*	*4.95*	*5.21*	*4.41*	*3.12*	*76. Titres à court terme*
77. Bonds	*6.39*	*6.18*	*6.16*	*6.00*	*6.00*	*8.39*	*9.92*	*9.06*	*9.74*	*9.46*	*77. Obligations*
78. Shares and participations	*3.26*	*3.32*	*3.37*	*4.40*	*4.23*	*3.95*	*4.00*	*4.12*	*4.21*	*4.35*	*78. Actions et participations*
79. Claims on non-residents	*7.82*	*7.28*	*7.92*	*8.02*	*12.66*	*21.29*	*17.42*	*19.62*	*18.56*	*17.22*	*79. Créances sur des non-résidents*
80. Liabilities to non-residents	*11.28*	*11.41*	*13.46*	*13.29*	*15.92*	*16.98*	*17.33*	*16.03*	*18.95*	*21.88*	*80. Engagements envers des non-résidents*

* See notes on previous pages.

* Voir les notes en pages précédentes.

SPAIN / ESPAGNE

Savings banks / Caisses d'épargne

	1988	1989	1990	1991	1992	1993	1994	1995	1996	1997	
Billion pesetas											*Milliards de pesetas*
INCOME STATEMENT											**COMPTE DE RESULTATS**
1. Interest income	1761	2151	2637	2782	3027	3461	3079	3375	3525	3122	1. Produits financiers
2. Interest expenses	989	1298	1693	1788	1920	2248	1806	2058	2136	1676	2. Frais financiers
3. Net interest income	773	853	944	994	1108	1213	1273	1316	1390	1446	3. Produits financiers nets
4. Non-interest income (net)	147	148	150	148	212	258	258	273	358	432	4. Produits non financiers (nets)
a. Fees and commissions receivable	*51*	*65*	*82*	*99*	*141*	*168*	*202*	*219*	*252*	*310*	*a. Frais et commissions à recevoir*
b. Fees and commissions payable	*13*	*20*	*25*	*33*	*24*	*29*	*32*	*36*	*41*	*48*	*b. Frais et commissions à payer*
c. Net profits or loss on financial operations	*54*	*43*	*35*	*31*	*40*	*74*	*20*	*33*	*98*	*110*	*c. Profits ou pertes nets sur opérations financières*
d. Other	*55*	*60*	*57*	*51*	*55*	*46*	*68*	*57*	*49*	*59*	*d. Autres*
5. Gross income	920	1001	1094	1142	1320	1471	1531	1589	1748	1878	5. Résultat brut
6. Operating expenses	683	678	723	722	790	881	927	988	1050	1106	6. Frais d'exploitation
a. Staff costs	*480*	*440*	*440*	*430*	*470*	*531*	*567*	*605*	*644*	*661*	*a. Dépenses en personnel*
b. Property costs	*194*	*233*	*277*	*289*	*317*	*347*	*356*	*373*	*395*	*433*	*b. Dépenses en immobilier*
c. Other	*9*	*6*	*6*	*3*	*3*	*4*	*3*	*9*	*11*	*12*	*c. Autres*
7. Net income	237	323	371	420	530	590	605	601	698	772	7. Résultat net
8. Provisions (net)	102	97	147	148	244	286	288	232	263	247	8. Provisions (nettes)
a. Provisions on loans	*59*	*37*	*57*	*123*	*175*	*282*	*207*	*190*	*166*	*133*	*a. Provisions sur prêts*
b. Provisions on securities	*2*	*3*	*29*	*4*	*46*	*-17*	*54*	*13*	*24*	*23*	*b. Provisions sur titres*
c. Other	*42*	*57*	*61*	*21*	*23*	*20*	*27*	*29*	*73*	*90*	*c. Autres*
9. Profit before tax	135	226	223	272	286	305	317	369	435	525	9. Bénéfices avant impôt
10. Income tax (1)	22	49	47	59	68	75	72	90	107	124	10. Impôt sur le revenu (1)
11. Profit after tax	113	178	176	213	218	229	245	279	328	401	11. Bénéfices après impôt
12. Distributed profit	43	50	47	47	50	62	60	68	86	102	12. Bénéfices distribués
13. Retained profit	70	128	129	166	168	167	185	212	242	299	13. Bénéfices mis en réserve
BALANCE SHEET											**BILAN**
Assets											**Actif**
14. Cash & balance with Central bank	2183	2698	2249	2418	2253	1928	1956	1640	1490	1461	14. Caisse & solde auprès de la Banque centrale
15. Interbank deposits	1800	2412	2827	3494	4923	5885	4822	5401	6268	6259	15. Dépôts interbancaires
16. Loans	7735	9482	10824	12319	14484	15724	17687	19234	21351	24829	16. Prêts
17. Securities	5762	6216	6736	5667	6039	5793	7850	8908	9879	10131	17. Valeurs mobilières
18. Other assets	1738	2139	2812	2927	3090	4320	4625	5189	4913	4575	18. Autres actifs
Liabilities											**Passif**
19. Capital & reserves	1408	1640	1987	2244	2493	2816	3188	3376	3808	4283	19. Capital et réserves
20. Borrowing from Central bank	39	559	294	329	1688	1077	1200	1362	953	837	20. Emprunts auprès de la Banque centrale
21. Interbank deposits	640	739	1210	1205	1567	1950	2421	2808	3244	3507	21. Dépôts interbancaires
22. Non-bank deposits	14886	17515	19086	20352	22531	25073	27631	29981	32726	34472	22. Dépôts non bancaires
23. Bonds	681	514	421	490	569	731	763	939	1079	1426	23. Obligations
24. Other liabilities	1565	1980	2449	2207	1940	2003	1737	1905	2092	2729	24. Autres engagements
Balance sheet total											**Total du bilan**
25. End-year total	19218	22947	25448	26825	30788	33650	36940	40372	43901	47254	25. En fin d'exercice
26. Average total	17597	21083	24198	26137	28807	32219	35295	38656	42137	45577	26. Moyen

SPAIN — ESPAGNE
Savings banks — Caisses d'épargne

	1988	1989	1990	1991	1992	1993	1994	1995	1996	1997	
Billion pesetas											*Milliards de pesetas*
Memorandum items											***Pour mémoire***
27. Short-term securities	*2335*	*3081*	*3556*	*2703*	*2960*	*2414*	*2770*	*2734*	*2864*	*2145*	*27. Titres à court terme*
28. Bonds	*3091*	*2700*	*2679*	*2432*	*2446*	*2619*	*4246*	*5141*	*5706*	*6049*	*28. Obligations*
29. Shares and participations	*336*	*435*	*501*	*532*	*633*	*760*	*835*	*1034*	*1309*	*1937*	*29. Actions et participations*
30. Claims on non-residents	*134*	*196*	*415*	*527*	*1065*	*2288*	*2286*	*2815*	*2518*	*2567*	*30. Créances sur des non-résidents*
31. Liabilities to non-residents	*399*	*450*	*699*	*758*	*804*	*961*	*1036*	*1060*	*1367*	*2290*	*31. Engagements envers des non-résidents*
Capital adequacy (1)											***Solvabilité (1)***
32. Tier 1 Capital	*905*	*1006*	*1312*	*1437*	*1669*	*1783*	*1980*	*2256*	*2568*	*2849*	*32. Fonds propres de base*
33. Tier 2 Capital	*168*	*193*	*230*	*268*	*297*	*435*	*441*	*394*	*515*	*633*	*33. Fonds propres complémentaires*
34. Supervisory deductions	-	-	-	-	-	*22*	*89*	*24*	*15*	*24*	*34. Eléments à déduire des fonds propres*
35. Total net capital resources	*1073*	*1199*	*1542*	*1705*	*1966*	*2195*	*2332*	*2626*	*3067*	*3458*	*35. Total net des ressources en capital*
36. Risk-weighted assets	*10141*	*11698*	*14387*	*15902*	*18617*	*17357*	*18678*	*20613*	*22834*	*26471*	*36. Actifs pondérés des risques*
SUPPLEMENTARY INFORMATION											**RENSEIGNEMENTS COMPLEMENTAIRES**
37. Number of institutions	79	78	66	57	54	52	52	51	51	51	37. Nombre d'institutions
38. Number of branches	14037	14944	15398	14031	14291	14485	14880	15214	16094	16636	38. Nombre de succursales
39. Number of employees (x 1000)	78	83	85	83	83	83	84	84	87	90	39. Nombre de salariés (x 1000)

1. Change in methodology.

Change in methodology

- As from 1992, Income tax (item 10) includes tax on domestic activities of resident entities rather than total tax.
- As from 1993, credit entities' branches from the European Union (EU) are not subject to capital requirements. As from 1994, credit entities' from non-EU members are also not subject to capital requirements if these countries have similar legislation.
- As from 1993, the means of calculating capital adequacy requirements has changed, as the gearing ratio and the additional surcharges relating to concentration have disappeared.
- As from 1994, trading portfolio price risk became subject to a different treatment than that of credit risk.

1. Changement méthodologique.

Changement méthodologique

- A partir de 1992, la rubrique Impôt sur le revenu (poste 10) inclut l'impôt sur les activités domestiques des entités résidentes plutôt que l'impôt total.
- A partir de 1993, les succursales des entités de crédit de l'Union Européenne (UE) ne sont pas soumises à des exigences de capital. A partir de 1994, les entités de crédit des pays non membres de l'UE ne sont pas non plus soumises à des exigences de capital si ces pays ont une législation semblable.
- A partir de 1993, les moyens de calcul pour la solvabilité exigée a changé, étant donné que le ratio d'effets de levier et les charges supplémentaires relatifs à la concentration ont disparus.
- A partir de 1994, le risque du prix du portefeuille de transactions a été sujet à une couverture différente que celle du risque de crédit.

SPAIN
Savings banks

ESPAGNE
Caisses d'épargne

Per cent	1988	1989	1990	1991	1992	1993	1994	1995	1996	1997	Pourcentage
INCOME STATEMENT ANALYSIS											**ANALYSE DU COMPTE DE RESULTATS**
% of average balance sheet total											**% du total moyen du bilan**
40. Interest income	10.01	10.20	10.90	10.64	10.51	10.74	8.72	8.73	8.37	6.85	40. Produits financiers
41. Interest expenses	5.62	6.16	7.00	6.84	6.67	6.98	5.12	5.32	5.07	3.68	41. Frais financiers
42. Net interest income	4.39	4.05	3.90	3.80	3.85	3.76	3.61	3.40	3.30	3.17	42. Produits financiers nets
43. Non-interest income (net)	0.84	0.70	0.62	0.57	0.74	0.80	0.73	0.71	0.85	0.95	43. Produits non financiers (nets)
a. Fees and commissions receivable	*0.29*	*0.31*	*0.34*	*0.38*	*0.49*	*0.52*	*0.57*	*0.57*	*0.60*	*0.68*	*a. Frais et commissions à recevoir*
b. Fees and commissions payable	*0.07*	*0.09*	*0.10*	*0.13*	*0.08*	*0.09*	*0.09*	*0.09*	*0.10*	*0.11*	*b. Frais et commissions à payer*
c. Net profits or loss on financial operations	*0.31*	*0.20*	*0.14*	*0.12*	*0.14*	*0.23*	*0.06*	*0.09*	*0.23*	*0.24*	*c. Profits ou pertes nets sur opérations financières*
d. Other	*0.31*	*0.28*	*0.24*	*0.20*	*0.19*	*0.14*	*0.19*	*0.15*	*0.12*	*0.13*	*d. Autres*
44. Gross income	5.23	4.75	4.52	4.37	4.58	4.57	4.34	4.11	4.15	4.12	44. Résultat brut
45. Operating expenses	3.88	3.22	2.99	2.76	2.74	2.73	2.63	2.56	2.49	2.43	45. Frais d'exploitation
a. Staff costs	*2.73*	*2.09*	*1.82*	*1.65*	*1.63*	*1.65*	*1.61*	*1.57*	*1.53*	*1.45*	*a. Dépenses en personnel*
b. Property costs	*1.10*	*1.11*	*1.14*	*1.11*	*1.10*	*1.08*	*1.01*	*0.96*	*0.94*	*0.95*	*b. Dépenses en immobilier*
c. Other	*0.05*	*0.03*	*0.02*	*0.01*	*0.01*	*0.01*	*0.01*	*0.02*	*0.03*	*0.03*	*c. Autres*
46. Net income	1.35	1.53	1.53	1.61	1.84	1.83	1.71	1.55	1.66	1.69	46. Résultat net
47. Provisions (net)	0.58	0.46	0.61	0.57	0.85	0.89	0.82	0.60	0.62	0.54	47. Provisions (nettes)
a. Provisions on loans	*0.34*	*0.18*	*0.24*	*0.47*	*0.61*	*0.88*	*0.59*	*0.49*	*0.39*	*0.29*	*a. Provisions sur prêts*
b. Provisions on securities	*0.01*	*0.01*	*0.12*	*0.02*	*0.16*	*-0.05*	*0.15*	*0.03*	*0.06*	*0.05*	*b. Provisions sur titres*
c. Other	*0.24*	*0.27*	*0.25*	*0.08*	*0.08*	*0.06*	*0.08*	*0.08*	*0.17*	*0.20*	*c. Autres*
48. Profit before tax	0.77	1.07	0.92	1.04	0.99	0.95	0.90	0.95	1.03	1.15	48. Bénéfices avant impôt
49. Income tax	0.13	0.23	0.19	0.23	0.24	0.23	0.20	0.23	0.25	0.27	49. Impôt sur le revenu
50. Profit after tax	0.64	0.84	0.73	0.81	0.76	0.71	0.69	0.72	0.78	0.88	50. Bénéfices après impôt
51. Distributed profit	0.24	0.24	0.19	0.18	0.17	0.19	0.17	0.18	0.20	0.22	51. Bénéfices distribués
52. Retained profit	0.40	0.61	0.53	0.64	0.58	0.52	0.52	0.55	0.57	0.66	52. Bénéfices mis en réserve
% of gross income											**% du total du résultat brut**
53. Net interest income	84.02	85.21	86.29	87.04	83.94	82.46	83.15	82.82	79.52	77.00	53. Produits financiers nets
54. Non-interest income (net)	15.98	14.79	13.71	12.96	16.06	17.54	16.85	17.18	20.48	23.00	54. Produits non financiers (nets)
a. Fees and commissions receivable	*5.54*	*6.49*	*7.50*	*8.67*	*10.68*	*11.42*	*13.19*	*13.78*	*14.42*	*16.51*	*a. Frais et commissions à recevoir*
b. Fees and commissions payable	*1.41*	*2.00*	*2.29*	*2.89*	*1.82*	*1.97*	*2.09*	*2.27*	*2.35*	*2.56*	*b. Frais et commissions à payer*
c. Net profits or loss on financial operations	*5.87*	*4.30*	*3.20*	*2.71*	*3.03*	*5.03*	*1.31*	*2.08*	*5.61*	*5.86*	*c. Profits ou pertes nets sur opérations financières*
d. Other	*5.98*	*5.99*	*5.21*	*4.47*	*4.17*	*3.13*	*4.44*	*3.59*	*2.80*	*3.14*	*d. Autres*
55. Operating expenses	74.24	67.73	66.09	63.22	59.85	59.89	60.55	62.18	60.07	58.89	55. Frais d'exploitation
a. Staff costs	*52.17*	*43.96*	*40.22*	*37.65*	*35.61*	*36.10*	*37.03*	*38.07*	*36.84*	*35.20*	*a. Dépenses en personnel*
b. Property costs	*21.09*	*23.28*	*25.32*	*25.31*	*24.02*	*23.59*	*23.25*	*23.47*	*22.60*	*23.06*	*b. Dépenses en immobilier*
c. Other	*0.98*	*0.60*	*0.55*	*0.26*	*0.23*	*0.27*	*0.20*	*0.57*	*0.63*	*0.64*	*c. Autres*
56. Net income	25.76	32.27	33.91	36.78	40.15	40.11	39.52	37.82	39.93	41.11	56. Résultat net
57. Provisions (net)	11.09	9.69	13.44	12.96	18.48	19.44	18.81	14.60	15.05	13.15	57. Provisions (nettes)
a. Provisions on loans	*6.41*	*3.70*	*5.21*	*10.77*	*13.26*	*19.17*	*13.52*	*11.96*	*9.50*	*7.08*	*a. Provisions sur prêts*
b. Provisions on securities	*0.22*	*0.30*	*2.65*	*0.35*	*3.48*	*-1.16*	*3.53*	*0.82*	*1.37*	*1.22*	*b. Provisions sur titres*
c. Other	*4.57*	*5.69*	*5.58*	*1.84*	*1.74*	*1.36*	*1.76*	*1.83*	*4.18*	*4.79*	*c. Autres*
58. Profit before tax	14.67	22.58	20.38	23.82	21.67	20.73	20.71	23.22	24.89	27.96	58. Bénéfices avant impôt
59. Income tax	2.39	4.90	4.30	5.17	5.15	5.10	4.70	5.66	6.12	6.60	59. Impôt sur le revenu
60. Profit after tax	12.28	17.78	16.09	18.65	16.52	15.57	16.00	17.56	18.76	21.35	60. Bénéfices après impôt
% of net income											**% du total du résultat net**
61. Provisions (net)	43.04	30.03	39.62	35.24	46.04	48.47	47.60	38.60	37.68	31.99	61. Provisions (nettes)
a. Provisions on loans	*24.89*	*11.46*	*15.36*	*29.29*	*33.02*	*47.80*	*34.21*	*31.61*	*23.78*	*17.23*	*a. Provisions sur prêts*
b. Provisions on securities	*0.84*	*0.93*	*7.82*	*0.95*	*8.68*	*-2.88*	*8.93*	*2.16*	*3.44*	*2.98*	*b. Provisions sur titres*
c. Other	*17.72*	*17.65*	*16.44*	*5.00*	*4.34*	*3.39*	*4.46*	*4.83*	*10.46*	*11.66*	*c. Autres*
62. Profit before tax	56.96	69.97	60.11	64.76	53.96	51.69	52.40	61.40	62.32	68.01	62. Bénéfices avant impôt
63. Income tax	9.28	15.17	12.67	14.05	12.83	12.71	11.90	14.98	15.33	16.06	63. Impôt sur le revenu
64. Profit after tax	47.68	55.11	47.44	50.71	41.13	38.81	40.50	46.42	46.99	51.94	64. Bénéfices après impôt

	1988	1989	1990	1991	1992	1993	1994	1995	1996	1997	
Per cent											*Pourcentage*
BALANCE SHEET ANALYSIS											**ANALYSE DU BILAN**
% of year-end balance sheet total											**% du total du bilan en fin d'exercice**
Assets											**Actif**
65. Cash & balance with Central bank	11.36	11.76	8.84	9.01	7.32	5.73	5.30	4.06	3.39	3.09	65. Caisse & solde auprès de la Banque centrale
66. Interbank deposits	9.37	10.51	11.11	13.03	15.99	17.49	13.05	13.38	14.28	13.25	66. Dépôts interbancaires
67. Loans	40.25	41.32	42.53	45.92	47.04	46.73	47.88	47.64	48.63	52.54	67. Prêts
68. Securities	29.98	27.09	26.47	21.13	19.61	17.22	21.25	22.06	22.50	21.44	68. Valeurs mobilières
69. Other assets	9.04	9.32	11.05	10.91	10.04	12.84	12.52	12.85	11.19	9.68	69. Autres actifs
Liabilities											**Passif**
70. Capital & reserves	7.33	7.15	7.81	8.37	8.10	8.37	8.63	8.36	8.67	9.06	70. Capital et réserves
71. Borrowing from Central bank	0.20	2.44	1.16	1.23	5.48	3.20	3.25	3.37	2.17	1.77	71. Emprunts auprès de la Banque centrale
72. Interbank deposits	3.33	3.22	4.75	4.49	5.09	5.79	6.55	6.96	7.39	7.42	72. Dépôts interbancaires
73. Non-bank deposits	77.46	76.33	75.00	75.87	73.18	74.51	74.80	74.26	74.54	72.95	73. Dépôts non bancaires
74. Bonds	3.54	2.24	1.65	1.83	1.85	2.17	2.07	2.33	2.46	3.02	74. Obligations
75. Other liabilities	8.14	8.63	9.62	8.23	6.30	5.95	4.70	4.72	4.77	5.78	75. Autres engagements
Memorandum items											***Pour mémoire***
76. Short-term securities	*12.15*	*13.43*	*13.97*	*10.08*	*9.61*	*7.17*	*7.50*	*6.77*	*6.52*	*4.54*	*76. Titres à court terme*
77. Bonds	*16.08*	*11.77*	*10.53*	*9.07*	*7.94*	*7.78*	*11.49*	*12.73*	*13.00*	*12.80*	*77. Obligations*
78. Shares and participations	*1.75*	*1.90*	*1.97*	*1.98*	*2.06*	*2.26*	*2.26*	*2.56*	*2.98*	*4.10*	*78. Actions et participations*
79. Claims on non-residents	*0.70*	*0.85*	*1.63*	*1.96*	*3.46*	*6.80*	*6.19*	*6.97*	*5.74*	*5.43*	*79. Créances sur des non-résidents*
80. Liabilities to non-residents	*2.08*	*1.96*	*2.75*	*2.83*	*2.61*	*2.86*	*2.80*	*2.63*	*3.11*	*4.85*	*80. Engagements envers des non-résidents*

* See notes on previous pages.

* Voir les notes en pages précédentes.

SPAIN
Co-operative banks

ESPAGNE
Banques mutualistes

	1988	1989	1990	1991	1992	1993	1994	1995	1996	1997	
Billion pesetas											*Milliards de pesetas*
INCOME STATEMENT											**COMPTE DE RESULTATS**
1. Interest income	167	186	221	256	281	324	296	338	366	320	1. Produits financiers
2. Interest expenses	88	97	122	143	156	182	151	179	194	144	2. Frais financiers
3. Net interest income	79	89	99	113	125	141	145	159	172	176	3. Produits financiers nets
4. Non-interest income (net)	4	5	6	7	7	11	12	9	14	23	4. Produits non financiers (nets)
a. Fees and commissions receivable	*3*	*4*	*6*	*7*	*11*	*15*	*18*	*20*	*25*	*30*	*a. Frais et commissions à recevoir*
b. Fees and commissions payable	*1*	*2*	*2*	*2*	*3*	*3*	*4*	*4*	*6*	*7*	*b. Frais et commissions à payer*
c. Net profits or loss on financial operations	-	*1*	-	-	*-1*	*2*	*1*	-	*4*	*8*	*c. Profits ou pertes nets sur opérations financières*
d. Other	*2*	*2*	*2*	*1*	*-1*	*-2*	*-3*	*-6*	*-9*	*-8*	*d. Autres*
5. Gross income	84	94	105	119	132	152	157	168	186	199	5. Résultat brut
6. Operating expenses	51	57	65	74	82	91	96	103	112	123	6. Frais d'exploitation
a. Staff costs	*33*	*35*	*39*	*44*	*48*	*52*	*56*	*60*	*65*	*70*	*a. Dépenses en personnel*
b. Property costs	*18*	*21*	*25*	*29*	*34*	*38*	*38*	*42*	*46*	*51*	*b. Dépenses en immobilier*
c. Other	*1*	*1*	*1*	*1*	*1*	*1*	*1*	*1*	*1*	*1*	*c. Autres*
7. Net income	32	37	40	45	50	61	61	66	74	76	7. Résultat net
8. Provisions (net)	9	7	10	11	13	27	20	15	14	10	8. Provisions (nettes)
a. Provisions on loans	*8*	*6*	*7*	*9*	*14*	*29*	*17*	*19*	*18*	*15*	*a. Provisions sur prêts*
b. Provisions on securities	-	*1*	*2*	*1*	*1*	-	*5*	-	-	-	*b. Provisions sur titres*
c. Other	*1*	*1*	-	*1*	*-1*	*-2*	*-2*	*-5*	*-4*	*-5*	*c. Autres*
9. Profit before tax	24	30	31	34	37	34	41	51	60	66	9. Bénéfices avant impôt
10. Income tax (1)	2	3	3	5	6	6	6	8	10	11	10. Impôt sur le revenu (1)
11. Profit after tax	22	27	27	29	31	28	35	42	50	55	11. Bénéfices après impôt
12. Distributed profit	5	7	8	9	10	10	11	12	13	14	12. Bénéfices distribués
13. Retained profit	17	20	19	20	21	18	25	30	37	41	13. Bénéfices mis en réserve
BALANCE SHEET											**BILAN**
Assets											**Actif**
14. Cash & balance with Central bank	207	253	269	265	219	197	193	188	177	168	14. Caisse & solde auprès de la Banque centrale
15. Interbank deposits	388	385	511	613	707	1011	883	1054	1101	1116	15. Dépôts interbancaires
16. Loans	706	800	910	1100	1296	1408	1649	1909	2219	2662	16. Prêts
17. Securities	260	247	225	225	205	192	410	517	577	560	17. Valeurs mobilières
18. Other assets	115	119	136	152	160	176	218	224	249	244	18. Autres actifs
Liabilities											**Passif**
19. Capital & reserves	181	204	234	269	296	342	390	432	492	557	19. Capital et réserves
20. Borrowing from Central bank	-	-	-	-	-	32	70	60	61	45	20. Emprunts auprès de la Banque centrale
21. Interbank deposits	98	87	112	104	127	119	125	161	195	295	21. Dépôts interbancaires
22. Non-bank deposits	1310	1431	1615	1889	2097	2415	2702	3133	3462	3780	22. Dépôts non bancaires
23. Bonds	9	1	1	-	-	-	-	-	-	-	23. Obligations
24. Other liabilities	78	80	89	93	67	76	66	108	113	73	24. Autres engagements
Balance sheet total											**Total du bilan**
25. End-year total	1676	1804	2050	2355	2587	2985	3353	3893	4323	4751	25. En fin d'exercice
26. Average total	1623	1740	1927	2203	2471	2786	3169	3623	4108	4537	26. Moyen

SPAIN / ESPAGNE

Co-operative banks / Banques mutualistes

	1988	1989	1990	1991	1992	1993	1994	1995	1996	1997	
Billion pesetas											*Milliards de pesetas*
Memorandum items											***Pour mémoire***
27. Short-term securities	*135*	*140*	*141*	*141*	*101*	*88*	*118*	*145*	*116*	*94*	*27. Titres à court terme*
28. Bonds	*117*	*99*	*71*	*70*	*86*	*81*	*262*	*315*	*380*	*398*	*28. Obligations*
29. Shares and participations	*8*	*8*	*13*	*15*	*18*	*23*	*30*	*58*	*82*	*68*	*29. Actions et participations*
30. Claims on non-residents	*1*	*1*	*1*	*2*	*15*	*27*	*31*	*13*	*24*	*18*	*30. Créances sur des non-résidents*
31. Liabilities to non-residents	*5*	*6*	*9*	*12*	*15*	*20*	*23*	*26*	*33*	*40*	*31. Engagements envers des non-résidents*
Capital adequacy (1)											***Solvabilité (1)***
32. Tier 1 Capital	*128*	*143*	*163*	*186*	*209*	*232*	*259*	*295*	*336*	*387*	*32. Fonds propres de base*
33. Tier 2 Capital	*1*	*1*	*2*	*2*	*2*	*2*	*2*	*2*	*14*	*10*	*33. Fonds propres complémentaires*
34. Supervisory deductions	*-*	*-*	*-*	*-*	*-*	*-*	*9*	*3*	*1*	*3*	*34. Eléments à déduire des fonds propres*
35. Total net capital resources	*129*	*144*	*164*	*187*	*210*	*234*	*252*	*294*	*349*	*394*	*35. Total net des ressources en capital*
36. Risk-weighted assets	*1043*	*1122*	*1256*	*1463*	*1640*	*1597*	*1759*	*2037*	*2390*	*2794*	*36. Actifs pondérés des risques*
SUPPLEMENTARY INFORMATION											**RENSEIGNEMENTS COMPLEMENTAIRES**
37. Number of institutions	117	110	107	106	101	100	99	97	97	97	37. Nombre d'institutions
38. Number of branches	3029	2890	2919	3018	3080	3072	3107	3195	3311	3468	38. Nombre de succursales
39. Number of employees (x 1000)	10	10	10	11	11	11	11	12	13	13	39. Nombre de salariés (x 1000)

1. Change in methodology.

Change in methodology

- As from 1992, Income tax (item 10) includes tax on domestic activities of resident entities rather than total tax.
- As from 1993, credit entities' branches from the European Union (EU) are not subject to capital requirements. As from 1994, credit entities' from non-EU members are also not subject to capital requirements if these countries have similar legislation.
- As from 1993, the means of calculating capital adequacy requirements has changed, as the gearing ratio and the additional surcharges relating to concentration have disappeared.
- As from 1994, trading portfolio price risk became subject to a different treatment than that of credit risk.

1. Changement méthodologique.

Changement méthodologique

- A partir de 1992, la rubrique Impôt sur le revenu (poste 10) inclut l'impôt sur les activités domestiques des entités résidentes plutôt que l'impôt total.
- A partir de 1993, les succursales des entités de crédit de l'Union Européenne (UE) ne sont pas soumises à des exigences de capital. A partir de 1994, les entités de crédit des pays non membres de l'UE ne sont pas non plus soumises à des exigences de capital si ces pays ont une législation semblable.
- A partir de 1993, les moyens de calcul pour la solvabilité exigée a changé, étant donné que le ratio d'effets de levier et les charges supplémentaires relatifs à la concentration ont disparus.
- A partir de 1994, le risque du prix du portefeuille de transactions a été sujet à une couverture différente que celle du risque de crédit.

SPAIN — ESPAGNE

Co-operative banks — Banques mutualistes

Per cent	1988	1989	1990	1991	1992	1993	1994	1995	1996	1997	Pourcentage
INCOME STATEMENT ANALYSIS											**ANALYSE DU COMPTE DE RESULTATS**
% of average balance sheet total											**% du total moyen du bilan**
40. Interest income	10.29	10.69	11.47	11.62	11.37	11.63	9.34	9.33	8.91	7.05	40. Produits financiers
41. Interest expenses	5.42	5.57	6.33	6.49	6.31	6.53	4.76	4.94	4.72	3.17	41. Frais financiers
42. Net interest income	4.87	5.11	5.14	5.13	5.06	5.06	4.58	4.39	4.19	3.88	42. Produits financiers nets
43. Non-interest income (net)	0.25	0.29	0.31	0.32	0.28	0.39	0.38	0.25	0.34	0.51	43. Produits non financiers (nets)
a. Fees and commissions receivable	*0.18*	*0.23*	*0.31*	*0.32*	*0.45*	*0.54*	*0.57*	*0.55*	*0.61*	*0.66*	*a. Frais et commissions à recevoir*
b. Fees and commissions payable	*0.06*	*0.11*	*0.10*	*0.09*	*0.12*	*0.11*	*0.13*	*0.11*	*0.15*	*0.15*	*b. Frais et commissions à payer*
c. Net profits or loss on financial operations	-	*0.06*	-	-	*-0.04*	*0.07*	*0.03*	-	*0.10*	*0.18*	*c. Profits ou pertes nets sur opérations financières*
d. Other	*0.12*	*0.11*	*0.10*	*0.05*	*-0.04*	*-0.07*	*-0.09*	*-0.17*	*-0.22*	*-0.18*	*d. Autres*
44. Gross income	5.18	5.40	5.45	5.40	5.34	5.46	4.95	4.64	4.53	4.39	44. Résultat brut
45. Operating expenses	3.14	3.28	3.37	3.36	3.32	3.27	3.03	2.84	2.73	2.71	45. Frais d'exploitation
a. Staff costs	*2.03*	*2.01*	*2.02*	*2.00*	*1.94*	*1.87*	*1.77*	*1.66*	*1.58*	*1.54*	*a. Dépenses en personnel*
b. Property costs	*1.11*	*1.21*	*1.30*	*1.32*	*1.38*	*1.36*	*1.20*	*1.16*	*1.12*	*1.12*	*b. Dépenses en immobilier*
c. Other	*0.06*	*0.06*	*0.05*	*0.05*	*0.04*	*0.04*	*0.03*	*0.03*	*0.02*	*0.02*	*c. Autres*
46. Net income	1.97	2.13	2.08	2.04	2.02	2.19	1.92	1.82	1.80	1.68	46. Résultat net
47. Provisions (net)	0.55	0.40	0.52	0.50	0.53	0.97	0.63	0.41	0.34	0.22	47. Provisions (nettes)
a. Provisions on loans	*0.49*	*0.34*	*0.36*	*0.41*	*0.57*	*1.04*	*0.54*	*0.52*	*0.44*	*0.33*	*a. Provisions sur prêts*
b. Provisions on securities	-	*0.06*	*0.10*	*0.05*	*0.04*	-	*0.16*	-	-	-	*b. Provisions sur titres*
c. Other	*0.06*	*0.06*	-	*0.05*	*-0.04*	*-0.07*	*-0.06*	*-0.14*	*-0.10*	*-0.11*	*c. Autres*
48. Profit before tax	1.48	1.72	1.61	1.54	1.50	1.22	1.29	1.41	1.46	1.45	48. Bénéfices avant impôt
49. Income tax	0.12	0.17	0.16	0.23	0.24	0.22	0.19	0.22	0.24	0.24	49. Impôt sur le revenu
50. Profit after tax	1.36	1.55	1.40	1.32	1.25	1.01	1.10	1.16	1.22	1.21	50. Bénéfices après impôt
51. Distributed profit	0.31	0.40	0.42	0.41	0.40	0.36	0.35	0.33	0.32	0.31	51. Bénéfices distribués
52. Retained profit	1.05	1.15	0.99	0.91	0.85	0.65	0.79	0.83	0.90	0.90	52. Bénéfices mis en réserve
% of gross income											**% du total du résultat brut**
53. Net interest income	94.05	94.68	94.29	94.96	94.70	92.76	92.36	94.64	92.47	88.44	53. Produits financiers nets
54. Non-interest income (net)	4.76	5.32	5.71	5.88	5.30	7.24	7.64	5.36	7.53	11.56	54. Produits non financiers (nets)
a. Fees and commissions receivable	*3.57*	*4.26*	*5.71*	*5.88*	*8.33*	*9.87*	*11.46*	*11.90*	*13.44*	*15.08*	*a. Frais et commissions à recevoir*
b. Fees and commissions payable	*1.19*	*2.13*	*1.90*	*1.68*	*2.27*	*1.97*	*2.55*	*2.38*	*3.23*	*3.52*	*b. Frais et commissions à payer*
c. Net profits or loss on financial operations	-	*1.06*	-	-	*-0.76*	*1.32*	*0.64*	-	*2.15*	*4.02*	*c. Profits ou pertes nets sur opérations financières*
d. Other	*2.38*	*2.13*	*1.90*	*0.84*	*-0.76*	*-1.32*	*-1.91*	*-3.57*	*-4.84*	*-4.02*	*d. Autres*
55. Operating expenses	60.71	60.64	61.90	62.18	62.12	59.87	61.15	61.31	60.22	61.81	55. Frais d'exploitation
a. Staff costs	*39.29*	*37.23*	*37.14*	*36.97*	*36.36*	*34.21*	*35.67*	*35.71*	*34.95*	*35.18*	*a. Dépenses en personnel*
b. Property costs	*21.43*	*22.34*	*23.81*	*24.37*	*25.76*	*25.00*	*24.20*	*25.00*	*24.73*	*25.63*	*b. Dépenses en immobilier*
c. Other	*1.19*	*1.06*	*0.95*	*0.84*	*0.76*	*0.66*	*0.64*	*0.60*	*0.54*	*0.50*	*c. Autres*
56. Net income	38.10	39.36	38.10	37.82	37.88	40.13	38.85	39.29	39.78	38.19	56. Résultat net
57. Provisions (net)	10.71	7.45	9.52	9.24	9.85	17.76	12.74	8.93	7.53	5.03	57. Provisions (nettes)
a. Provisions on loans	*9.52*	*6.38*	*6.67*	*7.56*	*10.61*	*19.08*	*10.83*	*11.31*	*9.68*	*7.54*	*a. Provisions sur prêts*
b. Provisions on securities	-	*1.06*	*1.90*	*0.84*	*0.76*	-	*3.18*	-	-	-	*b. Provisions sur titres*
c. Other	*1.19*	*1.06*	-	*0.84*	*-0.76*	*-1.32*	*-1.27*	*-2.98*	*-2.15*	*-2.51*	*c. Autres*
58. Profit before tax	28.57	31.91	29.52	28.57	28.03	22.37	26.11	30.36	32.26	33.17	58. Bénéfices avant impôt
59. Income tax	2.38	3.19	2.86	4.20	4.55	3.95	3.82	4.76	5.38	5.53	59. Impôt sur le revenu
60. Profit after tax	26.19	28.72	25.71	24.37	23.48	18.42	22.29	25.00	26.88	27.64	60. Bénéfices après impôt
% of net income											**% du total du résultat net**
61. Provisions (net)	28.13	18.92	25.00	24.44	26.00	44.26	32.79	22.73	18.92	13.16	61. Provisions (nettes)
a. Provisions on loans	*25.00*	*16.22*	*17.50*	*20.00*	*28.00*	*47.54*	*27.87*	*28.79*	*24.32*	*19.74*	*a. Provisions sur prêts*
b. Provisions on securities	-	*2.70*	*5.00*	*2.22*	*2.00*	-	*8.20*	-	-	-	*b. Provisions sur titres*
c. Other	*3.13*	*2.70*	-	*2.22*	*-2.00*	*-3.28*	*-3.28*	*-7.58*	*-5.41*	*-6.58*	*c. Autres*
62. Profit before tax	75.00	81.08	77.50	75.56	74.00	55.74	67.21	77.27	81.08	86.84	62. Bénéfices avant impôt
63. Income tax	6.25	8.11	7.50	11.11	12.00	9.84	9.84	12.12	13.51	14.47	63. Impôt sur le revenu
64. Profit after tax	68.75	72.97	67.50	64.44	62.00	45.90	57.38	63.64	67.57	72.37	64. Bénéfices après impôt

SPAIN / ESPAGNE

Co-operative banks / Banques mutualistes

	1988	1989	1990	1991	1992	1993	1994	1995	1996	1997	
Per cent											*Pourcentage*
BALANCE SHEET ANALYSIS											**ANALYSE DU BILAN**
% of year-end balance sheet total											**% du total du bilan en fin d'exercice**
Assets											**Actif**
65. Cash & balance with Central bank	12.35	14.02	13.12	11.25	8.47	6.60	5.76	4.83	4.09	3.54	65. Caisse & solde auprès de la Banque centrale
66. Interbank deposits	23.15	21.34	24.93	26.03	27.33	33.87	26.33	27.07	25.47	23.49	66. Dépôts interbancaires
67. Loans	42.12	44.35	44.39	46.71	50.10	47.17	49.18	49.04	51.33	56.03	67. Prêts
68. Securities	15.51	13.69	10.98	9.55	7.92	6.43	12.23	13.28	13.35	11.79	68. Valeurs mobilières
69. Other assets	6.86	6.60	6.63	6.45	6.18	5.90	6.50	5.75	5.76	5.14	69. Autres actifs
Liabilities											**Passif**
70. Capital & reserves	10.80	11.31	11.41	11.42	11.44	11.46	11.63	11.10	11.38	11.72	70. Capital et réserves
71. Borrowing from Central bank	-	-	-	-	-	1.07	2.09	1.54	1.41	0.95	71. Emprunts auprès de la Banque centrale
72. Interbank deposits	5.85	4.82	5.46	4.42	4.91	3.99	3.73	4.14	4.51	6.21	72. Dépôts interbancaires
73. Non-bank deposits	78.16	79.32	78.78	80.21	81.06	80.90	80.58	80.48	80.08	79.56	73. Dépôts non bancaires
74. Bonds	0.54	0.06	0.05	-	-	-	-	-	-	-	74. Obligations
75. Other liabilities	4.65	4.43	4.34	3.95	2.59	2.55	1.97	2.77	2.61	1.54	75. Autres engagements
Memorandum items											***Pour mémoire***
76. Short-term securities	*8.05*	*7.76*	*6.88*	*5.99*	*3.90*	*2.95*	*3.52*	*3.72*	*2.68*	*1.98*	*76. Titres à court terme*
77. Bonds	*6.98*	*5.49*	*3.46*	*2.97*	*3.32*	*2.71*	*7.81*	*8.09*	*8.79*	*8.38*	*77. Obligations*
78. Shares and participations	*0.48*	*0.44*	*0.63*	*0.64*	*0.70*	*0.77*	*0.89*	*1.49*	*1.90*	*1.43*	*78. Actions et participations*
79. Claims on non-residents	*0.06*	*0.06*	*0.05*	*0.08*	*0.58*	*0.90*	*0.92*	*0.33*	*0.56*	*0.38*	*79. Créances sur des non-résidents*
80. Liabilities to non-residents	*0.30*	*0.33*	*0.44*	*0.51*	*0.58*	*0.67*	*0.69*	*0.67*	*0.76*	*0.84*	*80. Engagements envers des non-résidents*

* See notes on previous pages.

* Voir les notes en pages précédentes.

Commercial banks — Banques commerciales

Million Swedish kroner	1988	1989	1990	1991	1992	1993	1994	1995	1996	1997	Millions de couronnes suédoises
INCOME STATEMENT											**COMPTE DE RESULTATS**
1. Interest income	70837	97962	130929	131201	122619	123005	101973	122322	106585	95113	1. Produits financiers
2. Interest expenses	51467	76559	105873	104914	96190	85426	66498	83939	71623	63943	2. Frais financiers
3. Net interest income	19370	21403	25056	26287	26429	37579	35475	38383	34962	31170	3. Produits financiers nets
4. Non-interest income (net)	7825	8565	8899	8848	17704	43796	20540	21246	26222	28461	4. Produits non financiers (nets)
a. Fees and commissions receivable	..	..	..	..	..	..	..	..	*14547*	*17973*	*a. Frais et commissions à recevoir*
b. Fees and commissions payable	..	..	..	..	..	..	..	..	*2254*	*2809*	*b. Frais et commissions à payer*
c. Net profits or loss on financial operations	..	..	..	..	..	..	..	..	*9415*	*2819*	*c. Profits ou pertes nets sur opérations financières*
d. Other	..	..	..	..	..	..	..	..	*4514*	*10478*	*d. Autres*
5. Gross income	27195	29968	33955	35135	44133	81375	56015	59629	61184	59630	5. Résultat brut
6. Operating expenses	15112	16736	26568	42353	64668	89359	45428	42665	39361	47203	6. Frais d'exploitation
a. Staff costs	*6254*	*7016*	*8308*	*9242*	*10442*	*13327*	*14117*	*16581*	*17442*	*18806*	*a. Dépenses en personnel*
b. Property costs	..	..	..	*341*	*181*	*440*	*512*	*499*	..	..	*b. Dépenses en immobilier*
c. Other	..	..	..	*32770*	*54045*	*75592*	*30799*	*25585*	..	..	*c. Autres*
7. Net income	12083	13232	7387	-7218	-20535	-7984	10587	16964	21823	12427	7. Résultat net
8. Provisions (net)	7397	8582	4786	-42895	-23564	-10050	-2948	-2026	94	649	8. Provisions (nettes)
a. Provisions on loans	*7602*	*3319*	*5680*	*-47814*	..	..	..	..	..	..	*a. Provisions sur prêts*
b. Provisions on securities	-	*5482*	*1154*	*-9236*	..	..	..	..	..	..	*b. Provisions sur titres*
c. Other	*-205*	*-219*	*-2048*	*14155*	..	..	..	..	..	..	*c. Autres*
9. Profit before tax	4686	4650	2601	35677	3029	2066	13535	18990	21729	11777	9. Bénéfices avant impôt
10. Income tax	2507	833	647	10576	510	1482	2120	3668	5004	3527	10. Impôt sur le revenu
11. Profit after tax	2179	3817	1954	25101	2519	584	11415	15322	16725	8250	11. Bénéfices après impôt
12. Distributed profit	1873	2082	2014	2014	1727	23	1076	4545	17356	6040	12. Bénéfices distribués
13. Retained profit	306	1735	-60	23087	792	561	10339	10777	-631	2210	13. Bénéfices mis en réserve
BALANCE SHEET											**BILAN**
Assets											**Actif**
14. Cash & balance with Central bank	21016	20754	29467	13756	20577	21982	7566	9192	18476	15128	14. Caisse & solde auprès de la Banque centrale
15. Interbank deposits	179948	189095	237934	194122	112209	127046	133139	219714	331813	400198	15. Dépôts interbancaires
16. Loans	450616	579838	676529	625661	670191	690861	644503	635926	650554	718030	16. Prêts
17. Securities	106185	125842	147546	316226	272689	431645	486676	520098	532871	635375	17. Valeurs mobilières
18. Other assets	77240	104792	173158	57982	77890	82295	72731	74429	196668	218265	18. Autres actifs
Liabilities											**Passif**
19. Capital & reserves	56944	65273	71307	65386	52898	73313	72486	86006	84965	105631	19. Capital et réserves
20. Borrowing from Central bank	19033	19946	14517	31415	60279	644	8	256	9563	31146	20. Emprunts auprès de la Banque centrale
21. Interbank deposits	314540	399495	526730	408906	300599	298288	294934	341201	419539	466468	21. Dépôts interbancaires
22. Non-bank deposits	325616	372914	440738	503993	535982	717766	731913	754923	788295	860671	22. Dépôts non bancaires
23. Bonds	39335	56383	85724	76723	89829	112966	107374	88391	161975	231892	23. Obligations
24. Other liabilities	79535	106310	125616	121325	113968	150854	137900	188582	266046	291188	24. Autres engagements
Balance sheet total											**Total du bilan**
25. End-year total	835005	1020321	1264632	1207745	1153554	1353830	1344615	1459359	1730382	1986996	25. En fin d'exercice
26. Average total	794416	994864	1202580	1254792	1209533	1383064	1383358	1431405	1670222	1897439	26. Moyen

SWEDEN
Commercial banks

SUEDE
Banques commerciales

	1988	1989	1990	1991	1992	1993	1994	1995	1996	1997	
Million Swedish kroner											*Millions de couronnes suédoises*
Memorandum items											***Pour mémoire***
27. Short-term securities	*2566*	*3705*	*9720*	*21402*	*136911*	*145151*	*153025*	*132114*	*91922*	*49841*	*27. Titres à court terme*
28. Bonds	*92876*	*108179*	*112899*	*86868*	*77073*	*156453*	*203784*	*262578*	*184562*	*136203*	*28. Obligations*
29. Shares and participations	*8386*	*13624*	*25071*	*35877*	*27575*	*39675*	*36584*	*42527*	*48542*	*68864*	*29. Actions et participations*
30. Claims on non-residents	*35366*	*65010*	*104230*	*303815*	*360649*	*380901*	*341671*	*482088*	*589093*	*595427*	*30. Créances sur des non-résidents*
31. Liabilities to non-residents	*50483*	*68976*	*103509*	*646684*	*563031*	*616819*	*568206*	*612010*	*668431*	*736462*	*31. Engagements envers des non-résidents*
Capital adequacy											***Solvabilité***
32. Tier 1 Capital	..	..	..	*58118*	*46540*	*68476*	*70224*	*82887*	*79975*	*86943*	*32. Fonds propres de base*
33. Tier 2 Capital (1)	..	..	..	*29195*	*28617*	*42747*	*42920*	*43152*	*46689*	*57976*	*33. Fonds propres complémentaires (1)*
34. Supervisory deductions	..	..	..	*446*	*1098*	*1331*	*1978*	*2303*	*4562*	*16349*	*34. Eléments à déduire des fonds propres*
35. Total net capital resources	..	..	..	*86867*	*74059*	*109892*	*111166*	*123736*	*122103*	*128570*	*35. Total net des ressources en capital*
36. Risk-weighted assets	..	..	..	*632179*	*693748*	*735779*	*671509*	*644835*	*749638*	*822877*	*36. Actifs pondérés des risques*
SUPPLEMENTARY INFORMATION											**RENSEIGNEMENTS COMPLEMENTAIRES**
37. Number of institutions	14	14	12	9	8	9	10	13	15	15	37. Nombre d'institutions
38. Number of branches	1394	1376	1345	1288	1872	2474	2327	2239	2202	2165	38. Nombre de succursales
39. Number of employees (x 1000)	25.4	25.4	25.0	25.1	28.4	37.2	39.1	39.0	39.0	39.2	39. Nombre de salariés (x 1000)

1. Beginning 1997, Tier 2 Capital (item 33) includes Tier 3 Capital.

Notes

- Average balance sheet totals (item 26) are based on thirteen end-month data.

Change in methodology

- For the year 1991, the Föreningsbankernas Bank is exceptionally included under Co-operative banks and not under Commercial banks.
- As from 1992, Co-operative banks, which merged into one single commercial bank, are included under Commercial banks.
- As from 1993, Commercial banks include what was formerly the largest savings bank.

1. A partir de 1997, les données de la rubrique Fonds propres complémentaires (poste 33) incluent les fonds propres surcomplémentaires.

Notes

- La moyenne du total des actifs/passifs (poste 26) est basée sur treize données de fin de mois.

Changement méthodologique

- Pour l'année 1991, la Föreningsbankernas Bank est comprise exceptionnellement dans les Banques mutualistes et non pas dans les Banques commerciales.
- Depuis 1992, les Banques mutualistes, ayant fusionnées en une seule banque commerciale, sont classées dans les données concernant les Banques commerciales.
- Depuis 1993, les Banques commerciales incluent ce qui était précedément la caisse d'épargne la plus grande.

SWEDEN
Commercial banks

SUEDE
Banques commerciales

	1988	1989	1990	1991	1992	1993	1994	1995	1996	1997	
Per cent											*Pourcentage*
INCOME STATEMENT ANALYSIS											**ANALYSE DU COMPTE DE RESULTATS**
% of average balance sheet total											**% du total moyen du bilan**
40. Interest income	8.92	9.85	10.89	10.46	10.14	8.89	7.37	8.55	6.38	5.01	40. Produits financiers
41. Interest expenses	6.48	7.70	8.80	8.36	7.95	6.18	4.81	5.86	4.29	3.37	41. Frais financiers
42. Net interest income	2.44	2.15	2.08	2.09	2.19	2.72	2.56	2.68	2.09	1.64	42. Produits financiers nets
43. Non-interest income (net)	0.99	0.86	0.74	0.71	1.46	3.17	1.48	1.48	1.57	1.50	43. Produits non financiers (nets)
a. Fees and commissions receivable	..	..	..	..	..	..	..	..	*0.87*	*0.95*	*a. Frais et commissions à recevoir*
b. Fees and commissions payable	..	..	..	..	..	..	..	..	*0.13*	*0.15*	*b. Frais et commissions à payer*
c. Net profits or loss on financial operations	..	..	..	..	..	..	..	..	*0.56*	*0.15*	*c. Profits ou pertes nets sur opérations financières*
d. Other	..	..	..	..	..	..	..	..	*0.27*	*0.55*	*d. Autres*
44. Gross income	3.42	3.01	2.82	2.80	3.65	5.88	4.05	4.17	3.66	3.14	44. Résultat brut
45. Operating expenses	1.90	1.68	2.21	3.38	5.35	6.46	3.28	2.98	2.36	2.49	45. Frais d'exploitation
a. Staff costs	*0.79*	*0.71*	*0.69*	*0.74*	*0.86*	*0.96*	*1.02*	*1.16*	*1.04*	*0.99*	*a. Dépenses en personnel*
b. Property costs	..	..	..	*0.03*	*0.01*	*0.03*	*0.04*	*0.03*	..	..	*b. Dépenses en immobilier*
c. Other	..	..	..	*2.61*	*4.47*	*5.47*	*2.23*	*1.79*	..	..	*c. Autres*
46. Net income	1.52	1.33	0.61	-0.58	-1.70	-0.58	0.77	1.19	1.31	0.65	46. Résultat net
47. Provisions (net)	0.93	0.86	0.40	-3.42	-1.95	-0.73	-0.21	-0.14	0.01	0.03	47. Provisions (nettes)
a. Provisions on loans	*0.96*	*0.33*	*0.47*	*-3.81*	..	..	..	..	..	..	*a. Provisions sur prêts*
b. Provisions on securities	-	*0.55*	*0.10*	*-0.74*	..	..	..	..	..	..	*b. Provisions sur titres*
c. Other	*-0.03*	*-0.02*	*-0.17*	*1.13*	..	..	..	..	..	..	*c. Autres*
48. Profit before tax	0.59	0.47	0.22	2.84	0.25	0.15	0.98	1.33	1.30	0.62	48. Bénéfices avant impôt
49. Income tax	0.32	0.08	0.05	0.84	0.04	0.11	0.15	0.26	0.30	0.19	49. Impôt sur le revenu
50. Profit after tax	0.27	0.38	0.16	2.00	0.21	0.04	0.83	1.07	1.00	0.43	50. Bénéfices après impôt
51. Distributed profit	0.24	0.21	0.17	0.16	0.14	-	0.08	0.32	1.04	0.32	51. Bénéfices distribués
52. Retained profit	0.04	0.17	-	1.84	0.07	0.04	0.75	0.75	-0.04	0.12	52. Bénéfices mis en réserve
% of gross income											**% du total du résultat brut**
53. Net interest income	71.23	71.42	73.79	74.82	59.88	46.18	63.33	64.37	57.14	52.27	53. Produits financiers nets
54. Non-interest income (net)	28.77	28.58	26.21	25.18	40.12	53.82	36.67	35.63	42.86	47.73	54. Produits non financiers (nets)
a. Fees and commissions receivable	..	..	..	..	..	..	..	..	*23.78*	*30.14*	*a. Frais et commissions à recevoir*
b. Fees and commissions payable	..	..	..	..	..	..	..	..	*3.68*	*4.71*	*b. Frais et commissions à payer*
c. Net profits or loss on financial operations	..	..	..	..	..	..	..	..	*15.39*	*4.73*	*c. Profits ou pertes nets sur opérations financières*
d. Other	..	..	..	..	..	..	..	..	*7.38*	*17.57*	*d. Autres*
55. Operating expenses	55.57	55.85	78.24	120.54	146.53	109.81	81.10	71.55	64.33	79.16	55. Frais d'exploitation
a. Staff costs	*23.00*	*23.41*	*24.47*	*26.30*	*23.66*	*16.38*	*25.20*	*27.81*	*28.51*	*31.54*	*a. Dépenses en personnel*
b. Property costs	..	..	..	*0.97*	*0.41*	*0.54*	*0.91*	*0.84*	..	..	*b. Dépenses en immobilier*
c. Other	..	..	..	*93.27*	*122.46*	*92.89*	*54.98*	*42.91*	..	..	*c. Autres*
56. Net income	44.43	44.15	21.76	-20.54	-46.53	-9.81	18.90	28.45	35.67	20.84	56. Résultat net
57. Provisions (net)	27.20	28.64	14.10	-122.09	-53.39	-12.35	-5.26	-3.40	0.15	1.09	57. Provisions (nettes)
a. Provisions on loans	*27.95*	*11.08*	*16.73*	*-136.09*	..	..	..	..	..	..	*a. Provisions sur prêts*
b. Provisions on securities	-	*18.29*	*3.40*	*-26.29*	..	..	..	..	..	..	*b. Provisions sur titres*
c. Other	*-0.75*	*-0.73*	*-6.03*	*40.29*	..	..	..	..	..	..	*c. Autres*
58. Profit before tax	17.23	15.52	7.66	101.54	6.86	2.54	24.16	31.85	35.51	19.75	58. Bénéfices avant impôt
59. Income tax	9.22	2.78	1.91	30.10	1.16	1.82	3.78	6.15	8.18	5.91	59. Impôt sur le revenu
60. Profit after tax	8.01	12.74	5.75	71.44	5.71	0.72	20.38	25.70	27.34	13.84	60. Bénéfices après impôt
% of net income											**% du total du résultat net**
61. Provisions (net)	61.22	64.86	64.79	..	114.75	125.88	-27.85	-11.94	0.43	5.22	61. Provisions (nettes)
a. Provisions on loans	*62.91*	*25.08*	*76.89*	..	..	..	..	..	..	..	*a. Provisions sur prêts*
b. Provisions on securities	-	*41.43*	*15.62*	..	..	..	..	..	..	..	*b. Provisions sur titres*
c. Other	*-1.70*	*-1.66*	*-27.72*	..	..	..	..	..	..	..	*c. Autres*
62. Profit before tax	38.78	35.14	35.21	..	-14.75	-25.88	127.85	111.94	99.57	94.77	62. Bénéfices avant impôt
63. Income tax	20.75	6.30	8.76	..	-2.48	-18.56	20.02	21.62	22.93	28.38	63. Impôt sur le revenu
64. Profit after tax	18.03	28.85	26.45	..	-12.27	-7.31	107.82	90.32	76.64	66.39	64. Bénéfices après impôt

SWEDEN

Commercial banks

SUEDE

Banques commerciales

	1988	1989	1990	1991	1992	1993	1994	1995	1996	1997	
Per cent											*Pourcentage*
BALANCE SHEET ANALYSIS											**ANALYSE DU BILAN**
% of year-end balance sheet total											**% du total du bilan en fin d'exercice**
Assets											**Actif**
65. Cash & balance with Central bank	2.52	2.03	2.33	1.14	1.78	1.62	0.56	0.63	1.07	0.76	65. Caisse & solde auprès de la Banque centrale
66. Interbank deposits	21.55	18.53	18.81	16.07	9.73	9.38	9.90	15.06	19.18	20.14	66. Dépôts interbancaires
67. Loans	53.97	56.83	53.50	51.80	58.10	51.03	47.93	43.58	37.60	36.14	67. Prêts
68. Securities	12.72	12.33	11.67	26.18	23.64	31.88	36.19	35.64	30.79	31.98	68. Valeurs mobilières
69. Other assets	9.25	10.27	13.69	4.80	6.75	6.08	5.41	5.10	11.37	10.98	69. Autres actifs
Liabilities											**Passif**
70. Capital & reserves	6.82	6.40	5.64	5.41	4.59	5.42	5.39	5.89	4.91	5.32	70. Capital et réserves
71. Borrowing from Central bank	2.28	1.95	1.15	2.60	5.23	0.05	-	0.02	0.55	1.57	71. Emprunts auprès de la Banque centrale
72. Interbank deposits	37.67	39.15	41.65	33.86	26.06	22.03	21.93	23.38	24.25	23.48	72. Dépôts interbancaires
73. Non-bank deposits	39.00	36.55	34.85	41.73	46.46	53.02	54.43	51.73	45.56	43.32	73. Dépôts non bancaires
74. Bonds	4.71	5.53	6.78	6.35	7.79	8.34	7.99	6.06	9.36	11.67	74. Obligations
75. Other liabilities	9.53	10.42	9.93	10.05	9.88	11.14	10.26	12.92	15.37	14.65	75. Autres engagements
Memorandum items											***Pour mémoire***
76. Short-term securities	*0.31*	*0.36*	*0.77*	*1.77*	*11.87*	*10.72*	*11.38*	*9.05*	*5.31*	*2.51*	*76. Titres à court terme*
77. Bonds	*11.12*	*10.60*	*8.93*	*7.19*	*6.68*	*11.56*	*15.16*	*17.99*	*10.67*	*6.85*	*77. Obligations*
78. Shares and participations	*1.00*	*1.34*	*1.98*	*2.97*	*2.39*	*2.93*	*2.72*	*2.91*	*2.81*	*3.47*	*78. Actions et participations*
79. Claims on non-residents	*4.24*	*6.37*	*8.24*	*25.16*	*31.26*	*28.14*	*25.41*	*33.03*	*34.04*	*29.97*	*79. Créances sur des non-résidents*
80. Liabilities to non-residents	*6.05*	*6.76*	*8.18*	*53.54*	*48.81*	*45.56*	*42.26*	*41.94*	*38.63*	*37.06*	*80. Engagements envers des non-résidents*

* See notes on previous pages.

* Voir les notes en pages précédentes.

SWEDEN / SUEDE

Foreign commercial banks / Banques commerciales étrangères

	1988	1989	1990	1991	1992	1993	1994	1995	1996	1997	
Million Swedish kroner											*Millions de couronnes suédoises*
INCOME STATEMENT											**COMPTE DE RESULTATS**
1. Interest income	1591	2708	2959	2440	2541	2296	1680	3610	4169	5452	1. Produits financiers
2. Interest expenses	1462	2562	2722	2273	2454	1978	1390	3240	3330	3873	2. Frais financiers
3. Net interest income	129	146	237	167	87	318	290	370	839	1579	3. Produits financiers nets
4. Non-interest income (net)	80	96	121	231	451	1394	127	100	428	947	4. Produits non financiers (nets)
a. Fees and commissions receivable	..	..	..	..	..	..	..	..	*192*	*501*	*a. Frais et commissions à recevoir*
b. Fees and commissions payable	..	..	..	..	..	..	..	..	*34*	*101*	*b. Frais et commissions à payer*
c. Net profits or loss on financial operations	..	..	..	..	..	..	..	..	*67*	*399*	*c. Profits ou pertes nets sur opérations financières*
d. Other	..	..	..	..	..	..	..	..	*204*	*149*	*d. Autres*
5. Gross income	209	242	358	398	538	1712	417	470	1267	2527	5. Résultat brut
6. Operating expenses	231	319	464	867	1369	538	316	639	1186	2210	6. Frais d'exploitation
a. Staff costs	*136*	*130*	*148*	*161*	*171*	*172*	*152*	*268*	*293*	*677*	*a. Dépenses en personnel*
b. Property costs	..	..	..	*1*	*1*	*4*	*2*	*2*	..	..	*b. Dépenses en immobilier*
c. Other	..	..	..	*705*	*1197*	*362*	*162*	*369*	..	..	*c. Autres*
7. Net income	-22	-77	-106	-469	-831	1174	101	-169	81	317	7. Résultat net
8. Provisions (net)	4	5	-38	-5	157	143	3	-74	85	108	8. Provisions (nettes)
a. Provisions on loans	*8*	*3*	*-6*	*13*	..	..	..	..	..	..	*a. Provisions sur prêts*
b. Provisions on securities	*4*	*10*	*-1*	*23*	..	..	..	..	..	..	*b. Provisions sur titres*
c. Other	*-8*	*-8*	*-31*	*-41*	..	..	..	..	..	..	*c. Autres*
9. Profit before tax	-26	-82	-68	-464	-988	1031	98	-95	-4	208	9. Bénéfices avant impôt
10. Income tax	1	-	-	1	42	35	19	1	-	46	10. Impôt sur le revenu
11. Profit after tax	-27	-82	-68	-465	-1030	996	79	-96	-4	162	11. Bénéfices après impôt
12. Distributed profit	4	-	-	5	8	95	135	-	65	92	12. Bénéfices distribués
13. Retained profit	-31	-82	-68	-470	-1038	901	-56	-96	-69	70	13. Bénéfices mis en réserve
BALANCE SHEET											**BILAN**
Assets											**Actif**
14. Cash & balance with Central bank	57	116	209	50	2794	147	1023	19	25	276	14. Caisse & solde auprès de la Banque centrale
15. Interbank deposits	8175	8963	6380	3959	6362	9651	10463	14015	18139	16786	15. Dépôts interbancaires
16. Loans	15337	18091	15564	13108	15732	11967	13416	15293	17333	44786	16. Prêts
17. Securities	1086	1744	580	3033	5111	6136	9271	13770	14477	14197	17. Valeurs mobilières
18. Other assets	2834	3633	2252	640	1991	1101	3490	6759	6313	8193	18. Autres actifs
Liabilities											**Passif**
19. Capital & reserves	942	890	835	528	664	1647	1401	1096	1175	3207	19. Capital et réserves
20. Borrowing from Central bank	326	603	377	169	5	-	7	3	961	3	20. Emprunts auprès de la Banque centrale
21. Interbank deposits	23726	28240	20687	16778	26951	22573	29637	39318	38456	44842	21. Dépôts interbancaires
22. Non-bank deposits	1383	1145	1517	2024	2916	3223	3996	4094	11272	26560	22. Dépôts non bancaires
23. Bonds	361	582	599	443	493	252	184	169	107	761	23. Obligations
24. Other liabilities	753	1086	970	850	960	1305	2438	5177	4316	8865	24. Autres engagements
Balance sheet total											**Total du bilan**
25. End-year total	27491	32547	24986	20793	31989	29000	37662	49857	56286	84239	25. En fin d'exercice
26. Average total	28052	28568	25507	23931	25834	31936	30835	44586	58078	77155	26. Moyen

SWEDEN
Foreign commercial banks

SUEDE
Banques commerciales étrangères

	1988	1989	1990	1991	1992	1993	1994	1995	1996	1997	
Million Swedish kroner											*Millions de couronnes suédoises*
Memorandum items											**Pour mémoire**
27. Short-term securities	*230*	*141*	*202*	*1961*	*10260*	*7393*	*10323*	*11655*	*7294*	*2902*	*27. Titres à court terme*
28. Bonds	*873*	*1515*	*140*	*90*	*100*	*606*	*1069*	*3705*	*1270*	*1098*	*28. Obligations*
29. Shares and participations	*17*	*132*	*117*	*12*	*4*	*5*	*4*	*15*	*2955*	*4530*	*29. Actions et participations*
30. Claims on non-residents	*1612*	*3582*	*2907*	*5769*	*6736*	*11612*	*8145*	*13307*	*16349*	*10118*	*30. Créances sur des non-résidents*
31. Liabilities to non-residents	*486*	*396*	*524*	*17898*	*27839*	*23285*	*26114*	*35970*	*32339*	*19765*	*31. Engagements envers des non-résidents*
Capital adequacy											**Solvabilité**
32. Tier 1 Capital	..	..	..	*544*	*1386*	*1429*	*789*	*763*	*1519*	*2323*	*32. Fonds propres de base*
33. Tier 2 Capital	..	..	..	*169*	*193*	*167*	*149*	-	-	*251*	*33. Fonds propres complémentaires*
34. Supervisory deductions	..	..	..	-	-	-	-	-	-	-	*34. Eléments à déduire des fonds propres*
35. Total net capital resources	..	..	..	*713*	*1579*	*1596*	*938*	*763*	*1519*	*2574*	*35. Total net des ressources en capital*
36. Risk-weighted assets	..	..	..	*9758*	*17619*	*11912*	*4946*	*2590*	*3846*	*10123*	*36. Actifs pondérés des risques*
SUPPLEMENTARY INFORMATION											**RENSEIGNEMENTS COMPLEMENTAIRES**
37. Number of institutions	10	9	9	8	8	8	12	13	21	22	37. Nombre d'institutions
38. Number of branches	1	-	-	-	10	10	11	13	21	54	38. Nombre de succursales
39. Number of employees (x 1000)	0.4	0.3	0.3	0.3	0.3	0.3	0.3	0.3	0.4	0.9	39. Nombre de salariés (x 1000)

Notes

- Average balance sheet totals (item 26) are based on thirteen end-month data.

Notes

- La moyenne du total des actifs/passifs (poste 26) est basée sur treize données de fin de mois.

Foreign commercial banks / Banques commerciales étrangères

	1988	1989	1990	1991	1992	1993	1994	1995	1996	1997	
Per cent											*Pourcentage*
INCOME STATEMENT ANALYSIS											**ANALYSE DU COMPTE DE RESULTATS**
% of average balance sheet total											**% du total moyen du bilan**
40. Interest income	5.67	9.48	11.60	10.20	9.84	7.19	5.45	8.10	7.18	7.07	40. Produits financiers
41. Interest expenses	5.21	8.97	10.67	9.50	9.50	6.19	4.51	7.27	5.73	5.02	41. Frais financiers
42. Net interest income	0.46	0.51	0.93	0.70	0.34	1.00	0.94	0.83	1.44	2.05	42. Produits financiers nets
43. Non-interest income (net)	0.29	0.34	0.47	0.97	1.75	4.36	0.41	0.22	0.74	1.23	43. Produits non financiers (nets)
a. Fees and commissions receivable	..	..	..	..	..	..	..	..	*0.33*	*0.65*	*a. Frais et commissions à recevoir*
b. Fees and commissions payable	..	..	..	..	..	..	..	..	*0.06*	*0.13*	*b. Frais et commissions à payer*
c. Net profits or loss on financial operations	..	..	..	..	..	..	..	..	*0.12*	*0.52*	*c. Profits ou pertes nets sur opérations financières*
d. Other	..	..	..	..	..	..	..	..	*0.35*	*0.19*	*d. Autres*
44. Gross income	0.75	0.85	1.40	1.66	2.08	5.36	1.35	1.05	2.18	3.28	44. Résultat brut
45. Operating expenses	0.82	1.12	1.82	3.62	5.30	1.68	1.02	1.43	2.04	2.86	45. Frais d'exploitation
a. Staff costs	*0.48*	*0.46*	*0.58*	*0.67*	*0.66*	*0.54*	*0.49*	*0.60*	*0.50*	*0.88*	*a. Dépenses en personnel*
b. Property costs	..	..	..	-	-	*0.01*	*0.01*	-	..	..	*b. Dépenses en immobilier*
c. Other	..	..	..	*2.95*	*4.63*	*1.13*	*0.53*	*0.83*	..	..	*c. Autres*
46. Net income	-0.08	-0.27	-0.42	-1.96	-3.22	3.68	0.33	-0.38	0.14	0.41	46. Résultat net
47. Provisions (net)	0.01	0.02	-0.15	-0.02	0.61	0.45	0.01	-0.17	0.15	0.14	47. Provisions (nettes)
a. Provisions on loans	*0.03*	*0.01*	*-0.02*	*0.05*	..	..	..	..	..	..	*a. Provisions sur prêts*
b. Provisions on securities	*0.01*	*0.04*	-	*0.10*	..	..	..	..	..	..	*b. Provisions sur titres*
c. Other	*-0.03*	*-0.03*	*-0.12*	*-0.17*	..	..	..	..	..	..	*c. Autres*
48. Profit before tax	-0.09	-0.29	-0.27	-1.94	-3.82	3.23	0.32	-0.21	-0.01	0.27	48. Bénéfices avant impôt
49. Income tax	-	-	-	-	0.16	0.11	0.06	-	-	0.06	49. Impôt sur le revenu
50. Profit after tax	-0.10	-0.29	-0.27	-1.94	-3.99	3.12	0.26	-0.22	-0.01	0.21	50. Bénéfices après impôt
51. Distributed profit	0.01	-	-	0.02	0.03	0.30	0.44	-	0.11	0.12	51. Bénéfices distribués
52. Retained profit	-0.11	-0.29	-0.27	-1.96	-4.02	2.82	-0.18	-0.22	-0.12	0.09	52. Bénéfices mis en réserve
% of gross income											**% du total du résultat brut**
53. Net interest income	61.72	60.33	66.20	41.96	16.17	18.57	69.54	78.72	66.22	62.49	53. Produits financiers nets
54. Non-interest income (net)	38.28	39.67	33.80	58.04	83.83	81.43	30.46	21.28	33.78	37.48	54. Produits non financiers (nets)
a. Fees and commissions receivable	..	..	..	..	..	..	..	..	*15.15*	*19.83*	*a. Frais et commissions à recevoir*
b. Fees and commissions payable	..	..	..	..	..	..	..	..	*2.68*	*4.00*	*b. Frais et commissions à payer*
c. Net profits or loss on financial operations	..	..	..	..	..	..	..	..	*5.29*	*15.79*	*c. Profits ou pertes nets sur opérations financières*
d. Other	..	..	..	..	..	..	..	..	*16.10*	*5.90*	*d. Autres*
55. Operating expenses	110.53	131.82	129.61	217.84	254.46	31.43	75.78	135.96	93.61	87.46	55. Frais d'exploitation
a. Staff costs	*65.07*	*53.72*	*41.34*	*40.45*	*31.78*	*10.05*	*36.45*	*57.02*	*23.13*	*26.79*	*a. Dépenses en personnel*
b. Property costs	..	..	..	*0.25*	*0.19*	*0.23*	*0.48*	*0.43*	..	..	*b. Dépenses en immobilier*
c. Other	..	..	..	*177.14*	*222.49*	*21.14*	*38.85*	*78.51*	..	..	*c. Autres*
56. Net income	-10.53	-31.82	-29.61	-117.84	-154.46	68.57	24.22	-35.96	6.39	12.54	56. Résultat net
57. Provisions (net)	1.91	2.07	-10.61	-1.26	29.18	8.35	0.72	-15.74	6.71	4.27	57. Provisions (nettes)
a. Provisions on loans	*3.83*	*1.24*	*-1.68*	*3.27*	..	..	..	..	..	..	*a. Provisions sur prêts*
b. Provisions on securities	*1.91*	*4.13*	*-0.28*	*5.78*	..	..	..	..	..	..	*b. Provisions sur titres*
c. Other	*-3.83*	*-3.31*	*-8.66*	*-10.30*	..	..	..	..	..	..	*c. Autres*
58. Profit before tax	-12.44	-33.88	-18.99	-116.58	-183.64	60.22	23.50	-20.21	-0.32	8.23	58. Bénéfices avant impôt
59. Income tax	0.48	-	-	0.25	7.81	2.04	4.56	0.21	-	1.82	59. Impôt sur le revenu
60. Profit after tax	-12.92	-33.88	-18.99	-116.83	-191.45	58.18	18.94	-20.43	-0.32	6.41	60. Bénéfices après impôt
% of net income											**% du total du résultat net**
61. Provisions (net)	-18.18	-6.49	35.85	1.07	-18.89	12.18	2.97	43.79	104.94	34.07	61. Provisions (nettes)
a. Provisions on loans	*-36.36*	*-3.90*	*5.66*	*-2.77*	..	..	..	..	..	..	*a. Provisions sur prêts*
b. Provisions on securities	*-18.18*	*-12.99*	*0.94*	*-4.90*	..	..	..	..	..	..	*b. Provisions sur titres*
c. Other	*36.36*	*10.39*	*29.25*	*8.74*	..	..	..	..	..	..	*c. Autres*
62. Profit before tax	118.18	106.49	64.15	98.93	118.89	87.82	97.03	56.21	-4.94	65.62	62. Bénéfices avant impôt
63. Income tax	-4.55	-	-	-0.21	-5.05	2.98	18.81	-0.59	-	14.51	63. Impôt sur le revenu
64. Profit after tax	122.73	106.49	64.15	99.15	123.95	84.84	78.22	56.80	-4.94	51.10	64. Bénéfices après impôt

Foreign commercial banks / Banques commerciales étrangères

	1988	1989	1990	1991	1992	1993	1994	1995	1996	1997	
Per cent											*Pourcentage*
BALANCE SHEET ANALYSIS											**ANALYSE DU BILAN**
% of year-end balance sheet total											**% du total du bilan en fin d'exercice**
Assets											**Actif**
65. Cash & balance with Central bank	0.21	0.36	0.84	0.24	8.73	0.51	2.72	0.04	0.04	0.33	65. Caisse & solde auprès de la Banque centrale
66. Interbank deposits	29.74	27.54	25.53	19.04	19.89	33.28	27.78	28.11	32.23	19.93	66. Dépôts interbancaires
67. Loans	55.79	55.58	62.29	63.04	49.18	41.27	35.62	30.67	30.79	53.17	67. Prêts
68. Securities	3.95	5.36	2.32	14.59	15.98	21.16	24.62	27.62	25.72	16.85	68. Valeurs mobilières
69. Other assets	10.31	11.16	9.01	3.08	6.22	3.80	9.27	13.56	11.22	9.73	69. Autres actifs
Liabilities											**Passif**
70. Capital & reserves	3.43	2.73	3.34	2.54	2.08	5.68	3.72	2.20	2.09	3.81	70. Capital et réserves
71. Borrowing from Central bank	1.19	1.85	1.51	0.81	0.02	-	0.02	0.01	1.71	-	71. Emprunts auprès de la Banque centrale
72. Interbank deposits	86.30	86.77	82.79	80.69	84.25	77.84	78.69	78.86	68.32	53.23	72. Dépôts interbancaires
73. Non-bank deposits	5.03	3.52	6.07	9.73	9.12	11.11	10.61	8.21	20.03	31.53	73. Dépôts non bancaires
74. Bonds	1.31	1.79	2.40	2.13	1.54	0.87	0.49	0.34	0.19	0.90	74. Obligations
75. Other liabilities	2.74	3.34	3.88	4.09	3.00	4.50	6.47	10.38	7.67	10.52	75. Autres engagements
Memorandum items											***Pour mémoire***
76. Short-term securities	*0.84*	*0.43*	*0.81*	*9.43*	*32.07*	*25.49*	*27.41*	*23.38*	*12.96*	*3.44*	*76. Titres à court terme*
77. Bonds	*3.18*	*4.65*	*0.56*	*0.43*	*0.31*	*2.09*	*2.84*	*7.43*	*2.26*	*1.30*	*77. Obligations*
78. Shares and participations	*0.06*	*0.41*	*0.47*	*0.06*	*0.01*	*0.02*	*0.01*	*0.03*	*5.25*	*5.38*	*78. Actions et participations*
79. Claims on non-residents	*5.86*	*11.01*	*11.63*	*27.74*	*21.06*	*40.04*	*21.63*	*26.69*	*29.05*	*12.01*	*79. Créances sur des non-résidents*
80. Liabilities to non-residents	*1.77*	*1.22*	*2.10*	*86.08*	*87.03*	*80.29*	*69.34*	*72.15*	*57.45*	*23.46*	*80. Engagements envers des non-résidents*

* See notes on previous pages.

* Voir les notes en pages précédentes.

SWEDEN
Savings banks

SUEDE
Caisses d'épargne

	1988	1989	1990	1991	1992	1993	1994	1995	1996	1997	
Million Swedish kroner											*Millions de couronnes suédoises*
INCOME STATEMENT											**COMPTE DE RESULTATS**
1. Interest income	20328	24461	32005	31956	49806	7551	6716	7251	6286	4903	1. Produits financiers
2. Interest expenses	12593	15744	20871	19994	37020	3585	3123	3584	2902	1698	2. Frais financiers
3. Net interest income	7735	8717	11134	11962	12786	3966	3593	3667	3384	3205	3. Produits financiers nets
4. Non-interest income (net)	2189	2371	2695	6210	19752	860	1184	1475	1300	1753	4. Produits non financiers (nets)
a. Fees and commissions receivable	..	..	..	..	..	..	..	..	*836*	*1000*	*a. Frais et commissions à recevoir*
b. Fees and commissions payable	..	..	..	..	..	..	..	..	*156*	*191*	*b. Frais et commissions à payer*
c. Net profits or loss on financial operations	..	..	..	..	..	..	..	..	*148*	*60*	*c. Profits ou pertes nets sur opérations financières*
d. Other	..	..	..	..	..	..	..	..	*472*	*884*	*d. Autres*
5. Gross income	9924	11088	13829	18172	32538	4826	4777	5142	4684	4957	5. Résultat brut
6. Operating expenses	7406	8531	11231	19919	28310	3741	3241	3417	2608	2644	6. Frais d'exploitation
a. Staff costs	*2088*	*3651*	*4237*	*4549*	*5203*	*1138*	*1154*	*1259*	*1261*	*1315*	*a. Dépenses en personnel*
b. Property costs	..	..	..	*229*	*480*	*93*	*94*	*97*	..	..	*b. Dépenses en immobilier*
c. Other	..	..	..	*15141*	*22627*	*2510*	*1993*	*2061*	..	..	*c. Autres*
7. Net income	2518	2557	2598	-1747	4228	1085	1536	1725	2075	2313	7. Résultat net
8. Provisions (net)	1731	2118	2448	-13356	-6458	-532	-583	41	304	250	8. Provisions (nettes)
a. Provisions on loans	*1748*	*1078*	*2035*	*-14692*	..	..	..	..	..	..	*a. Provisions sur prêts*
b. Provisions on securities	*5*	*1073*	*644*	*-2197*	..	..	..	..	..	..	*b. Provisions sur titres*
c. Other	*-22*	*-33*	*-231*	*3533*	..	..	..	..	..	..	*c. Autres*
9. Profit before tax	787	439	150	11609	10686	1617	2119	1684	1771	2063	9. Bénéfices avant impôt
10. Income tax	544	130	161	3587	549	485	510	510	446	560	10. Impôt sur le revenu
11. Profit after tax	243	309	-11	8022	10137	1132	1609	1174	1325	1503	11. Bénéfices après impôt
12. Distributed profit	-	-	-	-	-	-	-	-	-	-	12. Bénéfices distribués
13. Retained profit	243	309	-11	8022	10137	1132	1609	1174	1325	1503	13. Bénéfices mis en réserve
BALANCE SHEET											**BILAN**
Assets											**Actif**
14. Cash & balance with Central bank	2822	3225	4230	4592	16375	1168	998	1054	1056	972	14. Caisse & solde auprès de la Banque centrale
15. Interbank deposits	19708	20368	26163	17460	22127	9173	5471	6228	9293	6858	15. Dépôts interbancaires
16. Loans	140385	170524	203904	189497	214186	43009	44419	46551	43531	48294	16. Prêts
17. Securities	31320	31368	33334	52710	61489	16042	20844	19289	18420	15279	17. Valeurs mobilières
18. Other assets	6742	8727	9851	9640	18925	2421	2698	2645	2667	2557	18. Autres actifs
Liabilities											**Passif**
19. Capital & reserves	16179	17547	19242	16241	21519	7885	8464	10231	11628	13330	19. Capital et réserves
20. Borrowing from Central bank	-	-	-	88	8623	-	-	-	-	-	20. Emprunts auprès de la Banque centrale
21. Interbank deposits	30976	51737	73242	48353	48931	2458	2493	1560	1768	2261	21. Dépôts interbancaires
22. Non-bank deposits	145601	155530	170544	180318	197526	58016	59836	59935	59573	56334	22. Dépôts non bancaires
23. Bonds	2946	3826	3544	1139	21055	543	709	845	419	387	23. Obligations
24. Other liabilities	5274	5572	10909	27761	35448	2909	2930	3196	1579	1647	24. Autres engagements
Balance sheet total											**Total du bilan**
25. End-year total	200976	234212	277482	273898	333101	71813	74431	75767	74967	73959	25. En fin d'exercice
26. Average total	187376	217594	255847	275690	303500	..	73280	74126	71142	72419	26. Moyen

SWEDEN / SUEDE

Savings banks / Caisses d'épargne

	1988	1989	1990	1991	1992	1993	1994	1995	1996	1997	
Million Swedish kroner											*Millions de couronnes suédoises*
Memorandum items											**Pour mémoire**
27. Short-term securities	666	1426	4340	6846	38517	9783	10088	4044	..	..	27. Titres à court terme
28. Bonds	29388	31027	31037	24321	24190	6088	9165	11052	..	..	28. Obligations
29. Shares and participations	1869	1823	1890	1519	10920	1314	2640	1481	..	..	29. Actions et participations
30. Claims on non-residents	1026	3405	8186	9340	35000	347	480	-	..	..	30. Créances sur des non-résidents
31. Liabilities to non-residents	850	70	442	11407	74580	10	10	-	..	..	31. Engagements envers des non-résidents
Capital adequacy											**Solvabilité**
32. Tier 1 Capital	..	..	..	15483	20213	6701	7540	9155	10469	12436	32. Fonds propres de base
33. Tier 2 Capital	..	..	..	1619	5676	476	437	216	186	128	33. Fonds propres complémentaires
34. Supervisory deductions	..	..	..	425	1423	1392	1483	459	876	698	34. Eléments à déduire des fonds propres
35. Total net capital resources	..	..	..	16677	24466	5785	6494	8912	9779	11866	35. Total net des ressources en capital
36. Risk-weighted assets	..	..	..	164987	195636	38838	39582	39539	40177	43131	36. Actifs pondérés des risques
SUPPLEMENTARY INFORMATION											**RENSEIGNEMENTS COMPLEMENTAIRES**
37. Number of institutions	110	109	104	101	91	90	90	90	88	87	37. Nombre d'institutions
38. Number of branches	1190	1273	1124	1129	1028	351	352	349	307	303	38. Nombre de succursales
39. Number of employees (x 1000)	15.6	15.8	14.9	15.3	15.4	3.8	3.8	4.0	3.4	3.1	39. Nombre de salariés (x 1000)

Change in methodology

- As from 1993, what was formerly the largest savings bank is included in the category of Commercial banks.

Changement méthodologique

- Depuis 1993, ce qui était précedément la plus grande caisse d'épargne est incluse dans la catégorie Banques commerciales.

	1988	1989	1990	1991	1992	1993	1994	1995	1996	1997	
Per cent											*Pourcentage*
INCOME STATEMENT ANALYSIS											**ANALYSE DU COMPTE DE RESULTATS**
% of average balance sheet total											**% du total moyen du bilan**
40. Interest income	10.85	11.24	12.51	11.59	16.41	..	9.16	9.78	8.84	6.77	40. Produits financiers
41. Interest expenses	6.72	7.24	8.16	7.25	12.20	..	4.26	4.84	4.08	2.34	41. Frais financiers
42. Net interest income	4.13	4.01	4.35	4.34	4.21	..	4.90	4.95	4.76	4.43	42. Produits financiers nets
43. Non-interest income (net)	1.17	1.09	1.05	2.25	6.51	..	1.62	1.99	1.83	2.42	43. Produits non financiers (nets)
a. Fees and commissions receivable	..	..	..	..	..	..	..	..	*1.18*	*1.38*	*a. Frais et commissions à recevoir*
b. Fees and commissions payable	..	..	..	..	..	..	..	..	*0.22*	*0.26*	*b. Frais et commissions à payer*
c. Net profits or loss on financial operations	..	..	..	..	..	..	..	..	*0.21*	*0.08*	*c. Profits ou pertes nets sur opérations financières*
d. Other	..	..	..	..	..	..	..	..	*0.66*	*1.22*	*d. Autres*
44. Gross income	5.30	5.10	5.41	6.59	10.72	..	6.52	6.94	6.58	6.84	44. Résultat brut
45. Operating expenses	3.95	3.92	4.39	7.23	9.33	..	4.42	4.61	3.67	3.65	45. Frais d'exploitation
a. Staff costs	*1.11*	*1.68*	*1.66*	*1.65*	*1.71*	..	*1.57*	*1.70*	*1.77*	*1.82*	*a. Dépenses en personnel*
b. Property costs	..	..	..	*0.08*	*0.16*	..	*0.13*	*0.13*	..	..	*b. Dépenses en immobilier*
c. Other	..	..	..	*5.49*	*7.46*	..	*2.72*	*2.78*	..	..	*c. Autres*
46. Net income	1.34	1.18	1.02	-0.63	1.39	..	2.10	2.33	2.92	3.19	46. Résultat net
47. Provisions (net)	0.92	0.97	0.96	-4.84	-2.13	..	-0.80	0.06	0.43	0.35	47. Provisions (nettes)
a. Provisions on loans	*0.93*	*0.50*	*0.80*	*-5.33*	..	..	..	..	..	..	*a. Provisions sur prêts*
b. Provisions on securities	-	*0.49*	*0.25*	*-0.80*	..	..	..	..	..	..	*b. Provisions sur titres*
c. Other	*-0.01*	*-0.02*	*-0.09*	*1.28*	..	..	..	..	..	..	*c. Autres*
48. Profit before tax	0.42	0.20	0.06	4.21	3.52	..	2.89	2.27	2.49	2.85	48. Bénéfices avant impôt
49. Income tax	0.29	0.06	0.06	1.30	0.18	..	0.70	0.69	0.63	0.77	49. Impôt sur le revenu
50. Profit after tax	0.13	0.14	-	2.91	3.34	..	2.20	1.58	1.86	2.08	50. Bénéfices après impôt
51. Distributed profit	-	-	-	-	-	..	-	-	-	-	51. Bénéfices distribués
52. Retained profit	0.13	0.14	-	2.91	3.34	..	2.20	1.58	1.86	2.08	52. Bénéfices mis en réserve
% of gross income											**% du total du résultat brut**
53. Net interest income	77.94	78.62	80.51	65.83	39.30	82.18	75.21	71.31	72.25	64.66	53. Produits financiers nets
54. Non-interest income (net)	22.06	21.38	19.49	34.17	60.70	17.82	24.79	28.69	27.75	35.36	54. Produits non financiers (nets)
a. Fees and commissions receivable	..	..	..	..	..	..	..	..	*17.85*	*20.17*	*a. Frais et commissions à recevoir*
b. Fees and commissions payable	..	..	..	..	..	..	..	..	*3.33*	*3.85*	*b. Frais et commissions à payer*
c. Net profits or loss on financial operations	..	..	..	..	..	..	..	..	*3.16*	*1.21*	*c. Profits ou pertes nets sur opérations financières*
d. Other	..	..	..	..	..	..	..	..	*10.08*	*17.83*	*d. Autres*
55. Operating expenses	74.63	76.94	81.21	109.61	87.01	77.52	67.85	66.45	55.68	53.34	55. Frais d'exploitation
a. Staff costs	*21.04*	*32.93*	*30.64*	*25.03*	*15.99*	*23.58*	*24.16*	*24.48*	*26.92*	*26.53*	*a. Dépenses en personnel*
b. Property costs	..	..	..	*1.26*	*1.48*	*1.93*	*1.97*	*1.89*	..	..	*b. Dépenses en immobilier*
c. Other	..	..	..	*83.32*	*69.54*	*52.01*	*41.72*	*40.08*	..	..	*c. Autres*
56. Net income	25.37	23.06	18.79	-9.61	12.99	22.48	32.15	33.55	44.30	46.66	56. Résultat net
57. Provisions (net)	17.44	19.10	17.70	-73.50	-19.85	-11.02	-12.20	0.80	6.49	5.04	57. Provisions (nettes)
a. Provisions on loans	*17.61*	*9.72*	*14.72*	*-80.85*	..	..	..	..	..	..	*a. Provisions sur prêts*
b. Provisions on securities	*0.05*	*9.68*	*4.66*	*-12.09*	..	..	..	..	..	..	*b. Provisions sur titres*
c. Other	*-0.22*	*-0.30*	*-1.67*	*19.44*	..	..	..	..	..	..	*c. Autres*
58. Profit before tax	7.93	3.96	1.08	63.88	32.84	33.51	44.36	32.75	37.81	41.62	58. Bénéfices avant impôt
59. Income tax	5.48	1.17	1.16	19.74	1.69	10.05	10.68	9.92	9.52	11.30	59. Impôt sur le revenu
60. Profit after tax	2.45	2.79	-0.08	44.14	31.15	23.46	33.68	22.83	28.29	30.32	60. Bénéfices après impôt
% of net income											**% du total du résultat net**
61. Provisions (net)	68.75	82.83	94.23	..	-152.74	-49.03	-37.96	2.38	14.65	10.81	61. Provisions (nettes)
a. Provisions on loans	*69.42*	*42.16*	*78.33*	..	..	..	..	..	..	..	*a. Provisions sur prêts*
b. Provisions on securities	*0.20*	*41.96*	*24.79*	..	..	..	..	..	..	..	*b. Provisions sur titres*
c. Other	*-0.87*	*-1.29*	*-8.89*	..	..	..	..	..	..	..	*c. Autres*
62. Profit before tax	31.25	17.17	5.77	..	252.74	149.03	137.96	97.62	85.35	89.19	62. Bénéfices avant impôt
63. Income tax	21.60	5.08	6.20	..	12.98	44.70	33.20	29.57	21.49	24.21	63. Impôt sur le revenu
64. Profit after tax	9.65	12.08	-0.42	..	239.76	104.33	104.75	68.06	63.86	64.98	64. Bénéfices après impôt

SWEDEN — SUEDE

Savings banks — Caisses d'épargne

	1988	1989	1990	1991	1992	1993	1994	1995	1996	1997	
Per cent											*Pourcentage*
BALANCE SHEET ANALYSIS											**ANALYSE DU BILAN**
% of year-end balance sheet total											**% du total du bilan en fin d'exercice**
Assets											**Actif**
65. Cash & balance with Central bank	1.40	1.38	1.52	1.68	4.92	1.63	1.34	1.39	1.41	1.31	65. Caisse & solde auprès de la Banque centrale
66. Interbank deposits	9.81	8.70	9.43	6.37	6.64	12.77	7.35	8.22	12.40	9.27	66. Dépôts interbancaires
67. Loans	69.85	72.81	73.48	69.19	64.30	59.89	59.68	61.44	58.07	65.30	67. Prêts
68. Securities	15.58	13.39	12.01	19.24	18.46	22.34	28.00	25.46	24.57	20.66	68. Valeurs mobilières
69. Other assets	3.35	3.73	3.55	3.52	5.68	3.37	3.62	3.49	3.56	3.46	69. Autres actifs
Liabilities											**Passif**
70. Capital & reserves	8.05	7.49	6.93	5.93	6.46	10.98	11.37	13.50	15.51	18.02	70. Capital et réserves
71. Borrowing from Central bank	-	-	-	0.03	2.59	-	-	-	-	-	71. Emprunts auprès de la Banque centrale
72. Interbank deposits	15.41	22.09	26.40	17.65	14.69	3.42	3.35	2.06	2.36	3.06	72. Dépôts interbancaires
73. Non-bank deposits	72.45	66.41	61.46	65.83	59.30	80.79	80.39	79.10	79.47	76.17	73. Dépôts non bancaires
74. Bonds	1.47	1.63	1.28	0.42	6.32	0.76	0.95	1.12	0.56	0.52	74. Obligations
75. Other liabilities	2.62	2.38	3.93	10.14	10.64	4.05	3.94	4.22	2.11	2.23	75. Autres engagements
Memorandum items											***Pour mémoire***
76. Short-term securities	*0.33*	*0.61*	*1.56*	*2.50*	*11.56*	*13.62*	*13.55*	*5.34*	..	..	*76. Titres à court terme*
77. Bonds	*14.62*	*13.25*	*11.19*	*8.88*	*7.26*	*8.48*	*12.31*	*14.59*	..	..	*77. Obligations*
78. Shares and participations	*0.93*	*0.78*	*0.68*	*0.55*	*3.28*	*1.83*	*3.55*	*1.95*	..	..	*78. Actions et participations*
79. Claims on non-residents	*0.51*	*1.45*	*2.95*	*3.41*	*10.51*	*0.48*	*0.64*	-	..	..	*79. Créances sur des non-résidents*
80. Liabilities to non-residents	*0.42*	*0.03*	*0.16*	*4.16*	*22.39*	*0.01*	*0.01*	-	..	..	*80. Engagements envers des non-résidents*

* See notes on previous pages.

* Voir les notes en pages précédentes.

SWEDEN — SUEDE

Co-operative banks — Banques mutualistes

	1988	1989	1990	1991	
Million Swedish kroner					*Millions de couronnes suédoises*
INCOME STATEMENT					**COMPTE DE RESULTATS**
1. Interest income	5323	6340	8249	12157	1. Produits financiers
2. Interest expenses	3200	3857	4942	8427	2. Frais financiers
3. Net interest income	2123	2483	3307	3730	3. Produits financiers nets
4. Non-interest income (net)	391	472	602	1144	4. Produits non financiers (nets)
a. Fees and commissions receivable	..	..	..	..	*a. Frais et commissions à recevoir*
b. Fees and commissions payable	..	..	..	..	*b. Frais et commissions à payer*
c. Net profits or loss on financial operations	..	..	..	..	*c. Profits ou pertes nets sur opérations financières*
d. Other	..	..	..	..	*d. Autres*
5. Gross income	2514	2955	3909	4874	5. Résultat brut
6. Operating expenses	1838	2159	2981	5717	6. Frais d'exploitation
a. Staff costs	*799*	*888*	*1092*	*1377*	*a. Dépenses en personnel*
b. Property costs	..	..	..	*56*	*b. Dépenses en immobilier*
c. Other	..	..	..	*4284*	*c. Autres*
7. Net income	676	796	928	-843	7. Résultat net
8. Provisions (net)	497	616	711	-2856	8. Provisions (nettes)
a. Provisions on loans	-	*366*	*523*	*-3130*	*a. Provisions sur prêts*
b. Provisions on securities	*388*	*91*	*47*	*-818*	*b. Provisions sur titres*
c. Other	*109*	*159*	*141*	*1092*	*c. Autres*
9. Profit before tax	179	180	217	2013	9. Bénéfices avant impôt
10. Income tax	101	59	67	552	10. Impôt sur le revenu
11. Profit after tax	78	121	150	1461	11. Bénéfices après impôt
12. Distributed profit	-	-	-	-	12. Bénéfices distribués
13. Retained profit	78	121	150	1461	13. Bénéfices mis en réserve
BALANCE SHEET					**BILAN**
Assets					**Actif**
14. Cash & balance with Central bank	368	443	593	1453	14. Caisse & solde auprès de la Banque centrale
15. Interbank deposits	2572	1067	1515	5548	15. Dépôts interbancaires
16. Loans	32805	40411	47201	60019	16. Prêts
17. Securities	10009	10874	10828	23689	17. Valeurs mobilières
18. Other assets	1499	1960	2352	3093	18. Autres actifs
Liabilities					**Passif**
19. Capital & reserves	3407	4174	5035	4627	19. Capital et réserves
20. Borrowing from Central bank	-	-	-	982	20. Emprunts auprès de la Banque centrale
21. Interbank deposits	1533	3487	2540	20381	21. Dépôts interbancaires
22. Non-bank deposits	41028	45690	52980	58682	22. Dépôts non bancaires
23. Bonds	273	332	365	2396	23. Obligations
24. Other liabilities	1012	1073	1568	6733	24. Autres engagements
Balance sheet total					**Total du bilan**
25. End-year total	47253	54756	62488	93803	25. En fin d'exercice
26. Average total	45259	51406	57278	67395	26. Moyen

SWEDEN
Co-operative banks

SUEDE
Banques mutualistes

	1988	1989	1990	1991	
Million Swedish kroner					*Millions de couronnes suédoises*
Memorandum items					***Pour mémoire***
27. Short-term securities	*381*	*480*	*615*	*2217*	*27. Titres à court terme*
28. Bonds	*10062*	*10948*	*10479*	*9047*	*28. Obligations*
29. Shares and participations	*122*	*122*	*436*	*1458*	*29. Actions et participations*
30. Claims on non-residents	-	-	-	*1964*	*30. Créances sur des non-résidents*
31. Liabilities to non-residents	-	-	*6*	*9316*	*31. Engagements envers des non-résidents*
Capital adequacy					***Solvabilité***
32. Tier 1 Capital	..	..	..	*4289*	*32. Fonds propres de base*
33. Tier 2 Capital	..	..	..	*1844*	*33. Fonds propres complémentaires*
34. Supervisory deductions	..	..	..	*34*	*34. Eléments à déduire des fonds propres*
35. Total net capital resources	..	..	..	*6099*	*35. Total net des ressources en capital*
36. Risk-weighted assets	..	..	..	*57365*	*36. Actifs pondérés des risques*
SUPPLEMENTARY INFORMATION					**RENSEIGNEMENTS COMPLEMENTAIRES**
37. Number of institutions	12	12	12	12	37. Nombre d'institutions
38. Number of branches	391	383	373	332	38. Nombre de succursales
39. Number of employees (x 1000)	3.9	4.0	4.3	4.7	39. Nombre de salariés (x 1000)

Notes

- Average balance sheet totals (item 26) are based on thirteen end-month data.

Change in methodology

- For the year 1991, the Föreningsbankernas Bank is exceptionally included under Co-operative banks and not under Commercial banks.
- As from 1992, Co-operative banks, which merged into one single commercial bank, are included under Commercial banks.

Notes

- La moyenne du total des actifs/passifs (poste 26) est basée sur treize données de fin de mois.

Changement méthodologique

- Pour l'année 1991, la Föreningsbankernas Bank est comprise exceptionnellement dans les Banques mutualistes et non pas dans les Banques commerciales.
- Depuis 1992, les Banques mutualistes, ayant fusionnées en une seule banque commerciale, sont classées dans les données concernant les Banques commerciales.

SWEDEN — SUEDE

Co-operative banks — Banques mutualistes

	1988	1989	1990	1991	
Per cent					*Pourcentage*
INCOME STATEMENT ANALYSIS					**ANALYSE DU COMPTE DE RESULTATS**
% of average balance sheet total					**% du total moyen du bilan**
40. Interest income	11.76	12.33	14.40	18.04	40. Produits financiers
41. Interest expenses	7.07	7.50	8.63	12.50	41. Frais financiers
42. Net interest income	4.69	4.83	5.77	5.53	42. Produits financiers nets
43. Non-interest income (net)	0.86	0.92	1.05	1.70	43. Produits non financiers (nets)
a. Fees and commissions receivable	..	..	..	..	*a. Frais et commissions à recevoir*
b. Fees and commissions payable	..	..	..	..	*b. Frais et commissions à payer*
c. Net profits or loss on financial operations	..	..	..	..	*c. Profits ou pertes nets sur opérations financières*
d. Other	..	..	..	..	*d. Autres*
44. Gross income	5.55	5.75	6.82	7.23	44. Résultat brut
45. Operating expenses	4.06	4.20	5.20	8.48	45. Frais d'exploitation
a. Staff costs	*1.77*	*1.73*	*1.91*	*2.04*	*a. Dépenses en personnel*
b. Property costs	..	..	..	*0.08*	*b. Dépenses en immobilier*
c. Other	..	..	..	*6.36*	*c. Autres*
46. Net income	1.49	1.55	1.62	-1.25	46. Résultat net
47. Provisions (net)	1.10	1.20	1.24	-4.24	47. Provisions (nettes)
a. Provisions on loans	-	*0.71*	*0.91*	*-4.64*	*a. Provisions sur prêts*
b. Provisions on securities	*0.86*	*0.18*	*0.08*	*-1.21*	*b. Provisions sur titres*
c. Other	*0.24*	*0.31*	*0.25*	*1.62*	*c. Autres*
48. Profit before tax	0.40	0.35	0.38	2.99	48. Bénéfices avant impôt
49. Income tax	0.22	0.11	0.12	0.82	49. Impôt sur le revenu
50. Profit after tax	0.17	0.24	0.26	2.17	50. Bénéfices après impôt
51. Distributed profit	-	-	-	-	51. Bénéfices distribués
52. Retained profit	0.17	0.24	0.26	2.17	52. Bénéfices mis en réserve
% of gross income					**% du total du résultat brut**
53. Net interest income	84.45	84.03	84.60	76.53	53. Produits financiers nets
54. Non-interest income (net)	15.55	15.97	15.40	23.47	54. Produits non financiers (nets)
a. Fees and commissions receivable	..	..	..	..	*a. Frais et commissions à recevoir*
b. Fees and commissions payable	..	..	..	..	*b. Frais et commissions à payer*
c. Net profits or loss on financial operations	..	..	..	..	*c. Profits ou pertes nets sur opérations financières*
d. Other	..	..	..	..	*d. Autres*
55. Operating expenses	73.11	73.06	76.26	117.30	55. Frais d'exploitation
a. Staff costs	*31.78*	*30.05*	*27.94*	*28.25*	*a. Dépenses en personnel*
b. Property costs	..	..	..	*1.15*	*b. Dépenses en immobilier*
c. Other	..	..	..	*87.89*	*c. Autres*
56. Net income	26.89	26.94	23.74	-17.30	56. Résultat net
57. Provisions (net)	19.77	20.85	18.19	-58.60	57. Provisions (nettes)
a. Provisions on loans	-	*12.39*	*13.38*	*-64.22*	*a. Provisions sur prêts*
b. Provisions on securities	*15.43*	*3.08*	*1.20*	*-16.78*	*b. Provisions sur titres*
c. Other	*4.34*	*5.38*	*3.61*	*22.40*	*c. Autres*
58. Profit before tax	7.12	6.09	5.55	41.30	58. Bénéfices avant impôt
59. Income tax	4.02	2.00	1.71	11.33	59. Impôt sur le revenu
60. Profit after tax	3.10	4.09	3.84	29.98	60. Bénéfices après impôt
% of net income					**% du total du résultat net**
61. Provisions (net)	73.52	77.39	76.62	..	61. Provisions (nettes)
a. Provisions on loans	-	*45.98*	*56.36*	..	*a. Provisions sur prêts*
b. Provisions on securities	*57.40*	*11.43*	*5.06*	..	*b. Provisions sur titres*
c. Other	*16.12*	*19.97*	*15.19*	..	*c. Autres*
62. Profit before tax	26.48	22.61	23.38	..	62. Bénéfices avant impôt
63. Income tax	14.94	7.41	7.22	..	63. Impôt sur le revenu
64. Profit after tax	11.54	15.20	16.16	..	64. Bénéfices après impôt

SWEDEN / SUEDE

Co-operative banks / Banques mutualistes

	1988	1989	1990	1991	
Per cent					*Pourcentage*
BALANCE SHEET ANALYSIS					**ANALYSE DU BILAN**
% of year-end balance sheet total					**% du total du bilan en fin d'exercice**
Assets					**Actif**
65. Cash & balance with Central bank	0.78	0.81	0.95	1.55	65. Caisse & solde auprès de la Banque centrale
66. Interbank deposits	5.44	1.95	2.42	5.91	66. Dépôts interbancaires
67. Loans	69.42	73.80	75.54	63.98	67. Prêts
68. Securities	21.18	19.86	17.33	25.25	68. Valeurs mobilières
69. Other assets	3.17	3.58	3.76	3.30	69. Autres actifs
Liabilities					**Passif**
70. Capital & reserves	7.21	7.62	8.06	4.93	70. Capital et réserves
71. Borrowing from Central bank	-	-	-	1.05	71. Emprunts auprès de la Banque centrale
72. Interbank deposits	3.24	6.37	4.06	21.73	72. Dépôts interbancaires
73. Non-bank deposits	86.83	83.44	84.78	62.56	73. Dépôts non bancaires
74. Bonds	0.58	0.61	0.58	2.55	74. Obligations
75. Other liabilities	2.14	1.96	2.51	7.18	75. Autres engagements
Memorandum items					***Pour mémoire***
76. Short-term securities	*0.81*	*0.88*	*0.98*	*2.36*	*76. Titres à court terme*
77. Bonds	*21.29*	*19.99*	*16.77*	*9.64*	*77. Obligations*
78. Shares and participations	*0.26*	*0.22*	*0.70*	*1.55*	*78. Actions et participations*
79. Claims on non-residents	-	-	-	*2.09*	*79. Créances sur des non-résidents*
80. Liabilities to non-residents	-	-	*0.01*	*9.93*	*80. Engagements envers des non-résidents*

* See notes on previous pages.

* Voir les notes en pages précédentes.

SWITZERLAND | SUISSE

All banks | Ensemble des banques

	1988	1989	1990	1991	1992	1993	1994	1995	1996	1997	
Million Swiss francs											*Millions de francs suisses*
INCOME STATEMENT											**COMPTE DE RESULTATS**
1. Interest income	45836	59594	70944	75442	74255	68499	59284	58408	57324	65169	1. Produits financiers
2. Interest expenses	33563	46326	57257	58970	56246	47246	42638	41904	39990	45484	2. Frais financiers
3. Net interest income	12273	13268	13687	16472	18009	21253	16646	16504	17334	19685	3. Produits financiers nets
4. Non-interest income (net)	10900	13717	13049	16701	17301	20242	19528	21611	25618	30080	4. Produits non financiers (nets)
a. Fees and commissions receivable	*8103*	*9774*	*9198*	*10016*	*10851*	*13666*	*13541*	*12845*	*15407*	*19914*	*a. Frais et commissions à recevoir*
b. Fees and commissions payable	*473*	*658*	*631*	*607*	*632*	*760*	*756*	*891*	*1263*	*1734*	*b. Frais et commissions à payer*
c. Net profits or loss on financial operations	*2255*	*2565*	*2608*	*3383*	*3992*	*4662*	*3169*	*5575*	*6832*	*7679*	*c. Profits ou pertes nets sur opérations financières*
d. Other	*1015*	*2036*	*1874*	*3910*	*3090*	*2675*	*3574*	*4083*	*4642*	*4221*	*d. Autres*
5. Gross income	23174	26986	26737	33174	35310	41495	36174	38115	42952	49765	5. Résultat brut
6. Operating expenses	13386	14934	15939	17349	18408	20183	20124	21512	28407	31449	6. Frais d'exploitation
a. Staff costs	*8868*	*9828*	*10451*	*11419*	*11947*	*13184*	*12861*	*13401*	*14653*	*16269*	*a. Dépenses en personnel*
b. Property costs	..	..	..	..	..	..	..	..	..	..	*b. Dépenses en immobilier*
c. Other	..	..	..	..	..	..	..	..	..	..	*c. Autres*
7. Net income	9788	12052	10798	15825	16902	21312	16050	16603	14545	18316	7. Résultat net
8. Provisions (net)	4134	5104	5561	10127	11386	13270	10046	9641	13090	13663	8. Provisions (nettes)
a. Provisions on loans	..	..	..	..	..	..	..	..	..	..	*a. Provisions sur prêts*
b. Provisions on securities	..	..	..	..	..	..	..	..	..	..	*b. Provisions sur titres*
c. Other	..	..	..	..	..	..	..	..	..	..	*c. Autres*
9. Profit before tax	5654	6948	5237	5698	5516	8042	6004	6962	1455	4653	9. Bénéfices avant impôt
10. Income tax	1476	1535	1313	1382	1403	1752	1260	1219	1185	1022	10. Impôt sur le revenu
11. Profit after tax	4178	5413	3924	4316	4113	6290	4744	5743	270	3631	11. Bénéfices après impôt
12. Distributed profit	2523	3460	2715	2805	2829	3579	3396	3741	2652	5947	12. Bénéfices distribués
13. Retained profit	1655	1953	1209	1511	1284	2711	1348	2002	-2382	-2316	13. Bénéfices mis en réserve
BALANCE SHEET											**BILAN**
Assets											**Actif**
14. Cash & balance with Central bank	12360	12332	11876	11715	11818	11828	10996	11424	13255	14619	14. Caisse & solde auprès de la Banque centrale
15. Interbank deposits	226068	197365	196615	187439	196342	205946	196210	231577	287606	396740	15. Dépôts interbancaires
16. Loans	540796	621374	670261	711407	726741	738605	744490	730522	784362	827753	16. Prêts
17. Securities	88245	97684	105054	110906	121896	159059	164578	188218	234009	298402	17. Valeurs mobilières
18. Other assets	48342	49591	48973	51855	55417	62368	66507	138995	148227	209299	18. Autres actifs
Liabilities											**Passif**
19. Capital & reserves	58466	63925	67328	69368	72241	78005	80516	82893	87614	89686	19. Capital et réserves
20. Borrowing from Central bank (1)	..	..	..	..	..	..	..	..	..	..	20. Emprunts auprès de la Banque centrale (1)
21. Interbank deposits	183434	195673	210319	206978	211373	241193	231238	243249	298266	375317	21. Dépôts interbancaires
22. Non-bank deposits	467158	494038	510663	534720	557064	588258	613777	627153	713898	792987	22. Dépôts non bancaires
23. Bonds	151053	164228	181508	191779	194451	183602	174309	174346	167100	174893	23. Obligations
24. Other liabilities	55701	60482	62961	70476	77084	86747	82942	173094	200581	313932	24. Autres engagements
Balance sheet total											**Total du bilan**
25. End-year total	915812	978346	1032779	1073321	1112213	1177805	1182782	1300735	1467458	1746814	25. En fin d'exercice
26. Average total	886148	947079	1005563	1053050	1092767	1145009	1180294	1241759	1384097	1607136	26. Moyen

SWITZERLAND
All banks

SUISSE
Ensemble des banques

	1988	1989	1990	1991	1992	1993	1994	1995	1996	1997	
Million Swiss francs											*Millions de francs suisses*
Memorandum items											***Pour mémoire***
27. Short-term securities	*21328*	*25776*	*33898*	*29411*	*34438*	*34822*	*38926*	*46850*	*50271*	*71706*	*27. Titres à court terme*
28. Bonds	*53313*	*55961*	*56826*	*64916*	*68459*	*92633*	*86619*	*95346*	*119551*	*134025*	*28. Obligations*
29. Shares and participations	*13604*	*15947*	*14331*	*16579*	*18999*	*31605*	*39034*	*46021*	*57570*	*83533*	*29. Actions et participations*
30. Claims on non-residents	*337446*	*339306*	*354848*	*372834*	*392649*	*428143*	*415068*	*501797*	*648481*	*880071*	*30. Créances sur des non-résidents*
31. Liabilities to non-residents	*255951*	*270950*	*293525*	*314501*	*325954*	*351526*	*349274*	*428910*	*556828*	*780554*	*31. Engagements envers des non-résidents*
Capital adequacy											***Solvabilité***
32. Tier 1 Capital	..	..	..	..	..	..	..	*87652*	*86786*	*83610*	*32. Fonds propres de base*
33. Tier 2 Capital	..	..	..	..	..	..	..	*21992*	*24917*	*32402*	*33. Fonds propres complémentaires*
34. Supervisory deductions	..	..	..	..	..	..	..	*13821*	*14986*	*13877*	*34. Eléments à déduire des fonds propres*
35. Total net capital resources	*73423*	*81258*	*85494*	*88844*	*91362*	*99302*	*101483*	*95822*	*96717*	*102135*	*35. Total net des ressources en capital*
36. Risk-weighted assets	..	..	..	..	..	..	..	*912456*	*942040*	*959179*	*36. Actifs pondérés des risques*
SUPPLEMENTARY INFORMATION											**RENSEIGNEMENTS COMPLEMENTAIRES**
37. Number of institutions	454	455	457	444	434	419	393	382	370	360	37. Nombre d'institutions
38. Number of branches	4082	4130	4191	4190	4111	3991	3807	3727	3600	3395	38. Nombre de succursales
39. Number of employees (x 1000)	115.1	119.3	121.4	120.9	118.5	117.1	116.5	116.0	116.0	115.1	39. Nombre de salariés (x 1000)

1. Borrowing from Central bank (item 20) is included under Interbank deposits (item 21).

Notes

- All banks include Large commercial banks, Cantonal banks, Regional and savings banks, Loan associations and agricultural co-operative banks and Other Swiss and foreign commercial banks.

1. Emprunts auprès de la Banque centrale (poste 20) sont inclus sous Dépôts interbancaires (poste 21).

Notes

- L'Ensemble des banques comprend les Grandes banques commerciales, les Banques cantonales, les Banques régionales et caisses d'épargne, les Caisses de crédit mutuel et les banques mutualistes agricoles, et les Autres banques suisses et étrangères.

Per cent	1988	1989	1990	1991	1992	1993	1994	1995	1996	1997	Pourcentage
INCOME STATEMENT ANALYSIS											**ANALYSE DU COMPTE DE RESULTATS**
% of average balance sheet total											**% du total moyen du bilan**
40. Interest income	5.17	6.29	7.06	7.16	6.80	5.98	5.02	4.70	4.14	4.05	40. Produits financiers
41. Interest expenses	3.79	4.89	5.69	5.60	5.15	4.13	3.61	3.37	2.89	2.83	41. Frais financiers
42. Net interest income	1.38	1.40	1.36	1.56	1.65	1.86	1.41	1.33	1.25	1.22	42. Produits financiers nets
43. Non-interest income (net)	1.23	1.45	1.30	1.59	1.58	1.77	1.65	1.74	1.85	1.87	43. Produits non financiers (nets)
a. Fees and commissions receivable	*0.91*	*1.03*	*0.91*	*0.95*	*0.99*	*1.19*	*1.15*	*1.03*	*1.11*	*1.24*	*a. Frais et commissions à recevoir*
b. Fees and commissions payable	*0.05*	*0.07*	*0.06*	*0.06*	*0.06*	*0.07*	*0.06*	*0.07*	*0.09*	*0.11*	*b. Frais et commissions à payer*
c. Net profits or loss on financial operations	*0.25*	*0.27*	*0.26*	*0.32*	*0.37*	*0.41*	*0.27*	*0.45*	*0.49*	*0.48*	*c. Profits ou pertes nets sur opérations financières*
d. Other	*0.11*	*0.21*	*0.19*	*0.37*	*0.28*	*0.23*	*0.30*	*0.33*	*0.34*	*0.26*	*d. Autres*
44. Gross income	2.62	2.85	2.66	3.15	3.23	3.62	3.06	3.07	3.10	3.10	44. Résultat brut
45. Operating expenses	1.51	1.58	1.59	1.65	1.68	1.76	1.70	1.73	2.05	1.96	45. Frais d'exploitation
a. Staff costs	*1.00*	*1.04*	*1.04*	*1.08*	*1.09*	*1.15*	*1.09*	*1.08*	*1.06*	*1.01*	*a. Dépenses en personnel*
b. Property costs	..	..	..	..	..	..	..	..	..	..	*b. Dépenses en immobilier*
c. Other	..	..	..	..	..	..	..	..	..	..	*c. Autres*
46. Net income	1.10	1.27	1.07	1.50	1.55	1.86	1.36	1.34	1.05	1.14	46. Résultat net
47. Provisions (net)	0.47	0.54	0.55	0.96	1.04	1.16	0.85	0.78	0.95	0.85	47. Provisions (nettes)
a. Provisions on loans	..	..	..	..	..	..	..	..	..	..	*a. Provisions sur prêts*
b. Provisions on securities	..	..	..	..	..	..	..	..	..	..	*b. Provisions sur titres*
c. Other	..	..	..	..	..	..	..	..	..	..	*c. Autres*
48. Profit before tax	0.64	0.73	0.52	0.54	0.50	0.70	0.51	0.56	0.11	0.29	48. Bénéfices avant impôt
49. Income tax	0.17	0.16	0.13	0.13	0.13	0.15	0.11	0.10	0.09	0.06	49. Impôt sur le revenu
50. Profit after tax	0.47	0.57	0.39	0.41	0.38	0.55	0.40	0.46	0.02	0.23	50. Bénéfices après impôt
51. Distributed profit	0.28	0.37	0.27	0.27	0.26	0.31	0.29	0.30	0.19	0.37	51. Bénéfices distribués
52. Retained profit	0.19	0.21	0.12	0.14	0.12	0.24	0.11	0.16	-0.17	-0.14	52. Bénéfices mis en réserve
% of gross income											**% du total du résultat brut**
53. Net interest income	52.96	49.17	51.19	49.65	51.00	51.22	46.02	43.30	40.36	39.56	53. Produits financiers nets
54. Non-interest income (net)	47.04	50.83	48.81	50.34	49.00	48.78	53.98	56.70	59.64	60.44	54. Produits non financiers (nets)
a. Fees and commissions receivable	*34.97*	*36.22*	*34.40*	*30.19*	*30.73*	*32.93*	*37.43*	*33.70*	*35.87*	*40.02*	*a. Frais et commissions à recevoir*
b. Fees and commissions payable	*2.04*	*2.44*	*2.36*	*1.83*	*1.79*	*1.83*	*2.09*	*2.34*	*2.94*	*3.48*	*b. Frais et commissions à payer*
c. Net profits or loss on financial operations	*9.73*	*9.50*	*9.75*	*10.20*	*11.31*	*11.24*	*8.76*	*14.63*	*15.91*	*15.43*	*c. Profits ou pertes nets sur opérations financières*
d. Other	*4.38*	*7.54*	*7.01*	*11.79*	*8.75*	*6.45*	*9.88*	*10.71*	*10.81*	*8.48*	*d. Autres*
55. Operating expenses	57.76	55.34	59.61	52.30	52.13	48.64	55.63	56.44	66.14	63.20	55. Frais d'exploitation
a. Staff costs	*38.27*	*36.42*	*39.09*	*34.42*	*33.83*	*31.77*	*35.55*	*35.16*	*34.11*	*32.69*	*a. Dépenses en personnel*
b. Property costs	..	..	..	..	..	..	..	..	..	..	*b. Dépenses en immobilier*
c. Other	..	..	..	..	..	..	..	..	..	..	*c. Autres*
56. Net income	42.24	44.66	40.39	47.70	47.87	51.36	44.37	43.56	33.86	36.80	56. Résultat net
57. Provisions (net)	17.84	18.91	20.80	30.53	32.25	31.98	27.77	25.29	30.48	27.46	57. Provisions (nettes)
a. Provisions on loans	..	..	..	..	..	..	..	..	..	..	*a. Provisions sur prêts*
b. Provisions on securities	..	..	..	..	..	..	..	..	..	..	*b. Provisions sur titres*
c. Other	..	..	..	..	..	..	..	..	..	..	*c. Autres*
58. Profit before tax	24.40	25.75	19.59	17.18	15.62	19.38	16.60	18.27	3.39	9.35	58. Bénéfices avant impôt
59. Income tax	6.37	5.69	4.91	4.17	3.97	4.22	3.48	3.20	2.76	2.05	59. Impôt sur le revenu
60. Profit after tax	18.03	20.06	14.68	13.01	11.65	15.16	13.11	15.07	0.63	7.30	60. Bénéfices après impôt
% of net income											**% du total du résultat net**
61. Provisions (net)	42.24	42.35	51.50	63.99	67.36	62.27	62.59	58.07	90.00	74.60	61. Provisions (nettes)
a. Provisions on loans	..	..	..	..	..	..	..	..	..	..	*a. Provisions sur prêts*
b. Provisions on securities	..	..	..	..	..	..	..	..	..	..	*b. Provisions sur titres*
c. Other	..	..	..	..	..	..	..	..	..	..	*c. Autres*
62. Profit before tax	57.76	57.65	48.50	36.01	32.64	37.73	37.41	41.93	10.00	25.40	62. Bénéfices avant impôt
63. Income tax	15.08	12.74	12.16	8.73	8.30	8.22	7.85	7.34	8.15	5.58	63. Impôt sur le revenu
64. Profit after tax	42.68	44.91	36.34	27.27	24.33	29.51	29.56	34.59	1.86	19.82	64. Bénéfices après impôt

SWITZERLAND / SUISSE

All banks / Ensemble des banques

	1988	1989	1990	1991	1992	1993	1994	1995	1996	1997	
Per cent											*Pourcentage*
BALANCE SHEET ANALYSIS											**ANALYSE DU BILAN**
% of year-end balance sheet total											**% du total du bilan en fin d'exercice**
Assets											**Actif**
65. Cash & balance with Central bank	1.35	1.26	1.15	1.09	1.06	1.00	0.93	0.88	0.90	0.84	65. Caisse & solde auprès de la Banque centrale
66. Interbank deposits	24.68	20.17	19.04	17.46	17.65	17.49	16.59	17.80	19.60	22.71	66. Dépôts interbancaires
67. Loans	59.05	63.51	64.90	66.28	65.34	62.71	62.94	56.16	53.45	47.39	67. Prêts
68. Securities	9.64	9.98	10.17	10.33	10.96	13.50	13.91	14.47	15.95	17.08	68. Valeurs mobilières
69. Other assets	5.28	5.07	4.74	4.83	4.98	5.30	5.62	10.69	10.10	11.98	69. Autres actifs
Liabilities											**Passif**
70. Capital & reserves	6.38	6.53	6.52	6.46	6.50	6.62	6.81	6.37	5.97	5.13	70. Capital et réserves
71. Borrowing from Central bank	..	..	..	..	..	..	..	..	..	..	71. Emprunts auprès de la Banque centrale
72. Interbank deposits	20.03	20.00	20.36	19.28	19.00	20.48	19.55	18.70	20.33	21.49	72. Dépôts interbancaires
73. Non-bank deposits	51.01	50.50	49.45	49.82	50.09	49.95	51.89	48.22	48.65	45.40	73. Dépôts non bancaires
74. Bonds	16.49	16.79	17.57	17.87	17.48	15.59	14.74	13.40	11.39	10.01	74. Obligations
75. Other liabilities	6.08	6.18	6.10	6.57	6.93	7.37	7.01	13.31	13.67	17.97	75. Autres engagements
Memorandum items											***Pour mémoire***
76. Short-term securities	*2.33*	*2.63*	*3.28*	*2.74*	*3.10*	*2.96*	*3.29*	*3.60*	*3.43*	*4.10*	*76. Titres à court terme*
77. Bonds	*5.82*	*5.72*	*5.50*	*6.05*	*6.16*	*7.86*	*7.32*	*7.33*	*8.15*	*7.67*	*77. Obligations*
78. Shares and participations	*1.49*	*1.63*	*1.39*	*1.54*	*1.71*	*2.68*	*3.30*	*3.54*	*3.92*	*4.78*	*78. Actions et participations*
79. Claims on non-residents	*36.85*	*34.68*	*34.36*	*34.74*	*35.30*	*36.35*	*35.09*	*38.58*	*44.19*	*50.38*	*79. Créances sur des non-résidents*
80. Liabilities to non-residents	*27.95*	*27.69*	*28.42*	*29.30*	*29.31*	*29.85*	*29.53*	*32.97*	*37.95*	*44.68*	*80. Engagements envers des non-résidents*

* See notes on previous pages.

* Voir les notes en pages précédentes.

SWITZERLAND / SUISSE

Large commercial banks / Grandes banques commerciales

	1988	1989	1990	1991	1992	1993	1994	1995	1996	1997	
Million Swiss francs											*Millions de francs suisses*
INCOME STATEMENT											**COMPTE DE RESULTATS**
1. Interest income	25335	33228	37805	39353	37330	34051	30069	30007	31022	39176	1. Produits financiers
2. Interest expenses	18894	26427	31374	31220	27990	22748	21186	21786	21946	28430	2. Frais financiers
3. Net interest income	6441	6801	6431	8133	9340	11303	8883	8221	9076	10745	3. Produits financiers nets
4. Non-interest income (net)	5800	6879	6676	8544	9326	11508	10678	13143	15914	17436	4. Produits non financiers (nets)
a. Fees and commissions receivable	*4289*	*5139*	*4791*	*5393*	*5950*	*7438*	*7495*	*7230*	*8767*	*11293*	*a. Frais et commissions à recevoir*
b. Fees and commissions payable	*210*	*271*	*276*	*242*	*255*	*272*	*266*	*369*	*603*	*828*	*b. Frais et commissions à payer*
c. Net profits or loss on financial operations	*1389*	*1591*	*1634*	*2189*	*2720*	*3214*	*2028*	*4136*	*4855*	*5142*	*c. Profits ou pertes nets sur opérations financières*
d. Other	*331*	*421*	*527*	*1204*	*912*	*1128*	*1421*	*2147*	*2895*	*1829*	*d. Autres*
5. Gross income	12241	13680	13107	16677	18666	22811	19561	21364	24990	28181	5. Résultat brut
6. Operating expenses	7030	7849	8086	9023	9765	11168	11085	12386	18219	19738	6. Frais d'exploitation
a. Staff costs	*4700*	*5242*	*5410*	*6060*	*6455*	*7506*	*7164*	*7667*	*8668*	*9908*	*a. Dépenses en personnel*
b. Property costs	..	..	..	..	..	..	..	..	..	..	*b. Dépenses en immobilier*
c. Other	..	..	..	..	..	..	..	..	..	..	*c. Autres*
7. Net income	5211	5831	5021	7654	8901	11643	8476	8978	6772	8444	7. Résultat net
8. Provisions (net)	2177	2447	2280	4402	5650	7384	5112	5545	9037	9119	8. Provisions (nettes)
a. Provisions on loans	..	..	..	..	..	..	..	..	..	..	*a. Provisions sur prêts*
b. Provisions on securities	..	..	..	..	..	..	..	..	..	..	*b. Provisions sur titres*
c. Other	..	..	..	..	..	..	..	..	..	..	*c. Autres*
9. Profit before tax	3034	3384	2741	3252	3251	4259	3364	3433	-2265	-675	9. Bénéfices avant impôt
10. Income tax	823	827	682	803	795	881	592	520	396	4	10. Impôt sur le revenu
11. Profit after tax	2211	2557	2059	2449	2456	3378	2772	2913	-2661	-679	11. Bénéfices après impôt
12. Distributed profit	1432	1623	1576	1585	1584	1959	1955	2088	821	3086	12. Bénéfices distribués
13. Retained profit	779	934	483	864	872	1419	817	825	-3482	-3766	13. Bénéfices mis en réserve
BALANCE SHEET											**BILAN**
Assets											**Actif**
14. Cash & balance with Central bank	5523	5468	5189	5123	4889	4635	4478	4338	5897	6976	14. Caisse & solde auprès de la Banque centrale
15. Interbank deposits	142738	117329	110780	100290	103289	105729	101679	133775	181078	284325	15. Dépôts interbancaires
16. Loans	255872	302566	319625	344106	353135	356268	362606	344282	385678	413376	16. Prêts
17. Securities	47052	52822	59255	64030	73671	105712	109562	132430	173924	233984	17. Valeurs mobilières
18. Other assets	32313	31528	28678	29637	32297	39496	43664	115761	122794	182572	18. Autres actifs
Liabilities											**Passif**
19. Capital & reserves	29679	33203	33234	34185	35218	39452	42328	43926	41788	42422	19. Capital et réserves
20. Borrowing from Central bank (1)	..	..	..	..	..	..	..	..	..	..	20. Emprunts auprès de la Banque centrale (1)
21. Interbank deposits	116171	121935	127028	126874	128867	157226	147503	160358	209022	284892	21. Dépôts interbancaires
22. Non-bank deposits	247005	261719	271651	285212	303465	314050	335948	341877	404538	458373	22. Dépôts non bancaires
23. Bonds	57648	58710	58577	60272	59262	53765	52501	55074	56093	69762	23. Obligations
24. Other liabilities	32994	34146	33037	36645	40470	47347	43709	129351	157928	265783	24. Autres engagements
Balance sheet total											**Total du bilan**
25. End-year total	483497	509713	523526	543187	567281	611841	621989	730587	869370	1121233	25. En fin d'exercice
26. Average total	472125	496605	516620	533357	555234	589561	616915	676288	799979	995302	26. Moyen

SWITZERLAND
Large commercial banks

SUISSE
Grandes banques commerciales

	1988	1989	1990	1991	1992	1993	1994	1995	1996	1997	
Million Swiss francs											*Millions de francs suisses*
Memorandum items											***Pour mémoire***
27. Short-term securities	*16756*	*19541*	*26556*	*21777*	*26889*	*28279*	*30596*	*37617*	*39677*	*59849*	*27. Titres à court terme*
28. Bonds	*21059*	*22596*	*23619*	*30875*	*33756*	*53544*	*48148*	*57070*	*81185*	*97469*	*28. Obligations*
29. Shares and participations	*9237*	*10685*	*9080*	*11377*	*13026*	*23889*	*30819*	*37744*	*47091*	*70271*	*29. Actions et participations*
30. Claims on non-residents	*245803*	*242273*	*253852*	*267157*	*282046*	*308989*	*299813*	*386906*	*514175*	*735296*	*30. Créances sur des non-résidents*
31. Liabilities to non-residents	*193070*	*201479*	*220536*	*240443*	*248042*	*266879*	*266182*	*346690*	*456308*	*662478*	*31. Engagements envers des non-résidents*
Capital adequacy											***Solvabilité***
32. Tier 1 Capital	..	..	..	..	..	..	..	*43786*	*41053*	*35561*	*32. Fonds propres de base*
33. Tier 2 Capital	..	..	..	..	..	..	..	*16369*	*19143*	*26292*	*33. Fonds propres complémentaires*
34. Supervisory deductions	..	..	..	..	..	..	..	*12139*	*12894*	*11652*	*34. Eléments à déduire des fonds propres*
35. Total net capital resources	*38457*	*43721*	*43716*	*46180*	*47643*	*53224*	*55194*	*48015*	*47302*	*50201*	*35. Total net des ressources en capital*
36. Risk-weighted assets	..	..	..	..	..	..	..	*540686*	*558415*	*564447*	*36. Actifs pondérés des risques*
SUPPLEMENTARY INFORMATION											**RENSEIGNEMENTS COMPLEMENTAIRES**
37. Number of institutions	5	5	4	4	4	4	4	4	4	4	37. Nombre d'institutions
38. Number of branches	901	933	969	983	969	923	955	943	935	840	38. Nombre de succursales
39. Number of employees (x 1000)	60.8	62.9	62.4	62.5	61.9	61.2	62.0	63.0	64.0	63.0	39. Nombre de salariés (x 1000)

1. Borrowing from Central bank (item 20) is included under Interbank deposits (item 21).

1. Emprunts auprès de la Banque centrale (poste 20) sont inclus sous Dépôts interbancaires (poste 21).

SWITZERLAND — SUISSE

Large commercial banks — Grandes banques commerciales

	1988	1989	1990	1991	1992	1993	1994	1995	1996	1997	
Per cent											*Pourcentage*
INCOME STATEMENT ANALYSIS											**ANALYSE DU COMPTE DE RESULTATS**
% of average balance sheet total											**% du total moyen du bilan**
40. Interest income	5.37	6.69	7.32	7.38	6.72	5.78	4.87	4.44	3.88	3.94	40. Produits financiers
41. Interest expenses	4.00	5.32	6.07	5.85	5.04	3.86	3.43	3.22	2.74	2.86	41. Frais financiers
42. Net interest income	1.36	1.37	1.24	1.52	1.68	1.92	1.44	1.22	1.13	1.08	42. Produits financiers nets
43. Non-interest income (net)	1.23	1.39	1.29	1.60	1.68	1.95	1.73	1.94	1.99	1.75	43. Produits non financiers (nets)
a. Fees and commissions receivable	*0.91*	*1.03*	*0.93*	*1.01*	*1.07*	*1.26*	*1.21*	*1.07*	*1.10*	*1.13*	*a. Frais et commissions à recevoir*
b. Fees and commissions payable	*0.04*	*0.05*	*0.05*	*0.05*	*0.05*	*0.05*	*0.04*	*0.05*	*0.08*	*0.08*	*b. Frais et commissions à payer*
c. Net profits or loss on financial operations	*0.29*	*0.32*	*0.32*	*0.41*	*0.49*	*0.55*	*0.33*	*0.61*	*0.61*	*0.52*	*c. Profits ou pertes nets sur opérations financières*
d. Other	*0.07*	*0.08*	*0.10*	*0.23*	*0.16*	*0.19*	*0.23*	*0.32*	*0.36*	*0.18*	*d. Autres*
44. Gross income	2.59	2.75	2.54	3.13	3.36	3.87	3.17	3.16	3.12	2.83	44. Résultat brut
45. Operating expenses	1.49	1.58	1.57	1.69	1.76	1.89	1.80	1.83	2.28	1.98	45. Frais d'exploitation
a. Staff costs	*1.00*	*1.06*	*1.05*	*1.14*	*1.16*	*1.27*	*1.16*	*1.13*	*1.08*	*1.00*	*a. Dépenses en personnel*
b. Property costs	..	..	..	..	..	..	..	..	..	..	*b. Dépenses en immobilier*
c. Other	..	..	..	..	..	..	..	..	..	..	*c. Autres*
46. Net income	1.10	1.17	0.97	1.44	1.60	1.97	1.37	1.33	0.85	0.85	46. Résultat net
47. Provisions (net)	0.46	0.49	0.44	0.83	1.02	1.25	0.83	0.82	1.13	0.92	47. Provisions (nettes)
a. Provisions on loans	..	..	..	..	..	..	..	..	..	..	*a. Provisions sur prêts*
b. Provisions on securities	..	..	..	..	..	..	..	..	..	..	*b. Provisions sur titres*
c. Other	..	..	..	..	..	..	..	..	..	..	*c. Autres*
48. Profit before tax	0.64	0.68	0.53	0.61	0.59	0.72	0.55	0.51	-0.28	-0.07	48. Bénéfices avant impôt
49. Income tax	0.17	0.17	0.13	0.15	0.14	0.15	0.10	0.08	0.05	-	49. Impôt sur le revenu
50. Profit after tax	0.47	0.51	0.40	0.46	0.44	0.57	0.45	0.43	-0.33	-0.07	50. Bénéfices après impôt
51. Distributed profit	0.30	0.33	0.31	0.30	0.29	0.33	0.32	0.31	0.10	0.31	51. Bénéfices distribués
52. Retained profit	0.16	0.19	0.09	0.16	0.16	0.24	0.13	0.12	-0.44	-0.38	52. Bénéfices mis en réserve
% of gross income											**% du total du résultat brut**
53. Net interest income	52.62	49.71	49.07	48.77	50.04	49.55	45.41	38.48	36.32	38.13	53. Produits financiers nets
54. Non-interest income (net)	47.38	50.29	50.93	51.23	49.96	50.45	54.59	61.52	63.68	61.87	54. Produits non financiers (nets)
a. Fees and commissions receivable	*35.04*	*37.57*	*36.55*	*32.34*	*31.88*	*32.61*	*38.32*	*33.84*	*35.08*	*40.07*	*a. Frais et commissions à recevoir*
b. Fees and commissions payable	*1.72*	*1.98*	*2.11*	*1.45*	*1.37*	*1.19*	*1.36*	*1.73*	*2.41*	*2.94*	*b. Frais et commissions à payer*
c. Net profits or loss on financial operations	*11.35*	*11.63*	*12.47*	*13.13*	*14.57*	*14.09*	*10.37*	*19.36*	*19.43*	*18.25*	*c. Profits ou pertes nets sur opérations financières*
d. Other	*2.70*	*3.08*	*4.02*	*7.22*	*4.89*	*4.94*	*7.26*	*10.05*	*11.58*	*6.49*	*d. Autres*
55. Operating expenses	57.43	57.38	61.69	54.10	52.31	48.96	56.67	57.98	72.91	70.04	55. Frais d'exploitation
a. Staff costs	*38.40*	*38.32*	*41.28*	*36.34*	*34.58*	*32.91*	*36.62*	*35.89*	*34.69*	*35.16*	*a. Dépenses en personnel*
b. Property costs	..	..	..	..	..	..	..	..	..	..	*b. Dépenses en immobilier*
c. Other	..	..	..	..	..	..	..	..	..	..	*c. Autres*
56. Net income	42.57	42.62	38.31	45.90	47.69	51.04	43.33	42.02	27.10	29.96	56. Résultat net
57. Provisions (net)	17.78	17.89	17.40	26.40	30.27	32.37	26.13	25.95	36.16	32.36	57. Provisions (nettes)
a. Provisions on loans	..	..	..	..	..	..	..	..	..	..	*a. Provisions sur prêts*
b. Provisions on securities	..	..	..	..	..	..	..	..	..	..	*b. Provisions sur titres*
c. Other	..	..	..	..	..	..	..	..	..	..	*c. Autres*
58. Profit before tax	24.79	24.74	20.91	19.50	17.42	18.67	17.20	16.07	-9.06	-2.40	58. Bénéfices avant impôt
59. Income tax	6.72	6.05	5.20	4.82	4.26	3.86	3.03	2.43	1.58	0.01	59. Impôt sur le revenu
60. Profit after tax	18.06	18.69	15.71	14.68	13.16	14.81	14.17	13.64	-10.65	-2.41	60. Bénéfices après impôt
% of net income											**% du total du résultat net**
61. Provisions (net)	41.78	41.97	45.41	57.51	63.48	63.42	60.31	61.76	133.45	107.99	61. Provisions (nettes)
a. Provisions on loans	..	..	..	..	..	..	..	..	..	..	*a. Provisions sur prêts*
b. Provisions on securities	..	..	..	..	..	..	..	..	..	..	*b. Provisions sur titres*
c. Other	..	..	..	..	..	..	..	..	..	..	*c. Autres*
62. Profit before tax	58.22	58.03	54.59	42.49	36.52	36.58	39.69	38.24	-33.45	-7.99	62. Bénéfices avant impôt
63. Income tax	15.79	14.18	13.58	10.49	8.93	7.57	6.98	5.79	5.85	0.05	63. Impôt sur le revenu
64. Profit after tax	42.43	43.85	41.01	32.00	27.59	29.01	32.70	32.45	-39.29	-8.04	64. Bénéfices après impôt

SWITZERLAND
Large commercial banks

SUISSE
Grandes banques commerciales

	1988	1989	1990	1991	1992	1993	1994	1995	1996	1997	
Per cent											*Pourcentage*
BALANCE SHEET ANALYSIS											**ANALYSE DU BILAN**
% of year-end balance sheet total											**% du total du bilan en fin d'exercice**
Assets											**Actif**
65. Cash & balance with Central bank	1.14	1.07	0.99	0.94	0.86	0.76	0.72	0.59	0.68	0.62	65. Caisse & solde auprès de la Banque centrale
66. Interbank deposits	29.52	23.02	21.16	18.46	18.21	17.28	16.35	18.31	20.83	25.36	66. Dépôts interbancaires
67. Loans	52.92	59.36	61.05	63.35	62.25	58.23	58.30	47.12	44.36	36.87	67. Prêts
68. Securities	9.73	10.36	11.32	11.79	12.99	17.28	17.61	18.13	20.01	20.87	68. Valeurs mobilières
69. Other assets	6.68	6.19	5.48	5.46	5.69	6.46	7.02	15.84	14.12	16.28	69. Autres actifs
Liabilities											**Passif**
70. Capital & reserves	6.14	6.51	6.35	6.29	6.21	6.45	6.81	6.01	4.81	3.78	70. Capital et réserves
71. Borrowing from Central bank	..	..	..	..	..	..	..	..	..	..	71. Emprunts auprès de la Banque centrale
72. Interbank deposits	24.03	23.92	24.26	23.36	22.72	25.70	23.71	21.95	24.04	25.41	72. Dépôts interbancaires
73. Non-bank deposits	51.09	51.35	51.89	52.51	53.49	51.33	54.01	46.79	46.53	40.88	73. Dépôts non bancaires
74. Bonds	11.92	11.52	11.19	11.10	10.45	8.79	8.44	7.54	6.45	6.22	74. Obligations
75. Other liabilities	6.82	6.70	6.31	6.75	7.13	7.74	7.03	17.71	18.17	23.70	75. Autres engagements
Memorandum items											***Pour mémoire***
76. Short-term securities	*3.47*	*3.83*	*5.07*	*4.01*	*4.74*	*4.62*	*4.92*	*5.15*	*4.56*	*5.34*	*76. Titres à court terme*
77. Bonds	*4.36*	*4.43*	*4.51*	*5.68*	*5.95*	*8.75*	*7.74*	*7.81*	*9.34*	*8.69*	*77. Obligations*
78. Shares and participations	*1.91*	*2.10*	*1.73*	*2.09*	*2.30*	*3.90*	*4.95*	*5.17*	*5.42*	*6.27*	*78. Actions et participations*
79. Claims on non-residents	*50.84*	*47.53*	*48.49*	*49.18*	*49.72*	*50.50*	*48.20*	*52.96*	*59.14*	*65.58*	*79. Créances sur des non-résidents*
80. Liabilities to non-residents	*39.93*	*39.53*	*42.13*	*44.27*	*43.72*	*43.62*	*42.80*	*47.45*	*52.49*	*59.08*	*80. Engagements envers des non-résidents*

* See notes on previous pages.

* Voir les notes en pages précédentes.

SWITZERLAND
SUISSE

Other Swiss and foreign commercial banks
Autres banques commerciales suisses et étrangères

	1988	1989	1990	1991	1992	1993	1994	1995	1996	1997	
Million Swiss francs											*Millions de francs suisses*
INCOME STATEMENT											**COMPTE DE RESULTATS**
1. Interest income	7791	11134	13187	13228	12771	11989	9874	9967	8905	9587	1. Produits financiers
2. Interest expenses	5126	8100	9963	9633	9054	7480	6565	6455	5806	6228	2. Frais financiers
3. Net interest income	2665	3034	3224	3595	3717	4509	3309	3512	3099	3360	3. Produits financiers nets
4. Non-interest income (net)	3979	5560	4958	5825	5722	6602	6356	6192	7263	9596	4. Produits non financiers (nets)
a. Fees and commissions receivable	*3100*	*3808*	*3522*	*3684*	*3916*	*5063*	*4959*	*4659*	*5500*	*7104*	*a. Frais et commissions à recevoir*
b. Fees and commissions payable	*232*	*346*	*315*	*325*	*332*	*430*	*425*	*436*	*548*	*738*	*b. Frais et commissions à payer*
c. Net profits or loss on financial operations	*691*	*780*	*793*	*945*	*1021*	*1179*	*911*	*1069*	*1470*	*1930*	*c. Profits ou pertes nets sur opérations financières*
d. Other	*420*	*1318*	*958*	*1521*	*1117*	*790*	*911*	*900*	*841*	*1301*	*d. Autres*
5. Gross income	6644	8594	8182	9420	9439	11111	9665	9704	10361	12956	5. Résultat brut
6. Operating expenses	3762	4281	4728	4991	5135	5430	5394	5511	5959	6796	6. Frais d'exploitation
a. Staff costs	*2444*	*2732*	*3028*	*3180*	*3246*	*3415*	*3412*	*3477*	*3646*	*3957*	*a. Dépenses en personnel*
b. Property costs	..	..	..	..	..	..	..	..	..	..	*b. Dépenses en immobilier*
c. Other	..	..	..	..	..	..	..	..	..	..	*c. Autres*
7. Net income	2882	4313	3454	4429	4304	5681	4271	4193	4402	6160	7. Résultat net
8. Provisions (net)	1236	1794	2034	3003	2624	2859	2285	1703	1737	2102	8. Provisions (nettes)
a. Provisions on loans	..	..	..	..	..	..	..	..	..	..	*a. Provisions sur prêts*
b. Provisions on securities	..	..	..	..	..	..	..	..	..	..	*b. Provisions sur titres*
c. Other	..	..	..	..	..	..	..	..	..	..	*c. Autres*
9. Profit before tax	1646	2519	1420	1426	1680	2822	1986	2490	2665	4058	9. Bénéfices avant impôt
10. Income tax	487	542	407	410	454	723	536	566	643	852	10. Impôt sur le revenu
11. Profit after tax	1159	1977	1013	1016	1226	2099	1450	1924	2022	3206	11. Bénéfices après impôt
12. Distributed profit	571	1270	554	654	673	1018	862	1039	1203	2157	12. Bénéfices distribués
13. Retained profit	588	707	459	362	553	1081	588	885	819	1049	13. Bénéfices mis en réserve
BALANCE SHEET											**BILAN**
Assets											**Actif**
14. Cash & balance with Central bank	3201	3377	3135	2880	3046	3267	3150	3331	3454	3587	14. Caisse & solde auprès de la Banque centrale
15. Interbank deposits	51339	50703	57381	58495	61590	64281	63189	64199	73157	81723	15. Dépôts interbancaires
16. Loans	59906	67353	74007	76536	77108	80898	78090	76700	81899	88643	16. Prêts
17. Securities	20728	24400	24266	25062	26448	29945	31201	32428	36581	39463	17. Valeurs mobilières
18. Other assets	6918	7795	8947	9262	8532	8455	8486	9833	12526	15127	18. Autres actifs
Liabilities											**Passif**
19. Capital & reserves	16354	17583	19981	20597	21770	22887	22637	23130	25049	25315	19. Capital et réserves
20. Borrowing from Central bank (1)	..	..	..	..	..	..	..	..	..	..	20. Emprunts auprès de la Banque centrale (1)
21. Interbank deposits	50318	54111	58003	56446	59295	61617	60336	59609	65053	65929	21. Dépôts interbancaires
22. Non-bank deposits	55965	59633	63942	67664	69333	75551	76069	77913	90913	106380	22. Dépôts non bancaires
23. Bonds	10050	11307	14730	14675	13158	11853	10488	9549	8175	7217	23. Obligations
24. Other liabilities	9404	10993	11080	12854	13167	14937	14586	16289	18426	23701	24. Autres engagements
Balance sheet total											**Total du bilan**
25. End-year total	142091	153628	167737	172235	176723	186845	184116	186490	207617	228542	25. En fin d'exercice
26. Average total	134437	147860	160683	169986	174479	181784	185481	185303	197054	218080	26. Moyen

SWITZERLAND — SUISSE

Other Swiss and foreign commercial banks — Autres banques commerciales suisses et étrangères

	1988	1989	1990	1991	1992	1993	1994	1995	1996	1997	
Million Swiss francs											*Millions de francs suisses*
Memorandum items											***Pour mémoire***
27. Short-term securities	*3471*	*5328*	*6501*	*6875*	*6420*	*4825*	*6331*	*6540*	*7770*	*8826*	*27. Titres à court terme*
28. Bonds	*14587*	*15957*	*15068*	*15694*	*16689*	*20368*	*19548*	*20536*	*21021*	*19700*	*28. Obligations*
29. Shares and participations	*2670*	*3115*	*2698*	*2493*	*3339*	*4752*	*5321*	*5353*	*7495*	*10420*	*29. Actions et participations*
30. Claims on non-residents	*82017*	*87395*	*90756*	*95500*	*99193*	*105648*	*102717*	*100443*	*117911*	*128448*	*30. Créances sur des non-résidents*
31. Liabilities to non-residents	*57374*	*63889*	*66742*	*67487*	*71069*	*77797*	*76145*	*74396*	*91159*	*106148*	*31. Engagements envers des non-résidents*
Capital adequacy											***Solvabilité***
32. Tier 1 Capital	..	..	..	..	..	..	..	*23534*	*24394*	*24957*	*32. Fonds propres de base*
33. Tier 2 Capital	..	..	..	..	..	..	..	*2433*	*2365*	*2113*	*33. Fonds propres complémentaires*
34. Supervisory deductions	..	..	..	..	..	..	..	*1353*	*1662*	*1728*	*34. Eléments à déduire des fonds propres*
35. Total net capital resources	..	..	..	..	..	..	..	*24613*	*25096*	*25342*	*35. Total net des ressources en capital*
36. Risk-weighted assets	..	..	..	..	..	..	..	*127210*	*135621*	*142324*	*36. Actifs pondérés des risques*
SUPPLEMENTARY INFORMATION											**RENSEIGNEMENTS COMPLEMENTAIRES**
37. Number of institutions	205	209	218	222	227	230	226	225	222	214	37. Nombre d'institutions
38. Number of branches	527	549	587	607	592	578	561	564	553	550	38. Nombre de succursales
39. Number of employees (x 1000)	25.9	27.0	28.9	28.1	26.8	26.7	26.6	26.0	26.0	26.0	39. Nombre de salariés (x 1000)

1. Borrowing from Central bank (item 20) is included under Interbank deposits (item 21).

1. Emprunts auprès de la Banque centrale (poste 20) sont inclus sous Dépôts interbancaires (poste 21).

Notes

- Other Swiss and foreign commercial banks include Other Swiss commercial banks and Foreign commercial banks.

Notes

- Les Autres banques commerciales suisses et étrangères comprennent les Autres banques commerciales suisses et les Banques commerciales étrangères.

Other Swiss and foreign commercial banks / Autres banques commerciales suisses et étrangères

Per cent	1988	1989	1990	1991	1992	1993	1994	1995	1996	1997	Pourcentage
INCOME STATEMENT ANALYSIS											**ANALYSE DU COMPTE DE RESULTATS**
% of average balance sheet total											**% du total moyen du bilan**
40. Interest income	5.80	7.53	8.21	7.78	7.32	6.60	5.32	5.38	4.52	4.40	40. Produits financiers
41. Interest expenses	3.81	5.48	6.20	5.67	5.19	4.11	3.54	3.48	2.95	2.86	41. Frais financiers
42. Net interest income	1.98	2.05	2.01	2.11	2.13	2.48	1.78	1.90	1.57	1.54	42. Produits financiers nets
43. Non-interest income (net)	2.96	3.76	3.09	3.43	3.28	3.63	3.43	3.34	3.69	4.40	43. Produits non financiers (nets)
a. Fees and commissions receivable	*2.31*	*2.58*	*2.19*	*2.17*	*2.24*	*2.79*	*2.67*	*2.51*	*2.79*	*3.26*	*a. Frais et commissions à recevoir*
b. Fees and commissions payable	*0.17*	*0.23*	*0.20*	*0.19*	*0.19*	*0.24*	*0.23*	*0.24*	*0.28*	*0.34*	*b. Frais et commissions à payer*
c. Net profits or loss on financial operations	*0.51*	*0.53*	*0.49*	*0.56*	*0.59*	*0.65*	*0.49*	*0.58*	*0.75*	*0.88*	*c. Profits ou pertes nets sur opérations financières*
d. Other	*0.31*	*0.89*	*0.60*	*0.89*	*0.64*	*0.43*	*0.49*	*0.49*	*0.43*	*0.60*	*d. Autres*
44. Gross income	4.94	5.81	5.09	5.54	5.41	6.11	5.21	5.24	5.26	5.94	44. Résultat brut
45. Operating expenses	2.80	2.90	2.94	2.94	2.94	2.99	2.91	2.97	3.02	3.12	45. Frais d'exploitation
a. Staff costs	*1.82*	*1.85*	*1.88*	*1.87*	*1.86*	*1.88*	*1.84*	*1.88*	*1.85*	*1.81*	*a. Dépenses en personnel*
b. Property costs	..	..	..	..	..	..	..	..	..	..	*b. Dépenses en immobilier*
c. Other	..	..	..	..	..	..	..	..	..	..	*c. Autres*
46. Net income	2.14	2.92	2.15	2.61	2.47	3.13	2.30	2.26	2.23	2.82	46. Résultat net
47. Provisions (net)	0.92	1.21	1.27	1.77	1.50	1.57	1.23	0.92	0.88	0.96	47. Provisions (nettes)
a. Provisions on loans	..	..	..	..	..	..	..	..	..	..	*a. Provisions sur prêts*
b. Provisions on securities	..	..	..	..	..	..	..	..	..	..	*b. Provisions sur titres*
c. Other	..	..	..	..	..	..	..	..	..	..	*c. Autres*
48. Profit before tax	1.22	1.70	0.88	0.84	0.96	1.55	1.07	1.34	1.35	1.86	48. Bénéfices avant impôt
49. Income tax	0.36	0.37	0.25	0.24	0.26	0.40	0.29	0.31	0.33	0.39	49. Impôt sur le revenu
50. Profit after tax	0.86	1.34	0.63	0.60	0.70	1.15	0.78	1.04	1.03	1.47	50. Bénéfices après impôt
51. Distributed profit	0.42	0.86	0.34	0.38	0.39	0.56	0.46	0.56	0.61	0.99	51. Bénéfices distribués
52. Retained profit	0.44	0.48	0.29	0.21	0.32	0.59	0.32	0.48	0.42	0.48	52. Bénéfices mis en réserve
% of gross income											**% du total du résultat brut**
53. Net interest income	40.11	35.30	39.40	38.16	39.38	40.58	34.24	36.19	29.91	25.93	53. Produits financiers nets
54. Non-interest income (net)	59.89	64.70	60.60	61.84	60.62	59.42	65.76	63.81	70.10	74.07	54. Produits non financiers (nets)
a. Fees and commissions receivable	*46.66*	*44.31*	*43.05*	*39.11*	*41.49*	*45.57*	*51.31*	*48.01*	*53.08*	*54.83*	*a. Frais et commissions à recevoir*
b. Fees and commissions payable	*3.49*	*4.03*	*3.85*	*3.45*	*3.52*	*3.87*	*4.40*	*4.49*	*5.29*	*5.70*	*b. Frais et commissions à payer*
c. Net profits or loss on financial operations	*10.40*	*9.08*	*9.69*	*10.03*	*10.82*	*10.61*	*9.43*	*11.02*	*14.19*	*14.90*	*c. Profits ou pertes nets sur opérations financières*
d. Other	*6.32*	*15.34*	*11.71*	*16.15*	*11.83*	*7.11*	*9.43*	*9.27*	*8.12*	*10.04*	*d. Autres*
55. Operating expenses	56.62	49.81	57.79	52.98	54.40	48.87	55.81	56.79	57.51	52.45	55. Frais d'exploitation
a. Staff costs	*36.79*	*31.79*	*37.01*	*33.76*	*34.39*	*30.74*	*35.30*	*35.83*	*35.19*	*30.54*	*a. Dépenses en personnel*
b. Property costs	..	..	..	..	..	..	..	..	..	..	*b. Dépenses en immobilier*
c. Other	..	..	..	..	..	..	..	..	..	..	*c. Autres*
56. Net income	43.38	50.19	42.21	47.02	45.60	51.13	44.19	43.21	42.49	47.55	56. Résultat net
57. Provisions (net)	18.60	20.88	24.86	31.88	27.80	25.73	23.64	17.55	16.76	16.22	57. Provisions (nettes)
a. Provisions on loans	..	..	..	..	..	..	..	..	..	..	*a. Provisions sur prêts*
b. Provisions on securities	..	..	..	..	..	..	..	..	..	..	*b. Provisions sur titres*
c. Other	..	..	..	..	..	..	..	..	..	..	*c. Autres*
58. Profit before tax	24.77	29.31	17.36	15.14	17.80	25.40	20.55	25.66	25.72	31.32	58. Bénéfices avant impôt
59. Income tax	7.33	6.31	4.97	4.35	4.81	6.51	5.55	5.83	6.21	6.58	59. Impôt sur le revenu
60. Profit after tax	17.44	23.00	12.38	10.79	12.99	18.89	15.00	19.83	19.52	24.75	60. Bénéfices après impôt
% of net income											**% du total du résultat net**
61. Provisions (net)	42.89	41.60	58.89	67.80	60.97	50.33	53.50	40.62	39.46	34.12	61. Provisions (nettes)
a. Provisions on loans	..	..	..	..	..	..	..	..	..	..	*a. Provisions sur prêts*
b. Provisions on securities	..	..	..	..	..	..	..	..	..	..	*b. Provisions sur titres*
c. Other	..	..	..	..	..	..	..	..	..	..	*c. Autres*
62. Profit before tax	57.11	58.40	41.11	32.20	39.03	49.67	46.50	59.38	60.54	65.88	62. Bénéfices avant impôt
63. Income tax	16.90	12.57	11.78	9.26	10.55	12.73	12.55	13.50	14.61	13.83	63. Impôt sur le revenu
64. Profit after tax	40.22	45.84	29.33	22.94	28.49	36.95	33.95	45.89	45.93	52.05	64. Bénéfices après impôt

SWITZERLAND — SUISSE

Other Swiss and foreign commercial banks — Autres banques commerciales suisses et étrangères

	1988	1989	1990	1991	1992	1993	1994	1995	1996	1997	
Per cent											*Pourcentage*
BALANCE SHEET ANALYSIS											**ANALYSE DU BILAN**
% of year-end balance sheet total											**% du total du bilan en fin d'exercice**
Assets											**Actif**
65. Cash & balance with Central bank	2.25	2.20	1.87	1.67	1.72	1.75	1.71	1.79	1.66	1.57	65. Caisse & solde auprès de la Banque centrale
66. Interbank deposits	36.13	33.00	34.21	33.96	34.85	34.40	34.32	34.42	35.24	35.76	66. Dépôts interbancaires
67. Loans	42.16	43.84	44.12	44.44	43.63	43.30	42.41	41.13	39.45	38.79	67. Prêts
68. Securities	14.59	15.88	14.47	14.55	14.97	16.03	16.95	17.39	17.62	17.27	68. Valeurs mobilières
69. Other assets	4.87	5.07	5.33	5.38	4.83	4.53	4.61	5.27	6.03	6.62	69. Autres actifs
Liabilities											**Passif**
70. Capital & reserves	11.51	11.45	11.91	11.96	12.32	12.25	12.29	12.40	12.07	11.08	70. Capital et réserves
71. Borrowing from Central bank	..	..	..	..	..	..	..	..	..	..	71. Emprunts auprès de la Banque centrale
72. Interbank deposits	35.41	35.22	34.58	32.77	33.55	32.98	32.77	31.96	31.33	28.85	72. Dépôts interbancaires
73. Non-bank deposits	39.39	38.82	38.12	39.29	39.23	40.44	41.32	41.78	43.79	46.55	73. Dépôts non bancaires
74. Bonds	7.07	7.36	8.78	8.52	7.45	6.34	5.70	5.12	3.94	3.16	74. Obligations
75. Other liabilities	6.62	7.16	6.61	7.46	7.45	7.99	7.92	8.73	8.87	10.37	75. Autres engagements
Memorandum items											***Pour mémoire***
76. Short-term securities	*2.44*	*3.47*	*3.88*	*3.99*	*3.63*	*2.58*	*3.44*	*3.51*	*3.74*	*3.86*	*76. Titres à court terme*
77. Bonds	*10.27*	*10.39*	*8.98*	*9.11*	*9.44*	*10.90*	*10.62*	*11.01*	*10.12*	*8.62*	*77. Obligations*
78. Shares and participations	*1.88*	*2.03*	*1.61*	*1.45*	*1.89*	*2.54*	*2.89*	*2.87*	*3.61*	*4.56*	*78. Actions et participations*
79. Claims on non-residents	*57.72*	*56.89*	*54.11*	*55.45*	*56.13*	*56.54*	*55.79*	*53.86*	*56.79*	*56.20*	*79. Créances sur des non-résidents*
80. Liabilities to non-residents	*40.38*	*41.59*	*39.79*	*39.18*	*40.21*	*41.64*	*41.36*	*39.89*	*43.91*	*46.45*	*80. Engagements envers des non-résidents*

* See notes on previous pages.

* Voir les notes en pages précédentes.

SWITZERLAND

Other Swiss commercial banks

SUISSE

Autres banques commerciales suisses

	1988	1989	1990	1991	1992	1993	1994	1995	1996	1997	
Million Swiss francs											*Millions de francs suisses*
INCOME STATEMENT											**COMPTE DE RESULTATS**
1. Interest income	2557	3527	5547	5908	5737	5548	4509	4798	4216	4227	1. Produits financiers
2. Interest expenses	1454	2214	3945	4055	3817	3189	2809	2884	2469	2502	2. Frais financiers
3. Net interest income	1103	1313	1602	1853	1920	2359	1700	1914	1747	1724	3. Produits financiers nets
4. Non-interest income (net)	1659	2052	2295	2269	2574	2934	3042	3021	3353	4819	4. Produits non financiers (nets)
a. Fees and commissions receivable	*1349*	*1665*	*1730*	*1749*	*1874*	*2318*	*2422*	*2195*	*2558*	*3347*	*a. Frais et commissions à recevoir*
b. Fees and commissions payable	*125*	*167*	*178*	*191*	*191*	*212*	*229*	*221*	*253*	*320*	*b. Frais et commissions à payer*
c. Net profits or loss on financial operations	*277*	*325*	*374*	*416*	*465*	*553*	*414*	*560*	*773*	*1071*	*c. Profits ou pertes nets sur opérations financières*
d. Other	*158*	*229*	*369*	*295*	*426*	*275*	*435*	*487*	*275*	*720*	*d. Autres*
5. Gross income	2762	3365	3897	4122	4494	5293	4742	4935	5100	6543	5. Résultat brut
6. Operating expenses	1587	1860	2219	2329	2400	2467	2502	2604	2758	3125	6. Frais d'exploitation
a. Staff costs	*1000*	*1162*	*1407*	*1469*	*1510*	*1556*	*1573*	*1602*	*1671*	*1773*	*a. Dépenses en personnel*
b. Property costs	..	..	..	..	..	..	..	..	..	..	*b. Dépenses en immobilier*
c. Other	..	..	..	..	..	..	..	..	..	..	*c. Autres*
7. Net income	1175	1505	1678	1793	2094	2826	2240	2331	2341	3418	7. Résultat net
8. Provisions (net)	467	683	957	983	1216	1351	1132	829	883	957	8. Provisions (nettes)
a. Provisions on loans	..	..	..	..	..	..	..	..	..	..	*a. Provisions sur prêts*
b. Provisions on securities	..	..	..	..	..	..	..	..	..	..	*b. Provisions sur titres*
c. Other	..	..	..	..	..	..	..	..	..	..	*c. Autres*
9. Profit before tax	708	822	721	810	878	1475	1108	1502	1458	2461	9. Bénéfices avant impôt
10. Income tax	249	252	206	190	235	400	290	354	357	444	10. Impôt sur le revenu
11. Profit after tax	459	570	515	620	643	1075	818	1148	1101	2017	11. Bénéfices après impôt
12. Distributed profit	231	270	290	369	390	608	539	651	749	1443	12. Bénéfices distribués
13. Retained profit	228	300	225	251	253	467	279	497	353	573	13. Bénéfices mis en réserve
BALANCE SHEET											**BILAN**
Assets											**Actif**
14. Cash & balance with Central bank	1351	1261	1296	1128	1083	1361	1341	1500	1578	1467	14. Caisse & solde auprès de la Banque centrale
15. Interbank deposits	12107	12697	20466	21116	22526	23528	23920	25032	30205	33397	15. Dépôts interbancaires
16. Loans	28666	32209	39791	42316	42436	44418	43969	45241	46831	48862	16. Prêts
17. Securities	5663	6629	11232	10817	12212	12010	12493	14052	14665	16635	17. Valeurs mobilières
18. Other assets	2777	3076	4518	4585	4343	4300	4283	4591	5854	7007	18. Autres actifs
Liabilities											**Passif**
19. Capital & reserves	5520	6144	8190	7959	8574	8607	8601	9110	9918	9923	19. Capital et réserves
20. Borrowing from Central bank (1)	..	..	..	..	..	..	..	..	..	..	20. Emprunts auprès de la Banque centrale (1)
21. Interbank deposits	10180	11166	16847	16001	17215	17087	16927	18536	18899	18744	21. Dépôts interbancaires
22. Non-bank deposits	24975	26768	36031	38948	40147	43370	44920	47280	54148	60597	22. Dépôts non bancaires
23. Bonds	6244	7654	11218	11433	10476	9512	8528	7883	6769	5998	23. Obligations
24. Other liabilities	3645	4141	5017	5623	6189	7040	7030	7608	9399	12104	24. Autres engagements
Balance sheet total											**Total du bilan**
25. End-year total	50564	55872	77304	79963	82600	85616	86007	90416	99134	107366	25. En fin d'exercice
26. Average total	49228	53218	66588	78634	81281	84108	85812	88212	94775	103250	26. Moyen

SWITZERLAND

Other Swiss commercial banks

SUISSE

Autres banques commerciales suisses

	1988	1989	1990	1991	1992	1993	1994	1995	1996	1997	
Million Swiss francs											*Millions de francs suisses*
Memorandum items											***Pour mémoire***
27. Short-term securities	*1254*	*1711*	*4667*	*4596*	*4315*	*2771*	*4056*	*4009*	*4852*	*5640*	*27. Titres à court terme*
28. Bonds	*3297*	*3403*	*5288*	*4955*	*5858*	*7110*	*6232*	*7245*	*6416*	*6694*	*28. Obligations*
29. Shares and participations	*1111*	*1514*	*1277*	*1267*	*2039*	*2128*	*2205*	*2797*	*3212*	*3958*	*29. Actions et participations*
30. Claims on non-residents	*17047*	*19024*	*30140*	*32653*	*34826*	*36166*	*35054*	*33769*	*40515*	*42911*	*30. Créances sur des non-résidents*
31. Liabilities to non-residents	*12759*	*14484*	*21644*	*25164*	*26160*	*27918*	*27093*	*26542*	*31026*	*33225*	*31. Engagements envers des non-résidents*
Capital adequacy											***Solvabilité***
32. Tier 1 Capital	..	..	..	..	..	..	..	*9378*	*9501*	*9722*	*32. Fonds propres de base*
33. Tier 2 Capital	..	..	..	..	..	..	..	*1374*	*1466*	*1160*	*33. Fonds propres complémentaires*
34. Supervisory deductions	..	..	..	..	..	..	..	*656*	*855*	*938*	*34. Eléments à déduire des fonds propres*
35. Total net capital resources	..	..	..	..	..	..	..	*10096*	*10110*	*9944*	*35. Total net des ressources en capital*
36. Risk-weighted assets	..	..	..	..	..	..	..	*59351*	*61176*	*62635*	*36. Actifs pondérés des risques*
SUPPLEMENTARY INFORMATION											**RENSEIGNEMENTS COMPLEMENTAIRES**
37. Number of institutions	89	91	92	92	93	87	86	84	81	80	37. Nombre d'institutions
38. Number of branches	287	301	327	333	317	289	277	277	262	241	38. Nombre de succursales
39. Number of employees (x 1000)	11.2	11.8	13.9	13.6	12.9	12.6	12.5	12.6	12.0	12.0	39. Nombre de salariés (x 1000)

1. Borrowing from Central bank (item 20) is included under Interbank deposits (item 21).

1. Emprunts auprès de la Banque centrale (poste 20) sont inclus sous Dépôts interbancaires (poste 21).

Notes

- Other Swiss commercial banks are a sub-group of Other Swiss and foreign commercial banks.

Notes

- Les Autres banques commerciales suisses sont un sous-groupe des Autres banques commerciales suisses et étrangères.

Per cent	1988	1989	1990	1991	1992	1993	1994	1995	1996	1997	Pourcentage
INCOME STATEMENT ANALYSIS											**ANALYSE DU COMPTE DE RESULTATS**
% of average balance sheet total											**% du total moyen du bilan**
40. Interest income	5.19	6.63	8.33	7.51	7.06	6.60	5.25	5.44	4.45	4.09	40. Produits financiers
41. Interest expenses	2.95	4.16	5.92	5.16	4.70	3.79	3.27	3.27	2.61	2.42	41. Frais financiers
42. Net interest income	2.24	2.47	2.41	2.36	2.36	2.80	1.98	2.17	1.84	1.67	42. Produits financiers nets
43. Non-interest income (net)	3.37	3.86	3.45	2.89	3.17	3.49	3.54	3.42	3.54	4.67	43. Produits non financiers (nets)
a. Fees and commissions receivable	*2.74*	*3.13*	*2.60*	*2.22*	*2.31*	*2.76*	*2.82*	*2.49*	*2.70*	*3.24*	*a. Frais et commissions à recevoir*
b. Fees and commissions payable	*0.25*	*0.31*	*0.27*	*0.24*	*0.23*	*0.25*	*0.27*	*0.25*	*0.27*	*0.31*	*b. Frais et commissions à payer*
c. Net profits or loss on financial operations	*0.56*	*0.61*	*0.56*	*0.53*	*0.57*	*0.66*	*0.48*	*0.63*	*0.82*	*1.04*	*c. Profits ou pertes nets sur opérations financières*
d. Other	*0.32*	*0.43*	*0.55*	*0.38*	*0.52*	*0.33*	*0.51*	*0.55*	*0.29*	*0.70*	*d. Autres*
44. Gross income	5.61	6.32	5.85	5.24	5.53	6.29	5.53	5.59	5.38	6.34	44. Résultat brut
45. Operating expenses	3.22	3.50	3.33	2.96	2.95	2.93	2.92	2.95	2.91	3.03	45. Frais d'exploitation
a. Staff costs	*2.03*	*2.18*	*2.11*	*1.87*	*1.86*	*1.85*	*1.83*	*1.82*	*1.76*	*1.72*	*a. Dépenses en personnel*
b. Property costs	..	..	..	..	..	..	..	..	..	..	*b. Dépenses en immobilier*
c. Other	..	..	..	..	..	..	..	..	..	..	*c. Autres*
46. Net income	2.39	2.83	2.52	2.28	2.58	3.36	2.61	2.64	2.47	3.31	46. Résultat net
47. Provisions (net)	0.95	1.28	1.44	1.25	1.50	1.61	1.32	0.94	0.93	0.93	47. Provisions (nettes)
a. Provisions on loans	..	..	..	..	..	..	..	..	..	..	*a. Provisions sur prêts*
b. Provisions on securities	..	..	..	..	..	..	..	..	..	..	*b. Provisions sur titres*
c. Other	..	..	..	..	..	..	..	..	..	..	*c. Autres*
48. Profit before tax	1.44	1.54	1.08	1.03	1.08	1.75	1.29	1.70	1.54	2.38	48. Bénéfices avant impôt
49. Income tax	0.51	0.47	0.31	0.24	0.29	0.48	0.34	0.40	0.38	0.43	49. Impôt sur le revenu
50. Profit after tax	0.93	1.07	0.77	0.79	0.79	1.28	0.95	1.30	1.16	1.95	50. Bénéfices après impôt
51. Distributed profit	0.47	0.51	0.44	0.47	0.48	0.72	0.63	0.74	0.79	1.40	51. Bénéfices distribués
52. Retained profit	0.46	0.56	0.34	0.32	0.31	0.56	0.33	0.56	0.37	0.55	52. Bénéfices mis en réserve
% of gross income											**% du total du résultat brut**
53. Net interest income	39.93	39.02	41.11	44.95	42.72	44.57	35.85	38.78	34.25	26.35	53. Produits financiers nets
54. Non-interest income (net)	60.07	60.98	58.89	55.05	57.28	55.43	64.15	61.22	65.75	73.65	54. Produits non financiers (nets)
a. Fees and commissions receivable	*48.84*	*49.48*	*44.39*	*42.43*	*41.70*	*43.79*	*51.08*	*44.48*	*50.16*	*51.15*	*a. Frais et commissions à recevoir*
b. Fees and commissions payable	*4.53*	*4.96*	*4.57*	*4.63*	*4.25*	*4.01*	*4.83*	*4.48*	*4.96*	*4.89*	*b. Frais et commissions à payer*
c. Net profits or loss on financial operations	*10.03*	*9.66*	*9.60*	*10.09*	*10.35*	*10.45*	*8.73*	*11.35*	*15.16*	*16.37*	*c. Profits ou pertes nets sur opérations financières*
d. Other	*5.72*	*6.81*	*9.47*	*7.16*	*9.48*	*5.20*	*9.17*	*9.87*	*5.39*	*11.00*	*d. Autres*
55. Operating expenses	57.46	55.27	56.94	56.50	53.40	46.61	52.76	52.77	54.08	47.76	55. Frais d'exploitation
a. Staff costs	*36.21*	*34.53*	*36.10*	*35.64*	*33.60*	*29.40*	*33.17*	*32.46*	*32.76*	*27.10*	*a. Dépenses en personnel*
b. Property costs	..	..	..	..	..	..	..	..	..	..	*b. Dépenses en immobilier*
c. Other	..	..	..	..	..	..	..	..	..	..	*c. Autres*
56. Net income	42.54	44.73	43.06	43.50	46.60	53.39	47.24	47.23	45.90	52.24	56. Résultat net
57. Provisions (net)	16.91	20.30	24.56	23.85	27.06	25.52	23.87	16.80	17.31	14.63	57. Provisions (nettes)
a. Provisions on loans	..	..	..	..	..	..	..	..	..	..	*a. Provisions sur prêts*
b. Provisions on securities	..	..	..	..	..	..	..	..	..	..	*b. Provisions sur titres*
c. Other	..	..	..	..	..	..	..	..	..	..	*c. Autres*
58. Profit before tax	25.63	24.43	18.50	19.65	19.54	27.87	23.37	30.44	28.59	37.61	58. Bénéfices avant impôt
59. Income tax	9.02	7.49	5.29	4.61	5.23	7.56	6.12	7.17	7.00	6.79	59. Impôt sur le revenu
60. Profit after tax	16.62	16.94	13.22	15.04	14.31	20.31	17.25	23.26	21.59	30.83	60. Bénéfices après impôt
% of net income											**% du total du résultat net**
61. Provisions (net)	39.74	45.38	57.03	54.82	58.07	47.81	50.54	35.56	37.72	28.00	61. Provisions (nettes)
a. Provisions on loans	..	..	..	..	..	..	..	..	..	..	*a. Provisions sur prêts*
b. Provisions on securities	..	..	..	..	..	..	..	..	..	..	*b. Provisions sur titres*
c. Other	..	..	..	..	..	..	..	..	..	..	*c. Autres*
62. Profit before tax	60.26	54.62	42.97	45.18	41.93	52.19	49.46	64.44	62.28	72.00	62. Bénéfices avant impôt
63. Income tax	21.19	16.74	12.28	10.60	11.22	14.15	12.95	15.19	15.25	12.99	63. Impôt sur le revenu
64. Profit after tax	39.06	37.87	30.69	34.58	30.71	38.04	36.52	49.25	47.03	59.01	64. Bénéfices après impôt

SWITZERLAND
Other Swiss commercial banks

SUISSE
Autres banques commerciales suisses

	1988	1989	1990	1991	1992	1993	1994	1995	1996	1997	
Per cent											*Pourcentage*
BALANCE SHEET ANALYSIS											**ANALYSE DU BILAN**
% of year-end balance sheet total											**% du total du bilan en fin d'exercice**
Assets											**Actif**
65. Cash & balance with Central bank	2.67	2.26	1.68	1.41	1.31	1.59	1.56	1.66	1.59	1.37	65. Caisse & solde auprès de la Banque centrale
66. Interbank deposits	23.94	22.73	26.47	26.41	27.27	27.48	27.81	27.69	30.47	31.11	66. Dépôts interbancaires
67. Loans	56.69	57.65	51.47	52.92	51.38	51.88	51.12	50.04	47.24	45.51	67. Prêts
68. Securities	11.20	11.86	14.53	13.53	14.78	14.03	14.53	15.54	14.79	15.49	68. Valeurs mobilières
69. Other assets	5.49	5.51	5.84	5.73	5.26	5.02	4.98	5.08	5.91	6.53	69. Autres actifs
Liabilities											**Passif**
70. Capital & reserves	10.92	11.00	10.59	9.95	10.38	10.05	10.00	10.08	10.00	9.24	70. Capital et réserves
71. Borrowing from Central bank	..	..	..	..	..	..	..	..	..	..	71. Emprunts auprès de la Banque centrale
72. Interbank deposits	20.13	19.98	21.79	20.01	20.84	19.96	19.68	20.50	19.06	17.46	72. Dépôts interbancaires
73. Non-bank deposits	49.39	47.91	46.61	48.71	48.60	50.66	52.23	52.29	54.62	56.44	73. Dépôts non bancaires
74. Bonds	12.35	13.70	14.51	14.30	12.68	11.11	9.92	8.72	6.83	5.59	74. Obligations
75. Other liabilities	7.21	7.41	6.49	7.03	7.49	8.22	8.17	8.41	9.48	11.27	75. Autres engagements
Memorandum items											***Pour mémoire***
76. Short-term securities	*2.48*	*3.06*	*6.04*	*5.75*	*5.22*	*3.24*	*4.72*	*4.43*	*4.89*	*5.25*	*76. Titres à court terme*
77. Bonds	*6.52*	*6.09*	*6.84*	*6.20*	*7.09*	*8.30*	*7.25*	*8.01*	*6.47*	*6.23*	*77. Obligations*
78. Shares and participations	*2.20*	*2.71*	*1.65*	*1.58*	*2.47*	*2.49*	*2.56*	*3.09*	*3.24*	*3.69*	*78. Actions et participations*
79. Claims on non-residents	*33.71*	*34.05*	*38.99*	*40.84*	*42.16*	*42.24*	*40.76*	*37.35*	*40.87*	*39.97*	*79. Créances sur des non-résidents*
80. Liabilities to non-residents	*25.23*	*25.92*	*28.00*	*31.47*	*31.67*	*32.61*	*31.50*	*29.36*	*31.30*	*30.95*	*80. Engagements envers des non-résidents*

* See notes on previous pages.

* Voir les notes en pages précédentes.

SWITZERLAND — SUISSE

Foreign commercial banks — Banques commerciales étrangères

Million Swiss francs	1988	1989	1990	1991	1992	1993	1994	1995	1996	1997	Millions de francs suisses
INCOME STATEMENT											**COMPTE DE RESULTATS**
1. Interest income	5235	7607	7640	7320	7034	6442	5365	5169	4689	5360	1. Produits financiers
2. Interest expenses	3672	5886	6017	5578	5237	4291	3756	3571	3337	3725	2. Frais financiers
3. Net interest income	1563	1721	1623	1742	1797	2151	1609	1598	1351	1635	3. Produits financiers nets
4. Non-interest income (net)	2319	3508	2663	3558	3148	3666	3312	3170	3910	4778	4. Produits non financiers (nets)
a. Fees and commissions receivable	*1751*	*2143*	*1792*	*1935*	*2042*	*2745*	*2538*	*2465*	*2942*	*3757*	*a. Frais et commissions à recevoir*
b. Fees and commissions payable	*108*	*179*	*137*	*133*	*142*	*218*	*197*	*215*	*295*	*418*	*b. Frais et commissions à payer*
c. Net profits or loss on financial operations	*413*	*455*	*419*	*530*	*557*	*625*	*496*	*509*	*697*	*859*	*c. Profits ou pertes nets sur opérations financières*
d. Other	*263*	*1089*	*589*	*1226*	*691*	*514*	*475*	*412*	*566*	*580*	*d. Autres*
5. Gross income	3882	5229	4286	5300	4945	5817	4921	4768	5261	6413	5. Résultat brut
6. Operating expenses	2175	2421	2509	2662	2734	2963	2891	2907	3201	3671	6. Frais d'exploitation
a. Staff costs	*1444*	*1569*	*1621*	*1712*	*1736*	*1859*	*1839*	*1875*	*1976*	*2184*	*a. Dépenses en personnel*
b. Property costs	..	..	..	..	..	..	..	..	..	..	*b. Dépenses en immobilier*
c. Other	..	..	..	..	..	..	..	..	..	..	*c. Autres*
7. Net income	1707	2808	1777	2638	2211	2854	2030	1861	2060	2742	7. Résultat net
8. Provisions (net)	769	1112	1077	2021	1408	1508	1153	874	854	1145	8. Provisions (nettes)
a. Provisions on loans	..	..	..	..	..	..	..	..	..	..	*a. Provisions sur prêts*
b. Provisions on securities	..	..	..	..	..	..	..	..	..	..	*b. Provisions sur titres*
c. Other	..	..	..	..	..	..	..	..	..	..	*c. Autres*
9. Profit before tax	938	1696	700	617	803	1346	877	987	1206	1597	9. Bénéfices avant impôt
10. Income tax	238	290	201	220	219	323	247	212	286	408	10. Impôt sur le revenu
11. Profit after tax	700	1406	499	397	584	1023	630	775	920	1189	11. Bénéfices après impôt
12. Distributed profit	340	1000	264	285	283	409	323	387	455	714	12. Bénéfices distribués
13. Retained profit	360	406	235	112	301	614	307	388	465	475	13. Bénéfices mis en réserve
BALANCE SHEET											**BILAN**
Assets											**Actif**
14. Cash & balance with Central bank	1850	2116	1839	1753	1963	1906	1809	1830	1875	2120	14. Caisse & solde auprès de la Banque centrale
15. Interbank deposits	39232	38006	36915	37379	39064	40752	39269	39167	42951	48326	15. Dépôts interbancaires
16. Loans	31239	35144	34215	34220	34672	36481	34121	31459	35068	39781	16. Prêts
17. Securities	15065	17771	13034	14244	14236	17935	18708	18376	21916	22828	17. Valeurs mobilières
18. Other assets	4141	4719	4429	4677	4189	4155	4203	5242	6673	8120	18. Autres actifs
Liabilities											**Passif**
19. Capital & reserves	10834	11440	11791	12638	13197	14281	14036	14020	15131	15392	19. Capital et réserves
20. Borrowing from Central bank (1)	..	..	..	..	..	..	..	..	..	..	20. Emprunts auprès de la Banque centrale (1)
21. Interbank deposits	40137	42946	41156	40444	42081	44529	43409	41073	46154	47185	21. Dépôts interbancaires
22. Non-bank deposits	30990	32865	27910	28716	29186	32181	31149	30634	36765	45783	22. Dépôts non bancaires
23. Bonds	3806	3653	3512	3243	2682	2340	1959	1667	1406	1219	23. Obligations
24. Other liabilities	5759	6852	6063	7231	6978	7897	7556	8681	9028	11596	24. Autres engagements
Balance sheet total											**Total du bilan**
25. End-year total	91527	97756	90433	92272	94124	101229	98109	96074	108483	121175	25. En fin d'exercice
26. Average total	85209	94642	94095	91353	93198	97677	99669	97092	102279	114829	26. Moyen

SWITZERLAND
Foreign commercial banks

SUISSE
Banques commerciales étrangères

	1988	1989	1990	1991	1992	1993	1994	1995	1996	1997	
Million Swiss francs											*Millions de francs suisses*
Memorandum items											***Pour mémoire***
27. Short-term securities	*2217*	*3617*	*1834*	*2280*	*2105*	*2054*	*2275*	*2531*	*2918*	*3185*	*27. Titres à court terme*
28. Bonds	*11289*	*12554*	*9780*	*10739*	*10831*	*13257*	*13317*	*13291*	*14605*	*13007*	*28. Obligations*
29. Shares and participations	*1559*	*1601*	*1421*	*1226*	*1300*	*2623*	*3116*	*2555*	*4283*	*6463*	*29. Actions et participations*
30. Claims on non-residents	*64970*	*68371*	*60616*	*62847*	*64367*	*69482*	*67663*	*66674*	*77395*	*85538*	*30. Créances sur des non-résidents*
31. Liabilities to non-residents	*44614*	*49405*	*45098*	*42323*	*44909*	*49879*	*49052*	*47855*	*60132*	*72923*	*31. Engagements envers des non-résidents*
Capital adequacy											***Solvabilité***
32. Tier 1 Capital	..	..	..	..	..	..	..	*14156*	*14894*	*15235*	*32. Fonds propres de base*
33. Tier 2 Capital	..	..	..	..	..	..	..	*1059*	*899*	*954*	*33. Fonds propres complémentaires*
34. Supervisory deductions	..	..	..	..	..	..	..	*697*	*807*	*789*	*34. Eléments à déduire des fonds propres*
35. Total net capital resources	..	..	..	..	..	..	..	*14517*	*14986*	*15399*	*35. Total net des ressources en capital*
36. Risk-weighted assets	..	..	..	..	..	..	..	*67859*	*74444*	*79691*	*36. Actifs pondérés des risques*
SUPPLEMENTARY INFORMATION											**RENSEIGNEMENTS COMPLEMENTAIRES**
37. Number of institutions	116	118	126	130	134	143	140	141	141	134	37. Nombre d'institutions
38. Number of branches	240	248	260	274	275	289	284	287	291	309	38. Nombre de succursales
39. Number of employees (x 1000)	14.7	15.2	15.0	14.5	13.9	14.2	14.2	13.9	13.9	15.0	39. Nombre de salariés (x 1000)

1. Borrowing from Central bank (item 20) is included under Interbank deposits (item 21).

1. Emprunts auprès de la Banque centrale (poste 20) sont inclus sous Dépôts interbancaires (poste 21).

Notes

- Foreign commercial banks are a sub-group of Other Swiss and foreign commercial banks.

Notes

- Les Banques commerciales étrangères sont un sous-groupe des Autres banques commerciales suisses et étrangères.

SWITZERLAND — SUISSE

Foreign commercial banks — Banques commerciales étrangères

	1988	1989	1990	1991	1992	1993	1994	1995	1996	1997	
Per cent											*Pourcentage*
INCOME STATEMENT ANALYSIS											**ANALYSE DU COMPTE DE RESULTATS**
% of average balance sheet total											**% du total moyen du bilan**
40. Interest income	6.14	8.04	8.12	8.01	7.55	6.60	5.38	5.32	4.58	4.67	40. Produits financiers
41. Interest expenses	4.31	6.22	6.39	6.11	5.62	4.39	3.77	3.68	3.26	3.24	41. Frais financiers
42. Net interest income	1.83	1.82	1.72	1.91	1.93	2.20	1.61	1.65	1.32	1.42	42. Produits financiers nets
43. Non-interest income (net)	2.72	3.71	2.83	3.89	3.38	3.75	3.32	3.26	3.82	4.16	43. Produits non financiers (nets)
a. Fees and commissions receivable	*2.05*	*2.26*	*1.90*	*2.12*	*2.19*	*2.81*	*2.55*	*2.54*	*2.88*	*3.27*	*a. Frais et commissions à recevoir*
b. Fees and commissions payable	*0.13*	*0.19*	*0.15*	*0.15*	*0.15*	*0.22*	*0.20*	*0.22*	*0.29*	*0.36*	*b. Frais et commissions à payer*
c. Net profits or loss on financial operations	*0.48*	*0.48*	*0.45*	*0.58*	*0.60*	*0.64*	*0.50*	*0.52*	*0.68*	*0.75*	*c. Profits ou pertes nets sur opérations financières*
d. Other	*0.31*	*1.15*	*0.63*	*1.34*	*0.74*	*0.53*	*0.48*	*0.42*	*0.55*	*0.51*	*d. Autres*
44. Gross income	4.56	5.53	4.55	5.80	5.31	5.96	4.94	4.91	5.14	5.58	44. Résultat brut
45. Operating expenses	2.55	2.56	2.67	2.91	2.93	3.03	2.90	2.99	3.13	3.20	45. Frais d'exploitation
a. Staff costs	*1.69*	*1.66*	*1.72*	*1.87*	*1.86*	*1.90*	*1.85*	*1.93*	*1.93*	*1.90*	*a. Dépenses en personnel*
b. Property costs	..	..	..	..	..	..	..	..	..	..	*b. Dépenses en immobilier*
c. Other	..	..	..	..	..	..	..	..	..	..	*c. Autres*
46. Net income	2.00	2.97	1.89	2.89	2.37	2.92	2.04	1.92	2.01	2.39	46. Résultat net
47. Provisions (net)	0.90	1.17	1.14	2.21	1.51	1.54	1.16	0.90	0.83	1.00	47. Provisions (nettes)
a. Provisions on loans	..	..	..	..	..	..	..	..	..	..	*a. Provisions sur prêts*
b. Provisions on securities	..	..	..	..	..	..	..	..	..	..	*b. Provisions sur titres*
c. Other	..	..	..	..	..	..	..	..	..	..	*c. Autres*
48. Profit before tax	1.10	1.79	0.74	0.68	0.86	1.38	0.88	1.02	1.18	1.39	48. Bénéfices avant impôt
49. Income tax	0.28	0.31	0.21	0.24	0.23	0.33	0.25	0.22	0.28	0.36	49. Impôt sur le revenu
50. Profit after tax	0.82	1.49	0.53	0.43	0.63	1.05	0.63	0.80	0.90	1.04	50. Bénéfices après impôt
51. Distributed profit	0.40	1.06	0.28	0.31	0.30	0.42	0.32	0.40	0.44	0.62	51. Bénéfices distribués
52. Retained profit	0.42	0.43	0.25	0.12	0.32	0.63	0.31	0.40	0.45	0.41	52. Bénéfices mis en réserve
% of gross income											**% du total du résultat brut**
53. Net interest income	40.26	32.91	37.87	32.87	36.34	36.98	32.70	33.52	25.68	25.50	53. Produits financiers nets
54. Non-interest income (net)	59.74	67.09	62.13	67.13	63.66	63.02	67.30	66.48	74.32	74.50	54. Produits non financiers (nets)
a. Fees and commissions receivable	*45.11*	*40.98*	*41.81*	*36.51*	*41.29*	*47.19*	*51.57*	*51.70*	*55.92*	*58.58*	*a. Frais et commissions à recevoir*
b. Fees and commissions payable	*2.78*	*3.42*	*3.20*	*2.51*	*2.87*	*3.75*	*4.00*	*4.51*	*5.61*	*6.52*	*b. Frais et commissions à payer*
c. Net profits or loss on financial operations	*10.64*	*8.70*	*9.78*	*10.00*	*11.26*	*10.74*	*10.08*	*10.68*	*13.25*	*13.39*	*c. Profits ou pertes nets sur opérations financières*
d. Other	*6.77*	*20.83*	*13.74*	*23.13*	*13.97*	*8.84*	*9.65*	*8.64*	*10.76*	*9.04*	*d. Autres*
55. Operating expenses	56.03	46.30	58.54	50.23	55.29	50.94	58.75	60.97	60.84	57.24	55. Frais d'exploitation
a. Staff costs	*37.20*	*30.01*	*37.82*	*32.30*	*35.11*	*31.96*	*37.37*	*39.32*	*37.56*	*34.06*	*a. Dépenses en personnel*
b. Property costs	..	..	..	..	..	..	..	..	..	..	*b. Dépenses en immobilier*
c. Other	..	..	..	..	..	..	..	..	..	..	*c. Autres*
56. Net income	43.97	53.70	41.46	49.77	44.71	49.06	41.25	39.03	39.16	42.76	56. Résultat net
57. Provisions (net)	19.81	21.27	25.13	38.13	28.47	25.92	23.43	18.33	16.23	17.85	57. Provisions (nettes)
a. Provisions on loans	..	..	..	..	..	..	..	..	..	..	*a. Provisions sur prêts*
b. Provisions on securities	..	..	..	..	..	..	..	..	..	..	*b. Provisions sur titres*
c. Other	..	..	..	..	..	..	..	..	..	..	*c. Autres*
58. Profit before tax	24.16	32.43	16.33	11.64	16.24	23.14	17.82	20.70	22.92	24.90	58. Bénéfices avant impôt
59. Income tax	6.13	5.55	4.69	4.15	4.43	5.55	5.02	4.45	5.44	6.36	59. Impôt sur le revenu
60. Profit after tax	18.03	26.89	11.64	7.49	11.81	17.59	12.80	16.25	17.49	18.54	60. Bénéfices après impôt
% of net income											**% du total du résultat net**
61. Provisions (net)	45.05	39.60	60.61	76.61	63.68	52.84	56.80	46.96	41.46	41.76	61. Provisions (nettes)
a. Provisions on loans	..	..	..	..	..	..	..	..	..	..	*a. Provisions sur prêts*
b. Provisions on securities	..	..	..	..	..	..	..	..	..	..	*b. Provisions sur titres*
c. Other	..	..	..	..	..	..	..	..	..	..	*c. Autres*
62. Profit before tax	54.95	60.40	39.39	23.39	36.32	47.16	43.20	53.04	58.54	58.24	62. Bénéfices avant impôt
63. Income tax	13.94	10.33	11.31	8.34	9.91	11.32	12.17	11.39	13.88	14.88	63. Impôt sur le revenu
64. Profit after tax	41.01	50.07	28.08	15.05	26.41	35.84	31.03	41.64	44.66	43.36	64. Bénéfices après impôt

SWITZERLAND
Foreign commercial banks

SUISSE
Banques commerciales étrangères

	1988	1989	1990	1991	1992	1993	1994	1995	1996	1997	
Per cent											*Pourcentage*
BALANCE SHEET ANALYSIS											**ANALYSE DU BILAN**
% of year-end balance sheet total											**% du total du bilan en fin d'exercice**
Assets											**Actif**
65. Cash & balance with Central bank	2.02	2.16	2.03	1.90	2.09	1.88	1.84	1.90	1.73	1.75	65. Caisse & solde auprès de la Banque centrale
66. Interbank deposits	42.86	38.88	40.82	40.51	41.50	40.26	40.03	40.77	39.59	39.88	66. Dépôts interbancaires
67. Loans	34.13	35.95	37.83	37.09	36.84	36.04	34.78	32.74	32.33	32.83	67. Prêts
68. Securities	16.46	18.18	14.41	15.44	15.12	17.72	19.07	19.13	20.20	18.84	68. Valeurs mobilières
69. Other assets	4.52	4.83	4.90	5.07	4.45	4.10	4.28	5.46	6.15	6.70	69. Autres actifs
Liabilities											**Passif**
70. Capital & reserves	11.84	11.70	13.04	13.70	14.02	14.11	14.31	14.59	13.95	12.70	70. Capital et réserves
71. Borrowing from Central bank	..	..	..	..	..	..	..	..	..	..	71. Emprunts auprès de la Banque centrale
72. Interbank deposits	43.85	43.93	45.51	43.83	44.71	43.99	44.25	42.75	42.54	38.94	72. Dépôts interbancaires
73. Non-bank deposits	33.86	33.62	30.86	31.12	31.01	31.79	31.75	31.89	33.89	37.78	73. Dépôts non bancaires
74. Bonds	4.16	3.74	3.88	3.51	2.85	2.31	2.00	1.74	1.30	1.01	74. Obligations
75. Other liabilities	6.29	7.01	6.70	7.84	7.41	7.80	7.70	9.04	8.32	9.57	75. Autres engagements
Memorandum items											***Pour mémoire***
76. Short-term securities	*2.42*	*3.70*	*2.03*	*2.47*	*2.24*	*2.03*	*2.32*	*2.63*	*2.69*	*2.63*	*76. Titres à court terme*
77. Bonds	*12.33*	*12.84*	*10.81*	*11.64*	*11.51*	*13.10*	*13.57*	*13.83*	*13.46*	*10.73*	*77. Obligations*
78. Shares and participations	*1.70*	*1.64*	*1.57*	*1.33*	*1.38*	*2.59*	*3.18*	*2.66*	*3.95*	*5.33*	*78. Actions et participations*
79. Claims on non-residents	*70.98*	*69.94*	*67.03*	*68.11*	*68.39*	*68.64*	*68.97*	*69.40*	*71.34*	*70.59*	*79. Créances sur des non-résidents*
80. Liabilities to non-residents	*48.74*	*50.54*	*49.87*	*45.87*	*47.71*	*49.27*	*50.00*	*49.81*	*55.43*	*60.18*	*80. Engagements envers des non-résidents*

* See notes on previous pages.

* Voir les notes en pages précédentes.

SWITZERLAND / SUISSE

Cantonal banks / Banques cantonales

	1988	1989	1990	1991	1992	1993	1994	1995	1996	1997	
Million Swiss francs											*Millions de francs suisses*
INCOME STATEMENT											**COMPTE DE RESULTATS**
1. Interest income	7834	9504	12441	14496	15597	14889	13316	12367	11653	10966	1. Produits financiers
2. Interest expenses	5879	7387	9950	11531	12456	11241	10259	9193	8293	7414	2. Frais financiers
3. Net interest income	1955	2117	2491	2965	3141	3648	3057	3174	3361	3551	3. Produits financiers nets
4. Non-interest income (net)	740	845	937	1794	1616	1546	1818	1728	1825	2445	4. Produits non financiers (nets)
a. Fees and commissions receivable	*469*	*548*	*582*	*641*	*689*	*874*	*829*	*712*	*909*	*1197*	*a. Frais et commissions à recevoir*
b. Fees and commissions payable	*21*	*29*	*29*	*30*	*33*	*45*	*52*	*64*	*90*	*131*	*b. Frais et commissions à payer*
c. Net profits or loss on financial operations	*123*	*137*	*130*	*180*	*183*	*203*	*175*	*306*	*413*	*510*	*c. Profits ou pertes nets sur opérations financières*
d. Other	*169*	*189*	*254*	*1003*	*776*	*514*	*866*	*774*	*593*	*869*	*d. Autres*
5. Gross income	2695	2962	3428	4759	4757	5194	4875	4902	5186	5996	5. Résultat brut
6. Operating expenses	1636	1771	2006	2173	2312	2430	2594	2529	2966	3556	6. Frais d'exploitation
a. Staff costs	*1124*	*1210*	*1320*	*1455*	*1516*	*1576*	*1665*	*1619*	*1676*	*1702*	*a. Dépenses en personnel*
b. Property costs	..	..	..	..	..	..	..	..	..	..	*b. Dépenses en immobilier*
c. Other	..	..	..	..	..	..	..	..	..	..	*c. Autres*
7. Net income	1059	1191	1422	2586	2445	2764	2281	2373	2220	2440	7. Résultat net
8. Provisions (net)	468	546	732	1980	2236	2186	1779	1700	1539	1621	8. Provisions (nettes)
a. Provisions on loans	..	..	..	..	..	..	..	..	..	..	*a. Provisions sur prêts*
b. Provisions on securities	..	..	..	..	..	..	..	..	..	..	*b. Provisions sur titres*
c. Other	..	..	..	..	..	..	..	..	..	..	*c. Autres*
9. Profit before tax	591	645	690	606	209	578	502	673	681	819	9. Bénéfices avant impôt
10. Income tax	60	60	114	64	46	42	39	36	41	45	10. Impôt sur le revenu
11. Profit after tax	531	585	576	542	163	536	463	637	640	774	11. Bénéfices après impôt
12. Distributed profit	379	413	427	406	418	468	484	501	511	563	12. Bénéfices distribués
13. Retained profit	152	172	149	136	-255	68	-21	136	129	211	13. Bénéfices mis en réserve
BALANCE SHEET											**BILAN**
Assets											**Actif**
14. Cash & balance with Central bank	2146	2024	2080	2203	2311	2500	2136	2408	2456	2471	14. Caisse & solde auprès de la Banque centrale
15. Interbank deposits	23943	20976	19885	20112	22311	25069	22802	24134	25162	23211	15. Dépôts interbancaires
16. Loans	134904	152419	170371	182581	189022	198362	205616	207095	209883	214577	16. Prêts
17. Securities	13218	13513	14639	15121	15414	17221	18212	17926	18602	19903	17. Valeurs mobilières
18. Other assets	5490	6241	6904	8265	9773	9928	10515	9965	9754	8831	18. Autres actifs
Liabilities											**Passif**
19. Capital & reserves	7603	8078	8838	9182	9827	10471	10825	10917	15281	16351	19. Capital et réserves
20. Borrowing from Central bank (1)	..	..	..	..	..	..	..	..	..	..	20. Emprunts auprès de la Banque centrale (1)
21. Interbank deposits	10510	11931	15833	16031	17065	17171	18328	18023	19017	18942	21. Dépôts interbancaires
22. Non-bank deposits	100577	106657	109647	115245	117334	127706	131878	133061	139538	144734	22. Dépôts non bancaires
23. Bonds	51554	57677	66223	72846	77677	79506	78954	77944	73237	70109	23. Obligations
24. Other liabilities	9457	10830	13338	14978	16927	18226	19296	21582	18785	18858	24. Autres engagements
Balance sheet total											**Total du bilan**
25. End-year total	179701	195173	213879	228282	238830	253080	259281	261527	265858	268994	25. En fin d'exercice
26. Average total	173591	187437	204526	221081	233556	245955	256181	260404	263693	267426	26. Moyen

SWITZERLAND / SUISSE

Cantonal banks / Banques cantonales

	1988	1989	1990	1991	1992	1993	1994	1995	1996	1997	
Million Swiss francs											*Millions de francs suisses*
Memorandum items											***Pour mémoire***
27. Short-term securities	*932*	*712*	*660*	*588*	*992*	*1602*	*1896*	*2593*	*2741*	*2831*	*27. Titres à court terme*
28. Bonds	*11224*	*11396*	*12167*	*12653*	*12635*	*13480*	*14180*	*13129*	*13233*	*12820*	*28. Obligations*
29. Shares and participations	*1062*	*1405*	*1812*	*1880*	*1786*	*2139*	*2136*	*2204*	*2299*	*2286*	*29. Actions et participations*
30. Claims on non-residents	*8632*	*8620*	*9208*	*9342*	*10673*	*12763*	*11780*	*13754*	*15823*	*15800*	*30. Créances sur des non-résidents*
31. Liabilities to non-residents	*4475*	*4569*	*5283*	*5679*	*5854*	*5947*	*6139*	*7040*	*8457*	*10539*	*31. Engagements envers des non-résidents*
Capital adequacy											***Solvabilité***
32. Tier 1 Capital	..	..	..	..	..	..	..	*14445*	*14912*	*16293*	*32. Fonds propres de base*
33. Tier 2 Capital	..	..	..	..	..	..	..	*1677*	*1629*	*2134*	*33. Fonds propres complémentaires*
34. Supervisory deductions	..	..	..	..	..	..	..	*282*	*309*	*400*	*34. Eléments à déduire des fonds propres*
35. Total net capital resources	*9409*	*10055*	*11148*	*11478*	*11535*	*12601*	*13399*	*15840*	*16231*	*18028*	*35. Total net des ressources en capital*
36. Risk-weighted assets	..	..	..	..	..	..	..	*167741*	*170791*	*173249*	*36. Actifs pondérés des risques*
SUPPLEMENTARY INFORMATION											**RENSEIGNEMENTS COMPLEMENTAIRES**
37. Number of institutions	29	29	29	28	28	28	27	25	24	24	37. Nombre d'institutions
38. Number of branches	741	755	768	771	779	826	761	759	737	713	38. Nombre de succursales
39. Number of employees (x 1000)	17.3	18.0	18.8	19.5	19.3	19.8	19.6	18.9	18.0	18.0	39. Nombre de salariés (x 1000)

1. Borrowing from Central bank (item 20) is included under Interbank deposits (item 21).

1. Emprunts auprès de la Banque centrale (poste 20) sont inclus sous Dépôts interbancaires (poste 21).

SWITZERLAND / SUISSE

Cantonal banks / Banques cantonales

	1988	1989	1990	1991	1992	1993	1994	1995	1996	1997	
Per cent											*Pourcentage*
INCOME STATEMENT ANALYSIS											**ANALYSE DU COMPTE DE RESULTATS**
% of average balance sheet total											**% du total moyen du bilan**
40. Interest income	4.51	5.07	6.08	6.56	6.68	6.05	5.20	4.75	4.42	4.10	40. Produits financiers
41. Interest expenses	3.39	3.94	4.86	5.22	5.33	4.57	4.00	3.53	3.14	2.77	41. Frais financiers
42. Net interest income	1.13	1.13	1.22	1.34	1.34	1.48	1.19	1.22	1.27	1.33	42. Produits financiers nets
43. Non-interest income (net)	0.43	0.45	0.46	0.81	0.69	0.63	0.71	0.66	0.69	0.91	43. Produits non financiers (nets)
a. Fees and commissions receivable	*0.27*	*0.29*	*0.28*	*0.29*	*0.30*	*0.36*	*0.32*	*0.27*	*0.34*	*0.45*	*a. Frais et commissions à recevoir*
b. Fees and commissions payable	*0.01*	*0.02*	*0.01*	*0.01*	*0.01*	*0.02*	*0.02*	*0.02*	*0.03*	*0.05*	*b. Frais et commissions à payer*
c. Net profits or loss on financial operations	*0.07*	*0.07*	*0.06*	*0.08*	*0.08*	*0.08*	*0.07*	*0.12*	*0.16*	*0.19*	*c. Profits ou pertes nets sur opérations financières*
d. Other	*0.10*	*0.10*	*0.12*	*0.45*	*0.33*	*0.21*	*0.34*	*0.30*	*0.22*	*0.32*	*d. Autres*
44. Gross income	1.55	1.58	1.68	2.15	2.04	2.11	1.90	1.88	1.97	2.24	44. Résultat brut
45. Operating expenses	0.94	0.94	0.98	0.98	0.99	0.99	1.01	0.97	1.12	1.33	45. Frais d'exploitation
a. Staff costs	*0.65*	*0.65*	*0.65*	*0.66*	*0.65*	*0.64*	*0.65*	*0.62*	*0.64*	*0.64*	*a. Dépenses en personnel*
b. Property costs	..	..	..	..	..	..	..	..	..	..	*b. Dépenses en immobilier*
c. Other	..	..	..	..	..	..	..	..	..	..	*c. Autres*
46. Net income	0.61	0.64	0.70	1.17	1.05	1.12	0.89	0.91	0.84	0.91	46. Résultat net
47. Provisions (net)	0.27	0.29	0.36	0.90	0.96	0.89	0.69	0.65	0.58	0.61	47. Provisions (nettes)
a. Provisions on loans	..	..	..	..	..	..	..	..	..	..	*a. Provisions sur prêts*
b. Provisions on securities	..	..	..	..	..	..	..	..	..	..	*b. Provisions sur titres*
c. Other	..	..	..	..	..	..	..	..	..	..	*c. Autres*
48. Profit before tax	0.34	0.34	0.34	0.27	0.09	0.24	0.20	0.26	0.26	0.31	48. Bénéfices avant impôt
49. Income tax	0.03	0.03	0.06	0.03	0.02	0.02	0.02	0.01	0.02	0.02	49. Impôt sur le revenu
50. Profit after tax	0.31	0.31	0.28	0.25	0.07	0.22	0.18	0.24	0.24	0.29	50. Bénéfices après impôt
51. Distributed profit	0.22	0.22	0.21	0.18	0.18	0.19	0.19	0.19	0.19	0.21	51. Bénéfices distribués
52. Retained profit	0.09	0.09	0.07	0.06	-0.11	0.03	-0.01	0.05	0.05	0.08	52. Bénéfices mis en réserve
% of gross income											**% du total du résultat brut**
53. Net interest income	72.54	71.47	72.67	62.30	66.03	70.23	62.71	64.75	64.81	59.22	53. Produits financiers nets
54. Non-interest income (net)	27.46	28.53	27.33	37.70	33.97	29.77	37.29	35.25	35.19	40.78	54. Produits non financiers (nets)
a. Fees and commissions receivable	*17.40*	*18.50*	*16.98*	*13.47*	*14.48*	*16.83*	*17.01*	*14.52*	*17.53*	*19.96*	*a. Frais et commissions à recevoir*
b. Fees and commissions payable	*0.78*	*0.98*	*0.85*	*0.63*	*0.69*	*0.87*	*1.07*	*1.31*	*1.74*	*2.18*	*b. Frais et commissions à payer*
c. Net profits or loss on financial operations	*4.56*	*4.63*	*3.79*	*3.78*	*3.85*	*3.91*	*3.59*	*6.24*	*7.96*	*8.51*	*c. Profits ou pertes nets sur opérations financières*
d. Other	*6.27*	*6.38*	*7.41*	*21.08*	*16.31*	*9.90*	*17.76*	*15.79*	*11.43*	*14.49*	*d. Autres*
55. Operating expenses	60.71	59.79	58.52	45.66	48.60	46.78	53.21	51.59	57.19	59.31	55. Frais d'exploitation
a. Staff costs	*41.71*	*40.85*	*38.51*	*30.57*	*31.87*	*30.34*	*34.15*	*33.03*	*32.32*	*28.39*	*a. Dépenses en personnel*
b. Property costs	..	..	..	..	..	..	..	..	..	..	*b. Dépenses en immobilier*
c. Other	..	..	..	..	..	..	..	..	..	..	*c. Autres*
56. Net income	39.29	40.21	41.48	54.34	51.40	53.22	46.79	48.41	42.81	40.69	56. Résultat net
57. Provisions (net)	17.37	18.43	21.35	41.61	47.00	42.09	36.49	34.68	29.68	27.03	57. Provisions (nettes)
a. Provisions on loans	..	..	..	..	..	..	..	..	..	..	*a. Provisions sur prêts*
b. Provisions on securities	..	..	..	..	..	..	..	..	..	..	*b. Provisions sur titres*
c. Other	..	..	..	..	..	..	..	..	..	..	*c. Autres*
58. Profit before tax	21.93	21.78	20.13	12.73	4.39	11.13	10.30	13.73	13.13	13.66	58. Bénéfices avant impôt
59. Income tax	2.23	2.03	3.33	1.34	0.97	0.81	0.80	0.73	0.79	0.75	59. Impôt sur le revenu
60. Profit after tax	19.70	19.75	16.80	11.39	3.43	10.32	9.50	12.99	12.34	12.91	60. Bénéfices après impôt
% of net income											**% du total du résultat net**
61. Provisions (net)	44.19	45.84	51.48	76.57	91.45	79.09	77.99	71.64	69.32	66.43	61. Provisions (nettes)
a. Provisions on loans	..	..	..	..	..	..	..	..	..	..	*a. Provisions sur prêts*
b. Provisions on securities	..	..	..	..	..	..	..	..	..	..	*b. Provisions sur titres*
c. Other	..	..	..	..	..	..	..	..	..	..	*c. Autres*
62. Profit before tax	55.81	54.16	48.52	23.43	8.55	20.91	22.01	28.36	30.68	33.57	62. Bénéfices avant impôt
63. Income tax	5.67	5.04	8.02	2.47	1.88	1.52	1.71	1.52	1.85	1.84	63. Impôt sur le revenu
64. Profit after tax	50.14	49.12	40.51	20.96	6.67	19.39	20.30	26.84	28.83	31.72	64. Bénéfices après impôt

SWITZERLAND / SUISSE

Cantonal banks / Banques cantonales

	1988	1989	1990	1991	1992	1993	1994	1995	1996	1997	
Per cent											*Pourcentage*
BALANCE SHEET ANALYSIS											**ANALYSE DU BILAN**
% of year-end balance sheet total											**% du total du bilan en fin d'exercice**
Assets											**Actif**
65. Cash & balance with Central bank	1.19	1.04	0.97	0.97	0.97	0.99	0.82	0.92	0.92	0.92	65. Caisse & solde auprès de la Banque centrale
66. Interbank deposits	13.32	10.75	9.30	8.81	9.34	9.91	8.79	9.23	9.46	8.63	66. Dépôts interbancaires
67. Loans	75.07	78.09	79.66	79.98	79.14	78.38	79.30	79.19	78.95	79.77	67. Prêts
68. Securities	7.36	6.92	6.84	6.62	6.45	6.80	7.02	6.85	7.00	7.40	68. Valeurs mobilières
69. Other assets	3.06	3.20	3.23	3.62	4.09	3.92	4.06	3.81	3.67	3.28	69. Autres actifs
Liabilities											**Passif**
70. Capital & reserves	4.23	4.14	4.13	4.02	4.11	4.14	4.18	4.17	5.75	6.08	70. Capital et réserves
71. Borrowing from Central bank	..	..	..	..	..	..	..	..	..	..	71. Emprunts auprès de la Banque centrale
72. Interbank deposits	5.85	6.11	7.40	7.02	7.15	6.78	7.07	6.89	7.15	7.04	72. Dépôts interbancaires
73. Non-bank deposits	55.97	54.65	51.27	50.48	49.13	50.46	50.86	50.88	52.49	53.81	73. Dépôts non bancaires
74. Bonds	28.69	29.55	30.96	31.91	32.52	31.42	30.45	29.80	27.55	26.06	74. Obligations
75. Other liabilities	5.26	5.55	6.24	6.56	7.09	7.20	7.44	8.25	7.07	7.01	75. Autres engagements
Memorandum items											***Pour mémoire***
76. Short-term securities	*0.52*	*0.36*	*0.31*	*0.26*	*0.42*	*0.63*	*0.73*	*0.99*	*1.03*	*1.05*	*76. Titres à court terme*
77. Bonds	*6.25*	*5.84*	*5.69*	*5.54*	*5.29*	*5.33*	*5.47*	*5.02*	*4.98*	*4.77*	*77. Obligations*
78. Shares and participations	*0.59*	*0.72*	*0.85*	*0.82*	*0.75*	*0.85*	*0.82*	*0.84*	*0.86*	*0.85*	*78. Actions et participations*
79. Claims on non-residents	*4.80*	*4.42*	*4.31*	*4.09*	*4.47*	*5.04*	*4.54*	*5.26*	*5.95*	*5.87*	*79. Créances sur des non-résidents*
80. Liabilities to non-residents	*2.49*	*2.34*	*2.47*	*2.49*	*2.45*	*2.35*	*2.37*	*2.69*	*3.18*	*3.92*	*80. Engagements envers des non-résidents*

* See notes on previous pages.

* Voir les notes en pages précédentes.

SWITZERLAND — SUISSE

Regional and savings banks — Banques régionales et caisses d'épargne

	1988	1989	1990	1991	1992	1993	1994	1995	1996	1997	
Million Swiss francs											*Millions de francs suisses*
INCOME STATEMENT											**COMPTE DE RESULTATS**
1. Interest income	3666	4306	5606	6085	6053	5104	3761	3655	3343	3050	1. Produits financiers
2. Interest expenses	2708	3276	4402	4707	4677	3799	2828	2616	2238	1873	2. Frais financiers
3. Net interest income	958	1030	1204	1378	1376	1305	933	1039	1105	1177	3. Produits financiers nets
4. Non-interest income (net)	327	370	398	442	510	467	546	393	432	413	4. Produits non financiers (nets)
a. Fees and commissions receivable	*224*	*253*	*273*	*264*	*259*	*248*	*208*	*186*	*189*	*256*	*a. Frais et commissions à recevoir*
b. Fees and commissions payable	*9*	*9*	*8*	*7*	*8*	*8*	*6*	*10*	*13*	*19*	*b. Frais et commissions à payer*
c. Net profits or loss on financial operations	*46*	*49*	*44*	*56*	*56*	*55*	*43*	*51*	*74*	*81*	*c. Profits ou pertes nets sur opérations financières*
d. Other	*65*	*78*	*90*	*129*	*203*	*172*	*300*	*166*	*182*	*95*	*d. Autres*
5. Gross income	1285	1400	1602	1820	1886	1772	1479	1432	1536	1590	5. Résultat brut
6. Operating expenses	755	803	859	873	871	796	672	672	799	834	6. Frais d'exploitation
a. Staff costs	*489*	*519*	*553*	*566*	*558*	*500*	*424*	*427*	*431*	*442*	*a. Dépenses en personnel*
b. Property costs	..	..	..	..	..	..	..	..	..	..	*b. Dépenses en immobilier*
c. Other	..	..	..	..	..	..	..	..	..	..	*c. Autres*
7. Net income	530	597	743	947	1015	976	807	760	737	756	7. Résultat net
8. Provisions (net)	201	252	411	596	704	662	726	476	465	431	8. Provisions (nettes)
a. Provisions on loans	..	..	..	..	..	..	..	..	..	..	*a. Provisions sur prêts*
b. Provisions on securities	..	..	..	..	..	..	..	..	..	..	*b. Provisions sur titres*
c. Other	..	..	..	..	..	..	..	..	..	..	*c. Autres*
9. Profit before tax	329	345	332	351	311	314	81	284	272	326	9. Bénéfices avant impôt
10. Income tax	90	91	92	87	87	83	67	69	63	66	10. Impôt sur le revenu
11. Profit after tax	239	254	240	264	224	231	14	215	209	260	11. Bénéfices après impôt
12. Distributed profit	137	149	153	155	149	128	88	106	109	132	12. Bénéfices distribués
13. Retained profit	102	105	87	109	75	103	-74	109	100	128	13. Bénéfices mis en réserve
BALANCE SHEET											**BILAN**
Assets											**Actif**
14. Cash & balance with Central bank	1143	1108	1112	1119	1142	943	759	806	858	856	14. Caisse & solde auprès de la Banque centrale
15. Interbank deposits	4141	4382	4303	3841	4185	5516	3723	4027	3055	2460	15. Dépôts interbancaires
16. Loans	67342	73364	78230	77898	75047	67931	59348	60288	60881	61184	16. Prêts
17. Securities	7045	6725	6665	6464	6120	5938	5346	5169	4636	4716	17. Valeurs mobilières
18. Other assets	2743	3028	3284	3418	3447	3132	2473	1974	1841	1535	18. Autres actifs
Liabilities											**Passif**
19. Capital & reserves	4013	4205	4381	4467	4454	4164	3645	3749	4281	4306	19. Capital et réserves
20. Borrowing from Central bank (1)	..	..	..	..	..	..	..	..	..	..	20. Emprunts auprès de la Banque centrale (1)
21. Interbank deposits	4808	5519	7086	5307	3873	2745	2256	2414	2384	2348	21. Dépôts interbancaires
22. Non-bank deposits	44577	46076	45037	44756	43445	43414	38964	40103	41258	42700	22. Dépôts non bancaires
23. Bonds	25833	29091	32677	33547	33125	28362	22782	21603	19591	17663	23. Obligations
24. Other liabilities	3183	3715	4413	4664	5044	4775	4003	4394	3757	3732	24. Autres engagements
Balance sheet total											**Total du bilan**
25. End-year total	82414	88607	93595	92741	89941	83460	71650	72264	71271	70750	25. En fin d'exercice
26. Average total	79248	85511	91101	93168	91341	86701	77555	71957	71768	71011	26. Moyen

SWITZERLAND
Regional and savings banks

SUISSE
Banques régionales et caisses d'épargne

	1988	1989	1990	1991	1992	1993	1994	1995	1996	1997	
Million Swiss francs											*Millions de francs suisses*
Memorandum items											***Pour mémoire***
27. Short-term securities	*152*	*172*	*152*	*142*	*109*	*90*	*76*	*71*	*54*	*170*	*27. Titres à court terme*
28. Bonds	*6425*	*5994*	*5953*	*5676*	*5359*	*5225*	*4731*	*4599*	*4101*	*4023*	*28. Obligations*
29. Shares and participations	*468*	*559*	*560*	*646*	*652*	*623*	*539*	*499*	*459*	*328*	*29. Actions et participations*
30. Claims on non-residents	*994*	*1018*	*1032*	*834*	*738*	*743*	*758*	*694*	*571*	*503*	*30. Créances sur des non-résidents*
31. Liabilities to non-residents	*1032*	*1013*	*963*	*892*	*990*	*903*	*808*	*784*	*904*	*951*	*31. Engagements envers des non-résidents*
Capital adequacy											***Solvabilité***
32. Tier 1 Capital	..	..	..	..	..	..	..	*4216*	*4215*	*4284*	*32. Fonds propres de base*
33. Tier 2 Capital	..	..	..	..	..	..	..	*601*	*674*	*605*	*33. Fonds propres complémentaires*
34. Supervisory deductions	..	..	..	..	..	..	..	*47*	*104*	*79*	*34. Eléments à déduire des fonds propres*
35. Total net capital resources	..	..	..	..	..	..	..	*4770*	*4785*	*4809*	*35. Total net des ressources en capital*
36. Risk-weighted assets	..	..	..	..	..	..	..	*45546*	*44614*	*43880*	*36. Actifs pondérés des risques*
SUPPLEMENTARY INFORMATION											**RENSEIGNEMENTS COMPLEMENTAIRES**
37. Number of institutions	213	210	204	189	174	155	135	127	119	117	37. Nombre d'institutions
38. Number of branches	672	664	654	637	602	525	444	427	413	400	38. Nombre de succursales
39. Number of employees (x 1000)	8.2	8.4	8.5	8.2	7.9	6.7	5.5	5.2	5.2	5.2	39. Nombre de salariés (x 1000)

1. Borrowing from Central bank (item 20) is included under Interbank deposits (item 21).

1. Emprunts auprès de la Banque centrale (poste 20) sont inclus sous Dépôts interbancaires (poste 21).

	1988	1989	1990	1991	1992	1993	1994	1995	1996	1997	
Per cent											*Pourcentage*
INCOME STATEMENT ANALYSIS											**ANALYSE DU COMPTE DE RESULTATS**
% of average balance sheet total											**% du total moyen du bilan**
40. Interest income	4.63	5.04	6.15	6.53	6.63	5.89	4.85	5.08	4.66	4.30	40. Produits financiers
41. Interest expenses	3.42	3.83	4.83	5.05	5.12	4.38	3.65	3.64	3.12	2.64	41. Frais financiers
42. Net interest income	1.21	1.20	1.32	1.48	1.51	1.51	1.20	1.44	1.54	1.66	42. Produits financiers nets
43. Non-interest income (net)	0.41	0.43	0.44	0.47	0.56	0.54	0.70	0.55	0.60	0.58	43. Produits non financiers (nets)
a. Fees and commissions receivable	*0.28*	*0.30*	*0.30*	*0.28*	*0.28*	*0.29*	*0.27*	*0.26*	*0.26*	*0.36*	*a. Frais et commissions à recevoir*
b. Fees and commissions payable	*0.01*	*0.01*	*0.01*	*0.01*	*0.01*	*0.01*	*0.01*	*0.01*	*0.02*	*0.03*	*b. Frais et commissions à payer*
c. Net profits or loss on financial operations	*0.06*	*0.06*	*0.05*	*0.06*	*0.06*	*0.06*	*0.06*	*0.07*	*0.10*	*0.11*	*c. Profits ou pertes nets sur opérations financières*
d. Other	*0.08*	*0.09*	*0.10*	*0.14*	*0.22*	*0.20*	*0.39*	*0.23*	*0.25*	*0.13*	*d. Autres*
44. Gross income	1.62	1.64	1.76	1.95	2.06	2.04	1.91	1.99	2.14	2.24	44. Résultat brut
45. Operating expenses	0.95	0.94	0.94	0.94	0.95	0.92	0.87	0.93	1.11	1.17	45. Frais d'exploitation
a. Staff costs	*0.62*	*0.61*	*0.61*	*0.61*	*0.61*	*0.58*	*0.55*	*0.59*	*0.60*	*0.62*	*a. Dépenses en personnel*
b. Property costs	..	..	..	..	..	..	..	..	..	..	*b. Dépenses en immobilier*
c. Other	..	..	..	..	..	..	..	..	..	..	*c. Autres*
46. Net income	0.67	0.70	0.82	1.02	1.11	1.13	1.04	1.06	1.03	1.06	46. Résultat net
47. Provisions (net)	0.25	0.29	0.45	0.64	0.77	0.76	0.94	0.66	0.65	0.61	47. Provisions (nettes)
a. Provisions on loans	..	..	..	..	..	..	..	..	..	..	*a. Provisions sur prêts*
b. Provisions on securities	..	..	..	..	..	..	..	..	..	..	*b. Provisions sur titres*
c. Other	..	..	..	..	..	..	..	..	..	..	*c. Autres*
48. Profit before tax	0.42	0.40	0.36	0.38	0.34	0.36	0.10	0.39	0.38	0.46	48. Bénéfices avant impôt
49. Income tax	0.11	0.11	0.10	0.09	0.10	0.10	0.09	0.10	0.09	0.09	49. Impôt sur le revenu
50. Profit after tax	0.30	0.30	0.26	0.28	0.25	0.27	0.02	0.30	0.29	0.37	50. Bénéfices après impôt
51. Distributed profit	0.17	0.17	0.17	0.17	0.16	0.15	0.11	0.15	0.15	0.19	51. Bénéfices distribués
52. Retained profit	0.13	0.12	0.10	0.12	0.08	0.12	-0.10	0.15	0.14	0.18	52. Bénéfices mis en réserve
% of gross income											**% du total du résultat brut**
53. Net interest income	74.55	73.57	75.16	75.71	72.96	73.65	63.08	72.56	71.94	74.03	53. Produits financiers nets
54. Non-interest income (net)	25.45	26.43	24.84	24.29	27.04	26.35	36.92	27.44	28.13	25.97	54. Produits non financiers (nets)
a. Fees and commissions receivable	*17.43*	*18.07*	*17.04*	*14.51*	*13.73*	*14.00*	*14.06*	*12.99*	*12.30*	*16.10*	*a. Frais et commissions à recevoir*
b. Fees and commissions payable	*0.70*	*0.64*	*0.50*	*0.38*	*0.42*	*0.45*	*0.41*	*0.70*	*0.85*	*1.19*	*b. Frais et commissions à payer*
c. Net profits or loss on financial operations	*3.58*	*3.50*	*2.75*	*3.08*	*2.97*	*3.10*	*2.91*	*3.56*	*4.82*	*5.09*	*c. Profits ou pertes nets sur opérations financières*
d. Other	*5.06*	*5.57*	*5.62*	*7.09*	*10.76*	*9.71*	*20.28*	*11.59*	*11.85*	*5.97*	*d. Autres*
55. Operating expenses	58.75	57.36	53.62	47.97	46.18	44.92	45.44	46.93	52.02	52.45	55. Frais d'exploitation
a. Staff costs	*38.05*	*37.07*	*34.52*	*31.10*	*29.59*	*28.22*	*28.67*	*29.82*	*28.06*	*27.80*	*a. Dépenses en personnel*
b. Property costs	..	..	..	..	..	..	..	..	..	..	*b. Dépenses en immobilier*
c. Other	..	..	..	..	..	..	..	..	..	..	*c. Autres*
56. Net income	41.25	42.64	46.38	52.03	53.82	55.08	54.56	53.07	47.98	47.55	56. Résultat net
57. Provisions (net)	15.64	18.00	25.66	32.75	37.33	37.36	49.09	33.24	30.27	27.11	57. Provisions (nettes)
a. Provisions on loans	..	..	..	..	..	..	..	..	..	..	*a. Provisions sur prêts*
b. Provisions on securities	..	..	..	..	..	..	..	..	..	..	*b. Provisions sur titres*
c. Other	..	..	..	..	..	..	..	..	..	..	*c. Autres*
58. Profit before tax	25.60	24.64	20.72	19.29	16.49	17.72	5.48	19.83	17.71	20.50	58. Bénéfices avant impôt
59. Income tax	7.00	6.50	5.74	4.78	4.61	4.68	4.53	4.82	4.10	4.15	59. Impôt sur le revenu
60. Profit after tax	18.60	18.14	14.98	14.51	11.88	13.04	0.95	15.01	13.61	16.35	60. Bénéfices après impôt
% of net income											**% du total du résultat net**
61. Provisions (net)	37.92	42.21	55.32	62.94	69.36	67.83	89.96	62.63	63.09	57.01	61. Provisions (nettes)
a. Provisions on loans	..	..	..	..	..	..	..	..	..	..	*a. Provisions sur prêts*
b. Provisions on securities	..	..	..	..	..	..	..	..	..	..	*b. Provisions sur titres*
c. Other	..	..	..	..	..	..	..	..	..	..	*c. Autres*
62. Profit before tax	62.08	57.79	44.68	37.06	30.64	32.17	10.04	37.37	36.91	43.12	62. Bénéfices avant impôt
63. Income tax	16.98	15.24	12.38	9.19	8.57	8.50	8.30	9.08	8.55	8.73	63. Impôt sur le revenu
64. Profit after tax	45.09	42.55	32.30	27.88	22.07	23.67	1.73	28.29	28.36	34.39	64. Bénéfices après impôt

SWITZERLAND — SUISSE

Regional and savings banks — Banques régionales et caisses d'épargne

	1988	1989	1990	1991	1992	1993	1994	1995	1996	1997	
Per cent											*Pourcentage*
BALANCE SHEET ANALYSIS											**ANALYSE DU BILAN**
% of year-end balance sheet total											**% du total du bilan en fin d'exercice**
Assets											**Actif**
65. Cash & balance with Central bank	1.39	1.25	1.19	1.21	1.27	1.13	1.06	1.12	1.20	1.21	65. Caisse & solde auprès de la Banque centrale
66. Interbank deposits	5.02	4.95	4.60	4.14	4.65	6.61	5.20	5.57	4.29	3.48	66. Dépôts interbancaires
67. Loans	81.71	82.80	83.58	84.00	83.44	81.39	82.83	83.43	85.42	86.48	67. Prêts
68. Securities	8.55	7.59	7.12	6.97	6.80	7.11	7.46	7.15	6.50	6.67	68. Valeurs mobilières
69. Other assets	3.33	3.42	3.51	3.69	3.83	3.75	3.45	2.73	2.58	2.17	69. Autres actifs
Liabilities											**Passif**
70. Capital & reserves	4.87	4.75	4.68	4.82	4.95	4.99	5.09	5.19	6.01	6.09	70. Capital et réserves
71. Borrowing from Central bank	..	..	..	..	..	..	..	..	..	..	71. Emprunts auprès de la Banque centrale
72. Interbank deposits	5.83	6.23	7.57	5.72	4.31	3.29	3.15	3.34	3.34	3.32	72. Dépôts interbancaires
73. Non-bank deposits	54.09	52.00	48.12	48.26	48.30	52.02	54.38	55.50	57.89	60.35	73. Dépôts non bancaires
74. Bonds	31.35	32.83	34.91	36.17	36.83	33.98	31.80	29.89	27.49	24.97	74. Obligations
75. Other liabilities	3.86	4.19	4.71	5.03	5.61	5.72	5.59	6.08	5.27	5.27	75. Autres engagements
Memorandum items											***Pour mémoire***
76. Short-term securities	*0.18*	*0.19*	*0.16*	*0.15*	*0.12*	*0.11*	*0.11*	*0.10*	*0.08*	*0.24*	*76. Titres à court terme*
77. Bonds	*7.80*	*6.76*	*6.36*	*6.12*	*5.96*	*6.26*	*6.60*	*6.36*	*5.75*	*5.69*	*77. Obligations*
78. Shares and participations	*0.57*	*0.63*	*0.60*	*0.70*	*0.72*	*0.75*	*0.75*	*0.69*	*0.64*	*0.46*	*78. Actions et participations*
79. Claims on non-residents	*1.21*	*1.15*	*1.10*	*0.90*	*0.82*	*0.89*	*1.06*	*0.96*	*0.80*	*0.71*	*79. Créances sur des non-résidents*
80. Liabilities to non-residents	*1.25*	*1.14*	*1.03*	*0.96*	*1.10*	*1.08*	*1.13*	*1.08*	*1.27*	*1.34*	*80. Engagements envers des non-résidents*

* See notes on previous pages.

* Voir les notes en pages précédentes.

SWITZERLAND

Loan associations and agricultural co-operatives

SUISSE

Caisses de crédit mutuel et banques mutualistes agricoles

	1988	1989	1990	1991	1992	1993	1994	1995	1996	1997	
Million Swiss francs											*Millions de francs suisses*
INCOME STATEMENT											**COMPTE DE RESULTATS**
1. Interest income	1209	1422	1906	2280	2504	2466	2265	2411	2401	2390	1. Produits financiers
2. Interest expenses	955	1137	1567	1878	2070	1978	1799	1854	1707	1539	2. Frais financiers
3. Net interest income	254	285	339	402	434	488	466	557	694	852	3. Produits financiers nets
4. Non-interest income (net)	55	63	81	96	128	121	131	155	185	190	4. Produits non financiers (nets)
a. Fees and commissions receivable	*21*	*26*	*30*	*34*	*38*	*43*	*50*	*57*	*41*	*64*	*a. Frais et commissions à recevoir*
b. Fees and commissions payable	*1*	*2*	*3*	*3*	*3*	*5*	*8*	*12*	*8*	*18*	*b. Frais et commissions à payer*
c. Net profits or loss on financial operations	*6*	*8*	*7*	*11*	*12*	*12*	*13*	*13*	*21*	*16*	*c. Profits ou pertes nets sur opérations financières*
d. Other	*29*	*30*	*46*	*53*	*82*	*71*	*76*	*96*	*132*	*128*	*d. Autres*
5. Gross income	309	348	420	498	562	609	597	712	879	1041	5. Résultat brut
6. Operating expenses	203	230	259	291	325	359	380	415	464	525	6. Frais d'exploitation
a. Staff costs	*111*	*125*	*139*	*158*	*173*	*187*	*197*	*211*	*233*	*259*	*a. Dépenses en personnel*
b. Property costs	..	..	..	..	..	..	..	..	..	..	*b. Dépenses en immobilier*
c. Other	..	..	..	..	..	..	..	..	..	..	*c. Autres*
7. Net income	106	118	161	207	237	250	217	297	415	516	7. Résultat net
8. Provisions (net)	53	64	106	146	172	179	143	218	312	390	8. Provisions (nettes)
a. Provisions on loans	..	..	..	..	..	..	..	..	..	..	*a. Provisions sur prêts*
b. Provisions on securities	..	..	..	..	..	..	..	..	..	..	*b. Provisions sur titres*
c. Other	..	..	..	..	..	..	..	..	..	..	*c. Autres*
9. Profit before tax	53	54	55	61	65	71	74	79	103	126	9. Bénéfices avant impôt
10. Income tax	16	15	18	18	21	24	27	27	42	55	10. Impôt sur le revenu
11. Profit after tax	37	39	37	43	44	47	47	52	61	71	11. Bénéfices après impôt
12. Distributed profit	4	5	5	5	5	6	6	7	8	8	12. Bénéfices distribués
13. Retained profit	33	34	32	38	39	41	41	45	53	63	13. Bénéfices mis en réserve
BALANCE SHEET											**BILAN**
Assets											**Actif**
14. Cash & balance with Central bank	347	355	360	389	431	482	472	541	590	730	14. Caisse & solde auprès de la Banque centrale
15. Interbank deposits	3907	3975	4266	4700	4967	5351	4817	5442	5154	5022	15. Dépôts interbancaires
16. Loans	22773	25672	28028	30286	32429	35145	38831	42157	46020	49972	16. Prêts
17. Securities	204	223	229	229	244	244	257	265	267	337	17. Valeurs mobilières
18. Other assets	878	999	1159	1273	1368	1356	1369	1462	1311	1235	18. Autres actifs
Liabilities											**Passif**
19. Capital & reserves	807	845	885	926	964	1019	1067	1139	1214	1292	19. Capital et réserves
20. Borrowing from Central bank (1)	..	..	..	..	..	..	..	..	..	..	20. Emprunts auprès de la Banque centrale (1)
21. Interbank deposits	1627	2176	2369	2321	2273	2434	2816	2844	2790	3206	21. Dépôts interbancaires
22. Non-bank deposits	19034	19953	20386	21844	23487	27537	30919	34198	37651	40799	22. Dépôts non bancaires
23. Bonds	5968	7443	9301	10439	11229	10116	9584	10175	10004	10141	23. Obligations
24. Other liabilities	674	808	1101	1347	1485	1474	1360	1511	1684	1858	24. Autres engagements
Balance sheet total											**Total du bilan**
25. End-year total	28109	31225	34042	36876	39438	42579	45747	49868	53343	57296	25. En fin d'exercice
26. Average total	26748	29667	32634	35459	38157	41009	44163	47808	51606	55320	26. Moyen

SWITZERLAND / SUISSE

Loan associations and agricultural co-operatives / Caisses de crédit mutuel et banques mutualistes agricoles

	1988	1989	1990	1991	1992	1993	1994	1995	1996	1997	
Million Swiss francs											*Millions de francs suisses*
Memorandum items											***Pour mémoire***
27. Short-term securities	*18*	*24*	*28*	*29*	*28*	*25*	*27*	*31*	*28*	*29*	*27. Titres à court terme*
28. Bonds	*18*	*18*	*20*	*17*	*20*	*16*	*11*	*12*	*11*	*13*	*28. Obligations*
29. Shares and participations	*167*	*181*	*181*	*183*	*197*	*203*	*219*	*222*	*225*	*227*	*29. Actions et participations*
30. Claims on non-residents	..	..	..	..	..	..	..	..	..	..	*30. Créances sur des non-résidents*
31. Liabilities to non-residents	..	..	..	..	..	..	..	..	..	..	*31. Engagements envers des non-résidents*
Capital adequacy											***Solvabilité***
32. Tier 1 Capital	..	..	..	..	..	..	..	*1671*	*2212*	*2515*	*32. Fonds propres de base*
33. Tier 2 Capital	..	..	..	..	..	..	..	*912*	*1106*	*1258*	*33. Fonds propres complémentaires*
34. Supervisory deductions	..	..	..	..	..	..	..	-	*16*	*18*	*34. Eléments à déduire des fonds propres*
35. Total net capital resources	..	..	..	..	..	..	..	*2584*	*3301*	*3756*	*35. Total net des ressources en capital*
36. Risk-weighted assets	..	..	..	..	..	..	..	*31272*	*32610*	*35279*	*36. Actifs pondérés des risques*
SUPPLEMENTARY INFORMATION											**RENSEIGNEMENTS COMPLEMENTAIRES**
37. Number of institutions	2	2	2	2	2	2	1	1	1	1	37. Nombre d'institutions
38. Number of branches	1241	1229	1213	1192	1169	1139	1086	1034	962	892	38. Nombre de succursales
39. Number of employees (x 1000)	2.8	3.0	2.7	2.6	2.6	2.7	2.7	2.8	2.8	2.8	39. Nombre de salariés (x 1000)

1. Borrowing from Central bank (item 20) is included under Interbank deposits (item 21).

1. Emprunts auprès de la Banque centrale (poste 20) sont inclus sous Dépôts interbancaires (poste 21).

SWITZERLAND

Loan associations and agricultural co-operatives

SUISSE

Caisses de crédit mutuel et banques mutualistes agricoles

	1988	1989	1990	1991	1992	1993	1994	1995	1996	1997	
Per cent											*Pourcentage*
INCOME STATEMENT ANALYSIS											**ANALYSE DU COMPTE DE RESULTATS**
% of average balance sheet total											**% du total moyen du bilan**
40. Interest income	4.52	4.79	5.84	6.43	6.56	6.01	5.13	5.04	4.65	4.32	40. Produits financiers
41. Interest expenses	3.57	3.83	4.80	5.30	5.42	4.82	4.07	3.88	3.31	2.78	41. Frais financiers
42. Net interest income	0.95	0.96	1.04	1.13	1.14	1.19	1.06	1.17	1.34	1.54	42. Produits financiers nets
43. Non-interest income (net)	0.21	0.21	0.25	0.27	0.34	0.30	0.30	0.32	0.36	0.34	43. Produits non financiers (nets)
a. Fees and commissions receivable	*0.08*	*0.09*	*0.09*	*0.10*	*0.10*	*0.10*	*0.11*	*0.12*	*0.08*	*0.12*	*a. Frais et commissions à recevoir*
b. Fees and commissions payable	-	*0.01*	*0.01*	*0.01*	*0.01*	*0.01*	*0.02*	*0.03*	*0.02*	*0.03*	*b. Frais et commissions à payer*
c. Net profits or loss on financial operations	*0.02*	*0.03*	*0.02*	*0.03*	*0.03*	*0.03*	*0.03*	*0.03*	*0.04*	*0.03*	*c. Profits ou pertes nets sur opérations financières*
d. Other	*0.11*	*0.10*	*0.14*	*0.15*	*0.21*	*0.17*	*0.17*	*0.20*	*0.26*	*0.23*	*d. Autres*
44. Gross income	1.16	1.17	1.29	1.40	1.47	1.49	1.35	1.49	1.70	1.88	44. Résultat brut
45. Operating expenses	0.76	0.78	0.79	0.82	0.85	0.88	0.86	0.87	0.90	0.95	45. Frais d'exploitation
a. Staff costs	*0.41*	*0.42*	*0.43*	*0.45*	*0.45*	*0.46*	*0.45*	*0.44*	*0.45*	*0.47*	*a. Dépenses en personnel*
b. Property costs	..	..	..	..	..	..	..	..	..	..	*b. Dépenses en immobilier*
c. Other	..	..	..	..	..	..	..	..	..	..	*c. Autres*
46. Net income	0.40	0.40	0.49	0.58	0.62	0.61	0.49	0.62	0.80	0.93	46. Résultat net
47. Provisions (net)	0.20	0.22	0.32	0.41	0.45	0.44	0.32	0.46	0.60	0.70	47. Provisions (nettes)
a. Provisions on loans	..	..	..	..	..	..	..	..	..	..	*a. Provisions sur prêts*
b. Provisions on securities	..	..	..	..	..	..	..	..	..	..	*b. Provisions sur titres*
c. Other	..	..	..	..	..	..	..	..	..	..	*c. Autres*
48. Profit before tax	0.20	0.18	0.17	0.17	0.17	0.17	0.17	0.17	0.20	0.23	48. Bénéfices avant impôt
49. Income tax	0.06	0.05	0.06	0.05	0.06	0.06	0.06	0.06	0.08	0.10	49. Impôt sur le revenu
50. Profit after tax	0.14	0.13	0.11	0.12	0.12	0.11	0.11	0.11	0.12	0.13	50. Bénéfices après impôt
51. Distributed profit	0.01	0.02	0.02	0.01	0.01	0.01	0.01	0.01	0.02	0.01	51. Bénéfices distribués
52. Retained profit	0.12	0.11	0.10	0.11	0.10	0.10	0.09	0.09	0.10	0.11	52. Bénéfices mis en réserve
% of gross income											**% du total du résultat brut**
53. Net interest income	82.20	81.90	80.71	80.72	77.22	80.13	78.06	78.23	78.95	81.84	53. Produits financiers nets
54. Non-interest income (net)	17.80	18.10	19.29	19.28	22.78	19.87	21.94	21.77	21.05	18.25	54. Produits non financiers (nets)
a. Fees and commissions receivable	*6.80*	*7.47*	*7.14*	*6.83*	*6.76*	*7.06*	*8.38*	*8.01*	*4.66*	*6.15*	*a. Frais et commissions à recevoir*
b. Fees and commissions payable	*0.32*	*0.57*	*0.71*	*0.60*	*0.53*	*0.82*	*1.34*	*1.69*	*0.91*	*1.73*	*b. Frais et commissions à payer*
c. Net profits or loss on financial operations	*1.94*	*2.30*	*1.67*	*2.21*	*2.14*	*1.97*	*2.18*	*1.83*	*2.39*	*1.54*	*c. Profits ou pertes nets sur opérations financières*
d. Other	*9.39*	*8.62*	*10.95*	*10.64*	*14.59*	*11.66*	*12.73*	*13.48*	*15.02*	*12.30*	*d. Autres*
55. Operating expenses	65.70	66.09	61.67	58.43	57.83	58.95	63.65	58.29	52.79	50.43	55. Frais d'exploitation
a. Staff costs	*35.92*	*35.92*	*33.10*	*31.73*	*30.78*	*30.71*	*33.00*	*29.63*	*26.51*	*24.88*	*a. Dépenses en personnel*
b. Property costs	..	..	..	..	..	..	..	..	..	..	*b. Dépenses en immobilier*
c. Other	..	..	..	..	..	..	..	..	..	..	*c. Autres*
56. Net income	34.30	33.91	38.33	41.57	42.17	41.05	36.35	41.71	47.21	49.57	56. Résultat net
57. Provisions (net)	17.15	18.39	25.24	29.32	30.60	29.39	23.95	30.62	35.49	37.46	57. Provisions (nettes)
a. Provisions on loans	..	..	..	..	..	..	..	..	..	..	*a. Provisions sur prêts*
b. Provisions on securities	..	..	..	..	..	..	..	..	..	..	*b. Provisions sur titres*
c. Other	..	..	..	..	..	..	..	..	..	..	*c. Autres*
58. Profit before tax	17.15	15.52	13.10	12.25	11.57	11.66	12.40	11.10	11.72	12.10	58. Bénéfices avant impôt
59. Income tax	5.18	4.31	4.29	3.61	3.74	3.94	4.52	3.79	4.78	5.28	59. Impôt sur le revenu
60. Profit after tax	11.97	11.21	8.81	8.63	7.83	7.72	7.87	7.30	6.94	6.82	60. Bénéfices après impôt
% of net income											**% du total du résultat net**
61. Provisions (net)	50.00	54.24	65.84	70.53	72.57	71.60	65.90	73.40	75.18	75.58	61. Provisions (nettes)
a. Provisions on loans	..	..	..	..	..	..	..	..	..	..	*a. Provisions sur prêts*
b. Provisions on securities	..	..	..	..	..	..	..	..	..	..	*b. Provisions sur titres*
c. Other	..	..	..	..	..	..	..	..	..	..	*c. Autres*
62. Profit before tax	50.00	45.76	34.16	29.47	27.43	28.40	34.10	26.60	24.82	24.42	62. Bénéfices avant impôt
63. Income tax	15.09	12.71	11.18	8.70	8.86	9.60	12.44	9.09	10.12	10.66	63. Impôt sur le revenu
64. Profit after tax	34.91	33.05	22.98	20.77	18.57	18.80	21.66	17.51	14.70	13.76	64. Bénéfices après impôt

SWITZERLAND

Loan associations and agricultural co-operatives

SUISSE

Caisses de crédit mutuel et banques mutualistes agricoles

	1988	1989	1990	1991	1992	1993	1994	1995	1996	1997	
Per cent											*Pourcentage*
BALANCE SHEET ANALYSIS											**ANALYSE DU BILAN**
% of year-end balance sheet total											**% du total du bilan en fin d'exercice**
Assets											**Actif**
65. Cash & balance with Central bank	1.23	1.14	1.06	1.05	1.09	1.13	1.03	1.08	1.11	1.27	65. Caisse & solde auprès de la Banque centrale
66. Interbank deposits	13.90	12.73	12.53	12.75	12.59	12.57	10.53	10.91	9.66	8.77	66. Dépôts interbancaires
67. Loans	81.02	82.22	82.33	82.13	82.23	82.54	84.88	84.54	86.27	87.22	67. Prêts
68. Securities	0.73	0.71	0.67	0.62	0.62	0.57	0.56	0.53	0.50	0.59	68. Valeurs mobilières
69. Other assets	3.12	3.20	3.40	3.45	3.47	3.18	2.99	2.93	2.46	2.16	69. Autres actifs
Liabilities											**Passif**
70. Capital & reserves	2.87	2.71	2.60	2.51	2.44	2.39	2.33	2.28	2.28	2.25	70. Capital et réserves
71. Borrowing from Central bank	..	..	..	..	..	..	..	..	..	..	71. Emprunts auprès de la Banque centrale
72. Interbank deposits	5.79	6.97	6.96	6.29	5.76	5.72	6.16	5.70	5.23	5.60	72. Dépôts interbancaires
73. Non-bank deposits	67.71	63.90	59.88	59.24	59.55	64.67	67.59	68.58	70.58	71.21	73. Dépôts non bancaires
74. Bonds	21.23	23.84	27.32	28.31	28.47	23.76	20.95	20.40	18.75	17.70	74. Obligations
75. Other liabilities	2.40	2.59	3.23	3.65	3.77	3.46	2.97	3.03	3.16	3.24	75. Autres engagements
Memorandum items											***Pour mémoire***
76. Short-term securities	*0.06*	*0.08*	*0.08*	*0.08*	*0.07*	*0.06*	*0.06*	*0.06*	*0.05*	*0.05*	*76. Titres à court terme*
77. Bonds	*0.06*	*0.06*	*0.06*	*0.05*	*0.05*	*0.04*	*0.02*	*0.02*	*0.02*	*0.02*	*77. Obligations*
78. Shares and participations	*0.59*	*0.58*	*0.53*	*0.50*	*0.50*	*0.48*	*0.48*	*0.45*	*0.42*	*0.40*	*78. Actions et participations*
79. Claims on non-residents	..	..	..	..	..	..	..	..	..	..	*79. Créances sur des non-résidents*
80. Liabilities to non-residents	..	..	..	..	..	..	..	..	..	..	*80. Engagements envers des non-résidents*

* See notes on previous pages.

* Voir les notes en pages précédentes.

TURKEY — TURQUIE

Commercial banks — Banques commerciales

	1988	1989	1990	1991	1992	1993	1994	1995	1996	1997	
Billion Turkish liras											*Milliards de livres turques*
INCOME STATEMENT											**COMPTE DE RESULTATS**
1. Interest income	12165	20232	33243	63597	117540	207330	514052	885708	2101034	4808925	1. Produits financiers
2. Interest expenses	9177	17250	23803	42282	78163	121951	339317	628951	1433562	3344226	2. Frais financiers
3. Net interest income	2988	2982	9440	21315	39377	85379	174735	256757	667472	1464699	3. Produits financiers nets
4. Non-interest income (net) (1)	1098	2854	1963	-1956	-2471	-14022	-50508	11521	-95019	-11728	4. Produits non financiers (nets) (1)
a. Fees and commissions receivable(2)	*3003*	*2954*	*5464*	*19847*	*22002*	*47349*	*279493*	*329669*	*783875*	*1635959*	*a. Frais et commissions à recevoir (2)*
b. Fees and commissions payable(2)	*2260*	*1874*	*4602*	*20463*	*25086*	*62359*	*329816*	*349996*	*849730*	*1883809*	*b. Frais et commissions à payer (2)*
c. Net profits or loss on financial operations	*510*	*1305*	*1516*	*1614*	*4886*	*12131*	*14938*	*59403*	*91560*	*136275*	*c. Profits ou pertes nets sur opérations financières*
d. Other	*-265*	*446*	*-442*	*-2990*	*-4273*	*-11143*	*-15123*	*-27555*	*-120724*	*99847*	*d. Autres*
5. Gross income	4086	5836	11403	19359	36906	71357	124227	268278	572453	1452971	5. Résultat brut
6. Operating expenses (1)	1658	3014	5943	10896	20146	34504	60869	109526	217151	727099	6. Frais d'exploitation (1)
a. Staff costs	*1313*	*2420*	*4820*	*8353*	*15507*	*24943*	*42159*	*80914*	*163073*	*353052*	*a. Dépenses en personnel*
b. Property costs	*168*	*295*	*545*	*979*	*1790*	*3245*	*6082*	*14048*	*27672*	*29327*	*b. Dépenses en immobilier*
c. Other	*158*	*285*	*558*	*1533*	*2849*	*6316*	*12628*	*14564*	*26406*	*344720*	*c. Autres*
7. Net income	2428	2822	5460	8463	16760	36853	63358	158752	355302	725872	7. Résultat net
8. Provisions (net) (1)	841	947	1341	2430	2073	6785	21187	28849	62563	90132	8. Provisions (nettes) (1)
a. Provisions on loans	*654*	*671*	*861*	*1772*	*1438*	*3647*	*10954*	*12338*	*28406*	*71204*	*a. Provisions sur prêts*
b. Provisions on securities	-	-	*7*	*136*	*40*	*331*	*92*	*108*	*6007*	*3386*	*b. Provisions sur titres*
c. Other	*185*	*270*	*463*	*505*	*595*	*2807*	*10141*	*16403*	*28150*	*15542*	*c. Autres*
9. Profit before tax	1587	1875	4119	6033	14687	30068	42171	129903	292739	635740	9. Bénéfices avant impôt
10. Income tax	185	406	637	804	2134	6254	8765	11802	25620	180390	10. Impôt sur le revenu
11. Profit after tax	1402	1469	3482	5229	12553	23814	33406	118101	267119	455350	11. Bénéfices après impôt
12. Distributed profit	695	762	1788	2399	3848	9907	17719	32854	32269	153805	12. Bénéfices distribués
13. Retained profit	707	707	1694	2830	8705	13907	15687	85247	234850	301545	13. Bénéfices mis en réserve
BALANCE SHEET											**BILAN**
Assets											**Actif**
14. Cash & balance with Central bank	5331	7340	10349	16911	29766	54533	104892	199906	285441	577679	14. Caisse & solde auprès de la Banque centrale
15. Interbank deposits	8037	9733	14701	32039	85047	201809	316511	590727	1099571	2566086	15. Dépôts interbancaires
16. Loans	24496	38904	68887	111813	206434	388218	693028	1552477	3469960	7826158	16. Prêts
17. Securities	6987	12476	17111	34283	60357	112829	218776	421401	1375558	2908041	17. Valeurs mobilières
18. Other assets	16701	28229	41544	74912	128810	216203	521056	1038898	2174259	4457829	18. Autres actifs
Liabilities											**Passif**
19. Capital & reserves	2793	4517	6999	13635	23960	46326	83617	164774	340722	1600329	19. Capital et réserves
20. Borrowing from Central bank	2538	3088	3129	4013	8003	16969	12319	12303	8619	63771	20. Emprunts auprès de la Banque centrale
21. Interbank deposits	3222	4262	6837	8259	20435	78412	50306	181551	491220	3301434	21. Dépôts interbancaires
22. Non-bank deposits	35111	58141	88726	160595	285234	466751	1224806	2486483	5653896	11374370	22. Dépôts non bancaires
23. Bonds	54	389	413	704	6187	24525	16615	39686	28998	176314	23. Obligations
24. Other liabilities	17834	26285	46488	82752	166595	340609	466600	918612	1881334	1819575	24. Autres engagements
Balance sheet total											**Total du bilan**
25. End-year total	61552	96682	152592	269958	510414	973592	1854263	3803409	8404789	18335793	25. En fin d'exercice
26. Average total	49891	79117	124637	211275	390186	742003	1413928	2828836	6104099	13370291	26. Moyen

TURKEY
Commercial banks

TURQUIE
Banques commerciales

Billion Turkish liras	1988	1989	1990	1991	1992	1993	1994	1995	1996	1997	Milliards de livres turques
Memorandum items											**Pour mémoire**
27. Short-term securities	..	..	..	..	..	..	..	..	..	673002	27. Titres à court terme
28. Bonds	3961	9417	12579	19296	41965	90302	106754	209567	720312	1998183	28. Obligations
29. Shares and participations	1305	2666	4081	6370	11096	18116	34325	59410	123881	289554	29. Actions et participations
30. Claims on non-residents	6848	9208	13931	36108	81980	162573	393540	678256	1600055	2491477	30. Créances sur des non-résidents
31. Liabilities to non-residents	3578	5040	12821	22428	55466	144014	126322	329517	936479	3014155	31. Engagements envers des non-résidents
Capital adequacy											**Solvabilité**
32. Tier 1 Capital	..	..	..	..	..	64589	107703	256125	575104	1278674	32. Fonds propres de base
33. Tier 2 Capital	..	..	..	..	..	10769	21804	83170	162040	301347	33. Fonds propres complémentaires
34. Supervisory deductions	..	..	..	..	..	6096	14874	31069	79071	197551	34. Eléments à déduire des fonds propres
35. Total net capital resources	..	..	..	..	..	69262	114633	308226	658073	1382470	35. Total net des ressources en capital
36. Risk-weighted assets	..	..	..	..	..	628831	1202608	2365808	5387488	11569773	36. Actifs pondérés des risques
SUPPLEMENTARY INFORMATION											**RENSEIGNEMENTS COMPLEMENTAIRES**
37. Number of institutions	53	53	56	56	58	59	55	55	55	59	37. Nombre d'institutions
38. Number of branches	6517	6579	6543	6463	6188	6208	6085	6196	6385	6763	38. Nombre de succursales
39. Number of employees (x 1000)	149.4	151.1	152.0	150.8	144.6	141.7	136.8	139.0	141.0	149.8	39. Nombre de salariés (x 1000)

1. Change in methodology.
2. Fees and commissions receivable (item 4.a) includes gains on foreign-exchange claims and operations. Fees and commissions payable (item 4.b) includes losses on foreign-exchange liabilities and operations.

Notes

- The category Commercial banks covers all commercial banks operating in Turkey including foreign branches of domestic banks and foreign banks established in Turkey.

Change in methodology

- Iller Bankasi, although not being a full commercial bank, is included in the data until end-1988.
- Until 1992, the sub-items (a., b., c. and d.) of Non-interest income (item 4), Operating expenses (item 6) and net Provisions (item 8), exclude activities of foreign branches of domestic banks. These activities are included in the total item figure.

1. Changement méthodologique.
2. Les frais et commissions à recevoir (poste 4.a) comprennent les gains au titre de créances et d'opérations en devises. Les frais et commissions à payer (poste 4.b) comprennent les pertes au titre d'engagements et d'opérations en devises.

Notes

- La catégorie "Banques commerciales" regroupe toutes les banques commerciales en activité en Turquie y compris les succursales étrangères des banques domestiques ainsi que les banques étrangères basées en Turquie.

Changement méthodologique

- Iller Bankasi, bien que celle-ci ne soit pas à tous égards une banque commerciale, est incluse dans les données jusqu'en fin 1988.
- Jusqu'en 1992, les sous-catégories (a., b., c., et d.) des Produits non financiers (poste 4), des Frais d'exploitation (poste 6) et des Provisions nettes (poste 8) excluent les activités des succursales étrangères des banques locales. Ces activités sont incluses dans le résultat total.

Per cent	1988	1989	1990	1991	1992	1993	1994	1995	1996	1997	Pourcentage
INCOME STATEMENT ANALYSIS											**ANALYSE DU COMPTE DE RESULTATS**
% of average balance sheet total											**% du total moyen du bilan**
40. Interest income	24.38	25.57	26.67	30.10	30.12	27.94	36.36	31.31	34.42	35.97	40. Produits financiers
41. Interest expenses	18.39	21.80	19.10	20.01	20.03	16.44	24.00	22.23	23.49	25.01	41. Frais financiers
42. Net interest income	5.99	3.77	7.57	10.09	10.09	11.51	12.36	9.08	10.93	10.95	42. Produits financiers nets
43. Non-interest income (net)	2.20	3.61	1.57	-0.93	-0.63	-1.89	-3.57	0.41	-1.56	-0.09	43. Produits non financiers (nets)
a. Fees and commissions receivable	*6.02*	*3.73*	*4.38*	*9.39*	*5.64*	*6.38*	*19.77*	*11.65*	*12.84*	*12.24*	*a. Frais et commissions à recevoir*
b. Fees and commissions payable	*4.53*	*2.37*	*3.69*	*9.69*	*6.43*	*8.40*	*23.33*	*12.37*	*13.92*	*14.09*	*b. Frais et commissions à payer*
c. Net profits or loss on financial operations	*1.02*	*1.65*	*1.22*	*0.76*	*1.25*	*1.63*	*1.06*	*2.10*	*1.50*	*1.02*	*c. Profits ou pertes nets sur opérations financières*
d. Other	*-0.53*	*0.56*	*-0.35*	*-1.42*	*-1.10*	*-1.50*	*-1.07*	*-0.97*	*-1.98*	*0.75*	*d. Autres*
44. Gross income	8.19	7.38	9.15	9.16	9.46	9.62	8.79	9.48	9.38	10.87	44. Résultat brut
45. Operating expenses	3.32	3.81	4.77	5.16	5.16	4.65	4.30	3.87	3.56	5.44	45. Frais d'exploitation
a. Staff costs	*2.63*	*3.06*	*3.87*	*3.95*	*3.97*	*3.36*	*2.98*	*2.86*	*2.67*	*2.64*	*a. Dépenses en personnel*
b. Property costs	*0.34*	*0.37*	*0.44*	*0.46*	*0.46*	*0.44*	*0.43*	*0.50*	*0.45*	*0.22*	*b. Dépenses en immobilier*
c. Other	*0.32*	*0.36*	*0.45*	*0.73*	*0.73*	*0.85*	*0.89*	*0.51*	*0.43*	*2.58*	*c. Autres*
46. Net income	4.87	3.57	4.38	4.01	4.30	4.97	4.48	5.61	5.82	5.43	46. Résultat net
47. Provisions (net)	1.69	1.20	1.08	1.15	0.53	0.91	1.50	1.02	1.02	0.67	47. Provisions (nettes)
a. Provisions on loans	*1.31*	*0.85*	*0.69*	*0.84*	*0.37*	*0.49*	*0.77*	*0.44*	*0.47*	*0.53*	*a. Provisions sur prêts*
b. Provisions on securities	-	-	*0.01*	*0.06*	*0.01*	*0.04*	*0.01*	-	*0.10*	*0.03*	*b. Provisions sur titres*
c. Other	*0.37*	*0.34*	*0.37*	*0.24*	*0.15*	*0.38*	*0.72*	*0.58*	*0.46*	*0.12*	*c. Autres*
48. Profit before tax	3.18	2.37	3.30	2.86	3.76	4.05	2.98	4.59	4.80	4.75	48. Bénéfices avant impôt
49. Income tax	0.37	0.51	0.51	0.38	0.55	0.84	0.62	0.42	0.42	1.35	49. Impôt sur le revenu
50. Profit after tax	2.81	1.86	2.79	2.47	3.22	3.21	2.36	4.17	4.38	3.41	50. Bénéfices après impôt
51. Distributed profit	1.39	0.96	1.43	1.14	0.99	1.34	1.25	1.16	0.53	1.15	51. Bénéfices distribués
52. Retained profit	1.42	0.89	1.36	1.34	2.23	1.87	1.11	3.01	3.85	2.26	52. Bénéfices mis en réserve
% of gross income											**% du total du résultat brut**
53. Net interest income	73.13	51.10	82.79	110.10	106.70	119.65	140.66	95.71	116.60	100.81	53. Produits financiers nets
54. Non-interest income (net)	26.87	48.90	17.21	-10.10	-6.70	-19.65	-40.66	4.29	-16.60	-0.81	54. Produits non financiers (nets)
a. Fees and commissions receivable	*73.49*	*50.62*	*47.92*	*102.52*	*59.62*	*66.36*	*224.99*	*122.88*	*136.93*	*112.59*	*a. Frais et commissions à recevoir*
b. Fees and commissions payable	*55.31*	*32.11*	*40.36*	*105.70*	*67.97*	*87.39*	*265.49*	*130.46*	*148.44*	*129.65*	*b. Frais et commissions à payer*
c. Net profits or loss on financial operations	*12.48*	*22.36*	*13.29*	*8.34*	*13.24*	*17.00*	*12.02*	*22.14*	*15.99*	*9.38*	*c. Profits ou pertes nets sur opérations financières*
d. Other	*-6.49*	*7.64*	*-3.88*	*-15.45*	*-11.58*	*-15.62*	*-12.17*	*-10.27*	*-21.09*	*6.87*	*d. Autres*
55. Operating expenses	40.58	51.64	52.12	56.28	54.59	48.35	49.00	40.83	37.93	50.04	55. Frais d'exploitation
a. Staff costs	*32.13*	*41.47*	*42.27*	*43.15*	*42.02*	*34.96*	*33.94*	*30.16*	*28.49*	*24.30*	*a. Dépenses en personnel*
b. Property costs	*4.11*	*5.05*	*4.78*	*5.06*	*4.85*	*4.55*	*4.90*	*5.24*	*4.83*	*2.02*	*b. Dépenses en immobilier*
c. Other	*3.87*	*4.88*	*4.89*	*7.92*	*7.72*	*8.85*	*10.17*	*5.43*	*4.61*	*23.73*	*c. Autres*
56. Net income	59.42	48.36	47.88	43.72	45.41	51.65	51.00	59.17	62.07	49.96	56. Résultat net
57. Provisions (net)	20.58	16.23	11.76	12.55	5.62	9.51	17.06	10.75	10.93	6.20	57. Provisions (nettes)
a. Provisions on loans	*16.01*	*11.50*	*7.55*	*9.15*	*3.90*	*5.11*	*8.82*	*4.60*	*4.96*	*4.90*	*a. Provisions sur prêts*
b. Provisions on securities	-	-	*0.06*	*0.70*	*0.11*	*0.46*	*0.07*	*0.04*	*1.05*	*0.23*	*b. Provisions sur titres*
c. Other	*4.53*	*4.63*	*4.06*	*2.61*	*1.61*	*3.93*	*8.16*	*6.11*	*4.92*	*1.07*	*c. Autres*
58. Profit before tax	38.84	32.13	36.12	31.16	39.80	42.14	33.95	48.42	51.14	43.75	58. Bénéfices avant impôt
59. Income tax	4.53	6.96	5.59	4.15	5.78	8.76	7.06	4.40	4.48	12.42	59. Impôt sur le revenu
60. Profit after tax	34.31	25.17	30.54	27.01	34.01	33.37	26.89	44.02	46.66	31.34	60. Bénéfices après impôt
% of net income											**% du total du résultat net**
61. Provisions (net)	34.64	33.56	24.56	28.71	12.37	18.41	33.44	18.17	17.61	12.42	61. Provisions (nettes)
a. Provisions on loans	*26.94*	*23.78*	*15.77*	*20.94*	*8.58*	*9.90*	*17.29*	*7.77*	*7.99*	*9.81*	*a. Provisions sur prêts*
b. Provisions on securities	-	-	*0.13*	*1.61*	*0.24*	*0.90*	*0.15*	*0.07*	*1.69*	*0.47*	*b. Provisions sur titres*
c. Other	*7.62*	*9.57*	*8.48*	*5.97*	*3.55*	*7.62*	*16.01*	*10.33*	*7.92*	*2.14*	*c. Autres*
62. Profit before tax	65.36	66.44	75.44	71.29	87.63	81.59	66.56	81.83	82.39	87.58	62. Bénéfices avant impôt
63. Income tax	7.62	14.39	11.67	9.50	12.73	16.97	13.83	7.43	7.21	24.85	63. Impôt sur le revenu
64. Profit after tax	57.74	52.06	63.77	61.79	74.90	64.62	52.73	74.39	75.18	62.73	64. Bénéfices après impôt

TURKEY / TURQUIE

Commercial banks / Banques commerciales

	1988	1989	1990	1991	1992	1993	1994	1995	1996	1997	
Per cent											*Pourcentage*
BALANCE SHEET ANALYSIS											**ANALYSE DU BILAN**
% of year-end balance sheet total											**% du total du bilan en fin d'exercice**
Assets											**Actif**
65. Cash & balance with Central bank	8.66	7.59	6.78	6.26	5.83	5.60	5.66	5.26	3.40	3.15	65. Caisse & solde auprès de la Banque centrale
66. Interbank deposits	13.06	10.07	9.63	11.87	16.66	20.73	17.07	15.53	13.08	13.99	66. Dépôts interbancaires
67. Loans	39.80	40.24	45.14	41.42	40.44	39.87	37.37	40.82	41.29	42.68	67. Prêts
68. Securities	11.35	12.90	11.21	12.70	11.83	11.59	11.80	11.08	16.37	15.86	68. Valeurs mobilières
69. Other assets	27.13	29.20	27.23	27.75	25.24	22.21	28.10	27.31	25.87	24.31	69. Autres actifs
Liabilities											**Passif**
70. Capital & reserves	4.54	4.67	4.59	5.05	4.69	4.76	4.51	4.33	4.05	8.73	70. Capital et réserves
71. Borrowing from Central bank	4.12	3.19	2.05	1.49	1.57	1.74	0.66	0.32	0.10	0.35	71. Emprunts auprès de la Banque centrale
72. Interbank deposits	5.23	4.41	4.48	3.06	4.00	8.05	2.71	4.77	5.84	18.01	72. Dépôts interbancaires
73. Non-bank deposits	57.04	60.14	58.15	59.49	55.88	47.94	66.05	65.38	67.27	62.03	73. Dépôts non bancaires
74. Bonds	0.09	0.40	0.27	0.26	1.21	2.52	0.90	1.04	0.35	0.96	74. Obligations
75. Other liabilities	28.97	27.19	30.47	30.65	32.64	34.98	25.16	24.15	22.38	9.92	75. Autres engagements
Memorandum items											***Pour mémoire***
76. Short-term securities	..	..	..	..	..	..	..	..	..	*3.67*	*76. Titres à court terme*
77. Bonds	*6.44*	*9.74*	*8.24*	*7.15*	*8.22*	*9.28*	*5.76*	*5.51*	*8.57*	*10.90*	*77. Obligations*
78. Shares and participations	*2.12*	*2.76*	*2.67*	*2.36*	*2.17*	*1.86*	*1.85*	*1.56*	*1.47*	*1.58*	*78. Actions et participations*
79. Claims on non-residents	*11.13*	*9.52*	*9.13*	*13.38*	*16.06*	*16.70*	*21.22*	*17.83*	*19.04*	*13.59*	*79. Créances sur des non-résidents*
80. Liabilities to non-residents	*5.81*	*5.21*	*8.40*	*8.31*	*10.87*	*14.79*	*6.81*	*8.66*	*11.14*	*16.44*	*80. Engagements envers des non-résidents*

* See notes on previous pages.

* Voir les notes en pages précédentes.

UNITED KINGDOM — ROYAUME-UNI

Commercial banks — Banques commerciales

	1988	1989	1990	1991	1992	1993	1994	1995	1996	1997	
Million pounds sterling											*Millions de livres*
INCOME STATEMENT											**COMPTE DE RESULTATS**
1. Interest income	39998	56101	63140	57737	52004	44836	43005	50694	55421	60988	1. Produits financiers
2. Interest expenses	27121	41736	48286	42199	36550	28463	26490	32945	34459	38515	2. Frais financiers
3. Net interest income	12877	14365	14854	15538	15454	16373	16515	17749	20961	22474	3. Produits financiers nets
4. Non-interest income (net)	7300	8772	9474	10645	11407	13113	12539	13331	13138	14244	4. Produits non financiers (nets)
a. Fees and commissions receivable	..	..	..	..	..	..	*10396*	*10622*	*12325*	*13215*	*a. Frais et commissions à recevoir*
b. Fees and commissions payable	..	..	..	..	..	..	*1112*	*1207*	*1557*	*1916*	*b. Frais et commissions à payer*
c. Net profits or loss on financial operations	..	..	..	..	..	..	*3255*	*3916*	*2370*	*2945*	*c. Profits ou pertes nets sur opérations financières*
d. Other	..	..	..	..	..	..	-	-	-	-	*d. Autres*
5. Gross income	20177	23137	24328	26183	26861	29486	29054	31080	34099	36718	5. Résultat brut
6. Operating expenses	13159	14977	16021	17197	17761	18622	18620	19836	21254	22357	6. Frais d'exploitation
a. Staff costs	*7719*	*8658*	*9114*	*9519*	*9704*	*10272*	*10434*	*11068*	*11599*	*11935*	*a. Dépenses en personnel*
b. Property costs	..	..	..	..	..	..	*4135*	*4290*	*4536*	*4837*	*b. Dépenses en immobilier*
c. Other	..	..	..	..	..	..	*4051*	*4478*	*5118*	*5584*	*c. Autres*
7. Net income	7018	8160	8307	8986	9100	10864	10434	11244	12846	14361	7. Résultat net
8. Provisions (net)	1228	7325	4766	6885	7298	5814	2349	2304	1937	1953	8. Provisions (nettes)
a. Provisions on loans	..	..	..	..	..	..	..	..	..	..	*a. Provisions sur prêts*
b. Provisions on securities	..	..	..	..	..	..	..	..	..	..	*b. Provisions sur titres*
c. Other	..	..	..	..	..	..	..	..	..	..	*c. Autres*
9. Profit before tax	5790	835	3541	2101	1802	5050	8085	8940	10909	12408	9. Bénéfices avant impôt
10. Income tax	2113	550	1630	872	997	1847	2709	3037	3893	3827	10. Impôt sur le revenu
11. Profit after tax	3677	285	1911	1229	805	3203	5376	5903	7016	8581	11. Bénéfices après impôt
12. Distributed profit	949	1201	1262	1273	1238	1838	2188	3615	2933	4380	12. Bénéfices distribués
13. Retained profit	2728	-916	649	-44	-433	1365	3188	2288	4083	4201	13. Bénéfices mis en réserve
BALANCE SHEET (1)											**BILAN (1)**
Assets											**Actif**
14. Cash & balance with Central bank	6107	7433	7249	7057	5191	5252	5152	5614	5771	5946	14. Caisse & solde auprès de la Banque centrale
15. Interbank deposits	77191	79191	80039	79774	87921	102950	113393	111545	121256	143629	15. Dépôts interbancaires
16. Loans	257865	306456	319817	322240	376505	376115	375285	419637	561512	603607	16. Prêts
17. Securities	27986	34189	38401	45448	84290	110735	126055	148818	187550	226096	17. Valeurs mobilières
18. Other assets	52112	65416	69913	77832	92946	95074	102008	120372	138963	159063	18. Autres actifs
Liabilities											**Passif**
19. Capital & reserves	23833	24728	24614	24440	24518	26228	29520	31267	42570	46948	19. Capital et réserves
20. Borrowing from Central bank	-	-	-	-	-	-	-	-	-	-	20. Emprunts auprès de la Banque centrale
21. Interbank deposits (1)	..	..	..	..	..	..	123328	248663	130571	142337	21. Dépôts interbancaires (1)
22. Non-bank deposits	366372	429820	453145	465404	476173	493912	379619	303150	548559	599266	22. Dépôts non bancaires
23. Bonds	13941	16778	15077	16616	62101	75112	82619	90451	131452	156040	23. Obligations
24. Other liabilities	17115	21359	22583	25891	84062	94875	106806	132455	161900	193751	24. Autres engagements
Balance sheet total											**Total du bilan**
25. End-year total	421261	492685	515419	532351	646854	690127	721892	805986	1015053	1138341	25. En fin d'exercice
26. Average total	395652	456973	504052	523885	589603	668491	706010	763939	952651	1076697	26. Moyen

UNITED KINGDOM — ROYAUME-UNI

Commercial banks — Banques commerciales

	1988	1989	1990	1991	1992	1993	1994	1995	1996	1997	
Million pounds sterling											*Millions de livres*
Memorandum items											***Pour mémoire***
27. Short-term securities	*10718*	*15405*	*16403*	*17458*	*16519*	*21699*	*25498*	*29845*	*17305*	*23348*	*27. Titres à court terme*
28. Bonds	..	..	..	..	..	..	..	..	..	..	*28. Obligations*
29. Shares and participations	..	..	..	..	..	..	..	..	..	..	*29. Actions et participations*
30. Claims on non-residents	..	..	..	..	..	..	..	..	..	..	*30. Créances sur des non-résidents*
31. Liabilities to non-residents	..	..	..	..	..	..	..	..	..	..	*31. Engagements envers des non-résidents*
Capital adequacy											***Solvabilité***
32. Tier 1 Capital	..	..	..	..	..	..	..	*32068*	*43026*	*47064*	*32. Fonds propres de base*
33. Tier 2 Capital	..	..	..	..	..	..	..	*22985*	*25234*	*26934*	*33. Fonds propres complémentaires*
34. Supervisory deductions	..	..	..	..	..	..	..	*3275*	*5873*	*6196*	*34. Eléments à déduire des fonds propres*
35. Total net capital resources	..	..	..	..	..	..	..	*51778*	*62387*	*67802*	*35. Total net des ressources en capital*
36. Risk-weighted assets	..	..	..	..	..	..	..	*463888*	*541395*	*574938*	*36. Actifs pondérés des risques*
SUPPLEMENTARY INFORMATION											**RENSEIGNEMENTS COMPLEMENTAIRES**
37. Number of institutions	52	49	47	41	39	37	37	40	44	44	37. Nombre d'institutions
38. Number of branches	13702	13467	12994	12306	11751	11445	11075	10601	12070	11643	38. Nombre de succursales
39. Number of employees (x 1000)	402.6	414.2	411.5	399.9	401.2	371.7	386.5	382.7	414.8	412.1	39. Nombre de salariés (x 1000)

1. Change in methodology.

Notes

- Commercial banks comprises the world-wide operations of ten major British banking groups:

  Abbey National Group
  Alliance & Leicester Group (included in the coverage beginning 1996)
  Bank of Scotland Group
  Barclays Group
  Halifax Group (included in the coverage beginning 1996)
  Lloyds TSB Group
  Midland Group
  National Westminster Group
  Royal Bank of Scotland Group
  Woolwich Group (included in the coverage beginning 1996)

  Until 1996, the Standard Chartered Group was included.

Change in methodology:

- Until 1994, Interbank deposits (item 21) are included under Non-bank deposits (item 22).
- As from 1992, due to revised reporting requirements, balance-sheet data include long-term assurance funds.

1. Changement méthodologique.

Notes

- Les "Banques commerciales" regroupent les activités mondiales de dix grandes banques britaniques :

  Abbey National Group
  Alliance & Leicester Group (à partir des statistiques de 1996)
  Bank of Scotland Group
  Barclays Group
  Halifax Group (à partir des statistiques de 1996)
  Lloyds TSB Group
  Midland Group
  National Westminster Group
  Royal Bank of Scotland Group
  Woolwich Group (à partir des statistiques de 1996)

  Jusqu'en 1996, les activités du Standard Chartered Group ont été incluses.

Changement méthodologique :

- Jusqu'en 1994, les Dépôts interbancaires (poste 21) sont inclus sous la rubrique Dépôts non bancaires (poste 22).
- A compter de 1992, suite aux révisions du règlement en vigueur, les données de bilan comprennent les fonds d'assurance à long terme.

UNITED KINGDOM
Commercial banks

ROYAUME-UNI
Banques commerciales

	1988	1989	1990	1991	1992	1993	1994	1995	1996	1997	
Per cent											*Pourcentage*
INCOME STATEMENT ANALYSIS											**ANALYSE DU COMPTE DE RESULTATS**
% of average balance sheet total											**% du total moyen du bilan**
40. Interest income	10.11	12.28	12.53	11.02	8.82	6.71	6.09	6.64	5.82	5.66	40. Produits financiers
41. Interest expenses	6.85	9.13	9.58	8.06	6.20	4.26	3.75	4.31	3.62	3.58	41. Frais financiers
42. Net interest income	3.25	3.14	2.95	2.97	2.62	2.45	2.34	2.32	2.20	2.09	42. Produits financiers nets
43. Non-interest income (net)	1.85	1.92	1.88	2.03	1.93	1.96	1.78	1.75	1.38	1.32	43. Produits non financiers (nets)
a. Fees and commissions receivable	..	..	..	..	..	..	*1.47*	*1.39*	*1.29*	*1.23*	*a. Frais et commissions à recevoir*
b. Fees and commissions payable	..	..	..	..	..	..	*0.16*	*0.16*	*0.16*	*0.18*	*b. Frais et commissions à payer*
c. Net profits or loss on financial operations	..	..	..	..	..	..	*0.46*	*0.51*	*0.25*	*0.27*	*c. Profits ou pertes nets sur opérations financières*
d. Other	..	..	..	..	..	..	-	-	-	-	*d. Autres*
44. Gross income	5.10	5.06	4.83	5.00	4.56	4.41	4.12	4.07	3.58	3.41	44. Résultat brut
45. Operating expenses	3.33	3.28	3.18	3.28	3.01	2.79	2.64	2.60	2.23	2.08	45. Frais d'exploitation
a. Staff costs	*1.95*	*1.89*	*1.81*	*1.82*	*1.65*	*1.54*	*1.48*	*1.45*	*1.22*	*1.11*	*a. Dépenses en personnel*
b. Property costs	..	..	..	..	..	..	*0.59*	*0.56*	*0.48*	*0.45*	*b. Dépenses en immobilier*
c. Other	..	..	..	..	..	..	*0.57*	*0.59*	*0.54*	*0.52*	*c. Autres*
46. Net income	1.77	1.79	1.65	1.72	1.54	1.63	1.48	1.47	1.35	1.33	46. Résultat net
47. Provisions (net)	0.31	1.60	0.95	1.31	1.24	0.87	0.33	0.30	0.20	0.18	47. Provisions (nettes)
a. Provisions on loans	..	..	..	..	..	..	..	..	..	..	*a. Provisions sur prêts*
b. Provisions on securities	..	..	..	..	..	..	..	..	..	..	*b. Provisions sur titres*
c. Other	..	..	..	..	..	..	..	..	..	..	*c. Autres*
48. Profit before tax	1.46	0.18	0.70	0.40	0.31	0.76	1.15	1.17	1.15	1.15	48. Bénéfices avant impôt
49. Income tax	0.53	0.12	0.32	0.17	0.17	0.28	0.38	0.40	0.41	0.36	49. Impôt sur le revenu
50. Profit after tax	0.93	0.06	0.38	0.23	0.14	0.48	0.76	0.77	0.74	0.80	50. Bénéfices après impôt
51. Distributed profit	0.24	0.26	0.25	0.24	0.21	0.27	0.31	0.47	0.31	0.41	51. Bénéfices distribués
52. Retained profit	0.69	-0.20	0.13	-0.01	-0.07	0.20	0.45	0.30	0.43	0.39	52. Bénéfices mis en réserve
% of gross income											**% du total du résultat brut**
53. Net interest income	63.82	62.09	61.06	59.34	57.53	55.53	56.84	57.11	61.47	61.21	53. Produits financiers nets
54. Non-interest income (net)	36.18	37.91	38.94	40.66	42.47	44.47	43.16	42.89	38.53	38.79	54. Produits non financiers (nets)
a. Fees and commissions receivable	..	..	..	..	..	..	*35.78*	*34.18*	*36.14*	*35.99*	*a. Frais et commissions à recevoir*
b. Fees and commissions payable	..	..	..	..	..	..	*3.83*	*3.88*	*4.57*	*5.22*	*b. Frais et commissions à payer*
c. Net profits or loss on financial operations	..	..	..	..	..	..	*11.20*	*12.60*	*6.95*	*8.02*	*c. Profits ou pertes nets sur opérations financières*
d. Other	..	..	..	..	..	..	-	-	-	-	*d. Autres*
55. Operating expenses	65.22	64.73	65.85	65.68	66.12	63.16	64.09	63.82	62.33	60.89	55. Frais d'exploitation
a. Staff costs	*38.26*	*37.42*	*37.46*	*36.36*	*36.13*	*34.84*	*35.91*	*35.61*	*34.02*	*32.50*	*a. Dépenses en personnel*
b. Property costs	..	..	..	..	..	..	*14.23*	*13.80*	*13.30*	*13.17*	*b. Dépenses en immobilier*
c. Other	..	..	..	..	..	..	*13.94*	*14.41*	*15.01*	*15.21*	*c. Autres*
56. Net income	34.78	35.27	34.15	34.32	33.88	36.84	35.91	36.18	37.67	39.11	56. Résultat net
57. Provisions (net)	6.09	31.66	19.59	26.30	27.17	19.72	8.08	7.41	5.68	5.32	57. Provisions (nettes)
a. Provisions on loans	..	..	..	..	..	..	..	..	..	..	*a. Provisions sur prêts*
b. Provisions on securities	..	..	..	..	..	..	..	..	..	..	*b. Provisions sur titres*
c. Other	..	..	..	..	..	..	..	..	..	..	*c. Autres*
58. Profit before tax	28.70	3.61	14.56	8.02	6.71	17.13	27.83	28.76	31.99	33.79	58. Bénéfices avant impôt
59. Income tax	10.47	2.38	6.70	3.33	3.71	6.26	9.32	9.77	11.42	10.42	59. Impôt sur le revenu
60. Profit after tax	18.22	1.23	7.86	4.69	3.00	10.86	18.50	18.99	20.58	23.37	60. Bénéfices après impôt
% of net income											**% du total du résultat net**
61. Provisions (net)	17.50	89.77	57.37	76.62	80.20	53.52	22.51	20.49	15.08	13.60	61. Provisions (nettes)
a. Provisions on loans	..	..	..	..	..	..	..	..	..	..	*a. Provisions sur prêts*
b. Provisions on securities	..	..	..	..	..	..	..	..	..	..	*b. Provisions sur titres*
c. Other	..	..	..	..	..	..	..	..	..	..	*c. Autres*
62. Profit before tax	82.50	10.23	42.63	23.38	19.80	46.48	77.49	79.51	84.92	86.40	62. Bénéfices avant impôt
63. Income tax	30.11	6.74	19.62	9.70	10.96	17.00	25.96	27.01	30.31	26.65	63. Impôt sur le revenu
64. Profit after tax	52.39	3.49	23.00	13.68	8.85	29.48	51.52	52.50	54.62	59.75	64. Bénéfices après impôt

UNITED KINGDOM / ROYAUME-UNI

Commercial banks / Banques commerciales

	1988	1989	1990	1991	1992	1993	1994	1995	1996	1997	
Per cent											*Pourcentage*
BALANCE SHEET ANALYSIS											**ANALYSE DU BILAN**
% of year-end balance sheet total											**% du total du bilan en fin d'exercice**
Assets											**Actif**
65. Cash & balance with Central bank	1.45	1.51	1.41	1.33	0.80	0.76	0.71	0.70	0.57	0.52	65. Caisse & solde auprès de la Banque centrale
66. Interbank deposits	18.32	16.07	15.53	14.99	13.59	14.92	15.71	13.84	11.95	12.62	66. Dépôts interbancaires
67. Loans	61.21	62.20	62.05	60.53	58.21	54.50	51.99	52.07	55.32	53.03	67. Prêts
68. Securities	6.64	6.94	7.45	8.54	13.03	16.05	17.46	18.46	18.48	19.86	68. Valeurs mobilières
69. Other assets	12.37	13.28	13.56	14.62	14.37	13.78	14.13	14.93	13.69	13.97	69. Autres actifs
Liabilities											**Passif**
70. Capital & reserves	5.66	5.02	4.78	4.59	3.79	3.80	4.09	3.88	4.19	4.12	70. Capital et réserves
71. Borrowing from Central bank	-	-	-	-	-	-	-	-	-	-	71. Emprunts auprès de la Banque centrale
72. Interbank deposits	..	..	..	..	..	..	17.08	30.85	12.86	12.50	72. Dépôts interbancaires
73. Non-bank deposits	86.97	87.24	87.92	87.42	73.61	71.57	52.59	37.61	54.04	52.64	73. Dépôts non bancaires
74. Bonds	3.31	3.41	2.93	3.12	9.60	10.88	11.44	11.22	12.95	13.71	74. Obligations
75. Other liabilities	4.06	4.34	4.38	4.86	13.00	13.75	14.80	16.43	15.95	17.02	75. Autres engagements
Memorandum items											***Pour mémoire***
76. Short-term securities	*2.54*	*3.13*	*3.18*	*3.28*	*2.55*	*3.14*	*3.53*	*3.70*	*1.70*	*2.05*	*76. Titres à court terme*
77. Bonds	..	..	..	..	..	..	..	..	..	..	*77. Obligations*
78. Shares and participations	..	..	..	..	..	..	..	..	..	..	*78. Actions et participations*
79. Claims on non-residents	..	..	..	..	..	..	..	..	..	..	*79. Créances sur des non-résidents*
80. Liabilities to non-residents	..	..	..	..	..	..	..	..	..	..	*80. Engagements envers des non-résidents*

* See notes on previous pages.

* Voir les notes en pages précédentes.

UNITED STATES — ETATS-UNIS

Commercial banks — Banques commerciales

Million US dollars	1989	1990	1991	1992	1993	1994	1995	1996	1997	1998 p	Millions de dollars des EU
INCOME STATEMENT											**COMPTE DE RESULTATS**
1. Interest income	317046	320404	290692	256415	244742	257064	302336	313191	338171	359356	1. Produits financiers
2. Interest expenses	205078	204949	168492	122517	105615	110849	147939	150078	164481	178065	2. Frais financiers
3. Net interest income	111968	115454	122199	133899	139127	146214	154397	163113	173690	181290	3. Produits financiers nets
4. Non-interest income (net)	52711	56808	65219	71402	80986	76646	84355	96512	107542	127591	4. Produits non financiers (nets)
a. Fees and commissions receivable	..	..	*44725*	*49034*	*52693*	*56376*	*61721*	*69263*	*78120*	*92472*	*a. Frais et commissions à recevoir*
b. Fees and commissions payable (1)	..	..	..	..	..	..	..	..	..	..	*b. Frais et commissions à payer (1)*
c. Net profits or loss on financial operations	*4851*	*5328*	*8851*	*10230*	*12292*	*5689*	*6817*	*8650*	*9847*	*11051*	*c. Profits ou pertes nets sur opérations financières*
d. Other	..	..	*11643*	*12138*	*16001*	*14581*	*15817*	*18599*	*19575*	*24068*	*d. Autres*
5. Gross income	164679	172262	187418	205301	220113	222860	238752	259625	281232	308881	5. Résultat brut
6. Operating expenses	108993	116606	126665	132815	140523	144905	151114	162447	170925	193819	6. Frais d'exploitation
a. Staff costs	*49412*	*52111*	*53810*	*55484*	*58507*	*60904*	*64003*	*67802*	*72329*	*79511*	*a. Dépenses en personnel*
b. Property costs	*16697*	*17547*	*17984*	*18152*	*18578*	*18978*	*19757*	*20887*	*22076*	*24158*	*b. Dépenses en immobilier*
c. Other	*42885*	*46948*	*54871*	*59181*	*63439*	*65023*	*67355*	*73758*	*76517*	*90149*	*c. Autres*
7. Net income	55686	55656	60753	72486	79590	77955	87638	97178	110307	115062	7. Résultat net
8. Provisions (net)	31297	32282	34871	26813	16841	10993	12632	16205	19133	21570	8. Provisions (nettes)
a. Provisions on loans	*31297*	*32282*	*34871*	*26813*	*16841*	*10993*	*12632*	*16205*	*19133*	*21570*	*a. Provisions sur prêts*
b. Provisions on securities (2)	..	..	..	..	..	..	..	..	..	..	*b. Provisions sur titres (2)*
c. Other	-	-	-	-	-	-	-	-	-	-	*c. Autres*
9. Profit before tax	24389	23374	25882	45673	62749	66962	75006	80973	91174	93492	9. Bénéfices avant impôt
10. Income tax	9547	7749	8292	14450	19861	22430	26222	28438	31989	31926	10. Impôt sur le revenu
11. Profit after tax	14843	15626	17590	31224	42886	44542	48784	52535	59185	61567	11. Bénéfices après impôt
12. Distributed profit	14127	13965	15562	14226	22068	28164	31105	39618	42723	41295	12. Bénéfices distribués
13. Retained profit	716	1661	2028	16997	20816	16377	17680	12916	16462	20271	13. Bénéfices mis en réserve
BALANCE SHEET											**BILAN**
Assets											**Actif**
14. Cash & balance with Central bank	174866	176090	162506	161656	153816	173118	187166	193625	195126	196358	14. Caisse & solde auprès de la Banque centrale
15. Interbank deposits	172715	139029	140460	135532	118392	129543	118336	142073	159408	158457	15. Dépôts interbancaires
16. Loans	2143192	2191125	2139569	2129905	2241078	2443073	2718622	2903505	3147302	3420545	16. Prêts
17. Securities	598207	648782	754071	846728	950578	911215	916391	924088	1005947	1089917	17. Valeurs mobilières
18. Other assets	197381	217963	221387	218947	227303	331802	349298	387976	463837	514679	18. Autres actifs
Liabilities											**Passif**
19. Capital & reserves	204131	217683	230712	262440	295448	310918	348223	375127	414528	454242	19. Capital et réserves
20. Borrowing from Central bank	..	..	..	..	..	..	..	..	..	..	20. Emprunts auprès de la Banque centrale
21. Interbank deposits	53843	49582	50077	47908	45525	39083	44138	56706	50956	54239	21. Dépôts interbancaires
22. Non-bank deposits	2481024	2583071	2623572	2634951	2692578	2814594	2961770	3117974	3347923	3600542	22. Dépôts non bancaires
23. Bonds	19618	23737	24850	33521	37148	40580	43261	50938	61661	72145	23. Obligations
24. Other liabilities	527745	498916	488783	513952	620468	783576	892421	950522	1096552	1198788	24. Autres engagements
Balance sheet total											**Total du bilan**
25. End-year total	3286361	3372989	3417993	3492768	3691167	3988751	4289813	4551267	4971620	5379956	25. En fin d'exercice
26. Average total	3186541	3338091	3379178	3441557	3565707	3863398	4147609	4375996	4733704	5146532	26. Moyen

UNITED STATES
Commercial banks

ETATS-UNIS
Banques commerciales

	1989	1990	1991	1992	1993	1994	1995	1996	1997	1998 p	
Million US dollars											*Millions de dollars des EU*
Memorandum items											**Pour mémoire**
27. Short-term securities	..	..	..	..	..	..	..	..	..	..	*27. Titres à court terme*
28. Bonds	..	..	..	..	..	..	..	..	..	..	*28. Obligations*
29. Shares and participations	..	..	..	..	..	..	..	..	..	..	*29. Actions et participations*
30. Claims on non-residents	..	..	..	..	..	..	..	..	..	..	*30. Créances sur des non-résidents*
31. Liabilities to non-residents	..	..	..	..	..	..	..	..	..	..	*31. Engagements envers des non-résidents*
Capital adequacy											**Solvabilité**
32. Tier 1 Capital	..	*208389*	*216296*	*236533*	*266816*	*291740*	*311705*	*331248*	*355092*	*380354*	*32. Fonds propres de base*
33. Tier 2 Capital	..	*50300*	*54527*	*56950*	*64689*	*68634*	*74790*	*82349*	*92246*	*111687*	*33. Fonds propres complémentaires*
34. Supervisory deductions	..	..	..	..	..	..	..	..	..	..	*34. Eléments à déduire des fonds propres*
35. Total net capital resources	..	*258689*	*270823*	*293482*	*331505*	*360373*	*386495*	*413597*	*447339*	*492040*	*35. Total net des ressources en capital*
36. Risk-weighted assets	..	*2689945*	*2609917*	*2541125*	*2571692*	*2732787*	*3003012*	*3251292*	*3585078*	*4005377*	*36. Actifs pondérés des risques*
SUPPLEMENTARY INFORMATION											**RENSEIGNEMENTS COMPLEMENTAIRES**
37. Number of institutions	12728	12370	11950	11495	11001	10488	9983	9575	9187	8817	37. Nombre d'institutions
38. Number of branches	47390	49885	51514	52290	53123	55748	57610	..	..	..	38. Nombre de succursales
39. Number of employees (x 1000)	1529	1513	1484	1475	1490	1483	1479	1484	1530	1610	39. Nombre de salariés (x 1000)

1. Fees and commissions payable (item 4.b.) are included under Fees and commissions receivable (item 4.a.).

2. Provisions on securities (item 8.b.) are included under Provisions on loans (item 8.a.) .

Notes

- Income data have been adjusted to account for the effects of mergers on reported earnings.
- Non-interest income (item 4) includes extraordinary items and realized gains on investment account securities.
- Loans (item 16) are reported net of loss reserves and include federal funds sold and reverse repurchase agreements.
- Bonds (item 23) include subordinated notes and debentures and exclude senior debt.
- Average balance sheet totals (item 26) are based on the quarterly average levels.

1. Les Frais et commissions à payer (poste 4.b.) sont inclus sous Frais et commissions à recevoir (poste 4.a.)

2. Les Provisions sur titres (poste 8.b.) sont incluses sous Provisions sur prêts (poste 8.a.)

Notes

- Les données sur le revenu ont été ajustées pour rendre compte des effets de fusion en ce qui concerne les gains rapportés.
- La rubrique Produits non-financiers (item 4) comprend les profits exceptionnels et les revenus provenant des ventes de titres de placement
- Les données publiées dans la rubrique Prêts (items 16) sont nettes de réserves pour pertes et comprennent le solde des fonds fédéraux et les opérations de mise en pension.
- La rubrique Obligations (item 23) regroupe les créances et les certificats de dettes subordonnés et ne comprend pas la dette de premier rang.
- Le total moyen du bilan (item 26) est basé sur les moyennes trimestrielles.

	1989	1990	1991	1992	1993	1994	1995	1996	1997	1998 p	
Per cent											*Pourcentage*
INCOME STATEMENT ANALYSIS											**ANALYSE DU COMPTE DE RESULTATS**
% of average balance sheet total											**% du total moyen du bilan**
40. Interest income	9.95	9.60	8.60	7.45	6.86	6.65	7.29	7.16	7.14	6.98	40. Produits financiers
41. Interest expenses	6.44	6.14	4.99	3.56	2.96	2.87	3.57	3.43	3.47	3.46	41. Frais financiers
42. Net interest income	3.51	3.46	3.62	3.89	3.90	3.78	3.72	3.73	3.67	3.52	42. Produits financiers nets
43. Non-interest income (net)	1.65	1.70	1.93	2.07	2.27	1.98	2.03	2.21	2.27	2.48	43. Produits non financiers (nets)
a. Fees and commissions receivable	..	..	*1.32*	*1.42*	*1.48*	*1.46*	*1.49*	*1.58*	*1.65*	*1.80*	*a. Frais et commissions à recevoir*
b. Fees and commissions payable	..	..	..	..	..	..	..	..	..	..	*b. Frais et commissions à payer*
c. Net profits or loss on financial operations	*0.15*	*0.16*	*0.26*	*0.30*	*0.34*	*0.15*	*0.16*	*0.20*	*0.21*	*0.21*	*c. Profits ou pertes nets sur opérations financières*
d. Other	..	..	*0.34*	*0.35*	*0.45*	*0.38*	*0.38*	*0.43*	*0.41*	*0.47*	*d. Autres*
44. Gross income	5.17	5.16	5.55	5.97	6.17	5.77	5.76	5.93	5.94	6.00	44. Résultat brut
45. Operating expenses	3.42	3.49	3.75	3.86	3.94	3.75	3.64	3.71	3.61	3.77	45. Frais d'exploitation
a. Staff costs	*1.55*	*1.56*	*1.59*	*1.61*	*1.64*	*1.58*	*1.54*	*1.55*	*1.53*	*1.54*	*a. Dépenses en personnel*
b. Property costs	*0.52*	*0.53*	*0.53*	*0.53*	*0.52*	*0.49*	*0.48*	*0.48*	*0.47*	*0.47*	*b. Dépenses en immobilier*
c. Other	*1.35*	*1.41*	*1.62*	*1.72*	*1.78*	*1.68*	*1.62*	*1.69*	*1.62*	*1.75*	*c. Autres*
46. Net income	1.75	1.67	1.80	2.11	2.23	2.02	2.11	2.22	2.33	2.24	46. Résultat net
47. Provisions (net)	0.98	0.97	1.03	0.78	0.47	0.28	0.30	0.37	0.40	0.42	47. Provisions (nettes)
a. Provisions on loans	*0.98*	*0.97*	*1.03*	*0.78*	*0.47*	*0.28*	*0.30*	*0.37*	*0.40*	*0.42*	*a. Provisions sur prêts*
b. Provisions on securities	..	..	..	..	..	..	..	..	..	..	*b. Provisions sur titres*
c. Other	-	-	-	-	-	-	-	-	-	-	*c. Autres*
48. Profit before tax	0.77	0.70	0.77	1.33	1.76	1.73	1.81	1.85	1.93	1.82	48. Bénéfices avant impôt
49. Income tax	0.30	0.23	0.25	0.42	0.56	0.58	0.63	0.65	0.68	0.62	49. Impôt sur le revenu
50. Profit after tax	0.47	0.47	0.52	0.91	1.20	1.15	1.18	1.20	1.25	1.20	50. Bénéfices après impôt
51. Distributed profit	0.44	0.42	0.46	0.41	0.62	0.73	0.75	0.91	0.90	0.80	51. Bénéfices distribués
52. Retained profit	0.02	0.05	0.06	0.49	0.58	0.42	0.43	0.30	0.35	0.39	52. Bénéfices mis en réserve
% of gross income											**% du total du résultat brut**
53. Net interest income	67.99	67.02	65.20	65.22	63.21	65.61	64.67	62.83	61.76	58.69	53. Produits financiers nets
54. Non-interest income (net)	32.01	32.98	34.80	34.78	36.79	34.39	35.33	37.17	38.24	41.31	54. Produits non financiers (nets)
a. Fees and commissions receivable	..	..	*23.86*	*23.88*	*23.94*	*25.30*	*25.85*	*26.68*	*27.78*	*29.94*	*a. Frais et commissions à recevoir*
b. Fees and commissions payable	..	..	..	..	..	..	..	..	..	..	*b. Frais et commissions à payer*
c. Net profits or loss on financial operations	*2.95*	*3.09*	*4.72*	*4.98*	*5.58*	*2.55*	*2.86*	*3.33*	*3.50*	*3.58*	*c. Profits ou pertes nets sur opérations financières*
d. Other	..	..	*6.21*	*5.91*	*7.27*	*6.54*	*6.62*	*7.16*	*6.96*	*7.79*	*d. Autres*
55. Operating expenses	66.19	67.69	67.58	64.69	63.84	65.02	63.29	62.57	60.78	62.75	55. Frais d'exploitation
a. Staff costs	*30.01*	*30.25*	*28.71*	*27.03*	*26.58*	*27.33*	*26.81*	*26.12*	*25.72*	*25.74*	*a. Dépenses en personnel*
b. Property costs	*10.14*	*10.19*	*9.60*	*8.84*	*8.44*	*8.52*	*8.28*	*8.05*	*7.85*	*7.82*	*b. Dépenses en immobilier*
c. Other	*26.04*	*27.25*	*29.28*	*28.83*	*28.82*	*29.18*	*28.21*	*28.41*	*27.21*	*29.19*	*c. Autres*
56. Net income	33.81	32.31	32.42	35.31	36.16	34.98	36.71	37.43	39.22	37.25	56. Résultat net
57. Provisions (net)	19.00	18.74	18.61	13.06	7.65	4.93	5.29	6.24	6.80	6.98	57. Provisions (nettes)
a. Provisions on loans	*19.00*	*18.74*	*18.61*	*13.06*	*7.65*	*4.93*	*5.29*	*6.24*	*6.80*	*6.98*	*a. Provisions sur prêts*
b. Provisions on securities	..	..	..	..	..	..	..	..	..	..	*b. Provisions sur titres*
c. Other	-	-	-	-	-	-	-	-	-	-	*c. Autres*
58. Profit before tax	14.81	13.57	13.81	22.25	28.51	30.05	31.42	31.19	32.42	30.27	58. Bénéfices avant impôt
59. Income tax	5.80	4.50	4.42	7.04	9.02	10.06	10.98	10.95	11.37	10.34	59. Impôt sur le revenu
60. Profit after tax	9.01	9.07	9.39	15.21	19.48	19.99	20.43	20.23	21.04	19.93	60. Bénéfices après impôt
% of net income											**% du total du résultat net**
61. Provisions (net)	56.20	58.00	57.40	36.99	21.16	14.10	14.41	16.68	17.35	18.75	61. Provisions (nettes)
a. Provisions on loans	*56.20*	*58.00*	*57.40*	*36.99*	*21.16*	*14.10*	*14.41*	*16.68*	*17.35*	*18.75*	*a. Provisions sur prêts*
b. Provisions on securities	..	..	..	..	..	..	..	..	..	..	*b. Provisions sur titres*
c. Other	-	-	-	-	-	-	-	-	-	-	*c. Autres*
62. Profit before tax	43.80	42.00	42.60	63.01	78.84	85.90	85.59	83.32	82.65	81.25	62. Bénéfices avant impôt
63. Income tax	17.14	13.92	13.65	19.93	24.95	28.77	29.92	29.26	29.00	27.75	63. Impôt sur le revenu
64. Profit after tax	26.65	28.08	28.95	43.08	53.88	57.14	55.67	54.06	53.65	53.51	64. Bénéfices après impôt

UNITED STATES — ETATS-UNIS

Commercial banks — Banques commerciales

	1989	1990	1991	1992	1993	1994	1995	1996	1997	1998 p	
Per cent											*Pourcentage*
BALANCE SHEET ANALYSIS											**ANALYSE DU BILAN**
% of year-end balance sheet total											**% du total du bilan en fin d'exercice**
Assets											**Actif**
65. Cash & balance with Central bank	5.32	5.22	4.75	4.63	4.17	4.34	4.36	4.25	3.92	3.65	65. Caisse & solde auprès de la Banque centrale
66. Interbank deposits	5.26	4.12	4.11	3.88	3.21	3.25	2.76	3.12	3.21	2.95	66. Dépôts interbancaires
67. Loans	65.21	64.96	62.60	60.98	60.71	61.25	63.37	63.80	63.31	63.58	67. Prêts
68. Securities	18.20	19.23	22.06	24.24	25.75	22.84	21.36	20.30	20.23	20.26	68. Valeurs mobilières
69. Other assets	6.01	6.46	6.48	6.27	6.16	8.32	8.14	8.52	9.33	9.57	69. Autres actifs
Liabilities											**Passif**
70. Capital & reserves	6.21	6.45	6.75	7.51	8.00	7.79	8.12	8.24	8.34	8.44	70. Capital et réserves
71. Borrowing from Central bank	..	..	..	..	..	..	..	..	..	..	71. Emprunts auprès de la Banque centrale
72. Interbank deposits	1.64	1.47	1.47	1.37	1.23	0.98	1.03	1.25	1.02	1.01	72. Dépôts interbancaires
73. Non-bank deposits	75.49	76.58	76.76	75.44	72.95	70.56	69.04	68.51	67.34	66.93	73. Dépôts non bancaires
74. Bonds	0.60	0.70	0.73	0.96	1.01	1.02	1.01	1.12	1.24	1.34	74. Obligations
75. Other liabilities	16.06	14.79	14.30	14.71	16.81	19.64	20.80	20.88	22.06	22.28	75. Autres engagements
Memorandum items											***Pour mémoire***
76. Short-term securities	..	..	..	..	..	..	..	..	..	..	*76. Titres à court terme*
77. Bonds	..	..	..	..	..	..	..	..	..	..	*77. Obligations*
78. Shares and participations	..	..	..	..	..	..	..	..	..	..	*78. Actions et participations*
79. Claims on non-residents	..	..	..	..	..	..	..	..	..	..	*79. Créances sur des non-résidents*
80. Liabilities to non-residents	..	..	..	..	..	..	..	..	..	..	*80. Engagements envers des non-résidents*

* See notes on previous pages.

* Voir les notes en pages précédentes.

UNITED STATES — ETATS-UNIS

Large commercial banks — Grandes banques commerciales

	1989	1990	1991	1992	1993	1994	1995	1996	1997	1998 p	
Million US dollars											*Millions de dollars des EU*
INCOME STATEMENT											**COMPTE DE RESULTATS**
1. Interest income	166865	167797	145738	130968	130319	138252	166502	179489	212077	237936	1. Produits financiers
2. Interest expenses	116574	116005	90006	67889	62847	65521	87701	91160	108448	123526	2. Frais financiers
3. Net interest income	50292	51794	55732	63077	67472	72731	78800	88331	103629	114412	3. Produits financiers nets
4. Non-interest income (net)	33482	35683	40035	45222	52627	49316	55150	66658	77966	95503	4. Produits non financiers (nets)
a. Fees and commissions receivable	..	..	*25995*	*29491*	*31742*	*34131*	*38029*	*45374*	*54853*	*68185*	*a. Frais et commissions à recevoir*
b. Fees and commissions payable (1)	..	..	..	..	..	..	..	..	..	..	*b. Frais et commissions à payer (1)*
c. Net profits or loss on financial operations	*4309*	*4952*	*7243*	*8358*	*10956*	*6165*	*6543*	*8202*	*9420*	*10395*	*c. Profits ou pertes nets sur opérations financières*
d. Other	..	..	*6797*	*7373*	*9929*	*9020*	*10578*	*13082*	*13693*	*16923*	*d. Autres*
5. Gross income	83774	87477	95767	108299	120099	122047	133950	154989	181595	209915	5. Résultat brut
6. Operating expenses	55134	59998	65451	69786	76503	80265	85598	98407	110924	133338	6. Frais d'exploitation
a. Staff costs	*25329*	*27204*	*28156*	*29152*	*31857*	*33710*	*36331*	*40658*	*46132*	*53095*	*a. Dépenses en personnel*
b. Property costs	*8995*	*9613*	*9855*	*9981*	*10527*	*10897*	*11510*	*12833*	*14427*	*16615*	*b. Dépenses en immobilier*
c. Other	*20809*	*23180*	*27438*	*30655*	*34119*	*35657*	*37757*	*44915*	*50367*	*63627*	*c. Autres*
7. Net income	28640	27479	30316	38513	43596	41782	48352	56582	70671	76577	7. Résultat net
8. Provisions (net)	21277	18222	21014	16463	10323	6324	6335	9137	12042	15188	8. Provisions (nettes)
a. Provisions on loans	*21277*	*18222*	*21014*	*16463*	*10323*	*6324*	*6335*	*9137*	*12042*	*15188*	*a. Provisions sur prêts*
b. Provisions on securities (2)	..	..	..	..	..	..	..	..	..	..	*b. Provisions sur titres (2)*
c. Other	-	-	-	-	-	-	-	-	-	-	*c. Autres*
9. Profit before tax	7363	9257	9302	22050	33273	35458	42017	47445	58629	61389	9. Bénéfices avant impôt
10. Income tax	4305	3454	3069	6898	10427	12061	15218	17104	21127	21651	10. Impôt sur le revenu
11. Profit after tax	3057	5806	6235	15150	22846	23398	26800	30343	37503	39738	11. Bénéfices après impôt
12. Distributed profit	6372	5641	6186	6009	10549	15906	17418	24189	27393	26444	12. Bénéfices distribués
13. Retained profit	-3316	163	50	9140	12297	7492	9383	6155	10112	13295	13. Bénéfices mis en réserve
BALANCE SHEET											**BILAN**
Assets											**Actif**
14. Cash & balance with Central bank	101996	103545	94222	93742	91737	104679	115351	129992	143520	150827	14. Caisse & solde auprès de la Banque centrale
15. Interbank deposits	108129	83432	86832	87829	77928	91907	80017	101520	124810	122943	15. Dépôts interbancaires
16. Loans	1092996	1124969	1096605	1109360	1201840	1346936	1541373	1772315	2111099	2377865	16. Prêts
17. Securities	244293	261258	315286	375440	458419	438566	461164	495883	599081	675156	17. Valeurs mobilières
18. Other assets	126865	139182	139783	141105	153676	252388	269104	309640	387623	435340	18. Autres actifs
Liabilities											**Passif**
19. Capital & reserves	85072	92661	99831	123521	147015	158195	180622	210899	258860	298424	19. Capital et réserves
20. Borrowing from Central bank	..	..	..	..	..	..	..	..	..	..	20. Emprunts auprès de la Banque centrale
21. Interbank deposits	32716	30701	28664	27043	25369	23021	26842	38818	37825	41242	21. Dépôts interbancaires
22. Non-bank deposits	1166507	1218492	1236868	1252133	1326244	1448840	1547985	1763736	2082859	2330627	22. Dépôts non bancaires
23. Bonds	16666	21027	22412	30722	33887	36889	38903	46796	58584	68697	23. Obligations
24. Other liabilities	373318	349507	344953	374057	451085	567532	672657	749101	928004	1023142	24. Autres engagements
Balance sheet total											**Total du bilan**
25. End-year total	1674279	1712386	1732728	1807476	1983600	2234476	2467009	2809350	3366133	3762131	25. En fin d'exercice
26. Average total	1632951	1720137	1722970	1777490	1900706	2152902	2389212	2639565	3118481	3565737	26. Moyen

UNITED STATES
Large commercial banks

ETATS-UNIS
Grandes banques commerciales

	1989	1990	1991	1992	1993	1994	1995	1996	1997	1998 p	
Million US dollars											*Millions de dollars des EU*
Memorandum items											***Pour mémoire***
27. Short-term securities	..	..	..	..	..	..	..	..	..	..	*27. Titres à court terme*
28. Bonds	..	..	..	..	..	..	..	..	..	..	*28. Obligations*
29. Shares and participations	..	..	..	..	..	..	..	..	..	..	*29. Actions et participations*
30. Claims on non-residents	..	..	..	..	..	..	..	..	..	..	*30. Créances sur des non-résidents*
31. Liabilities to non-residents	..	..	..	..	..	..	..	..	..	..	*31. Engagements envers des non-résidents*
Capital adequacy											***Solvabilité***
32. Tier 1 Capital	..	*87373*	*92089*	*105946*	*127613*	*144290*	*157880*	*177241*	*209990*	*237730*	*32. Fonds propres de base*
33. Tier 2 Capital	..	*35486*	*39320*	*41859*	*49222*	*52251*	*57428*	*65131*	*76822*	*95495*	*33. Fonds propres complémentaires*
34. Supervisory deductions	..	..	..	..	..	..	..	..	..	..	*34. Eléments à déduire des fonds propres*
35. Total net capital resources	..	*122859*	*131409*	*147805*	*176835*	*196541*	*215308*	*242372*	*286811*	*333225*	*35. Total net des ressources en capital*
36. Risk-weighted assets	..	*1545530*	*1502880*	*1473085*	*1523372*	*1637900*	*1841934*	*2092638*	*2505717*	*2937849*	*36. Actifs pondérés des risques*
SUPPLEMENTARY INFORMATION											**RENSEIGNEMENTS COMPLEMENTAIRES**
37. Number of institutions	100	100	100	100	100	100	100	100	100	100	37. Nombre d'institutions
38. Number of branches	..	..	..	..	..	..	..	..	..	..	38. Nombre de succursales
39. Number of employees (x 1000)	661	659	646	668	693	696	721	781	879	986	39. Nombre de salariés (x 1000)

1. Fees and commissions payable (item 4.b.) are included under Fees and commissions receivable (item 4.a.).
2. Provisions on securities (item 8.b.) are included under Provisions on loans (item 8.a.) .

Notes

- Large commercial banks refer to the 100 largest Commercial banks.
- Income data have been adjusted to account for the effects of mergers on reported earnings.
- Non-interest income (item 4) includes extraordinary items and realized gains on investment account securities.
- Loans (item 16) are reported net of loss reserves and include federal funds sold and reverse repurchase agreements.
- Bonds (item 23) include subordinated notes and debentures and exclude senior debt.
- Average balance sheet totals (item 26) are based on the quarterly average levels.

1. Les Frais et commissions à payer (poste 4.b.) sont inclus sous Frais et commissions à recevoir (poste 4.a.).
2. Les Provisions sur titres (poste 8.b.) sont incluses sous Provisions sur prêts (poste 8.a.).

Notes

- Les Grandes banques commerciales font référence aux 100 plus grandes Banques commerciales.
- Les données sur le revenu ont été ajustées pour rendre compte des effets de fusion en ce qui concerne les gains rapportés.
- La rubrique Produits non-financiers (item 4) comprend les profits exceptionnels et les revenus provenant des ventes de titres de placement.
- Les données publiées dans la rubrique Prêts (items 16) sont nettes de réserves pour pertes et comprennent le solde des fonds fédéraux et les opérations de mise en pension.
- La rubrique Obligations (item 23) regroupe les créances et les certificats de dettes subordonnés et ne comprend pas la dette de premier rang.
- Le total moyen du bilan (item 26) est basé sur les moyennes trimestrielles.

UNITED STATES — ETATS-UNIS

Large commercial banks — Grandes banques commerciales

Per cent	1989	1990	1991	1992	1993	1994	1995	1996	1997	1998 p	Pourcentage
INCOME STATEMENT ANALYSIS											**ANALYSE DU COMPTE DE RESULTATS**
% of average balance sheet total											**% du total moyen du bilan**
40. Interest income	10.22	9.75	8.46	7.37	6.86	6.42	6.97	6.80	6.80	6.67	40. Produits financiers
41. Interest expenses	7.14	6.74	5.22	3.82	3.31	3.04	3.67	3.45	3.48	3.46	41. Frais financiers
42. Net interest income	3.08	3.01	3.23	3.55	3.55	3.38	3.30	3.35	3.32	3.21	42. Produits financiers nets
43. Non-interest income (net)	2.05	2.07	2.32	2.54	2.77	2.29	2.31	2.53	2.50	2.68	43. Produits non financiers (nets)
a. Fees and commissions receivable	..	..	*1.51*	*1.66*	*1.67*	*1.59*	*1.59*	*1.72*	*1.76*	*1.91*	*a. Frais et commissions à recevoir*
b. Fees and commissions payable	..	..	..	..	..	..	..	..	..	..	*b. Frais et commissions à payer*
c. Net profits or loss on financial operations	*0.26*	*0.29*	*0.42*	*0.47*	*0.58*	*0.29*	*0.27*	*0.31*	*0.30*	*0.29*	*c. Profits ou pertes nets sur opérations financières*
d. Other	..	..	*0.39*	*0.41*	*0.52*	*0.42*	*0.44*	*0.50*	*0.44*	*0.47*	*d. Autres*
44. Gross income	5.13	5.09	5.56	6.09	6.32	5.67	5.61	5.87	5.82	5.89	44. Résultat brut
45. Operating expenses	3.38	3.49	3.80	3.93	4.02	3.73	3.58	3.73	3.56	3.74	45. Frais d'exploitation
a. Staff costs	*1.55*	*1.58*	*1.63*	*1.64*	*1.68*	*1.57*	*1.52*	*1.54*	*1.48*	*1.49*	*a. Dépenses en personnel*
b. Property costs	*0.55*	*0.56*	*0.57*	*0.56*	*0.55*	*0.51*	*0.48*	*0.49*	*0.46*	*0.47*	*b. Dépenses en immobilier*
c. Other	*1.27*	*1.35*	*1.59*	*1.72*	*1.80*	*1.66*	*1.58*	*1.70*	*1.62*	*1.78*	*c. Autres*
46. Net income	1.75	1.60	1.76	2.17	2.29	1.94	2.02	2.14	2.27	2.15	46. Résultat net
47. Provisions (net)	1.30	1.06	1.22	0.93	0.54	0.29	0.27	0.35	0.39	0.43	47. Provisions (nettes)
a. Provisions on loans	*1.30*	*1.06*	*1.22*	*0.93*	*0.54*	*0.29*	*0.27*	*0.35*	*0.39*	*0.43*	*a. Provisions sur prêts*
b. Provisions on securities	..	..	..	..	..	..	..	..	..	..	*b. Provisions sur titres*
c. Other	-	-	-	-	-	-	-	-	-	-	*c. Autres*
48. Profit before tax	0.45	0.54	0.54	1.24	1.75	1.65	1.76	1.80	1.88	1.72	48. Bénéfices avant impôt
49. Income tax	0.26	0.20	0.18	0.39	0.55	0.56	0.64	0.65	0.68	0.61	49. Impôt sur le revenu
50. Profit after tax	0.19	0.34	0.36	0.85	1.20	1.09	1.12	1.15	1.20	1.11	50. Bénéfices après impôt
51. Distributed profit	0.39	0.33	0.36	0.34	0.56	0.74	0.73	0.92	0.88	0.74	51. Bénéfices distribués
52. Retained profit	-0.20	0.01	-	0.51	0.65	0.35	0.39	0.23	0.32	0.37	52. Bénéfices mis en réserve
% of gross income											**% du total du résultat brut**
53. Net interest income	60.03	59.21	58.20	58.24	56.18	59.59	58.83	56.99	57.07	54.50	53. Produits financiers nets
54. Non-interest income (net)	39.97	40.79	41.80	41.76	43.82	40.41	41.17	43.01	42.93	45.50	54. Produits non financiers (nets)
a. Fees and commissions receivable	..	..	*27.14*	*27.23*	*26.43*	*27.97*	*28.39*	*29.28*	*30.21*	*32.48*	*a. Frais et commissions à recevoir*
b. Fees and commissions payable	..	..	..	..	..	..	..	..	..	..	*b. Frais et commissions à payer*
c. Net profits or loss on financial operations	*5.14*	*5.66*	*7.56*	*7.72*	*9.12*	*5.05*	*4.88*	*5.29*	*5.19*	*4.95*	*c. Profits ou pertes nets sur opérations financières*
d. Other	..	..	*7.10*	*6.81*	*8.27*	*7.39*	*7.90*	*8.44*	*7.54*	*8.06*	*d. Autres*
55. Operating expenses	65.81	68.59	68.34	64.44	63.70	65.77	63.90	63.49	61.08	63.52	55. Frais d'exploitation
a. Staff costs	*30.23*	*31.10*	*29.40*	*26.92*	*26.53*	*27.62*	*27.12*	*26.23*	*25.40*	*25.29*	*a. Dépenses en personnel*
b. Property costs	*10.74*	*10.99*	*10.29*	*9.22*	*8.77*	*8.93*	*8.59*	*8.28*	*7.94*	*7.92*	*b. Dépenses en immobilier*
c. Other	*24.84*	*26.50*	*28.65*	*28.31*	*28.41*	*29.22*	*28.19*	*28.98*	*27.74*	*30.31*	*c. Autres*
56. Net income	34.19	31.41	31.66	35.56	36.30	34.23	36.10	36.51	38.92	36.48	56. Résultat net
57. Provisions (net)	25.40	20.83	21.94	15.20	8.60	5.18	4.73	5.90	6.63	7.24	57. Provisions (nettes)
a. Provisions on loans	*25.40*	*20.83*	*21.94*	*15.20*	*8.60*	*5.18*	*4.73*	*5.90*	*6.63*	*7.24*	*a. Provisions sur prêts*
b. Provisions on securities	..	..	..	..	..	..	..	..	..	..	*b. Provisions sur titres*
c. Other	-	-	-	-	-	-	-	-	-	-	*c. Autres*
58. Profit before tax	8.79	10.58	9.71	20.36	27.70	29.05	31.37	30.61	32.29	29.24	58. Bénéfices avant impôt
59. Income tax	5.14	3.95	3.20	6.37	8.68	9.88	11.36	11.04	11.63	10.31	59. Impôt sur le revenu
60. Profit after tax	3.65	6.64	6.51	13.99	19.02	19.17	20.01	19.58	20.65	18.93	60. Bénéfices après impôt
% of net income											**% du total du résultat net**
61. Provisions (net)	74.29	66.31	69.32	42.75	23.68	15.14	13.10	16.15	17.04	19.83	61. Provisions (nettes)
a. Provisions on loans	*74.29*	*66.31*	*69.32*	*42.75*	*23.68*	*15.14*	*13.10*	*16.15*	*17.04*	*19.83*	*a. Provisions sur prêts*
b. Provisions on securities	..	..	..	..	..	..	..	..	..	..	*b. Provisions sur titres*
c. Other	-	-	-	-	-	-	-	-	-	-	*c. Autres*
62. Profit before tax	25.71	33.69	30.68	57.25	76.32	84.86	86.90	83.85	82.96	80.17	62. Bénéfices avant impôt
63. Income tax	15.03	12.57	10.12	17.91	23.92	28.87	31.47	30.23	29.89	28.27	63. Impôt sur le revenu
64. Profit after tax	10.67	21.13	20.57	39.34	52.40	56.00	55.43	53.63	53.07	51.89	64. Bénéfices après impôt

UNITED STATES
Large commercial banks

ETATS-UNIS
Grandes banques commerciales

	1989	1990	1991	1992	1993	1994	1995	1996	1997	1998 p	
Per cent											*Pourcentage*
BALANCE SHEET ANALYSIS											**ANALYSE DU BILAN**
% of year-end balance sheet total											**% du total du bilan en fin d'exercice**
Assets											**Actif**
65. Cash & balance with Central bank	6.09	6.05	5.44	5.19	4.62	4.68	4.68	4.63	4.26	4.01	65. Caisse & solde auprès de la Banque centrale
66. Interbank deposits	6.46	4.87	5.01	4.86	3.93	4.11	3.24	3.61	3.71	3.27	66. Dépôts interbancaires
67. Loans	65.28	65.70	63.29	61.38	60.59	60.28	62.48	63.09	62.72	63.21	67. Prêts
68. Securities	14.59	15.26	18.20	20.77	23.11	19.63	18.69	17.65	17.80	17.95	68. Valeurs mobilières
69. Other assets	7.58	8.13	8.07	7.81	7.75	11.30	10.91	11.02	11.52	11.57	69. Autres actifs
Liabilities											**Passif**
70. Capital & reserves	5.08	5.41	5.76	6.83	7.41	7.08	7.32	7.51	7.69	7.93	70. Capital et réserves
71. Borrowing from Central bank	..	..	..	..	..	..	..	..	..	..	71. Emprunts auprès de la Banque centrale
72. Interbank deposits	1.95	1.79	1.65	1.50	1.28	1.03	1.09	1.38	1.12	1.10	72. Dépôts interbancaires
73. Non-bank deposits	69.67	71.16	71.38	69.28	66.86	64.84	62.75	62.78	61.88	61.95	73. Dépôts non bancaires
74. Bonds	1.00	1.23	1.29	1.70	1.71	1.65	1.58	1.67	1.74	1.83	74. Obligations
75. Other liabilities	22.30	20.41	19.91	20.69	22.74	25.40	27.27	26.66	27.57	27.20	75. Autres engagements
Memorandum items											***Pour mémoire***
76. Short-term securities	..	..	..	..	..	..	..	..	..	..	*76. Titres à court terme*
77. Bonds	..	..	..	..	..	..	..	..	..	..	*77. Obligations*
78. Shares and participations	..	..	..	..	..	..	..	..	..	..	*78. Actions et participations*
79. Claims on non-residents	..	..	..	..	..	..	..	..	..	..	*79. Créances sur des non-résidents*
80. Liabilities to non-residents	..	..	..	..	..	..	..	..	..	..	*80. Engagements envers des non-résidents*

* See notes on previous pages.

* Voir les notes en pages précédentes.

UNITED STATES
Savings institutions

ETATS-UNIS
Institutions d'épargne

	1989	1990	1991	1992	1993	1994	1995	1996	1997	1998 p	
Million US dollars											*Millions de dollars des EU*
INCOME STATEMENT											**COMPTE DE RESULTATS**
1. Interest income	134178	117208	97602	77652	66138	63470	70995	72270	69174	71059	1. Produits financiers
2. Interest expenses	109572	90942	69463	45852	34518	33411	42259	42171	40559	41888	2. Frais financiers
3. Net interest income	24606	26266	28139	31800	31620	30059	28736	30099	28615	29171	3. Produits financiers nets
4. Non-interest income (net)	9580	7319	6642	6311	6416	6123	7121	7493	7029	9200	4. Produits non financiers (nets)
a. Fees and commissions receivable	*6552*	*5066*	*5328*	*4745*	*4741*	*4838*	*5028*	*4848*	*4990*	*5356*	*a. Frais et commissions à recevoir*
b. Fees and commissions payable	..	..	..	..	..	..	..	..	..	..	*b. Frais et commissions à payer*
c. Net profits or loss on financial operations	..	..	..	..	..	..	..	..	..	..	*c. Profits ou pertes nets sur opérations financières*
d. Other	*3029*	*2255*	*1334*	*1582*	*1675*	*1285*	*2091*	*2645*	*2043*	*3844*	*d. Autres*
5. Gross income	34186	33585	34781	38111	38036	36182	35857	37592	35644	38371	5. Résultat brut
6. Operating expenses	30803	28473	26454	28232	24898	23231	21835	25700	21072	23545	6. Frais d'exploitation
a. Staff costs	*11497*	*10813*	*9849*	*9632*	*9964*	*9756*	*9584*	*10140*	*9925*	*10861*	*a. Dépenses en personnel*
b. Property costs	*5368*	*5052*	*4565*	*4281*	*4080*	*3968*	*4004*	*4097*	*3788*	*4283*	*b. Dépenses en immobilier*
c. Other	*13939*	*12614*	*12085*	*11369*	*10854*	*9507*	*8243*	*11464*	*7359*	*8401*	*c. Autres*
7. Net income	3383	5112	8327	9879	13138	12951	14022	11892	14572	14826	7. Résultat net
8. Provisions (net)	-6277	-4163	7003	5184	4312	2481	2110	2534	2159	1958	8. Provisions (nettes)
a. Provisions on loans	*-6277*	*-4163*	*7003*	*5184*	*4312*	*2481*	*2110*	*2534*	*2159*	*1958*	*a. Provisions sur prêts*
b. Provisions on securities (1)	..	..	..	..	..	..	..	..	..	..	*b. Provisions sur titres (1)*
c. Other	-	-	-	-	-	-	-	-	-	-	*c. Autres*
9. Profit before tax	9660	9275	1324	4695	8826	10470	11912	9358	12413	12868	9. Bénéfices avant impôt
10. Income tax	1186	1360	2812	3755	3858	3780	4159	3037	4852	5269	10. Impôt sur le revenu
11. Profit after tax (2)	8474	7915	-1488	940	4968	6690	7753	6321	7561	7599	11. Bénéfices après impôt (2)
12. Distributed profit	1566	1288	1818	2107	2293	2598	4083	5810	4890	6577	12. Bénéfices distribués
13. Retained profit	6908	6627	-3306	-1167	2675	4092	3670	511	2671	1022	13. Bénéfices mis en réserve
BALANCE SHEET											**BILAN**
Assets											**Actif**
14. Cash & balance with Central bank	-	-	-	-	-	-	-	-	-	-	14. Caisse & solde auprès de la Banque centrale
15. Interbank deposits	5580	15081	13431	12230	10060	6179	11228	10102	9237	14720	15. Dépôts interbancaires
16. Loans	915561	812146	723734	647917	626380	635061	647908	681328	691760	713986	16. Prêts
17. Securities	357836	285320	252942	267585	275773	290276	288582	262356	248679	269246	17. Valeurs mobilières
18. Other assets	148535	146631	122895	102482	88674	77048	78023	74503	76510	89732	18. Autres actifs
Liabilities											**Passif**
19. Capital & reserves	69371	67535	68628	74350	78421	79934	86063	85790	89332	94427	19. Capital et réserves
20. Borrowing from Central bank	-	-	-	-	-	-	-	-	-	-	20. Emprunts auprès de la Banque centrale
21. Interbank deposits	63327	46966	25964	26585	33767	52809	55288	52248	50713	62847	21. Dépôts interbancaires
22. Non-bank deposits	1059506	964667	881972	801071	774157	737180	741907	727920	670907	663344	22. Dépôts non bancaires
23. Bonds	4675	4331	3524	3056	2533	2395	2581	2401	2935	2812	23. Obligations
24. Other liabilities	230633	175679	132914	125152	112009	136246	139902	159930	212299	264254	24. Autres engagements
Balance sheet total											**Total du bilan**
25. End-year total	1427512	1259178	1113002	1030214	1000887	1008564	1025741	1028289	1026186	1087684	25. En fin d'exercice
26. Average total	1517001	1343345	1186090	1071608	1015551	1004726	1017153	1027015	1027238	1056935	26. Moyen

UNITED STATES
Savings institutions

ETATS-UNIS
Institutions d'épargne

	1989	1990	1991	1992	1993	1994	1995	1996	1997	1998 p	
Million US dollars											*Millions de dollars des EU*
Memorandum items											***Pour mémoire***
27. Short-term securities	..	..	..	..	..	..	..	..	..	..	*27. Titres à court terme*
28. Bonds	..	..	..	..	..	..	..	..	..	..	*28. Obligations*
29. Shares and participations	..	..	..	..	..	..	..	..	..	..	*29. Actions et participations*
30. Claims on non-residents	..	..	..	..	..	..	..	..	..	..	*30. Créances sur des non-résidents*
31. Liabilities to non-residents	..	..	..	..	..	..	..	..	..	..	*31. Engagements envers des non-résidents*
Capital adequacy											***Solvabilité***
32. Tier 1 Capital	..	*58341*	*61819*	*70034*	*74252*	*76979*	*79337*	*79250*	*80542*	*83997*	*32. Fonds propres de base*
33. Tier 2 Capital	..	*9507*	*9106*	*8696*	*7891*	*7487*	*7759*	*7796*	*7931*	*8645*	*33. Fonds propres complémentaires*
34. Supervisory deductions	..	-	-	-	-	-	-	-	-	-	*34. Eléments à déduire des fonds propres*
35. Total net capital resources	..	*67848*	*70925*	*78730*	*82143*	*84466*	*87096*	*87046*	*88473*	*92642*	*35. Total net des ressources en capital*
36. Risk-weighted assets	..	*773376*	*673237*	*576129*	*544492*	*542416*	*556747*	*575681*	*584756*	*615113*	*36. Actifs pondérés des risques*
SUPPLEMENTARY INFORMATION											**RENSEIGNEMENTS COMPLEMENTAIRES**
37. Number of institutions	3087	2815	2561	2390	2262	2152	2030	1924	1780	1684	37. Nombre d'institutions
38. Number of branches	20562	18792	17016	15407	14599	14644	13436	13740	12656	12451	38. Nombre de succursales
39. Number of employees (x 1000)	..	345.3	305.3	295.9	286.6	261.5	250.3	252.7	244.8	236.6	39. Nombre de salariés (x 1000)

1. Provisions on securities (item 8.b.) are included under Provisions on loans (item 8.a.)

2. Change in methodology.

Notes

- Savings institutions include Savings banks and Savings and loan associations.

Change in methodology

- Until 1996, Profit after tax (item 11) reflects extraordinary items and realized gains on assets and securities taken into account when calculating net income.

1. Les Provisions sur titres (poste 8.b.) sont incluses sous Provisions sur prêts (poste 8.a.)

2. Changement méthodologique.

Notes

- Les Institutions d'épargne comprennent les Caisses d'épargne et les Associations d'épargne et de prêts.

Changement méthodologique

- Jusqu'en 1996, la rubrique Bénéfices après impôts (poste 11) représente les profits exceptionnels et les revenus provenant des actifs et valeurs mobilières pris en compte lors du calcul du résultat net.

UNITED STATES — ETATS-UNIS

Savings institutions — Institutions d'épargne

	1989	1990	1991	1992	1993	1994	1995	1996	1997	1998 p	
Per cent											*Pourcentage*
INCOME STATEMENT ANALYSIS											**ANALYSE DU COMPTE DE RESULTATS**
% of average balance sheet total											**% du total moyen du bilan**
40. Interest income	8.84	8.73	8.23	7.25	6.51	6.32	6.98	7.04	6.73	6.72	40. Produits financiers
41. Interest expenses	7.22	6.77	5.86	4.28	3.40	3.33	4.15	4.11	3.95	3.96	41. Frais financiers
42. Net interest income	1.62	1.96	2.37	2.97	3.11	2.99	2.83	2.93	2.79	2.76	42. Produits financiers nets
43. Non-interest income (net)	0.63	0.54	0.56	0.59	0.63	0.61	0.70	0.73	0.68	0.87	43. Produits non financiers (nets)
a. Fees and commissions receivable	*0.43*	*0.38*	*0.45*	*0.44*	*0.47*	*0.48*	*0.49*	*0.47*	*0.49*	*0.51*	*a. Frais et commissions à recevoir*
b. Fees and commissions payable	..	..	..	..	..	..	..	..	..	..	*b. Frais et commissions à payer*
c. Net profits or loss on financial operations	..	..	..	..	..	..	..	..	..	..	*c. Profits ou pertes nets sur opérations financières*
d. Other	*0.20*	*0.17*	*0.11*	*0.15*	*0.16*	*0.13*	*0.21*	*0.26*	*0.20*	*0.36*	*d. Autres*
44. Gross income	2.25	2.50	2.93	3.56	3.75	3.60	3.53	3.66	3.47	3.63	44. Résultat brut
45. Operating expenses	2.03	2.12	2.23	2.63	2.45	2.31	2.15	2.50	2.05	2.23	45. Frais d'exploitation
a. Staff costs	*0.76*	*0.80*	*0.83*	*0.90*	*0.98*	*0.97*	*0.94*	*0.99*	*0.97*	*1.03*	*a. Dépenses en personnel*
b. Property costs	*0.35*	*0.38*	*0.38*	*0.40*	*0.40*	*0.39*	*0.39*	*0.40*	*0.37*	*0.41*	*b. Dépenses en immobilier*
c. Other	*0.92*	*0.94*	*1.02*	*1.06*	*1.07*	*0.95*	*0.81*	*1.12*	*0.72*	*0.79*	*c. Autres*
46. Net income	0.22	0.38	0.70	0.92	1.29	1.29	1.38	1.16	1.42	1.40	46. Résultat net
47. Provisions (net)	-0.41	-0.31	0.59	0.48	0.42	0.25	0.21	0.25	0.21	0.19	47. Provisions (nettes)
a. Provisions on loans	*-0.41*	*-0.31*	*0.59*	*0.48*	*0.42*	*0.25*	*0.21*	*0.25*	*0.21*	*0.19*	*a. Provisions sur prêts*
b. Provisions on securities	..	..	..	..	..	..	..	..	..	..	*b. Provisions sur titres*
c. Other	-	-	-	-	-	-	-	-	-	-	*c. Autres*
48. Profit before tax	0.64	0.69	0.11	0.44	0.87	1.04	1.17	0.91	1.21	1.22	48. Bénéfices avant impôt
49. Income tax	0.08	0.10	0.24	0.35	0.38	0.38	0.41	0.30	0.47	0.50	49. Impôt sur le revenu
50. Profit after tax	0.56	0.59	-0.13	0.09	0.49	0.67	0.76	0.62	0.74	0.72	50. Bénéfices après impôt
51. Distributed profit	0.10	0.10	0.15	0.20	0.23	0.26	0.40	0.57	0.48	0.62	51. Bénéfices distribués
52. Retained profit	0.46	0.49	-0.28	-0.11	0.26	0.41	0.36	0.05	0.26	0.10	52. Bénéfices mis en réserve
% of gross income											**% du total du résultat brut**
53. Net interest income	71.98	78.21	80.90	83.44	83.13	83.08	80.14	80.07	80.28	76.02	53. Produits financiers nets
54. Non-interest income (net)	28.02	21.79	19.10	16.56	16.87	16.92	19.86	19.93	19.72	23.98	54. Produits non financiers (nets)
a. Fees and commissions receivable	*19.17*	*15.08*	*15.32*	*12.45*	*12.46*	*13.37*	*14.02*	*12.90*	*14.00*	*13.96*	*a. Frais et commissions à recevoir*
b. Fees and commissions payable	..	..	..	..	..	..	..	..	..	..	*b. Frais et commissions à payer*
c. Net profits or loss on financial operations	..	..	..	..	..	..	..	..	..	..	*c. Profits ou pertes nets sur opérations financières*
d. Other	*8.86*	*6.71*	*3.84*	*4.15*	*4.40*	*3.55*	*5.83*	*7.04*	*5.73*	*10.02*	*d. Autres*
55. Operating expenses	90.10	84.78	76.06	74.08	65.46	64.21	60.89	68.37	59.12	61.36	55. Frais d'exploitation
a. Staff costs	*33.63*	*32.20*	*28.32*	*25.27*	*26.20*	*26.96*	*26.73*	*26.97*	*27.84*	*28.31*	*a. Dépenses en personnel*
b. Property costs	*15.70*	*15.04*	*13.12*	*11.23*	*10.73*	*10.97*	*11.17*	*10.90*	*10.63*	*11.16*	*b. Dépenses en immobilier*
c. Other	*40.77*	*37.56*	*34.75*	*29.83*	*28.54*	*26.28*	*22.99*	*30.50*	*20.65*	*21.89*	*c. Autres*
56. Net income	9.90	15.22	23.94	25.92	34.54	35.79	39.11	31.63	40.88	38.64	56. Résultat net
57. Provisions (net)	-18.36	-12.40	20.13	13.60	11.34	6.86	5.88	6.74	6.06	5.10	57. Provisions (nettes)
a. Provisions on loans	*-18.36*	*-12.40*	*20.13*	*13.60*	*11.34*	*6.86*	*5.88*	*6.74*	*6.06*	*5.10*	*a. Provisions sur prêts*
b. Provisions on securities	..	..	..	..	..	..	..	..	..	..	*b. Provisions sur titres*
c. Other	-	-	-	-	-	-	-	-	-	-	*c. Autres*
58. Profit before tax	28.26	27.62	3.81	12.32	23.20	28.94	33.22	24.89	34.82	33.54	58. Bénéfices avant impôt
59. Income tax	3.47	4.05	8.08	9.85	10.14	10.45	11.60	8.08	13.61	13.73	59. Impôt sur le revenu
60. Profit after tax	24.79	23.57	-4.28	2.47	13.06	18.49	21.62	16.81	21.21	19.80	60. Bénéfices après impôt
% of net income											**% du total du résultat net**
61. Provisions (net)	-185.55	-81.44	84.10	52.47	32.82	19.16	15.05	21.31	14.82	13.21	61. Provisions (nettes)
a. Provisions on loans	*-185.55*	*-81.44*	*84.10*	*52.47*	*32.82*	*19.16*	*15.05*	*21.31*	*14.82*	*13.21*	*a. Provisions sur prêts*
b. Provisions on securities	..	..	..	..	..	..	..	..	..	..	*b. Provisions sur titres*
c. Other	-	-	-	-	-	-	-	-	-	-	*c. Autres*
62. Profit before tax	285.55	181.44	15.90	47.53	67.18	80.84	84.95	78.69	85.18	86.79	62. Bénéfices avant impôt
63. Income tax	35.06	26.60	33.77	38.01	29.37	29.19	29.66	25.54	33.30	35.54	63. Impôt sur le revenu
64. Profit after tax	250.49	154.83	-17.87	9.52	37.81	51.66	55.29	53.15	51.89	51.25	64. Bénéfices après impôt

UNITED STATES / ETATS-UNIS

Savings institutions / Institutions d'épargne

	1989	1990	1991	1992	1993	1994	1995	1996	1997	1998 p	
Per cent											*Pourcentage*
BALANCE SHEET ANALYSIS											**ANALYSE DU BILAN**
% of year-end balance sheet total											**% du total du bilan en fin d'exercice**
Assets											**Actif**
65. Cash & balance with Central bank	-	-	-	-	-	-	-	-	-	-	65. Caisse & solde auprès de la Banque centrale
66. Interbank deposits	0.39	1.20	1.21	1.19	1.01	0.61	1.09	0.98	0.90	1.35	66. Dépôts interbancaires
67. Loans	64.14	64.50	65.03	62.89	62.58	62.97	63.16	66.26	67.41	65.64	67. Prêts
68. Securities	25.07	22.66	22.73	25.97	27.55	28.78	28.13	25.51	24.23	24.75	68. Valeurs mobilières
69. Other assets	10.41	11.64	11.04	9.95	8.86	7.64	7.61	7.25	7.46	8.25	69. Autres actifs
Liabilities											**Passif**
70. Capital & reserves	4.86	5.36	6.17	7.22	7.84	7.93	8.39	8.34	8.71	8.68	70. Capital et réserves
71. Borrowing from Central bank	-	-	-	-	-	-	-	-	-	-	71. Emprunts auprès de la Banque centrale
72. Interbank deposits	4.44	3.73	2.33	2.58	3.37	5.24	5.39	5.08	4.94	5.78	72. Dépôts interbancaires
73. Non-bank deposits	74.22	76.61	79.24	77.76	77.35	73.09	72.33	70.79	65.38	60.99	73. Dépôts non bancaires
74. Bonds	0.33	0.34	0.32	0.30	0.25	0.24	0.25	0.23	0.29	0.26	74. Obligations
75. Other liabilities	16.16	13.95	11.94	12.15	11.19	13.51	13.64	15.55	20.69	24.30	75. Autres engagements
Memorandum items											***Pour mémoire***
76. Short-term securities	..	..	..	..	..	..	..	..	..	..	*76. Titres à court terme*
77. Bonds	..	..	..	..	..	..	..	..	..	..	*77. Obligations*
78. Shares and participations	..	..	..	..	..	..	..	..	..	..	*78. Actions et participations*
79. Claims on non-residents	..	..	..	..	..	..	..	..	..	..	*79. Créances sur des non-résidents*
80. Liabilities to non-residents	..	..	..	..	..	..	..	..	..	..	*80. Engagements envers des non-résidents*

* See notes on previous pages.

* Voir les notes en pages précédentes.

Part II

GENERAL TABLES

TABLEAUX GÉNÉRAUX

STRUCTURE OF THE FINANCIAL SYSTEM
STRUCTURE DU SYSTEME FINANCIER
end-June 1997 - fin juin 1997

	Number of institutions / Nombre d'institutions	Number of branches / Nombre de succursales	Number of employees / Nombre de salariés	Total assets or liabilities / Total des actifs ou des passifs	Total financial assets / Total des actifs financiers		
				million A$ / $A	million A$ / $A	%	
Central bank	*1*	*6*	*1304*	*48807*	*48323*	..	*Banque centrale*
Other monetary institutions	*50*	*13113*	..	*548854*	*543942*	..	*Autres institutions monétaires*
Commercial banks (1)	29	13072	..	508736	503896	..	Banques commerciales (1)
Foreign-owned banks (2)	21	41	..	40118	40046	..	Banques étrangères (2)
Other financial institutions	*1886*	..	..	*178361*	..	..	*Autres institutions financières*
Mortgage credit institutions (3)	23	1229	2889	10582	10373	..	Institutions de crédit hypothécaire (3)
Credit co-operatives	271	1922	8121	16929	..		Coopératives de crédit
Finance companies (4)	173	..	..	50236	..	..	Sociétés financières (4)
Others	1419	..	..	100614	..	..	Autres
Insurance institutions	*151676*	..	..	*499519*	..	..	*Institutions d'assurance*
Insurance companies (5)	*212*	..	..	*208145*	..	..	Sociétés d'assurance (5)
Pension funds and foundations (6)	150800	..	..	199755	..	..	Fonds de pension et fondations (6)
Others (7)	664	..	..	91619	..	..	Autres (7)
All financial institutions	*153613*	..	..	*1275541*	..	..	*Ensemble des institutions financieres*

1. Includes 12 banks authorised as subsidiaries of foreign banks. Total assets of foreign subsidiary banks was $A 49 827 million at June 1997. Data refers to Australian operations of banks.
2. Refers to banks authorised as foreign branch banks. Data refers to the Australian operations of these banks.
3. Co-operative building societies.
4. General financiers and other finance companies.
5. Life and General Insurance companies.
6. Non-life superannuation.
7. Public unit trusts, trustee companies and friendly societies.

1. Y compris 12 banques agréées comme filiales de banques étrangères. Le total des actifs des filiales bancaires étrangères était de 49 827 millions de $A en juin 1997. Les données se réfèrent aux transactions australiennes des banques.
2 Comprend les banques agréées comme succursales bancaires étrangères. Les données se réfèrent aux opérations australiennes de ces banques.
3. Mutuelles de crédit immobilier.
4. Financiers et autres sociétés financières.
5. Compagnies d'assurance et d'assurance vie.
6. Cotisations non-vie.
7. Fonds commun de placement, compagnies fiduciaires et sociétés de prévoyance.

RESIDENT/NON-RESIDENT AND DOMESTIC/FOREIGN CURRENCY CLASSIFICATION OF BANK ASSETS AND LIABILITIES (1)

RESIDENT/NON RESIDENT ET MONNAIE NATIONALE/ETRANGERE CLASSIFICATION DE L'ACTIF ET DU PASSIF DES BANQUES (1)

Million Australian dollars — *Millions de dollars australians*

	Residents / Résidents	Non-residents / Non résidents	Total / Total	
Assets				*Actif*
Domestic currency	507207	10063	517270	Monnaie nationale
Foreign currencies	18035	13549	31584	Monnaies étrangères
Total	525242	23612	548854	Total
Liabilities (2)				*Passif (2)*
Domestic currency	402595	22076	424671	Monnaie nationale
Foreign currencies	13036	62956	75992	Monnaies étrangères
Total	415631	85032	500663	Total

1. Figures refer to balances reported on the Australian books of locally incorporated banks and banks authorised as branches of foreign banks. They exclude banks' overseas branch and overseas bank subsidiary operations and domestic and overseas non-bank subsidiaries.
2. Liabilities exclude shareholders' funds of banks.

1. Les chiffres se réfèrent aux bilans présentés dans les comptes australiens des banques inscrites localement et des banques agrées comme succursales des banques étrangères. Ils excluent les opérations des succursales étrangères et celles des filiales bancaires étrangères ainsi que les filiales non bancaires nationales et étrangères.
2. Les fonds des actionnaires des banques sont exclus du passif.

STRUCTURE OF THE FINANCIAL SYSTEM
STRUCTURE DU SYSTEME FINANCIER

1997

	Number of institutions / Nombre d'institutions	Number of branches / Nombre de succursales	Number of employees / Nombre de salariés	Total assets or liabilities / Total des actifs ou des passifs	Total financial assets / Total des actifs financiers		
				million Sch / S	*million Sch / S*	*%*	
Central bank	*1*	*8*	..	*374543*	*342593*	*4.6*	*Banque centrale*
Other monetary institutions	*893*	*4473*	..	*5035914*	*5004969*	*66.8*	*Autres institutions monétaires*
Commercial banks	37	780	..	1552378	1547914	*20.7*	Banques commerciales
Foreign-owned banks (1)	26	..	..	157014	156226	*2.1*	Banques étrangères (1)
Savings banks	73	1465	..	1848456	1840578	*24.6*	Caisses d'épargne
Co-operative banks	757	2228	..	1478066	1460251	*19.5*	Banques mutualistes
Other financial institutions	*97*	*182*	..	*964313*	*960662*	*12.8*	*Autres institutions financières*
Mortgage credit institutions	9	156	..	321563	319872	*4.3*	Institutions de crédit hypothécaire
Others (2)	88	26	..	642750	640790	*8.6*	Autres (2)
Insurance institutions	*710*	-	..	*1230565*	*1182321*	*15.8*	*Institutions d'assurance*
Insurance companies	71	-	..	619469	571477	*7.6*	Sociétés d'assurance
Pension funds and foundations	14	-	..	43655	43403	*0.6*	Fonds de pension et fondations
Others (3)	625	-	..	567441	567441	*7.6*	Autres (3)
All financial institutions	*1701*	*4663*	..	*7605335*	*7490545*	*100.0*	*Ensemble des institutions financières*

1. Foreign-owned bank branches are included with those of Commercial banks
2. Special purpose credit institutions.
3. Investment funds.

1. Les succursales des Banques étrangères sont incluses avec celles des Banques commerciales
2. Institutions de crédit specialisées.
3. Fonds d'investissement.

RESIDENT/NON-RESIDENT AND DOMESTIC/FOREIGN CURRENCY CLASSIFICATION OF BANK ASSETS AND LIABILITIES

RESIDENT/NON RESIDENT ET MONNAIE NATIONALE/ETRANGERE CLASSIFICATION DE L'ACTIF ET DU PASSIF DES BANQUES

Million schillings *Millions de schillings*

	Residents / Résidents	Non-residents / Non résidents	Total / Total	
Assets				*Actif*
Domestic currency	4377862	347166	4725028	Monnaie nationale
Foreign currencies	351920	923281	1275201	Monnaies étrangères
Total	4729782	1270447	6000229	Total
Liabilities				*Passif*
Domestic currency	3815283	145562	3960846	Monnaie nationale
Foreign currencies	421619	1617764	2039383	Monnaies étrangères
Total	4236902	1763327	6000229	Total

STRUCTURE OF THE FINANCIAL SYSTEM
STRUCTURE DU SYSTEME FINANCIER

1997

	Number of institutions / Nombre d'institutions	Number of branches / Nombre de succursales	Number of employees / Nombre de salariés	Total assets or liabilities / Total des actifs ou des passifs	Total financial assets / Total des actifs financiers		
				million BF / FB	million BF / FB	%	
Central bank	*1*	*14*	*2805*	*1042137*	*1021316*	..	*Banque centrale*
Credit institutions	*131*	*17259*	*76939*	*29205310*	*27526307*	..	*Etablissements de crédit*
7 large credit institutions governed by Belgian law	7	..	..	19715231	18497014	..	7 grands établissements de crédit de droit belge
Other credit institutions governed by Belgian law	86	..	..	5438974	5140439	..	Autres établissements de crédit de droit belge
Branches of credit institutions governed by foreign law	38	..	..	4051106	3888854	..	Succursales d'établissements de crédit de droit étranger
Collective investment institutions	*330*	..	..	*2831300*	..	..	*Organismes de placement collectif*
Securities dealers	*57*	..	..	*94632*	*93043*	..	*Sociétés de bourse*
Mortgage companies	..	..	..	..	..	..	*Sociétés hypothécaires*
Insurance institutions	*475*	..	..	*3506397*	*2891382*	..	*Entreprises d'assurance*
Insurance companies	168	..	26877	3073508	2462585	..	Compagnies d'assurance
Pension funds	307	..	..	432889	428797	..	Fonds de pension
All financial institutions	..	..	..	..	..	..	*Ensemble des institutions financières*

RESIDENT/NON-RESIDENT AND DOMESTIC/FOREIGN CURRENCY CLASSIFICATION OF CREDIT INSTITUTIONS ASSETS AND LIABILITIES

RESIDENT/NON RESIDENT ET MONNAIE NATIONALE/ETRANGERE CLASSIFICATION DE L'ACTIF ET DU PASSIF DES ETABLISSEMENTS DE CREDIT

Million Belgian francs *Millions de francs belges*

	Residents / Résidents	Non-residents / Non résidents	Total / Total	
Assets				*Actif*
Domestic currency	15116216	1278760	16394976	Monnaie nationale
Foreign currencies	1530798	11279536	12810334	Monnaies étrangères
Total	16647014	12558296	29205310	Total
Liabilities				*Passif*
Domestic currency	14027108	2042851	16069959	Monnaie nationale
Foreign currencies	1546481	11588870	13135351	Monnaies étrangères
Total	15573589	13631721	29205310	Total

STRUCTURE OF THE FINANCIAL SYSTEM
STRUCTURE DU SYSTEME FINANCIER

1998 p

	Number of institutions / Nombre d'institutions	Number of branches / Nombre de succursales	Number of employees / Nombre de salariés	Total assets or liabilities / Total des actifs ou des passifs	Total financial assets / Total des actifs financiers		
				million C$ / $Can	million C$ / $Can	%	
Central bank	*1*	*1*	..	*33935*	*33625*	*1.6*	*Banque centrale*
Other monetary institutions	*2354*	..	..	*1078354*	*1063951*	*49.8*	*Autres institutions monétaires*
Commercial banks	9	..	..	866378	854388	*40.0*	Banques commerciales
Foreign-owned banks	45	..	..	93488	93116	*4.4*	Banques étrangères
Savings banks							Caisses d'épargne
Co-operative banks	2300	..	..	118488	116447	*5.5*	Banques mutualistes
Other financial institutions	*42090*	..	..	*473937*	*451574*	*21.1*	*Autres institutions financières*
Mortgage credit institutions	*45*	..	..	60019	58324	*2.7*	Institutions de crédit hypothécaire
Development credit institutions	*20*	..	..	51247	47259	*2.2*	Institutions de crédit de développement
Finance companies	*25*	..	..	46897	46676	*2.2*	Sociétés financières
Others	*42000*	..	..	315774	299315	*14.0*	Autres
Insurance institutions	*3660*	..	..	*610460*	*586328*	*27.5*	*Institutions d'assurance*
Insurance companies	*160*	..	..	172556	161753	*7.6*	Sociétés d'assurance
Pension funds and foundations	3500	..	..	437904	424575	*19.9*	Fonds de pension et fondations
All financial institutions	*48105*	..	..	*2196686*	*2135478*	*100.00*	*Ensemble des institutions financières*

1. The data are for 31 December and cover only booked-in Canada business.

1. Les données se rapportent au 31 décembre et concernent uniquement les opérations enregistrées au Canada.

STRUCTURE OF THE FINANCIAL SYSTEM
STRUCTURE DU SYSTEME FINANCIER

1997

	Number of institutions / Nombre d'institutions	Number of branches / Nombre de succursales	Number of employees / Nombre de salariés	Total assets or liabilities / Total des actifs ou des passifs	Total financial assets / Total des actifs financiers		
				million Ck / KC	million Ck / KC	%	
Central bank	*1*	*9*	*1698*	*655083*	..	..	*Banque centrale*
Other monetary institutions	*50*	*1557*	*53121*	*2321178*	..	..	*Autres institutions monétaires*
Commercial banks (1)	20	1496	48184	1735663	..	..	Banques commerciales(1)
Foreign-owned banks(2)	24	61	3759	518511	..	..	Banques étrangères (2)
Savings banks (3)	6	-	1178	67004	..	..	Caisses d'épargne (3)
Co-operative banks	-	-	-	-	..	..	Banques mutualistes
Other financial institutions	*508*	*13*	*4141*	..	..	..	*Autres institutions financières*
Mortgage credit institutions	1	13	438	9656	..	..	Institutions de crédit hypothécaire
Development credit institutions	..	..	..	..	..	..	Institutions de crédit de développement
Finance companies	507	..	3703	..	..	..	Sociétés financières
Insurance institutions	*117*	..	*20690*	..	..	..	*Institutions d'assurance*
Insurance companies	*35*	..	*20184*	..	..	..	Sociétés d'assurance
Pension funds and foundations	38	..	237	..	..	..	Fonds de pension et fondations
Others (4)	44	23	269	..	..	..	Autres (4)
All financial institutions	676	*1602*	*79650*	..	..	..	*Ensemble des institutions financières*

1. Includes 5 banks with special statute.
2. Banks with more than 50% foreign capital and branches of foreign banks
3. Building savings institutions.
4. Assistance companies in the Insurance sector.

1. Y inclus 5 banques avec régime spécial.
2. Banques avec plus de 50 % de capital étranger et succursales de banques étrangères
3. Institutions d'épargne immobilière.
4. Compagnies d'assistance dans le secteur de l'Assurance

RESIDENT/NON-RESIDENT AND DOMESTIC/FOREIGN CURRENCY CLASSIFICATION OF BANK ASSETS AND LIABILITIES (1)

RESIDENT/NON RESIDENT ET MONNAIE NATIONALE/ETRANGERE CLASSIFICATION DE L'ACTIF ET DU PASSIF DES BANQUES (1)

Million Czech koruna *Million de couronnes tchèques*

	Residents / Résidents	Non-residents / Non résidents	Total / Total	
Assets				*Actif*
Domestic currency	1904055	77330	1981385	Monnaie nationale
Foreign currencies	255275	244850	500125	Monnaies étrangères
Total	2159330	322180	2481510	Total
Liabilities				*Passif*
Domestic currency	1789876	61203	1851079	Monnaie nationale
Foreign currencies	210832	268923	479755	Monnaies étrangères
Total	2000708	330126	2481510	Total

1. Includes adjustments and depreciation in the amount of Ck 150676 million

1. Y compris des ajustements et des dépréciations d'un montant de 150676 millions de KC.

STRUCTURE OF THE FINANCIAL SYSTEM
STRUCTURE DU SYSTEME FINANCIER

1997

	Number of institutions / Nombre d'institutions	Number of branches / Nombre de succursales	Number of employees / Nombre de salariés	Total assets or liabilities / Total des actifs ou des passifs	Total financial assets / Total des actifs financiers		
				million DKr / KrD	*million DKr / KrD*	*%*	
Central bank	*1*	-	*600*	*209817*	..	..	*Banque centrale*
Other monetary institutions	*107*	..	..	..	..	..	*Autres institutions monétaires*
Commercial banks (1)	92	2178	42483	1288570	..	..	Banques commerciales(1)
Foreign-owned banks	15	..	..	..	..	..	Banques étrangères
Savings banks	..	..	..	..	..	..	Caisses d'épargne
Co-operative banks	..	..	..	..	..	..	Banques mutualistes
Other financial institutions	..	..	..	..	..	..	*Autres institutions financières*
Mortgage credit institutions	8	..	4347	1066589	..	..	Institutions de crédit hypothécaire
Development credit institutions	..	..	..	..	..	..	Institutions de crédit de développement
Finance companies	..	..	..	..	..	..	Sociétés financières
Insurance institutions	*301*	..	*15328*	*782560*	..	..	*Institutions d'assurance*
Insurance companies	238	..	*15283*	745050	..	..	Sociétés d'assurance
Pension funds and foundations	63	..	45	37510	..	..	Fonds de pension et fondations
All financial institutions	..	..	..	..	..	..	*Ensemble des institutions financières*

1. Includes banks, savings banks, and credit co-operatives with a minimum working capital of DKr 250 million.

1. Comprend les banques, les caisses d'épargne et les institutions coopératives de crédit disposant d'un fond de roulement minimum de 250 millions de KrD.

STRUCTURE OF THE FINANCIAL SYSTEM
STRUCTURE DU SYSTEME FINANCIER

1997

	Number of institutions / Nombre d'institutions	Number of branches / Nombre de succursales	Number of employees / Nombre de salariés	Total assets or liabilities / Total des actifs ou des passifs	Total financial assets / Total des actifs financiers		
				million Mk / MkF	million Mk / MkF	%	
Central bank	*1*	*4*	*776*	*62159*	*62159*	*4.6*	*Banque centrale*
Other monetary institutions	*348*	*1306*	*25692*	*672676*	*665612*	*49.0*	*Autres institutions monétaires*
Commercial banks	9	547	16584	479583	475928	*35.1*	Banques commerciales
Foreign-owned banks	5	12	479	48610	48532	*3.6*	Banques étrangères
Savings banks	40	211	1651	26627	25994	*1.9*	Caisses d'épargne
Co-operative banks	294	536	6978	117856	115158	*8.5*	Banques mutualistes
Other financial institutions	..	..	..	..	*193557*	*14.3*	*Autres institutions financières*
Other credit institutions	23	19	1648	115215	..	..	Autres institutions de crédit
Mutual funds and fund companies	78	..	..	19397	..	..	Fonds communs de placement et entreprises de placement
Asset management companies	3	8	507	30678	..	..	Entreprises de gestion de portefeuille
Financial auxiliaries	..	..	..	..	*2537*	*0.2*	*Auxiliaires financiers*
Insurance institutions (1)	..	..	..	..	*433388*	*31.9*	*Institutions d'assurance (1)*
Insurance companies	..	..	..	..	130960	*9.6*	Sociétés d'assurance
Pension funds and foundations (2)	..	..	..	..	302428	*22.3*	Fonds de pension et fondations (2)
All financial institutions	..	..	..	..	*1357253*	*100.0*	*Ensemble des institutions financières*

1. Provisional figures.
2. Employment pension schemes, which are now a part of social security funds.

1. Données provisoires.
2. Régimes de retraites, qui font maintenant partie des fonds de sécurité sociale.

RESIDENT/NON-RESIDENT AND DOMESTIC/FOREIGN CURRENCY CLASSIFICATION OF BANK ASSETS AND LIABILITIES

RESIDENT/NON RESIDENT ET MONNAIE NATIONALE/ETRANGERE CLASSIFICATION DE L'ACTIF ET DU PASSIF DES BANQUES

Million markkaa *Millions de markkas*

	Residents / Résidents	Non-residents / Non résidents	Total / Total	
Assets				*Actif*
Domestic currency	479872	30399	510271	Monnaie nationale
Foreign currencies	35384	127021	162405	Monnaies étrangères
Total	515256	157420	672676	Total
Liabilities				*Passif*
Domestic currency	499391	16646	516037	Monnaie nationale
Foreign currencies	33607	123032	156639	Monnaies étrangères
Total	532998	139678	672676	Total

STRUCTURE OF THE FINANCIAL SYSTEM (1)
STRUCTURE DU SYSTEME FINANCIER (1)

1997

	Number of institutions / Nombre d'institutions (2)	Number of branches / Nombre de succursales (2)	Number of employees / Nombre de salariés (3)	Total assets or liabilities / Total des actifs ou des passifs	Total financial assets / Total des actifs financiers		
				million FF	million FF	%	
Central bank	*1*	*211*	*17386*	*591200*	..	..	*Banque centrale*
Other monetary institutions	*567*	25385	345965	*14205415*	..	..	*Autres institutions monétaires*
Commercial banks	406	10309	187078	9425896	..	..	Banques commerciales
Foreign-owned banks(4)	..	..	..	..	..	..	Banques étrangères (4)
Savings banks	34	4220	36249	1509943	..	..	Caisses d'épargne
Co-operative banks	127	10856	122638	3269576	..	..	Banques mutualistes
Other financial institutions	*732*	*79*	*30314*	*3160649*	..	..	*Autres institutions financières*
Finance companies	682	..	21540	2099929	..	..	Sociétés financières
Specialised financial institutions	29	..	7549	1047993	..	..	Institutions financières spécialisées
Municipal credit institutions	21	79	1225	12727	..	..	Caisses de crédit municipal
Insurance institutions	..	..	..	..	..	..	*Institutions d'assurance*
All financial institutions (5)	*1300*	*25675*	*393665*	*17957264*	..	..	*Ensemble des institutions financières (5)*

1. The data provided cover exclusively activities in France, including the overseas departments and territories.
2. Number of institutions and branches are taken from the "Rapport annuel du Comité des établissements de crédit".
3. Number of employees encompasses all staff, without deductions in the case of part-time staff
4. Data for Foreign-owned banks is included in Commercial bank figures.
5. All credit institutions.

1. Les données répertoriées concernent uniquement l'activité en métropole et dans les départements et territoires d'Outre-Mer.
2. Le nombre d'établissements et de guichets sont repris dans le "Rapport annuel du Comité des établissements de crédit".
3. En ce qui concerne les effectifs, il s'agit des effectifs sans déduction éventuelle des temps partiels
4. Les données pour les Banques étrangères sont comprises dans celles des Banques commerciales.
5. Ensemble des institutions de crédit.

RESIDENT/NON-RESIDENT AND DOMESTIC/FOREIGN CURRENCY CLASSIFICATION OF BANK ASSETS AND LIABILITIES (1)

RESIDENT/NON RESIDENT ET MONNAIE NATIONALE/ETRANGERE CLASSIFICATION DE L'ACTIF ET DU PASSIF DES BANQUES (1)

Million French francs *Millions de francs français*

	Residents / Résidents	Non-residents / Non résidents	Total / Total	
Assets				*Actif*
Domestic currency	1211124	1104976	13316100	Monnaie nationale
Foreign currencies	776735	3273231	4049966	Monnaies étrangères
Total	12987859	4378207	17366065	Total
Liabilities				*Passif*
Domestic currency	12485736	938907	13424643	Monnaie nationale
Foreign currencies	816242	3125180	3941422	Monnaies étrangères
Total	13301978	4064087	17366065	Total

1. Data are for activities in France and its overseas departments and territories as of 31 December 1997.

1. Il s'agit de données relatives à l'activité en métropole, dans les départements et territoires d'Outre-Mer au 31 décembre 1997.

STRUCTURE OF THE FINANCIAL SYSTEM
STRUCTURE DU SYSTEME FINANCIER

1997

	Number of institutions / Nombre d'institutions	Number of branches / Nombre de succursales	Number of employees / Nombre de salariés (x 1000)	Total assets or liabilities / Total des actifs ou des passifs	Total financial assets / Total des actifs financiers		
				billion / milliards DM	billion / milliards DM	%	
Central bank	*1*	*163*	*16*	*381*	*377*	..	*Banque centrale*
Other monetary institutions	*3422*	*43311*	..	..	..	..	*Autres institutions monétaires*
Commercial banks	249	7030	216	2809	2796	..	Banques commerciales
Foreign-owned banks	155	768	..	..	..	..	Banques étrangères
Savings banks	598	18751	288	1692	1664	..	Caisses d'épargne
Co-operative banks	2420	16762	172	979	960	..	Banques mutualistes
Other financial institutions	..	..	..	..	..	..	*Autres institutions financières*
Mortgage credit institutions	35	290	12	1318	1316	.. ..	Institutions de crédit hypothécaire
Development credit institutions	..	..	..	..	..	..	Institutions de crédit de développement
Finance companies	..	..	..	..	..	..	Sociétés financières
Others	..	..	..	..	..	..	Autres
Insurance institutions	..	..	..	..	..	..	*Institutions d'assurance*
All financial institutions	..	..	..	..	..	..	*Ensemble des institutions financières*

RESIDENT/NON-RESIDENT AND DOMESTIC/FOREIGN CURRENCY CLASSIFICATION OF BANK ASSETS AND LIABILITIES

RESIDENT/NON RESIDENT ET MONNAIE NATIONALE/ETRANGERE CLASSIFICATION DE L'ACTIF ET DU PASSIF DES BANQUES

Billion DM *Milliards de DM*

	Residents / Résidents	Non-residents / Non résidents	Total / Total	
Assets				*Actif*
Domestic currency	5744	553	6297	Monnaie nationale
Foreign currencies	79	1533	1612	Monnaies étrangères
Total	5823	2086	7909	Total
Liabilities				*Passif*
Domestic currency	6091	483	6574	Monnaie nationale
Foreign currencies	73	1262	1335	Monnaies étrangères
Total	6164	1745	7909	Total

STRUCTURE OF THE FINANCIAL SYSTEM
STRUCTURE DU SYSTEME FINANCIER

1997

	Number of institutions / Nombre d'institutions	Number of branches / Nombre de succursales (1)	Number of employees / Nombre de salariés	Total assets or liabilities / Total des actifs ou des passifs	Total financial assets / Total des actifs financiers		
				million Dr	*million Dr*	%	
Central bank	*1*	*28*	*3174*	*10760013*	*10728897*	*17.7*	*Banque centrale*
Other monetary institutions	*51*	*2258*	*54463*	*37122538*	*36676731*	*60.4*	*Autres institutions monetaires*
Commercial banks (2)	43	2109	52976	34032899	33595463	55.3	Banques commerciales (2)
Foreign-owned banks (3)	23	103	3712	6176991	6142547	10.1	Banques etrangeres (3)
Savings banks	1	128	1320	3007398	3000629	4.9	Caisses d'epargne
Co-operative banks	7	21	167	82241	80639	0.1	Banques mutualistes
Other financial institutions	*200*	*128*	*2863*	*12065304*	*11953557*	*19.7*	*Autres institutions financieres*
Mortgage credit institutions (4)	2	110	1742	2576910	2553228	4.2	Institutions de credit hypothecaire (4)
Development credit institutions (4)	2	14	691	833737	768150	1.3	Institutions de credit de developpement (4)
Deposits and loan fund (4)	1	4	430	859527	855112	1.4	Depots et prets (4)
Others (5)	195	..	..	7795130	7777067	12.8	Autres (5)
Insurance institutions	*131*	..	..	*1426676*	*1395759*	*2.3*	*Institutions d'assurance*
Insurance companies	131	..	..	1426676	1395759	2.3	Societes d'assurance
All financial institutions	*383*	*2414*	*60500*	*61374531*	*60754944*	*100.0*	*Ensemble des institutions financieres*

1. Including head office.
2. Including the Agricultural Bank of Greece.
3. Foreign-owned banks are a subgroup of commercial banks.
4. These institutions are monetary institutions.
5. Not including venture capital companies for which data are not available.

1. Y compris le siege central.
2. Y compris la Banque Agricole de Grece.
3. Les banques etrangeres sont un sous-groupe des banques commerciales.
4. Cettes institutions sont des institutions monetaires.
5. Non inclues les sociétés de capital-risque pour lesquelles il n' y a pas de donnees disponibles.

RESIDENT/NON-RESIDENT AND DOMESTIC/FOREIGN CURRENCY CLASSIFICATION OF BANK ASSETS AND LIABILITIES (1)

RESIDENT/NON RESIDENT ET MONNAIE NATIONALE/ETRANGERE CLASSIFICATION DE L'ACTIF ET DU PASSIF DES BANQUES (1)

Million drachmas *Millions de drachmes*

	Residents / Résidents	Non-residents / Non résidents	Total / Total	
Assets				*Actif*
Domestic currency	..	..	24762162	Monnaie nationale
Foreign currencies	..	..	9270737	Monnaies etrangeres
Total	..	..	34032899	Total
Liabilities				*Passif*
Domestic currency	..	..	22126140	Monnaie nationale
Foreign currencies	..	..	11906759	Monnaies etrangeres
Total	..	..	34032899	Total

1. The data concern commercial banks (including the Agricultural Bank of Greece).

1. Les données concernent les banques commerciales (y compris la Banque Agricole de Grèce).

STRUCTURE OF THE FINANCIAL SYSTEM
STRUCTURE DU SYSTEME FINANCIER

1997

	Number of institutions / Nombre d'institutions	Number of branches / Nombre de succursales	Number of employees / Nombre de salariés (x 1000)	Total assets or liabilities / Total des actifs ou des passifs (1)	Total financial assets / Total des actifs financiers		
				million Ft	million Ft	%	
Central bank	*1*	*8*	*1468*	*5270314*	..	..	*Banque centrale*
Other monetary institutions	*294*	..	*39904*	*5980390*	..	..	*Autres institutions monétaires*
Commercial banks (2)	43	..	32441	5681066	..	..	Banques commerciales (2)
Foreign-owned banks	..	..	..	..	..	..	Banques étrangères
Savings banks	..	..	..	..	..	..	Caisses d'épargne
Co-operative banks	251	..	7463	299324	..	..	Banques mutualistes
Other financial institutions	..	..	..	..	..	..	*Autres institutions financières*
Insurance institutions	..	..	..	..	..	..	*Institutions d'assurance*
Insurance companies	20	..	*17256*	346553	..	..	Sociétés d'assurance
Pension funds and foundations	..	..	..	..	..	..	Fonds de pension et fondations
Others (3)	27	..	69	6825	..	..	Autres (3)
All financial institutions	..	..	..	..	..	..	*Ensemble des institutions financières*

1. Excluding National Bank of Hungary bond buy-backs.
2. Includes commercial banks, foreign-owned banks and savings banks.
3. Insurance associations.

1. Hors opérations de rachat d'obligations de la Banque nationale de Hongrie.
2. Comprend les banques commerciales, les banques étrangères, et les caisses d'épargne.
3. Associations d'assurance.

RESIDENT/NON-RESIDENT AND DOMESTIC/FOREIGN CURRENCY CLASSIFICATION OF BANK ASSETS AND LIABILITIES

RESIDENT/NON RESIDENT ET MONNAIE NATIONALE/ETRANGERE CLASSIFICATION DE L'ACTIF ET DU PASSIF DES BANQUES

Million forints — *Millions de forints*

	Residents / Résidents	Non-residents / Non résidents	Total / Total	
Assets				*Actif*
Domestic currency	..	..	3831862	Monnaie nationale
Foreign currencies	1326275	522929	1849204	Monnaies étrangères
Total	..	..	5681066	Total
Liabilities				*Passif*
Domestic currency	..	..	3593191	Monnaie nationale
Foreign currencies	1090148	997727	2087875	Monnaies étrangères
Total	..	..	5681066	Total

STRUCTURE OF THE FINANCIAL SYSTEM
STRUCTURE DU SYSTEME FINANCIER

1997

	Number of institutions / Nombre d'institutions	Number of branches / Nombre de succursales (1)	Number of employees / Nombre de salariés	Total assets or liabilities / Total des actifs ou des passifs million IKr / Krl	Total financial assets / Total des actifs financiers million IKr / Krl	%	
Central bank	*1*	*1*	*129*	*64411*	*64411*	..	*Banque centrale*
Other monetary institutions	*31*	*182*	*2603*	*360486*	*348374*	..	*Autres institutions monétaires*
Commercial banks	4	132	2131	290071	279948	..	Banques commerciales
Foreign-owned banks	-	-	-	-	-	..	Banques étrangères
Savings banks	27	50	472	70415	68426	..	Caisses d'épargne
Co-operative banks	-	-	-	-	-	..	Banques mutualistes
Other financial institutions	*18*	*18*	*290*	*410926*	*409920*	..	*Autres institutions financières*
Mortgage credit institutions	3	3	56	255919	255703	..	Institutions de crédit hypothécaire
Development credit institutions	1	2	29	7175	6910	..	Institutions de crédit de développement
Finance companies	13	13	183	109308	108836	..	Sociétés financières
Others	1	-	22	38524	38471	..	Autres
Insurance institutions	*80*	*80*	*571*	*404515*	..	..	*Institutions d'assurance*
Insurance companies	14	14	463	51825	..	..	Sociétés d'assurance
Pension funds and foundations	66	66	108	352690	352057	..	Fonds de pension et fondations
Others	-	-	-	-	-	-	Autres
All financial institutions	*130*	*281*	*3593*	*1240338*	..	..	*Ensemble des institutions financières*

1. The number of branches includes the number of head offices shown in the first column

1. Le nombre de filiales comprend le nombre de sièges sociaux apparaissant dans la première colonne

RESIDENT/NON-RESIDENT AND DOMESTIC/FOREIGN CURRENCY CLASSIFICATION OF BANK ASSETS AND LIABILITIES (1)

RESIDENT/NON RESIDENT ET MONNAIE NATIONALE/ETRANGERE CLASSIFICATION DE L'ACTIF ET DU PASSIF DES BANQUES (1)

Million Icelandic krónur — *Millions de couronnes islandaises*

	Residents / Résidents	Non-residents / Non résidents	Total / Total	
Assets				*Actif*
Domestic currency	285138	2519	287657	Monnaie nationale
Foreign currencies	60907	10591	71498	Monnaies étrangères
Total	346045	13110	359155	Total
Liabilities				*Passif*
Domestic currency	284780	2381	287161	Monnaie nationale
Foreign currencies	36900	35094	71994	Monnaies étrangères
Total	321680	37475	359155	Total

1. Commercial and savings banks.

1. Banques commerciales et caisses d'épargne.

STRUCTURE OF THE FINANCIAL SYSTEM
STRUCTURE DU SYSTEME FINANCIER

1997

	Number of institutions / Nombre d'institutions	Number of branches / Nombre de succursales	Number of employees / Nombre de salariés	Total assets or liabilities / Total des actifs ou des passifs	Total financial assets / Total des actifs financiers		
				million Ir£	million £Ir	%	
Central bank	1	2	620	6515	6491	..	*Banque centrale*
Credit institutions (1)	71	1500	44000	125192	124185	..	*Institutions de crédit (1)*
Other financial institutions	..	..	..	..	..	..	*Autres institutions financières*
Insurance institutions	..	..	..	..	..	..	*Institutions d'assurance*
Life insurance	31	..	5303	17594	17321	..	Assurance vie
Industrial insurance	83	..	4728	5043	4949	..	Assurance des entreprises
Pension funds and foundations	..	..	..	..	..	..	Fonds de pension et fondations
All financial institutions	..	..	..	..	..	..	*Ensemble des institutions financières*

1. Data refer to within-the-State offices of credit institutions and domestic interbank positions are netted out. The corresponding data inclusive of the interbank component are Irish pounds million 145 548 and 144 541 for Total assets and Total financial assets respectively.

1. Les données font référence aux agences sur le territoire de la République d'Irlande des établissements de crédit et les positions interbancaires intérieures sont indiquées en chiffres nets. Les données correspondantes comprenant la composante interbancaire s'élèvent à 145 548 et 144 541 millions de livres irlandaises pour le Total des actifs et les Actifs financiers respectivement.

RESIDENT/NON-RESIDENT AND DOMESTIC/FOREIGN CURRENCY CLASSIFICATION OF BANK ASSETS AND LIABILITIES (1)

RESIDENT/NON RESIDENT ET MONNAIE NATIONALE/ETRANGERE CLASSIFICATION DE L'ACTIF ET DU PASSIF DES BANQUES (1)

Million Irish pounds *Millions de livres irlandaises*

	Residents / Résidents	Non-residents / Non résidents	Total / Total	
Assets				*Actif*
Domestic currency	54473	3736	58209	Monnaie nationale
Foreign currencies	19302	68037	87339	Monnaies étrangères
Total	73775	71773	145548	Total
Liabilities				*Passif*
Domestic currency	50996	8284	59280	Monnaie nationale
Foreign currencies	19582	66686	86268	Monnaies étrangères
Total	70578	74970	145548	Total

1. Data refer to within-the-State offices of credit institutions. Domestic interbank positions are not netted out.

1. Les données font référence aux agences sur le territoire de la République d'Irlande des établissements de crédit. Les positions interbancaires intérieures sont indiquées en chiffres bruts.

STRUCTURE OF THE FINANCIAL SYSTEM
STRUCTURE DU SYSTEME FINANCIER

1997

	Number of institutions / Nombre d'institutions	Number of branches / Nombre de succursales	Number of employees / Nombre de salariés	Total assets or liabilities / Total des actifs ou des passifs	Total financial assets / Total des actifs financiers		
				billion / milliards L	billion / milliards L	%	
Central bank	*1*	*99*	*8956*	*3309021*	..	..	*Banque centrale*
Other monetary institutions	*935*	*25250*	*346778*	*3017484*	..	..	*Autres institutions monétaires*
Commercial banks	222	18124	268455	2305149	..	..	Banques commerciales
Foreign-owned banks	55	82	2909	152580	..	..	Banques étrangères
Co-operative banks (1)	652	7016	73871	516653	..	..	Banques mutualistes (1)
Central credit and refinancing	6	28	1543	43102	..	..	Organismes de crédit et de refinancement
Other financial instituti. (2)	*392*	..	*29904*	*189166*	..	..	*Autres institut. financières(2)*
Insurance institutions	*421*	..	..	*396902*	..	..	*Institutions d'assurance*
Insurance companies	261	..	..	295656	..	..	Sociétés d'assurance
Pension funds and foundations	160	..	..	101246	..	..	Fonds de pension et fondations
All financial institutions	*1749*	..	..	*6912573*	..	..	*Ensemble des institutions financières*

1. Co-operative banks (banche popolari) and mutual banks (banche di credito cooperativo)
2. Leasing and factoring companies, consumer credit, securities firms and other financial institutions.

1. Banques coopératives (banche popolari) et mutuelles (banche di credito cooperativo)
2. Sociétés de crédit-bail et d'affacturage, crédit à la consommation, maisons de titres et autres institutions financières

RESIDENT/NON-RESIDENT AND DOMESTIC/FOREIGN CURRENCY CLASSIFICATION OF BANK ASSETS AND LIABILITIES

RESIDENT/NON RESIDENT ET MONNAIE NATIONALE/ETRANGERE CLASSIFICATION DE L'ACTIF ET DU PASSIF DES BANQUES

Billion lire *Milliards de lires*

	Residents / Résidents	Non-residents / Non résidents	Total / Total	
Assets				*Actif*
Domestic currency	2712347	186647	2898994	Monnaie nationale
Foreign currencies	153640	157435	311075	Monnaies étrangères
Total	2865987	344082	3210069	Total
Liabilities				*Passif*
Domestic currency	2714503	149583	2864086	Monnaie nationale
Foreign currencies	90419	255565	345983	Monnaies étrangères
Total	2804921	405148	3210069	Total

STRUCTURE OF THE FINANCIAL SYSTEM
STRUCTURE DU SYSTEME FINANCIER

1997

(fiscal year ending 31 March 1998)
(exercice financier se terminant le 31 mars 1998)

	Number of institutions / Nombre d'institutions	Number of branches / Nombre de succursales	Number of employees / Nombre de salariés (x 1000)	Total assets or liabilities / Total des actifs ou des passifs	Total financial assets / Total des actifs financiers		
				100 million ¥	100 million ¥	%	
Ordinary Banks	136	14395	367	6964910	6870752	..	*Banques ordinaires*
City Banks	9	2955	128	4272198	4219850	..	City banks
Regional Banks	64	7108	158	1999975	1969541	..	banques régionales
Regional Banks II	63	4332	79	692735	681360	..	banques Sogo
Long-Term Credit Banks	3	103	11	839899	835240	..	*Banques de crédit à long terme*
Banking Departments of Trust Banks	33	-	-	639618	633084	..	*Départements bancaires des banques de gestion de patrimoine*
Trust Departments of Banks	53	-	-	2272128	2244629	..	*Départements de gestion de patrimoine des banques*
Credit Associations (Shinkin Banks)	401	8267	148	1113331	1094168	..	*Associations de crédit (Shinkin banks)*
Labor Credit Associations	47	622	11	115013	113877	..	*Associations de crédit aux travailleurs*
Credit Co-operatives	351	2402	36	258867	253970	..	*Coopératives de crédit*
Agricultural Co-operatives	1984	13559	290	-	704446	..	*Coopératives agricoles*
Fishery Co-operatives	1121	362	14	-	22413	..	*Coopératives de la pêche*
Central Co-operative Bank for Agriculture & Forestry (Norinchukin Bank)	1	32	2	572710	570466	..	*Banque centrale coopérative pour l'agriculture et la sylviculture (Norinchukin Bank)*
Central Bank for Commercial & Industrial Co-operatives (Shoko Chukin Bank)	1	94	5	146191	145568	..	*Banque centrale des coopératives commerciales et industrielles (Shokochukin Bank)*
Insurance institutions							*Institutions d'assurance*
Insurance companies	76	-	-	2212283	2092170	..	Compagnies d'assurance
Postal saving system	1	24680	64	2472487	2472487	..	*Système d'épargne postale*
Government financial Institutions	11	284	11	..	..	..	*Institutions financières gouvernementales*
All financial institutions	4219	..	..	..	..	..	*Ensemble des institutions financières*

STRUCTURE OF THE FINANCIAL SYSTEM
STRUCTURE DU SYSTEME FINANCIER

1997

	Number of institutions / Nombre d'institutions	Number of branches / Nombre de succursales	Number of employees / Nombre de salariés	Total assets or liabilities / Total des actifs ou des passifs	Total financial assets / Total des actifs financiers		
				billion / milliards W	billion / milliards W	%	
Central bank	*1*	*16*	*2894*	*112420.0*	*110150.0*	*13.2*	*Banque centrale*
Other monetary institutions	*79*	*4791*	*116574*	*458610.7*	*434035.1*	*52.0*	*Autres institutions monétaires*
Commercial banks	26	4723	113994	417824.6	401125.0	48.1	Banques commerciales
Foreign-owned banks	53	68	2580	40786.1	32910.1	3.9	Banques étrangères
Development institutions	*3*	*98*	*4280*	*87704.8*	*87419.5*	*10.5*	*Institutions de développement*
Investment institutions	*62*	*348*	*10104*	*83887.0*	*73942.0*	*8.9*	*Institutions d'investissement*
Savings institutions	*231*	*110*	*9975*	*36253.0*	*33978.0*	*4.1*	*Institutions d'épargne*
Insurance institutions	*50*	*16898*	*83304*	*111846.0*	*94936.0*	*11.4*	*Institutions d'assurance*
All financial institutions	*426*	*22261*	*227131*	*890721.5*	*834460.6*	*100.0*	*Ensemble des institutions financières*

Note: Number of branches and employees exclude overseas branches. Total assets exclude guarantees and the accounts of their overseas branches.

Note : Les succursales étrangères sont exclues du nombre d'institutions et du nombre de succursales. L'ensemble des actifs exclut les garanties et les comptes de leurs succursales étrangères.

STRUCTURE OF THE FINANCIAL SYSTEM
STRUCTURE DU SYSTEME FINANCIER

1998 p

	Number of institutions / Nombre d'institutions	Number of branches / Nombre de succursales	Number of employees / Nombre de salariés	Total assets or liabilities / Total des actifs ou des passifs	Total financial assets / Total des actifs financiers		
				billion / milliards LF / F Lux	billion / milliards LF / F Lux	%	
Banks and savings institutions	*209*	*289*	*19814*	*21814*	..	..	*Établissements bancaires et d'épargne*
of which:							*dont :*
Bodies set up under Luxembourg public law	2	101	1781	1137	..	..	Établissements de droit public luxembourgeois
Sociétés anonymes set up under Luxembourg law	139	188	17040	17183	..	..	Sociétés anonymes de droit luxembourgeois
Foreign companies	68	-	820	3494	..	..	Sociétés de droit étranger
Savings banks and credit unions organised in the form of agricultural associations or co-operative societies	*54*	..	..	..	..	..	*Caisses d'épargne et de crédit organisées sous forme d°associations agricoles ou de sociétés coopératives*
of which:							*dont :*
Co-operative societies set up under Luxembourg law	1	-	16	..	..	..	Sociétés coopératives de droit luxembourgeois
Central savings banks	1	-	157	..	..	..	Caisses centrales
Local rural savings banks	35	..	..	..	..	..	Caisses rurales locales
Non-bank financial institutions	*83*	-	*2337*	*24*	..	..	*Établissements financiers non bancaires*

RESIDENT/NON-RESIDENT AND DOMESTIC/FOREIGN CURRENCY CLASSIFICATION OF BANK ASSETS AND LIABILITIES

RESIDENT/NON RESIDENT ET MONNAIE NATIONALE/ETRANGERE CLASSIFICATION DE L'ACTIF ET DU PASSIF DES BANQUES

Million Luxembourg francs — *Millions de francs luxembourgeois*

	Residents / Résidents	Non-residents / Non résidents	Total / Total	
Assets				*Actif*
Domestic currency	746663	2235516	2982180	Monnaie nationale
Foreign currencies	2753958	16077902	18831860	Monnaies étrangères
Total	3500621	18313419	21814040	Total
Liabilities				*Passif*
Domestic currency	1404493	1738706	3143199	Monnaie nationale
Foreign currencies	4354289	14316552	18670841	Monnaies étrangères
Total	5758781	16055259	21814040	Total

Note: Local rural savings banks not included in this table.

Note : Les caisses ruarles locales ne sont pas pris en compte dans ce tableau.

STRUCTURE OF THE FINANCIAL SYSTEM
STRUCTURE DU SYSTEME FINANCIER

1998 p

	Number of institutions / Nombre d'institutions	Number of branches / Nombre de succursales	Number of employees / Nombre de salariés	Total assets or liabilities / Total des actifs ou des passifs	Total financial assets / Total des actifs financiers		
				million Mex$ / $Mex	*million Mex$ / $Mex*	*%*	
Central bank	*1*	..	..	..	..	..	*Banque centrale*
Other monetary institutions	*39*	*6563*	*119250*	*1217492*	..	..	*Autres institutions monétaires*
Commercial banks	19	5684	104852	1018529	..	..	Banques commerciales
Foreign-owned banks	20	879	14398	198963	..	..	Banques étrangères
Savings banks	-	-	-	-	..	..	Caisses d'épargne
Co-operative banks	-	-	-	-	..	..	Banques mutualistes
Other financial institutions	*325*	..	..	*504288*	..	..	*Autres institutions financières*
Mortgage credit institutions	25	..	..	11293	..	..	Institutions de crédit hypothécaire
Development credit institutions	6	615	18836	460961	..	..	Institutions de crédit de développement
Finance companies	-	-	-	-	..	..	Sociétés financières
Others (1)	294	..	..	32034	..	..	Autres (1)
Insurance institutions	*68*	*168*	*21451*	*63712*	..	..	*Institutions d'assurance*
Insurance companies	68	168	21451	63712	..	..	Sociétés d'assurance
All financial institutions	*433*	..	..	*1785492*	..	..	*Ensemble des institutions financières*

1. Includes leasing companies, factoring companies, foreign exchange houses and credit unions.

1. Y compris les sociétés de crédit-bail, les sociétés d'affacturage, les sociétés de change et les caisses de crédit mutuel.

RESIDENT/NON-RESIDENT AND DOMESTIC/FOREIGN CURRENCY CLASSIFICATION OF BANK ASSETS AND LIABILITIES

RESIDENT/NON RESIDENT ET MONNAIE NATIONALE/ETRANGERE CLASSIFICATION DE L'ACTIF ET DU PASSIF DES BANQUES

Million pesos *Million de pesos*

	Residents / Résidents	Non-residents / Non résidents	Total / Total	
Assets				*Actif*
Domestic currency	734547	-	734547	Monnaie nationale
Foreign currencies	316449	166497	482946	Monnaies étrangères
Total	1050996	166497	1217492	Total
Liabilities				*Passif*
Domestic currency	763595	-	763595	Monnaie nationale
Foreign currencies	291954	161944	453898	Monnaies étrangères
Total	1055549	161944	1217492	Total

STRUCTURE OF THE FINANCIAL SYSTEM
STRUCTURE DU SYSTEME FINANCIER
1997

	Number of institutions / Nombre d'institutions	Number of branches / Nombre de succursales (1)	Number of employees / Nombre de salariés (1)	Total assets or liabilities / Total des actifs ou des passifs	Total financial assets / Total des actifs financiers		
				billion / milliards Gld / Fl	billion / milliards Gld / Fl	%	
Central bank	*1*	..	*1721*	*82.0*	*81.4*	..	*Banque centrale*
Other monetary institut. (2)	*99*	*7026*	*120054*	*1578.5*	*1561.1*	..	*Autres institut. monétaires(2)*
Universal banks (3)	86	5179	78091	1238.1	1226.2	..	Banques universelles (3)
Co-operative banks(4)	1	1823	41390	334.8	329.4	..	Banques mutualistes (4)
Savings banks	4	16	125	2.9	2.9	..	Caisses d'épargne
Security credit institutions	8	8	448	2.7	2.6	..	Institutions de crédit de valeurs mobilières
Other financial institutions	..	..	..	..	..	..	*Autres institutions financières*
Mortgage credit institutions (2)	1	1	25	0.9	0.9	..	Institutions de crédit hypothécaire (2)
Insurance institutions	*125*	..	..	*1032.3*	*967.8*	..	*Institutions d'assurance*
Insurance companies	7	..	..	344.5	325.9	..	Sociétés d'assurance
Pension funds and foundations	98	..	..	681.1	635.5	..	Fonds de pension et fondations
Others	20	..	..	6.7	6.4	..	Autres
All financial institutions	..	..	..	..	..	..	*Ensemble des institutions financières*

1. The figures for number of branches and employees are from *Banks and Brokers in the Netherlands, 1998/99,* Netherlands Institute for the Banking and Stockbroking Industry. The branch figures except for Co-operative banks (Rabobank) are estimates.
2. Data reflect the credit institutions which have consolidated their domestic bank (and non-bank) subsidiaries. This implies that the data of universal banks, savings banks, security credit institutions and mortgage credit institutions do not correspond to the groups as registered in the Register of the Act on the Supervision of the Credit System 1992. For example, a large number of savings banks have merged - or been taken over - and the parent saving bank has become a universal bank.
3. Branch figures include local post offices which are jointly owned by the Royal Dutch Post and the ING Bank.
4. The Rabobanken comprises 1 central institution, which reports as a group, with 481 members and a total of 1823 offices .

1. Les chiffres pour le nombre de succursales et de salariés proviennent de *Les banques et courtiers dans les Pays-Bas, 1998/99,* Institut néerlandais pour la banque et l'industrie du commerce des valeurs en Bourse. Les chiffres qui se réfèrent aux succursales sont des estimations, sauf dans le cas des Banques mutualistes (Rabobank).
2. Les données reflètent les institutions de crédit qui ont consolidé leurs filiales bancaires (et non-bancaires) nationales. Ceci implique que les données des banques universelles, des banques d'épargne, des institutions de crédit et de crédit hypothécaire ne correspondent pas aux groupes répertoriés en tant que tel dans le Register of the Act on the Supervision of the Credit System de 1992. Par exemple un grand nombre de banques d'épargne ont fusionné - ou ont été absorbées - et la banque d'épargne mère est devenue une banque universell
3. Les chiffres pour les succursales comprennent les bureaux de poste locaux appartenant conjointement à la Royal Dutch Post et à la banque IN
4. La Rabobanken comprend 1 institution centrale, qui en tant que groupe comprend 481 membres et a au total 1823 agences.

RESIDENT/NON-RESIDENT AND DOMESTIC/FOREIGN CURRENCY CLASSIFICATION OF BANK ASSETS AND LIABILITIES(1)

RESIDENT/NON RESIDENT ET MONNAIE NATIONALE/ETRANGERE(1) CLASSIFICATION DE L'ACTIF ET DU PASSIF DES BANQUES

Billion guilders *Milliards de florins*

	Residents / Résidents	Non-residents / Non résidents	Total / Total	
Assets				*Actif*
Domestic currency	1002.2	64.4	1066.6	Monnaie nationale
Foreign currencies	44.6	467.3	511.9	Monnaies étrangères
Total	1046.8	531.7	1578.5	Total
Liabilities				*Passif*
Domestic currency	931.3	98.8	1030.1	Monnaie nationale
Foreign currencies	55.2	493.2	548.4	Monnaies étrangères
Total	986.5	592.0	1578.5	Total

1. Monetary institutions, excluding the Central bank.

1. Les institutions monétaires à l'exclusion de la Banque centrale.

STRUCTURE OF THE FINANCIAL SYSTEM
STRUCTURE DU SYSTEME FINANCIER

1997

	Number of institutions / Nombre d'institutions	Number of branches / Nombre de succursales	Number of employees / Nombre de salariés	Total assets or liabilities / Total des actifs ou des passifs	Total financial assets / Total des actifs financiers		
				million NZ$ / $ NZ	million NZ$ / $ NZ	%	
Central bank	*1*	*3*	*289*	*8834.0*	*8772.0*	..	*Banque centrale*
Other monetary institutions	*18*	*1560*	*24240*	*130164.0*	*116682.0*	..	*Autres institutions monétaires*
Other financial institutions		..	..	*87425.7*	..	..	*Autres institutions financières*
Insurance institutions	..	..	..	*15742.7*	..	..	*Institutions d'assurance*
All financial institutions	..	..	..	*242166.4*	..	..	*Ensemble des institutions financières*

Sources: Reserve Bank of New Zealand and Statistics New Zealand.

Sources: Banque de réserve de Nouvelle-Zélande et Statistiques Nouvelle-Zélande.

RESIDENT/NON-RESIDENT AND DOMESTIC/FOREIGN CURRENCY CLASSIFICATION OF BANK ASSETS AND LIABILITIES (1)

RESIDENT/NON RESIDENT ET MONNAIE NATIONALE/ETRANGERE CLASSIFICATION DE L'ACTIF ET DU PASSIF DES BANQUES (1)

Million New Zealand dollars *Millions de dollars de Nouvelle-Zélande*

	Residents / Résidents	Non-residents / Non résidents	Total / Total	
Assets				*Actif*
Domestic currency	122576.0	3335.8	125911.8	Monnaie nationale
Foreign currencies	1902.5	454.9	2357.4	Monnaies étrangères
Total	124478.5	3790.7	128269.2	Total
Liabilities				*Passif*
Domestic currency	90840.8	2820.7	93661.5	Monnaie nationale
Foreign currencies	18483.3	16124.5	34607.8	Monnaies étrangères
Total	109324.0	18945.2	128269.2	Total

1. Data are based on the Reserve Bank of New Zealand's quarterly survey of M3 institutions. The data cover local activities of banks registered in New Zealand and exclude business conducted from their non New Zealand operations.

1. Les données se réfèrent à l'enquête trimestrielle des institutions de M3. Il s'agit des données relatives aux activités locales des banques répertoriées en Nouvelle-Zélande, sont exclues les activités de leurs agences à l'étranger.

STRUCTURE OF THE FINANCIAL SYSTEM
STRUCTURE DU SYSTEME FINANCIER

1997

	Number of institutions / Nombre d'institutions	Number of branches / Nombre de succursales	Number of employees / Nombre de salariés (1)	Total assets or liabilities / Total des actifs ou des passifs	Total financial assets / Total des actifs financiers		
				million NKr / KrN	*million NKr / KrN*	*%*	
Central bank	*1*	*12*	*1154*	*318715*	*316567*	*15.5*	*Banque centrale*
Other monetary institutions	*154*	*1586*	*24977*	*979384*	*969036*	*47.5*	*Autres institutions monétaires*
Commercial banks	14	454	13727	570154	563441	*27.6*	Banques commerciales
Foreign-owned banks	7	16	586	47215	47145	*2.3*	Banques étrangères
Savings banks	133	1116	10664	362015	358450	*17.6*	Caisses d'épargne
Co-operative banks	-	-	-	-	-	-	Banques mutualistes
Other financial institutions	*60*	*39*	*1662*	*344324*	*343817*	*16.8*	*Autres institutions financières*
Mortgage credit institutions	9	2	281	105167	105008	*5.1*	Institutions de crédit hypothécaire
Development credit institutions	-	-	-	-	-	-	Institutions de crédit de développement
Finance companies	46	37	1381	41568	41362	*2.0*	Sociétés financières
Others (2)	5	..	..	197589	197447	*9.7*	Autres (2)
Insurance institutions	*448*	..	..	*437570*	*412266*	*20.2*	*Institutions d'assurance*
Insurance companies	117	..	9905	361810	338538	*16.6*	Sociétés d'assurance(3)
Pension funds and foundations	329	..	..	74751	72719	*3.6*	Fonds de pension et fondations
Others (3)	2	-	-	1009	1009	-	Autres (4)
All financial institutions	*663*	..	..	*2079993*	*2041686*	*100.0*	*Ensemble des institutions financières*

1. Man-labour years, except for the Central bank.
2. State lending institutions exclusive of the Guarantee Institute for Export Credit (GIEK).
3. Joint scheme for collective agreement-based pensions (FTP) and Agreement-based pensions (AFP).

1. Travail-années, sauf pour la Banque centrale.
2. Institutions de prêts de l'état à l'exclusion de l'Institut de garantie pour le crédit à l'exportation (GIEK)
3. FTP et AFP.

RESIDENT/NON-RESIDENT AND DOMESTIC/FOREIGN CURRENCY CLASSIFICATION OF BANK ASSETS AND LIABILITIES

RESIDENT/NON RESIDENT ET MONNAIE NATIONALE/ETRANGERE CLASSIFICATION DE L'ACTIF ET DU PASSIF DES BANQUES

Million Norwegian kroner — *Millions de couronnes norvégiennes*

	Residents / Résidents	Non-residents / Non résidents	Total / Total	
Assets				*Actif*
Domestic currency	860025	14670	874695	Monnaie nationale
Foreign currencies	50189	54502	104691	Monnaies étrangères
Total	910214	69172	979386	Total
Liabilities				*Passif*
Domestic currency	754185	37433	791618	Monnaie nationale
Foreign currencies	37490	150278	187768	Monnaies étrangères
Total	791675	187711	979386	Total

STRUCTURE OF THE FINANCIAL SYSTEM
STRUCTURE DU SYSTEME FINANCIER

1998 p

	Number of institutions / Nombre d'institutions	Number of branches / Nombre de succursales	Number of employees / Nombre de salariés (1)	Total assets or liabilities / Total des actifs ou des passifs	Total financial assets / Total des actifs financiers		
				million PLN	*million PLN*	*%*	
Central bank (2)	*1*	*14*	*6348*	*130855*	..	..	*Banque centrale(2)*
Other monetary institutions	*1272*	*1864*	*174056*	*320679*	..	..	*Autres institutions monétaires*
Commercial banks	83	1864	149067	306977	..	..	Banques commerciales
- Banks with a majority of Polish capital	52	1572	131266	253972	..	..	- Banques ayant une majorité de capitaux polonais
- Banks with a majority of foreign capital	31	292	17801	53005	..	..	- Banques ayant une majorité de capitaux étrangers
Co-operative banks	1189	..	24989	13702	..	..	Banques mutualistes
Other financial institutions	..	..	..	..	..	..	*Autres institutions financières*
Finance companies (3)	38	..	..	1744	1744	..	Sociétés financières (3)
Insurance institutions	..	..	..	..	..	..	*Institutions d'assurance*
Insurance companies (4)	53	..	26325	18938	15256	..	Sociétés d'assurance (4)
All financial institutions	..	..	..	..	..	..	*Ensemble des institutions financières*

1. Number of full-time contracts.
2. Central bank branches: 13 regional branches, 1 chief branch of foreign exchange.
3. Finance company figures refer to open-end (trust) funds. Data are for end-June 1998
4. Data refer to insurance companies submitting financial statements to the supervisory office. Number of employees: average employment excluding brokers. Figures are for end-September 1998.

1. Nombre de contrats à plein temps.
2. Succursales de la Banque centrale : 13 succursales régionales, 1 succursale principale de change.
3. Les données pour les Sociétés financières concernent les fonds à capital. Les chiffres se rapportent à fin juin 1998.
4. Les données se réfèrent aux compagnies d'assurance qui soumettent leurs comptes au bureau de surveillance. Le nombre d'employés : nombre moyen excluant les courtiers. Les chiffres se rapportent à fin septembre 1998.

RESIDENT/NON-RESIDENT AND DOMESTIC/FOREIGN CURRENCY CLASSIFICATION OF BANK ASSETS AND LIABILITIES

RESIDENT/NON RESIDENT ET MONNAIE NATIONALE/ETRANGERE CLASSIFICATION DE L'ACTIF ET DU PASSIF DES BANQUES

Million zlotys *Millions de zlotys*

	Residents / Résidents	Non-residents / Non résidents	Total / Total	
Assets				*Actif*
Domestic currency	271008	1497	272505	Monnaie nationale
Foreign currencies	42240	17459	59699	Monnaies étrangères
Total	313248	18955	332203(1)	Total
Liabilities				*Passif*
Domestic currency	261721	2401	264122	Monnaie nationale
Foreign currencies	40290	16266	56557	Monnaies étrangères
Total	302011	18667	320679	Total

1. Includes provisions, accumulated depreciation and valuation allowances in the amount of ZL 11 524.6 million, for which the breakdown by currencies and resident/non-resident is not available.

1. Y compris des provisions, de l'amortissement cumulé et dotations de réévaluation d'un montant de 11 524.6 millions de ZL, pour lequel la ventilation par monnaie et par résident/non-résident n'est pas disponible.

STRUCTURE OF THE FINANCIAL SYSTEM
STRUCTURE DU SYSTEME FINANCIER

1997

	Number of institutions / Nombre d'institutions	Number of branches / Nombre de succursales	Number of employees / Nombre de salariés	Total assets or liabilities / Total des actifs ou des passifs	Total financial assets / Total des actifs financiers		
				million Esc	million Esc	%	
Central bank	*1*	*11*	*1811*	*4605936*	*4530493*	..	*Banque centrale*
Other monetary institutions	*237*	*4745*	*64595*	*43985054*	*37393205*	..	*Autres institutions monétaires*
Commercial banks (1)	44	4121	59646	41362075	34905314	..	Banques commerciales(1)
Foreign-owned banks(2)	17	98	1103	1100271	1028957	..	Banques étrangères (2)
Savings banks	6	13	161	53023	48921	..	Caisses d'épargne
Co-operative banks	170	513	3685	1469685	1410013	..	Banques mutualistes
Other financial institutions(3)	*291*	*538*	..	..	..	..	*Autres institutions financières financières (3)*
Insurance institutions	*128*	..	..	*5091489*	*4625410*	..	*Institutions d'assurance*
Insurance companies	99	1016	12334	3074560	2635573	..	Sociétés d'assurance
Pension funds and foundations	29	..	..	2016929	1989837	..	Fonds de pension et fondations
All financial institutions	*657*	..	..	..	..	..	*Ensemble des institutions financières*

1. Banks with head-offices in Portuguese territory.
2. Branches of foreign banks located in Portuguese territory.
3. Other financial institutions registered at the Banco de Portugal.

1. Banques dont le siège social se situe en territoire portugais.
2. Filiales de banques étrangères situées en territoire portugais.
3. Autres institutions financières répertoriées à la Banco de Portugal.

RESIDENT/NON-RESIDENT AND DOMESTIC/FOREIGN CURRENCY CLASSIFICATION OF BANK ASSETS AND LIABILITIES (1)

RESIDENT/NON RESIDENT ET MONNAIE NATIONALE/ETRANGERE CLASSIFICATION DE L'ACTIF ET DU PASSIF DES BANQUES (1)

Million escudos *Millions d'escudos*

	Residents / Résidents	Non-residents / Non résidents	Total / Total	
Assets				*Actif*
Domestic currency	..	..	..	Monnaie nationale
Foreign currencies	..	..	..	Monnaies étrangères
Total	32149603	9212472	41362075	Total
Liabilities				*Passif*
Domestic currency	..	..	..	Monnaie nationale
Foreign currencies	..	..	..	Monnaies étrangères
Total	32122751	9239324	41362075	Total

1. Domestic/foreign currency breakdown not available.

1. La ventilation par monnaie nationale/étrangère n'est pas disponible

STRUCTURE OF THE FINANCIAL SYSTEM
STRUCTURE DU SYSTEME FINANCIER

1997

	Number of institutions / Nombre d'institutions	Number of branches / Nombre de succursales	Number of employees / Nombre de salariés	Total assets or liabilities / Total des actifs ou des passifs	Total financial assets / Total des actifs financiers		
				billion / milliards Ptas	billion / milliards Ptas	%	
Central bank	*1*	*53*	*3228*	*16664*	*16624*	*10.7*	*Banque centrale*
Other monetary institutions	*307*	*37634*	*242155*	*134954*	*131375*	*84.5*	*Autres institutions monétaires*
Commercial banks	105	17403	135831	73879	72283	46.5	Banques commerciales
Foreign-owned banks	54	127	3367	9070	9039	5.8	Banques étrangères
Savings banks	51	16636	90153	47254	45450	29.2	Caisses d'épargne
Co-operative banks	97	3468	12804	4751	4603	3.0	Banques mutualistes
Other financial institutions	*109*	*405*	*5206*	*7613*	*7547*	*4.9*	*Autres institutions financières*
Development credit institutions	1	1	270	4346	4324	2.8	Institutions de crédit de développement
Specialised credit institutions	108	404	4936	3267	3223	2.1	Institutions spécialisées de crédit
Insurance institutions(1)	..	..	..	..	..	..	*Institutions d'assurance(1)*
All financial institutions	*417*	*38092*	*250589*	*159231*	*155546*	*100.0*	*Ensemble des institutions financières*

1. Insurance institutions are included in 'Other resident sectors' in the Spanish money and banking statistics.

1. Les institutions d'assurance sont incluses dans "Autres secteurs résidents" dans les statistiques monétaires et bancaires espagnols.

RESIDENT/NON-RESIDENT AND DOMESTIC/FOREIGN CURRENCY CLASSIFICATION OF BANK ASSETS AND LIABILITIES

RESIDENT/NON RESIDENT ET MONNAIE NATIONALE/ETRANGERE CLASSIFICATION DE L'ACTIF ET DU PASSIF DES BANQUES

Billion pesetas *Milliards de pesetas*

	Residents / Résidents	Non-residents / Non résidents	Total / Total	
Assets				*Actif*
Domestic currency	113130	6734	119864	Monnaie nationale
Foreign currencies	4957	10132	15089	Monnaies étrangères
Total	118087	16866	134953	Total
Liabilities				*Passif*
Domestic currency	110650	5816	116466	Monnaie nationale
Foreign currencies	3820	14667	18487	Monnaies étrangères
Total	114470	20483	134953	Total

STRUCTURE OF THE FINANCIAL SYSTEM
STRUCTURE DU SYSTEME FINANCIER

1997

	Number of institutions / Nombre d'institutions	Number of branches / Nombre de succursales	Number of employees / Nombre de salariés	Total assets or liabilities / Total des actifs ou des passifs	Total financial assets / Total des actifs financiers		
				million SKr / KrS	million SKr / KrS	%	
Central bank	*1*	*11*	*670*	*189169*	*188469*	*3.1*	*Banque centrale*
Other monetary institutions	*124*	*2522*	*43202*	*2145194*	*2131331*	*34.7*	*Autres institutions monétaires*
Commercial banks	15	2165	39193	1986996	1977534	32.2	Banques commerciales
Foreign-owned banks	22	54	936	84239	81264	1.3	Banques étrangères
Savings banks	87	303	3073	73959	72533	1.2	Caisses d'épargne
Other financial institutions	*560*	..	..	*2113380*	*2111339*	*34.4*	*Autres institutions financières*
Mortgage credit institutions	11	..	1915	1216815	1216482	19.8	Institutions de crédit hypothécaire
Development credit institutions	12	..	281	219581	219405	3.6	Institutions de crédit de développement
Finance companies	60	..	2040	118042	117772	1.9	Sociétés financières
Securities brokerage companies	80	..	1841	21140	20892	0.3	Sociétés de courtage
Mutual funds	368	..	..	363915	363915	5.9	Fonds communs de placement
Others	29	..	..	173887	172873	2.8	Autres
Insurance institutions	*111*		..	*1759903*	*1703152*	*27.8*	*Institutions d'assurance*
Insurance companies	110	..	..	1211822	1155071	18.8	Sociétés d'assurance
Pension funds and foundations	1	..	..	548081	548081	8.9	Fonds de pension et fondations
All financial institutions	*796*	..	..	*6207646*	*6134291*	*100.0*	*Ensemble des institutions financières*

RESIDENT/NON-RESIDENT AND DOMESTIC/FOREIGN CURRENCY CLASSIFICATION OF BANK ASSETS AND LIABILITIES (1)

RESIDENT/NON RESIDENT ET MONNAIE NATIONALE/ETRANGERE CLASSIFICATION DE L'ACTIF ET DU PASSIF DES BANQUES (1)

Million Swedish kroner — *Millions de couronnes suèdoises*

	Residents / Résidents	Non-residents / Non résidents	Total / Total	
Assets				*Actif*
Domestic currency	1248282	157415	1405697	Monnaie nationale
Foreign currencies	117378	538760	656138	Monnaies étrangères
Total	1365660	696175	2061835	Total
Liabilities				*Passif*
Domestic currency	1162246	142701	1304947	Monnaie nationale
Foreign currencies	62533	694355	756888	Monnaies étrangères
Total	1224779	837056	2061835	Total

1. Swedish banks.

1. Banques suèdoises.

STRUCTURE OF THE FINANCIAL SYSTEM
STRUCTURE DU SYSTEME FINANCIER

1997

	Number of institutions / Nombre d'institutions	Number of branches / Nombre de succursales (1)	Number of employees / Nombre de salariés	Total assets or liabilities / Total des actifs ou des passifs million SF / FS	
1. Central bank	*1*	*8*	*621*	*75905*	*1. Banque centrale*
2. Other monetary institutions					*2. Autres institutions monétaires*
2.1 Banks Total of which:	394	3439	119691	1782213	2.1 Banques - total dont :
2.1.1 Cantonal banks	24	713	17842	268994	2.1.1 Banques cantonales
2.1.2 Large banks (2)	4	840	63090	1121233	2.1.2 Grandes banques (2)
2.1.3 Regional and Savings Banks	117	400	5228	70750	2.1.3 Banques régionales et caisses d'épargne
2.1.4 Loan Associations and Agricultural Credit Co operatives	1	892	3154	57296	2.1.4 Caisses de crédit mutuel et caisses Raiffeisen
2.1.5 Other banks	214	550	26100	228542	2.1.5 Autres banques
of which: Swiss	80	241	11560	107367	dont : en mains suisses
of which: foreign controlled	134	309	14540	121175	dont : en mains étrangères
2.1.6 Branches of foreign banks	18	25	1529	23906	2.1.6 Succursales de banques étrangères
2.1.7 Private bankers	16	19	2748	11494	2.1.7 Banquiers privés
2.2 Post Office System	1	..	59661	..	2.2 Services postaux
3. Other financial institutions	..	..	..	..	*3. Autres institutions financières*
4. Memorandum: Banks with special statute					*4. Pour mémoire:* Banques à statut particulier
4.1 Central mortgage bond issuing houses of Swiss cantonal banks	1	..	..	19067	4.1 Centrales de lettres de gage des banques cantonales suisses
4.2 Mortgage bond issuing houses of Swiss mortgage loan banks	1	..	5	14301	4.2 Banques des lettres de gage d'Etablissements suisses de Crédit hypothécaire
4.3 Central bank of the Swiss Union of agricultural credit banks	1	..	735	11712	4.3 Banque centrale de l'Union suisse des Caisses Raiffeisen
4.4 Clearing centre of regional banks and savings banks	1	..	31	1754	4.4 Centrale de Clearing des Banques Régionales et Caisses d'Epargne suisses
4.5 Intersettle	1	..	103	864	4.5 Intersettle

1. Excluding receiving outlets and representative offices.
2. Balance Sheet Total (SF million)

Union de Banques Suisses	437071
Société de Banques Suisses	371144
Crédit Suisse First Boston	195584
Crédit Suisse	117434

1. Sans les bureaux de recettes et représentations.
2. Total du bilan (millions de francs)

Union de Banques Suisses	437071
Société de Banques Suisses	371144
Crédit Suisse First Boston	195584
Crédit Suisse	117434

RESIDENT/NON-RESIDENT AND DOMESTIC/FOREIGN CURRENCY CLASSIFICATION OF BANK ASSETS AND LIABILITIES

RESIDENT/NON RESIDENT ET MONNAIE NATIONALE/ETRANGERE CLASSIFICATION DE L'ACTIF ET DU PASSIF DES BANQUES

1997

Million Swiss francs *Millions de francs suisses*

	Residents / Résidents	Non-residents / Non résidents	Total / Total	
Assets				*Actif*
Domestic currency	815083	78100	893183	Monnaie nationale
Foreign currencies	51660	801971	853631	Monnaies étrangères
Total	866743	880071	1746814	Total
Liabilities				*Passif*
Domestic currency	834202	76949	911151	Monnaie nationale
Foreign currencies	132058	703605	835663	Monnaies étrangères
Total	966260	780554	1746814	Total

STRUCTURE OF THE FINANCIAL SYSTEM
STRUCTURE DU SYSTEME FINANCIER

1997

	Number of institutions / Nombre d'institutions	Number of branches / Nombre de succursales	Number of employees / Nombre de salariés	Total assets or liabilities / Total des actifs ou des passifs	Total financial assets / Total des actifs financiers		
				billion / milliards TL / LT	billion / milliards TL / LT	%	
Central bank	*1*	*21*	*6880*	*6837288*	..	..	*Banque centrale*
Other monetary institutions	..	..	..	..	..	..	*Autres institutions monétaires*
Commercial banks	59	6763	149792	18335793			Banques commerciales
Foreign-owned banks (1)	..	..	..	..	..	..	Banques étrangères (1)
Savings banks	..	..	..	..	..	..	Caisses d'épargne
Co-operative banks	..	..	..	..	..	..	Banques mutualistes
Other financial institutions	..	..	..	..	..	..	*Autres institutions financières*
Insurance institutions	..	..	..	..	..	..	*Institutions d'assurance*
All financial institutions	..	..	..	..	..	..	*Ensemble des institutions financières*

1. Data for Foreign-owned banks is included in Commercial bank figures.

1. Les données pour les Banques étrangères sont comprises dans celles des Banques commerciales.

RESIDENT/NON-RESIDENT AND DOMESTIC/FOREIGN CURRENCY CLASSIFICATION OF BANK ASSETS AND LIABILITY

RESIDENT/NON RESIDENT ET MONNAIE NATIONALE/ETRANGER CLASSIFICATION DE L'ACTIF ET DU PASSIF DES BANQUES

Billion Turkish liras — *Milliards de livres turques*

	Residents / Résidents	Non-residents / Non résidents	Total / Total	
Assets				*Actif*
Domestic currency	..	..	10226955	Monnaie nationale
Foreign currencies	..	..	8108838	Monnaies étrangères
Total	..	..	18335793	Total
Liabilities				*Passif*
Domestic currency	..	..	9187454	Monnaie nationale
Foreign currencies	..	..	9148339	Monnaies étrangères
Total	..	..	18335793	Total

STRUCTURE OF THE FINANCIAL SYSTEM
STRUCTURE DU SYSTEME FINANCIER

1997

	Number of institutions / Nombre d'institutions	Number of branches / Nombre de succursales	Number of employees / Nombre de salariés	Total assets or liabilities / Total des actifs ou des passifs	Total financial assets / Total des actifs financiers		
				billion / milliards £	billion / milliards £	%	
Central bank	*1*	..	*3700*	34.1	..	..	*Banque centrale*
Other monetary institutions	*468*	*14000*	*444800*	2449.1	..	..	*Autres institutions monétaires*
Commercial banks	214	13000	385200	1112.3	..	..	Banques commerciales
Foreign-owned banks	254	1000	59400	1336.8	..	..	Banques étrangères
Savings banks	..	..	..	..	..	..	Caisses d'épargne
Co-operative banks	..	..	..	..	..	..	Banques mutualistes
Other financial institutions	..	..	*259200*	366.0	..	..	*Autres institutions financières*
Mortgage credit institutions	..	*2500*	*39600*	138.4	..	..	Institutions de crédit hypothécaire
Development credit institutions	..	..	..	53.8	..	..	Institutions de crédit de développement
Finance companies	..	..	..	25.6	..	..	Sociétés financières
Others	..	..	..	148.2	..	..	Autres
Insurance institutions	..	..	*352000*	*1432.1*	..	..	*Institutions d'assurance*
Insurance companies	..	..	235100	677.8	..	..	Sociétés d'assurance
Pension funds and foundations	..	..	..	656.9	..	..	Fonds de pension et fondations
Others	..	..	..	97.4	..	..	Autres
All financial institutions	..	..	*1059700*	*4281.3*	..	..	*Ensemble des institutions financières*

RESIDENT/NON-RESIDENT AND DOMESTIC/FOREIGN CURRENCY CLASSIFICATION OF BANK ASSETS AND LIABILITIES

RESIDENT/NON RESIDENT ET MONNAIE NATIONALE/ETRANGERE CLASSIFICATION DE L'ACTIF ET DU PASSIF DES BANQUES

Million pounds sterling *Millions de livres*

	Residents / Résidents	Non-residents / Non résidents	Total (1)/ Total (1)	
Assets				*Actif*
Domestic currency	1023145	118372	1192263	Monnaie nationale
Foreign currencies	271388	905931	1256850	Monnaies étrangères
Total	1294533	1024303	2449113	Total
Liabilities				*Passif*
Domestic currency	772958	134434	1197858	Monnaie nationale
Foreign currencies	203348	817508	1251258	Monnaies étrangères
Total	976306	951942	2449116	Total

1. Includes capital and unclassified (net), for which breakdown by resident/non-resident is not available
1. Y inclus Capital et le non classé (net),pour lequel la ventilation par monnaie et par résident/non-résident n'est pas disponible

STRUCTURE OF THE FINANCIAL SYSTEM
STRUCTURE DU SYSTEME FINANCIER

1997

	Number of institutions / Nombre d'institutions	Number of branches / Nombre de succursales	Number of employees / Nombre de salariés	Total assets or liabilities / Total des actifs ou des passifs	Total financial assets / Total des actifs financiers		
				million $ US	*million $ US*	%	
Central bank (1)	*1*	*37*	*24457*	*519163*	*517317*		*Banque centrale*
Other monetary institutions	..	..	..	..	..	..	*Autres institutions monétaires*
Commercial banks (2)	9176	60320	1531000	4976456	4512592	..	Banques commerciales (2)
Foreign-owned banks					..	..	Banques étrangères
Savings institutions	1780	12656	244800	1026186	..	..	Institutions d'épargne
Co-operative banks					..	..	Banques mutualistes
Other financial institutions	..	..	..	..	..	..	*Autres institutions financières*
Insurance institutions	..	..	..	..	..	..	*Institutions d'assurance*
All financial institutions	..	..	..	..	..	..	*Ensemble des institutions financières*

1. Data are aggregated across the Board of Governors, the 12 District Banks, and their 25 branches. Financial assets exclude property, buildings, and equipment.
2. Employees are indicated in man-labour years. Financial assets are cash, balances with central bank, interbank deposits, loans, and securities.

1. Les données sont agrégées à l'échelle globale du Conseil des gouverneurs, des 12 Banques de réserve fédérale et de leurs 25 succursales. Les actifs financiers excluent les biens immobiliers, les bâtiments et biens d'équipement.
2. Le nombre de salariés est indiqué en équivalent plein-temps. Les actifs financiers recouvrent les espèces, les avoirs auprès de la banque centrale, les dépôts interbancaires, les prêts et les valeurs mobilières.

Did you Know?

This publication is available in electronic form

Many OECD publications and data sets are now available in electronic form to suit your needs at affordable prices.

For our statistical publications we use powerful software platforms (Ivation's Beyond 20/20 or STATWISE) that allow you to get the maximum value from the data. Other publications are available using the simple Acrobat/PDF presentation. **Delivery platforms** range from magnetic tape through CD-Rom and diskettes to online via internet. **Stand alone and network** versions are offered for many titles.

For more information about electronic editions of this publication, or to ask for a catalogue of all our electronic publications, contact your nearest OECD Centre (see overleaf).

Le saviez-vous ?

La version électronique de cette publication est disponible !

Désormais, afin de mieux répondre à vos besoins, un grand nombre de publications et de données de l'OCDE sont disponibles sous forme électronique à des prix très abordables.

Nos études statistiques sont présentées sur des logiciels puissants (Beyond 20/20 ou Statwise) permettant d'optimiser les données au maximum. Certaines publications sont également disponibles sur Acrobat/PDF.

Par ailleurs, **un éventail très large de supports** vous est proposé : bande magnétique, Cédérom, disquette et interrogation en ligne via Internet. De nombreux titres sont également proposés en **versions monoposte et réseau.**

Pour de plus amples informations sur les versions électroniques de cette publication ou pour obtenir le catalogue de nos éditions électroniques, n'hésitez pas à contacter le Centre OCDE le plus proche (voir verso).

Beyond 20/20™

OECD-OCDE

A POTENT INSTRUMENT OF GLOBAL CHANGE

UN INSTRUMENT PUISSANT DE CHANGEMENT ET DE REFORME DANS LE MONDE

Where to send your request:

Où envoyer votre demande:

In Austria, Germany and Switzerland / En Allemagne, en Autriche et en Suisse

OECD CENTRE BONN / CENTRE OCDE DE BONN
August-Bebel-Allee 6,
D-53175 Bonn
Tel.: (49-228) 959 1215
Fax: (49-228) 959 1218
E-mail: bonn.contact@oecd.org
Internet: www.oecd.org/bonn

In Latin America / En Amérique latine

OECD CENTRE MEXICO / CENTRE OCDE DE MEXICO
Edificio INFOTEC
Av. San Fernando No. 37
Col. Toriello Guerra
Tlalpan C.P. 14050,
Mexico D.F.
Tel.: (525) 528 10 38
Fax: (525) 606 13 07
E-mail: mexico.contact@oecd.org
Internet: rtn.net.mx/ocde/

In the United States / Aux États-Unis

OECD CENTER WASHINGTON / CENTRE OCDE DE WASHINGTON
2001 L Street N.W., Suite 650
Washington, DC 20036-4922
Tel.: (202) 785 6323
Toll free / Numéro vert : (800) 456-6323
Fax: (202) 785 0350
E-mail: washington.contact@oecd.org
Internet: www.oecdwash.org

In Asia / En Asie

OECD CENTRE TOKYO / CENTRE OCDE DE TOKYO
Landic Akasaka Bldg.
2-3-4 Akasaka, Minato-ku,
Tokyo 107-0052
Tel.: (81-3) 3586 2016
Fax: (81-3) 3584 7929
E-mail : center@oecdtokyo.org
Internet: www.oecdtokyo.org

In the rest of the world / Dans le reste du monde
OECD PARIS CENTRE / CENTRE OCDE DE PARIS
2 rue André-Pascal, 75775 Paris Cedex 16, France
Orders / Commandes : Fax: 33 (0)1 49 10 42 76

Enquiries / Renseignements : Tel: 33 (0)1 45 24 81 22 Fax: 33 (0) 1 45 24 19 50
E-mail : sales@oecd.org

Online Ordering: www.oecd.org/publications *(secure payment with credit card)*
Commande en ligne : www.oecd.org/publications *(paiement sécurisé par carte de crédit)*

OECD Main Switchboard / Standard OCDE : 33 (0) 1 45 24 82 00

Internet: www.oecd.org

OECD PUBLICATIONS, 2, rue André-Pascal, 75775 PARIS CEDEX 16
PRINTED IN FRANCE
(21 1999 04 3 P) ISBN 92-64-05857-5 – No. 50780 1999